Claude Lévi-Strauss

# Claude Lévi-Strauss

## A Critical Study of His Thought

Maurice Godelier

Translated by Nora Scott

VERSO
London • New York

This work was published with the help of the French Ministry of Culture – Centre national du livre

Ouvrage publié avec le concours du Ministère français chargé de la culture – Centre national du livre

Centre de Recherche et
R
E
D
O sur l' Océanie
de Documentation

This English-language edition first published by Verso 2018
First published as *Lévi-Strauss*
© Éditions du Seuil 2013
Translation © Nora Scott 2018

1 3 5 7 9 10 8 6 4 2

**Verso**
UK: 6 Meard Street, London W1F 0EG
US: 20 Jay Street, Suite 1010, Brooklyn, NY 11201

versobooks.com

Verso is the imprint of New Left Books

ISBN-13: 978-1-78478-707-3
ISBN-13: 978-1-78478-706-6 (HB)
ISBN-13: 978-1-78478-709-7 (US EBK)
ISBN-13: 978-1-78478-708-0 (UK EBK)

**British Library Cataloguing in Publication Data**
A catalogue record for this book is available from the British Library

**Library of Congress Cataloging-in-Publication Data**

Names: Godelier, Maurice, author.
Title: Claude Levi-Strauss : a critical study of his thought / by Maurice
   Godelier ; translated by Nora Scott.
Other titles: Levi-Strauss. English
Description: London ; Brooklyn, NY : Verso, 2018. | Includes bibliographical
   references and index.
Identifiers: LCCN 2018012500| ISBN 9781784787066 (hardback) | ISBN
   9781784787073 () | ISBN 9781784787097 (U.S. ebook) | ISBN 9781784787080
   (U.K. ebook)
Subjects: LCSH: Lāevi-Strauss, Claude. | Structural anthropology. | BISAC:
   BIOGRAPHY & AUTOBIOGRAPHY / Social Scientists & Psychologists. | SOCIAL
   SCIENCE / Anthropology / Cultural. | SOCIAL SCIENCE / Customs & Traditions.
Classification: LCC GN21.L4 G6313 2018 | DDC 301– dc23
LC record available at https://lccn.loc.gov/2018012500

Typeset in Minion by Hewer Text UK Ltd, Edinburgh
Printed and bound by CPI Group (UK) Ltd, Croydon CR0 4YY

# Contents

# Preface

On 30 October 2009, death brought to a close the final chapter of the life and work of Claude Lévi-Strauss. He had produced an immense body of work – scientific and literary, multifaceted, uncommonly powerful and creative – and his bold hypotheses, irritatingly rigorous demonstrations, and surprising and dazzling conclusions over more than half a century had shaken up and enriched not only anthropology, his own discipline, but the entire field of the human and social sciences.

In 1945, Lévi-Strauss was still an unfamiliar name, especially in France, when he published his first major theoretical article.[1] In it he boldly challenged the status quo of all these disciplines by declaring that the use of the principles and methods of structural analysis would soon deeply modify our understanding of kinship, myths, art, social organizations and so on – just as they had recently done in the field of linguistics.

In 1947, the promise was kept and the challenge met, with the publication of the French edition of *The Elementary Structures of Kinship*. Then, over the space of five decades, a succession of essential works of reference attested time and again to the same creative power: *The Savage Mind* (published in French in 1962), the Mythology series (four volumes 1964–1971, titled variously Mythologiques or Introduction to the

---

1 C. Lévi-Strauss, 'Structural Analysis in Linguistics and in Anthropology', in *Structural Anthropology*, trans. C. Jacobson and B. Grundfest Schoepf (New York, Basic Books, 1963), pp. 31–54.

Science of Mythology, the initial title), *The Way of the Masks* (French, 1975), *The Jealous Potter* (French, 1985) and *The Story of Lynx* (French, 1984), to cite only a few of the some twenty books, not to mention the 200 articles.

Lévi-Strauss quickly became famous in France, where he had chosen to pursue his career in research and teaching, and even more quickly won international celebrity, as attested by the many debates, quarrels, symposia and publications in all languages that greeted the appearance of each new work.

Looking back, it is clear that Lévi-Strauss's fame – the status and impact of his work on the scientific and literary community, but also on the general public – breaks down into two phases: the first from 1945 to around 1980, and the second to 2000 or slightly later.

During the first phase, his renown grew quickly, and his publications had an impact on an increasing number of areas and circles, and in a growing number of Western countries. He was seen as providing new foundations for not only anthropology and the social sciences, but also the criticism of literature and art. It was in this period that Lévi-Strauss would twice expose the principles and demonstrate the effectiveness of structural analysis, by publishing first of all *Structural Anthropology* (French, 1958) and then *Structural Anthropology, Volume 2* (French, 1973), which he saw as manifestos.

Ten years later, in 1983, he dropped the title 'Anthropologie structurale trois' for a new book, which would become *The View from Afar*. In 1988, he explained himself in an interview with Didier Eribon, who asked him the reason for this decision:

> in the meantime, the word 'structuralism' had become so degraded and was the victim of such abuse that no one had any idea what it meant. I continued to know, but I'm not sure that this would have been true of my readers . . . The educated public in France is bulimic. For a while, it fed on structuralism. People thought it carried a message. That fashion has passed . . . Simply because structuralism was – and continues to be – a type of inquiry far removed from the major occupations of our contemporaries.[2]

2 C. Lévi-Strauss and D. Eribon, *Conversations with Claude Lévi-Strauss*, trans. P. Wissing (Chicago and London, University of Chicago Press, 1991), pp. 91–2.

It may be that Lévi-Strauss already no longer believed, as he had written in 1956, that anthropology,

> after the aristocratic humanism of the Renaissance and the bourgeois humanism of the nineteenth century . . . marks the advent, for the finite world which our planet has become, of a double universal humanism . . . a democratic humanism in opposition to those preceding it and created from privileged civilizations for the privileged classes, [and which] calls for the reconciliation of man and nature in a generalized humanism.[3]

Despite these declarations, Lévi-Strauss would never cease to send out messages to humanity. Some were positive, like certain passages in the three lectures he gave in Japan in 1986, published only after his death, as *Anthropology Confronts the Problems of the Modern World* (French, 2011); others negative and pessimistic, like the closing passage of *The Naked Man* (French, 1971), or his praise of Montaigne and the duty to live 'as though life had meaning', in the penultimate chapter of *The Story of Lynx* (French, 1991). In the conclusion to the present work, I will analyse the various positions Lévi-Strauss adopted over his lifetime on history and on the future of humankind.

But, as early as 1965, Lévi-Strauss had remarked on the deep misunderstanding that had grown up between structuralism and literary criticism:

> The fundamental vice of literary criticism with structuralist pretensions stems from its too often being limited to a play of mirrors . . . The work studied and the analyst's thought reflect each other, and we are deprived of any means of sorting out what is simply received from the one and what the other puts into it.[4]

Gradually, criticism of structuralism grew as fascination with it waned, until, in 1979, in his book *The Postmodern Condition*,[5] Jean-François

---

3 C. Lévi-Strauss, 'Answers to Some Investigations: The Three Humanisms', in *Structural Anthropology, Volume 2*, trans. M. Layton (Chicago, University of Chicago Press, 1983), p. 274.

4 C. Lévi-Strauss, 'Answers to Some Investigations: Structuralism and Literary Criticism', in *Structural Anthropology, Volume 2*, p. 275.

5 J.-F. Lyotard, *The Postmodern Condition: A Report on Knowledge*, trans. G. Bennington and B. Massumi, foreword by F. Jameson (Manchester, Manchester University Press, 1984).

Lyotard launched an attack on structuralism and Marxism, accusing Marx and Lévi-Strauss of being, each in his own way, producers, under cover of science and objective truths, of 'grand narratives', 'meta-narratives with universal claims concerning the nature of man, history, differences between cultures, etc., rife with the arrogance of the West in the face of the rest of the world'.

War had been declared on the search for structures and invariants. And though, at one time, Lévi-Strauss had joined with Althusser, Barthes and Foucault in announcing the 'death of the Subject' – a formula which, when taken out of context, sounded like pure scientism – from the 1980s we would see the triumphal return of the subject and the individual in social sciences and literary criticism. The return was both predictable and necessary, for the subject exists and individuals are, each in their own right, the actors of their own history and actors, however small, of history writ large.

Over the next twenty years, more and more scholars came to espouse 'postmodern' views and attacked the social and human sciences, deconstructing them one after the other in an attempt to bring to light the ideological biases embedded in their production, the common source of which was Western thought and its claim to universality and therefore to hegemony.[6] Not all was negative in this critical endeavour, however: it often extended the criticisms long addressed to sociologists, historians, economists, etc. by thinkers paradoxically inspired by Marxism or structuralism. Postmodernism was also intended to provide a new understanding of humankind by paying attention to all the voices present within societies and cultures that had previously been ignored, overlooked or disdained. It posited that each of these voices would contribute its own truth, which, taken together with all the others, would constitute the many-facetted reason of humanity. These voices and discourses too would have to be deconstructed so as to reveal their own ideological biases, formed well before Western domination had overwhelmed them. The 'postmoderns' did not do this. In short, it is not easy to be rid of the problems raised by the search for objectivity in the human sciences.

---

6 Of course, this work of theoretical deconstruction and even demolition never took on nuclear physics, molecular biology, mathematics, etc., in sum the so-called 'hard' sciences, most of which arose and developed in the West.

Between the 1980s and 2000, Lévi-Strauss's fame and the status of his work underwent a change. He was now perceived as a great scholar continuing his academic work on kinship, with *Anthropology and Myth* (French, 1984); Amerindian myths, with *The Story of Lynx*; or art, with *Look, Listen, Read* (French, 1993). Although the scholar was motivated, as always by desire as well as pleasure, to understand, he now declared he was convinced, like Montaigne, that 'we have no communication with Being'.[7]

Lastly, in order to grasp the nature and concatenation of the two periods characterizing this half century – without any claim to make the rapid succession of events in the world at this time, the principal reason for the rise or fall of the various intellectual trends in the West – we can assert without great risk that the geopolitical context of these events had something to do with it.

Let us cast our minds back. In 1945, the West, with the powerful help of the USSR, had just conquered a coalition of three countries – Germany, Italy and Japan – each of which claimed the right to expand their 'living space', to the detriment of their neighbours, in the name of the superiority of their race and ideologies. These ideologies – Nazism, fascism or Japanese imperialism – all combatted or rejected the idea of democracy. In the aftermath of the war, one of the most pressing needs of many researchers was therefore to understand the 'objective reasons', most often transfigured by ideology, that had led to this conflict. The individual could not be the main object of this research. How could the origin of World War II be explained by Hitler's action and Chamberlain's or Daladier's inaction alone?

The immediate consequence of the war was a new world division driven by the USSR. Communist regimes invoking Marx, Lenin and Stalin would seize power in several countries in Europe, Asia, Africa and then Latin America, and ultimately cover half the globe. Through its criticism of capitalism and Western imperialism, the 'socialist camp', as it was called in those days, attracted the sympathy of Western colonies that were now demanding their independence.

As of 1950, the conflict was openly engaged between the two economic and political systems now splitting the world. The West already felt a sustained ideological threat from the socialist countries. Communist ideology held up the virtues of a planned, centralized economy in the

---

7 C. Lévi-Strauss, *The Story of Lynx*, trans. C. Tihanyi (Chicago, University of Chicago Press, 1995), p. 214.

service of the people and its needs, as opposed to the market economy motivated by profit-seeking and the accumulation of capital, and it presented socialism as the only path that would ensure continued progress for humanity.

The West thus found itself threatened from the outside, by the countries of the 'socialist camp', and from the inside, by those in the West who wanted rapid independence for former colonies, who continued to see the USSR as the first country in history where a revolution had brought the workers and the people to power – rather than as the dictatorship of a party over the masses.

All these issues divided intellectual circles and encouraged them increasingly to think in terms of systems, of objectives, of structural contradictions that kept one or the other of the two world systems, according to their proponents, from responding to the needs of humankind and enabling human progress. For many social scientists, the primary focus was not the individual but class relations, the nature of the state, etc.

It is therefore easy to see why two post-war decades provided a context that particularly favoured the influence of Marxism and structuralism, neither of which relied on the individual to explain the nature of societies. And yet the individual was not absent. It was present at the heart of Sartre's philosophy, which held that the world was 'absurd' but at the same time posited that each individual was endowed with absolute freedom, capable by his or her acts of giving this world meaning. Sartre himself had chosen as his personal path of freedom to be a fellow traveller of the French Communist Party.

The rest is known. In 1989, after many fissures and cracks, the Berlin Wall finally crumbled, and the socialist camp imploded, forced to abandon Europe and the old USSR. The capitalist market economy rapidly came to dominate the world economy, including that of countries such as China and Vietnam, where communist parties are still in power. Marxism ceased to be a reference for the social sciences, and by the early 1990s the very name of Marx had almost fallen into oblivion. For Lévi-Strauss, whose name was neither associated with such a political force, as were those of Marxists, nor present, by way of structuralism, in the major social clashes, his fame would be above all that of a major scientist, the only fame he had ever aspired to.

By the year 2000, history apparently no longer had a reason to change its verdict, and some pronounced its 'end'. The capitalist system, the first to have become a true world system, would go on developing indefinitely. Crises, should they arise, could only be a passing phenomenon – since the system was capable of self-regulation – and would be followed by still more prosperity for more people. Individuals had only to learn to govern themselves in order to capture a share of this prosperity.

But things did not go according to plan. In 2007, two years before Lévi-Strauss's death, a global crisis erupted that is still not over. Clearly self-regulation had reached its limits; any further and the system would spawn negative 'systemic effects' that would affect millions of people who had not caused them. The cause lay in the very nature of the system and could not be detached from it, since the cause was inherent in the system's functioning. Another, undesirable but predictable, consequence was that accession to the world capitalist system by China, India, Brazil and other, formerly 'underdeveloped', countries would bring about the end of Western economic hegemony and cultural domination.[8]

This rapid overview of half a century of world history – seen from France – is intended only to show the context and the milestones that illuminate the ebb and flow of the questions debated from 1945 among social scientists and literary critics, as well as the theoretical approaches they proposed for their resolution. In the first decades of this period, the study of social systems and their comparison was the privileged object of reflection. From the 1980s on, one of the two world systems being on the verge of disappearing, interest shifted to the individual as actor and subject.

In reality, the two domains cannot be separated. Each is the negative template of the other and calls it into existence. Every human being is born and grows up in a social system they have neither created nor chosen, which existed before their birth and which they will have to reproduce in order to ensure their own conditions of social, material and spiritual existence. They will have to learn to hunt if born into a society of hunters, to sell something if born into a market society. Of course, at some point in life, an individual may wish to contest, alone or with others, the system in which they live, and struggle to institute other kinds of social relations

---

8  The first of the three lectures Lévi-Strauss gave in Japan in 1986 was entitled 'The End of the West's Cultural Supremacy'; it was published only after his death (in French in 2011 and in English in 2013), in *Anthropology Confronts the Problems of the Modern World*, foreword by M. Olender, trans. J. M. Todd (Cambridge, MA and London, The Belknap Press of Harvard University Press, 2013), pp. 1–44.

more in keeping with their desires and interests; nevertheless, the success of such undertakings will never depend on the individual alone, but on the social forces he or she is able to mobilize, and the degree of resistance advocates of the old system are capable of mounting.

To discover the internal working logic of social systems and the structures that explain this logic, to analyse the conditions in which these systems have or have not managed to reproduce or transform themselves, and to measure the actual role played by the individuals belonging to these systems in their emergence, reproduction or disappearance: these are some of the basic goals that constitute the common ambition and horizon of the research conducted separately by the different social and human sciences, whatever fashions may accompany their development. It is in this way that *la mode* condemned Lévi-Strauss's work to a sort of scientific death, by first glorifying and then rejecting and forgetting it, without this glory or neglect ever having rested on a true effort at scientific evaluation.

The preceding explains why I wrote this book. To my mind, Lévi-Strauss is one of the twentieth-century thinkers who made the greatest strides toward discovering and analysing the structures of the human mind and those of several domains of social life – kinship relations, rites and myths, art, etc. From the outset, he went to the heart of the relationship between systems and individuals as subjects, always emphasizing the role of structures rather than that of subjects. For this he was criticized, and the criticism was necessary. But a large portion of his theses and conclusions constitute an achievement on which we can build if we want to continue to progress in our knowledge of humankind. It is true, however, that other aspects of his work are no longer admissible as they stand. It is to this critical evaluation that the present book is also devoted, and I will base my re-reading on the two domains with which I am most familiar: the study of kinship and that of myths and mythical thought.

The corpus of Lévi-Strauss's work forms a very long braid, with five interlacing strands that traverse time to the tune of some 200 articles and twenty-one books that make up this oeuvre. The five strands reflect the five domains he incessantly explored. They are:

– kinship
– myths and mythical thought
– art

– the principles and methods of structural analysis, as well as the relations entertained by structural anthropology with linguistics, history, philosophy, mathematics, but also with Marx, Freud, Rousseau, Gobineau, etc.

– the history and assessment of the future of humanity.

These five strands have never ceased to be intertwined even though, depending on the era, one sometimes assumes more importance than others, for instance the study of kinship during the first part of his career, or that of myths and mythical thought in the second part.

Of these five domains, I will leave aside art, for I claim no competence that would allow me to assess, for instance, what Lévi-Strauss wrote about music in general and Wagner and Rameau in particular, about serial music, or his negative comments on Picasso and modern painting, among others.[9] A few bibliographic references will suffice to indicate his continued interest in art. In one of his first major articles, concerning 'Split Representation in the Art of Asia and America', published in the United States in the journal *Renaissance* in 1945, he compared the style and motifs of ancient Chinese bronzes, Maori carvings and those of Northwest American Indians, boldly advancing the hypothesis that there had existed a very ancient cradle of culture common to the populations that had reached America from Asia and those that had left South China and the region of Taiwan to settle the Pacific islands and become what are now known as Polynesians.[10] The last book published

9 In a text published in *Arts*, n° 60 (1966), for the opening of the exhibition 'Hommage à Picasso' at the Grand and Petit Palais in Paris, Lévi-Strauss, after declaring Picasso 'a painter whose genius must be acknowledged', confessed his irritation with 'a work which, rather than contributing an original message, gives itself over to a sort of breaking down of the code of painting' and attests to 'the deeply rhetorical nature of contemporary art' (*Structural Anthropology, Volume 2*, pp. 276, 277, 278).

10 *Renaissance* 2 and 3 (1944–45), pp. 168–86; also 'Split Representation in the Art of Asia and America', in *Structural Anthropology*, pp. 245–68. Lévi-Strauss's fascination with Northwest American Indian art goes back to his discovery of the collections in the American Museum of Natural History and the period when he haunted New York's antique shops with Max Ernst, André Breton and Georges Duthuit: 'The almost carnal bond I had contracted with the art of the Northwest never relaxed itself'. In a note added in 1958 to the reprinted version of his article, Lévi-Strauss announced the recent discovery in a little museum in southeast Taiwan – where the Austronesian populations had been driven back by Chinese immigration – of a carving of three figures, 'two of which were in the pure Maori style' while the third resembled the art of the Northwest American Indians. He went on to posit the existence of a very old 'cradle' of culture common to

during his lifetime, *Look, Listen, Read* (French, 1993) analysed the music of Rameau and the painting of Poussin.

In the meantime, the publisher Skira brought out a superb book entitled *La Voie des masques* (1975), later published in English as *The Way of the Masks*, to which I will return, for it was in attempting to define the nature of the kinship systems in the societies that made and used these masks – the Kwakiutl, Tlingit, Nootka, Tsimshian, Haida, etc., the complexity of whose systems had nearly defeated Franz Boas – that Lévi-Strauss came to develop the concept of 'house'. He would later look for 'house' systems on all continents and continued to develop his analysis from 1976 to 1982, the year of his final lesson at the Collège de France. For this reason, *The Way of the Masks* serves as an introduction to the texts published in *Anthropology and Myth* (French, 1984), which sum up his thinking.

The fourth strand of the braid is composed of the texts in which Lévi-Strauss exposed the principles and methods of structural analysis, collected or dispersed in four works: *Structural Anthropology* (French, 1968), *The Savage Mind* (French, 1962), *Structural Anthropology, volume II* (French, 1973) and *The View from Afar* (French, 1983). To these we can add *Conversations with Claude Lévi-Strauss* (French, 1961), edited by Georges Charbonnier,[11] and another *Conversations with Claude Lévi-Strauss* conducted and edited by Didier Eribon (1988, expanded 2001). These texts are indispensable for anyone wishing to understand what structural analysis is and what it purports to contribute, and I will refer to them often in the course of this book.

The fifth and last strand of the braid unrolls the sequence of texts in which Lévi-Strauss conducted a critical re-examination of the notions of race, culture, progress, Western supremacy, and resistance to development, as well as the notions of human condition, history and the future of humanity.

---

those groups that had left Asia to settle in America or the Pacific Islands. This hypothesis has today been largely confirmed by Serge Dunis, whose research has shown the presence of the same myth patterns and the same symbols in the art of the Austronesians of Taiwan, in Polynesian peoples throughout the Pacific and in several South and North American tribes. See S. Dunis, *L'Île aux femmes. Mythologie transpacifique* (Paris, CNRS Éditions, 2016).

11 G. Charbonnier, ed., *Conversations with Claude Lévi-Strauss*, trans. J. and D. Weightman (London, Jonathan Cape, 1969).

In 'Race and History', first published in 1952, Lévi-Strauss was already analysing the notion of progress, and he demonstrated the absence of objective criteria that would allow one to compare and judge all societies from all periods. He was also developing the distinction between cumulative history and stationary history.[12] In 1954, he defined anthropology as the study of 'those forms of social life – of which the so-called primitive societies are merely the most readily identifiable and most developed examples – whose degree of authenticity is estimated according to the scope and variety of the concrete relations between individuals'.[13] This distinction between 'authentic societies' and 'unauthentic societies' (societies of modern man) would be found again in a short book published posthumously, *Anthropology Confronts the Problems of the Modern World* (French, 2011).

In 1956 the idea appeared that anthropology would be the bearer of a new, democratic and generalized humanism insofar as it would imply, in addition to respect for human beings, respect for nature.[14] In 1963, Lévi-Strauss raised the problem of cultural discontinuities and the sources of resistance to development found among many peoples subjected by the West.[15] In 1971, *The Naked Man* ended on a vision of what will remain of humans and their works, namely 'nothing'.[16] In 1986, the first of three lectures he gave in Japan announced 'the end of Western cultural supremacy', and he saw in the example of Japan, which combined tradition and industrial modernity, the promise of a possible revival of humanity's cultural diversity. In 2001 he explored the relationship between 'productivity and the human condition',[17] and in 2003, the last article he wrote would remind us once again that 'the experience of nature is a fundamental need'.[18] Given the same man asserted, as early as

12 C. Lévi-Strauss, 'Race and History', in *Structural Anthropology, Volume 2*, , pp. 323–62.

13 C. Lévi-Strauss, 'The Place of Anthropology in the Social Sciences', in *Structural Anthropology*, p. 369.

14 'Answers to Some Investigations: The Three Humanisms', pp. 271–4.

15 C. Lévi-Strauss, 'Cultural Discontinuity and Economic and Social Development', in *Structural Anthropology, Volume II*, pp. 312–22.

16 C. Lévi-Strauss, *The Naked Man*, Mythologiques, volume 4, trans. J. and D. Weightman (Chicago, University of Chicago Press, 1981), p. 621.

17 C. Lévi-Strauss, 'Productivité et condition humaine', *Études rurales*, nos 159–160 (2001), pp. 129–44.

18 C. Lévi-Strauss, 'Le Sentiment de la nature. Un besoin fondamental', *Ethnies*, nos 29–30 (2003), pp. 88–94.

1973, that 'structuralism did not carry a message' and his research 'was far removed from the major preoccupations of our contemporaries', he was no doubt right to remark to Maurice Olender, in 1976, that 'one is the last to know oneself'.[19] I will return in my conclusion to the (increasingly pessimistic and negative) messages that Lévi-Strauss conveyed at the end of his life on the future of humanity.

But now let us turn to the heart of our reflection, the analysis of kinship, on the one hand, and that of myths and of mythical thought, on the other.

---

19  Interview with Lévi-Strauss by Maurice Olender in 1976, after the publication of *The Way of the Masks*, published in *Le Point*, 30 September 2010, pp. 75–7.

# PART ONE
# Kinship

*The Elementary Structures of Kinship,* originally published in French in 1947, was Lévi-Strauss's first major work and it rapidly earned him an international audience and fame. In France, with the exception of an article by Simone de Beauvoir in *Les Temps modernes,* the work attracted little attention. However, subsequently and throughout his life Lévi-Strauss would continually be at the centre of research on kinship, discovering new problems, developing new concepts, responding to attacks and criticisms, and revisiting and enriching certain theses dear to his heart. An overview of his research and publications in this area reveals four periods.

The first period, from 1943 to 1956, weighs heavily on his later trajectory. It began in 1943, with a short text in which Lévi-Strauss analysed the social use of kin terms among the Nambikwara Indians of the Brazilian state of Matto Grosso, with whom he had stayed during his expeditions into Amazonia before World War II.[1] Here we already find the idea of the importance, in a system where marriages are contracted between cross cousins, of the exchange of women between groups and of the maternal uncle. In 1945 he laid out the principles of structural analysis in his first major theoretical article, published in the journal *Word*; it was at this time, too, that the notion of 'atom of kinship' first appeared.[2]

---

1 C. Lévi-Strauss, 'The Social Use of Kinship Terms among Brazilian Indians', *American Anthropologist* 45, n° 3 (1943), pp. 398–409.

2 C. Lévi-Strauss, 'L'Analyse structurale en linguistique et en anthropologie', *Word* 1, n° 2 (1945), pp. 1–12.

But the dominant work of this period is clearly *The Elementary Structures of Kinship*, which he completed in New York on 24 February 1947. I will devote lengthy analysis to it in these pages.[3] The book would be completed in 1956 by a very important analysis of the theoretical status of the family in the functioning of kinship systems.[4] The article reviews various forms of family found in Asia, among American Indians, etc., which are very different from the Western European monogamous family. He raises the possibility that it may actually be the women who exchange men, and then rejects it in view of the facts. Furthermore, one part of the famous *Introduction to the Work of Marcel Mauss* (French edition, 1949–1950),[5] that dealing with the appearance of symbolic thought – the source, according to *The Elementary Structures*, of the incest taboo and explanation of the fact that it is the women who are exchanged by the men and not the other way around – is an indispensable extension and complement to *The Elementary Structures of Kinship*.

The second period (1965–1967) centres on the text of the 1965 Huxley Memorial Lecture, given before the Royal Anthropological Institute of Great Britain and Ireland, and entitled 'The Future of Kinship Studies'. In it, Lévi-Strauss answers his Anglo-Saxon colleagues, who had criticized his use of the notions of structure and model in *The Elementary Structures*.[6] But above all, he urges anthropologists to analyse the transitional forms between elementary and complex structures, what he calls 'semi-complex structures' of kinship, whose operating rules he defines and illustrates by an example from what are known as the Crow-Omaha systems; I will examine this question later in the present book. These new developments can be found again in 1967, in the Preface to the second French edition of The Elementary Structures of Kinship.[7] Here Lévi-Strauss declares he is forgoing his plans to write a book on the

---

3 C. Lévi-Strauss, *The Elementary Structures of Kinship*, trans. and ed. J. H. Bell, J. R. von Sturmer and R. Needham (Boston, Beacon Press, 1969).

4 C. Lévi-Strauss, 'The Family', in H. L. Shapiro, ed., *Man, Culture and Society* (New York, Oxford University Press, 1956), pp. 261–85.

5 C. Lévi-Strauss, *Introduction to the Work of Marcel Mauss*, trans. F. Baker (London, Routledge & Kegan Paul, 1987).

6 C. Lévi-Strauss, 'The Future of Kinship Studies', *Proceedings of the Royal Anthropological Institute of Great Britain and Ireland* (1965), pp. 13–20.

7 Preface to the second edition of *The Elementary Structures of Kinship*, pp. xxiv–xlii.

complex structures of kinship, but, in response to popular demand, is nevertheless publishing a new edition of *The Elementary Structures*, whose documentation seems to him twenty years later somewhat out of date even though it 'required [him] to consult more than 7,000 books and articles'; and, above all, because he considers the entire part devoted to China and India to have been 'outstripped by the progress of anthropology'.[8] A few chapters were nevertheless reworked: those dealing with the Kachin system, for instance, for which Lévi-Strauss was strongly taken to task by Edmund Leach.

The third period (1973–1986) is dominated by the discovery of the both theoretical and historical importance of one form of kinship organization, the 'house' (as in the expression 'the house of Windsor'), a concept he developed in *The Way of the Masks* to illuminate the nature of the Kwakiutl and Tlingit kinship systems and those of other peoples of the American Northwest and Canada, which Boas had never managed to characterize. However, the notion of 'house' in this sense was already used by historians of the European Middle Ages or of Japan in analysing aristocratic marriage strategies.[9] For the next nearly ten years, until his last year at the Collège de France (1982), he concentrated on identifying this form of kinship organization in Melanesia, Polynesia, Africa, Madagascar and Indonesia, where paradoxically it was widespread, not only in certain Melanesian groups that used to be listed among the 'primitive societies', but also in strongly ranked societies headed by paramount chiefs (Polynesia), kings (Africa, Madagascar, Europe) and even emperors (Japan). Increasingly, the anthropology of kinship was to look to history, feed on it and seek in it the reasons for these transformations.

His findings would appear in 1984, in *Anthropology and Myth*,[10] of which they constitute a major part. But in 1973, before having discovered the importance of 'houses', Lévi-Strauss had returned to his analysis of the notion of atom of kinship, which appeared in his 1945 article in *Word*. And in the same year as he published the French edition of *Anthropology and Myth* (1984), he parried the objections raised to his

---

8 Ibid., p. xxvii.

9 C. Lévi-Strauss, *The Way of the Masks*, trans. S. Modelski (Seattle, University of Washington Press, 1982), pp. 163–87.

10 C. Lévi-Strauss, *Anthropology and Myth: Lectures 1951–1982*, trans. R. Willis (Oxford and New York, Blackwell, 1987), pp. 151–84.

theory of women being exchanged by their father or their brothers by marriages between children of the same father or the same mother – as practiced in Ancient Athens or Sparta, but also in other periods or in other parts of the world (Egypt, Polynesia, Peru, etc.). His response was the article published in *L'Homme*, 'Du mariage dans un degré rapproché'.[11]

In his next work, which is worth pausing over, Lévi-Strauss rebounded with a further contribution to the domain of kinship studies. In the spring of 1985, he visited Japan for the fourth time and gave three remarkable lectures, which would be published only after his death, in the form of a small book translated into English as *Anthropology Confronts the Problems of the Modern World*.[12] In the second of these lectures, he takes a stand on some of the most debated questions of the day in the Western world, in the domain of kinship: surrogate mothers, same-sex parents, medically assisted reproduction, etc. He was very open to legal, social and other solutions, an attitude some of his disciples had not yet adopted, persuaded as they were that, when it came to kinship, everything had already been invented. But Lévi-Strauss reminds us that all societies must maintain themselves over time and are thus obliged to find remedies for sterility or the death of childless couples, and that these means are indispensable to the continuity of a family line and name. He goes on to describe seven customs invented by various peoples in Africa or the Americas, some of which are the equivalent of insemination with a donor's sperm. Unfortunately, these analyses remained unknown to the general public as well to anthropologists, and therefore had no impact on the debates that continue to rage in Western media, parliamentary commissions, religious circles and public opinion.

From 1998 to 2000, in the last years of his life, Lévi-Strauss battled on in defence of his theses, in particular that of kinship as the exchange of women by men. He refuted the hypothesis advanced by certain 'evolutionist' anthropologists, according to whom the loss of

---

11 C. Lévi-Strauss, 'Du mariage dans un degré rapproché', in J.-C. Galey, ed., *Différences, valeurs, hiérarchie. Textes offerts à Louis Dumont* (Paris, Éditions de l'EHESS, 1984), pp. 79–89.

12 C. Lévi-Strauss, *Anthropology Confronts the Problems of the Modern World*, foreword M. Olender, trans. J. M. Todd (Cambridge, MA & London, The Belknap Press of Harvard University Press, 2013).

oestrus or its dissimulation in the ancestors of the human female allowed women to retain men by exchanging sexual favours for food brought back to camp by the men, and for protection for themselves and their children, summed up by the formula 'sex for food and care'. Men's attachment to women, and hence to the human family, it was argued, stems from the capacity of humans to make love at any time. Lévi-Strauss would treat this hypothesis with irony and disdain, first of all in a text published in Italian in *La Repubblica* and then in an article in *Les Temps modernes*.[13]

There was one last controversy. In his 'Apologue des amibes',[14] published in 2000, Lévi-Strauss concedes that Tylor's formula, which had served him well in *The Elementary Structures* and in the article 'The Family' – namely that early on, men had no other choice than 'marrying out or being killed out' – was merely a mythic view of an imaginary past. Years after having asserted that all society rests on the exchange of women, signs and their meanings (culture), he conceded that 'not everything in society can be exchanged', but went on to state the obvious, that 'if there were no exchange, there would be no society.'

The final act was the publication, also in 2000, of the afterword to a special issue of *L'Homme* devoted to kinship. Lévi-Strauss writes of being struck by the 'uneasiness that appears here concerning the exchange of women'.[15] Once again he repeats that it is indifferent from the standpoint of theory whether it is the men who exchange the women or the women who exchange the men. He goes on to add a few words about the controversial problem of so-called 'Arab' marriage. Finally, he revisits the distinction developed in *The Elementary Structures* between restricted and generalized exchange, and emphasizes that as far as he is concerned – he had modified his initial positions years earlier – he now considers restricted exchange as a 'special case of generalized exchange'. I will return to this question later, but only after having examined the whole work, text by text.

---

13 C. Lévi-Strauss, 'La Sexualité humaine et l'origine de la société', *Les Temps modernes*, n° 598 (1998), pp. 78–84.

14 C. Lévi-Strauss, 'Apologue des amibes', in J.-L. Jamard, M. Xanthakou and E. Terray, eds, *En substances. Textes pour Françoise Héritier* (Paris, Fayard, 2000), pp. 493–6.

15 C. Lévi-Strauss, afterword to *L'Homme*, nos° 154–55 (April–September 2000), special issue: *Question de parenté*, pp. 713–20.

This rough outline of the evolution of Lévi-Strauss's theory of kinship reveals two clear character traits: first, his passion to understand; and second, his feistiness, his readiness to respond to criticism, to reply to attacks and to defend, to the end, some of the theses he had developed in his first texts on kinship and whose validity he took for granted.

# 1

# The Beginnings (1943–1945): What Came Before *The Elementary Structures of Kinship*

We will not dwell on the 1943 *American Anthropologist* article analysing the social and political importance of the use of the term 'brother-in-law' among the Nambikwara Indians. Simply put, Lévi-Strauss outlines a kinship system with marriage between cross cousins that today would be classed as Dravidian. He indicates the existence of the possibility for a man to marry one of his older sister's daughters and the importance of the maternal uncle. He would find this form of 'oblique' marriage again in Asia, and would mention it in *The Elementary Structures*. One originality of the text is his use of observations contained in the accounts of sixteenth-century French travellers and Portuguese missionaries, such as Jean de Léry, Yves d'Évereux or Soares de Sousa, who describe in great detail the exchange of sisters between men and the authority they exercise over their nieces. Throughout his life, Lévi-Strauss would pay the greatest attention to such testimony as well as to historical sources in general.

It was in his first major theoretical article, in 1945, that Lévi-Strauss – convinced for several years already by his scientific exchanges with Roman Jakobson that modern linguistics was the single social science 'which can truly claim to be a science and which has achieved both the formulation of an empirical method and an understanding of the nature of the data submitted to its analysis' – wrote that structural analysis is the only method that would enable anthropology to progress and gradually stand as a science.[1]

---

1 C. Lévi-Strauss, 'Structural Analysis in Linguistics and in Anthropology', in *Structural Anthropology*, trans. C. Jacobson and B. Grundfest Schoepf (New York, Basic Books, 1963), p. 31.

By modern linguistics, he of course meant the school of thought inaugurated by Ferdinand de Saussure, but above all the 'revolution' of structural phonology, illustrated by the work of its founder, Nikolaï Troubetzkoy, and the Prague circle of linguists, of which Jakobson was a member. In 1933, Troubetzkoy had reduced the structural method as practiced in phonology to four basic operations. Indeed, reading them, it is easy to understand why this summary corresponded to the programme Lévi-Strauss then and there set for himself in anthropology. The first operation shifts from the study of *conscious* linguistic phenomena to that of their *unconscious* infrastructure; the second invites us to base the analysis on the *relations* between the terms and never to treat the terms as independent entities; the third consists in supposing that 'phonemes are always part of a system'; and fourth, the analysis should aim to discover 'general laws either by induction "or by logical deduction, which would give them an absolute character"'. [2]

Lévi-Strauss's application of this last principle – to discover general laws by logical deduction – explains the approach he takes in *The Elementary Structures*, something shocking and alien for the Anglo-Saxon anthropologists and sociologists of the time, since he begins the book by positing the universality of the incest taboo and then goes on to deduce the reasons for the exchange of women and the basis of cross-cousin marriage, etc. It is only in Chapter Eleven that he begins to analyse specific cases – the Australian kinship systems as typical examples of restricted exchange, and then the systems of China, India and peripheral regions as typical of generalized exchange.

Of course, Europe did not wait until the twentieth century (that is, for Saussure, followed by Troubetzkoy and Jakobson) to discover that people's relations with one another and with the natural environment form systems, that these systems differ in their structures, that these structures explain the logic behind the particular way each system works, and that these structures are not directly visible to the naked eye, but must be discovered by analysis and reconstructed in and through theory. For this reason, coming to know the structures of a system cannot be reduced to the representations of it held by the individuals

---

2 Ibid., p. 33; citing N. Troubetzkoy, 'La phonologie actuelle', in Henri Delacroix et al., *Psychologie du langage* (Paris: Félix Alcan, 1933).

and groups who make up this system and ensure its and their own reproduction. Because social systems are sets of interlocking relations, it is the very nature of these relations and of their articulation that determines the position and signification of the components (moieties, clans, castes, classes, religious groups, etc.) in the system.

The reader will have recognized in the foregoing the theoretical approach that Marx defined in his text on method included in his *Contribution to the Critique of Political Economy* (1859),[3] and developed later in *Capital.*[4] There he showed that, in the capitalist system, capital and labour are bound together by relations that are at once complementary and opposed, and that the wages paid by the owners of capital in exchange for the use of the workers' manual and intellectual labour is not what it is supposed to seem – the equivalent of the market value created by this use – but represents only part of this value. To wages, a category indispensable to the practical functioning of the capitalist system (based principally on the generalization and exploitation of wage labour) are thus attached representations that obscure and contradict, when it comes to theory, the real process by which the value of material and immaterial commodities are produced as reconstructed by the analyst. Marx had already clearly set out the methodological principle according to which one cannot study the genesis of a system until one knows its structure, thus repudiating historicism, as Lévi-Strauss would in turn do a century later.

Lévi-Strauss was certainly not unaware of Marx. As a student, he had read part of *Capital* and had devoted a text to it. But in 1945, structural linguistics, unlike *Capital*, was not the object of scientific or ideological controversy. More particularly, in his article Lévi-Strauss's only aim was to apply structural analysis to the study of the relation between two components of all kinship systems: on the one hand, the system of terms expressing the different kinship relations (father, maternal uncle, etc.), and, on the other, the system of attitudes and behaviours that individuals using these terms feel obliged to display toward those they are addressing – respect or familiarity, affection or hostility, etc.

---

3 K. Marx, *A Contribution to the Critique of Political Economy*, ed. and intro. M. Dobb (New York, International Publishers, 1970).

4 K. Marx, *Capital*, intro. E. Mandel, trans. B. Fowkes (New York, Vintage Books, 1977).

In any event, Lévi-Strauss would show there is no term-for-term correlation between these two systems, although there is interdependence, and that the key to understanding a system of attitudes is the behaviour prescribed toward, say, a maternal uncle and the behaviour expected of him in return. That is the starting point of his hypothesis of the existence of an 'atom of kinship', which combines four types of relationships:[5]

– between husband and wife (Hu–Wi)
– between brother and sister (B–Z)
– between maternal uncle and sister's son (MB–ZS)
– between father and son (F–S).

The atom of kinship is thus a structure with four components made up of individuals from two generations, between whom, in each generation, two pairs of correlative oppositions are divided. For example, among the Trobriand Islanders of Melanesia, who have a matrilineal kinship system, relations between father and son are free and familiar (+), relations between maternal uncle and nephew are respectful and antagonistic (-), those between husband and wife are intimate and affectionate (+), and those between brother and sister are heavily tabooed (-). Lévi-Strauss represents this system in the following way.

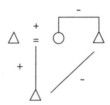

*System of attitudes in the Trobriand Islands*

Lévi-Strauss shows that these oppositions are not directly governed by the patrilineal or matrilineal descent principle, since among the Siuai, a matrilineal society in the Solomon Islands, the oppositions are distributed differently: relations between brother and sister are intimate, between maternal uncle and nephew they are antagonistic, between father and son they are familiar and between husband and wife they are tense.

---

5  Hu = husband; Wi = wife; Z = sister; S = son, etc.

We see that two of the relationships – between husband and wife and between brother and sister – have changed their sign and nature, and are the inverse of each other; on the other hand, two relationships remain the same and once again underscore the importance of the maternal uncle in matrilineal societies, since the uncle transmits to his sister's son, and not to his own, the rights, duties and status attaching to his clan.

For Lévi-Strauss, these two examples, and others not retained here, constitute 'a law which can be formulated as follows: in both groups, the relation between maternal uncle and nephew is to the relation between brother and sister as the relation between father and son is to that between husband and wife. Thus if we know one pair of relations, it is always possible to infer the other',[6] to deduce it from a law that has been discovered and is based on relations of correlation and opposition between the components of a structure. From then on Lévi-Strauss worked with structural analysis to achieve surprising results. Nevertheless, he conceded that his construction of the 'atom of kinship' was deliberately simplistic: 'clusters of attitudes' can exist among the four individuals occupying the kin positions that make up this structure, and not only those he had chosen; the institution of avunculate is not found in all kinship systems, whether matrilineal or patrilineal, and so on.

But he wanted to take his theory further. He wanted to show, contrary to Radcliffe-Browne, that the biological family was not the starting point for the development of kinship systems in the various societies. Kinship exists, he argued, not because it preserves the state of nature but because it separates us from it. And what produces the separation is the institution of the prohibition of incest, which is universal. The incest taboo has as its consequence that a man can obtain a wife only from another man, who cedes her to him in the form of his sister or his daughter.

That is the case because 'in human society it is the men who exchange the women, and not vice versa'. Lévi-Strauss admits that 'this is certainly a theoretical possibility. But it is immediately eliminated on empirical grounds . . . It remains for further research to determine whether certain cultures have not tended to create a kind of fictitious

---

6 'Structural Analysis in Linguistics and in Anthropology', p. 42.

image of this symmetrical structure. Such cases would surely be uncommon.'[7]

Yet such cases do exist. Granted, they are uncommon, but they are nonetheless not 'fictitious images' but real societies. The incest taboo thus obliges families to intermarry in order to continue. Kinship is established or perpetuated only through definite forms of alliance, in other words, the exchange of women among men. Hence the importance of the maternal uncle, the wife's brother, as the giver of a woman. Hence the tie between him and his sister's husband. Hence the presence of the child born of this marriage within the atom of kinship –yet Lévi-Strauss goes on to say the child is not there because he 'perpetuates the race', or a line of descent, but because of 'the fact that the disequilibrium . . . between the group that gives the woman and the group that receives her can be stabilized only by counter-prestations in following generations'.[8]

Lévi-Strauss advances here a fundamental thesis: that of the secondary character of forms of descent and filiation with respect to the principles organizing alliance in the workings of kinship systems. This thesis would bring him into head-on conflict with Anglo-Saxon anthropologists, most of whom held the various descent modes to be the main axis of kinship systems. Although the debate is not closed, perhaps the present book may contribute to terminating it.

The article ends with two equally important observations. First, the idea that 'the kinship system does not have the same importance in all cultures. For some cultures it provides the active principle regulating all or most of the social relationships. In other groups, as in our own society, this function is either absent altogether or greatly reduced. In still others . . . it is only partially fulfilled.'[9] Here we recognize the all-too-widespread idea that kinship is the basis of societies without a state, castes or classes, in sum, of those that the Anglo-Saxon manuals term 'kin-based societies'. In reality, although the importance of kinship relations differs with the nature of different societies, nowhere do they form the foundation of society. It falls to other types of social relations to ensure that a certain number of human groups form a

---

7 Ibid., p. 47.
8 Ibid.
9 Ibid.

'society'; these are what in the West are called 'political-religious' relations.[10]

The last idea exposed in this article is that kinship systems are systems of symbols and therefore imply the existence of symbolic thought, whose emergence in humans needs to be explained. According to Lévi-Strauss, although it is legitimate, at least initially, to fall back on a naturalist interpretation of this emergence, later the nature of the explanation must 'change as radically as the newly appeared phenomenon differs from those which have preceded and prepared it'.[11] In this statement, we detect the seeds of the idea that symbolic thought emerged like a sort of 'big bang', which would be developed in the final chapter of *The Elementary Structures* and in the *Introduction to the Work of Marcel Mauss* (first published in French in 1950). The consequence, as we know, was that it is the women who are exchanged and not the men.

A last word about the circumstances surrounding the project to write *The Elementary Structures of Kinship*. Fleeing anti-Semitic persecution by the Nazis and the Vichy regime in France, many artists and academics found themselves in New York when war broke out. At the behest of the jurist Boris Mirkine-Guetzévitch, the École Libre des Hautes Études de New York was founded in 1941. Jakobson was giving a course on structural linguistics and Lévi-Strauss, one on kinship. Each attended the other's lectures. It was Jakobson who one day told Lévi-Strauss that he should 'write about it'. The idea had not occurred to Lévi-Strauss. Thus in 1943 he began work on *The Elementary Structures of Kinship*, which he finished in New York, on 23 February 1947.[12]

---

10 I developed this thesis in two books: *The Metamorphoses of Kinship*, trans. N. Scott (London and New York, Verso, 2012; French edition, 2004), and again in *In and Out of the West: Reconstructing Anthropology*, trans. N. Scott (Charlottesville, University of Virginia Press and London and New York, Verso, 2009; French edition, 2007).

11 'Structural Analysis in Linguistics and in Anthropology', p. 51.

12 See C. Lévi-Strauss and D. Eribon, ed., *Conversations with Claude Lévi-Strauss*, trans. P. Wissing (Chicago, University of Chicago Press, 1991), pp. 42–3.

# 2

## The Elementary Structures of Kinship (New York, 1947; Paris, 1949)

Before we begin, a preliminary remark is in order. Lévi-Strauss wrote *The Elementary Structures of Kinship* in view of his *thèse d'État*, defended before a jury of sociologists none of whom were kinship specialists. The book constituted what was called at the time the '*grande thèse*', which was to be completed by a '*petite thèse*' – this was *La Vie familiale et sociale des Indiens Nambikwara*,[1] published in 1948, a year before *The Elementary Structures* came out in France (1949).

The specific object of the thesis was the analysis of the 'elementary structures' of kinship, which Lévi-Strauss defined in the opening lines of his preface:

Elementary structures of kinship are those systems in which the nomenclature permits the immediate determination of the circle of kin and that of affines, that is, those systems which prescribe marriage with a certain type of relative, or, alternatively, those which, while defining all members of the society as relatives, divide them into two categories, viz., possible spouses and prohibited spouses. The term 'complex structures' is reserved for systems which limit themselves to defining the circle of relatives and leave the

1  C. Lévi-Strauss, 'La Vie familiale et sociale des Indiens Nambikwara', *Journal de la Société des Américanistes* 37, n° 1 (1948), pp. 1–132.

determination of the spouse to other mechanisms, economic or psychological.[2]

Lévi-Strauss then goes on to clarify these definitions with some examples. A kinship system that makes cross cousins the prescribed or preferred spouses is an elementary structure. A system in which the spouse is acquired by the transfer of wealth or is the object of free choice is a complex system.

But even with elementary structures there is room for choice, for several individuals may belong to the category of possible spouses; conversely, in complex structures not everything is possible, for the prohibition of incest excludes a certain number of Ego's kin from marriage and/or sexual relations – mother or daughter for example. It is to be noted that, in the first definition in the French edition, Lévi-Strauss uses the word '*groupe*' in the sense of 'society' – all members of the society are 'related' to each other in various degrees. In the second definition, the term 'relatives' or 'kin' (in French, *parents*) designates only those we call 'consanguineous' kin, to the exclusion of affines.

Of course, the question is a bit more complex than these definitions suggest; Lévi-Strauss was keeping things simple. Some kinship systems, such as the so-called 'Iroquois' systems, have separate kin terms for parallel and cross cousins, at the same time as different and specific terms for affines (spouse's relatives). This means two things: on the one hand, that in these systems the exchange of women is the general marriage rule, which gives rise in the following generation to the distinction between cross and parallel cousins; and, on the other hand, that marriage between cousins is neither prescribed nor preferred. In each generation, it is possible to exchange women from different lineages. But there is no obligation to repeat alliances. The system is open. The possible spouses are all individuals of the opposite sex who belong to lineages with which Ego's lineage has never yet exchanged women, or had done so several generations before. Hence the existence of a special vocabulary for new affines who are, to some extent, outsiders.[3]

---

2 C. Lévi-Strauss, *The Elementary Structures of Kinship*, trans. J. H. Bell, J. R. von Sturmer and R. Needham, eds, (Boston, Beacon Press, 1969), p. xxiii.

3 This is the case among the Baruya of New Guinea, among whom I have lived and worked.

On the other hand, in a so-called 'Dravidian' kinship system, as found in South India, Amazonia and Australia, marriage with a cross cousin is often the rule, and alliances are repeated regularly.[4] In the kin terminology of these systems, a single term subsumes several relations that, in the present-day European system, would correspond to consanguineous relations or to affinal relations. In this case, the term for mother's brother (MB), the maternal uncle, for a man designates wife's father (WiF), and for a woman, husband's father (HuF), which is written: MB = WiF = HuF.

In symmetrical fashion, the father's sister (FZ), the paternal aunt, is at the same time the wife's mother (WiM) and, for a woman, the husband's mother (HuM): FZ = WiM = HuM. These terms immediately show that in $G^{+1}$ there was an exchange of sisters between two men belonging to two separate kin groups (lines, lineages, sections, clans). Ego's father's sister became the wife of Ego's mother's brother, and the sister of Ego's mother's brother became the wife of Ego's father, i.e. his mother. But since the alliances were repeated in the following generation, the maternal uncle (MB) becomes Ego's father-in-law (WiF or HuF). In systems like these, it is most often the case that there is no separate vocabulary for affinal kin; affinity and consanguinity overlap. Lévi-Strauss's definition covers this type of system.

In fact, the distinction between Iroquois and Dravidian systems was not clearly established until 1964; this was done by Floyd G. Lounsbury in a sensational article,[5] of which Lévi-Strauss was completely unaware at the time he wrote *The Elementary Structures*.[6]

In 1947, when Lévi-Strauss completed *The Elementary Structures*, little had been written in France on the question of kinship since

---

4 Cross cousins can be of the first, second or third degree, and alliances are renewed after one, two or three generations.

5 F. G. Lounsbury, 'The Structural Analysis of Kinship Semantics', in H. G. Lunt, ed., *Proceedings of the Ninth International Congress of Linguistics* (The Hague, Mouton, 1964), pp. 1073–83.

6 In 1949, George Peter Murdock had constructed a typology of known kinship systems based on those proposed by Lowie (1928) and Kirchhoff (1932), in which the Iroquois system appeared, to which he had added the Crow-Omaha system. But since he used only the terms present in $G^{+1}$ to compare them, and since in $G^{+1}$ the terminologies of the Dravidian and Iroquois systems are largely similar, their difference escaped him. G. P. Murdock, *Social Structure* (New York, Free Press, 1949); R. M. Lowie, 'A Note on Relationship Terminologies', *American Anthropologist*, n° 30 (1928), pp. 263–7; P. Kirchhoff, 'Verwandschaftsbezeichnungen und Verwandtenheirat', *Zeitschrift für Ethnologie* 64 (1932), pp. 41–72.

Durkheim's article on 'La Prohibition de l'inceste et ses origines', published in the first volume of *L'Année sociologique*, in 1898, and a few remarks by Mauss on moiety systems. The noteworthy exception was the sinologist Marcel Granet, who, although not himself an anthropologist, published in 1939 an attempt at reconstructing the kinship system of Ancient China, which already contained the distinction Lévi-Strauss would develop between two forms of the exchange of women: restricted exchange and generalized exchange.[7]

While Lévi-Strauss recognized that Marcel Granet had 'succeed[ed] in arriving at theoretical truths of a greater and more general significance',[8] he devoted three chapters of *The Elementary Structures* to a critique of Granet's hypotheses, which he described in the end as 'an ideological construction with no objective basis'.[9] Many would see this judgment as unfair and the expression of a thinly disguised rivalry.[10] I will return to the question later.

Lévi-Strauss dedicated his book to Lewis H. Morgan, regarded as the founder of kinship studies and, at the time, if not forgotten in the United States and Great Britain, at least disdained since Boas's critiques. In point of fact, Morgan's work has two sides. He was the first to have organized a vast survey of the forms of kinship found throughout the world in his time. The result was the monumental *Systems of Consanguinity and Affinity of the Human Family* (1871),[11] which is still useful; and it was in tribute to this book that Lévi-Strauss dedicated *The Elementary Structures* to Morgan. Then in a second book, *Ancient Society* (1877), Morgan attempted to establish a correspondence between each of these kinship systems and a state in the development of humanity, from a primitive savage state through the barbarian state and finally to the civilized state, the paramount embodiment of which was the

---

7 M. Granet, *Catégories matrimoniales et relations de proximité dans la Chine ancienne* (Paris, Alcan, 1939).

8 *The Elementary Structures of Kinship*, p. 311. Marcel Granet died in 1940, deeply affected by the German victory and Pétain's capitulation to Hitler. See Y. Goudineau, 'Lévi-Strauss, la Chine de Granet, l'ombre de Durkheim. Retour aux sources de l'analyse structurale de la parenté', *Cahiers de L'Herne*, n° 82 (2004), pp. 165–78.

9 *The Elementary Structures of Kinship*, p. 324.

10 See F. Héran, 'De Granet à Lévi-Strauss', *Social Anthropology* 6, n° 1 (1998), pp. 1–60; vol. 6, n° 2, pp. 169–201; vol. 6, n° 3, pp. 309–30.

11 L. H. Morgan, *Systems of Consanguinity and Affinity of the Human Family* (Washington DC, Smithsonian Institution, 1871).

European-American kinship system and the monogamous nuclear family.[12] It was this book, inspired by the evolutionist doctrines of the time, which drew Boas's criticism. For anthropology to progress, it was necessary to shun the second Morgan, and it was not to this Morgan that Lévi-Strauss dedicated his *Elementary Structures*.

In the period between the two world wars and during the second, while Lévi-Strauss found himself in the United States, a great deal of fieldwork and theoretical debates appeared, the bulk of which were the work of American, British and Australian anthropologists together with a few Russians. These anthropologists, including Boas, Rivers, Lowie, Kroeber, Hocart, Malinowski and many others, had collected a mass of facts and documents that did not exist in France and which were introduced by *The Elementary Structures*. Lévi-Strauss claimed to have read some 7,000 books and articles in order to write this book, yet twenty years later, preparing the new edition in 1967, he regarded this documentation as already 'old-fashioned', stressing that the work on kinship had grown at a dizzying pace since the initial version.

In his Preface to the first edition, Lévi-Strauss presents the work as a study in 'comparative sociology'. The expression is Durkheim's, but at the time in France the word 'anthropology' was not yet current. 'Ethnology' was the term employed. He presents his book as 'properly speaking . . . an introduction to a general theory of kinship systems'. And he announces two studies to come, intended to complete *The Elementary Structures*: one on complex kinship structures and the next, or third, on 'those family attitudes expressing or overcoming, by conventional behaviour, conflicts or contradictions inherent in the logical structure such as are revealed in the system of nomenclature'.[13] This is a clear allusion to his article published in *Word* (1945) on the 'atom of kinship'. But in 1967, Lévi-Strauss would announce that he had abandoned the idea of writing on complex structures. The third book never saw the light of day, either, but Lévi-Strauss returned to the analysis of the atom of kinship on two occasions: once in 1973 in response to criticisms made by Luc de Heusch in 1958 – this would be the article

---

12  L. H. Morgan, *Ancient Society, or, Research in the Lines of Human Progress from Savagery through Barbarism to Civilization* (Tucson, University of Arizona Press, 1985; First edition 1887).

13  *The Elementary Structures of Kinship*, p. xxiv.

'Réflexions sur l'atome de parenté'[14] – and a second time, in 1983, with an article entitled 'An Australian "atom of kinship"', re-issued in translation in *The View from Afar*.[15]

We now come to two important points: the architecture of the book and therefore of its content. Until now, little attention has been paid to what Lévi-Strauss said about his approach in the Preface to his book. He singles out two stages. First, he sets out his hypotheses, illustrates principles and follows his intuition. Given the phenomena surveyed in this first part are 'universal and simple', the examples amassed will be used to illustrate rather than to demonstrate. For – which may seem surprising – Lévi-Strauss asserts that 'comparison with the subject's own experience as a member of a social group is almost always enough to restore the content'.[16] This is the method followed by the author in the first ten chapters. Then, in the second stage, he applies his analytical grid to a detailed examination of four groups of societies. He begins with Australia, the classic land of restricted exchange, excepting the system of the Murngin and their neighbours – a form of generalized exchange whose principle Lévi-Strauss defines. He next provides an overview of three vast groups of kinship systems and societies.[17] The first group follows an axis running from Burma in the south to Siberia in the north. Two systems illustrate this axis: that of the Kachin in the south and that of the Gilyak in the north. He then spends three chapters on the Chinese system and four on India. There he analyses the forms of marriage with the matrilateral cross cousin (MBD), and opposes them to the systems

---

14 *L'Homme* 13, n° 3 (1973), pp. 5–30.

15 C. Lévi-Strauss, *The View from Afar*, trans. J. Neugroschel and P. Hoss (Chicago, University of Chicago Press, 1985), pp. 63–72.

16 *The Elementary Structures of Kinship*, 'Preface to the first edition', p. xxv.

17 The three cover a considerable geographical area encompassing a large number of societies. Lévi-Strauss justifies his choice in the conclusion to *The Elementary Structures*: 'The area to which we have been spontaneously confined in the course of our analysis has an extraordinary density of kinship systems answering to the definition of elementary structures. It allows all types to be considered and gives several examples of each type. These examples are the richest and most lucid, and approximate most closely to the demands of a theoretical demonstration' (p. 461). In 1988, in conversation with Didier Eribon, looking back on *The Elementary Structures* he says: 'First of all, I wouldn't write it. As I've gotten older, I have become too prudent to undertake vast synthetic works' (C. Lévi-Strauss and D. Eribon, ed., *Conversations with Claude Lévi-Strauss*, trans. P. Wissing [Chicago and London, University of Chicago Press, 1991], p. 101).

with a preference for the patrilateral cross cousin (FZD), which he calls an 'abortive form', 'the Cheap-Jack, in the scale of marriage transactions'.[18]

The book ends on two points. First, a chapter outlines a reflection on the conditions of the passage from elementary to complex structures. Lévi-Strauss sees the widespread African practice of 'marriage by purchase' as a transformation of the generalized exchange formula, which transcends its limits and makes it possible to multiply alliances well beyond those allowed by generalized exchange. Furthermore, he sees in one of the eight marriage formulas present in the ancient Indian Laws of Manu – *swayamvara* marriage, in which the woman freely chooses her husband – the origin of 'the three basic characteristics of modern European marriage: freedom to choose the spouse within the limit of the prohibited degrees; equality of the sexes in the matter of marriage vows; and finally, emancipation from relatives and the individualization of the contract'.[19]

In the final chapter, Lévi-Strauss exposes the 'principles of kinship', an occasion for him to return to the nature of the incest prohibition, to Freud's *Totem and Taboo*, and to the exchange of women by men as a consequence of the appearance of symbolic thought, an exchange he compares to the circulation of signs in and by language.

Let us now make our way through the book so as to follow the subtleties of the theoretical argument. The first surprise comes when, having announced on the opening page of his Preface to the first edition that the book's purpose is to study the elementary structures of kinship and to define them, Lévi-Strauss starts off by addressing a problem that has little to do with this aim: that of the relationship between nature and culture and, more specifically, the passage from one to the other. And he promptly asserts that the answer to this question lies in the prohibition of incest, which he calls 'the fundamental step because of which, by which, but above all in which the transition from nature to culture is accomplished'.[20]

This passage did not consist in the superposition of culture on nature, but in a transformation of nature by culture: 'if man is a domesticated animal, he is the only one who has domesticated himself'.[21] 'Before [the

---

18 *The Elementary Structures of Kinship*, p. 449.
19 Ibid., p. 477.
20 Ibid., p. 24.
21 Ibid., p. 5.

prohibition of incest] culture is still nonexistent; with it, nature's sovereignty over man is ended. The prohibition of incest is where nature transcends itself.'[22]

These are superb formulations, whose breadth of vision broke masterfully with over a century of speculation on the origin of this prohibition. It is worth noting the philosophical postulate explicitly present in these formulations: it is nature that transcends itself in man by giving him the capacity to domesticate himself, to transform himself. There is no vision of divine creation, but instead a 'naturalist' vision, which is in fact 'materialist'.

Paradoxically, Lévi-Strauss does not go on to define incest. He leaves us with the common, almost intuitive idea that incest is, for an individual, the fact of uniting sexually with those who are 'forbidden' sexual partners – mother, sisters, daughters. There is as yet no question of exchange, and even less of the obligation to give the woman one has renounced. Furthermore, incest is mentioned only in relation to a man, not to a woman, for whom the prohibition of incest signifies conversely the prohibition on uniting sexually with and marrying her father, brother, son, etc. And yet the two sets of prohibitions obey the same principle. They are the two sides of a coin. But Lévi-Strauss does not place them on the same footing because, once the prohibition of incest has been established and exchange has become both possible and necessary, it is the men who will exchange the women and not vice versa.

We see that this both commonplace and almost intuitive definition of incest fits perfectly within the bounds of the 'atom of kinship' constructed by Lévi-Strauss in his *Word* article as being the foundation, the basic elementary cog in the whole kinship system, whether these structures are elementary or complex. Indeed, all the protagonists of exchange are present in the atom of kinship: a man and his sister, a father and a mother, and their male and female children.

Let us look at the status Lévi-Strauss lends to the notion of the incest taboo in these opening pages. Since it is by means of and in this prohibition that the transition from nature to culture is accomplished, the prohibition must therefore logically have preceded the appearance of kinship relations among human ancestors, since it was the condition of these relations. But for the prohibition of incest to have meaning,

---

22 Ibid., p. 25.

kinship relations must already exist; for women to be forbidden because they are someone's – a man's – sisters, daughters (Lévi-Strauss will even add mother), they must already be tied to him by relations of kinship, of descent (father–daughter), or of siblingship (brother–sister). We have here a paralogism.

Lévi-Strauss assigns the prohibition of incest a double role in his logic. It is at once the cause and the effect of this cause. It conditions the appearance of kinship relations (and, for Lévi-Strauss, that of culture as a whole) and is inscribed in them; it is the starting point for the construction and articulation of all the other pieces of kinship systems. It springs from and becomes the centrepiece, as it were, of the internal structure of any kinship system of whatever kind. But the prohibition of sexual intercourse between certain members of a human group has meaning only if this group already constitutes something like a group of related people.

The incest prohibition must therefore not be thought or posited as a static starting point, but as a complex dynamic process that was at once universal, since Lévi-Strauss believes it to have brought the human species as a whole from its animal to its human state, and transhistoric, since, once this prohibition appeared, it would remain present in all periods of human history. Thinking the incest prohibition comes down to thinking a process that fulfilled two different functions at two periods in the protohistory and then the history of humankind: to explain the genesis of kinship relations in protohumans, and to explain the reproduction in humans of these relations once they had appeared.

It was from the prohibition of incest as the cause and the effect of this cause that Lévi-Strauss would go on logically to deduce and articulate the other concepts he needed in order to analyse kinship systems – exogamy, exchange, alliance, and so on. In sum, by positing the prohibition of incest as both the cause and the effect of this cause, Lévi-Strauss made the concept the equivalent of a mathematical postulate. For if the consequences derived from a postulate do not explain its genesis, it is nevertheless from it that they derive their mathematical existence and their logical articulation. The prohibition of incest thus operates like a logical sociological postulate which resembles a paralogism, that is like an effect that is its own cause or vice versa.

And so Lévi-Strauss set out to discover whether the animal kingdom displays rudiments of the elements that make up culture everywhere

– language, tools, social institutions – and for this he turned to the great apes, only to conclude that 'research on the great apes during the last thirty years has been particularly discouraging in this respect.' He is struck by 'the irremediable lack of language and the total incapacity to treat sounds uttered or heard as signs'. Even more important is the fact that 'the social life of monkeys does not lend itself to the formulation of any norm . . . in sexual life as in other forms of activity.' He concludes that 'no empirical analysis . . . can determine the point of transition between natural and cultural facts, nor how they are connected.'[23] And he deduces that, wherever there are rules, we are in a state of culture. He then explains how he intends to proceed in order to advance his argument:

> Failing a real analysis, the double criterion of norm and universality provides the principle for an ideal analysis which, in certain cases and within certain limits, may allow the natural to be isolated from the cultural elements which are involved in more complex syntheses.[24]

He then submits that, in principle, everything that is universal in man relates to the natural order, and everything that is subject to a norm is cultural and particular. Applying these criteria to the incest taboo, he observes that it constitutes a rule but, alone of all the social norms, it possesses a universal character. And he asks: is this rule really universally observed by humans? Are there no groups that did or do not have any prohibition on incest, Ancient Egypt for example, Inca Peru, the Hawaiian chiefdoms, the Malagasy royal houses? He concludes that there is no exception to this prohibition, for the absence of prohibition attributed to these groups is merely the viewpoint of another group, whose rule is defined and applied differently.[25]

Lévi-Strauss was right about this. There is no group that does not apply some form of incest taboo. Nor is there any group that accepts all sexual acts. Sexual practices, and not only those that are authorized or forbidden within marriage, are everywhere subject to rules. As for Lévi-Strauss's claims concerning the lack of language and tools

---

23  Ibid., pp. 6–8.
24  Ibid.
25  Ibid., p. 9.

among monkeys, and even the absence of social institutions, it must be said that they have all been refuted by discoveries made by ethologists and primatologists after 1947, the year Lévi-Strauss finished his book.

With regard to brother–sister marriages in Ancient Egypt or among the Inca, Lévi-Strauss saw these as being 'more disturbing', because his whole theoretical endeavour consisted in showing that kinship is based on the exchange of women – sisters or daughters – by men – their brothers or father. He would 'get around' this, as it were, by citing a certain papyrus, which appears to mention the possibility of a brother marrying his older sister and not the younger. The theory was thus 'half' salvaged. What Lévi-Strauss was unable or unwilling to see in the existing documentation was that marriage between a brother and a sister in Egypt or Persia *did not constitute incest*. It was the *most valued* form of social union in these groups, insofar as it was a *sacred* act by which humans imitated the gods and thus collaborated to preserve the social and cosmic orders. This was also the case of the marriage between brother and sister (but also exceptionally between father and daughter) in Ancient Iran, which was by no means the preserve of an elite.[26] This type of marriage was performed by a Mazdean priest who had himself married his sister. According to this theology, the son born of a *xwetodas* (sibling) marriage possesses within himself the optimum balance of male and female principles, which are at the same time opposite and complementary. He is the man best equipped to fight evil in the universe and in society, and to foster good. The union of such close blood relatives as a brother and sister, and sometimes even a father and daughter, far from being a pornographic or incestuous act, would be the most sacred form of marriage. This custom was combatted by Christianity and eliminated by Islam.[27]

Accepting that the prohibition of incest is the only truly universal rule among all the customs and beliefs held by humankind, Lévi-Strauss goes on to explain this universality by the fact that it applies to sexual life – which is the highest expression of man's 'animal nature'. The sexual

26 See C. Herrenschmidt, 'Le xwêtôdas ou "mariage incestueux" en Iran ancien', in P. Bonte, ed., *Épouser au plus proche. Inceste, prohibition et stratégies matrimoniales autour de la Méditerranée* (Paris, Éditions de l'EHESS, 1994).

27 Cf. M. Godelier, *The Metamorphoses of Kinship*, trans. N. Scott (London and New York, Verso, 2012), pp. 380–5, 461.

instinct, he argues, is the only instinct 'requiring the stimulation of another person'.[28]

From this Lévi-Strauss deduces that *'the change [from nature to culture] can and must* necessarily take place in the field of sexual life above any other.'[29] Once again, we cannot accept such a claim. We now know that, long before the appearance of *Homo sapiens sapiens* (120,000 BCE) and even before that of Neanderthal man (around 300,000 BCE), fire had already been domesticated by the ancestors of these species. And fire is the first sign of the radical separation between the animal state and protohumans.

Animals eat their food raw and are afraid of fire. Fire is a weapon and a tool. It enabled protohumans to protect themselves from animals and from the cold, and to penetrate new regions and exploit plants and animals that are inedible until they have been cooked. But above all, fire encouraged the ancestors of man to create, around their hearths, places where food was cooked and distributed, places of sharing and therefore reciprocity. All that must have had enormous consequences for the organization of protohuman groups, adding to the effects of the domestication of the 'sexual instinct', subject to rules and taboos. But in 1947, Lévi-Strauss was not ready to write the first volumes of his Mythology series (1964), or to carry out the structural analysis of the Amerindian myths concerning the origin of fire.

Lévi-Strauss goes on to examine the explanations for the origin of the incest taboo advanced by his predecessors. These he divides into three groups. First, those who, like Morgan or H. J. S. Maine, thought that the prohibition stems from social and rational reflection on the harmful consequences of consanguineal unions. He rejects this explanation, underscoring that these consequences are not recognized or understood by the innumerable peoples practicing marriage between very close relatives. Furthermore, since the end of the Paleolithic era, in aid of improving the vegetable or animal species they have domesticated, they

---

28 *The Elementary Structures of Kinship*, p. 12. This claim should have led him to examine both heterosexual and homosexual forms of desiring others. Lévi-Strauss did not do this because including homosexuality would have contributed nothing to his demonstration. In addition, children's survival depends on the intervention of others, of the adults that feed and care for them. The sexual instinct is therefore not the only instinct that requires 'another person'.

29 Ibid.; my emphasis.

have cross-bred very closely related individuals. It is not from this type of experience that humanity could have acquired the notion of prohibiting incest.

The second group, represented primarily by Edvard Westermarck and Havelock Ellis, had developed the thesis that there was in human nature an instinctive reaction of horrified repugnance at the idea of sexual congress with close relatives. So, Lévi-Strauss asks himself: why the ubiquitous laws against something that human nature already finds repugnant? And, referring to psychoanalysis, he recalls that it would be just the opposite, since everyone can spontaneously feel incestuous desires.

There remains the third group of authors, like Spencer or John Lubbock; but Émile Durkheim is the main target here, because he alone explained the origin of the incest taboo by purely social causes, like Lévi-Strauss. For Durkheim, this prohibition was a holdover from archaic beliefs that can still be found among the Aboriginal peoples of Australia. To them blood is the sacred symbol of a shared clan and totemic identity. These beliefs mean that the menstrual blood of the clan's women is subject to very powerful taboos. This would have obliged men to look for a wife in the other clans, where the women's blood and the clan totem were not taboo to them. For Durkheim, then, the prohibition of incest derived from the necessity of exogamy.

For Lévi-Strauss, it is the opposite. It is the prohibition of incest that forces men to look outside the family for a possible spouse, whether or not there are clans and inter-clan exchanges. Furthermore, Lévi-Strauss wonders, how could such particular beliefs – referring, according to Durkheim, to a very distant time in human evolution, of which the Australian Aborigines were for him the last vestiges – explain the universal presence of the incest taboo in societies and at times that do not share these beliefs? Since these pseudo-historical and psychological explanations are not based on evidence of any kind, it remains 'to discover what profound and omnipresent causes could account for the regulation of the relationships between the sexes in every society and age'.[30]

The causes of the prohibition of incest can be found only by exploring 'those functions which are still current and are verifiable by observation'.[31]

---

30  Ibid., p. 23.
31  Ibid.

Lévi-Strauss thus spends the next eight chapters defining these functions, challenging himself, as it were, to explain that which all scholars before him – anthropologists, sociologists, philosophers – had failed to understand and which most anthropologists had even given up trying to explain.[32]

Lévi-Strauss's explanation can be summed up in the following theses:

– the prohibition of incest results in exogamous social groups;

– exogamy makes it necessary to exchange. Exchange is therefore based on the prohibition of incest;

– the prohibition of incest being imposed on everyone, exchange between families must of necessity be reciprocal;

– reciprocal exchange is thus the common basis of all modes of marriage and of the family institution;

– but what is exchanged? The basic fact is that it is the men who exchange the women, and not vice versa. A tie of reciprocity is created between the men by means of women, who are not partners in this exchange but the objects exchanged.

This is, to my mind, the heart of the theory of kinship as developed by Lévi-Strauss at that time. It constitutes a core of theoretical propositions that have nurtured kinship theory down to the present day and brought research to take an irreversible step forward. For more than half a century they have influenced the entire field of kinship studies, through the discoveries they have promoted as well as the criticisms they have prompted, some of which, as we will see, have been completely justified.

But Lévi-Strauss continued his demonstration into a second phase. This time he would use an example that would allow him to fit into his theory such well-known facts as cross-cousin marriage, which would receive a new meaning – the true meaning, according to Lévi-Strauss. The example he used was that of dual organization, found in numerous parts of the world. The simplest formula for a society organized

---

32 Lévi-Strauss is referring to Robert Lowie, who in his famous work, *Primitive Society*, ultimately renounced giving an explanation of the incest taboo, writing that 'it is not a function of the ethnologist but of the biologist and psychologist to explain why man has so deep-rooted a horror of incest.' Lévi-Strauss also quotes Brenda Seligman, who said: 'It may be that it is impossible to explain or to trace the origin of any human custom that is universal; perhaps the most we can do is to correlate it with certain other conditions' ('The Incest Taboo as a Social Regulation', *Sociological Review* 27, n° 1 [1935], pp. 75–93). See *The Elementary Structures of Kinship*, pp. 24–5.

according to a dual principle is that of a society divided into two exogamous moieties that exchange women with each other from one generation to the next. Men in moiety A marry women in moiety B, and vice versa: men in moiety B marry the sisters or daughters of men in moiety A.

These systems – and they are not the only ones – divide cousins into two categories. The first contains the children of Ego's father's brothers and those of Ego's mother's sisters, as well as Ego and Ego's brothers and sisters. Anthropologists call these parallel cousins (//) and they are said to be assimilated to siblings (// = Si). Because they are (as) brothers and sisters, they cannot be spouses. On the other hand, children of the father's sister (FZ) and of the mother's brother (MB) are classified as what we call cross cousins, and these are potential spouses. In a society divided into two exogamous moieties where the same alliances are repeated from one generation to the next, cross cousins are not only possible spouses, they are the prescribed spouses.

We see, then, that the children of two brothers or two sisters cannot marry each other because they are also each other's brothers and sisters, and their union would come under the incest taboo.[33] But the children of a brother and a sister can marry each other. How does the distinction between these two categories of cousin come about, what is it based on? It depends on the fact of starting with Ego, and changing sexes or not when going from the direct line to the collateral line.[34] If there is no change of sex (father's brother, mother's sister), the cousins are assimilated to brothers and sisters. If there is a change of sex (father's sister, mother's brother), they become potential affines before becoming real ones. Marriage between cross cousins is thus a privileged example, because it makes it possible directly to see that 'reciprocity is behind all marriages'.[35] It demonstrates the social – and not the biological or psychological – reasons for the prohibition of incest, since from a genetic point of view,

---

33  In a great many kinship systems that distinguish in $G^0$ between Ego's parallel and cross cousins, kinship terminology in $G^{+1}$ uses the same term for father and father's brothers (FB=F), and the same term for mother and mother's sisters (MZ=M). Which means that in $G^0$, the children of Ego's fathers and mothers are Ego's brothers and sisters, parallel cousins being assimilated to siblings.

34  *The Elementary Structures of Kinship*, pp. 128–9.

35  Ibid., p. 143.

parallel and cross cousins stand at the same genetic distance from Ego, and yet the first are forbidden spouses while the second are preferred if not prescribed. A biological equivalence is not a social equivalence.

The connection between the prohibition of incest and cross-cousin marriage can thus be seen directly. The prohibition determines whom one cannot marry, but also whom one can and even must marry.[36] The two principles, one negative and the other positive, are closely linked. One has no meaning without the other. Both are pieces of a global structure. The conclusion must then be drawn that parallel cousins are forbidden and cross cousins prescribed for the same reason. And the reason for these complementary oppositions and reciprocal exclusions is that they are the conditions of exchange. Exchange is thus the basis of these oppositions, which have a *structural* character.[37] In the final analysis, exchange is the *raison d'être* of the incest prohibition. It reveals its true nature because it is at once the origin and the purpose.

It is in this way that cross-cousin marriage appears as 'the elementary formula for marriage by exchange',[38] and this will illuminate all the analyses Lévi-Strauss devotes to his study of the 'elementary structures of kinship', that is, of the kinship systems that use the formulas of restricted exchange or generalized exchange, all of which entail one form or another of cross-cousin marriage. Cross-cousin marriage thus shows that, when it comes to marriage, one must always give and receive, give in order to receive.[39] If I can obtain a wife (I = a man), it is always because another man, in the position of father or brother, has given her up.[40] And that is true in all societies and at all times, including our time and 'modern societies'.[41]

At the end of his analysis of cross-cousin marriage, Lévi-Strauss would feel justified in saying that, before him, 'its full significance ha[d]

---

36  Ibid., p. 119.

37  Ibid., pp. 128–9. Lévi-Strauss stresses that 'the idea that kinship must be interpreted as a structural phenomenon, and not simply as the result of a juxtaposition of terms and customs, is not new. Goldenweiser asserted it' (pp. 124–5); cf. A. Goldenweiser, 'Remarks on the Social Organization of the Crow', *American Anthropologist* 15 (1913).

38  Ibid., p. 129.

39  Ibid., p. 131.

40  Ibid., p. 62.

41  Ibid., pp. 129–30.

never been clearly perceived,[42] since his analysis had made it possible to discover – without resorting to speculation about the evolution of humanity – the true nature of the prohibition of incest and the very essence of marriage which, in all its forms, is marriage by exchange. And he would reiterate his method:

> we have been careful to eliminate all historical speculation, all research into origins, and all attempts to reconstruct a hypothetical order in which institutions succeeded one another. By according cross-cousin marriage the prime position in our demonstration we have postulated neither its former universality nor its relative anteriority with respect to other forms of marriage.[43]

Lévi-Strauss would go on to underscore the idea that cross-cousin marriage is a specific feature of not only dual organizations and systems with exogamous moieties. The parallel–cross distinction is present in numerous types of kinship systems that do not have moieties. The parallel–cross distinction merely needs to exist for exchange to be possible, without the necessity to re-group into exogamous moieties. The reciprocity principle can thus function in two forms: either in the form of the simple selection of certain kinship relations that authorize or forbid marriage between the individuals, or in the form of the constitution of two groups that function as 'marriage classes' with reciprocal exchange of spouses.

It will no doubt be clear that the analysis was conducted without taking into account the second component of any kinship system, which

---

42 Ibid., p. 121. Before Lévi-Strauss, some, like Rivers, went as far as to say that cross-cousin marriage is a meaningless institution, considering it as an unexplained relic from the past. Cf. W. H. R. Rivers, 'Marriage of Cousins in India', *Journal of the Royal Asiatic Society of Great Britain and Ireland* (July 1907), pp. 623–4; cf. *The Elementary Structures of Kinship*, p. 450.

43 Ibid., pp. 142–3. Frazer had intuited the relationship between cross-cousin marriage and marriage by sister exchange, but he believed they were two stages in the forms of society that followed each other once humans had renounced the sexual promiscuity of their primitive animal state. This promiscuity, he believed, was followed by marriage between consanguineous kin and then marriage between groups, followed by marriage by exchange and finally marriage between cross-cousins in 'dual organizations'. We can see why the evolutionism of anthropology's founders, Morgan and Tylor, quickly brought the development of the discipline to a halt.

is the calculation of descent. All kinship systems combine the two axes, descent and alliance. It will be remembered that, before Lévi-Strauss, Anglo-Saxon anthropologists had stressed the analysis of descent modes while often neglecting modes of alliance. Lévi-Strauss stepped into the breach and, from his demonstration that every kinship system rests on some form of exchange, concluded that 'the nature of descent is a secondary characteristic of kinship systems',[44] underlining that 'the mode of descent never constitutes an essential feature of a kinship system.'[45] The crucial component of alliance is exchange, and not descent. Whether the mode of calculation is patrilineal or matrilineal, the formal structure of the systems remains the same.

That is a fundamental point in the theory, with which I deeply disagree and to which I will return. But what was meant in France at the time by '*filiation*' (the word Lévi-Strauss originally uses )? Two different things. On the one hand, the relation within the family between children and their parents, their father and mother. And on the other hand, where there are broader groups of kin than the family, extending to lineages, clans, moieties, etc., the ties of the members of these groups to a founding ancestor – either a man or a woman, and depending on one case or the other, descent was supposed to go through one line and along one axis, through the men or through the women, and therefore formed a patrilineal or a matrilineal system.

The Anglo-Saxons used the term 'descent' for what the French called '*filiation*'. Circa 1950, however, they increasingly began to use two words to designate the two meanings of the French word. 'Descent' was reserved for the modes connecting the descendants of a common ancestor through the men, through the women or through both, and 'filiation' was pressed into service to designate the ties between children and their father and mother within the family where they were born and raised.

Lévi-Strauss, for his part, continued to use the term '*filiation*' with its two meanings, which earned him Leach's unusual and inappropriate accusation of confusing the one with the other. Lévi-Strauss's sharply disdainful response was published in *L'Homme* in 1977.

Having cleared up this point, we understand what Lévi-Strauss was talking about when he said that the mode of descent (*filiation*) *never*

---

44  Ibid., p. 404.
45  Ibid., p. 408.

*constitutes an essential feature of a kinship system.* He rapidly mentions the two most widely known descent principles of his time: patrilineal and matrilineal. Referring to Swanton,[46] he stresses that, in either case, the line not chosen for the calculation of descent always plays a role, without going so far as to formulate the notion of 'complementary filiation' that would be developed a few years later by Meyer Fortes. He also mentions the notion of 'double descent' first advanced by Murdock in 1942,[47] considering that it was a catch-all notion but that some cases did exist.[48] He notes that, in human groups, patri- and matrilineal systems are not equivalent, except on a formal level. In human society 'they have neither the same place nor the same rank . . . To be unmindful of this would be to overlook the basic fact that it is men who exchange women, and not vice versa . . . [It is] a complete misappreciation of the initial situation, which includes women among the objects in the men's transactions.'[49]

The universal political and social superiority of men over women would explain two empirical observations, according to Lévi-Strauss. On the one hand, the very small number of societies that are both matrilineal and matrilocal, plus the preponderance of patrilocal residence, attesting to the fundamental asymmetry between the sexes. And on the other hand, the fact that 'societies attaining this level [where political power takes precedence over other forms of organization] of political organization tend to generalize the paternal right.'[50] He says nothing about the stage in which societies 'accede' to political organization. As there is no society without some form of government, in the absence of further explanation Lévi-Strauss's vision of the political is not only unclear, it is disputable.

Here we already see appearing clearly one of the major limits of Lévi-Strauss's theory of kinship: his incapacity or refusal to recognize that

---

46 J. R. Swanton, 'The Social Organization of American Tribes', *American Anthropologist*, vol. 7, n°1905; Lévi-Strauss, *The Elementary Structures of Kinship*, p. 104.

47 G. P. Murdock, 'Double Descent', *American Anthropologist* 42, n° 4 (1942), pp. 555–61; *The Elementary Structures of Kinship*, pp. 104–5.

48 In the second edition of *The Elementary Structures*, Lévi-Strauss would consider this an erroneous assessment. But paradoxically, while he mentions the new importance of cognatic systems with undifferentiated descent reckoning in kinship studies, he has little to say about bilineal systems.

49 *The Elementary Structures of Kinship*, pp. 115, 117.

50 Ibid., p. 116.

descent plays a role that is different, to be sure, from alliance, but which is just as crucial to the functioning of kinship systems, to the interplay and the stakes entailed in the kinship relations they produce. The descent axis is the axis of transmission, and it does more than ensure the reproduction from one generation to the next of former alliances or the production of new ones. It is the axis of transmission because it ensures the formation and continuity of the different types of kin groups (lineages, clans, houses, etc.) engendered by the application of the various descent principles that have been identified and which are now recognized; these principles, once installed, become the internal mental armatures of these groups and thus serve to produce and reproduce them. The armatures support and convey the transmission of the statuses, functions, and immaterial and material assets that will circulate between the generations and be divided among the descendants in different ways, depending on whether one is dealing with men or women, with first-born or last-born, and so on. For instance, land rights will perhaps be passed on through the women and religious functions through the men, or vice versa, as in the case of ambilineal systems, among the Yakö of Africa, for example.

To posit that 'something' that comes from a founding ancestor 'descends', that it circulates between the generations *only* through the women (matrilineal principle) or *only* through the men (patrilineal principle) is a cultural coup and a source of imaginary representations that will serve as norms for the production of social relations; the latter, on the other hand, will not be purely imaginary. Nevertheless, all the kinship relations engendered by the application of a descent principle will be 'marked', imbued with the *imaginary* character of this principle. For instance, in the Trobriand Islands, a 'matrilineal' society, the blood that flows in the bodies of both men and women is 'female' blood, which comes from the founding woman ancestor of the clan into which these men and women were born. In this case, only the women engender children; the men's semen merely nourishes the foetus, it does not engender it. When the child is born, it belongs to its mother's clan and is placed under the authority of the mother's brother, the maternal uncle. In contrast, for the Baruya of New Guinea, a patrilineal society, the child belongs to its father's clan. The man's semen makes the foetal bones and flesh, with the exception of the nose and the fingers and toes, which are completed in the mother's womb by the Sun, a god. For the Baruya, women do not engender their children. Their uterus is a 'bag' into which the man projects his semen. He alone (together with the Sun) is the genitor of his children. Of course, there is no biological 'truth' in these representations.

Descent principles are thus, in their very essence, cultural constructions and just as 'artificial' and no more or less 'arbitrary' than the division of cousins into two categories, parallel and cross, whose purpose and consequence is that the first are not permitted spouses and the second are. Their aim and effect are to engender groups of individuals related by kin ties, along with the attendant rights and obligations, which are key issues in the lives of individuals and the group to which they belong and which they are responsible for continuing.

So why does Lévi-Strauss so underrate the importance of descent? Why does he turn a blind eye to it in his theoretical analysis? The answer lies in the role he assigns to the incest taboo in the transition from the state of nature to that of culture, which leads him to shift descent (*filiation* for Lévi-Strauss) to the side of nature and biology. Here is what he says:

> But culture, although it is powerless before descent, becomes aware of its rights, and of itself, with the completely different phenomenon of [alliance], in which nature for once has not already had the last word.[51]

Descent is thus pulled toward 'consanguinity', in the sense of a set of biological relations between humans which lie in the domain of nature. That could correspond to one of the senses of the word *filiation* as used by Lévi-Strauss, to the biological ties that connect children to the man and woman who conceived them. But it has nothing to do with the imaginary relationships men and women are supposed to have with their common ancestor. Let us continue:

> the incest prohibition expresses the transition from the natural fact of consanguinity to the cultural fact of alliance.[52]

---

51 Ibid., p. 31. This is a finely turned phrase, but it would be futile to look to Lévi-Strauss for all the phenomena on which nature has had the final word.

52 Ibid., p. 30.

As I have just shown, the invention and implementation of a descent principle correspond precisely to a passage from the natural fact of consanguinity to a fact of culture, namely to the attribution of a different role – attached to one sex rather than the other – in the transmission of a key component, most often imaginary and therefore impossible to verify, of the identity of individuals and of a group. Moreover, Lévi-Strauss himself showed that 'the transition from nature to culture is determined by man's ability to think of biological relationships as systems of oppositions: opposition between the men who own and the women who are owned; opposition among the latter between wives who are acquired and sisters and daughters who are given away.'[53]

We see that the ability to imbue biological relations with opposite social meanings here merely serves to demonstrate once again that this ability is restricted to men, since in the text the word 'man' obviously does not mean mankind, made up of men and women. But before looking at what Lévi-Strauss has to say about the superiority of men to women, let us come back to the deep-seated reasons for his blindness to the key role of descent. This failure is the direct consequence of the role he attributed to the prohibition of incest. This prohibition, he declares, is 'the fundamental step because of which, by which, but above all in which, the transition from nature to culture is accomplished . . . Before it, culture is still nonexistent; with it, nature's sovereignty over man is ended. It brings about and is in itself the advent of a new order.'[54]

Having recourse exclusively to the prohibition of incest to explain the passage from nature to culture and the 'hold' of culture over nature, Lévi-Strauss could no longer 'see', could no longer observe the specific cultural role descent principles play in turning biological relations into social and cultural realities. A second consequence was that he could no longer see that incest subverts and destroys descent and alliance relations alike. Because of this, many of his criticisms of Malinowski's and Brenda Seligman's explanations of incest are invalid. One example will suffice. A man who has sexual intercourse with his daughter in a modern-day European monogamous family not only places his daughter and his wife in the position of rivals and damages the intergenerational relations of solidarity and authority that ensure family cohesion, but, by devaluing

---

53  Ibid., p. 136.
54  Ibid., pp. 24–5.

his wife in favour of his daughter, he also compromises relations with his wife's family, in other words the alliance he had contracted with this family through marriage.

In short, incest subverts at the same time and in equal proportion relations of alliance between families and relations within the family, what are called relations of 'consanguinity'. Lévi-Strauss has shown this for alliance, Malinowski demonstrated it for 'consanguinity'. The two theories are complementary – and both are necessary.

Lévi-Strauss's partial approach consequently produced an innovative but partial theory of kinship. If today we were to venture a general theory of kinship, as was his aim in 1947, we would need to keep his analysis of the fundamental features of alliance and add, among other things, an analysis of the fundamental characteristics of the descent principles as well as an analysis of representations of the process by which children are conceived, in which each society expresses the way it represents to itself what a child receives from its ascendants and their alliances.

Because the descent axis involves specific and fundamental stakes, we can explain why kinship terminologies have the same structure whatever the descent principle, patrilineal, matrilineal or other. Let us take the example of the so-called 'Iroquois' terminologies, which distinguish parallel and cross-cousins in $G^0$ and in $G^{+1}$ and merge father and father's brothers under the same term, the same being true for mother and mother's sisters, under a different same term. But, unlike the Dravidian and Australian systems, which also distinguish parallel and cross-cousins, this terminology does not have any rule indicating that marriage between cross-cousins is prescribed or preferred.

This type of terminology is widespread in Melanesia and North America. Yet the Iroquois have a matrilineal descent principle, whereas in Melanesia, among the Baruya for instance, whose kinship terminology has the same structure as that of the Iroquois, the descent rule is patrilineal. That proves descent carries other social stakes than simply alliance, and is even largely independent of the latter. But descent cannot be disconnected from alliance – owing to the fact of the incest taboo – any more than alliance can be disconnected from descent, since the latter ensures that at each generation it will be possible to contract new alliances or renew old ones.

Alliances enable descent, and descent imposes alliances. Far from being a secondary characteristic of kinship, as Lévi-Strauss claimed, descent is therefore just as much a 'universal rule' of kinship as the incest taboo, which he set forth as the 'only universal rule', the only one that permitted the passage from nature to culture, the only one that could transform nature into culture. Descent is the second universal rule, because a descent principle must necessarily be at work for there to be a kinship system.

There are very few descent rules, but there must always be *one* in order for a kinship system to come into existence. Likewise, however the prohibition of incest may be defined and whatever may be its field of application, there must always be *one* form of incest taboo at work for a kinship system to exist. It is only on condition that both principles are held to be equally crucial that a general theory of kinship is possible. The prohibition of incest plays a positive role because of what it excludes, which creates the obligation to exchange. Descent plays a positive role because of what it includes, which channels and regulates transmissions.

One of the essential stakes involved in descent is to determine to whom belong the children to be born of the alliances between one group of descendants and other groups: will the children belong to their mother's group or to that of their father? In other words, will it be the daughters who will produce new members for the group, or will it be their brothers? Will the children of a brother and those of a sister inherit the same or different things? Each time, it is the society's conception of the role and contributions of the man and the woman to its functioning and perpetuation that is engaged, and this conception has an existential value for all members of the society. Clearly, the choice of a descent principle structures kin groups that its implementation contributes to engender and reproduce, and thus serves as a line for the transmission, to one generation after another, of the different components of society – material, immaterial, or (in the eyes of other cultures) imaginary – the combination of which defines the social and cultural identity of these groups in their own eyes.

Having shown that descent is a constant that is just as universal as the prohibition of incest, and that both are basic rules of all known (or possible) kinship systems, we can now resume our examination of *The Elementary Structures of Kinship* and benefit from the analyses Lévi-Strauss devoted to the 'universe of rules'. But I will 'expand' his conclusions so as to include our discussion of descent, for culture, contrary to what he claimed, was not 'powerless before descent'.

For the production of kinship relations to have been and to be possible, there must be mental operations that call upon 'certain fundamental structures of the human mind', structures that are present in all humans, at all times and in all societies, and therefore structures that are universal and verifiable by one and all. According to Lévi-Strauss, it is necessary that:

– the notion of *rule* be understood, and that people's relations with each other and with nature be governed by rules;

– the notion of *reciprocity* be understood, and serve as a principle for the exchange of gifts;

– the *synthetic character of gift-giving* be recognized, that is, 'that the agreed transfer of a valuable from one individual to another makes these individuals partners, and adds a new quality to the valuable transferred'.

These notions are universal because they belong to a 'common basis of mental structures and schemes of sociability for all cultures, each of which draws on certain elements for its own particular model'.[55] And because they are universal and depend on fundamental structures of the human mind, these mental schemata of sociability are found in every child that is born, each of whom will use them in the way its specific culture demands. In an eloquent passage, Lévi-Strauss writes:

> Every newborn child comes equipped, in the form of adumbrated mental structures, with all the means ever available to mankind to define its relations to the world in general and its relations to others. But these structures are exclusive . . . each type of social organization represents a choice, which the group [society] imposes and perpetuates.[56]

In positing the existence of mental structures and sociability schemata common to all humans, Lévi-Strauss shows that the diversity of forms of society and culture, each relative to its own time and place, does not exclude, but on the contrary, presupposes, the universality of the fundamental structures of the human mind. Absolute relativism is

---

55 Ibid., pp. 84–5.

56 Ibid., p. 93. In this passage, Lévi-Strauss rejects all those who, like Lévy-Bruhl, asserted that the adult mind of primitive humans corresponded roughly to the infantile mind of children in civilized societies.

meaningless here, for, above and beyond whatever distinguishes and separates cultures and forms of society, there are mental structures and schemata of sociability at work in all societies and at all times. This means that each society presents a singular combination of universal and particular structures, which are not opposed, since the first are the condition of existence of the second and are at the same time the particular form these assume when they turn into social realities.

Let us examine the three conditions set out above:

1. The first condition is that the notion of *rule* must be understood in order to live together, and that life in society must be governed by rules. That much is obvious; the prohibition of incest as the only universal rule is not. We have seen that, for the production of any kinship system, two universal rules must exist and work together. But many other rules are necessary as well, and these make up the conditions of human social and cultural life. We need only to mention the rules of the division of labour between the sexes, the rules of language, etc. Some rules are a matter of common consent; others are not, or not completely. We will leave aside for the time being the problem of the 'unconscious' nature of these rules.

2. The second condition necessary for exchange is, as we have said, that the notion of *reciprocity* be understood and that it serve as the principle for the exchange of gifts between humans. Here Lévi-Strauss continues the analyses presented by Mauss in his essay *The Gift*,[57] but his use is partial. Mauss showed that a gift cannot be understood in isolation. A gift is always the first act in a sequence of three acts that each time establishes a different relationship between two partners, who can be individuals and/or groups. To give is to detach something of oneself in order to offer it to another. It is to share something of oneself with another. But it can be a gift only if the other accepts. If the other refuses, the gift is not made and the rejection of the gift can give rise to a negative, hostile relationship between the two parties involved. But if the gift is accepted, a new relationship is created between the two actors. By accepting, the receiver finds himself in the obligation to give in turn. To give in turn is the third moment in this three-act sequence that constitutes gift-giving. But to give in turn does not mean to 'pay back', as

---

57 M. Mauss, *The Gift: The Form and Reason for Exchange in Archaic Societies*, trans. W. D. Halls, foreword by M. Douglas (New York and London, W. W. Norton, 1990).

many assert when they project the logic of commercial transactions onto that of gift-giving.

To give in turn is to create for the original giver a debt that re-establishes the social equivalence of the two partners even as it obliges them subsequently to engage in the reciprocal giving of gifts and/or services, which are not meant to erase the debt. All that is expected is that the debt will 'die out' over time. The creation of reciprocal debts means that each party is at once superior to the other as giver (>) and indebted to the other as receiver (<):

$$(a \Rightarrow b) \rightarrow (a \approx b)$$

Commodities that are bought and sold are detached from the seller and attached to the buyer and are therefore fully alienated. By contrast, things given are both alienated – because they have been transferred to someone else – and not alienated, because something of the giver remains attached to the thing given and entails the obligation in the person who accepts the gift to give in turn to the one who made the original gift.

Following this analysis of the basic structure of gift exchange, Mauss goes on to distinguish between non-agonistic and agonistic giving, such as the practice of potlatch among the Indians of the American Northwest (Kwakiutl, Tlingit, etc.) described by Boas, or the *Kula* among the Melanesian Trobriand Islanders and their neighbours, described by Malinowski. Mauss was interested especially in agonistic gifts; the rest interested him less. He glosses over, as examples of non-agonistic gifts, exchanges of women, goods and ritual services between the two moieties that make up certain societies in Australia and North America, and leaves it at that. Lévi-Strauss, by contrast, was interested in non-agonistic gifts insofar as, for him, kinship is based on the exchange of women between and for men, who are the social and political powerholders.

The logic of agonistic giving is not the same because the aim is not the same. In the case of potlatch, for example, several clans vie by means of their headman or chief for a function, a title, a rank held by another clan but which has come up for grabs owing to the death of its holder. The goal is to occupy a hierarchical rank. Giving thus becomes a weapon of 'war' in an all-out competition at the end of which one clan will come out on top and the others will be subordinated to it. The logic is to give more than any rival can possibly give in turn, or to give in turn more than the other or others have given. ('More' is both a quantitative and a qualitative notion; it can for example mean the sacrifice of slaves or the ostentatious destruction of valuables, etc.) Here giving is not designed, as before, to re-establish the balance and equality of status between the partners, but to crush one's rivals and show their non-equivalence. Agonistic giving is thus practised in societies based at once on reciprocal relations and on relations of hierarchy and subordination. Lévi-Strauss could have used Mauss's analyses of agonistic giving to shed light on the hierarchical relations between nobles, commoners, slaves, etc. in chiefdoms and societies based on generalized exchange such as the Kachin, the Naga, etc. But he did not do this.

One last point here. Mauss indicates in passing that, in potlatch societies, sacred things never entered into the potlatch and were kept as clan treasures. And then he drops the subject, even though it is of crucial importance – something I analysed in *The Enigma of the Gift*.[58] These material and immaterial goods that are neither given nor sold are kept, to be transmitted. They are withheld or even withdrawn from circulation in view of being given to existing or potential descendants. And what is kept for transmission carries and conveys from one generation to the next the basic elements of the identity of a person and/or a group, and attests to its origin – historical or mythical, imaginary or real. These descent relations are the principal vectors of gifts and passages. Lévi-Strauss neglected their importance for as long as he made alliance the only basis of kinship. But when in 1975 he took a closer look at a form of kinship whose existence he had glimpsed, without taking much interest in it – the 'house' system – he was led to recognize that to transmit means keeping in order to give; to exchange means giving in order to receive.

3. We still need to examine the last condition presented by Lévi-Strauss as a prerequisite for the exchange of women between men, but also for all non-agonistic giving. These reciprocal exchanges imply the understanding that giving makes the giver and receiver partners, and adds this new, purely social value to the value of the object of the gift. His analysis of this point is thoroughly pertinent and requires no further comment.

---

58 M. Godelier, *The Enigma of the Gift*, trans. N. Scott (Chicago, University of Chicago Press; Cambridge, Polity Press, 1998).

But he goes even further. For him, and he is right, the social is inseparable from the *mental*, and no social relation can exist without the intervention of thought processes, which spring from the fundamental structures
of the human mind. When discussing the incest taboo or the division of
cousins into parallel and cross, we saw that biological relations are
conceived as oppositions. To oppose is simultaneously to exclude and
include on the basis of the very principles that structure the system of
oppositions. Individuals acquire the characteristic of being available or
unavailable spouses, not from the fact that they possess a particular essence
that is different, but because they stand in 'a certain system of antithetical
relationships, the role of which is to establish inclusions by means of exclusions, and vice versa, because this is precisely the one means of establishing
reciprocity, which is the reason for the whole undertaking'.[59]

But to think is not only to perceive existing relations or to imagine
ones that do not yet exist, it is also to apprehend or imagine relationships between relationships. It is this process that engenders the bipar-
tite division of cousins into parallel and cross.

> Before the institutions, and as a condition of their existence, there is
> in fact the apprehension of a relationship, or more exactly the appre-
> hension of the opposition between two relationships [which] concern
> both the direct line and the collateral line, and the difference emerges
> from the fact that these two lines can be linked through relatives of
> the one sex, or relatives of different sexes. Why is this difference seen
> as an opposition? Positive and negative phenomena mean nothing by
> themselves, but form parts of a whole . . . cross-cousins are recom-
> mended for the same reasons that parallel cousins are excluded.[60]

For Lévi-Strauss, relationships take precedence over the terms they
bring together, and the representation of these relationships logically
precedes their realization. What was a logical condition then becomes a
part of the immanent structure of the imagined relationships, and if
these come about, it becomes a part of the immanent structure of the
real relationships. 'Kinship must be interpreted as a structural phenomenon, and not simply as the result of a juxtaposition of terms and

---

59 *The Elementary Structures of Kinship*, p. 114.
60 Ibid., p. 129.

customs.'[61] The formula applies not only to kinship but to all human institutions, which are 'structures whose whole – in other words the regulating principle – can be given before the parts'.[62]

To take the example of kinship again: 'What should [be] done . . . [is] to treat cross-cousin marriage, rules of exogamy, and dual organization as so many examples of one basic structure. This structure should [be] interpreted in terms of its total characteristics, instead of being broken up into bits and pieces and set alongside one another in a juxtaposition which . . . would have no intrinsic significance.'[63]

We have seen that exchange was the *raison d'être* of these oppositions and institutions. The exchange relationship was therefore given in advance and independently of the persons or things exchanged. 'We see exchange as a mere aspect of a total structure of reciprocity which (in circumstances still to be specified) was immediately and intuitively apprehended by social man.'[64]

But exchange can be immediately apprehended only because it calls on abstract structures of the human mind. 'Duality, alternation, opposition and symmetry, whether presented in definite forms or in imprecise forms, are basic and immediate data of mental and social reality which should be the starting-point of any attempt at explanation.'[65]

We must therefore go back to deeper structures of the human mind and to more abstract levels: 'The further we penetrate towards the deeper levels of mental life, the more we are presented with structures diminishing in number but increasing in strictness and simplicity.'[66]

At these levels, there can be no differences between the modes of thinking of so-called primitive peoples and those of 'civilized' peoples. This position would guide Lévi-Strauss in his analysis of the structures of mythical thought (as we will see when we examine this aspect of his work). But Lévi-Strauss is not content with affirming the immanence in the human mind of a certain number of fundamental structures that are therefore identical in all human beings. He goes further and, crossing the boundaries of the human and social sciences, asserts that 'the laws of

---

61  Ibid., p. 124.
62  Ibid., p. 100.
63  Ibid., p. 123.
64  Ibid., p. 137.
65  Ibid., p. 136.
66  Ibid., p. 94.

thought – primitive or civilized – are the same as those which are expressed in physical reality and in social reality, which is itself only one of its aspects.' [67]

Generalizations or positions of this sort are normally characteristic of a philosophical undertaking. In adopting this approach, Lévi-Strauss is thus affirming his materialism, which explains the fact that he incorporates a quotation from Friedrich Engels's *Dialectic of Nature*,[68] in which he writes: 'It is, therefore, from the history of nature and human society that the laws of dialectics are abstracted. For they are nothing but the most general laws of these two aspects of historical development, as well as of thought itself.'[69]

The analyses and theses developed by Lévi-Strauss in *The Elementary Structures* lead to a fundamental problem of which he was perfectly aware, that of explanation in the social sciences. What is the role of conscious thought – which is always the thought of singular individuals – and that of the fundamental structures of the human mind – which are shared by everyone – in the elaboration and production of the relationships humans entertain with one another and with their environment, changing relationships which are accompanied by beliefs and customs expressed in the words of many different languages?

Because for social relations to be reproduced by the men and women involved in them, their 'regulating principles' – their logic – must be understood and present in their mind, in their head, in a mental (what in French I term *idéel*) and ideological form, in other words as a set of rules along with beliefs that legitimize these rules. It is through these forms of consciousness and because of them that the principles of a social system present themselves as rules of conduct and action to be followed by those who belong to this system. This mental and ideological form cannot have been placed fully developed in the consciousness of the members of a society by their unconscious. It must have been prepared and 'developed', and that is why it functions as 'a sort of

---

67  Ibid., p. 451.

68  F. Engels, *Dialectic of Nature* (New York, 1940), pp. 26–7. An unfinished work not published in its author's lifetime, a first version, based on photocopies of the manuscripts, was published in the Soviet Union in 1925 in German and in Russian. The French version appeared in 1968 (Paris, Éditions Sociales).

69  *The Elementary Structures of Kinship*, p. 451. Lévi-Strauss was already anxious to point out that his approach was a refutation of 'associationism and idealism' (p. 100).

rationalization,'[70] in the words of Lévi-Strauss, of the solutions this society has chosen (through the theoretical work of certain of its members) in response to the problems it had to solve in order to exist as a society. Therefore, the mental and ideological representations that, in a society, serve to transform the principles regulating its social system into rules of conduct for each of its members cannot but bear the marks of the culture and period in which they were developed.

But why did the same type of kinship system appear several times over in the course of human history, in societies that have never come into historical or geographical contact with each other? As examples, we can cite the case of what are known as 'Dravidian' systems present in South India, Amazonia and Australia; or the so-called 'Eskimo' systems found among the Inuit (the term that has replaced the word 'Eskimo', which the Inuit felt to be derogatory), the Garia of New Guinea, in certain islands of the Indonesian archipelago, in Western Europe and in the European or Europeanized populations of North and South America.

Of course, the appearance several times in the course of history of these different systems implies the implementation everywhere of fundamental structures of the human mind, since these are common to all human beings. But because they are a common feature of all humans, they do not suffice to explain why some humans 'chose' to live in a Dravidian system and others in an 'Eskimo' system. And even less do they explain the fact that several societies made the same choice without ever having come in contact. Did they face the same problems, which led them to choose the same solutions? But what similar problems could have led both the inhabitants of South India and the Amazonian Indians to develop a Dravidian-type system, which distinguishes between parallel and cross-cousins, and prescribes marriage with a matrilateral cross-cousin in India and a bilateral or matrilateral cross-cousin in Amazonia? Anthropological research has made no progress on these questions since *The Elementary Structures*.

There remains the problem of the role played by conscious thought in the development of the principles that gave rise to kinship relations and which took the form of systems. For all anthropologists having spent enough time in the field to understand the nature and functioning of the kinship relations found in the society in which they lived, conscious

---

70  Ibid., p. 108.

thought plays a large role. Lévi-Strauss, who favours Boas's position – that 'social phenomena (language, beliefs, customs, techniques, etc.) had the common characteristic of having been developed by the mind at the level of unconscious thought' – wonders about the truth value of 'some local theory which has been developed by the native as a formulation of his own problems'.[71]

It goes without saying that these 'indigenous' theories do not seek to discover the universal basis of all kinship systems, such as, for example, the prohibition of incest and descent principles. That is not their purpose. But these indigenous theories usually make very clear the regulating principles of the kinship system as it operates in their society. Lévi-Strauss gives several, already well-known examples. Indeed, anthropologists working in Australia at that time were able to observe the spread of section and/or subsection systems among the tribes in the Australian interior. It was around 1932 that this type of system reached the Pintupi,[72] and slightly later arrived among the Ngaanyatjarra.[73] Stanner, who had witnessed the diffusion of the system among the Murinbata, wrote the following, which Lévi-Strauss quotes:

> In fact, it is partly as a theoretical formula that subsections are carried intertribally ... Those who doubt the Aborigines' power of such abstract reasoning can never have heard them expounding to their tribe's fellows how subsections should work, by inference from the theory to the case under attention. In this way an abstraction becomes a flesh-and-blood reality.[74]

The other famous example, also cited by Lévi-Strauss, is that of the people of Ambrym, who twice drew diagrams on the ground to show the anthropologist, Arthur B. Deacon, how a very complex system of apparently six marriage classes worked.[75]

---

71 Ibid.

72 F. Meyers, *Pintupi Country, Pintupi Self: Sentiment, Place and Politics among Western Aborigines* (Washington, DC, Smithsonian Institution Press, 1986).

73 L. Dousset, *Assimilating Identities: Social Networks and the Diffusion of Sections* (Sydney, University of Sydney, 2005; Oceania Monograph, n° 57).

74 W. E. H. Stanner, 'Murinbata Kinship and Totemism', *Oceania* 7, n° 2 (1936–37), p. 202; cf. *The Elementary Structures of Kinship*, p. 125.

75 A. B. Deacon, 'The Regulation of Marriage in Ambrym', *Journal of the Royal Anthropological Institute* 57 (1927), p. 329; cf. *The Elementary Structures of Kinship*, pp.

These two examples suffice to show that the conscious work of the mind plays a major role in the development and diffusion of kinship systems, which are never made up of bits and pieces but are coherent sets of social relationships constructed on the basis of their own logic, which is immanent from the outset. Since the number of types of kinship systems in the world is very limited (around ten),[76] and since all known societies have a kinship system, the hundreds of kinship systems inventoried and described by anthropologists are simply local varieties of one or another of this handful of types of systems known to date.

Finally, I will discuss the last point in Lévi-Strauss's reasoning. Owing to the prohibition of incest, kinship always implies exchange, and it is women who are exchanged by men, never vice versa. This thesis has sparked so much controversy – even today – that I would like to go back and reconstruct the author's demonstration as accurately as possible, so as to clearly bring out its strengths and weaknesses.

Lévi-Strauss starts from what he assumes to be a universal fact: 'political authority, or simply social authority, always belongs to men and ... this masculine priority appears constant ... it ... imposes its model on all aspects of social life.'[77]

Or again: 'But although there is ... this primacy of relationships over the terms which they unite, it should never be overlooked that these terms are human beings, and that the relationship between the sexes is never symmetrical ... To be unmindful of this would be to overlook the basic fact that it is men who exchange women, and not vice versa.'[78]

What are women in regard to men? 'Women are not primarily a sign of social value, but a natural stimulant; and the stimulant of the only instinct the satisfaction of which can be deferred, and consequently the only one for which, in the act of exchange ... the transformation from the stimulant to the sign can take place and, defining by this fundamental process the transformation from nature to culture, assume the character of an institution.'[79]

---

124–6. Lévi-Strauss reproduced one of these diagrams and planned to study the Ambrym system elsewhere. But he never did.

76 Cf. M. Godelier, *Metamorphoses of Kinship*, trans. N. Scott (London and New York, Verso, 2012), pp. 507–9.

77 *The Elementary Structures of Kinship*, pp. 116–17.

78 Ibid., pp. 114–15.

79 Ibid., pp. 62–3.

The woman goes from being a sexual stimulant to being a sign. She is 'on the one hand ... the object of personal desire, thus exciting sexual and proprietorial instincts; and on the other ... the subject of the desire of others ... i.e. the means of binding others through alliance with them.'[80] A sexual stimulant, a sign, the woman is also a valuable asset. Women 'are the most precious possession'.[81] They are even 'the supreme gift among those that can only be obtained in the form of reciprocal prestations'.[82]

Owing to the division of labour between the sexes, marriage, 'in most primitive societies (and also, but to a lesser extent, in the rural classes of our own society) ... is of an entirely different importance, not erotic, but economic'.[83] In such societies, being unmarried or an orphan is a 'calamity'; 'marriage is of vital importance for every individual.'[84]

Nowhere, it should be noted, in *The Elementary Structures* is the woman credited with making children and taking the responsibility for providing descendants, either for her kin group or for that of her husband. She is important because of her participation in the production of material means of existence (food, for instance) and because she can be exchanged to form alliances. She is 'valued' because she is the means of alliance, but not because she is also the means of having descendants. She is of rare value for two reasons. In the first place, because of men's inherent polygamous tendencies, and, in the second place, because 'not all women are equally desirable'. In effect, 'social and biological observation combine to suggest that, in man, [polygamous] tendencies are natural and universal, and that only limitations born of the environment and culture are responsible for their suppression. Consequently, to our eyes, monogamy is not a positive institution, but merely incorporates the limit of polygamy.'[85]

This deep-seated polygamous tendency which exists among all men 'always makes the number of available women seem insufficient';[86] and

---

80  Ibid., p. 496.

81  Ibid., p. 62.

82  Ibid., p. 65. But also realized through purchase, he says elsewhere (p. 139).

83  Ibid., p. 38. Food is another value whose allocation is controlled by the group: 'between [food] and women there is a whole system of real and symbolic relationships' (p. 33).

84  Ibid., p. 39.

85  Ibid., p. 37.

86  Ibid., p. 38.

doubly so because not all the available women are, as I have said, equally desirable. From this, Lévi-Strauss concludes that women can be likened 'to commodities, not only scarce but essential to the life of the group'.[87] Because of this, their distribution among the men requires the intervention of the social group. By establishing a general rule of obedience, 'the group asserts its jural authority over what it legitimately considers an essential valuable'.[88] Such a rule exists, and it organizes relations between the sexes: this is the prohibition of incest. It is a rule 'advantageous' to men since, by obliging them to renounce certain immediately available women – daughters or sisters – it gives them a right to lay claim to a number of women 'which theoretically is as large as possible'.[89]

The prohibition of incest, like exogamy, 'which is its widened social application', means that 'the woman whom one does not take, and whom one may not take, is, for that very reason, offered up'.[90] The women now available for other men – as a consequence of the prohibition of incest – can now be offered in marriage, in other words as gifts, as objects of exchange. '[The] prohibition of marriage within prohibited degrees tends to ensure the total and continuous circulation of the group's most important assets, its wives and its daughters'.[91]

Men thus find themselves in a relationship of domination and opposition with respect to women: 'opposition between the men who own and the women who are owned; opposition among the latter between wives who are acquired and sisters and daughters who are given away; opposition between two types of bond, i.e., bonds of alliance and bonds of kinship'.[92]

Since the exchange of women is the common and fundamental basis of all forms of marriage alliance, what place does the woman have in these exchanges?

The total relationship of exchange which constitutes marriage is not established between a man and a woman, where each owes and

---

87 Ibid., p. 36.
88 Ibid., p. 42.
89 Ibid.
90 Ibid., p. 51.
91 Ibid., p. 479.
92 Ibid., p. 136.

receives something, but between two groups of men, and the woman figures only as one of the objects in the exchange, not as one of the partners between whom the exchange takes place. This remains true even when the girl's feelings are taken into consideration . . . The relationship of reciprocity which is the basis of marriage is not established between men and women, but between men by means of women, who are merely the occasion of this relationship.[93]

Lévi-Strauss goes on to stress the point: 'This view must be kept in all strictness, even with regard to our own society, where marriage appears to be a contract between persons.'

The incest taboo exists in our Western societies as well, of course, and makes marriage (or unions) impossible within the forbidden degrees; but that is a sociological constant and in no way means that marriage is only apparently a contract between the persons involved. But what, for Lévi-Strauss, is the underlying reason for the fact that it is women who are exchanged and not men?

The emergence of symbolic thought must have required that women, like words, should be things that were exchanged . . . But woman could never become just a sign and nothing more, since even in a man's world *she is still a person*, and since in so far as she is defined as a sign she must be recognized as a generator of signs . . . In contrast to words, which have wholly become signs, woman has remained at once a sign and a value.[94]

Since the emergence of symbolic thought is associated with the development of the hominid brain and then that of *Homo sapiens sapiens*, male domination and the exchange of women are both grounded in nature, deep in human nature; hence the following assertion, which is consistent with what was said before:

there is nothing in the exchange of women faintly resembling a reasoned solution to an economic problem (although it can acquire this function in societies which have already learnt in some other way

93  Ibid., pp. 115–16.
94  Ibid., p. 496; my emphasis.

what purchase and sale are). It is *a primitive and indivisible act of awareness* which sees *the daughter or sister* as a *valuable which is offered*, and vice versa the daughter and sister of someone else as a *valuable which may be demanded.*[95]

The exchange of women by men is thus an immediate given of a mind capable of symbolic thought. But since women apparently have the same brain as men and are capable of the same symbolic thought – since as signs, they are also producers of signs (language, judgments, concepts, etc.) – is it thinkable and even possible that the women could exchange the men?

> Even supposing a very hypothetical marriage system in which the man and not the woman were exchanged, it would only be necessary to reverse all the signs in the diagram and the [global] structure would remain unchanged.[96]

This is a very strange remark coming from a sociologist. For even if the formal structure of the exchange relationship were to remain the same, its social structure and content would, on the other hand, be profoundly different. In addition, there is nothing hypothetical about women exchanging men; we know of several matrilineal societies where women exchange their brothers with other women: the Tetum of Timor, the Rhade people in Vietnam, the Nagovisi on Bougainville. Lévi-Strauss should have been pleased about this, for, once again, it is the prohibition of incest that creates the possibility and the necessity to exchange human beings, this time men, between matrilineages. But Lévi-Strauss could not see the possibility that men could be exchanged by women as a real one, since the exchange of women is a primitive and indivisible conscious act associated with the emergence of symbolic thought in the human species. Hence his ironic tone at the idea – or the memory – of a 'reign of women':

> The men's house, by reuniting husbands and brothers-in-law in a ritual and political collaboration, resolves the conflict between 'owners' and strangers. The 'reign of women' is remembered only in

---

95  Ibid., pp. 139–40; my emphasis.
96  Ibid., p. 132.

mythology, an age, perhaps more simply, when men had not resolved the antinomy which is always likely to appear between their roles as takers of wives and givers of sisters.[97]

It should therefore come as no surprise that twenty years later, in the second edition of *The Elementary Structures*, confronted with the accumulation of facts that contradicted his affirmations, Lévi-Strauss came up with a formula that gave him the upper hand once again:

> Certain tribes of South-East Asia, which provide [an approximate] picture of [an] inverse situation, can undoubtedly be used as an example. This would not be to say that in such societies it is the women who exchange the men, but [at best] that men exchange other men by means of women.[98]

His honour was saved; and yet this is not an 'approximate picture', but well and truly the inverse situation, as described by anthropologists having lived and worked in these societies.

To conclude: no one can deny the fact of male domination in probably all known societies, and particularly in the areas of politics and religion. The forms assumed by this domination vary immensely; some are highly oppressive, like those I observed in New Guinea among the Baruya,[99] while others have more to do with complementarity than with dominant-submissive relations. The case of the Na[100] in China or the Nagovisi on Bougainville can be mentioned here. Among the Nagovisi people, the women own the land, they deal with problems of village life and take part in male initiations, something that would be unthinkable for the Baruya. The two activities in which Nagovisi women did not take part before the European colonization were war and long-distance trade – highly dangerous because far from home, besides the risk of being killed and sometimes eaten.[101]

---

97 Ibid., p. 118.

98 Ibid., p. 115, n. 1.

99 M. Godelier, *The Making of Great Men: Male Domination and Power among the New Guinea Baruya*, trans. R. Swyer (Cambridge, Cambridge University Press, 1986).

100 C. Hua, *Une société sans père ni mari. Les Na de Chine* (Paris, Presses Universitaires de France, 1997).

101 J. Nash, *Matriliny and Modernization: The Nagovisi of South Bougainville* (Canberra, Australian National University Press, 1974).

Which brings us to the essential issue. If the final (or the initial) reason for the exchange of women by and for men is the direct and immediate consequence of the emergence of symbolic thought, Lévi-Strauss's argument collapses. Unless we suppose that women do not have the same brain as men, and that they transmit the capacity for symbolic thought only to their sons, not to their daughters. But if this is not the case, and it is not men (nor humankind) that endowed themselves with a brain capable of symbolic thought, then women could and should, in a primitive and indivisible act of consciousness, have apprehended their sons or their brothers as a value to offer, and vice versa, the son and brother of other women as a value to be demanded. And once again, this is not a hypothesis. Some did.

Falling back on the argument of the emergence of symbolic thought thus appears as a coup without any true scientific basis,[102] drawing on the new theories of information and communication in circulation at the time.[103] Hence, we read: 'women themselves are treated as *signs*, which are *misused* when not put to the use reserved to signs, which is to be communicated . . . In this way, language and exogamy represent two solutions to one and the same fundamental situation.'[104]

That being said, we again find ourselves confronted with the same state of affairs: the existence of a relationship of inequality between men and women to the benefit of the men, always and everywhere as far as we know. If the reasons for this are to be found, it is therefore elsewhere than in the fact that we speak and think by means of symbols. Nor can we seek the reason for the inequalities between men and women in the sexual division of labour, which exists in all societies. There are two reasons for this. One is that we must first explain the reasons for the division of labour between the sexes in any society, before advancing this fact as an explanation. The other is that the division of labour between men and women is only one aspect of the roles and functions fulfilled by each sex in the totality of social relations and activities that go into the functioning and reproduction of a given society, and which

---

102 This argument, by no means a scientific one, can have no other origin than an aspect of its author's subjectivity.

103 Lévi-Strauss often referred to Norbert Weiner's work on cybernetics and communication theory. See especially his *Cybernetics: or, Control and Communication in the Animal and the Machine* (Cambridge, MA and New York, John Wiley & Sons, 1948).

104 *The Elementary Structures of Kinship*, p. 496; original emphasis.

characterize it. What we must try to understand in the first place are the reasons for women's exclusion from, or relegation to a minor participation in, two essential functions of social life: governing the society and representing it to neighbouring, friendly and/or hostile societies.[105]

To govern is to exercise in and over society a regime of power, and therefore a form of sovereignty over a territory, its resources and its inhabitants.[106] The form of sovereignty differs according to whether or not there is some form of State to exercise it, but all forms of sovereignty implement what we call, in abstract terms, political-religious relations.

Before the European Enlightenment, no one anywhere could have governed a society without calling on the gods or Heaven for help. And no one anywhere could have governed without the use of armed violence or the threat of its use. Furthermore, the weapons used for hunting or warfare have always been a male monopoly. It is in these directions that we need to look for the grounds of men's universal domination of women.

But the modern era has shown – and continues to show – that change is possible, even if it is slow and partial and always subject to reversals. And if situations change, it is because they are not embedded for all eternity in the lobes of the human brain. Let us not forget that men have had – and still have – the monopoly of armed violence; women have – and will have for a long time to come – the monopoly of making babies (in their bodies) and bringing them into the world. We see that one issue in the control of women, but also in the violence committed against them, is the child: the child that is kept so that it will perpetuate the group's existence, and the child that is given to seal alliances, which also contribute to perpetuating the group. In distinct forms, then, alliance and descent both work to the same end. Later we will see that, faced with the particular form of kin group known as 'houses', Lévi-Strauss will be led to acknowledge this interplay of alliance and descent as being the basis for this type of kinship system at least.

After a systematic examination of the first ten chapters of *The Elementary Structures*, which is necessary if we are to understand the nature of the

---

105 To be sure, there is no ignoring the role played, for instance, by Catherine the Great, Queen Victoria or Indira Gandhi, but it must be remembered that all three governed with the help of men.

106 M. Godelier, *In and Out of the West: Reconstructing Anthropology*, trans. N. Scott (Charlottesville, University of Virginia Press and Verso, 2009).

theoretical approach adopted, we will pass more quickly over the use Lévi-Strauss made of it in analysing the kinship systems of Australia, Birmano-Siberian Asia, China and India. This is a huge geographical zone of incredible sociological and historical diversity, which he chose because he considered it to have 'an extraordinary density of kinship systems answering to the definition of elementary structures. It allows all types to be considered and gives several examples of each type. These examples are the richest and most lucid, and approximate most closely to the demands of a theoretical demonstration.'[107] A bold wager, as I have said. But whatever the limitations of his book, it continues to be read as an essential reference for the study of kinship.

Lévi-Strauss begins his study of the Australian systems by acknowledging his tremendous debt to the work done on Australia by Radcliffe-Brown and his colleagues at the journal *Oceania*, in particular Elkin, Lawrence, Webb and of course Spencer and Gillen before them. Like his predecessors, Lévi-Strauss chooses to base his study on the Kariera and Aranda systems in order to clarify the systems with four sections (Kariera) and eight subsections (Aranda). He says he will attempt to explain the workings of the Murngin system (with eight sections, but which functions like a system with four), which had until then remained unintelligible because it had been interpreted as being governed by restricted exchange whereas, as Lévi-Strauss sets out to show in the following chapter, the Murngin system operates on the principle of generalized exchange.

Before coming to this problem, though, we see Lévi-Strauss pause several times over the nature of sections and subsections. Are they 'marriage classes', as they had been called since Morgan, regulating the exchange of women between the classes and therefore mediating alliance? Or did they, as Radcliffe-Brown claimed, have nothing to do with marriage, prompting his refusal to go on calling them 'marriage classes' and his proposal to call them quite simply moieties, sections and subsections, whose functions he sees as of a more ritual nature?

Let me rapidly review the characteristics of the Kariera and Aranda systems. The Kariera society, a 'tribe' living on the west coast of the Australian continent, has always been divided into two intermarrying moieties, A and B, and two patrilineal moieties, 1 and 2; and each moiety is divided into two sections. Each moiety combines a matrilineal and a

---

107 *The Elementary Structures of Kinship*, p. 461.

patrilineal principle, which yields four sections [(A1) + (A2)] [(B1) + (B2)], each of which has a name: Banaka, Karimera, Burung and Palyeri. Women are exchanged reciprocally between A1 and B2 and between A2 and B1. The men in A1 marry women in B2, and the men in B2 marry women in A1, and so on.

When a man from A1 marries a woman from B2, their children belong to a different section from their parents but which is in the same matrilineal moiety as their mother, in the present case B1. At the same time, they belong to their father's patrilineal moiety, namely A1. Since their children belong to B1, they must marry men and women from A2, and their children will engender children who once again belong to A1 (marriage between a B1 man and an A2 woman) and to B2 (marriage between an A2 man and a B1 woman). The system comes full circle from one cycle to the next. The simplest way to explain this is to draw a diagram, where the arrows indicate the mother–child relationship; the equals sign (=), the alliance between sections; the rectangles, the matrilineal and patrilineal moieties.

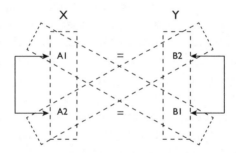

– A man from A1 marries a woman from B2; his children are B1.
– A man from B1 marries a woman from A2; his children are A1.
– Etc.
Matrilineal moieties [A1 + A2]; [B1 + B2] = X and Y.
Patrilineal moieties [A1 + B1]; [B2 + A2] = four sections.
If we replace the letters and numbers by the names the Kariera used to designate their sections, we obtain the following diagram:

Each section thus contains, with respect to a given individual, a number of kin categories linked to him or her by distinct kin ties and genealogical paths. Let us take for example a woman from B1 who marries a man from A2:

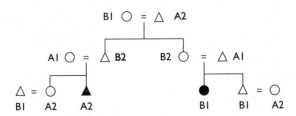

In marrying B1, A2 marries his father's sister's daughter (FZD), his patrilateral cross-cousin, while B1, in marrying A2, marries her mother's brother's son (MBS), her matrilateral cross-cousin. A2 belongs to the same moiety as his mother (A1) and to his father's moiety B2. The mother transmits her blood and flesh to her children; the father transmits his membership of a local group that exploits the resources of a territory; but at the same time, if the children are boys, he also transmits responsibilities concerning certain sacred sites and totemic places.[108]

Looking at the last diagram, there would seem to be a close match between two ways of expressing the same social relationships, one using the language of sections, and the other the language of real or classificatory kin ties. It was for this reason that, on several occasions, Lévi-Strauss expressed his admiration for these systems, which were both simple in terms of their principles and complex in the functions they served. He even praised their 'crystalline beauty'. Nor was he

---

108 Cf. L. Dousset, *Australian Aboriginal Kinship* (Marseille, Pacific-Credo Publications, 2011), p. 108. By dividing the sections in two, we create an eight-section system whose prototype is the kinship system of the Aranda, a nomadic people in the southwestern part of the Northern Territory. The same principles govern both alliance and descent. Cf. *The Elementary Structures of Kinship*, pp. 162–4.

If a man in subsection / marries a woman in subsection / their children belong to
A1 = B1 → D2
A2 = B2 → D1
B1 = A1 → C1
B2 = A2 → C2
C1 = D1 → B1
C2 = D2 → B2
D1 = C1 → A2
D2 = C2 → A1

unaware that many Australian systems had neither sections nor subsections, and that their marriage formula was nevertheless identical to that found in section systems: marriage with the cross-cousin. He was also aware that the systems with sections and subsections were in the process of spreading, before the very eyes of anthropologists, among tribes in which these were formerly unknown, some of which adopted and adapted them, while others tried them out and rejected them. This raises two questions.

First question: before the arrival and adoption (or rejection) of sections and subsections, these tribes had other kinship systems: so, *of what kind were they*? Lévi-Strauss does not ask this question directly, but he knows these societies practised cross-cousin marriage. The new systems therefore have also to distinguish between parallel and cross cousins and, in order to do so, father and father's brothers must be merged under the same term (FB = F) as must mother and mother's sisters under another term (MZ = M). This means that the system preceding the arrival of sections must have been 'bifurcate merging',[109] a feature that characterizes not only the Australian systems, but also Dravidian and Iroquois types.

However, in 1947, the structural difference between Dravidian and Iroquois systems had not yet been identified, and the two types were lumped together. It was not until 1964, with Floyd Lounsbury's famous article, that this confusion was dispelled.[110] Then new field-work by new generations of anthropologists and linguists was needed to discover that, before the invention of sections and subsections, the Australian systems were in fact of the Dravidian type, and that they had continued as such in all groups where the section system had not yet arrived or where it no longer existed after having been 'tried out' and rejected in favour of the former system. Still other groups, like the Ngaanyatjarra, kept a Dravidian-type system solely in order to use

---

109 'Merging' refers to the use of the same term for father and father's brothers and another same term for mother and mother's sisters. 'Bifurcate' refers to the distinction between Ego's collaterals, the distinction between parallel and cross kin, which results from merging the terms for father and father's brothers, on the one hand, and for mother and mother's sisters, on the other.

110 F. G. Lounsbury, 'A Formal Account of Crow-Omaha Type Kinship Terminologies', in W. H. Goodenough, ed., *Explorations in Cultural Anthropology: Essays in Honor of George Peter Murdock* (New York, McGraw Hill, 1964), pp. 331–43.

it as a common idiom for communicating with certain formerly unknown tribes with which they had kept in touch in the camps or the cities, and which had, in their case, adopted a section system for their own use.

Second question: if in earlier times sections and subsections did not exist and the Australian kinship systems did not need them in order to function, why invent them? What did they add? But if they were invented, why was this done, where and by whom? And if the sections and subsections did not arrive until sometime around 1930, among the Pintupi, who nomadized in the southern part of Western Australia near the Northern Territory, along what routes were they disseminated and at what rate?

Lévi-Strauss was aware that moiety and section systems were not present everywhere in Australia and that they were continuing to spread.[111] He knew, too, that tribes without sections occupied certain coastal zones of Australia. And, like Elkin, he regarded the groups of the southern desert, which Elkin had named the Aluridja, as 'aberrant'. Apparently, these groups did not distinguish between parallel and cross cousins, and allowed marriage between classificatory brothers and sisters, in disregard therefore of the incest taboo. Lastly, they did not have exogamous moieties but endogamous generational moieties. Concerning exogamous moieties and sections, Lévi-Strauss quotes Elkin: 'Moieties and sections are not universal and inevitable developments from the kinship-system and associated marriage-rules.'[112]

And Lévi-Strauss goes on to give the reason for this: 'All the effects of the different forms of marriage class systems may occur when there are no such systems, by the appropriate determination of the underlying relationships.'

This confirms that systems without sections practiced cross-cousin marriage, just like systems with sections and subsections. Lévi-Strauss therefore asks: are organizations without classes more, or less, primitive than those with classes? To which he replies:

---

111 *The Elementary Structures of Kinship*, p. 152: 'recent observations have revealed the rapid diffusion of marriage systems from one group to another, and efforts at adaptation between different systems, all of which supposes a good deal of original invention.'

112 Cited in ibid., p. 203.

For the time being . . . there is nothing to prove that . . . it is necessary to give to systems without classes and to systems with classes an obsolete position in time. They have the same result but employ different methods, based sometimes on the notion of class and sometimes on that of relation.[113]

He was right to be cautious at the time, but today no doubt remains. We now know that the section systems were invented sometime during the first millennium CE along the southwest coast of Australia, and spread first of all northward along traditional intertribal trade routes and then toward the Central Desert. Lévi-Strauss notes, however, that 'these two methods never correspond exactly and that . . . inter-individual relationships must be always taken into consideration. Nonetheless, . . . there should be at least a certain degree of equivalence between the two systems. Not all the members of the class [i.e. section] are possible spouses, and even between possible and preferred spouses there are differences which can only be explained in terms of consanguinity, *whereas such differences are non-apparent in terms of class.* Nevertheless, no possible spouse is to be found outside the class, and this alone indicates that from the point of view of marriage rules the class does have a function.'[114]

And he concludes, correctly:

It does not follow from the mechanism of marriage classes [i.e. sections] that their end or even their result is the automatic determination of the prescribed spouse. Indeed the opposite is true, since a class may contain both permitted and prohibited spouses . . . but the natives regard the violation of class exogamy with the same horror as they regard marriage with a relative of a forbidden consanguineous relationship.[115]

In the end, Lévi-Strauss writes that the relationship between 'section' and 'kin ties or kinship relations' 'remains to be clarified'. Radcliffe-Brown, who invented the words 'section' and 'subsection' to avoid using

---

113  Ibid., pp. 151–2.
114  Ibid., p. 159; my emphasis.
115  Cited in ibid., pp. 165–6.

the term 'marriage class' because he refused to see sections as a means of regulating marriages, surely carried his refusal too far, for it is a fact that there is no possible (prescribed or preferred) spouse outside the section. But if the primary purpose of sections is not to regulate marriage, and accompany alliances, what is their use? Once again, Lévi-Strauss cites Elkin, who poses the question in the following terms: 'We do know, however, that sections and subsections and moieties are frequently totemic in nature, and that in some sections at least, they have spread or are spreading as a system of totemism.'[116]

In reality, the tie between section and totem does exist, but it is rare. The ceremonies and rituals addressed to the mythological heroes of the Dreamtime and to totemic places, the rituals for multiplying the species, and the male and female initiations all existed before the sections came into being, and were based on the endogamous generational moieties present in all Australian systems. The sections and subsections brought together part of these pre-existing ritual functions. We understand more clearly now why sections spread easily and were very often accepted. They did not modify the existing kinship rules, particularly marriage with the cross cousin – a basic principle of the previous Dravidian systems – and they improved the existing ritual structures.

For sections are at once social and cosmological categories, which divide all humans together with all beings in the universe – sun, moon, reptiles, birds, cold-blooded animals, warm-blooded animals, etc. – into complementary and opposing categories. Sections are constructed according to a basic dualist principle that operates at all levels of the universe and society. Research by the linguist Carl Georg von Brandenstein on the meaning of section names has clearly shown that belonging to a section endows humans with qualities that align them with the elements of the universe in their section. For instance, he showed that, for the Kariera, the *pannaga* and the *purungu* sections are associated with 'cold blood', and the *karimarra* and *paltjarri* sections with 'warm blood'. In consequence, reptiles are part of the *pannaga* and *purungu* sections, whose human members can communicate with and act ritually on them. The sun and fire, on the other hand, are *karimarra* and *paltjarri*, and so on.

---

116 A. P. Elkin, 'Sections and Kinship in Some Desert Tribes', *Man* 40 (1940), p. 24, cited in *The Elementary Structures of Kinship*, pp. 200–1.

Another essential point is that sections are sociocentric and not egocentric categories. They do not start from male or female human ancestors, and they divide up all individuals without reference to this kind of genealogy. Once they are applied to kinship, they bring kin terms into line with categories. Their use now makes it possible to reconstruct, if need be, the genealogical ties between individuals, but also to bypass this reconstruction. It is in terms of kin categories and not of genealogical positions that the three basic components of kinship – incest, alliance and descent – are defined. Another advantage is that, whereas generational moieties do not distinguish consanguines from affines, sections create this distinction within each generational moiety by dividing it into two categories: those who can be or are affines, and those who cannot be and are not potential marriage partners. Sections thus produce information that simplifies the calculation of kinship and lies at the junction between the reproduction of the group for the group, ensured by the generational moieties, and the reproduction of relations with other groups (affines, outsiders, etc.).[117]

At the same time, being sociocentric, sections provide a remarkable means of communication between tribes, or between Aboriginal peoples who do not know each other and come in contact for the first time, or are today required to live together in camps or on the outskirts of town. Such encounters existed before the Europeans arrived, but they have become more numerous since. It is because of their usefulness in such intertribal exchanges that groups like the Ngaanyatjarra, after having 'tried out' a section system and then reverted to their former system, nevertheless kept the new system for use in their intertribal relations, which thus take place under cover of fictitious kinship relations.

Lastly, there remains the problem of the Aluridja systems. Laurent Dousset has shown that there is nothing 'aberrant' about them, as Lévi-Strauss thought, instead they function normally as Dravidian systems divided into two endogamous generational moieties. Generational

---

117

| A1 Mother, mother's brothers and sisters. Ego's children: girls | B2 Father, father's brothers and sisters. Ego's children: boys |
|---|---|
| A2 (Ego), Ego's brothers and sisters, father's brothers' children (// cousins), mother's sisters' children (// cousins) | B1 mother's brother's children (X cousins), father's sister's children (X cousins) |

Note: 'Sections et Catégories de Parenté', in L. Dousset, *Assimilating Identities*, p. 16.

moieties have nothing to do with people's age. They place in the same generation, Ego, Ego's brothers and sisters, Ego's parallel and cross cousins ($G^0$) but also Ego's grandparents ($G^{+2}$) and Ego's grandchildren ($G^{-2}$). The other moiety contains Ego's parents, father's sisters, father's sisters' husbands, mother's brothers, mother's brothers' wives, father-in-law and mother-in-law, etc., ($G^{+1}$) and at the same time Ego's children, Ego's brothers' and sisters' children, etc. ($G^{-1}$). Between individuals in these two moieties, different conducts are imposed: respect toward those in generation $G^{+1}$, authority over those in $G^{-1}$, intimacy and affection with those in $G^{+2}$ and $G^{-2}$.

All these individuals belong to biologically and chronologically different generations, but they call each other brothers and sisters because of their mutual belonging to the same endogamous moiety. A reciprocal flow of goods, services, attentions and emotions circulates constantly among them, and all are held to share the same identity due to the fact that the generations are merged.

Alternatively, in the moiety opposite that of Ego, the generations are distinguished and correspond to the distinction between those who engender ($G^{+1}$) and those who are engendered ($G^{-1}$). To address these persons, Ego will use the terms 'father' and 'mother' for those in $G^{+1}$, and 'son' and 'daughter' for those in $G^{-1}$. It is therefore only in the framework of generational moieties that cross cousins in Ego's generation ($G^0$) are called 'brothers' and 'sisters', and that cross kin in generation $G^{+1}$ are addressed as 'fathers' and 'mothers'. That is where the picture became blurred for Elkin, because he had mistaken endogamous generational moieties for exogamous 'marriage classes'.

Generational moieties served and continue to serve to organize rites among the Ngaanyatjarra. One of the moieties is called 'shade side' (facing west) and the other 'sun side' (facing east), terms that designate the place occupied by each person during the rites. But what happens when the time comes for a Ngaanyatjarra to get married? The prescribed spouse is a cross kinsperson who is geographically and genealogically remote. The rule prohibits renewing the same alliance before a certain number of generations have elapsed, and drives each group of nomads to find allies further afield. The result is that a man will marry in his generation at least a second-degree if not a third-degree cross cousin. But she must also be a bilateral cross cousin, in other words the daughter of both a classificatory mother's brother (MBD) and a classificatory father's sister (FZD), which is the basic rule of a Dravidian system. But a man can also marry a cross kinswoman in $G^{+2}$ and $G^{-2}$ who belongs, with the cross cousins of his generation ($G^0$), to his endogamous moiety. He can therefore marry a classificatory father's mother or a classificatory daughter's daughter. His first- and second-degree female cross cousins, who are prohibited spouses, continue to be addressed as 'sisters'. This explains the difficulty in understanding that it was prescribed to marry cross cousins but that this was forbidden when they were as brothers and sisters.

This 'aberrant' system was therefore perfectly normal, providing one recognized the underlying nature of the Australian systems, which is of the Dravidian type, and the ritual importance of endoga-mous generational moieties. That became possible only thirty years after the publication of *The Elementary Structures of Kinship*. We now know that sections are a recent invention dating to the first millen-nium after Christ, which arose within groups living in two regions, one that went from the coastal zone of Pilbara to the Kimberley Mountains and the other lying further to the southwest. From there, sections moved into the Western Desert along the traditional inter-tribal trade routes; there they encountered another system with sections, which is thought to have come from south of Darwin. This encounter gave rise to new combinations, like the systems with subsections characteristic of the deserts. The question Lévi-Strauss posed concerning the historical priority of systems without sections and systems with 'marriage classes' (= sections) is thus answered. The first predated the second. And these were (and still are for numerous groups) Dravidian-type systems with generational moieties, which feature in ritual practices. These are the true 'classical' Australian systems.

Another important conclusion: sections and subsections were not invented to regulate marriage, since the alliance system worked very well without them and was based on cross-cousin marriage. Sections and subsections are first and foremost ceremonial group-ings composed of various categories of kin.[118] That they were

---

118  Lévi-Strauss, writing about the Murinbata system in the wake of Stanner, who had studied them, has this to say: 'The question of whether the subsections are basically totemic groups or marriage classes is meaningless' (*The Elementary Structures of Kinship*, p. 153).

invented confirms once again the primacy of ritual and what in the West are known as 'political-religious' relations over kinship when it comes to running societies.

Rites are charged with liberating, in a sacred place connected with a mythical totemic hero, the spirits of the animal and plant species associated with it so that they may reproduce on the territory of the group's clan, but also on the territory of neighbouring groups that do not have the same species for totems.

> Rites thus make up a vast system of ritual cooperation between tribes and between groups, as services rendered and received, vital for the reproduction of the society . . .
> Within the group the men conduct ritual exchanges with the women of game for children . . . then, outside the group, they exchange some of these children for potential game that is *ritually* reproduced.[119]

These rites for the conservation and multiplication of the species useful to humans are performed by liberating the spirits that 'fecundate' them. They are the men's responsibility and are taboo for the women. The presence of women is even more strictly forbidden during the rites the men perform to call a 'spirit child' to enter their wife's body and there to become a human being. In these rites, the men attract and feed with their blood – which they cause to flow from their penis or a vein in their arm – the spirits that, after having dwelled in an animal or plant species, will enter a woman's body and grow there.

It happens that in Australia – except among the Murngin and related groups – blood is transmitted by women. The men therefore put into circulation for the reproduction of the society the blood received from their mother, while at the same time eliminating 'women's power of auto-procreation by the simple fact of a spirit-child entering their body'. In Australia women take part in male initiations as well as having their own initiations, but men are 'the actors in the exchanges that organize social relations', and they do this 'by manipulating blood, the life-substance, and the children, both of which come from the women'.[120]

---

119 L. Dousset, 'Production et reproduction en Australie. Pour un tableau de l'unité des tribus aborigènes', *Social Anthropology* 4, n° 3 (1996), pp. 281–98; p. 290.

120 Ibid., p. 291.

The ritual management of the universe is thus directly bound up with kinship relations – descent (women's blood), alliance (exchange of game and women) – but it has primacy over kinship relations because it is the (cultural) basis for the overall reproduction of Australian societies – of each one, but at the same time of all of them together. Kinship relations are not the ultimate foundation of society for Australian Aboriginal peoples, however, no more than they are elsewhere, despite all appearances to the contrary. The relations that do make a certain number of human groups into a society must be sought elsewhere than in kinship. They are what in the West are called political-religious relations, as I have said, to which we can add the generational moieties and the sections as ritual and totemic groupings. Without them, the overall structure of Australian societies could not exist, and that is clearly confirmed by the following fact. Among Australian Aboriginal societies, as in many others, men and women cannot marry unless they have been initiated.[121] On the other hand, because in Australia it is men who control the most important and secret rites – conceived as ensuring the reproduction of the natural species, of humans and of society as a whole, including its exchanges with the other societies – it is clear that this primacy of the men is what explains that it is they who exchange the women and 'not vice versa'.[122]

We now come to the last Australian kinship system analysed by Lévi-Strauss, the Murngin system, characterized by a set of groups living in the north of Australia in Arnhem Land, today known as the Yolngu. At present, we know that these groups were pushed back and confined in Arnhem Land by waves of immigration into Australia circa 3000 BCE, around the time the dog appeared there. The Murngin/Yolngu groups speak languages belonging to the Pama-Nyungan family, one of the twenty-eight language families recorded in Australia and that occupies the better part of south Australia. The Pama-Nyungan groups probably belonged to the first wave of

---

121 Three conditions must be fulfilled for a man to get married in Australia: the woman must belong to the category of possible spouses, the man must have certain rights on this woman, and he must have been initiated; cf. ibid.

122 Yet, given that men's preferred tool for establishing and justifying their pre-eminence is the manipulation of totemic spirits and totemism itself, we will have to confront these facts with the criticism Lévi-Strauss would later make of the very notion of totemism.

immigration that entered Australia (around 30,000 BCE), and it was the other migrations that cut off the Yolngu and confined them in north-eastern Arnhem Land.

The Murngin system was described in 1931 by Lloyd Warner, who indicated that the rule there was to marry the mother's brother's daughter, or matrilateral cross cousin (MBD); but that this rule did not fit the logic of the system, which had eight subsections and was therefore, for him, of the Aranda type. However, marriage with the matrilateral cross cousin is forbidden in an Aranda system. Two years later, in 1933, Theodore Webb, a missionary living with the Murngin, contributed another important piece of information: where he lived, a man had the choice of a spouse from two other specific sections, but normally married a woman from just one of these, and only exceptionally from the other. On the basis of this information, Elkin tried in 1933 to reconstruct the logic of the Murngin system, but was unsuccessful.

Lévi-Strauss decided to tackle the problem himself, and it was then that he made an important discovery. The Murngin have a system with eight subsections, like an Aranda system, but the eight 'classes' function as though there were only four, as in a Kariera system. He posited that the Murngin system 'is the result of a sort of compromise between a pre-existing marriage rule and a fully developed class system introduced from outside'.[123] The system worked like an Aranda system with eight subsections, eliminating marriage with the patrilateral cross cousin, but it continued to allow marriage with the matrilateral cross cousin, as in a system with four sections.

That produces a system oriented in a single direction. The men of one section marry women in another section but the relation between the sections is no longer reciprocal, as in a Kariera system. It is one-way. The men in A marry women in B, the men in B marry women in C, the men in C marry women in D and the men in D marry women in A, coming full circle.

Now, the formula $[A{\rightarrow}B{\rightarrow}C{\rightarrow}D{\rightarrow}A]$ is the formula for generalized exchange. Furthermore, as Lévi-Strauss showed, 'in a four-class [= sections] system of generalized exchange there are always two explicit or implicit patrilineal moieties, but no matrilineal moiety'.[124]

---

123  *The Elementary Structures of Kinship*, p. 176.
124  Ibid., p. 179.

The Murngin are patrilineal. Lévi-Strauss assumes then that the arrival of a system with subsections, which they wanted to adopt, obliged them to create the matrilineal moieties they did not have, the addition of which gave the system the appearance of one with restricted exchange of the Aranda type – which it is not – and explains the presence of the two marriage rules.

Lévi-Strauss concludes that: 'the theory of the Murngin system will not be brought to a conclusion until there is precise information on the way in which the marriage cycles are closed . . . a definitive interpretation of the Murngin system still eludes us because [of] our ignorance of, firstly, the number of "local lines" at any one time, and, secondly, the extent of the networks of alliances uniting them.'[125]

We will end our exploration of this subject here, but the question is not closed. An additional remark must however be made. Whereas in all other Australian groups patrilineal descent reckoning defines one's belonging to a territory, to a pathway and to sacred places associated with mythical heroes, and matrilineal descent reckoning, which is the flesh and blood that are transmitted from one generation to the next through lineages, defines an individual's social identity, for the Murngin and the groups covered by this term, matters are very different.

> Blood, the life-substance, is not transmitted through the women. The spirits responsible for the clan's continuation are located in the sacred places connected with the man's ancestors, such that patrilineal descent is both physical and spiritual.[126]

In addition, the Murngin do not perform rites for the reproduction of species and their totems are not associated with spirit-child sites. Their rites are limited to accompanying and interpreting the cycle of the seasons.

A final point. When Lévi-Strauss was to deal further on in *The Elementary Structures* with the systems of generalized exchange found massively in Asia, he would stress that generalized exchange allows the circulation of women between local groups which might even have different customs and descent principles. It is therefore possible that

125  Ibid., pp. 192, 194.
126  Dousset, 'Production et reproduction en Australie', p. 292.

groups driven toward north-eastern Arnhem Land by new immigrants may have wanted to exchange women among themselves, given their shared language and culture, but without significantly modifying the internal organization of each group.

The analysis of restricted exchange systems in *The Elementary Structures* ends with a chapter in which Lévi-Strauss distinguishes two types of regimes that combine variously descent rules and residence rules. He calls 'harmonic regimes' those in which the two principles run parallel, namely patrilineal and patrilocal, matrilineal and matrilocal. And he calls 'disharmonic regimes' those in which the two rules are separate and opposed, namely matrilineal and patrilocal, and patrilineal and matrilocal. He invokes universal male domination to explain the fact that matrilineal matrilocal regimes are very rare compared to matrilineal patrilocal regimes. In the four existing matrilineal matrilocal systems, the men's situation after marriage, according to Lévi-Strauss, is highly precarious and a source of tension with their affines. But he cites too few examples, with too few details, for this conclusion to be convincing. And above all, he speaks too broadly when he asserts that restricted exchange systems are disharmonic and generalized exchange systems are harmonic. Since, according to him, Australia is the classic land of restricted exchange, the data we have today do not permit us to say that the overwhelming majority of Australian regimes are disharmonic.

The last chapter in this sequence devoted to restricted exchange systems is an appendix comprising an algebraic study of the Murngin system, developed by the mathematician André Weil at the behest of Lévi-Strauss. Weil wanted to show 'how algebra and the theory of groups of substitutions can facilitate [the] study and classification [of marriage laws]'.[127] He won the wager and since then the number of logical-mathematical studies of kinship systems has grown apace.

The second part of *The Elementary Structures* is devoted to the study of the kinship systems known at the time of writing in the three major cultural areas of Asia: the first stretching from Burma in the south to Siberia in the north, and then China and India. To this Lévi-Strauss adds a brief detour into Melanesia before going on to consider the problem of the transition to complex systems. The total area covered is immense and

---

127 *The Elementary Structures of Kinship*, p. 221.

takes in hundreds of very different societies, from the Gold of the Amur River to the Manchu, from the Munda of India to the Gilyak of Siberia. In each case, except for the studies of the Kachin and the Chinese systems, the analysis is very short and simply shows that he is indeed dealing with a kinship system which dictates that a man marries his matrilateral cross cousin. Unlike symmetrical dual systems, which prescribe marriage with the bilateral cross cousin, the Kachin systems and others of the same type are asymmetrical and prescribe marriage with the matrilateral cross cousin (MBD), forbidding marriage with the patrilateral cross cousin (FZD) and therefore even with the bilateral cross cousin.

Lévi-Strauss acknowledges that Hodson pointed out these differences in structure as early as 1922.[128] But his intention is to certify the manifold presence of the generalized exchange formula in this whole zone, and to show how this formula often combines in these societies with restricted exchange formulas, which continue to regulate matrimonial exchanges in portions of their population – commoners, peasants, younger sons of aristocratic families, etc.

The Burma–Siberia axis is based on two exceptionally rich ethnographic studies, one on the Burmese Kachin by Gilhodes, and the other by Leo Shternberg on the Siberian Gilyak (1912).[129] These societies practice generalized exchange and therefore distinguish between wife-givers and wife-takers. Group B gives its women to group C and receives its wives from group A.

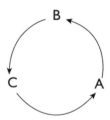

The generalized exchange formula therefore implies a minimum of three local groups between which the women circulate and, in order to

128  Ibid., p. 234; T. C. Hodson, *The Primitive Culture of India* (London, Royal Asiatic Society, 1922; James G. Furlong Fund, vol. 1).

129  C. Gilhodes, *The Kachins: Religion and Customs* (Kolkata, 1922); L. I. Shternberg, 'The Social Organization of the Gilyak', *Anthropological Papers of the American Museum of Natural History*, n° 82 (June 1999). The original was in Russian.

come full circle, C must give its women to A, according to the formula [A→B→C→A]. The circle thus works in one direction only, but it can open up to integrate other groups into the '*connubium*', that is into the cycles in which women circulate between the groups.

Each local group is thus at the same time a giver and a taker of women. The men give their daughters and sisters to other groups, and take and receive as wives the daughters and sisters of other groups. The exchanges are not reciprocal, as they are in the Australian systems with moieties and sections. Translated into the idiom of kinship, we thus have the following scheme: as a man, I marry my matrilateral cross cousin (MBD), who belongs therefore to the group of my givers, and my sister marries my father's sister's son (FZS), my patrilateral cross cousin, with respect to whom we are wife-givers.

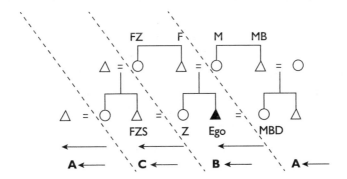

However, women are never 'given' without countergifts. Takers hand over great quantities of 'male' wealth to their givers, who in return give them 'female' goods. The Kachin use two words to distinguish givers (*mayu*) and takers (*dama*). Lévi-Strauss – much as Leach, a specialist of the Kachin in the wake of Gilhodes, would do later in his book published after *The Elementary Structures*[130] – showed that women are not 'exchanged' for these goods, and that these gifts of goods do not signify that the women are sold or purchased. Everyone knows, because every-one belongs to a circle that exchanges women, that for a woman given there will always be, when the time comes, a woman received, unless one of the partners leaves the circle or disappears.

---

130 E. Leach, *Political Systems of Highland Burma: A Study of Kachin Social Structure* (Cambridge MA, Harvard University Press, 1954).

Lévi-Strauss then analyses what he calls the limits on the functioning of these systems. Ideally, generalized exchange supposes equality of status and prestige between the exchanging groups A, B and C. Ideally the relation (C→A) should be equivalent to the relation (B→C). A woman from A should be worth a woman from B, who should be worth a woman from C, who should be worth a woman from A.[131] In reality, however, many factors intervene to create inequalities of wealth and status between the exchanging groups. These inequalities engender marriages between spouses of different status, relations of hypergamy and hypogamy (which Lévi-Strauss brackets together under the term *anisogamie*).

Kachin society was thus divided into 'noble houses' and commoners and slaves,[132] and was characterized by a high degree of political instability, which Leach's later work would elucidate by showing that the Kachin swung between two forms of social organization: a more egalitarian form called *gumlao* and a hierarchical form with 'feudal tendencies', called *gumsa*. Lévi-Strauss was unaware of the existence of dual political forms, and when he discovered it in Leach's book, he immediately concluded that this swing was predictable and based on the conflict 'between the egalitarian conditions of generalized exchange, and its aristocratic consequences.'[133] Lévi-Strauss goes on to compare the Kachin system with a number of other ranked Southeast Asian societies ruled by a tribal aristocracy: the Lushai, the Sema Naga, etc; and this comparison seems still to be justified. Similarly, his hypothesis of a Burma–Siberia and a Kachin–Gilyak axis along which systems of generalized exchange predominate has been confirmed.

The same is not true, however, of his suggestion that this type of kinship system must also have characterized the Inca society of pre-Columbian Peru, in which 'an organization based originally on clans had a system of lineages, increasingly feudal in character, gradually superimposed upon it.'[134] Lévi-Strauss advances the argument of the *yanacona* system. These were individuals torn away from their original communities and attached for life to members of the Inca's lineage and

---

131 *The Elementary Structures of Kinship*, p. 266.
132 Between the categories of commoner and slave lay an intermediate category made up of descendants of unions between a free man and a slave woman.
133 *The Elementary Structures of Kinship*, p. 267.
134 Ibid., p. 246.

to noble families close to the emperor. It is therefore hard to compare the structure of the multi-ethnic Inca Empire with the Kachin political system floating between its egalitarian *gumlao* and its hierarchical *gumsa* systems. Furthermore, the use of the term 'feudal' to describe a ranked society in which a tribal aristocracy holds sway – a phenomenon still frequent when Lévi-Strauss was writing his *Elementary Structures* – is no longer admissible today.

This particular study ends with a hypothesis that Lévi-Strauss returns to in the final chapter of his book, devoted to the problem of the transition to complex structures. Generalized exchange, he writes, is an organizational scheme

> of an exceptional clarity and richness, a formula which can be widened indefinitely ... The dangers which threaten it come from outside, from concrete characteristics and not from the formal structure of the group. *Marriage by purchase* ... then provides a new formula which, while safeguarding the principle of the formal structure, furnishes the means of integrating those irrational factors which arise from chance and from history, factors which the evolution of human society shows to follow ... the logical structures which are elaborated by unconscious thought, access to which is often more easily gained through very primitive forms of organization.[135]

Marriage by the pure and simple purchase of women, he hypothesizes, replaced generalized exchange, which imposed marriage with the matrilateral cross cousin and a reciprocal flow of male and female wealth between wife-givers and -takers. Marriage by purchase, according to his hypothesis, shook off these kinship relations and spread to several continents, but especially to Africa. In reality one does not buy a woman, unless she is a slave, and 'bridewealth', or goods given in exchange for a freewoman, is by no means the same as the 'price' of a commodity. But what is striking in the preceding quotation is the vision Lévi-Strauss already had at this time (1947) of the struggle between humans to amass power, wealth and prestige, which he sets on the side of 'those irrational factors which arise from chance and from history', in opposition to primitive societies that are still relatively unopen to history and are

---

135  Ibid., p. 268; my emphasis.

based on 'logical' structures elaborated by 'unconscious thought'. Let us skip over this vision of history placed on the side of irrational factors; but we have just seen how the Australian Aborigines had consciously elaborated their section and subsection systems using the logical principle of reciprocal relations between two elements that are both complementary and opposed. We should not forget, as Stanner stressed in 1937 when writing about the Murinbata, that 'it is partly as a theoretical formula that subsections are carried intertribally'.[136] Not only do they carry the system, but they also find a way each time of articulating it with the pre-existing Dravidian systems. This owes little to unconscious thought. At the same time, Stanner's praise of the unconscious contradicts what Lévi-Strauss himself has to say about the Aborigines in his criticism of Granet's theses:

> Today we know that the archaic nature of the material culture of the Australian aborigines has no correspondence in the field of social institutions. By contrast, their social institutions are the result of a long series of deliberate elaborations and systematic reforms. In short, the Australian sociology of the family is . . . a 'planned sociology'.[137]

I can only approve of this thinking, however it does not demonstrate the fundamental role of the unconscious.

We now come to the two last groups of societies and cultures whose kinship system Lévi-Strauss examined: China and India. I will not dwell on them, though, in line with Lévi-Strauss's own judgment on this part of his work, reached twenty years after the first publication of *The Elementary Structures* (1966). He sees them as 'begging the reader to take them for what they are, as stages outstripped by the progress of anthropology', for 'sinologists and Indianists, in pursuing these studies, rely on a body of historical and philological knowledge which a cursory comparative approach cannot fully grasp'.[138]

Reading Chapters Nineteen and Twenty, devoted to an examination of Granet's theory on the nature of the Chinese kinship system and on the *chao mu* order of mourning grades imposed by the imperial state on

---

136 Cited in ibid., p. 125.
137 Ibid., p. 314.
138 Ibid., 'Preface to the second edition', p. xxviii.

the whole of the Han population, I feel both perplexed and slightly uneasy. I cannot help thinking that Lévi-Strauss only reluctantly awards the great sinologist a few crumbs of praise, so sharp is his criticism; this is a radical departure from the obvious respect he showed for Radcliffe-Brown, Rivers or Elkin, even when he happened to criticize them. Only Edmund Leach would later receive similar treatment.

Marcel Granet, a disciple of Durkheim and friend of Mauss, was the pre-eminent French sinologist of the first half of the twentieth century; he died in 1940, overcome by emotion when Pétain's government submitted to the diktats of Nazi Germany. Several of his general works on Chinese civilization or thought are regularly reissued.[139] His earliest study already dealt with kinship systems in Chinese society, and in 1920 he published *La Polygynie sororale et le sororat dans la Chine féodale. Étude sur les formes anciennes de la polygamie chinoise.* After the publication of his major panoramas, he once again undertook to examine Chinese kinship, this time in an effort to reconstruct it as a whole. In 1939 a long study came out in *Annales sociologiques*, published the same year by Alcan, under the title *Catégories matrimoniales et relations de proximité en Chine ancienne.* Granet died the following year, but would probably have been a member of Lévi-Strauss's thesis jury (in 1949) had he lived on.

Granet was not acquainted with the work of Hodson and Held who, before Lévi-Strauss, had already developed the distinction between restricted exchange formulas and 'generalized' exchange. But Granet reinvented this distinction on his own when he spoke of symmetrical exchanges reproduced from one generation to the next, which he called '*chassé-croisé*', or crossover exchanges, and one-way systems of circulation of women with a separation between wife-givers and wife-takers and continuance of the alliance between them – which he called 'deferred exchanges'. *Chassé-croisé* exchanges are reciprocal exchanges entailing marriage with the female bilateral cross cousin. Exchanges with 'deferred returns' involve marriage with the female matrilateral cross cousin. Here we recognize Lévi-Strauss's later distinction between restricted exchange and generalized exchange. Granet knew the nature of the classical Australian systems, if only from reading Durkheim, and

---

139 M. Granet, *La Civilisation chinoise* (Paris, Albin Michel, 1994; First edition, 1929); *La pensée chinoise* (Paris, Albin Michel, 1988; First edition, 1934).

he was familiar with the work of Gilhodes, who had revealed the circulation of Kachin women between wife-givers and wife-takers; this is the same Gilhodes whose work would be much used by Lévi-Strauss. Granet stressed that deferred alliances were a 'gamble', an idea that Lévi-Strauss would pursue, citing Granet.

Unlike Durkheim, Granet posited the prohibition of incest, not as a consequence of exogamy, but as its founding principle, which is also Lévi-Strauss's basic thesis; and he proposed that the fact that descent is reckoned patri- or matrilineally is independent of the marriage formula. For Lévi-Strauss, descent would be a 'secondary' feature of kinship systems.

François Héran devoted three very thorough critical articles, which appeared in *Social Anthropology*[140] and in his book *Figures de la parenté*,[141] to an inventory of Granet's analyses and theories that have their equivalent in *The Elementary Structures*. In all he found twenty-five.

In reality, Lévi-Strauss minimized Granet's work, and only forty years later recognized his importance in the elaboration of his own work.[142] The reason for this reluctance to acknowledge his debt and the importance of his predecessor probably lies in Lévi-Strauss' deep-seated conviction that he was identifying general theories, in other words revealing the foundations common to a multitude of kinship systems, not only that of China. Granet had noted when analysing the old Chinese treatise, *Her Ya*, that the early Chinese kin terms suggested the existence of reciprocal exchanges of women between exogamous groups and marriage with the female bilateral cross cousin. The term *fu* was used for both father and father's brothers (FB = F), and the term *gu* designated at the same time father's sister (FZ), mother's brother's wife (MBWi), wife's mother (WiM) and husband's mother (HuM). This term therefore expressed the existence of an exchange of spouses in $G^{+1}$ and in $G^0$. He had also noted the existence of alternating generations, the consequence of which was that grandfather and grandson belonged to the same category, and father and son to opposite categories, all features that are found in the *chao mu* order of mourning grades.

---

140  F. Héran, 'De Granet à Lévi-Strauss', *Social Anthropology* 6, n° 1, pp. 1–60; n° 2, pp. 169–201; n° 3, pp. 309–30.

141  F. Héran, *Figures de la parenté* (Paris, Presses Universitaires de France, 2009), pp. 395–482; especially chapter X, 'Lévi-Strauss lecteur de Granet ou la dette refoulée'.

142  Lévi-Strauss and Eribon, *Conversations with Claude Lévi-Strauss*, p. 99.

Based on these observations, Granet imagined that the ancient Chinese kinship system was like one of the Australian systems, that of the Kariera. This system, he posited, must have disappeared over time with the development of what he called Chinese 'feudalism'. To ensure its marriage alliances, the nobility had then installed a system of deferred exchanges, while commoners, especially the peasantry, must have continued to practise the reciprocal exchange (*chassé-croisé*) of women between village communities. Things must have changed again when the emperor established the *chao mu* order, which imposed on the population an ordered series of funeral rites and mourning conduct according to the degree of proximity or remoteness of the deceased and his or her descendants. The rites were celebrated by the eldest son of the clan-founder's lineage, and the ancestors of the four ascending generations were honoured, each differently, by their descendants in both direct and collateral lines.

Granet posited that the imposition of the *chao mu* order must have transformed Chinese kinship terminology by multiplying the number of kin terms in order to designate the ascendants and descendants of the four generations in both direct and collateral lines, thereby becoming the most perfect and accurate descriptive kinship system of its kind.[143] This system, which is reminiscent of that of Ancient Rome, has been known since Murdock as a Sudanese-type kinship system because it is still found in certain tribes in Sudan. The technical term for such a system is 'bifurcate collateral': there are different terms for father, father's brothers, mother, mother's sisters, father's sister and mother's brother. At the time Granet was writing his book, a Chinese anthropologist, Han Yi Feng,[144] whom Lévi-Strauss cites and who, like Granet, had analysed the ancient treatises on ritual, the *Li*, had concluded that Chinese kinship terminology had been decreed by a Confucian scholarly élite in the service of the emperor. But we will now leave these debates and return to Lévi-Strauss's assessment of Granet's work.

Lévi-Strauss pays 'tribute' to Granet for having classified kinship systems into '*chassé-croisé*' and 'deferred exchange', which Lévi-Strauss shows to be 'the only possible positive basis for the study of kinship

143  *The Elementary Structures of Kinship*, p. 327.
144  Ibid., p. 325 ff; H. Yi Feng, 'The Chinese Kinship System', *Harvard Journal of Asiatic Studies* 2, n° 2 (1937).

systems ("restricted exchange" and "generalized exchange")'. He even
credits him with having unwittingly reinvented the Murngin system and
having understood that descent reckoning does not affect the structure
of a marriage system.[145]

Then he quickly moves on to his criticisms. He felt that Granet, like
Durkheim, saw the Australians as relics of a very ancient era, and dealt
likewise with the archaic Chinese kinship system.[146] Starting from the
already complex Kariera system, he supposed Granet to have constructed
systems so complex that 'they are no longer verified by the facts'.[147] His
method is 'essentially ideological'. His interpretations 'seem confused
and contradictory, and sinologists have received them suspiciously, even
when their own analyses were not contrary to them'. Granet believed
that his knowledge of the Australian data was sufficient; it was not.
Finally, what he lacked, in Lévi-Strauss's opinion, was 'an adequate
familiarity with kinship problems, not only in China but in the rest of
the world'. Furthermore, the 'evolutionist distortion . . . prevents Granet
from seeing that restricted exchange and generalized exchange are two
elementary modalities, and not two stages in the one process'.[148]

Lévi-Strauss advances another hypothesis. Instead of abandoning its
original nomenclature, the Chinese system, he argues, kept it and
included it in the more complex system decreed by a scholarly élite
when they developed the system of mourning grades designed to
maintain internal clan solidarity. But this explanation does not suffice to
account for all aspects of the new system, in particular its 'obliqueness',
such as the seigneurial practice of marrying women from two different
generations. At this point, Lévi-Strauss compares the feudal Chinese
system to the 'oblique' system of the North American Miwok, and even
that of the Inca.

Let us pause here for a moment. I obviously cannot speak for Granet
and answer Lévi-Strauss's criticisms, some of which do not seem well
founded. I will therefore content myself with a few words. Granet, for

---

145 *The Elementary Structures of Kinship*, p. 323. 'One of Granet's main contributions to the general theory of kinship is to have shown that marriage rules are not
dependent on the idea of unilateral descent . . .'

146 Ibid., pp. 358–73.

147 Ibid., pp. 314, 350. Granet had imagined a Kariera-type system with eight
marriage classes.

148 Ibid., pp. 319, 311, 313, 320.

instance, did not place the existence in China of cross-cousin marriage at a time in ancient history, but at the end of the first millennium before Christ. The term *sheng* designated both patrilateral cross cousins (FZS) and matrilateral cross cousins (MBS), together with wife's brother (WiB) and sister's husband (ZHu);[149] this implies at once an exchange of sisters in $G^{+1}$ and marriage between cross cousins in $G^0$. Mikhail Kryukov, a specialist of Chinese and Southeast Asian kinship systems, has since shown that, according to the ancient texts, there was in China, alongside an egocentric Dravidian-type system, a sociocentric division of local societies into four categories resembling the Australian 'sections', which probably corresponded to ritual divisions in the society. The four divisions may also have served to regulate marriage alliances according to a principle of symmetrical reciprocal exchange.[150] These four categories were called *bo* (A), *shu* (B), *zhong* (C) and *ji* (D). A and D exchanged women, and their children belonged to categories B and C; B and C exchanged women, and their children belonged to categories A and D. Descent was reckoned patrilinearily, and it was the father's breath that was transmitted to the children, not the mother's blood as in Australia.

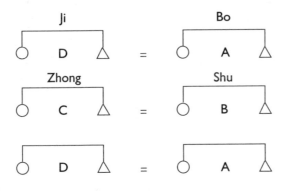

$D \times a = C$
$A \times d = B$
$C \times b = D$
$B \times c = A$

---

149 Ibid., p. 317. Lévi-Strauss summarizes Granet's hypothesis, deeming it possible but not verified. Yet it is: cf. M.V. Kryukov, 'Development of the Chinese Kinship System', in M. Godelier, F. Tjon Sie Fat and T. Trautmann, *Transformations of Kinship*, trans. N. Scott (Washington DC, Smithsonian Institution Press, 1998), pp. 296–8.

150 Kryukov, 'Development of the Chinese Kinship System'.

According to Kryukov, the system was transformed with the differentiation of kin into direct and collateral lines, and the distinction between consanguines and affines. In the fifth century BCE, wife's mother was no longer designated as *gu* – which also meant father's sister and mother's brother's wife (FZ, MBWi) – but by a separate term, *po*. Father's brother is distinguished from father; mother's sister from mother; wife's father from mother's uncle; and wife's mother from father's sister (FB ≠ F; MZ ≠ M; WF ≠ MB; WM ≠ FZ). In the second century CE, another kinship vocabulary, *shiming*, recorded a new change in the Chinese kinship nomenclature. The old term for patrilateral and matrilateral cross cousins (FZS, MBS), *sheng*, changed meaning and now designated father's son (FS). A new term, *shang*, appeared to designate wife's father (WF). The old Dravidian-type system with sister exchange and cross-cousin marriage had disappeared, at least among the dominant classes of Chinese society, while in the countryside and depending on the region, the old system of reciprocal exchange of wives between villages and communities continued to thrive.

In 1967, Lévi-Strauss therefore had reason to think the kinship systems of China, India and Southeast Asia should be re-examined on the basis of new information. This was the burden of his chapter entitled 'Peripheral Systems', presenting a rapid analysis of the Tibetan, Manchu, Lolo, Tungus, etc. systems, which offered the same mixture of restricted and generalized exchange; Lévi-Strauss suggested that 'generalized exchange was the most archaic form, and that restricted exchange appear[ed] subsequently'.[151]

Here, too, recent research does not substantiate the latter hypothesis, which would make generalized exchange the formula underlying all kinship systems from India to China and Southeast Asia. To take but one example – the evolution of the groups formerly known as Lolo and today Ji, who belong to the Tibeto-Burman groups of Yunnan Province – Chinese archaeological research has shown that, at the end of the Bronze Age, the ancestors of the Lolo groups split up, some settling in the west around Deli and the rest around Kumming. After their separation, the two groups evolved differently.

Using Chinese documents going back several centuries, dictionaries compiled in the nineteenth century and his own fieldwork, Kryukov

---

151 *The Elementary Structures of Kinship*, p. 388.

was able to show that, in the west, the groups that originally used a Dravidian terminology with cross-cousin marriage and no (developed) vocabulary for affines substituted an Iroquois-type terminology that still distinguished between parallel and cross kin, but had no rule prescribing marriage with a cross cousin, hence the development of a terminology for affines. In the east, among the Sasupo, their originally Dravidian-type terminology, which was therefore symmetrical and prescriptive (marriage with the bilateral cross cousin), gave way to an asymmetric-prescriptive system, retaining marriage with only one of the cross cousins, the matrilateral one. This was very similar to the Kachin system in Burma, but without any of the Omaha features of the Kachin system. So, there was indeed a shift from a Dravidian-type system with restricted exchange to a system with generalized exchange, and not the other way around. We find the same transformation among the Hmong-Khmer groups of Vietnam, which in their case are matrilineal and prescribe marriage with the female matrilateral cross cousin (MBD), with equations that cancel generational differences between certain kin positions, thus producing Crow-like oblique features.[152]

Now to India, with its immense chequerboard of several hundreds of different local groups, most of which adhere to the caste system, while a small minority belong to tribal formations.[153] In the space of three chapters, Lévi-Strauss mentions nearly one hundred groups, extending from the foothills of the Himalayas to the southern tip of India with the Tamils. He underscores the exceptional interest presented by South India, because that is where we find the three forms of marriage with the female cross cousin – the majority with the bilateral cross cousin, then with the matrilateral cross cousin and finally, in a few groups, with the patrilateral cross cousin. He emphasizes that, in the South, a man can claim one of his elder sister's daughters for a wife, and compares this custom with identical cases he observed in Amazonia.[154]

I will restrict myself here to looking at some of the hypotheses or assertions Lévi-Strauss advanced at the time (1947) and which today are

---

152  M. V. Kryukov, personal communication. Kryukov had used G. Condominas's work among the Hmong-Gar of South Vietnam.

153  The 1971 Linguistic Survey of India counted 1,652 languages.

154  *The Elementary Structures of Kinship*, pp. 422, 429.

no longer admissible on the basis, first, of Louis Dumont's findings,[155] and later those of Thomas Trautmann,[156] who, using Sanskrit and other texts covering several hundreds of years, reconstructed the logic underlying the Indian Dravidian systems and their development over the centuries. Robert Parkin's publications on the Munda, but also on the Indo-European-type systems of North India, shed new light on the Munda systems in the Himalayan zone.[157] Nick Allen, for his part, revisited the analysis of Sherpa and Byansi kinship systems.[158] I will summarize some of their contributions later.

The first invalid hypothesis is that there exists an archaic kinship system common to India and China, and founded on generalized exchange. Another is that India has been characterized since protohistory by a belief held in common with the peoples of Siberia, Tibet and Central Asia: that bones come from the father and flesh from the mother. Yet in fact these beliefs are found exclusively in North India, around the Himalayan zone, and nowhere else. Another hypothesis is that the caste system arises from the transformation of originally exogamous castes into endogamous castes. Within the endogamous castes there would have been two exogamous groups: on the one hand, the *sapinda*, groups of the deceased's paternal and maternal kin-gathered together for the funeral rites; this would result in the prohibition of new alliances between these two groups for three and sometimes five generations. And on the other hand, the *gotra*, which Lévi-Strauss describes as exogamous patrilineal groups, schools specialized in rituals, as it were, originally founded by Brahmins and then imitated by the other castes. Finally, when analysing the eight types of marriage listed in the Laws of Manu, Lévi-Strauss expresses surprise that the authorized forms of marriage are apparently regarded as unreciprocated 'gifts', with no countergift expected. Invoking the authority of Lowie and Mauss, he declares the hypothesis to be unfounded. How could a society function without

---

155  L. Dumont, *Dravidien et Kariera. L'Alliance de mariage dans l'Inde du Sud et en Australie* (Paris, Mouton, 1975).

156  T. R. Trautmann, *Dravidian Kinship* (Cambridge, Cambridge University Press, 1981).

157  R. Parkin, *The Munda of Central India: An Account of their Social Organization* (Delhi, Oxford University Press, 1992).

158  N. Allen, 'Sherpa Kinship Terminology in Diachronic Perspective', *Man* 11 (1976), pp. 569–97.

reciprocity? And so, Lévi-Strauss struggles to fit the Indian marriages 'by gift' into the category of exchanges between wife-takers and wife-givers: in a generalized exchange system, wife-givers do not receive women back from the givers, they receive goods.

None of these hypotheses or assertions is sustainable today. Clans are kin groups, and cannot in any way turn into castes. Castes are an overarching structure which encompassed and organized all the local societies that constituted pre-colonial India: hundreds of kingdoms and thousands of village organizations. This global structure reproduced at every level of the society the religious and political hierarchy dominated by the Brahmins, who were responsible for rites, and the Kshatriya, the warrior group that supplied the rajas who ruled the hundreds of kingdoms in question. This global structure, based on Vedic texts, is not governed by kinship relations. It encompasses and subordinates them for its own reproduction, hence caste endogamy and within each caste and subcaste (*jati*) the exogamy of the *gotra* and the *sapinda*. The *sapinda* are in fact only temporarily exogamous, since they allow the same alliances to be renewed after three, and sometimes five, generations. The *gotra* are exogamous patrilineal clans that refer to fictional divine and cosmic ancestors (the Sun, for example) and exchange women with the lineages of other clans from the same caste or subcaste. Their origin is therefore not associated with the formation of Brahminical religious schools subsequently imitated by the lower castes.

Lastly, marriage by 'gift without a countergift' – the possibility of which was rejected by Lowie, and which had led Mauss to think that India was the exception to his theory that a gift always entails the 'obligation to give in turn'. In his essay *The Gift*, Mauss writes: 'The cunning Brahmins in fact entrusted the gods and the shades with the task of returning gifts that had been made to themselves.' Here again, it is for religious reasons that the wife-takers are superior to the wife-givers when the latter give a daughter for one of their sons. But they accept the gift of this girl, who must be a virgin, only after carefully checking out the family's status within the caste and the astrological compatibility of the spouses, and above all after fiercely negotiating the dowry the bride will bring.

Apparently, the gift of a virgin, to which must be added a dowry that often bankrupts her family, is a gift without countergift, material or other. But this is not the case if one considers the religious and ritual backdrop of the marriage. From the Hindu standpoint, woman's nature is evil. She is sexually insatiable and therefore dangerous for men and for society.[159] Her body is polluted by the blood that she periodically sheds during menstruation. It is therefore a father's duty to keep his sons and marry off his daughters as soon as they reach puberty, if not before. Failing which, the ancestors could become so angry that they quaff the menstrual blood of the girl in guise of an offering. Women are therefore a permanent source of impurity in a social and cosmic order that ranks and divides castes and individuals according to their degrees of purity and impurity.

There is a countergift the wife-takers make to their givers, but it is on a religious, cosmic level, since they 'take on' the source of the pollution carried by this girl who has just begun to menstruate. Through a series of ritual acts, the takers accept responsibility for the inauspicious omens that accompany the transfer of this woman into their family, thereby ensuring their givers' future well-being. But at the time Mauss and then Lévi-Strauss were writing, this was not known.[160] Lowie was therefore right. Among humans there is no such thing as a gift without a counter-gift (if only an imaginary one).

It was only in 1964 that Lounsbury demonstrated the radical difference in nature between Dravidian systems and Iroquois systems,[161] which, until then, had been regarded as variants of Iroquois-type systems. Likewise, it was only in 1953, with the work of Louis Dumont and Irawati Karve,[162] and then in 1981 with the monumental study by Thomas Trautmann, *Dravidian Kinship*, that the inventory of India's kinship systems was systematized, and it became possible to compare South Indian Dravidian with Kariera systems, as well as with other section and subsection systems found in Australia.

---

159  Mauss, *The Gift*, p. 147, n. 61.

160  It was G. G. Raheja's book that enabled this step forward: *The Poison in the Gift. Ritual, Prestation and the Dominant Caste in a North Indian Village* (Chicago, University of Chicago Press, 1988); cf. Godelier, *Metamorphoses of Kinship*, p. 168.

161  Lounsbury, 'The Structural Analysis of Kinship Semantics'. The two types of system are confused in George Peter Murdock's book, *Social Structure* (New York, Free Press, 1949), published the year Lévi-Strauss's *Elementary Structures of Kinship* came out in France.

162  L. Dumont, 'The Dravidian Kinship Terminology as an Expression of Marriage', *Man* 53, n° 54 (1953), pp. 34–9; Dumont, *Dravidien et Kariera*; I. Karve, *Kinship Organization in India* (Bombay, Asia Publishing House, 1953).

Today the table of Indian kinship systems has become much more legible. If we leave aside a certain number of local tribal systems, India is divided into three types of kinship systems, associated with three major language groups: in the North, the Indo-European languages; in the South, the Dravidian languages; and in the Centre and the East, the Munda languages, which belong to the Austronesian family.

The Indo-Aryan system is structured by the opposition between wife-givers and wife-takers, which differentiate the affines on each side. The bride and the taking group must be not related, and the dowry accompanying the gift of the girl is not reciprocated materially. This type of marriage is founded on the Sanskrit texts governing the 'gift of a virgin' (*kanyadana*), which is a religious act, a gift without a material counterpart, unlike non-religious gifts and countergifts. These kinship systems distinguish between consanguines and affines, and do not distinguish between parallel and cross cousins. Since these alliances are not reciprocal, they always go in one direction only. This is reflected in the Hindi terminologies.

In Dravidian systems, particularly the Tamil system analysed by Louis Dumont, consanguines and affines are subsumed under the same terms: individuals are either parallel or cross kin – possible or impossible spouses. Cross-cousin marriage is the rule structuring the system and is inscribed in the terminology.

The Munda kinship system is by far in the minority if we compare it with the two other systems, the Indo-Aryan and the Dravidian. We now have Robert Parkin's major comparative study (1992) of the variants of these systems.[163] The Munda system distinguishes between parallel and cross kin, but marriage between cross cousins is forbidden, and in $G^0$, the parallel/cross distinction disappears. All consanguineal kin in that generation are brothers and sisters. A separate terminology is used for affines, as in the Indo-Aryan terminologies. Alliances are contracted between groups and are repeated, as in the Dravidian systems, but only after a lapse of several generations, so that the alliances are contracted between cousins separated by several degrees. These are thus bilateral alliances that are repeated after a certain span of time; the system also has a rule that underpins the edifice: the existence of alternate

163 Parkin, *The Munda of Central India*.

generations, as in certain Dravidian groups in central India and in Australia.[164]

We thus see that neither in India nor elsewhere is kinship capable of providing society with an overall structure. In India, the necessary over-arching structure is provided by from the division of society into four ranked categories, the *varna*, which are themselves divided into hundreds of endogamous castes and subcastes (*jati*). This structure is made up of a gigantic system of religious and political relations which encompasses all castes and individuals, and assigns them their place and role, complementary to the roles and place all the other castes and their members occupy in the *varna* hierarchy.

It is furthermore because the South Indian Dravidian systems are subordinated to a caste system that runs through them and structures them that the alliances they prescribe are, as Louis Dumont so clearly saw, 'marriage alliances' between lineages inherited from one generation to the next and not prescribed alliances between categories of individuals, as is the case with Australian sections. But in 1953 and even in 1975, Dumont could not know that sections were a relatively recent invention, and had not originally been designed to define whom one could marry. They were conceived, as we have seen, as ceremonial groupings of related individuals, and because of this they simplified, by 'improving', the functioning of the egocentric Dravidian systems that existed well before. Had he known this, Dumont would have had another argument in support of his theses.

The theoretical conclusion that must therefore be drawn is that, whenever the documentation allows it, we must combine 'structural' analysis, which reveals the principles governing the functioning of the systems, with historical analysis, which sees them appear and change over time and space. Lévi-Strauss was wary of the pitfalls of evolutionism and had rejected all historical considerations.[165] The lesson is clear. If we are to advance the state of our knowledge today, we must use both approaches so as to illuminate the question from two angles.

---

164 The foregoing is based on Trautmann's overview 'India and the Study of Kinship Terminologies', *L' Homme*, n^os 154–5 (September 2000), pp. 559–72.

165 *The Elementary Structures of Kinship*, p. 142: 'We have been careful to eliminate all historical speculation, all research into origins, and all attempts to reconstruct a hypothetical order in which institutions succeeded one another.'

The last two chapters of the book, which continue those devoted to China and India and precede the conclusion, examine asymmetrical structures – those that prescribe marriage with a matrilateral or a patrilateral cross cousin, the one excluding the other and of course excluding the bilateral cross cousin. Lévi-Strauss emphasizes that kinship theory needed to explain two enigmas concerning cousins:[166] the division between parallel and cross cousins, and the division among cross cousins between those who are prescribed spouses and those who are excluded. He notes that, in systems prescribing the reciprocal exchange of spouses, marriage is prescribed with the bilateral cross cousin, while the two other cross cousins, patrilateral and matrilateral, are regarded as equivalents of a bilateral cross cousin.

This is not the case with many systems, such as the Kachin, which is governed by a generalized exchange where marriage with the matrilateral cross cousin excludes marriage with the patrilateral cross cousin. An 'elective'[167] and ideological fission thus occurs here between cross cousins, which expresses the generative formula of the alliance, in other words the distinction between wife-givers and wife-takers, and the one-way direction of their relations. And once a unilateral preference intervenes, consideration of the degrees of kinship between the possible spouses moves to the fore.

Lévi-Strauss then shows that, while all cross-cousin marriage systems engender a structure of reciprocity, the systems entailing marriage with the matrilateral or the patrilateral cross cousin are not equivalent. In the second case, marriage with the father's sister's daughter (FZD) engenders a short cycle and constitutes a discontinuous change. My father gave a sister – no woman was given in return; my father's sister's first daughter will be my wife. Marriage with a matrilateral cross cousin, on the other hand, gives rise to two forms of continuous reciprocity. For Lévi-Strauss, marriage with the patrilateral cross cousin is the 'cheapjack' of the various forms of matrimonial transaction.[168] It is 'an abortive form [*sic*] . . . because it precipitately closes the cycle of reciprocity and consequently prevents the latter from ever being extended to the whole group'. To this form he opposes two others, which organize 'a vast cycle of reciprocity

---

166 Ibid., p. 438.
167 Ibid., p. 423.
168 Ibid., p. 449.

between all generations and lineages . . . as harmonious and ineluctable as any physical or biological law . . . In one case, the overall cycle of reciprocity is co-extensive with the group itself both in time and in space . . . In the other case, the multiple cycles which are continually created fracture and distort the unity of the group.'[169]

These assertions are odd because there is no such thing as a cheapjack system, no more than there are any 'aberrant' systems in Australia. I myself lived and worked for nearly seven years among the Baruya, a population in the New Guinea Highlands that practiced marriage with the patrilateral cross cousin whenever there had been no exchange of women between two lineages in $G^{+1}$.

One lineage gives a woman to another lineage without receiving a woman in exchange. The first daughter born to this woman must marry a man from her mother's lineage. The basic rule, then, was the direct exchange of women between two lineages, with a ban on reproducing this alliance for several generations, unless there had been no return gift for the woman given. The logic of the system was thus to multiply alliances, since a son could not take a wife in his mother's lineage – which would reproduce his father's marriage – and two brothers could not take wives in the same lineage. This set of rules, both positive (direct 'sister' exchange and marriage with the patrilateral cross cousin) and negative (prohibition on marrying one's matrilateral cross cousin, and, for brothers, on marrying in the same lineage, and for everyone, the obligation to wait two if not three generations before reproducing the same alliances), made for a flexible system, which was not repetitive over the short term and was in no way an 'abortive' system of exchange.[170]

In truth, Lévi-Strauss's judgments, which attribute to generalized exchange or to reciprocal exchange repeated from one generation to the next the capacity to engender 'a vast cycle of reciprocity between all generations and lineages . . . as harmonious and ineluctable as any physical or biological law', express a theoretical a priori on the part of their author: the idea that kinship relations in primitive societies as well as in many other social formations may potentially serve as a foundation for society, engendering a cycle of reciprocity that binds together all kin groups.

---

169  Ibid., pp. 448, 450.
170  Godelier, *Metamorphoses of Kinship*, pp. 23–85.

Such an overarching framework exists among the Baruya, but it is provided by relations other than those of kinship, namely, the political-religious relations that underpin the male and female initiations and which involve everyone according to age and sex, independently of lineage or village. And yet not just any clan can perform the initiation rites. Not all clans have their place in the performance of these rites, and those that hold the responsibility for the initiations are in a hierarchical relationship that has nothing to do with the kinship or alliance relations they have with each other. The same is true of India, where it is the caste system that provides the overall framework of reciprocities, complementarities and oppositions between castes (in accordance with the degrees of impurity and purity connected with each caste's activities), and not one or the other of the three kinship systems we have discussed: Indo-Aryan, Munda and Dravidian.

We now come to the conclusion of the book. This is divided into two parts. The penultimate chapter poses the problem of the passage to complex structures of kinship. The final chapter sums up one last time what kinship principles are for Lévi-Strauss, in the perspective he announced at the outset, which was to produce an introduction to a general theory of kinship.[171]

Lévi-Strauss justifies his choice of the immense zone, stretching from Siberia to Assam and from India to Melanesia, from which he draws the materials for his analyses. All types of restricted and generalized exchanges were represented there. But he reminds his readers that he was not looking for these systems' origins and paths of diffusion, because 'the three elementary structures of exchange, viz., bilateral, matrilateral and patrilateral, are always present to the human mind, at least in an unconscious form, and . . . it cannot evoke one of them without thinking of this structure in opposition to – but also in correlation with – the two others.'[172]

In reality, what is unconscious is not the exchange *formula*, be it bilateral or other. It is the intellectual conditions enabling the imagining of possible forms, of what can be done when one is forbidden to unite with 'close' kin and must therefore unite with others. These others can have been appropriated by violence, by abduction, or equally without

---

171 *The Elementary Structures of Kinship*, p. xxiv.
172 Ibid., p. 464.

violence, through reciprocal exchanges. The very limited number of possible forms of exchange explains the presence of the same types of kinship systems in societies that have never come into either geographical or historical contact with one another.

Lévi-Strauss then posits that complex structures can be explained by the development or combination of elementary structures. These contain a certain number of negative marriage rules connected with the prohibition of incest, but do not propose any positive indications for choosing a possible spouse – or more accurately, the latter come from outside the kinship system. There are prohibitions on marrying someone from another religion or another social class or someone of a different colour, among others. Lévi-Strauss thus sets aside for a later time his examination of the so-called Crow-Omaha systems, which do not prescribe a particular spouse but nevertheless combine principles of restricted and generalized exchange. In 1947, he did not yet define Crow-Omaha systems as being semi-complex – something he would do in 1965 in the Huxley Memorial Lecture, entitled 'The Future of Kinship Studies', which he gave at Oxford; and he would entrust the younger generations with studying them. This task would be taken up by Françoise Héritier and Élisabeth Copet-Rougier, together with numerous other researchers.

In an enigmatic formula, Lévi-Strauss mentions 'that wide zone of breakdown of kinship structures which is the Polynesian world'.[173] This assessment is meaningless today. It probably reflects the fact that Lévi-Strauss was as yet unaware of the importance and nature of the workings of 'undifferentiated' cognatic systems, organized not into clans but into what Raymond Firth christened 'demes'. In such systems, an individual's membership of a cognatic group goes through both men and women, and is maintained only if the individual continues to reside on their territory and to cultivate it. These systems, sometimes known as 'Hawaiian', are characteristic of the Polynesian zone and are by no means the effects of a 'wide zone of breakdown of kinship structures'.

Lévi-Strauss next turns to Africa and advances a hypothesis on the nature of the transition from elementary to complex structures. For him, Africa is the 'elected territory' of marriage by purchase, which 'in its very essence, relates to this elementary structure [generalized

---

173  Ibid., p. 466.

exchange], and, in a way, constitutes a supple and developed form of it'.[174]

To illustrate his hypothesis, he analyses the practice of *lobola* among the Bantu peoples of South Africa (Zulu, Herero, etc.) and similar customs observed among the Nilotic peoples in Sudan (Shilluk, etc.).[175]

I will isolate two crucial elements of this analysis. Firstly, in these predominantly pastoral groups, the relationship between men and their cattle, between each clan and its herd, is conceived of as a true 'substantial identity', and 'cattle are the most important medium for all ritual relations between human groups'.[176] Cattle are a sacrificial offering by men to the gods or the ancestors. Between humans themselves, cattle are used to seal marriages as well as political alliances.

Secondly, the principle at work in marriage exchanges is that the cattle received in exchange for a wife enable her brother to marry in turn: the cattle received from wife-takers is not kept, but transferred to wife-givers. The circulation of women and cattle is a new form of generalized exchange, but it is free of the constraint that exists among the Kachin, which dictates that the woman must already be linked to the man who marries her by a precise kinship relation – she must be his matrilateral cross cousin. Marriage by purchase dissociates the exchange structure from the obligation to choose a prescribed spouse within the field of kin ties. Such prescription as exists will come from the obligation to marry within one's religion, one's rank or one's ethnic group, or all three at once, as well as other obligations.

These analyses of marriage 'by purchase' – a far too ethnocentric and loaded term – had an impact that Lévi-Strauss could not foresee in 1947. The interior of New Guinea was still unexplored. Since then, dozens of monographs have revealed an opposition between two groups of societies, those practicing various of forms of so-called sister exchange (restricted exchange) – Baruya, Yafar, etc. – and those forbidding direct exchange and practising a formula like that found in Africa, namely the exchange of valuables – pigs, shells, etc. – for women. There, too, pigs are regarded as substitutes for human beings: the pigs received as

---

174  Ibid.

175  Ibid., pp. 468–9. Lévi-Strauss is using A. Hoernlé's work (1925) devoted to the Bantu, and that of C. Seligman and B. Seligman (1932) on the Nilotic peoples.

176  Ibid., p. 466.

compensation for a sister are in turn given to procure a wife for her brother (among the Chimbu, the Melpa, etc.). I showed the existence of these two systems in Melanesia in a collective volume edited with a Cambridge colleague, Marilyn Strathern.[177]

Lévi-Strauss then extends his hypothesis to Europe, suggesting that generalized exchange may have been the marriage formula practised in the Middle Ages or among the inhabitants of Tacitus's Germania. Lévi-Strauss raises another hypothesis, that of Hocart, but rejects it. In 1928, Hocart had suggested that the ancient Indo-Europeans might have practiced marriage between bilateral cross cousins, and therefore – in modern terms – their system may have been of a Dravidian type with cross-cousin marriage.[178] It would have been only later that it became – somewhat like what happened in ancient China – a so-called 'Sudanese'-type system, rich in descriptive terms (grandfather, grand-son, great-grandson, etc.), like the system of the Latins under the Republic. In reality, no Indo-European system makes a distinction between parallel and cross cousins, with one group being possible spouses and the other not, which is the precondition for cross-cousin marriage. Fresh light was thrown on these questions by Georges Dumézil in 1979, when he published his book on Indo-European wedlock.[179] But the problem remained unresolved, owing to the lack of any documentation as complete as the data provided by the *Annales* of China.

In the end, it was in India, and already then thanks to Dumézil, that in 1947 Lévi-Strauss would find a form of marriage that, for him, prefigured the traits of the modern European marriage system (and beyond, including Euro-American marriage). This was the *swayamvara* marriage, to which the Mahabharata devotes an entire section,[180] but which is not among the eight marriage formulas described in the Laws of Manu. The *swayamvara* marriage is a staple of courtly novels and epic poetry, where several princes in love with the same princess, the daughter of a raja, compete to win her hand with feats of valour. The

177 M. Godelier and M. Strathern, *Big Men and Great Men: Personifications of Power in Melanesia* (Cambridge, Cambridge University Press, 1991; new ed. 2008).

178 A. M. Hocart, 'The Indo-European Kinship System', *Ceylon Journal of Science*, section G, vol. 1 (1928), pp. 203 ff.; cf. *The Elementary Structures of Kinship*, p. 472.

179 G. Dumézil, *Mariages indo-européens* (Paris, Payot, 1979).

180 G. Dumézil, *Naissance d'archanges* (Paris, Gallimard, 1945).

princess makes her own choice. Her royal father does not oppose her. In the end the marriage depends on the partners' mutual wish.

Lévi-Strauss interprets this form of marriage as the consequence of the 'hypergamic' structure of Indo-European societies. Since a king's daughter can never find a spouse worthy of her, she is free to choose the suitor who outperforms the others in the tests set for him; she therefore marries a man of inferior rank, even if this rank is that of the Kshatriya nobility. And Lévi-Strauss comments: 'the lower classes have a major interest in the *swayamvara*'.[181]

In reality, the *swayamvara* formula is the aristocratic, princely and accepted form of another type of marriage by mutual choice: this kind, listed in the Laws of Manu and placed under the sign of the demons, is condemned. I am talking about *gandharva* marriage, the 'democratic' but negative form of *swayamvara* marriage, which is 'aristocratic' and positive. *Gandharva* marriage is the union of a man and a woman who desire each other and marry without their families' consent. It is condemned – as is *asura* marriage, or marriage by purchase – as irreligious because it is not the freely given, unreciprocated gift of a virgin and therefore carries all the impurities of a business transaction. In freely choosing to marry, the woman rejects the authority of the men in her family. She no longer represents her family, and forfeits the right to their support or to a dowry. This form of marriage occupies a growing place in the imaginations and aspirations of recent generations. It appears as the 'modern' form of marriage, as opposed to traditional marriage strategies, preoccupied with maintaining or raising the status of wife-givers and wife-takers within the caste and subcaste hierarchy.[182]

It is therefore *gandharva* marriage, rather than the princely *swayamvara* form, that anticipated and already displayed what, for Lévi-Strauss, were the three basic features of modern European marriage: 'freedom to choose the spouse within the limit of the prohibited degrees; equality of the sexes in the matter of marriage vows; and finally, emancipation from [kindred] and the individualization of the contract'.[183] One can only

---

181 *The Elementary Structures of Kinship*, p. 486.

182 For an analysis of the eight forms of marriage – four placed under the sign of the gods and four under the sign of demons – listed in the Laws of Manu, see Godelier, *Metamorphoses of Kinship*, pp. 139–41.

183 *The Elementary Structures of Kinship*, p. 477. The three principles are 'ideals'. In reality each can be circumvented – and therefore cancelled.

agree with this definition, which corresponds to the French Civil Code and to the marital state as it could be observed, at least in France, until the 1960s. Nevertheless, one reservation must be made. Modern European marriage is not modelled on an ancient, disparaged Indian ancestor. It descends straight from the ancient, imposed and extolled Christian marriage, a union freely consented between a man and a woman (monogamous marriage), which is a religious act, a sacrament, the joining before God, through God and in God of two persons of opposite sex, who will thenceforth be united for life since they are forbidden to divorce. Since the French Revolution and the Napoleonic Code (promulgated in 1801), a change has set in that began gradually but has gained speed and depth since the twentieth century.

The final chapter of *The Elementary Structures* is entitled 'The Principles of Kinship'. In it, Lévi-Strauss marshals his major theses and hypotheses. It is therefore important to join him in this inventory, since it is this book that deeply transformed the study of kinship, more than the few articles he wrote over the course of the fifty years following its publication. Here is how the theory unfolds.

All forms of marriage are forms of exchange. The exchange can be direct or indirect, continuous or discontinuous, immediate or deferred, closed or open, local or global, concrete or symbolic.

Exogamy 'provides the fundamental and immutable rule ensuring the existence of the group as a group' (*group* here meaning society). For there are two threats hanging over any society: the practice of consanguineous marriages would split the society into 'a multitude of families, forming so many closed systems or sealed monads which no pre-established harmony could prevent from proliferating or from coming into conflict'.

But the exogamy rule in itself does not suffice to prevent two families, or two groups organized according to a dual principle, from isolating themselves as 'an indefinitely self-sufficient pair, closely united by a succession of intermarriages'.[184] These two dangers are therefore eliminated only when the moieties are subdivided into sections or subsections, or when generalized exchange binds the growing number of local groups into the same '*connubium*' and creates alliances among them. Consanguineous marriages thus do not pose a biological threat but

184 Ibid., pp. 478–9.

rather a social threat. Everything begins with the establishment of the prohibition of incest as a universal taboo and the basic rule of all societies. The prohibition of incest is of crucial importance because it is the 'rule of giving par excellence', and the rule of giving women, which are the asset par excellence. Hence the famous formula: 'The prohibition of incest is less a rule prohibiting marriage with the mother, sister or daughter, than a rule obliging the mother, sister or daughter to be given to others.'[185] And this assertion, which might surprise a few psychoanalysts: 'There is nothing in the sister, mother, or daughter which disqualifies them as such.'[186]

Lévi-Strauss thus rejects Malinowski's thesis that 'incest would mean the upsetting of age distinctions, the mixing up of generations, the disorganization of sentiments and a violent exchange of roles', as exhibiting a 'naïve egocentrism [that is] far from being new or original'.[187] And he mocks it by showing the reader a few types of non-European families in which a man can marry a girl when she is still a child, whom he raises as a father before making her his wife. He cites pell-mell: 'incest à l'égyptienne', the Arapesh of New Guinea, the Tupi-Kawahiva of central Brazil, and so on, who, to be sure, do not live in the nuclear families characteristic of Christian Europe. But he fails to convince. The prohibition of incest rests on not one but two, complementary, foundations: on the one hand, the necessity for kin groups to form alliances in order to reproduce themselves and therefore to exchange some of their members with other groups; and on the other, the necessity, within these kin groups, to maintain relations of authority and solidarity between the generations and between the sexes, failing which the group will self-destruct. No society can tolerate confusion of the roles it prescribes to blood relatives, and even less their negation. This was what Malinowski was reminding us of, and rightly so. Culture imposes its order on nature, but it does so by the institution of two rules, not one: to form alliances in order to reproduce, and to reproduce in order to

---

185 Ibid., p. 481. It is difficult to marry or exchange one's mother if she is still the wife of one's father, but the formula is there purely for the beauty of it. The idea is fundamental, that of a double game, of a twofold effect of the prohibition – and not only the repressive aspect of the taboo.

186 Ibid., p. 485.

187 B. Malinowski, *Sex and Repression in Savage Society* (New York, Harcourt, Brace & Co., 1927), p. 251; *The Elementary Structures of Kinship*, p. 486.

transmit and to form new alliances. Descent principles are every bit as fundamental as alliance rules and are in no way, as Lévi-Strauss claimed at the time, a 'secondary aspect of kinship'. I believe I have demonstrated this in the foregoing. To impose on relations between the sexes, on humankind's biological nature, social forms determined by rules of descent and alliance is to reproduce kinship, a component of every human society. For humans are not content simply to live in society, as other primates such as chimpanzees and bonobos do; they produce society in order to live. And societies are at the same time cultures.

In his final chapter, Lévi-Strauss refers for the first time to Freud, and most courteously. To be sure, he criticizes *Totem and Taboo*, in which Freud explained the incest taboo and the exchange of women by a singular event that forever left its mark on the human collective unconscious. This was the sons' murder of their tyrannical father, who monopolized for his own enjoyment sexual access to the women of his horde; the sons then renounced their own access to the women, to avoid the risk of killing each other for the same reason. The forbidden women thus became available for other men and could be exchanged for their daughters and sisters, and so on.

For Lévi-Strauss, on the other hand, the prohibition of incest cannot be the inexhaustible consequence of a unique act that occurred in a mythical protohistoric past. It is an ongoing act, repeated in every era and in every society: the production by men of one of the components of every human society, kinship relations built on sexual relations between the sexes.

The continual production of this condition of our social existence has its own conditions of possibility, residing in the permanent intervention of a human mind universally capable of imagining reciprocal or univocal relations, complementary and opposing relations, etc. The origin of the incest taboo is therefore present within us at every turn. It is co-present at every moment in human history. It runs through all eras, since it is one of the immanent conditions of that history.

Lévi-Strauss's theoretical position seems irrefutable to me. Nevertheless, it needs to be completed, for alone it cannot account for the status of the child in the functioning of kinship systems. Another thesis, which is just as fundamental, must be added: in every era and in all forms of society, rules are needed to define to which group of adults (men and women) the children born of their unions, or adopted, belong, and towards which of these adults they have duties and rights. As a result, the rule that defines this belonging engenders the axis of transmission – and thus of *sharing* between the generations and individuals connected by this rule – of the various material and immaterial, concrete and imaginary components of their shared identity. To pose and impose a descent rule is therefore, and to the same extent as the incest taboo, a continual and ongoing act, repeated in every era and in every society, of producing the conditions of existence of the specific relations known as kinship relations.

In the end, Lévi-Strauss credits Freud with having revealed that 'the desire for the mother or the sister, the murder of the father and the son's repentance . . . perhaps . . . symbolically express an ancient and lasting dream . . . the permanent desire for disorder, or rather counter-order.' But in his view, instead of founding the taboo on an origin myth, psychoanalysis should adopt a 'more modern and scientifically more solid attitude, which expects a knowledge of its future and past from an analysis of the present.' For Lévi-Strauss, the only social science that has managed to conjugate a synchronic with a diachronic explanation 'is linguistics, regarded as a phonological study'. Lévi-Strauss comes back to the analysis he developed in 1945, in his article published in *Word*, of the relationship between structural linguistics and anthropology. He claims to have managed to reduce a mass of apparently complicated and arbitrary phenomena to a small number of simple forms, elementary structures of kinship that 'are constructed by means of two forms of exchange [restricted and generalized]; and these two forms of exchange themselves depend upon a single differential characteristic, namely the harmonic or disharmonic character of the regime considered.'[188] Systems with moieties, sections or subsections, systems with deferred exchange, are all built on one or the other form of exchange; but the relation between descent rule and residence rule, which would give rise to harmonic or disharmonic regimes, in no way acts as the automatic differential entailing a specific kinship system, as Lévi-Strauss believed at the time.

He nevertheless persisted in this belief all his life. But structural linguistics was not only an appropriate model for endowing anthropology with a scientific status. It also explained why it is men who exchange

---

188  *The Elementary Structures of Kinship*, pp. 491–3.

women and not the reverse. How could Lévi-Strauss provide a foundation for this thesis? Let us follow his reasoning. The prohibition of incest founds exogamy; yet 'exogamy and language . . . have fundamentally the same function – communication and integration with others'. We can imagine relations between the sexes as one of the modalities of a ' "great communication function" which also includes language'.[189] But language and the other forms of communication suppose the existence of symbolic thought. Therefore, it was the emergence of symbolic thought that would explain why it was women and not men that were exchanged.

> The emergence of symbolic thought must have required that women, like words, should be things that were exchanged . . . this was the only means of overcoming the contradiction by which the same woman was seen under two incompatible aspects: on the one hand, as the object of personal desire, thus exciting sexual and proprietorial instincts; and, on the other, as the subject of the desire of others, and seen as such, i.e., as the means of binding others through alliance with them. But woman could never become just a sign and nothing more, since even in a man's world she is still a person, and since in so far as she is defined as a sign she must be recognized as a generator of signs. In the matrimonial dialogue of men, woman is never purely what is spoken about . . . In contrast to words, which have wholly become signs, woman has remained at once a sign and a value.[190]

Paradoxically, Lévi-Strauss, who was always seeking to show that culture modifies nature and subordinates it, makes men's domination of women a fact grounded in nature. Clearly, it was not humans who endowed themselves with a brain capable of producing forms of thought that gave meaning to the world around us and to ourselves who inhabit and transform it. To give meaning is always to think with symbols, and it is because of these symbols – words, gestures, acts, institutions – that we can communicate our thoughts. 'We' designates both men and women and, unless we suppose that men and women do not have identical brains and do not enjoy the same capacity to think with symbols, Lévi-Strauss's demonstration has no basis in science: it is subjective and a

---

189  Ibid., pp. 493–4.
190  Ibid., p. 496.

fantasy of the author. Not that men's domination and women's subordination in many areas of social life are not, to varying degrees, social *facts*. The fact is there and it is indisputable. What is disputable, however, is the explanation Lévi-Strauss provides, and which he would never question.

The final words of this powerful book are also marked by subjectivity. Down to our day, Lévi-Strauss explains, humankind has dreamed and continues to dream of a time when it was still possible to win without losing, to finesse the law of exchange. It was a time when 'in that atmosphere of feverish excitement and sensitivity symbolic thought appeared and social life, which is its collective form', and when one could still dream that it was possible to 'enjoy without sharing'.[191] This fantasised vision of the moment when symbolic thought and social life appeared clearly did not stem from any form of 'structural analysis'. It was the pervasive, intimate vision of a secret world that would soon find expression, this time in a more invasive form, in *Tristes Tropiques* (1995) and which he would never renounce.

For if it is true that, during over 90 per cent of its existence – certainly more than 100,000 years – our species, *Homo sapiens sapiens*, made its livelihood from hunting, fishing, gathering, in short, by scarcely transforming the surrounding environment which offered its resources, all anthropological and archaeological studies prove that humankind did not dream of enjoying without sharing. Countless testimonies show that hunters do not generally consume the game they bring back to camp, or if they keep some for themselves, it is only after the others have taken their share ('taken' because they have the *right* to do so even if they have not personally participated in the hunt). A fundamental principle is asserted in these forms of sharing that structured the whole of social life, not only kinship relations. An individual can neither survive nor live without others. This constraint, which structures all aspects of life in society, this implicit obligation to give in turn, directly or indirectly, immediately or at a later time, is not based primarily in thought. It is immanent to the fact that no individual can exist without society, or develop their latent possibilities without society's permission, and its bestowal (or refusal) of the means to do so.

---

191 Ibid., p. 497.

Reciprocity is not only a principle of thought applied to life in society and contributing at the same time to its creation. The 'principle of reciprocity' is not the abstract expression, elaborated by the mind, of this rule embodied in our essence as a species that 'exists in society and produces society'. It is the same principle as appears in more concrete forms in the many proverbs, myths, tales, novels and poems that express it and are part of humanity's treasury of oral and written literatures. Thought did not invent the principle of reciprocity in order to apply it to social life in the form of a rule, a norm to be obeyed. The principle of reciprocity is merely the abstract representation of a constraint that pervades our existence: namely, that people cannot exist unless other humans contribute to make them exist and to sustain their existence. And this universal constraint is inscribed as much in the body as in the mind.

The reciprocity principle is therefore not a product of the unconscious, but of our 'way of relating to the world', our 'existing in the world'. The unconscious is that inaccessible place where part of the mind dwells and acts beyond the realm of conscious thought. Thought cannot be present at its own birth in us. It is born along with the capacity to represent relations between objects, ideas and so on, but also relations between relations. It therefore arises in each of us already endowed with structures that enable us to imagine and produce the mental armatures of kinship relations, of power relations, of the institutions that implement them, and endowed also with the capacity to imagine gods, myths or geometrical treatises. It is these capacities, rooted in the structures of the human mind, and therefore structures shared by all humans, that remain unconscious when we use them to analyse the world around us and to produce society.

The time has now come to take stock of *The Elementary Structures of Kinship*, a unique work of exceptional scientific import, completed on 23 February 1947 in New York and published for the first time in France in 1949.

I will proceed in two parts. The first reviews the aspects of the book that have made it unsurpassed and unsurpassable when it comes to explaining one of the two components of kinship, namely alliance. Next come the fundamental criticisms of certain theoretical positions that hinder further progress in the field. Finally, I will add a few clarifications.

But first, why is this such a powerful, great and unique book? In his Preface, Lévi-Strauss had made it clear that his goal was to lay the foundations of a general theory of kinship. He won his wager, even if his contribution did not cover the entire theory but one of its crucial domains: alliance. In making this choice, Lévi-Strauss was pursuing an aim that was both tactical and theoretical. It was tactical because his thorough knowledge of the work of English and American anthropologists, who were well ahead of their European colleagues in this area, had led him to identify a major flaw in their approach. Their work had been devoted above all to the inventory and analysis of the various descent modes, without according the same attention to modes of alliance. Furthermore, their distinctions between cross and parallel cousins as well as cross-cousin marriage were still somewhat obscure and continued to be the object of controversy. To be sure, the evolutionist view of human institutions, which characterized the birth of anthropology (Morgan, Tylor) and the historical fictions it had engendered, had practically vanished from the scientific debate. Anglo-Saxon anthropologists were less interested in the past than in the present state of non-Western societies, in other words in the way they worked, since they were for the most part locked into colonial systems and 'world empires' created by the European 'powers', or shut away on 'reservations' like those imposed on the Indians by the American Federal Government.

In terms of theory, after evolutionism, the time had come for functionalism, an approach to facts starting from this simple hypothesis: that the institutions of a society form a whole of which they are the complementary parts; and the explanation for their existence must primarily be sought in the context in which each society lives and reproduces itself, this context being ecological, ethnic and colonial. Nothing in common, then, with a project for the structural analysis of social systems that claimed to explain by the *same* principles *both* the similarities and the differences between social systems and the societies that reproduce them.

This was a tactical choice, then, that would place its author at the top of the international ranking of anthropologists and among the specialists of kinship, the privileged object of anthropology. But it was above all a strategic choice, for in focusing on the analysis of alliance, Lévi-Strauss was tackling a fundamental and universal component of kinship. In order to flesh out his project, Lévi-Strauss used a method that had never been practiced before. It is this method that organizes the first ten chapters of *The Elementary Structures*. Yet, while it is the source of the scientific content of the work, few critics have dwelled on it. Let me summarize.

Lévi-Strauss begins by examining the relationship between nature and culture. He then posits the prohibition of incest as the condition for the passage from the one to the other, with the insertion of a social rule in the relations between men and women. In so doing, he posits as the starting point of his analyses a universal social and cultural fact which he has deliberately stripped of its specific modalities. No sociologist or anthropologist of the time would have dared to do this, would have been so . . . reckless. Having posited this universal fact, Lévi-Strauss proceeds to deduce logically (in terms of mental and social logic) a whole series of consequences for society, shown by his theory to correspond to real, known institutions. The universal prohibition on uniting with close kin obliges a group to turn to exogamy, and creates both the possibility and the necessity to exchange women. Lévi-Strauss does not find his definitions of the facts of kinship in any handbook. He produces them as he goes, as he analyses the facts; and these definitions then form logical sequences, illuminated one after another by the universal meaning of the point of departure of their emergence and succession: the prohibition of incest. Thus the obligation to exchange women begets the analysis of dual organizations and then the distinction between parallel and cross cousins, which itself begets a typology of the possible forms of exchange – direct, indirect, immediate, deferred and so on. And in the end, all these facts, now elucidated and explained, are subsumed in two general categories: restricted exchange systems and generalized exchange systems. These are in turn subsumed in the all-encompassing category of 'elementary structures of kinship', in opposition to another all-encompassing category, but one that is practically empty at the close of the book, that of complex structures of kinship. In this category, we find only marriage by purchase, an emancipated form of generalized exchange, and modern marriage, that is, the Euro-American form.

Lévi-Strauss develops his general theory of kinship by deduction, starting from the analysis of a universal fact; and this general theory (or these initial elements of a general theory) was entirely new. No one had come up with it before, not even Morgan, to whom he pays tribute, as I said, by dedicating the book to him.

Another aspect of Lévi-Strauss's approach also helped lend a universal character to his analyses and their results: he showed that the production of kinship relations implied mental operations that are rooted in the deep structures of the human mind. In positing that every human mind possesses the same deep structures, regardless of era and society, Lévi-Strauss gave his results an importance that is valid for all historical periods and frees them from the limits and objections with which cultural and historical relativism meets all general assertions. Do not separate the mental from the social, and identify the universal structures at work within particular structures: these are the precepts that make for the enduring grandeur and power of this work.

Among the other positive but less far-reaching elements, is the hypothesis that the Murngin system had as its 'generating principle' a simple form of generalized exchange of the type $[A \rightarrow B \rightarrow C \rightarrow D \rightarrow A]$, which took the guise of an Aranda-type system with eight subsections. The hypothesis seems to have since been confirmed. In passing I would note that the effectiveness of structural analysis for unravelling sets of structures that have become intertwined over the course of history worked wonders here, reducing complexity by the discovery of the underlying generating principles, which are always few in number.

I must also stress the richness of the information with which Lévi-Strauss worked. He made available to generations of French anthropologists after him a considerable amount of data, debates and disputes that British, American, Australian and other anthropologists had amassed between the two world wars. Before the First World War, the group of sociologists that had gathered in France around Durkheim, Mauss and later Granet and others, certainly knew and discussed all the anthropological publications in English, German, Russian and Swedish – and in some cases Chinese. They had read the works of Boas, Malinowski and the first texts of Max Weber soon after they appeared. Mauss had gone to the United States. He corresponded in particular with Radcliffe-Brown. But in France, kinship was not at the top of anthropologists' list of interests in the interwar period. *The Elementary Structures*, appearing as it did in 1949, filled a gap and encouraged French anthropologists to continue to work in close collaboration with their English and American colleagues and to use and enrich the same database.

Despite the power of the book, though, it has its limitations. When it comes to theory, as we have seen, the major weakness of *The Elementary Structures* is not to have recognized the role of descent in structuring the way kinship systems work. Whatever the nature of the descent principle chosen by a society, there must be one in order for a kinship system and kin groups to exist. Whether descent is traced through the men, through the women or through both but differently, its principles are just as 'culturally artificial' as the alliance principles, and equally few in number, which reduces the immense diversity of kinship systems to the varied application of these few principles. Alliance is gift; descent is sharing and transmission. And if the same terminology is often used even where the descent principles associated with it are different, it is simply because human groups have for the most part imagined descent independently from alliance.

However, this relative independence in no way proves that descent is not an essential aspect of kinship. Descent involves the representations and values societies attach to the man and the woman, to their roles in society and to what each can transmit through their children. And these representations and values are much more complex and varied than the simple fact of contracting alliances. Every aspect of the evolution of kinship relations in Europe over the past thirty years argues against Lévi-Strauss's devaluation of descent. Today's forms of alliance are increasingly flexible and varied: marriage, cohabitation, civil partnerships, etc. But the importance of children and the measures society (the state) sets in place to protect them in the event of the parents' separation or the dissolution of their alliance have also grown stronger. Of course, whether families are based on cohabitation or marriage, or are recomposed following divorces or separations, the prohibition of incest still applies, even with the children of a previous marriage who come with the new partner and who, despite lacking a genetic tie with the other partner, are supposed to be treated as his or her 'own' children, and therefore excluded from sexual relations. In sum, the incest taboo is not the rule par excellence – and even less the only rule. It is one of the two rules that transformed nature into culture and effected the passage from one to the other, but only where relations between the sexes and appropriation of the resulting children are concerned.

Another criticism I have already mentioned and to which I will return is the 'disguised naturalization' of men's domination of women and their monopoly of power and authority in society. I use the word 'naturalization' because this domination is presented as the effect of the emergence of symbolic thought, in other words as the result of brain development. Women's subordination to men, in this view, is thus the direct consequence of the human brain and its cognitive capacities. I ask again: was the female brain so different, then, from that of men? Unsuited to language and symbols?

Finally, like many anthropologists even today, Lévi-Strauss believed that primitive societies were kin-based, that kinship relations determined their overall structure, and that this capacity diminished and disappeared as the societies 'opened up to history'. But open to history or not, societies are always historical realities that extend over a larger or smaller territory; and what makes these societies concretely exist is not the tangle of kinship relations between the constituent groups but relations of another order, which encompass and pervade kinship relations and kin groups, and subordinate them to their reproduction. These relations are those that define their sovereignty over their territory and its resources, and over themselves; in the West they are, I repeat, called 'political-religious relations'. Although – following Gilhodes for the Kachin and Granet for Ancient China – Lévi-Strauss mentioned the existence of feudal or semi-feudal structures in this part of the world, he did not pursue the analysis of the relations between political power and kinship. To conclude, I will add that the theoretical importance Lévi-Strauss attributed to the existence of a harmonic or disharmonic relation between descent reckoning and residence has not been corroborated.

I will rapidly mention a certain number of limitations attaching to *The Elementary Structures* that are not the consequence of Lévi-Strauss's theoretical positions, but derive from the limits of the material at his disposal. In 1945–47, the difference in nature between Dravidian- and Iroquois-type systems was not known. The two were lumped together under the label 'Iroquois'. It was not until 1964 that Lounsbury demonstrated the difference between them; and in 1965 Lévi-Strauss took this into account in his Huxley Memorial Lecture on 'The Future of Kinship Studies'. Likewise, in 1945–47, the study of the Polynesian systems was still in its infancy. Firth and Goodenough had merely scratched the surface. Lévi-Strauss would again take their findings into consideration in the second edition of *The Elementary Structures*, published in 1967. He would no longer talk about the 'collapse of kinship' in Polynesia but about 'undifferentiated' systems, that is, cognatic systems, which were the prevailing form there.

In 1947, Lévi-Strauss was perfectly aware that systems with sections and subsections were still spreading among the Aboriginal groups of Australia a few years before he wrote his chapters on Australian kinship systems. These were, in his opinion, 'classic' restricted exchange systems. Oddly enough, he did not ask himself what kinship systems were in force before the groups adopted sections and subsections. Had he done so, he could have avoided describing Elkin's 'Aluridja' systems as 'aberrant'. In addition, Lévi-Strauss did not yet have a clear picture of the kinship systems found in India, from the Himalayas to the southern tip of Tamil country and Sri Lanka. Hence the limits of his analysis.

Lastly, while affirming that there can be no family without society, Lévi-Strauss remains ambiguous concerning the status of what he calls 'consanguineous' families, closed groups tempted by incest. Is he referring to a time when humankind had not yet emerged from its animal state, a time when the incest taboo, the prohibition on uniting with close kin, had not yet come into being? If so, this humanity before the prohibition of incest would look a lot like Freud's imaginary horde, in which the father would be murdered, thus giving rise to the exchange of the women.[192]

---

192  M. Godelier, 'Meurtre du père ou sacrifice de la sexualité', in J. Hassoun and M. Godelier, eds, Meurtre du père, sacrifice de la sexualité. Approches anthropologiques et psychanalytiques (Paris, Arcanes, 1996), pp. 21–52.

# 3

## *The Elementary Structures of Kinship*: Complements (1949–1959)

Although *The Elementary Structures of Kinship* received a luke-warm welcome in France, it sparked lively interest in Great Britain and the United States, and immediately became the target of criti-cism and a welter of controversy. Lévi-Strauss's approach to theo-retical questions, his way of defining facts and stringing together definitions and his conclusions all were designed to clash head-long with the functionalist empirical school of thought prevailing in France at the time.[1] Lévi-Strauss was immediately taxed with 'intellectualism' *à la française*, 'idealism', etc. One of the quarrels concerned the nature of the *structures* he had described. Had he meant to set out a simplified model of reality? Was 'structure' a mental entity, or an immanent aspect of reality that he was propos-ing to analyse?

Another bone of contention was the question of whether the cross-cousin marriage rule was really prescriptive – in which case no one was exempt – or merely preferential? Furthermore, it was hardly easy to understand what Lévi-Strauss meant by 'deep struc-tures' of the human mind, and to verify whether a 'model'

---

1 Cf. M. Bloch, 'Lévi-Strauss chez les Britanniques', *Cahiers de L'Herne*, n° 82 (2004), pp. 349–56. 'To British anthropologists, any mention of the "spirit" is tinged with fuzzy metaphysics'. The turnaround was slow and due to two eminent personalities: E. Leach and R. Needham.

constructed to visualize the complexity of an empirical reality coincided more or less, or not at all, with this reality was a permanently open question. We will return to all these issues later.

Between 1949 and 1959, Lévi-Strauss wrote five new texts on kinship. For the most part, they repeated the ideas developed in *The Elementary Structures*, and enriched certain points. But they also opened new avenues of inquiry, concerning Arab Muslim marriage for instance, which raises the more general issue of endogamous marriages and therefore of marriages between close kin. In 1955, we also find Lévi-Strauss giving a lesson in Marxism to the great Islam specialist Maxime Rodinson, and affirming that his analysis of kinship systems in classless societies is entirely in line with Marx and Engels's dialectical materialism.

The following texts were written during this period:

– *Introduction to the Work of Marcel Mauss*, 1950[2]
– 'La notion de structure en ethnologie', 1952[3]
– Letter to the editor-in-chief of *La Nouvelle Critique*, 25 November 1955[4]
– 'The Family', 1956[5]
– 'Le Problème des relations de parenté', 1959.[6]

We will examine them in order.

2  C. Lévi-Strauss, *Introduction to the Work of Marcel Mauss*, trans. F. Baker (London, Routledge & Kegan Paul, 1987).

3  C. Lévi-Strauss, 'Social Structure', presented at the Wenner-Gren Foundation International Symposium on Anthropology, New York, 1952, in A. L. Kroeber, ed., *Anthropology Today* (Chicago, University of Chicago Press, 1953), pp. 524–53; also in Lévi-Strauss, *Structural Anthropology*, trans. C. Jacobson and B. Grundfest Schoepf (New York, Basic Books, 1963), pp. 277–323.

4  *Structural Anthropology*, pp. 343–5.

5  C. Lévi-Strauss, 'The Family', in H. L. Shapiro, ed., *Man, Culture, and Society* (London, Oxford University Press, 1956), pp. 332–57.

6  C. Lévi-Strauss, 'Le Problème des relations de parenté', in *Systèmes de parenté. Entretiens multidisciplinaires sur les sociétés musulmanes* (Paris, École des Hautes Études, 6th section, 1959; mimeo), pp. 13–20.

## Introduction to the Work of Marcel Mauss (1950)

This text focuses on Lévi-Strauss's view of nature and the role of symbolic thought in the emergence of life in society. For Lévi-Strauss, any culture is a set of symbolic systems 'headed by language, marriage rules, economic relations, art, science and religion'. This list does not include power relations, i.e. politics. And in his view, these systems 'remain incommensurable'.[7] The question therefore arises of the relations obtaining among these relations. But, in his inquiry, Lévi-Strauss performs a fundamental theoretical about-face with respect to Mauss: 'Mauss still thinks it possible to develop a sociological theory of symbolism, whereas it is obvious that what is needed is a symbolic origin of society.'[8]

The origin of society, he writes, is connected with the appearance of symbolic thought and language, and this could only have occurred in the form of a 'big bang'.

> Whatever may have been the moment and the circumstances of its appearance in the ascent of animal life, language can only have arisen all at once. Things cannot have begun to signify gradually. In the wake of a transformation which is not a subject of study for the social sciences, but for biology and psychology, a shift occurred from a stage when nothing had a meaning to another stage when everything had meaning ... at the moment when the entire universe all at once became *significant*, it was none the better known for being so.[9]

This formula is already an introduction to the study of mythical thought. Through myths, the universe becomes symbolically 'significant' without being truly 'known'.[10] At the same time, as soon as it appeared, symbolic thought had to effect a 'synthesis immediately given to, and given by,

---

7 *Introduction to the Work of Marcel Mauss*, pp. 16–17.

8 Ibid., p. 21.

9 Ibid., pp. 59–60.

10 Ibid., p. 58. 'The universe signified long before people began to know what it signified' (p. 61). Hence the famous formula: 'symbols are more real than what they symbolise, the signifier precedes and determines the signified' (p. 37). The signified is what man imagines, but the imaginary is only part of what he imagines, the rest continues to be more real than what one imagines.

symbolic thought' that would overcome the contradiction by virtue of which one perceives things in terms of self and others, and at the same time grasps the social value of gifts and countergifts. This is the thesis he developed in *The Elementary Structures*.

The 'big bang' theory of the appearance of symbolic thought is obviously no longer accepted today, if it ever was. We know that the separation of our protohuman ancestors from the animal kingdom began well before the appearance of spoken language. There is little doubt that there were proto-languages, and some 500,000 years before our era, *Homo erectus* domesticated and utilized fire. Animals eat their food raw and are afraid of fire. The discovery, use and preservation of fire had therefore already transformed the social, intellectual and emotional relations among the distant ancestors of the Neanderthals, a branch of *Homo sapiens* older than our own that coexisted with *Homo sapiens sapiens* for several millennia before dying out.

For Lévi-Strauss, symbolic thought is rooted in the unconscious, and it is at this level that the 'opposition' between self and others could be surmounted. A part of the same mind, whose deep structures are the same in all humans, the unconscious, 'would be the mediating term between self and others'. The encounter with others would thus take place initially without moving outside ourselves, but would follow 'itineraries traced once and for all in the innate structure of the human mind'.[11]

The unconscious of which Lévi-Strauss is speaking here is not the repository of repressed desires. It is not the unconscious explored by psychoanalysts, whose methods are unable to capture the image of a society's structure. It is a cognitive rather than an affective unconscious, which must be explored using 'a *differently* intellectualist psychology, the generalised expression of the laws of human thought, of which the individual manifestations, in different sociological contexts, are simply the various modes'. That is why the aim of anthropology is to contribute, as Mauss but also Lévi-Strauss strove to do, to 'an enlargement of the scope of human reason'.[12] A superb formula that attests to his deeply held and ceaselessly proclaimed conviction that anthropology is a 'humanism'.

---

11  Ibid., pp. 34–6.
12  Ibid., p. 65.

## 'The Notion of Social Structure in Anthropology' (1952)

This is an important text for understanding Lévi-Strauss's approaches to theory and method. It is a sort of second structuralist manifesto, following the important article he published in *Word* in 1945. This long article, written in English, was aimed primarily at British and American anthropologists. It was first published in the collective work edited by A. L. Kroeber in 1953, whose title encapsulates the contributors' intention to review the state of anthropology after World War II.[13]

I will concentrate on the passages in which the author defines the notions of structure and model, as well as those that complete his analyses of kinship and the reasons for which it is the women who are exchanged and not the men.

He opens with a hard-hitting statement: 'The term "social structure" has nothing to do with empirical reality but with models which are built up after it . . . social relations consist of the raw materials out of which the models making up the social structure are built.'[14]

In any given society, we find social relations. These are the relations that make up the society, but the *structure* of these relations is not to be found in the field of observed reality. It must be reconstructed in the mind. The reconstruction takes the shape of a model, and it is these models that constitute the object of structural analysis. This kind of analysis is applicable to many fields, of which anthropology is one. Drawing on the then-recent work (1944) of John von Neumann and Oskar Morgenstern in game theory and information systems, but also on research by Norbert Wiener and Claude Shannon (1948),[15] Lévi-Strauss went on to define the four conditions models must meet in order to qualify as representations of structures:[16]

---

13 Kroeber, ed., *Anthropology Today*, pp. 524–53; also published in *Structural Anthropology*, pp. 277–323. These texts were presented at an international symposium organized in 1952 by the Wenner-Gren Foundation on the topic of 'Social Structure'.

14 *Structural Anthropology*, p. 279.

15 J. von Neumann and O. Morgenstern, *Theory of Games and Economic Behavior* (Princeton, Princeton University Press, 1944); N. Wiener, *Cybernetics or Control and Communication in the Animal and the Machine* (Cambridge, MIT Press, 1948); C. Shannon and W. Weaver, *The Mathematical Theory of Communication* (Urbana, University of Illinois Press, 1949).

16 *Structural Anthropology*, pp. 279–80.

First, the structure exhibits the characteristics of a system. It is made up of several elements, none of which can undergo a change without effecting changes in all the other elements.

Second, for any given model there should be a possibility of ordering a series of transformations resulting in a group of models of the same type.

Third, the above properties make it possible to predict how the model will react if one or more of its elements are submitted to certain modifications.

Finally, the model should be constituted so as to make immediately intelligible all the observed facts.[17]

We immediately see that this is not an anthropological definition but an epistemological one. It concerns all the sciences dealing with nature and society. It is the common base. The best model, the one that has the best chance of being 'true', will be the simplest one, even though it is based on no other facts than those it must account for; but it must account for them all.

There are many kinds of models, 'conscious or unconscious, depending on the level at which they operate'. Among the conscious models, there are those already constructed by societies to explain themselves. These indigenous models are often flawed or incomplete owing to their function, which is to 'perpetuate beliefs and customs rather than to expose their workings'. Let us recall that Marx likewise showed that the notion of 'wages', as the price of labour, concealed the added value created by labour as well as the true mechanism behind the production of commodity value and the source of the profit produced by capital.

Nevertheless, for Lévi-Strauss, certain indigenous models can help us discover structures, and they are deserving of the utmost attention. This is the case of the models of kinship systems with sections and subsections, passed on in the form of theoretical rules from tribe to tribe by the Australian Aboriginal groups themselves. I discussed this problem when I emphasized that, in order for a social system to be reproduced,

---

17 Applying these principles, Lévi-Strauss revisited his analysis of Chinese kinship in an attempt to explain certain elements, for example the addition of tecnonyms to kin terms.

the conscious forms by which it is represented for those who are going to reproduce it must attach themselves to something in its structure. Failing this, their acts would lose all meaning and the system would fall apart.

In his *Introduction to the Work of Marcel Mauss*, Lévi-Strauss even ventured the idea that the integral explanation of an object must account simultaneously for its own structure and for the representations by means of which we apprehend its features, or, 'to put it another way, we can never be sure of having reached the meaning and the function of an institution if we are not in a position to relive its impact on an individual consciousness. As . . . that impact is an integral part of the institution.'[18]

Let us face it: anthropology is as yet no more able than the other social sciences to explain why and how given social relations are represented in given ways – by representations which, once they have appeared and been shaped into a symbolic system, constantly affect the way these relations are experienced, and therefore have an impact on and within the subjectivity of those who experience them.

To return to Lévi-Strauss's argument, he also stresses that there is no necessary connection between the notions of measure and structure. The search for structures bears first of all on qualitative aspects of reality, and therefore can call upon set theory, group theory and mathematical logic, which do not give a measurable solution to the problems they address.[19] But when it comes to measuring, for example, how it is that, in a society with a known population, a given form of marriage comes to be practised, one can always call on either mechanical models (if the population is small) or statistical models (if one is dealing with large groups).

Lévi-Strauss then set a more ambitious goal for structural research, which he strove to achieve in his analyses of Amerindian myths. Once he had isolated the levels of reality that were of strategic value for the research, and constructed models to represent them, his ambition was

---

18 *Introduction to the Work of Marcel Mauss*, p. 28; or again, 'Any valid interpretation must bring together the objectivity of historical or comparative analysis and the subjectivity of the lived experience' (ibid.). This was already Marx's position in his famous theses on Feuerbach.

19 Hence the article Lévi-Strauss published in 1954: 'Les Mathématiques de l'homme', *Bulletin international des sciences sociales* 6, n° 4, pp. 653–76.

to compare the formal properties of these models *independently* of the nature of their components – kinship relations, economic relations and so on. To advance on this path, Lévi-Strauss adopted the theoretical position taken by Kurt Goldstein,[20] and (paradoxically) urged anthropologists attached to the comparative model 'to limit [themselves] to a thorough study of a small number of cases, thus proving that in the last analysis one well-done experiment is sufficient to make a demonstration.'[21] And he was right.

In my own case, it was only when I extended my analysis of the Baruya society to the question of whether, in a society with neither classes nor castes and which had recently become subordinate to a colonial state, kinship relations and kin groups indeed formed the foundation of this society, as prevailing anthropological theory encouraged us to think, that I discovered that what had made this society what it is – a local human group claiming its own identity and territory – was not kinship, but the production of political-religious relations. And this theoretical conclusion, obtained by analysing particular cases, turned out to be generalizable and capable of illuminating the forms of sovereignty exercised by societies at different points in time and in different geographical locations.[22]

To achieve this, Lévi-Strauss urged including anthropology in a framework of sciences in the process of construction. Such a framework would combine social anthropology, economics and linguistics into a single discipline, that of the science of communication. For, to his way of thinking, 'in any society, communication operates on three different levels: communication of women, communication of goods and services, communication of messages. Therefore, kinship studies, economics and linguistics approach the same kinds of problems on different strategic levels.'[23]

For Lévi-Strauss, in the context of marriage, women are at once signs, values and persons. In the case of economic exchanges, goods and services are values and not persons. These statements are obviously

20  K. Goldstein, *La Structure de l'organisme* (Paris, Gallimard, 1951), pp. 8–25.
21  *Structural Anthropology*, p. 288.
22  M. Godelier, *In and Out of the West: Reconstructing Anthropology,* trans. N. Scott (Charlottesville, University of Virginia Press, and Verso, 2009).
23  *Structural Anthropology*, p. 196.

debatable. In economic relations, persons and groups do the producing, exchanging and communicating. To be sure, marriage strategies are amenable to an analysis in terms of game strategies, but these are employed within a pre-existing structure: they do not produce it, rather they use it to achieve their goals. This is the flaw in Bourdieu's theory as developed in *Outline of a Theory of Practice*, in which he claims that, as they weave together, the strategies of individuals and groups engender the social structures in which they live and act.[24]

Lévi-Strauss then poses the problem of the relations between structures of communication and structures of subordination, only to reiterate his already familiar analysis of matrimonial exchanges among the Kachin or in India, where these exchanges take place between groups ranked according to political power or economic wealth, thus giving rise to strategies of hypergamy and hypogamy. Yet he takes advantage of a long footnote to repeat, in opposition to Schneider and Homans,[25] that there is no necessary link between a patrilineal or matrilineal descent rule and marriage with the matrilateral cross cousin, something he had already underscored. But the reason is not the one he advances. The disconnect between descent rule and marriage rule within a kinship system does not mean that descent is a secondary aspect of the system; on the contrary, it is just as essential as – though independent of – alliance.

Lévi-Strauss ends his article with this basic question: is there an order of orders, a structure of relations between structures? Meyer Fortes had attempted a reply in 1949, in the 'Mélanges' in homage to Radcliffe-Brown.[26] But Lévi-Strauss suggests in a roundabout way that the problem of the order of orders should be approached from the standpoint of Marx's distinction between base and superstructure, a language that, at the time, was fairly new to British and American anthropologists.

---

24  P. Bourdieu, *Outline of a Theory of Practice*, trans. R. Nice (Cambridge, Cambridge University Press, 1977).

25  G. C. Homans and D. M. Schneider, *Marriage, Authority and Final Causes: A Study of Unilateral Cross-Cousin Marriage* (Glencoe, IL, Free Press, 1955).

26  M. Fortes, ed., *Social Structure* (Oxford, Oxford University Press, 1949).

## Letter to the Editor-in-Chief of *La Nouvelle Critique* (1955)

The reader will therefore be less surprised to learn that in 1955, in response to two articles by the eminent Marxian specialist of Islam, Maxime Rodinson, who had criticized him in the journal *La Nouvelle Critique*, Lévi-Strauss reaffirmed his adhesion and fidelity to the ideas of Marx and Engels.

> I regret, however, since so much attention was paid to me, that he did not think it profitable to inquire into my endeavours to reintegrate the anthropological knowledge acquired during the last fifty years into the Marxian tradition . . . He would have discovered – in addition to a Marxian hypothesis on the origins of writing – two studies dedicated to Brazilian tribes (the Caduveo and the Bororo), which are efforts to interpret native superstructures based upon dialectic materialism. The novelty of this approach in the Western anthropological literature perhaps deserves more attention and sympathy.[27]

Lévi-Strauss goes on to cite, as he was to do frequently in later writings, a letter Engels wrote to Marx, dated 8 December 1882, and another to Kautsky, dated 10 February 1883, who had asked him about the meaning of the *Origin of the Family, Private Property and the State* (1883), written after reading Morgan's *Ancient Society*. Engels answered Kautsky as follows: 'It is not barbarism that establishes the primitive character of a society, but, rather, the degree of integrity of the old blood ties in the tribe. It is these blood ties which must be demonstrated in each particular instance, before drawing conclusions for this and that tribe from isolated phenomena.' And Lévi-Strauss adds: 'What have I done in *The Elementary Structures*, if not to demonstrate, "in each particular instance," the nature of the [old] "blood ties", "for this and that tribe"?'[28]

Reading these declarations, we understand better why Lévi-Strauss would affirm in *The Savage Mind*,[29] written in 1962, the primacy of the

---

27 Lévi-Strauss, 'Letter to the Editor-in-Chief of *La Nouvelle Critique*', dated 25 November 1955, which the journal did not publish; *Structural Anthropology*, p. 343–4, n. 31.

28 Ibid., p. 345, n. 48.

29 C. Lévi-Strauss, *The Savage Mind* (Chicago, University of Chicago Press, 1966), pp. 126, 178.

base, and why this thesis would be constantly reaffirmed throughout the four volumes of his series devoted to Amerindian mythology.

## 'The Family' (1956)

'The Family' is a didactic text written as a complement to *The Elementary Structures of Kinship.* In it, Lévi-Strauss advances the idea that families are both the condition and the negation of a society. When they close in on themselves, they threaten that society. Alternatively, by ensuring the birth of children and contracting alliances they guarantee the permanence of the society. These remarks may seem trite, but they contain the implicit judgment that it is alliance that binds families together and makes a society.

Lévi-Strauss then describes what the ideal family is for someone from Western Europe. It is a husband, a wife and the children born of their union. The members of the family are bound together by legal ties, by rights and obligations of an economic, religious or other nature, by sexual rights and duties, and by a variety of sentiments such as love, affection and respect.[30]

He goes on to compare this Western version of the family with other forms of family based on different principles: polygynous or polyandrous families, the south-Slavic *zadruga*, the French *maisnie* and so on. He recalls that in Africa, high-ranking women could marry a woman of lower rank and have her 'bear children through the services of acknowledged male lovers'.[31] The female husband then became the 'father' of these children and transmitted to them her name, rank, possessions, etc. Forty years later, in 1986, Lévi-Strauss would come back to these facts, which are familiar to anthropologists, to explain to a Japanese audience that humankind had long ago already invented the means to remedy the sterility of couples or the premature death of the spouse who leaves a widow or widower without descendants. This lecture places him at the very heart of current debates on surrogate mothers, gay parenting, and so on. But the 1986 texts did not appear in France until April 2011, a year and a half after

---

30 'The Family', p. 339.
31 Ibid., p. 345.

the author's death, on 30 October 2009.[32] His very open-minded positions on these controversial questions – more open than those of many of his disciples – have had no real social or intellectual impact on the debates raging in our societies for the last thirty years. It nevertheless remains that, in 1956, Lévi-Strauss considered that each society attributes a different value to the temporary union, resulting from love or violence, and the union resulting from marriage, whether this be the outcome of free choice, is imposed by the family, or stems from a 'purchase'. Whatever the case may be, for Lévi-Strauss a marriage is originated not by individuals but by groups, who bind themselves to each other 'before and above the individuals'.[33] Marriage, for him, never is and can never be a 'private business'.[34] The conjugal family is probably the most widespread form, but 'monogamy is not inscribed in the nature of man',[35] a thesis he had already developed in *The Elementary Structures*.

What renders the family necessary for Lévi-Strauss is primarily the division of labour between the sexes, which establishes mutual dependence between men and women. Aside from the 'solid ground of women's biological specialization in the production of children',[36] this division of tasks is largely of cultural, social, origin and therefore artificial: in some societies, it is the women who weave; in others it is the men. The division of labour stems from a reciprocal prohibition on performing certain tasks, in the image of the prohibition of incest, which stems from a division of marriage rights among families.[37]

For there to be a society, there must be a plurality of families that acknowledge that there are other links than consanguineous ones, and that 'the natural process of filiation can only be carried on through the social process of affinity'. The opposition between a purported 'natural' filiation and alliance as a wholly cultural invention is in no way founded,

---

32 C. Lévi-Strauss, *Anthropology Confronts the Problems of the Modern World*, Foreword M. Olender, trans. J. M. Todd (Cambridge, MA and London, The Belknap Press of Harvard University Press, 2013), pp. 45–87.

33 'The Family', p. 341.

34 Ibid., p. 342.

35 Ibid., p. 340.

36 Ibid., p. 347.

37 Ibid., p. 349.

as we have seen, but Lévi-Strauss nevertheless hammers home the principle:

> If social organization had a beginning, this could only have consisted in the incest prohibition. It is there, and only there, that we find a passage from nature to culture, from animal to human life, and that we are in a position to understand the very essence of their articulation.[38]

Here is the most famous passage in this article, which, from a quasi-scientific explanation in 1956, would, in his last article on kinship, written in 2000, morph into a simple myth about the origins of society.

> As Tylor has shown almost a century ago, the ultimate explanation is probably that mankind has understood very early that, in order to free itself from a wild struggle for existence, it was confronted with the very simple choice of 'either marrying-out or being killed-out'. The alternative was between biological families living in juxtaposition and endeavouring to remain closed, self-perpetuating units, over-ridden by their fears, hatreds and ignorances, and the systematic establishment, through the incest prohibition, of links of intermarriage between them, thus succeeding to build, out of the artificial bonds of affinity, a true human society, despite, and even in contradiction with the isolating influence of consanguinity.[39]

Here is a dismal picture of humankind before it shook off its animal state by forbidding sexual relations within the consanguineous family. We are no longer far from Freud's sinister picture of the primal horde, emerging from the animal state through the murder of a despotic father and his devouring by his sons. Of course, for Lévi-Strauss it was not sexual desire and the refusal to keep on murdering each other that drove humankind to take upon itself the prohibition of incest. It was a rational decision aimed at living a better life, ceasing to be afraid, desisting from hatred and killing. But once again, as in Freud's story, it was to break free of an imaginary, sinister protohistory.

---

38 Ibid., p. 350.
39 Ibid.

Then Lévi-Strauss sums up, for his Anglo-Saxon audience, his interpretation of cross-cousin marriage and his distinction between parallel
and cross kin. He goes on to oppose restricted and generalized forms of
exchange, and ends by once again justifying the fact that it is the men
who exchange the women and not the other way around. But this time,
Lévi-Strauss's explanation is tinged with mordant irony:

> The female reader, who may be shocked to see womankind treated
> as a commodity submitted to transactions between male opera-
> tors, can easily find comfort in the assurance that the rules of the
> game would remain unchanged should it be decided to consider
> the men as being exchanged by women's groups. As a matter of
> fact, some very few societies, of a highly developed matrilineal
> type, have to a limited extent attempted to express things that way.
> And both sexes can be comforted from a still different (but in that
> case slightly more complicated) formulation of the game, whereby
> it would be said that the consanguineous groups consisting of both
> men and women are engaged in exchanging together bonds of
> relationships.[40]

The two hypotheses evoked here are new. Since writing *The Elementary
Structures*, Lévi-Strauss had learned that the women of the Rhade group
in Vietnam exchanged their brothers. He therefore acknowledges this,
but without revising the final argument in his book: the exchange of
women by men remains associated with the emergence of symbolic
thought.

In passing, Lévi-Strauss raises an unresolved problem for kinship
theory: how to interpret the Crow-Omaha systems. It was only in 1965,
in his Huxley Memorial Lecture, that he tackled this issue.

## 'Le Problème des relations de parenté' (1959)

In 1959, Jacques Berque, a professor at the Collège de France and an
expert on Islam and Muslim societies, organized a debate on the topic of
so-called Arab kinship systems, which allowed and often imposed the

---

40  Ibid., p. 356.

rule that a man must marry a father's brother's daughter. In the front ranks of participants in this debate was Lévi-Strauss, who had just received a professorship at the Collège de France. In addition to Berque, the other participants were Raoul Makarius (the Arab world), Sayed Younes (Lebanon) and Abdel Gawad (Egypt).

Lévi-Strauss acknowledged that the interpretation of this type of kinship system presented him with a problem, insofar as they are highly endogamous and do not seem to practise the exchange of a woman for a woman, since the wife belongs to the same lineage as her husband. As a result, and because there is no exchange of women, he declares these systems to be a 'sort of aberration'. The marriage is 'made at a loss', unless there are other benefits, such as political advantage. Lévi-Strauss points out the paucity of studies providing further information on the way these systems actually work, and cites the two most recent publications of which he is aware: those by Fredrik Barth on the Swat Pathan (Pashtuns) of Afghanistan, and Robert F. Murphy and Leonard Kasdan on the Bedouins. As he sees it, these two interpretations of marriage with a patrilateral cross cousin are opposed, but both seek the explanation of the phenomenon beyond the field of kinship, in that of political relations.

For Barth, by giving his daughters to his brothers' sons, the head of a lineage binds them to himself, thus obtaining their political allegiance within a society in which there is intense competition for political power between the various clans and lineages that compose it.

For Murphy, Bedouins live, to be sure, in a tribal society where there is strong political rivalry between lineages and clans, but this rivalry implies the need constantly to rebuild solidarities between lineages at the level at which the rivals confront each other. The logic of these confrontations is perfectly summed up by the Arab saying: 'I against my brother, my brother and I against my cousin, my cousin, my brother and I against a stranger'. In these tribal societies made up of clans and lineages perpetually threatened by ruptures, scissions and shifting allegiances, marriage with the father's brother's daughter, according to Murphy, allows each lineage to consolidate its bonds in view of confronting other groups at the same level.

Ultimately, Lévi-Strauss emphasizes that there is still insufficient ethnographic and historical material available to permit a choice between the two interpretations, and he briefly discusses the research needed to complete the interpretation. He further recalls that the existence of marriage between very close relatives is attested in Antiquity, in Egypt and Greece, but also in a vast region extending from India to the Mediterranean. These marriages pose a problem for him, since, according to his theory, kinship is based on the exchange of women, who must be ceded in order to contract alliances with others, rather than be kept to forge internal alliances.

But he affirms that here we are dealing with 'a set of societies that seems to have broken away from the mainstream in order to get around ['*ruser*'] the law of exchange and to practice marriage with close relatives insofar as it is compatible with the existence of a social system.'[41]

Already, in *The Elementary Structures*, the so-called Aluridja Australian systems were declared to be 'aberrant'. It is now the turn of 'Arab' marriage to be depicted as a *ruse*, aimed at getting around the law (posited by Lévi-Strauss) that kinship rests on the exchange of the women by the men and not the other way around.

In reality, no kinship system is 'aberrant'. All are normal social facts, relations produced in response to what societies imagine their interest to be, and which have meaning for them. Brother–sister marriages in ancient Egypt or Persia never endangered their social system. On the contrary, they were one of its crucial pieces. They gave marriage within a close degree of consanguinity a religious and cosmic dimension, as well as moral and social value.

And yet, reading Lévi-Strauss's commentaries on Barth's and Murphy's analyses of Arab-Muslim close marriages, we see that an avenue already lay open which would have allowed him to go on affirming that kinship always entails an exchange, while at the same time acknowledging that this exchange is not always an exchange of women by men.

In the two societies he cites, even if there is no exchange of women within the same lineage, the gift of a woman still intervenes to strengthen the pre-existing bonds of consanguinity through an alliance. This reinforcement of bonds, this mixing and close intertwining of relations of consanguinity and alliance make the solidarity of lineage members an indivisible bloc of strengths and increase their political weight within their society. The benefits of such endogamous alliances for all involved

---

41 'Le Problème des relations de parenté'.

are clear, and in no way a *ruse* to get around the laws of kinship. This is all the more true in Arab-Muslim societies, since one does not marry one's sister even if one marries the closest woman to one's sister in a patrilineal system, namely, one's patrilateral parallel cousin. There is indeed a prohibition of incest, and no one gets around it. (Marriage with the closest cousin is not regarded as incest, as it would be in Christian societies.)

Let us not forget either that this reiteration of kinship ties is not original, since, in systems of restricted or generalized exchange, when one marries a matrilateral cross cousin, one is marrying the daughter of a man who is at once one's mother's brother and the father of one's wife.

In the years following the publication of this text, the study of societies practicing highly endogamous unions developed very slowly, and the researchers often approached these systems with Lévi-Strauss's negative judgments in mind. It was not until 1976 that Claude Lefébure reminded his colleagues of 'the geographical extension and the considerable historical weight of societies practicing agnatic unions'. Lévi-Strauss had chosen not to speak of these in *The Elementary Structures of Kinship*,[42] even though, as early as 1962, Jean Cuisenier had published an article in *L'Homme*, the journal founded by Lévi-Strauss in 1961, entitled 'Endogamie et exogamie dans le mariage arabe'.[43] Since then, fieldwork and debates on this subject have flourished.[44] Let us mention the work of Pierre Bonte, Édouard Conte, Sophie Caratini, Dominique Casajus, Hélène Claudot, Sophie Ferchiou, Raymond Jamous and, of course, outside France, of Fredrik Barth, Ernest Gellner, Gideon Kressel, Robert Murphy and Leonard Kasdan, Emrys Peters, and many more. Laurent

---

42 C. Lefébure, 'Le Mariage des cousins parallèles patrilatéraux et l'endogamie de lignée agnatique. L'anthropologie de la parenté face à la question de l'endogamie', in C.-H. Breteau and C. Lacoste-Dujardin, eds, *Production, pouvoir et parenté dans le monde méditerranéen de Sumer à nos jours* (Paris, AECLAS, Librairie Orientaliste Paul Geuthner, 1981; with the support of CNRS), pp. 195–207.

43 J. Cuisenier, 'Endogamie et exogamie dans le mariage arabe', *L'Homme* 2, n° 2 (1962), pp. 80–105.

44 P. Bonte, ed., *Épouser au plus proche. Inceste, prohibition et stratégies matrimoniales autour de la Méditerranée* (Paris, Éditions de l'École des Hautes Études en Sciences Sociales, 1994).

Barry, in a comparative perspective, has found over fifty societies practicing a high degree of agnatic endogamy, in Africa and Madagascar, and well beyond the zones where Islam is the dominant or influential religion.[45] Much remains to be done, but the 'Arab marriage' is no longer regarded as a mystery.

45  L. Barry, 'Les Modes de composition de l'alliance, le mariage arabe', L'Homme 38, n° 147 (1988), pp. 17–50; 'L'Union endogame en Afrique et à Madagascar', L'Homme, nos 154–155 (2000), pp. 67–100. Lévi-Strauss later took an interest in the findings of Sophie Caratini and Sophie Ferchiou, who demonstrated that Arab marriage often entailed a hierarchical relation between givers and takers, the latter being superior to the former. S. Caratini, 'À propos du mariage "arabe". Discours endogames et pratiques exogames: l'exemple des Rgayb'at du Nord-Ouest saharien', L'Homme 29, n° 110 (1989), pp. 30–49; S. Ferchiou, Hasab wa nasab. Parenté, alliance et patrimoine en Tunisie (Paris, CNRS Éditions, 1992).

# 4

# The Invention of Semi-Complex Systems (1965–1973)

## 'The Future of Kinship Studies' (1965)

In 1965, Lévi-Strauss was invited by the Royal Anthropological Institute to give the prestigious Huxley Memorial Lecture. He decided to expose, before an audience containing the biggest names in British anthropology – Edmund Leach, Rodney Needham, Raymond Firth and many others – the research programme that would be needed in order to continue the analysis of the elementary structures of kinship, and to go on to the complex structures. He did not intend the programme for himself, however, for, since 1955, Lévi-Strauss had been devoted almost exclusively to the study of myths and mythical thought.[1] In 1958 he had published 'The Story of Asdiwal', in 1962 *Totemism* and *The Savage Mind*, in 1964, *The Raw and the Cooked*, the first volume in the four-volume mythology series also known as 'Mythologiques' (a name he did not particularly like) and 'Introduction to a Science of Mythology'. By 1965 he was in the thick of the second volume, *From Honey to Ashes*, which would appear in 1967.[2]

---

1 C. Lévi-Strauss, 'The Structural Study of Myth', *Journal of American Folklore* 68, n° 270 (1955), pp. 428–44.

2 'The Story of Asdiwal', in *Structural Anthropology, vol. 2*, trans. M. Layton (Chicago, University of Chicago Press, 1976), pp. 146–97; *Totemism*, trans. R. Needham (Boston, Beacon Press, 1963); *The Savage Mind* (no translator mentioned), (Chicago, University of Chicago Press, 1966); *The Raw and the Cooked: Introduction to a Science of Mythology*

In 1965, then, when the Royal Anthropological Institute invited him to give the Huxley Memorial Lecture, Lévi-Strauss knew he would not be writing the book on the complex structures of kinship that he had announced in the Preface and the Conclusion of *The Elementary Structures of Kinship*. Instead, he chose to outline the path that others could (or should) follow in his wake to analyse the complex forms of kinship typically found in contemporary societies, but not only there. This led him to draft one of the most remarkable texts in terms of rigour and creative power ever written on kinship. He wrote the original in English, but included long passages in the 1967 preface to the French second edition of *The Elementary Structures*.

In his lecture, Lévi-Strauss begins by reminding the audience that kinship systems have internal consistency, that they pursue one or several aims and that they are meaningful for those who live under and reproduce them; in this sense, they are teleological systems. And he goes on to say that he feels close to the neo-Darwinian biologists on this point. But the heart of the matter lies elsewhere. He had recently discovered the crucial articles by Lounsbury (1964) and Buchler (1964), which we have already discussed and which, for the first time, made it possible to distinguish Dravidian from Iroquois systems, whereas the two had previously been lumped together. However, he says nothing about the Dravidian systems and merely reports the need to reinterpret the Iroquois systems in the wake of Lounsbury's analyses. He also mentions that the so-called Hawaiian systems must be studied anew with the same methodological rigor, but that is all.

After criticizing the psychological and sociological interpretations of kinship systems advanced by Pitt-Rivers and Radcliffe-Brown, Lévi-Strauss reasserts his theoretical doctrine that 'the function of a kinship system is to generate marriage possibilities or impossibilities ... the primary function of a kinship system is to define categories from which to set up a certain type of marriage regulation.'[3]

No more than in previous work is the descent axis, the second pillar of any kinship system, mentioned, whereas the semi-complex systems

---

*1*, trans. J. and D. Weightman (Harmondsworth, Penguin, 1986); *From Honey to Ashes: Introduction to a Science of Mythology 2*, trans. J. and D. Weightman (Chicago, University of Chicago Press, 1973).

3 C. Lévi-Strauss, 'The Future of Kinship Studies. Huxley Memorial Lecture', in *Proceedings of the Royal Institute of Great Britain and Ireland*, 1965, p. 14.

he proposes to analyse – the Crow and the Omaha – are generally matrilineal (Crow) and patrilineal (Omaha). Then Lévi-Strauss launches into a sort of self-critique, declaring that, in his earlier work, he had been somewhat hasty in invoking the unconscious processes of the human mind, as though 'the so-called primitive could not be granted the power to use his intellect otherwise than unknowingly'.[4] It must be admitted, he says, that in every era, highly sophisticated forms of theoretical thought have been developed by a minority of individuals gifted with this capacity.

The speaker must certainly have surprised his audience when next he began to elaborate on the idea that mythology in its own way also deals with issues of kinship. He had just published *The Raw and the Cooked*, which analyses certain South American Indian myths on the origin of fire, cooking and meat. And he was in the midst of writing what was to become *From Honey to Ashes*, in which he analyses myths dealing with the origin of agriculture and the conflicts arising from the growth of populations and their dispersal, as well as from the diversification of languages and customs. Both sets of myths tell of conflicts between individuals bound by marriage, but the nature of those joined in the alliance differs from one group to the next.

The myths dealing with the acquisition of fire and meat show affines who are either a wife's brother (WiB) or a husband's sister (HuZ). In myths dealing with the origin of agriculture, we have either a wife's sister (WiZ) or a husband's brother (HuB). Two types of affines thus intervene. The first are directly concerned by the exchange of women between men (the wife's brother has exchanged her for the husband's sister); they are 'cross' affines. The second are parallel affines: the wife's sister or the husband's brother, who are not partners in the exchange but can endanger the contracted union by seducing their brother's wife or their husband's brother.

Lévi-Strauss gives the name 'Paleolithic' to the kinship model found in the myths of the origin of fire and cooking, and 'Neolithic' to the model involved in the myths of the origin of agriculture, but 'without loading these terms with historical content'.[5] The reason for this is

---

4  Ibid., p. 15.
5  Ibid., p. 16.

probably that these two groups of myths coexist within the same populations; one set does not come from the time when fire was domesticated but deals with it, just as the other set does not come from the time when agriculture was invented but talks about it in a different way. Yet at the end of the four volumes of his series (1971), Lévi-Strauss repeats several times that myths hark back to the mists of time, 'hundreds of millions of years back', that they speak within him and have become part of his very self.

Lévi-Strauss adds the idea that the 'Paleolithic' myths serve to explain the origin of culture, while the 'Neolithic' myths deal with society at a time when it had already become difficult to govern, owing to the overgrowth of populations and the haphazard distribution of resources. To be sure, Lévi-Strauss is not suggesting that culture preceded life in society, for there is no culture without society or society without culture. But we can already see the tip of the idea – which would fully emerge in *Tristes Tropiques* (1955) – that humanity's difficulties began with the success of the Neolithic, the domestication of plants and animals, the birth of writing, the appearance of towns, and that the greatest threat to the future of humanity has always been population growth. On this point, Lévi-Strauss is closer to the positions of Malthus than to those of Marx.

After this lyric flight on the embedding of kinship in myths – myths that go back to the Paleolithic era – Lévi-Strauss returns to the debates and quarrels that *The Elementary Structures of Kinship* ignited among his British and American colleagues. In particular, they had pressed him to say whether the marriage rules contained in the kinship systems were 'prescriptions' or 'preferences'. Since he had already answered this question in 1960, in a short article published in the Dutch journal *Bijdragen* in response to Maybury-Lewis,[6] he simply summarizes here. He explains that he is talking not about empirical realities but about models constructed to account for the logic of kinship systems, such as the terminologies and rules defining alliance and the descent principles that were the mental representations of these. This is different from seeing how things happened on the ground and whether they correspond directly, indirectly or not at all to the model described by informants or

6 C. Lévi-Strauss, 'On Manipulated Sociological Models', *Bijdragen tot de Taal-, Land-, en Volkenkunde* 116, n° 1 (1960), pp. 45–54.

reconstructed by anthropologists. We observe social relations; we reconstruct structures.

Finally, having set aside as secondary the question of how to distinguish prescription from preference, he comes to the object of his lecture. Can modern societies be included within the anthropologist's sphere of analysis? And if so, what tools can be brought to bear on the forms of kinship that characterize modern societies? These forms come under the heading of complex structures of kinship, in which the spouse is not determined by the structure of the kinship system but by external criteria. One marries within one's class and/or one's religion, or for some other subjective or collective reason, but not because the future spouse is a cross cousin and thus a permissible marriage partner.

How do we move from elementary structures to complex structures? What obstacles must be overcome to get there? Lévi-Strauss begins with an important remark, which immediately enriches the theory developed in *The Elementary Structures*:

> All systems of kinship and marriage contain an 'elementary' core which manifests itself in the incest prohibition. Similarly, all systems have a 'complex' aspect, deriving from the fact that more than one individual can usually meet the requirements of even the most prescriptive systems, thus allowing for a certain freedom of choice.[7]

He goes on to assert that we cannot say what kinship 'really' is until we have analysed how it work in all forms of society, and discovered if and how it changes the way it works when one goes from 'simple' to complex societies. Lévi-Strauss then moves on to the problem of the analysis of complex structures, announcing that the way is blocked, and we will get no farther until the analysis of a type of kinship system, which he dubs 'semi-complex', has been resolved. These systems that stand in the way include those that anthropologists have christened 'Crow-Omaha' types. It will be recalled that, in *The Elementary Structures*, Lévi-Strauss had stated he was leaving the Crow-Omaha systems to one side but that he would come back to them later; here he keeps his promise.

The details he adds in the previous statement are important from a theoretical standpoint because they immediately show the existence of a

---

7 'The Future of Kinship Studies', p. 18.

structural continuity between elementary and complex structures of kinship. In all kinship systems, there exists the prohibition of incest – which can take different forms and extensions – as well as a wide or narrow field of choices open to those seeking to contract a socially legitimate union.

But why do the Crow-Omaha systems appear as lying midway between elementary and complex structures? First of all, because they forbid, for example, a man to take a wife in the clans of his father (F), his mother (M), his father's mother (FM) and his mother's mother (MM); and they forbid renewing alliances before several generations. Each marriage therefore modifies the field of alliances possible in the following generations. To the diversity of alliances in space is added their diversity over time. As we saw earlier with the Baruya, an identical strategy of diversity and mobility of alliances can be pursued in an Iroquois-type kinship system, which systematically practices the exchange of women between two lineages, with a ban on repeating these alliances before several (three or four) generations have elapsed, and the prohibition on two brothers marrying women from the same lineage.

But there is another structural aspect that is specific to Crow-Omaha systems: they obey what is known as a 'skewing principle'. This system posits the formal equivalence between two (or more) types of kin belonging to two (or more) different generations, and thus cancels the difference between generations for a certain number of kin positions. I will explain.

In Crow-Omaha systems, siblings (SI) and parallel cousins (P) are equivalent (SI = P), as they are in Dravidian, Australian and Iroquois systems; this links the Crow-Omaha systems to elementary structures. It is an important feature, which Lévi-Strauss had not mentioned in his lecture and which immediately shows that these systems are transformations of systems with elementary structures. However, the status of cross cousins is not the same as in the Australian, Dravidian and Iroquois systems. This is where the skewing principle comes in: it cancels the difference between generations. In Omaha systems (most but not all of which are patrilineal), matrilateral cross cousins (mXc) are classified in the generation above Ego, and patrilateral cross cousins (pXc) in the generation below. In Crow systems (most but not all of which are matrilineal), the opposite is the case: patrilateral cross cousins (pXc) are raised a generation, while matrilateral cross cousins are lowered a generation.

In an Omaha system, the father's sister's son (FZS), a patrilateral cross cousin, is lowered one generation and becomes a son for Ego (FZS = S); the mother's brother's son (MBS) becomes a maternal uncle (MBS = MB); and the mother's brother's daughter (MBD) becomes a mother for Ego (MBD = M). In a Crow system, it is the inverse: my father's sister's son (FZS) is a father for me (FZS = F), and my mother's brother's son is a son for me (MBS = S), and so on.

Briefly, in these systems the paternal and maternal sides see-saw around Ego, raising or lowering cross kin by one or sometimes several generations. This means that a whole series of individuals belonging to chronologically and biologically distinct generations are merged into one category. All become sons, mothers, fathers, maternal uncles, etc. This is why the principle that generates these mergers and the raising and lowering around Ego has been christened the 'skewing principle'.

The patrilineal descent principle (Omaha) or the matrilineal principle (Crow) directly affect the way the system works, since in a Crow system, the skewing applies to the paternal side while, in an Omaha system, it applies to the maternal side. Owing to the raising and lowering of Ego's cross cousins, certain of these cousins become daughters for Ego, and others mothers; these women will therefore be forbidden spouses for him, because of the incest prohibition. Ego will therefore have to turn to other clans or lineages to find a wife. It is precisely this which distinguishes Crow-Omaha systems from the asymmetrical Kachin-type systems, which prescribe marriage with the matrilateral cross cousin (MBD), but prohibit marriage with the patrilateral cross cousin (FZS). As he had already done in *The Elementary Structures*, Lévi-Strauss insists on the fact that Crow-Omaha systems are by no means to be confused with asymmetrical systems. Later research would show that Lévi-Strauss had been a bit hasty here, for forms of skewing can be found in numerous asymmetrical systems.[8]

Lévi-Strauss then goes on to define the opposition he believes he has found between these two types of system, in a formula he would use

---

8 T. R. Trautmann, 'Crossness and Crow-Omaha', in T. R. Trautmann and P. M. Whiteley, eds, *Crow-Omaha. New Light on a Classic Problem of Kinship Analysis* (Tucson, University of Arizona Press, 2012), pp. 31–50.

again two years later (1967) in his Preface to the second edition of *The Elementary Structures of Kinship*: 'Thus, an asymmetrical system endeavours to turn kinsmen into affines, whereas a Crow-Omaha system takes the opposite stand by turning affines into kinsmen.'[9]

In the first case, kinship and affinity are mutually inclusive; in the second, they are mutually exclusive. Why then do the Crow-Omaha systems occupy for Lévi-Strauss such a strategic position in the theory of kinship and marriage? To which he replies: 'In fact the Crow-Omaha systems still belong to the elementary structures from the point of view of the marriage prohibitions they frame in sociological terms, but they already belong to the complex structures from the point of view of the probabilist alliance network which they produce.'[10]

They are, for these reasons, the pivotal point between systems based on elementary structures and those based on complex structures. To establish the 'pivotal' character of the Crow-Omaha systems, Lévi-Strauss makes use of only two aspects of these systems, which fall into the category of alliance: the prohibition of incest and the ban on marriage in a certain number of ascending lines. He leaves aside the fact that these systems pose the equivalence of siblings and parallel cousins, as do systems based on elementary structures, and therefore presuppose the existence of cross cousins. But the latter are cancelled and prohibited as spouses in different and opposing ways, depending on whether descent is reckoned patri- or matrilineally. The descent rule thus intervenes directly in the way cross cousins are turned into fathers, mothers, sons or daughters, and become impossible spouses.

Lévi-Strauss ends his lecture affirming that, to advance our understanding of the Crow-Omaha systems, it would be necessary to enlist the aid of mathematicians, and especially statisticians. With the help of mathematician Bernard Jaulin, he had already calculated the list of types of marriage possible for an individual in the case where only two clans, father's and mother's, were forbidden in a society having seven clans. The number would come to 23,436 possible choices, and 3,766,140 if the society had fifteen clans. Of course, the number would

---

9 'The Future of Kinship Studies', p. 19; Lévi-Strauss, 'Preface to the second edition', *The Elementary Structures of Kinship*, trans. J. H. Bell and J. R. von Sturmer and R. Needham, ed., (Boston, Beacon Press, 1969), p. xxxix.

10 'The Future of Kinship Studies', p. 19; 'Preface', p. xxvix.

be even larger in a contemporary European society where prohibitions on marriage are limited to a few degrees of kinship (at the minimum mother, daughter, sister, or father, son, brother), and where the number of possible partners (in the case of free unions) is virtually unlimited.

Lévi-Strauss concedes that things are not necessarily as complex as they seem, for the population of societies with Crow-Omaha kinship systems is generally very small, between 5,000 and 10,000 individuals (the Cherokee or the matrilineal Hopi, for instance). In this case, in changing direction with each generation, clans and lineages are sooner or later forced to repeat the same alliances. There is also the fact that not all the local clans or groups have the same social status, the same degree of wealth, the same functions; and these realities, too, intervene in the choosing of marriage partners by individuals and the groups to which they belong.

Finally, Lévi-Strauss ends his lecture on two lyrical flights, predicting that the analysis of semi-complex systems would demand a conceptual transformation of the same magnitude as that which made it possible to conceive quantum mechanics. Yet none of this happened. He also predicted that future theoretical developments would increasingly align anthropologists with the native theories of kinship, whether expressly formulated as such or hidden in myths, rites or other symbolic representations that would need to be identified.

In sum, in 1965, the Crow-Omaha case was brilliantly re-opened . . . and handed over to others. The Iroquois and Hawaiian systems briefly mentioned as types of semi-complex systems would not come up again. And yet Lounsbury had just produced a veritable theoretical revolution by identifying the structural differences – but also the proximity – between Dravidian and Iroquois systems, and had also just returned to the analysis of Crow-Omaha systems, of which he had shown the existence of eight distinct forms – four for the Crow systems and four for the Omaha.[11] From his point of view – which would be adopted by Thomas Trautmann, the eminent specialist of Indian Dravidian systems, by Robert Barnes,

---

11 F. G. Lounsbury, 'A Formal Account of the Crow and Omaha Kinship Terminologies', in W. Goodenough, ed., *Explorations in Cultural Anthropology: Essays in Honor of George Peter Murdock* (New York, McGraw-Hill, 1964), pp. 352–94; F. G. Lounsbury, 'The Structural Analysis of Kinship Semantics', in *Proceedings of the Third International Congress of Linguists* (Cambridge and The Hague, Mouton, 1962), pp. 1073–93.

specialist precisely of the Omaha kinship system, by Franklin Tjon Sie Fat, Viveiros de Castro and a number of others – it would appear that exploration of the Crow-Omaha systems, if we were to obtain a clear idea of how they worked, would require first of all to understand the different meanings behind the 'crossness' of certain kinship relations and the 'parallelness' of others in the three types of systems containing this distinction – Dravidian, Iroquois and Crow-Omaha.

The story begins in 1859. When Morgan was making his survey of the North American kinship systems, he was shocked to find that the Iroquois used the same term for father and father's brothers, who were all fathers, and did likewise on the mother's side, since all mother's sisters were also mothers. Therefore, logically speaking, the sons and daughters of all these fathers and all these mothers were brothers and sisters, and could not marry each other. He had just discovered that societies classified cousins into two categories, which anthropologists would later call 'parallel' and 'cross'. Unlike European systems, then, the Iroquois merged certain collaterals with kin in the direct line.

In 1859, already accustomed to finding this type of kinship terminology in the tribes he visited, Morgan came to the Kaw, a tribe living in the present North American state of Kansas, and here he received a second shock: in effect, he discovered what would later be called an Omaha-type terminology. The Kaw, Osage, Omaha, Otoe and other Indian groups all shared this type of terminology.

> I first discovered this deviation from the typical form while working out the system of the Kaws in Kansas in 1859. The Kaw chief from whom I obtained it, through a perfectly competent interpreter, insisted upon the verity of these relationships against all doubts and questionings; and when the work was done I found it proved itself through the correlative relationships. Afterwards in 1860, while at the Iowa reservation in Nebraska, I had an opportunity to test it fully, both in Iowa and Otoe, through White Cloud, a native Iowa well versed in English. While discussing these relationships he pointed out a boy near us, and remarked that he was his uncle, and the son of his mother's brother who was also his uncle.[12]

-------

12 L. H. Morgan, *Systems of Consanguinity and Affinity of the Human Family* (Washington DC, Smithsonian Institution, 1871), p. 179, n. 1.

Morgan next visited the Plains Indians, the Crow, the Pawnee, etc., and then, farther south the Choctaw, the Cherokee, etc., and discovered the same system, but operating the other way around. We will trace the rest of the story by summing up the recent analysis made by Thomas Trautmann and Peter Whiteley.[13] Trautmann and Whiteley distinguish two distinctly different periods in the analysis of the Crow-Omaha systems, one running from Morgan to Lévi-Strauss and the other from Lévi-Strauss to our day.

In the first period, Crow-Omaha systems were associated with unilineal kinship systems, since it seems the Omaha systems were always associated with patrilineal descent principles and the Crow systems with matrilineal principles. Reverend James Owen Dorsey had published a book in 1884 entitled *Omaha Sociology*, which prompted a legal scholar, Joseph Kohler, to examine and compare the Omaha- and Crow-type systems (he called the latter Choctaw). Kohler was the first to try to explain the types of terminologies by deriving them from unilineal descent principles. In 1887 he published his book, *On the Prehistory of Marriage* (published in English only in 1975),[14] which Durkheim reviewed in glowing terms in a long article that appeared in 1898 in *L'Année sociologique*.[15] Kohler had also advanced the hypothesis that this type of system was probably linked to the existence of clans, and to the inheritance of various forms of property or functions in the father's line (Omaha) or the mother's line (Chocktaw, Crow). This hypothesis was adopted by many sociologists, from Durkheim to Radcliffe-Brown.[16] The latter primarily stressed the existence of descent groups; others underscored the existence of strategies of succession – from father to son to grandson, or from mother to daughter to granddaughter, etc. – to functions, and to tangible or intangible material goods.[17]

The hypothesis of a direct link between Crow-Omaha terminologies and unilineal descent principles quickly drew criticism. First of all, owing

---

13 Cf. Trautmann and Whiteley, eds, *Crow-Omaha*, chapter I: 'A Classic Problem', pp. 1–27.

14 J. Kohler, *On the Prehistory of Marriage, Totemism, Group Marriage, Mother Right* (Chicago and London, University of Chicago Press, 1975; 1st ed.,1897).

15 É. Durkheim, 'Compte rendu de *Zur Urgeschichte der Ehe. Prof. J. Kohler*', *L'Année sociologique* 1 (1898), pp. 306–19.

16 A. R. Radcliffe-Brown, 'The Study of Kinship Systems', *Journal of the Royal Anthropological Institute* 71, n° 1 (1941), pp. 1–18.

17 This is what Lounsbury did in his famous article published in 1964.

to the fact that many unilineal descent systems do not use Crow-Omaha terminology – if only the Iroquois-type, which are either matrilineal (Iroquois) or patrilineal (Baruya). But the chief objection was the example of the Fox Indians, who use an Omaha-type terminology but do not have unilineal descent groups,[18] or the Yuchi, who have an Omaha terminology and matrilineal descent groups.[19] There was thus room for doubt: was this type of terminology as strongly linked to the existence of unilineal descent groups as Radcliffe-Brown or Leslie White claimed?

A second problem had also arisen. It had been noticed that there were elements of Crow-Omaha terminology in another variety of kinship systems, those of the Kachin type, which prescribe marriage with the matrilateral cross cousin (MBD), but forbid marriage with the patrilateral cross cousin (FZD). These systems, to be able to function, imply the existence of at least three descent groups: those of Ego, of Ego's mother (the group that gave her) and of Ego's father's sister's husband (the group to which Ego's group gives wives). Indeed Kachin terminology does have some Omaha features.[20] But in the chapters of The Elementary Structures devoted to the Kachin, Gilyak, etc. systems as typifying systems of generalized exchange (A gives to B, B to C, C to D, D to A, and so on), Lévi-Strauss had completely neglected this aspect.[21] Yet, while the North American Crow-Omaha systems prohibit marriage in several clans without prescribing marriage in others, Kachin-type systems are asymmetrical, since they prohibit marriage with the patrilateral cross cousin, but prescribe it with the matrilateral cross cousin; for this reason they are called prescriptive asymmetric systems.[22]

That is where matters stood in 1964, when Lounsbury showed that the Dravidian and Iroquois systems differed, whereas they had previously

---

18 S. Tax, 'The Social Organization of the Fox Indians', in F. Eggan, ed., *Social Anthropology of North American Tribes* (Chicago, University of Chicago Press, 1937), pp. 243–84.

19 A. Lesser, 'Kinship Origins in the Light of Some Distributions', *American Anthropologist* 31, n° 4 (1929), pp. 710–30.

20 The Kachin system analysed by Leach was known at the time as Jinghpaw. E. Leach, 'Jinghpaw Kinship Terminology', *Journal of the Royal Anthropological Institute* 75 (1945), pp. 59–72; E. Leach, 'The Structural Implications of Matrilateral Cross-Cousin Marriage', *Journal of the Royal Anthropological Institute* 81 (1951), pp. 23–55.

21 *The Elementary Structures of Kinship*, chaps. XIV–XVII.

22 B. S. Lane, 'Structural Contrasts between Symmetric and Asymmetric Marriage Systems: A Fallacy', *South Western Journal of Anthropology* 17, n° 1 (1961), pp. 49–55.

been lumped together under the label 'Iroquois' (cf. Murdock, 1949), as we have seen. The difference was threefold: (1) The distinction between cross and parallel is not the same (in Iroquois systems, it exists only in $G^0$; in Dravidian systems it extends over several ascending and descending generations). (2) Dravidian systems include in their terminology a marriage rule (with the bilateral cross cousin [FZD = MBD = Wi]), whereas the Iroquois terminology does not. (3) Because of this, Dravidian systems do not have a specific vocabulary for affines (or do not have terms reserved for father-in-law and mother-in-law), whereas the Iroquois systems have a specific set of terms for affines.

In short, thanks to Lounsbury the structural differences between the two systems were now clear. At the same time, the presence of the cross/parallel distinction in both systems appeared as a manifestation of their deep structure, which could take several forms depending on whether several or a single generation were concerned (Dravidian or Iroquois, respectively). Lounsbury's second contribution was to show the existence of different forms of Crow-Omaha systems – four Omaha and four Crow – depending on the way crossness was defined.

At this point, based on traditional debates and on Lounsbury's recent discoveries (1964), Lévi-Strauss stepped in and upset the status quo by giving the 1965 Huxley Memorial Lecture in front of his British colleagues. He pointed out a fundamental aspect of the Crow-Omaha systems that had been hitherto neglected, and advised re-examining the problems from that standpoint: namely, there had been a failure to take into account the marriage rules associated with the systems in question. Once again, Lévi-Strauss had spotted a flaw. True to the Anglo-Saxon tradition, alliance had been relegated to the background – or forgotten – in favour of descent.

But, as we have seen, the marriage rules associated with Crow-Omaha systems are negative. There is no positive rule in the terminology that prescribes marriage with a particular kin position. For Lévi-Strauss, then, this type of system should be the focus if we wanted profitably to undertake the study of the complex systems typical of our modern societies, and build a unified model of all known kinship systems. Because Crow-Omaha systems state marriage prohibitions in terms of kin groups (father's, mother's, mother's father's, father's mother's, etc. clans or lineages), they can be classified as elementary structures, but because they have no rule prescribing a certain category of kin for potential spouses, they are already close to complex systems. For these reasons, Lévi-Strauss calls them 'semi-complex' and assigns them a new theoretical value, that of marking the transition between elementary and complex systems.[23] And he adds that, as he sees it, the Iroquois and Hawaiian systems also ensure this transition, but he would never again bring up the matter.

His approach had two consequences. On the one hand, it prompted new analyses and discoveries, as illustrated by the work and publications of Françoise Héritier on the Omaha system or the Samo in Burkina Faso, and by Élisabeth Copet-Rougier on the Omaha kinship system of the Mkako of Cameroon. But, on the other hand, the Kachin-type systems were classified in a completely different category, even though their terminologies often contained skewing features of a Crow or Omaha type.

The asymmetrical systems that had also previously been classified with the Crow-Omaha systems were placed in separate categories because their structure and terminology carry a positive rule for choosing a spouse, which means they still belong among the elementary structures of kinship. Given these conditions, the terminological features that caused them to be taken for Crow-Omaha systems needed to be re-analysed. For, in an asymmetrical system, all male members of the mother's lineage, that is, members of the wife-giver group, are for this very reason uniformly considered as 'fathers-in-law', and all members of the wife-taker group are 'sons-in-law'. In 1965, despite certain similarities between the two sets of terminologies, the two categories of systems were now for Lévi-Strauss 'as widely dissimilar as, say, fish and whale'.[24] In short, by placing the emphasis exclusively on marriage rules, Lévi-Strauss had half-obscured the *skewing principle* present in what had become true Crow-Omaha systems and vehicles of the transition to complex systems. But are they really? We will see that they are not.

But let us first consider the domains in which Lévi-Strauss's approach in terms of marriage rules renewed and enriched kinship theory, as well as our knowledge of these societies. Héritier's work is one of the best

---

23 These systems are classified as 'complex' in Lévi-Strauss's theory, whereas they are very 'simple' from the standpoint of their structures. Or at least the modern European and American systems are.

24 'The Future of Kinship Studies', p. 18.

illustrations. She made a detailed study of the kinship system of the Samo, a group with over 150,000 members, living in Burkina Faso in the vicinity of the Mossi. The Mossi had come from Ghana sometime around the sixteenth century and had invaded and subjected the peasant populations of the White Volta River Valley. The Samo lived in villages, and a number of local groups formed a network of intermarrying patrilineal clans and lineages. Relations within a network were in principle peaceful, but it could often find itself at war with other networks composed of neighbouring villages.

The Samo have an Omaha-type kinship system with the following marriage prohibitions: a man cannot marry a woman from his father's lineage, from his mother's lineage, from his father's mother's lineage or from his mother's mother's lineage, to which must be added any lineage in which a real or classificatory father or a real or classificatory brother (and therefore from the same patriarchal clan) has taken a wife. Furthermore, he cannot take a second wife from his wife's lineage or from the lineages of his wife's mother, his wife's mother's mother or his wife's father's mother (W, WM, WMM, WFM).[25]

Having compiled a vast and highly detailed database of genealogies and marriages in three Samo villages in the canton of Kowy, Héritier sought to reconstruct the marriage strategies adopted by the lineages and, on the basis of these strategies, to uncover the structures governing alliance among the Samo.

Yet, while it is clear the existence of so many prohibitions forces the groups to spread their alliances and to renew them only after a certain number of generations (often five), are these alliances as random as Lévi-Strauss claimed? And if they are not, and forms of reciprocal, direct exchange exist despite the prohibitions, in what way are these Omaha systems 'in transition', on their way to becoming complex systems?

---

25 Marriage prohibitions in the Samo system are in part similar to those of the Omaha system. These forbid marriage in the clans of the father, mother, father's mother and mother's mother, like the Samo system, but also in the subclan of the father's mother's mother (FMM), and the subclan of the mother's mother's mother (MMM), which are not forbidden by the Samo. Cf. R. Barnes, 'Omaha and "Omaha"', in Trautmann and Whiteley, eds, *Crow-Omaha*. pp. 69–82. Because of these differences between the prohibitions set by 'real' Omaha Indians and those of the same and other groups classified as having 'Omaha systems', Barnes rejects the very idea of the existence of any such category.

Françoise Héritier's work allowed us to answer these questions. Her studies showed that this set of prohibitions combined those created by being born into a paternal lineage and those arising from the principle of sharing the same 'maternal' lineages.[26] The result is that, in this type of system defined by a unilineal descent rule (patrilineal in this case), consanguineous cognatic kin are recognized but implicitly forbidden.[27] Unilineal descent and bilateral consanguinity together thus structure the field of alliance. And yet, 'agnatic belonging takes precedence over the sharing of the same maternal and grand-maternal lineages.'[28]

A second factor, revealed by the analysis of Samo genealogies and therefore by the marriages they contracted, led Héritier to advance the hypothesis that 'people marry as "close as possible" once marriage prohibitions are no longer in effect'. An alliance is therefore not contracted at random, since it is repeated with the same lineages as soon as the prohibitions on these lineages of former affines who have become remote consanguines have been lifted. In other words, marriages will be contracted 'as close as possible to that which the kinsmen of the spouses considered to be incestuous for themselves'. And these close alliances are not only possible but 'sought, and not in a random manner'.[29]

This last aspect of Samo alliance strategies places us in the presence of a principle belonging to the elementary structures of kinship, namely that 'nothing forbids a sister marrying there where her brother cannot. The effect of this non-reciprocity principle is therefore to authorize direct exchanges between the same family lines.'[30] This feature, discovered by Élisabeth Copet-Rougier among the Cameroon Mkako, who have an Omaha-type system, is also found among the Samo.[31] Repetition of alliances is therefore possible and practiced by opposite-sex consanguines (a brother and a sister) but is forbidden for same-sex consanguines (two brothers or two sisters). Finally, a man (and therefore a lineage) who has received a woman from another lineage, can, in the

---

26 F. Héritier, *L'Exercice de la parenté* (Paris, Gallimard/Seuil, 1981), p. 100.

27 Ibid., p. 105.

28 Ibid., p. 114.

29 Ibid., pp. 109, 114, 122.

30 É. Copet-Rougier, 'Mariage et inceste. L'Endogamie dans une société à fortes prohibitions matrimoniales', *Bulletin de la Société d'anthropologie du Sud-Ouest* 15, n° 1 (1980), pp. 13–53.

31 Héritier, *L'Exercice de la parenté*, p. 128.

following generation, give this lineage a daughter born of a wife other than the one he received in the preceding generation.[32] The girl is thus given to the same lineage but not to the same family line.

Last of all, nothing, in our opinion, allows us to conclude that the Samo system is in transition to anything whatsoever. It is a system that combines, within an endogamous network made up of a certain number of villages living peacefully together, a policy of spreading alliances and repeating the same alliances after a given number of generations. Its particularity with respect to Iroquois-type systems, which have the same policy of spreading alliances and repeating the same alliances after several generations,[33] is that the men do not exchange women directly between lineages in the same generation in which another alliance was contracted between these lineages (= $G^0$).

It goes without saying that such strategies entail two consequences, which shape the structure of the Omaha systems: first, the distinction between cross and parallel cousins is cancelled in $G^0$, which makes all cross cousins in $G^0$ prohibited spouses; and second, there is a special vocabulary for affines, since the alliances are contracted with lineages or clans that are no longer or have never been connected with Ego's lineage or clan.

In these two respects the Crow-Omaha and the Iroquois systems, with their multiple prohibitions on the repetition of alliances, are similar. The difference resides in the fact that Iroquois systems always involve the merging of same-sex consanguines in $G^{+1}$ (FB = F; MZ = M) and a direct exchange of women, which generates the distinction between parallel and cross cousins, the latter being in principle permissible spouses. But, in order for the exchange of women not to be repeated in $G^0$, they need to cancel the distinction between parallel and cross cousins in $G^0$, and make all cousins siblings between whom marriage is forbidden. The marriage will therefore have to be made with cross

---

32 Ibid., p. 123.

33 This is the case of the kinship systems of the Yafar of New Guinea, the Red-Knife Indians of North America, the Aguaruna Indians of South America, and others. On all these points, see M. Godelier, *Metamorphoses of Kinship*, trans. N. Scott (London and New York, Verso, 2012), pp. 211–12. As well as M. Godelier, 'Afterword. Transformations and Lines of Evolution', in M. Godelier, F. Tjon Sie Fat and T. Trautmann, eds, *Transformations of Kinship*, trans. N. Scott (Washington DC, Smithsonian Institution Press), pp. 386–413.

cousins of the second, third or even fourth degree, or with lineages having no previous ties with Ego's. Crow-Omaha systems thus appear as a transformation of Iroquois-type systems, in which the principle of the direct exchange of women in $G^0$ has disappeared and the number of alliance prohibitions with 'consanguineous' lineages (father, mother, father's mother, mother's mother, etc.) has been multiplied. But all these systems are based on the same deep structure: this structure entails some form of 'crossness', which must be either used or neutralized for the marriage to take place.

All these possibilities, which imply the presence and implementation of the distinction between cross and non-cross kin, now appear as the consequences of various transformations in Dravidian systems, where the rule of marriage with the bilateral cousin – which supposes the exchange of women generation after generation between two kin groups, two moieties (Australia), two clans, two lineages (South India) – has been abolished. When that rule disappears, the system becomes open to other forms of alliance; or to put it another way, when societies have looked for other forms of alliance, the rule has disappeared and the system has changed.

Let us take the example of the transformation of a Dravidian system into an Iroquois system as Alf Hornborg reconstructed it.[34] If the principle continues to be the exchange of women between groups but there is no longer the obligation to repeat the exchange of women between the same groups, then the cross/parallel distinction is limited to $G^0$, which stems from an exchange of women in $G^{+1}$. Because it is forbidden to repeat this alliance, Ego, who belongs to $G^0$, must contract an alliance with other groups, either with those with which his group contracted an alliance several generations earlier, or with those with which it has never made an alliance. In this case, Ego will marry either a cross cousin in the second, third or even fourth degree, or will contract an alliance with a kin group that has not yet exchanged women with his lineage or his clan. Hence the need for a specific vocabulary to distinguish affines who are or are not (or no longer) cross kin. And if the principle of the direct exchange of women in $G^0$ disappears, while keeping the repetition of alliances after a certain number of generations, we are on the way to the

---

34  A. Hornborg, 'Social Redundancy in Amazonian Social Structure', in Godelier et al., *Transformations of Kinship*, pp. 168–86.

Crow-Omaha systems. We can see the advantages, in certain historical and sociological circumstances, of opening (diversifying but also multiplying) alliances within a globally closed network of exchanges, in other words an endogamous network.

All these kinship systems are, in our opinion, elementary systems in the process of various transformations from the original Dravidian systems. These are replaced by other systems, and, in most cases, the transformations are irreversible, but we cannot say they constitute forms of transition to complex structures of kinship. Furthermore, these systems, we repeat, are not complex in terms of their structure. What is complex is the number of determining factors from outside the area of kinship that intervene in the choice of the individuals desiring to unite by marriage or any other form of bond ('free' union, common-law marriage, etc.). These determinations have to do with religion, wealth, prestige of a name, etc. and can intervene more or less consciously in the choice of a partner. Even in our Western societies, such choices are never made entirely at random.

Let us come back to the list of known forms of transformation of elementary systems entailing the presence and action of relations of cross kinship which must be implemented (or on the contrary eliminated) in order to contract various forms of alliance. This is where we will once again find the problem of the presence or absence of a skewing principle in a number of kin positions, which is a characteristic feature of Crow-Omaha systems, but also of numerous systems that are neither Crow nor Omaha.

In the Kariera- or Aranda-type Dravidian systems of Australia, we do not find a Crow- or Omaha-type terminology. One marries the first-degree (Kariera) or second-degree (Aranda) bilateral cross cousin, and patrilateral and matrilateral cross cousins are considered equivalents of the bilateral cross cousin (resulting from marriage of the father's sister [FZ] with the mother's brother [MB]). This is a case of restricted exchange.

Alternatively, in the Murngin-type systems of Australia and in Kachin- or Gilyak-type systems, which come under the heading of generalized exchange, we find terminologies that are partially of the Omaha type.

Why? Because these systems prescribe marriage with one cross cousin, more specifically, with the matrilateral cross cousin, but prohibit marriage with the patrilateral cross cousin. Of the two types of cross cousin, one is therefore eliminated and the reciprocal exchange of women between givers and takers is forbidden. We have here the family of kinship systems that Lévi-Strauss had ejected from the set of systems classified, before him, as Crow-Omaha. This is the family of prescriptive asymmetric systems.

In these conditions, the system allows a large number of clans and lineages to form a chain of exchanging groups that comes full circle after a certain number of exchanges. It should be noted that, insofar as each group can be part of several chains, it is able to receive women from several groups and to give women to several groups, at the same time.

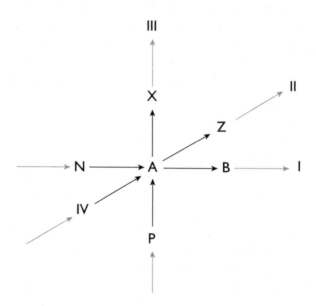

The system thus makes it possible to diversify and multiply alliances, while ensuring for each group that the alliances in question will be repeated generation after generation. What has disappeared with respect to Dravidian systems is the principle of the reciprocal exchange of women. What has been retained is the principle of repeating the same alliances generation after generation for as long as ties with the partner groups have not been broken. Here we have one of the possible transformations of a Dravidian system into a prescriptive asymmetric system. Such is the case of the Murngin system (Australia), the Kachin system (Burma), and so on.

Another possible transformation is the one we have already described, following Hornborg, and which, starting from a Dravidian system, wound up as an Iroquois system. Contrary to other asymmetrical systems, this one keeps the Dravidian rule of reciprocal exchange of women (or children), which produces in the following generation Ego's cross and parallel cousins, the first being possible spouses and the second forbidden. In this case, Ego has the option of marrying either a cross cousin of the first degree or, if that is forbidden, a cross cousin of the second or third degree. In this case, in $G^0$, all cross cousins now forbidden to marry are transformed into parallel cousins, in other words into forbidden 'brothers and sisters'. This transformation of all cousins into siblings in $G^0$ results in what is called the 'Hawaiianization' of the systems in $G^0$ because, in so-called Hawaiian systems, all cousins are 'brothers and sisters'. Iroquois systems, like Dravidian systems, work on the principle of the direct exchange of women but, unlike Dravidian systems, they have no rule prescribing marriage with cross cousins, except when a woman has been given by a lineage that has not received a woman in return. In this case, as with the Baruya of New Guinea, the first daughter born to the unreciprocated woman must marry a man from her mother's lineage. A male Ego therefore marries his patrilateral cross cousin, his father's sister's daughter (FZD). Crow-Omaha systems, on the other hand, forbid the direct exchange of women, which is a feature shared by both Dravidian and Iroquois systems. The distinction between parallel and cross kin disappears. And since Ego cannot take a woman either in his own lineage or in lineages with which his own has contracted alliances in the past two or three generations, he must turn elsewhere.

It is therefore no accident if, in North America, tribes with a Crow or Omaha system are found in the vicinity of tribes with an Iroquois system.[35] Nor should we forget that Iroquois systems can have either a matrilineal (the Iroquois themselves) or a patrilineal (the Baruya) descent principle. These systems can therefore transform either into a matrilineal Crow system or a patrilineal Omaha system. But Iroquois

---

35 T. Trautmann and R. Barnes, ' "Dravidian", "Iroquois" and "Crow-Omaha" in North American Perspective', in Godelier et al., *Transformations of Kinship*, pp. 27–58; more recently, P. Whiteley, 'Crow-Omaha Kinship in North American: A Pueblo Perspective', in Trautmann and Whiteley, eds, *Crow-Omaha*, pp. 83–108.

systems themselves are found in the neighbourhood of Dravidian systems, which, as we have seen in the case of the Australian systems, combine one principle that goes through the men and another that goes through the women.

Here we are in the presence of a family of systems all of which stem from the Dravidian type. This hypothesis, advanced by Kryukov and by ourselves in his wake,[36] sheds some light on these transformations. But if the latter all originate from the same type of system, they diverge among themselves depending on whether they keep the parallel/cross distinction or cancel it partially or totally, and whether they keep the principle of exchanging women but forbid repetition of the exchange with the same allies for a given number of generations, and so on. In short, systems with a complete or partial Crow-Omaha terminology appear or disappear as a function of these choices for, in addition to completely or partially cancelling crossness and making cross kin consanguines, for a certain number of kin positions, they cancel the generational differences that separate them and subsume these positions under the same term. In so doing, they assert that these kin are all in the same relation to Ego, and that this equivalence takes precedence over and erases the generational difference between them and Ego.

At this point, we must mention, for the third time, certain 'skewed' terminologies, such as the Crow or Omaha type, which are no longer associated with alliance strategies but with strategies for the accession to 'rights', 'functions', privileges, and so on. The most spectacular case is that of the Fante, an Akan group of over a million persons, closely related to the Ashanti people of Ghana studied by Rattray and Fortes. The Fante have two sets of kin terms, a Crow-type system used in certain social contexts and another that resembles that of the North American Cheyenne Indians, based on a matrilineal descent principle. The latter is a matrilineal Iroquois system with, in $G^0$, cancellation of all cross cousins, who are treated as Ego's brothers and sisters, as are Ego's parallel cousins; in this case, we speak of Hawaiianization in $G^0$, which can lead to confusion, we should recall in passing, with true Hawaiian systems.[37]

36  Godelier, 'Afterword', pp. 386–413.

37  F. Tjon Sie Fat, 'On the Formal Analysis of Dravidian, Iroquois and Generational Varieties as Nearly Associative Combinations', in Godelier et al., *Transformations of Kinship*, pp. 50–93.

David Kronenfeld, a specialist of the Fante, has shown that they used their matrilineal terminology for everyday matters and in discussing marriage alliances. Yet in certain contexts they used the same terminology but modified to a Crow type by the application of a skewing principle. All his informants stressed that they used the Crow-type terminology to determine, for instance, which man in a matriline should succeed the man in charge of important rites. In other contexts involving the transmission of various forms of property, Crow terminology was also used.

This use produces a twofold effect. On the one hand, skewing deletes the equivalence posed in the non-Crow system between paternal and maternal grandparents ($G^{+2}$), and does the same in $G^{+1}$. It thus gives more importance to the maternal side, in other words to the matrilineal descent principle that generates the matrilineages. Furthermore, the skewing acts on cross cousins without affecting parallel cousins, whereas in the non-Crow system, and therefore in everyday life, the cross/parallel distinction does not play any particular role.[38]

Kronenfeld concludes from this that the Fante's Crow terminology is an 'overlay', superimposed on the everyday matrilineal system to bring out the existence of matrilineages and their importance in succession and transmission. We must not forget that transmission in these systems does not follow a straight line from father to son, but is skewed obliquely, from maternal uncle (MB) to uterine nephew (ZS). Kronenfeld generalizes this conclusion and advances the hypothesis that all Crow-Omaha terminologies are merely overlays introduced as a result of certain historical contexts into systems that function in daily life without the need to raise or lower kin positions around Ego, thus cancelling the difference between the generations and merging under the same term a certain number of persons of the same sex and from the same lineage. These individuals are thereby defined as equivalents of one another, whatever their age.

The question then becomes: with respect to what, and therefore why, is this equivalence posited? The Fante case shows that the passage from one terminology to another corresponds to social goals: it has a function. In this case, 'overlay' seems an inadequate term to account for it. A

---

38 D. Kronenfeld, 'Crow- (and Omaha-) Type Kinship Terminology: The Fanti Case', in Trautmann and Whiteley, *Crow-Omaha*, chapter VIII.

terminology, of whatever type, is a tool, a 'social technology' known and used by all members of a society to solve certain problems.

We can ultimately distinguish two different contexts in which a Crow-Omaha terminology is used, and other contexts where terminologies that are not structurally of a Crow-Omaha type take on some Crow or Omaha features.

The first context is that in which Crow or Omaha terminologies are utilized to regulate marriage alliances, at once through a process of forbidding unions with a certain number of lineages to which Ego is related, and through the possibility of repeating past alliances as soon as the required number of generations has elapsed. These are the Omaha systems, like those of the Samo and the Mkako in Africa, and the Crow systems, like those of the Hopi in North America, and so on.

The second context is that in which a Crow- or Omaha-type terminology exists, but is not associated with a policy of marriage alliances. It is used for other purposes: transmission of functions, of tangible or intangible property, etc. In these cases, the skewing of several kin positions located at different genealogical levels emphasizes the internal unity of a kin group along a chosen axis, and asserts the equivalence of all those who occupy the same position along this axis. It was these facts that led Radcliffe-Brown and certain of his predecessors to associate Crow-Omaha terminologies with the existence of unilineal (patrilineal or matrilineal) descent systems and with policies of succession and transmission in these unilineal groups. This was also the position of Lounsbury (1966) and of Kronenfeld (1973). But if the Crow-Omaha terminology does not regulate alliances, there must be another one, in the same society, that does. This is the case of the Fante.[39]

In this third context, terminologies can have some Crow-Omaha features even though they are associated with a positive marriage rule and contain a principle distinguishing parallel and cross kin. This is the case of the prescriptive asymmetric systems, like the Murngin, Kachin, etc. But since the rule prescribes marriage with the matrilateral cross cousin, the mother's brother's daughter, and forbids it with the father's sister's daughter (with the group of wife-takers), the cross/parallel

39 D. Kronenfeld, 'Fanti Kinship: The Structure of Terminology and Behaviour', *American Anthropologist*, n° 75 (1973), pp. 1577–95; *Fanti Kinship and the Analysis of Kinship Terminologies* (Urbana and Chicago, University of Illinois Press, 2009).

distinction is maintained on the maternal side but disappears on the paternal side. A skewing process is thus set in place. Around Ego, the maternal kin are raised as 'in-laws', wife-givers, while the paternals are lowered as wife-takers. This asymmetrical treatment generates Omaha features in the terminology.

We could even add a fourth system to those we have just examined. It is a system that Elkin, and Lévi-Strauss after him, had declared to be 'aberrant':[40] it is the system found in the Australian societies of the Western Desert, whose kinship system is of the Aluridja type. In everyday life, cross cousins in Ego's generation ($G^0$) are classified as brothers and sisters, and are treated as such. The reason is that they all belong to the same generational moiety, which identifies all individuals in $G^0$ with those in the two alternate generations $G^{+2}$ and $G^{-2}$. The other generational moiety includes all individuals belonging to generations $G^{+1}$ and $G^{-1}$, in other words those who engendered those in $G^0$ and those $G^0$ will engender. For the generational moieties of the social groups whose members, whatever their generation (their age), are 'brothers' and 'sisters' for each other, the members of the other generational moiety are 'fathers' and 'mothers'. The moieties are therefore both sociocentric and ego-centred.[41]

Alternatively, when it comes to marriage and choosing a spouse, the distinction between siblings and parallel and cross cousins reappears. Marriage always takes place with a cross cousin who is neither genealogically nor geographically close, in other words a third- or even fourth-degree cross cousin. We are in the presence of what Laurent Dousset has called a 'horizontal skewing', as opposed to the 'oblique skewing' of the Crow-Omaha systems. The neutralization or, on the contrary, the underscoring of crossness thus corresponds to sociological contexts and to the different collective and individual aims. It is impossible to discover these facts and the reason for their existence without spending a long time living with and observing a group. Elkin, and Tindale after him, spent too little time in the field to have had a chance to discover them.

---

40 Cf. L. Dousset, 'On the Misinterpretation of the Aluridja Kinship System Type', *Social Anthropology* 11, n° 1 (2003), pp. 43–61.

41 L. Dousset, '"Horizontal" and "Vertical" Skewing: Similar Objectives, Two Solutions?' in Trautmann and Whiteley, eds, *Crow and Omaha*, chapter XIII.

Yet the reasons for this 'horizontal skewing' are quite clear, and of great importance for societies that exploit erratic resources in one of the most arid deserts on earth. Imposing marriage with a third-degree cross cousin in a band nomadizing in other parts of the desert gives the new family and its band ties and affiliations, both ritual and material, with a greater number of groups spread over a vast area, and allows them potentially to expand the resources that will enable them to survive.

In the end, all kinship systems are dynamic systems that accompany individuals throughout their life, together with the groups created by these kinship relations. Kinship terminologies are part and parcel of these systems. They are neither 'aberrant' nor 'unnecessary'; they are coherent and effective. They are coherent when we discover the social purposes they are associated with. They are effective because they act as a guide, as a memorizable formula and even a recipe to be applied when one wishes to achieve these goals. They are not 'overlays' able to adapt to any or almost any kinship system. They are sets of rules and symbols that are an integral part of the abstract structure of kinship systems, and enable these to be implemented.

We are now prepared to measure the impact of the Huxley Memorial Lecture on our knowledge of kinship. It set the cat among the flock of true and false problems. It sparked a wealth of fruitful studies down to our day, studies based as much on the structural approach as on regional fieldwork.[42] Dravidian systems have been discovered in South Africa,[43] systems with direct exchange of women in other parts of Africa, not to mention the many Omaha systems found in West Africa and Cameroon. The harvest has been just as rich when it comes to North and South America or to New Guinea. Terms for cross cousins have even been discovered in the kinship systems of western Polynesia – the famous Hawaiian systems – which suggests these systems, too, resulted from the transformation of what were probably Dravidian systems since the remote ancestors of the Polynesian

---

42 Cf. the series of publications entitled *Les Complexités de l'alliance*, edited by É. Copet-Rougier and F. Héritier in 1990 (vol. 1) and 1991 (vol. 2) (Paris, Éditions des archives contemporaines).

43 P. Hage, 'Dravidian Kinship Systems', *L'Homme*, Nos 177–8 (2006), pp. 395–408.

populations left Taiwan and perhaps South China. For it seems that, in the last millennium before our era, there were still kinship systems in that region involving the direct or deferred exchange of women, which were associated, probably for ritual purposes, with sociocentric moieties.

Little work has so far been done on the Sudanese-type systems, which are very close to the ancient Latin system and can be found today in some Slavic groups or in China, while closer study of the partially endogamous systems, in particular the so-called 'Arab' systems, is presently getting under way. Meanwhile the Eskimo-type systems, characteristic of Western Europe and 'Europeanized' America, have commanded little attention.

Lévi-Strauss was right, then. The systems grouped under the 'Crow-Omaha' heading needed to be subjected to a new analysis, beginning with the marriage rules associated with them, which had been neglected. But cutting the old category of terminologies in two would make it harder to discover the common factor underlying all those systems, namely, the ubiquitous presence of the distinction between cross and parallel kin characteristic of elementary structures, whether they come under the heading of restricted or generalized exchange.[44] It is an effective presence, continually operating either positively, as in systems of restricted exchange, or negatively, since it had to be neutralized either completely, in order to create a maximum diversity of alliances, or partially, as in Crow-Omaha systems, in order to organize them into one or several chains that might be extended and thus tie a greater number of groups into the interplay of kinship relations. But these chains had also to terminate somewhere, to come full circle, as in the prescriptive asymmetric systems. Crow-Omaha terminologies everywhere, whether highly developed or reduced to a few features, presuppose the existence and the social effectiveness of the cross/non-cross distinction that, according to Lévi-Strauss, defines the elementary structures of kinship. This distinction is one of the chief

---

44 F. Tjon Sie Fat showed there are sixteen possible variants of the cross/parallel opposition, and the Iroquois formula is the farthest from the Dravidian formula if one constructs the hypercube with these sixteen variants. See Godelier et al., *Transformations of Kinship*, pp. 11, 59–93. E. Viveiros de Castro has compared several of these variants, which he found in five different kinship systems; see, in the same volume, 'Dravidian and Related Kinship Systems', pp. 332–85.

consequences of the prohibition of incest and the obligation to exchange between groups those members with whom one cannot unite.

If the deep structure of all these systems is the same – whether it appears on the surface or is masked – then we have not really left the elementary structures behind with the Crow-Omaha systems. Those Lévi-Strauss singled out as 'true' Crow-Omaha systems, endowed, in the *grande théorie* of kinship, with the property of epitomizing systems that ensure the transition to complex systems, would therefore in no way lead anywhere beyond themselves. Such systems resolve clearly defined problems in specific sociological contexts – contexts in which there are kin groups structured by unilineal or cognatic descent principles.

One day, we will have seriously to re-examine the notion of 'complex structures' of kinship, for if the choice of a spouse or partner, in our type of society, clearly has a certain randomness about it, that does not suffice to label a system with a simple structure, like the European kinship system, a '*complex*' system. From this standpoint, the definitions of elementary and complex need to be reviewed. And until we either rethink them from scratch or abandon them for another typology, the issue will remain blurred.

One last point. In the Huxley Memorial Lecture, Lévi-Strauss concluded his analysis of Crow-Omaha systems by suggesting that with their advent 'history comes to the foreground in the life of simple socie-ties'.[45] It is difficult to say that the Kachin were a 'simple' society. In *The Elementary Structures of Kinship*, basing his reflection on Wehrli's and Gilhodes's published work on the Chingpaw (Kachin),[46] Lévi-Strauss describes them as a ranked society in which commoners are ruled by an aristocracy of noble 'houses'. At the bottom of the society are the slaves, or those born of the union between a freeman and a slave. Even if the nobles all claim a mythic common ancestor associated with the creation of the world, thus inscribing their existence in a time that predates human history, it is the social transformations that occurred in the course of their history that generated this division of the society into

45 'The Future of Kinship Studies', p. 20.
46 C. Gilhodes, *The Kachins, Religion and Customs* (Calcutta, Catholic Mission Press, 1922).

ranked groups. Lévi-Strauss describes this society as 'feudal' and compares it to the Inca society of pre-Columbian Peru. Here we have the paradox of a 'simple', multi-ethnic society forming an empire under a strongly centralized State.[47]

## Preface to the Second Edition of *The Elementary Structures of Kinship* (1967)

In 1967, Lévi-Strauss published *From Honey to Ashes*, the second volume in his Mythology series. And, after having been solicited for several years, he published a new edition of *The Elementary Structures of Kinship*, which had been out of print for some time. Although he made very few changes to this new edition, he did add a new preface (written in 1966). The Preface to the second edition shows the evolution of his thinking on several important points, and confirms the options he had asserted in The Huxley Memorial Lecture concerning the necessity of studying the Crow-Omaha systems if ever one was to understand the complex structures of kinship.[48] He also reiterates his surprise at having seen so many debates arise among his British and American colleagues about the difference between preferential and prescriptive marriages.

Lévi-Strauss emphasized that so much new material had become available since 1947, and kinship theory had become so complex, he would have had to rewrite his text completely. But he contented himself with merely rewriting the chapter on the Murngin systems (XIII) and the three chapters (XV–XVII) devoted to the Kachin. These he altered because of the criticisms voiced by Leach, a specialist of the Kachin.[49] Leach was to become the target of Lévi-Strauss's reaction, but that is not the most important.

The crucial development lies in the evolution of Lévi-Strauss's thinking concerning the distinction and opposition between nature and culture, which was the starting point of the analyses in *The Elementary*

---

47 *The Elementary Structures of Kinship*, pp. 246–8.

48 *The Elementary Structures of Kinship*, 'Preface to the Second Edition', p. xxxvi. Lévi-Strauss reminds us that, in 1947–48, he was contemplating approaching the study of complex systems in a second volume, 'but which doubtless I shall never write'.

49 E. Leach, *Rethinking Anthropology* (London, Athlone Press, 1961).

*Structures* and served as a presupposition for the emergence of the incest taboo, from which all the analyses in the book flow.

> As far as the contrast between nature and culture is concerned . . . My proposal [in 1947] was to trace the line of demarcation between the two orders guided by the presence or absence of articulated speech . . . But . . . the appearance of certain phenomena has made this line of demarcation, if not less real, then certainly more tenuous and tortuous than was imagined twenty years ago.[50]

Lévi-Strauss cites three orders of phenomenon that make the line of demarcation between humanity and the animal kingdom 'more tenuous'. In the first place, complex processes of communication had been discovered in birds, fish and mammals, some of which 'bring true symbols into play'. In second place was the fact that some birds and mammals 'can fashion and use tools', notably chimpanzees in the wild. Last came the fact that, in the lower Paleolithic, 'different genera of hominoids, fashioners of stone and bone, seem to have lived together on the same sites'.

Lévi-Strauss was therefore led to wonder 'just how far the contrast between nature and culture may be pushed', since it appears no longer as 'a concrete aspect of universal order' but rather as 'an artificial creation of culture'. He goes on to bring serious charges against our species, *Homo sapiens,* inspired 'as it presumably was some hundreds of thousands of years or more ago by the same obtuse and destructive spirit which today impels it to destroy other living forms, having annihilated so many human societies'.[51] The critique of the human species already present in *Tristes Tropiques* (1955) resurfaces here. It would not cease to permeate Lévi-Strauss's work until his death.

From these new facts, Lévi-Strauss draws the conclusion that, to understand culture in its essence, we must proceed differently:

> We would have to trace it back to its source and run counter to its forward trend and retie all the broken threads by seeking out their loose ends in other animal and even vegetable families. Ultimately we

---

50 'Preface to the Second Edition', p. xxix.
51 Ibid.

shall perhaps discover that the interrelationship between nature and culture does not favour culture to the extent of being hierarchically superimposed on nature and irreducible to it. Rather it takes the form of a *synthetic duplication* of mechanisms already in existence but which the animal kingdom shows only in disjointed form and dispersed variously among its members.[52]

We would draw attention to the expression 'synthetic duplication', because this notion opens new perspectives on the passage from nature to culture that the 'big bang' theory of the appearance of symbolic thought did not offer. But in 1967, these potentials could not yet be exploited. The fact that chimpanzees and bonobos, our closest relatives in the animal kingdom, communicate through complex processes, going so far as to understand symbols, and that they furthermore make and use tools (although they do not make tools to make tools), means that they have significant cognitive capacities. But the crucial factor of this passage from nature to culture, for Lévi-Strauss, is still missing, and that is the prohibition of incest – the subordination of individual sexuality to social rules that exclude sexual unions with closely related persons.

In 1969, however, little was actually known about the sexual behaviour of man's closest primate relatives, whereas it 'does give one reason why the change [from nature to culture] can and must necessarily take place in the field of sexual life above any other'.[53] He therefore concludes: 'I still believe that the prohibition of incest is to be explained entirely in terms of sociological causes. Certainly, however, I have treated the genetic aspect in too casual a manner.'[54]

Twenty years later, when he was confronted with the data amassed by primatologists on what they at the time called biological mechanisms of 'incest avoidance' and even 'exchange of females' between bands of chimpanzees, Lévi-Strauss, in his conversation with Didier Eribon (published in 1988), would not even go to the trouble of actually analysing their data and ridding them of the over-loose metaphors that many primatologists had borrowed from the concepts used by anthropologists in analysing kinship.

---

52  Ibid., p. xxx.
53  *The Elementary Structures of Kinship*, chapter II: 'The Problem of Incest', p. 12.
54  'Preface to the Second Edition', pp. xxviii–xxix.

All of this, I admit, leaves me somewhat skeptical. Not concerning the data that have been observed but their interpretation, which too often has an anthropomorphic tinge to it. That there exists a general tendency to expel the young from the group when they reach puberty – sometimes males, sometimes females, depending on the species under consideration – can be explained in various ways, the most likely of which seems to be competition for food. Nothing leads us to think that the dispersion of the young is the result of a so-called incest prohibition in the animal realm.[55]

In reality, food competition is the least likely explanation. Nor is it probable that these biological and social mechanisms serve to avoid some kind of 'incest' between related individuals, nor does the fact that females leave their original band at puberty and disperse to neighbouring bands in any way constitute an 'exchange' of females between the males of these bands.[56] Rather, it is when a new generation of primates, both male and female, reaches puberty and will really enter into competition with the adults of their band – which have heretofore had priority access to sex and food – that *the reproduction of the band as such* (as a group of males and females depending on each other to individually or collectively exploit the resources of their territory and defend it against intrusions from neighbouring bands), which forms a 'society', *comes under threat.*[57] The females' departure and dispersal is therefore both a biological and a social regulating mechanism. Since this mechanism divides the society into two groups – the adult males and females that joined the band at puberty and gave birth to the young males that will remain, and the young females that will leave – it is one of the threads that link the human species to certain animal species, to those primates

55  C. Lévi-Strauss and D. Eribon, ed., *Conversations with Claude Lévi-Strauss*, trans. P. Wissing (Chicago, University of Chicago Press, 1991), pp. 100–1.

56  B. Deputte, 'L'Évitement de l'inceste chez les primates non humains', *Nouvelle Revue d'ethnopsychiatrie*, n° 3 (1985), pp. 41–72.

57  Cf. J. Moore and R. Ali, 'Are Dispersal and Inbreeding Avoidances Related?', *Animal Behaviour*, n° 32 (1984), pp. 94–112. Any society, animal or human, is, for the individuals in it – according to the definition of the biologist François Jacob in *La Logique du vivant* (Paris, Gallimard, 1970) – the necessary environment for individuals to reach full development. Environment in this sense means not only their surroundings and its resources, but an organization of the individuals' social existence according to sex and age.

that are our closest relatives.[58] The young males that remain in the band are the sons of the adult males, but no one has yet discovered any sign that the males recognize the sons and daughters they have engendered with a given receptive female.[59] On the other hand, continual and reciprocal signs of recognition have been observed between a female and the sons and daughters she has borne. But after infancy and continuing into adolescence, the mothers endeavour gradually to detach their offspring from themselves, using more aggressive tactics with the sons than with the daughters. In short, these mechanisms do not serve the biological reproduction of individuals and society in such a way as to prevent the deleterious effects of consanguineous unions. They are biological mechanisms that serve the *social* reproduction of the species, the reproduction of the kind of society that ensures this species' reproduction.

Lévi-Strauss arrived at another theoretical conclusion in the first edition of *The Elementary Structures* that could have bolstered an interpretation, in line with his thinking, of the new data gathered by primatologists. In effect, in a statement that has given rise to much commentary, and which we have already quoted, Lévi-Strauss had asserted that: 'The prohibition of incest is less a rule prohibiting marriage with the mother, sister or daughter, than a rule obliging the mother, sister or daughter to be given to others.'[60] These are conscious rules and stem from symbolic thought, the only process capable of ascribing a social sense to differences and relations between the sexes. But in the closest primate relatives of humans, two opposing forces are clearly at play: those that repel and those that attract sexual desires between the male and female members of the bands that make up their form of society. One set of forces drives the young males and females of the band to detach themselves from their mother, who has ensured their development from birth, whereas the males play no role in this development; the other draws them to members of their band who attract them or whom they attract. As for the young males that stay in the band while their 'sisters' leave, and that see young females come in from other bands that are more attractive because unfamiliar, we find

---

58 Today it is thought that the ancestor of all hominians split off from the ancestors we share with chimpanzees and bonobos some six million years ago. The ancestors of chimpanzees and bonobos separated some four million years ago.

59 On all these points, see our analysis in *Metamorphoses of Kinship*, pp. 431–47.

60 *The Elementary Structures of Kinship*, p. 481.

that it is precisely when their sexual desires might come into direct competition with those of the adult males in the band that such drives are inhibited, and remain so until they have garnered a place in the hierarchy of the band's males and thus won access to the receptive females. The temporary inhibition of their sexuality is therefore linked to the relations of domination and subordination obtaining between the males, but also between the females and, of course, between males and females. These mechanisms thus contribute to reproduce the social form of existence characteristic of these primates and, indirectly, to the natural selection that operates in the evolution of all species.

Absent in chimpanzees and bonobos is not only the males' recognition of their role in the birth of offspring but also cooperation between adult males and females in raising the young, as well as transmission of particular rights and duties that go with the reproduction of kinship relations. There are no kin groups in chimpanzee societies; there are simply male lines of descendants which recognize each other if they were raised by the same mother.

The passage from nature to culture is today seen as a both continuous and discontinuous transition between the social life of the very remote ancestors of the Neanderthals (now extinct), still in their animal-like state, and that of our own species, *Homo sapiens sapiens*. The incest prohibition may have consisted in a duplication and mutation, elaborated in the minds of *Homo sapiens sapiens*, of biological mechanisms operating in the natural state to ensure the reproduction of the primate form of social existence: a band controlling a territory and its useful resources through relations of both subordination and cooperation between individuals, on the basis of age and sex.

Duplication and mutation signify both continuity and discontinuity. But men's cooperation with women, made necessary by the sexual division of labour and the establishment of relations of appropriation and control with regard to the children born of their unions, constituted a break with the social structures of their remote ancestors. Let us not forget that some 500,000 years ago these remote ancestors had already domesticated fire and definitively split off from the protohuman species of the animal kingdom, which continue to include chimpanzees and bonobos. Now, fire, which makes it possible to eat cooked food, which needs to be tended, which keeps animals at bay, protects from the cold, etc., creates new solidarities at once material, social and affective, between the sexes and between the generations: young children cannot cook their own food and must receive it from the adults, who are thus obliged to share it. Yet this does not mean the new place assigned to children in the society, and the evolution of adult male behaviour with respect to them, can be explained by the development of feelings of 'love'. Instead, it may be attributed to the fact that the child is now the bearer of new social relations, and that it will fall to him to reproduce these relations when he in turn reaches adulthood. The child thus became a social investment before becoming an object of love.

Humankind did not invent society. It received this mode of existence from nature, at the same time as the capacity to transform what it had received. We are, in effect, the only species that not only lives in society, like other social species, but also produces new forms of social existence, and therefore of culture, in order to continue to live. By contrast, chimpanzees or bonobos have never yet been seen to transform their social organization. They have been observed *adapting* to environments, but not modifying the social structures in which they live.

In conclusion: there is no mechanism for 'avoiding incest' in primates. Nor is there any 'exchange' of females between bands. There is no such thing as 'patrilineages' in chimpanzees or 'matrilineages' in Japanese macaques, where it is the males that leave the band and disperse at puberty and the females that spend their life in their birth band. There are male lines (chimpanzees) or female lines (macaques). But these lines are not lineages; a patrilineage or a matrilineage in human kinship is a group made up of *both* men and women (brothers and sisters, sons and daughters) who share or claim to share a common ascendance along with mutual rights and duties. Nothing of the sort exists in man's closest primate relatives. What does exist are biological mechanisms that operate differentially in the two sexes, by dispersal of the pubescent females and inhibition of the pubescent males, to ensure that the conflicts between generations, which increase when the 'young' of a group reach adulthood, do not imperil the existence of the band as a necessary environment for the existence and survival of each individual, whichever its sex.

What should be retained here is that nature provides mechanisms to regulate the sexuality of individuals by subordinating these drives to the reproduction of their society. These mechanisms operate by separating the sexes and dividing the children born to one mother, with the ones leaving their birth band and the others staying. It is conceivable therefore that these separations and divisions in primate society, the consequences of an unconscious mechanism regulating sexuality, may have constituted one of the threads linking humankind with the animal species most closely related to us. These mechanisms may then have served as the matter and starting point for, according to Lévi-Strauss's remarkable formula, their 'synthetic duplication . . . permitted by the emergence of certain cerebral structures which themselves belong to nature'.[61] These structures then may have led to the conscious formulation of norms designed to subordinate individuals' sexuality to the reproduction of the society as a whole. To be sure it was sexuality-as-desire, a polymorphous and polytropic drive proper to humans, that had to be subordinated, in other words repressed, restricted, amputated and even proscribed, depending on the social and religious orders that set out to subject it.[62]

Generalized sexual permissiveness is incompatible with the existence of human society. Nor does it exist in the primates most closely related to humans. Not to be able to do everything with sex is, to be sure, a form of amputation, but it is also the condition for the advancement of humankind in its capacity to produce society in order to (continue to) live. To produce society, and not simply to reproduce it: this is the radical difference between ourselves and our closest primate relatives. This is specific to humans.

## 'Reflections on the Atom of Kinship' (1973)

By 1971, Lévi-Strauss had finished his four-volume 'Mythologiques' with the publication of *The Origin of Table Manners* in 1968 and *The Naked Man* in 1971. In 1971 he also resumed his kinship seminars at the Collège de France and, in 1971–72, returned to the 'atom of kinship'.

In 1973 he published his new 'Réflexions sur l'atome de parenté' in the journal *L'Homme*.[63] The article was a very belated response to the

---

61 'Preface to the Second Edition', p.xxx.

62 Alternatively, it could be extolled by other forms of religion provided that sexual pleasure was placed at the service of the family's well-being, as in Hinduism. Cf. M. Godelier, 'Meurtre du père ou sacrifice de la sexualité?' in M. Godelier and J. Hassoun, eds, *Meurtre du père, sacrifice de la sexualité. Approches anthropologiques et psychanalytiques* (Paris, Arcanes, 1995).

63 *L'Homme* 13, n° 3 (1973), pp. 5–30, and in C. Lévi-Strauss, *Structural Anthropology, Volume 2*, trans. M. Layton (Chicago, University of Chicago Press, 1983), pp. 82–112.

objections Luc de Heusch had raised in 1958, 1965 and finally in 1971, in his book *Pourquoi l'épouser? et autres essais*,[64] to the notion of 'atom of kinship', which Lévi-Strauss had first set out in his 1945 article, analysed earlier.[65] Taken up by writing his mythology series, Lévi-Strauss had not found the time to respond. The publication of *Pourquoi l'épouser?*, in which de Heusch voiced his criticisms for the third time, prompted a reply.

Let us pause and recall Lévi-Strauss's theoretical aim when he initially developed the notion of 'atom of kinship'. This was the first blow struck at the edifice of Anglo-American anthropology, and most particularly at the theories of kinship focused exclusively on descent rules, at the expense of alliance. He wanted to show that kinship could not be reduced to relations between a father, a mother and their children (what at the time he termed the 'biological family'). The simplest kinship structure, the atom of kinship, must include the wife's brother – the children's maternal uncle, the man who had given his sister to the one who became his brother-in-law. This structure, the simplest in his eyes, combined relations of consanguinity, alliance and filiation, in other words the relationship between a brother and sister (B–Z), between a husband and wife (Hu–Wi), between a father and son (F–S) and between a maternal uncle and his nephew (MB–ZS).

He then went on to posit that, in all societies, these four relationships correspond to formalized attitudes that work in pairs, balancing two positive relationships against a negative pair. It can therefore be expected that, in a matrilineal system, since children belong to their mother's clan, the relationship between mother's brother and his nephew (in other words, between the maternal uncle and nephew) will be marked by authority (to which Lévi-Strauss assigns a minus sign -), and the relationship between father and son, marked by affection (to which Lévi-Strauss assigns a plus sign +). Alternatively, the relationship between husband and wife can be tense (-), while that between brother and sister will be affectionate (see diagram below). We are therefore

64 L. de Heusch, *Essais sur le symbolisme de l'inceste royal en Afrique* (Brussels, Éditions de l'Université libre de Bruxelles, 1958); *Pourquoi l'épouser? et autres essais* (Paris, Gallimard, 1971).

65 C. Lévi-Strauss, 'L'Analyse structurale en linguistique et en anthropologie', *Word* 1, n° 1 (1945).

dealing with two pairs entertaining relations of correlation and opposition, which keep the structure of the 'atom' in balance.

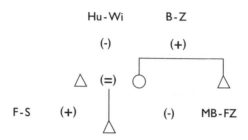

However, Lévi-Strauss had already made it clear in 1945 that the avuncular relationship (maternal uncle–nephew) was not governed by descent rules. He had also made it clear that, in systems with more complex structures, the avunculate not only ceased to play an important role but could be completely obliterated or merged with other roles. Finally, Lévi-Strauss reminded his critic that he had already written, in 1945, that 'the positive and negative symbols . . . represent an oversimplification, useful only as a part of the demonstration . . . In many systems the relationship between two individuals is often expressed not by a single attitude, but by several attitudes which together form, as it were, a bundle of attitudes.'[66]

He then insists on the fact that the content that can be assigned to one attitude or another adopted by individuals in the specific kinship relation that binds them matters less than the opposition discerned between the two pairs of attitudes. Ultimately, we would not even need to know what these contents are: 'What these attitudes are in themselves, the affective contents they mask, does not have, from the particular point of view of our argument, any intrinsic meaning.'[67]

Having recalled the passages from his 1945 text which invalidated Luc de Heusch's reiterated objections in advance, Lévi-Strauss deals the *coup de grâce* when he accuses de Heusch of having ('momentarily' as he says, to soften the blow) forgotten a fundamental rule of structural analysis, which is that 'the analysis can never consider the terms only

---

66 C. Lévi-Strauss, *Structural Anthropology*, trans. C. Jacobson and B. Grundfest Schoepf (New York, Basic Books, 1963), p. 49.

67 *Structural Anthropology, Volume 2*, p. 86.

but must, beyond the terms, apprehend their interrelations. These alone constitute its true object.'[68]

The issue is neither secondary nor innocent for Lévi-Strauss. Let us not forget that, in his Preface to the first edition of *The Elementary Structures of Kinship*, he announced his project of constituting the general theory of kinship systems in three stages and three volumes. The first, devoted to the elementary structures, had been written and published; the second, dealing with complex structures, had been abandoned but suggested as a research programme for others, once the structural analysis of the semi-complex systems had been completed. This prospective second book had become the 1965 Huxley Memorial Lecture. The third volume was to be on 'those family attitudes expressing or overcoming, by conventional behaviour, conflicts or contradictions inherent in the logical structure such as are revealed in the system of nomenclature.'[69]

The 1973 text, 'Reflections on the Atom of Kinship', is a thirty-two-page article written in place of the projected third volume. In it, Lévi-Strauss embarks on a dazzling counter-analysis of the three examples Luc de Heusch had cited in support of his objections: the case of the Lambumbu, a group living in the interior of Malekula Island in what is today Vanuatu;[70] the case of the Lele of the Kasai, in Africa, studied by Mary Douglas; and finally, the case of the Mundugumor, a people living in the Sepik region of New Guinea, studied by Margaret Mead. We will merely summarize these analyses.

The Lambumbu case is simple; its diagram shows it to be the exact opposite of our earlier construction:

---

68 Ibid., p. 83.

69 *The Elementary Structures of Kinship*, 'Preface to the first edition', p. xxiv.

70 A. B. Deacon, *Malekula: A Vanishing People in the New Hebrides* (London, C. Wedgwood, 1934), pp. 103–4, 159–71.

The Mundugumor case is more complicated, because descent is traced matrilineally for the boys and patrilineally for the girls. Marriage is by exchange. There is rivalry between a father and his sons, and similar rivalry between the sons; there is strong tension between a mother and her daughters. On the other hand, relations between the maternal uncle and his nephew are friendly.

The father's mother (FM) has close ties with her granddaughter (rope 2), and the mother's father (MF) with his grandson (rope 1). A grandchild carries the name of his/her grandparent and is 'socially identical' with him or her. Father's mother and mother's father therefore have their place in the atom of kinship, as well as the father's sister in regard to the mother, and the daughter in regard to the son.[71] All the oblique links corresponding to ropes are positive, as are the relations between father's sister (FZ) and father's brother's son (BS), and between mother's brother (MB) and her sister's daughter (ZD). All other links, vertical and horizontal, are negative (husband–wife, brother–sister, father–son, mother–daughter, brother-in-law–brother-in-law). The whole 'economy of the system' thus rests on the opposition between diagonal and straight (horizontal and vertical) links, and so on.

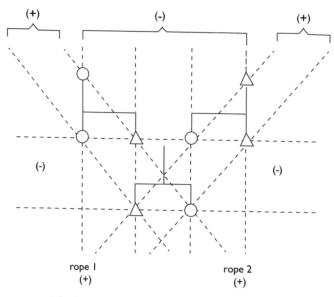

The heavy atom of Mundugumor kinship

71 *Structural Anthropology, Volume 2*, p. 91.

At the end of this demonstration, Lévi-Strauss concludes that this 'heavy atom' satisfies the three conditions set out in his initial hypothesis, namely: that an elementary structure of kinship (here among the Mundugumor) combines relations of alliance and of consanguinity; that the avuncular relation is independent from the descent rule; and that in such a structure, attitudes are opposed but form a balanced whole.

He next tackles the Lele case, and goes on to show that the Mundugumor and Lele systems are both based on a common deep structure, which he characterizes as having alternate generations that are opposed to consecutive generations. He then enquires into the role alternate generations can play in attributing different statuses in each generation to men and to women, to brothers and to sisters. In passing, he mentions various Amazonian systems with alternate generations and sex affiliations, and concludes by positing that all these systems could be 'states of a same group of transformation'.[72] This is one of the first times he alludes to that notion in analysing kinship systems, whereas it had already provided a hypothetical basis for analysing the relations between Amerindian myths on which he had just spent over six years.

All in all, 'Reflections on the Atom of Kinship' presented the public with a synopsis of the analyses Lévi-Strauss had proposed in his course at the Collège de France in 1971–72. A course abstract can be found in *Anthropology and Myth*, which sums up his lectures at the École Pratique des Hautes Études and then at the Collège de France. This oral cycle ended in 1982. *Anthropology and Myth* appeared in French, under the title *Paroles données*, in 1983. In the summary of the 1971–72 course devoted to the atom of kinship, alongside the analyses offered in the article we have just examined, we find some important ideas he had never before expressed, or which he expressed here in a new form.

As we have seen, Lévi-Strauss had shown that the system of attitudes is not correlated with a patri- or matrilineal rule of descent, that the avuncular relationship can disappear, that the notion of atom of kinship is therefore not universally applicable and that finally it can be merged with others. 'My hypothesis', he wrote, 'would require only that, in every elementary structure of kinship, the position of donor be effectively filled'; but, whatever the number of constituents, 'it is necessary only

---

72  Ibid., p. 111.

that the relations uniting them be of the same type and that the forces composing them form a balanced system.'[73]

If the position of giver is not occupied by the maternal uncle (MB), then it is filled by another relative, and, in this case, we have a 'heavy atom' of kinship. Lévi-Strauss goes on to criticize Radcliffe-Brown for the 'naturalism' that led him to derive kinship from biological considerations alone, the union of a man and a woman thus forming a consanguineous family. That is to overlook, Lévi-Strauss reminds us, that this union supposes an alliance: 'Social alliance . . . There and there only, is the universal principle announced in the 1945 text and of which *The Elementary Structures of Kinship* proposed to provide the proof.'[74] And he adds, 'It would be incorrect to assume that the kinship system constitutes the principal means of regulating interpersonal relationships in all societies. Even in societies where the kinship system does function as such, it does not fulfil that role everywhere to the same extent.'[75]

The problem with this quotation is that it suggests there might be societies where kinship really was the *principal* means of regulating all relations between individuals. We are entitled to doubt this, for, even in Australian societies with Dravidian-type kinship systems and where everyone is related to everyone else in varying degrees, a whole series of inter-individual relations goes through positions that each individual – depending on sex, age and membership in endogamous generational moieties and in exogamous sections – must or must not occupy, in the performance of rites on totemic sites for the multiplication of the species and the attraction of spirit children to fertilize the women, and so on. These inter-individual relations are determined by the contribution each individual can and must make, as a function of age, sex, etc., to ensure the reproduction of a metaphysical world – the world set in place by the mythological heroes of the Dreamtime, a world that is shared by all Aborigines.

This metaphysical world common to all Australian societies (except those with a Murngin-type kinship system) envelops them and bestows

---

73 C. Lévi-Strauss, *Anthropology and Myth: Lectures, 1951–1982*, trans. R. Willis (Oxford, Basil Blackwell, 1987), p. 139.

74 Ibid., p. 139.

75 Ibid., p 136. Also in *Structural Anthropology*, p. 38.

a joint cultural identity that transcends *tribal* boundaries, a shared identity that kinship relations cannot produce but can only participate in. And as we have seen, it is for the better management of this metaphysical world, and to articulate this management with the kinship relations in each local group, that sections and cross-sections were invented sometime during the first millennium of our era.

It is therefore surprising to read in this summary the following assertions about the origin and nature of sections in Australia, which no longer tally with what he was saying in 1947:

> Since about 1930 all the authorities on Australia have repeatedly said that the sections and subsections related to a division of the natural and social worlds into categories and *did not play a major part in the ordering of marriage*, which was essentially based on genealogical considerations . . . we prefer to adhere to the more complex notion we have always had about the role of the sections and subsections: that of a code which is doubtless simplified, but easy to use when faced with questions of equivalence between several dialects or languages and which, to fulfil its function, can in no way contradict the more complex coding that expresses itself through, in and by the kinship system.[76]

But this 'nuanced' conception applies to only one aspect of the problem. In the years preceding the writing of *The Elementary Structures*, most anthropologists – with the exception of Radcliffe-Brown, who claimed that sections had nothing to do with the regulation of marriages – believed just the opposite, and they were right. In 1945–47, when he was writing *The Elementary Structures*, Lévi-Strauss asserted that to regulate marriages on the basis of kinship relations between the individuals involved or on the basis of their membership of 'marriage classes' (or sections) amounted to the same thing, except that in the section where a man must take his wife there are also women he may not marry. And he, too, was right. But he should then have asked himself: what use other than the regulation of marriage could sections have, if, in the same section, one found individuals who were permissible spouses and others who were forbidden? That might have led him

---

76 *Anthropology and Myth*, pp. 142–3; my emphasis.

to ask himself two more questions: what type of kinship system did these tribes have before they adopted or rejected the section system? What was the function of sections if they were not involved *primarily* in the regulation of marriages? The answers to these questions would have shaped a 'nuanced conception of the role of sections'. But he did not ask them.

# 5

# The Concept of 'House': Theory
# Makes New Strides (1976–1987)

It is to Lévi-Strauss's passion for the art of the Indians of the Pacific Northwest that we owe his interest in the nature of the social organization of tribes that produced or used the masks that had again delighted him on his second visit to British Columbia, in 1974: the *swaihwe* masks with their protuberant eyes and the *dzunukwa* masks with their sunken orbs, representing supernatural beings, big-breasted monsters. These tribes bear the names Kwakiutl, Bella Bella, Nimpkish, Lillooet, Squamish.

Lévi-Strauss had two deep bonds with this region. One, an old tie, dated from the period between the wars; it was an 'almost physical bond' with the art of these Indians, which 'never slackened'. He confessed that on seeing such masks worn during initiations, he felt within himself the 'omnipresence of the supernatural and the swarming of the myths'. When he lived in New York, during and after World War II, this passion drove him to haunt antique dealers in the company of Max Ernst and André Breton and to purchase some of these masks, which interested almost no one at the time.

But another, equally deep, more intellectual and scientific tie bound him to this region of North America. After having completed *From Honey to Ashes* in 1967, Lévi-Strauss began to explore the North American Indian myths in an attempt to track the myth of the Bird-Nester (Myth 1 in his Mythology series), which he had first identified in South America. This is a Bororo myth that he found among the Ge

(M7–M12) and then repeatedly in a variety of transformations, from one tribe to the next, one linguistic group to the next, from southern Brazil to northern Guyana. This northerly trek gave rise to the first two volumes of his Mythology series: *The Raw and the Cooked* (French edition, 1964) and *From Honey to Ashes*.

But as he moved to the world of North American Indian mythology in search of the myth and its series of transformations, he gradually discovered – to his great surprise – that not only was the myth present in North America, but the central character and nearly all the other mythic patterns encountered in the course of his search seemed to converge in a very small region of North America, and more precisely on the Northwest coast. Sandwiched between the shores of the Pacific Ocean and a chain of mountains running from northern Washington State to southern Oregon, beyond which lies the Columbia plateau, stretching to the Rockies, this region has been inhabited from the earliest times, as attested by archaeological remains. It was populated by some one hundred small tribes, whose languages, cultures and forms of social organization were highly varied. The region thus appeared to him as a sort of sanctuary for the myths of the Indians of both North and South America.

In short, on returning from his second trip to British Columbia, Lévi-Strauss undertook to analyse the meaning of the opposition between the masks with protuberant eyes and those with sunken eyes. To this end, he proposed to use structural analysis, which, when applied to Amerindian myths after having been used on kinship systems, he believed would illuminate their meaning.

> Each type of mask is linked to myths whose objective is to explain its legendary or supernatural origin and to lay the foundation for its role in ritual, in the economy, and in the society. My hypothesis, then, which extends to works of art (which, however, are more than works of art) a method validated in the study of myths (which are also works of art), will be proven right if, in the last analysis, we can perceive, between the origin myths for each type of mask, transformation relations homologous to those that, from a purely plastic point of view, prevail among the masks themselves.[1]

1 C. Lévi-Strauss, *The Way of the Masks*, trans. S. Modelski (Seattle, University of Washington Press, 1982), p. 14.

In 1975, Lévi-Strauss therefore wrote and published an initial version of *The Way of the Masks*. But along the way, he realized he had great difficulty characterizing the social organization of the groups that produced these masks and myths: the Kwakiutl, the Tlingit, the Bella Coola, etc. Once the book appeared, he returned to his data, seeking to resolve this problem. It would occupy him between 1976 and 1977, as can be seen from the abstract of his Collège de France course, in which the notion of 'house' appears for the first time, and would become the primary topic of his kinship seminar, until the time of his retirement in 1982.

Having defined the 'house' as a kin-based structure, in 1976, Lévi-Strauss would spend the next five years combing dozens of monographs in an attempt to find 'houses' in other parts of the world, with the exception of Asia and China. It will be remembered that, in *The Elementary Structures of Kinship*, he had mentioned in passing the Kachin 'seigneury houses' or the aristocratic 'houses' of the Naga. He does not come back to these, but year after year analyses the ethnological literature on a certain number of countries. His course abstracts, published in 1984 and translated as *Anthropology and Myth*, provide the list:

1976–77: The notion of 'house'
1977–78: Considerations on Indonesia
1978–79: The problems of Melanesia
1979–80: Melanesia (continued) and Polynesia
1980–81: Comparisons: New Zealand, Madagascar, Micronesia
1981–82: Considerations on Africa

In 1979, Lévi-Strauss published the second edition of *The Way of the Masks*. This was a revised version with three additional excursuses, including a renewed analysis of Kwakiutl social organization; it was the first text in which he presented the notion of 'house' to the reading public.

The same text was enriched on the occasion of the fifth Marc Bloch Lecture, given by Lévi-Strauss at the Sorbonne on 2 June 1983, a year after he retired. The contents of the lecture were published in the journal *Annales* under the title 'Histoire et ethnologie'; it is an important article, which defines his conception of history at the time and launches a ringing appeal for cooperation between historians and anthropologists.

In 1984 he published, as mentioned above, the abstracts of his courses in *Anthropology and Myth*. In 1987 he granted an interview on the notion of 'house' to Pierre Lamaison, an anthropologist specialized in the European rural world. The interview appeared in the journal *Terrain* in October of the same year. As far as we know, this was his final word on the subject.

In analysing this notion, which was new to anthropology when Lévi-Strauss introduced it (the concept of 'house' had long been employed by historians, as well as by such great chroniclers of the French monarchy as Saint-Simon), I have chosen to use the text of the second edition of *The Way of the Masks* (1979), alongside that of the Marc Bloch Lecture (1983), both of which expand on the abstract of the 1976 course.

It is hard to say much about the approximately forty societies of Melanesia, Polynesia, Indonesia, Madagascar and Africa that feature in the course abstracts between 1977 and 1982. Sometimes, the allusion to a tribe and the anthropologist who studied it boils down to a few lines; in other cases, an African kingdom or a Polynesian chiefdom gets a long paragraph – all of which is interrupted by theoretical conclusions for which we do not have the developed argument. I am therefore reduced to doing my best in the following summary.

It all began with Lévi-Strauss's desire to understand the nature of Kwakiutl kinship and social organization. In 1975, in the first version of *The Way of the Masks*, he had written:

> Most writers estimate that these Indians had [cognatic] descent, inflected by a quite pronounced patrilineal bias. I believe, however, that the true nature of Kwakiutl institutions has not been understood by observers and analysts, and that, within them, the matrilineal and patrilineal principles are in active competition at all levels. The problem is too vast to be dealt with here.[2]

This conclusion led to the seminar he gave in 1976, where we find his first definition of the notion of 'house' as 'a moral person possessing a domain, perpetuated by transmission of its name, wealth and titles

2 Ibid., p. 92.

through a real or fictitious descent line which is recognized as legitimate as long as the continuity can be expressed in the language of descent or alliance or, most often, of both together'.[3]

The important point here is that the 'house' is an abstract social unit that is not to be confused with those who belong to it. A 'corporate' or 'legal entity', in the terms of Henry Maine, the nineteenth-century founder of comparative law;[4] an 'entité fétiche', or fetishized entity, as Lévi-Strauss would say in his 1977–78 seminar, borrowing from Marx's discussion of 'commodity fetishism'.[5]

In order to perpetuate itself, this social unit manipulates the two forms of kinship, descent and alliance; but it also makes use of forms of fictitious kinship, such as adoption. In the absence of male heirs, transmission can take place through sisters or daughters, who act as 'the bridge and the plank', according to the terms of Salic Law. A second component of the dossier is his comparison with medieval Europe and its noble, but also peasant, 'houses'. Later, Lévi-Strauss would extend the notion to medieval Japan, the great chiefdoms of Fiji or Polynesia, the ancient kingdoms of Madagascar, and so on.

Lévi-Strauss saw 'house' societies as combining social principles that are usually mutually exclusive: descent and residence, exogamy and endogamy and, in medieval terms, a law based on 'race' and name, as opposed to a law founded on election by one's peers. Permanent tensions resulted, but no explosions.

Finally, in order to explain the recurring presence of this kinship structure down through time and the world over, Lévi-Strauss posited that it originated in 'a structural state where political and economic interests tending to invade the social field did not yet have distinct languages at their disposal and, being obliged to express themselves in the only language available, which is that of kinship, inevitably subverted it'.[6]

---

3 C. Lévi-Strauss, *Anthropology and Myth: Lectures, 1951–1982*, trans. R. Willis (Oxford, Basil Blackwell, 1987), p. 152.

4 H. J. S. Maine, *Ancient Law: Its Connection with the Early History of Society, and Its Relation to Modern Ideas* (London, John Murray, 1861).

5 K. Marx, *Capital*, vol. 1, chap. II; M. Godelier, 'Économie marchande, fétichisme, magie et science selon Marx dans *Le Capital*', *Nouvelle Revue de psychanalyse* 2 (1970), pp. 197–213.

6 *Anthropology and Myth*, p. 152.

This is probably the weakest point in his approach. The political-religious sphere in all societies – be they with or without classes or castes, or a State – is never confused with kinship relations and their exercise, even where the government of the society and its worship of gods and spirits of nature rely on individuals and groups which themselves are organized by kinship relations. For it is not these relations that explain why certain individuals and their ascendants claim to have descended from the rice goddess (the Chinese imperial family), or from the Polynesian paramount god Tangaloa (the Tu'i Tonga, the 'supreme' chief of the kingdom of Tonga).

Throughout human history, political power has borrowed more from the language of 'religion' than from that of kinship in order to express and legitimize itself. Of course, once the power was in place, with or without the help of the gods, it still had to be transmitted and consolidated, unless it was redistributed within each new generation. However, recognition of the power and rank of certain tribal or clan chiefs is not a matter of kinship but of politics, as can be seen in the Kwakiutl practice of potlatch. Politics does not invade the social field at a certain moment in time, as though kinship had until then filled all the political and economic functions necessary to the existence of societies. If that were the case, kinship, thus stripped of some of its functions, would have been reduced to serving as a language and an ornament so that these functions might develop under cover, until they were capable of shedding the disguise of kinship and openly speaking their own language. We will return to this crucial point, which attests to the way Lévi-Strauss conceived of politics.

The 1977–78 and the 1978–79 seminars examined the various monographic studies recently published on Indonesia (1977–78), then Melanesia, and New Guinea in particular (1978–79). Finally, in 1979 Lévi-Strauss got down to resolving the enigma of the social organization of the Kwakiutl and their neighbours. For this he went back to the work of Boas,[7] who, in a half-century of publications and repeated bouts of fieldwork, had amassed a unique documentation on the Kwakiutl yet never managed to formulate what he felt to be a satisfactory definition of their kinship system.

---

7 Franz Boas published first in German in the 1880s, and from then on in English, until his death in 1942.

Boas thought that the Kwakiutl system was initially patrilineal, like that of the Salish to the south and the east, and that it had subsequently evolved into a matrilineal system, like that of their neighbours to the north, the Tsimshian, the Haida and the Tlingit. He gave up the idea of using Morgan's term, 'gens', to designate patrilineal descent groups and instead adopted the word 'sept', which in ancient Ireland had designated a bilateral kin group; ultimately he settled on 'clan'. Durkheim and Mauss, after reading Boas, challenged the idea that a patrilineal system could give way to one that was matrilineal. In their view, the transformation of a matrilineal system and its replacement by a patrilineal principle were possible, but not vice versa.

In 1920 Boas finally renounced his effort to define the Kwakiutl kinship system, because it was like no other. Instead of speaking of septs, clans, etc., he simply used the Kwakiutl word *numaym* to designate the social units that made up this society, dominated by a tribal aristocracy who headed these *numaym*.

The difficulty arose from the fact that there were two lines of succession in the aristocracy: one that went from father to eldest son (primogeniture) when it came to the names, titles and ranks that could not leave the lineage; and the other, used for the titles a father transmitted to his daughters and which settled on his sons-in-law. When a man married, he could no longer carry these aristocratic names and emblems, and adopted those of his wife, which he in turn transmitted to his daughters, and so on. In short, there was indeed a line of transmission through the women, which had suggested to some that the system was matrilineal. However, residence after marriage was patrilocal, not uxorilocal or matrilocal. The great names whose mythic origin founded the appearance of the tribes and kin groups were always transmitted in direct line from father to eldest son, and a man never succeeded his mother's brother.

Finally, after Boas's death (in 1942), several unpublished texts were brought together, and appeared in 1966; these reveal the final state of his thinking on the *numaym*.

> The structure of the *numayma* is best understood if we disregard the living individuals and rather consider the *numayma* as consisting of a certain number of positions to each of which belong a name, a 'seat'

or 'standing place', that means rank, and privileges. Their number is limited, and they form a ranked nobility.[8]

This definition compared the *numaym* to the European aristocratic houses, but Boas was unable to conceive the articulation between the patrilineal and the matrilineal principles that together structured the kinship regime of these houses. Furthermore, he was unaware of the existence of undifferentiated cognatic systems, which made it possible to mobilize these principles in a flexible manner when it suited the political, religious or economic interests of the kin group. He therefore thought he was dealing with a wholly original system. But Lévi-Strauss would show that equivalent systems abounded the world over.

For Boas, the crux of the matter was that the flexibility of the cognatic systems allowed them to 'disguise all sorts of socio-political maneuvers under the veneer of kinship'.[9]

Returning to the analyses formulated in his 1976–77 seminar on the Yurok as studied by Alfred Kroeber, whose population was divided into fifty-four cities each of which was divided into 'houses' (in their own words), Lévi-Strauss again advanced the idea that these 'houses' were 'moral persons' that act as true subjects of rights and obligations through the individuals and families that compose them.

Lévi-Strauss was well aware that the concept of 'moral person' had been borrowed from Maine – by Meyer Fortes, Jack Goody and other English and American anthropologists – largely in order to define patrilineal or matrilineal clans as so many 'corporate groups'. But in 1977–78, he undertook a meticulous critical examination of the definitions of 'corporate groups' proposed by Fortes and his colleagues. According to Lévi-Strauss, Fortes had merely produced a tautology: a 'corporate group', in this case, was a moral person because it was allowed to amend rights and obligations – in other words, because it was a moral person. Others, like Goody, founded the definition on joint ownership of the land or other assets, and still others on co-residence, as among the Iban of Borneo, studied by Derek Freeman.[10]

---

8  *The Way of the Masks*, p. 169; cited in F. Boas, *Kwakiutl Ethnography* (Chicago, University of Chicago Press, 1967), pp. 50 ff.

9  *The Way of the Masks*, p. 171.

10  D. Freeman, 'The Family of Iban of Borneo', in J. Goody, ed., *The Development Cycle in Domestic Groups* (New York, Cambridge University Press, 1958); 'On the Concept of the Kindred', *Journal of the Royal Anthropological Institute of Great Britain and Ireland* 91, n° 2 (1961), pp. 192–220.

In sum, these explanations, each of which rested on different criteria, could not, in Lévi-Strauss's opinion, constitute a theory. To advance, it was necessary to return to the definitions formulated by certain historians of the Middle Ages, such as Karl Schmid,[11] whom he had already discussed in his first course on the 'notion of house'. The 'house' was once again defined as 'a corporate body holding an estate made up of both material and immaterial wealth, which perpetuates itself through the transmission of its name, its goods, and its titles down a real or imaginary line, considered legitimate as long as this continuity can express itself in the language of kinship or of affinity and, most often, of both.'[12]

Here we have the same definition as in 1976, except that the domain of application is specified. It is the 'material and immaterial wealth' that is the property of this corporate body, the 'house'. Lévi-Strauss would not modify his definition further, and would propose the same definition again in his 1983 Marc Bloch Lecture and in the interview with Pierre Lamaison in 1987. In the latter, he went into somewhat more detail about what he meant by material and immaterial, assembling information that had been scattered through his earliest texts.

> By material, I mean the possession of a real estate that can be expressed, as among the Northwest Coast Indians who were my essential reference, by fishing sites that are the traditional property of the house, or hunting territories owned by the estate. By immaterial I mean everything having to do with the traditions. The immaterial includes names belonging to the houses, legends that also belong to the houses, the exclusive right to perform certain dances or rituals, all of which, in different respects concern complex as well as primitive societies, in particular in Europe and in the nobility whose model (the 'house of Bourbon', etc.) inevitably guided me.[13]

Lamaison, a specialist of traditional social structures in northern and especially southern European peasant cultures, suggested another type

---

11 K. Schmid, 'Zur Problematik von Familie, Sippe und Geschlecht, Haus und Dynastie beim mittelalterlichen Adel', *Zeitschrift für die Geschichte des Oberrheins* 105, n° 1 (1957), pp. 56 ff. Cf. *The Way of the Masks*, p. 169.

12 *The Way of the Masks*, p. 174.

13 P. Lamaison, 'La Notion de maison. Entretien avec Claude Lévi-Strauss', *Terrain*, n° 9 (October 1987), p. 34.

of 'house', which could still be found less than a century ago in the South of France: this was the *oustau*, in the historical Gévaudan area,[14] or, in Catalonia, the *casa*, found more particularly in the mountainous regions. Here, the economy was based on a combination of agriculture, practiced on privately owned lands, and grazing, on communal lands, which were the joint property of all the 'houses' that made up the village community. To each of these 'houses' a name was attached, regardless of the owners' patronym. Depending on their size, their wealth in terms of agricultural lands and livestock, but also their role in the community's history, these 'houses' had more or less say in the management of community affairs and lands. Each also had its own pew in the parish church, and its position in religious processions.

In order for each house to reproduce itself, the system demanded that it be transmitted intact – land, rank, traditions, etc. – to a single descendant, who would live there and run it. Generally speaking, it was the eldest son who inherited, but if there was no son it fell to the eldest of the daughters, whose husband would move into the 'house' and take its name. The 'house' thus did not belong to those who lived there, rather those who lived there belonged to the 'house'. One could therefore not carry the name of a 'house' or inherit it without residing there and managing it. (Residing in this case means more than simply living there; it means being present in the community and acting to reproduce it, in the same manner and to the same extent as one acts to reproduce the 'house'.[15]) Such 'house' systems thus implied a twofold hierarchy: that between the 'houses' and, within them, that between those who would inherit and those who must be excluded from the succession (usually the younger sons and the daughters). Furthermore, owing to the hierarchy between the 'houses', the heir (male or female) to a house was obliged to marry someone of the same rank on pain of facing problems of hypo- or hypergamy (according to the respective ranks of the 'houses' to which the spouses belonged). In addition, since the spouse chosen was usually someone who belonged to the same village community, after a few generations, the marriages necessarily entailed sequences of

---

14  P. Maurice, *La Famille en Gévaudan au XVe siècle (1380–1483)* (Paris, Publications de la Sorbonne, 1988).

15  See G. Augustins, *Comment se perpétuer? Devenir des lignées et destins des patri-moines dans les paysanneries européennes* (Nanterre, Société d'Ethnologie, 1989).

alliances between 'houses', unless the respective ranks of the 'houses' had changed in the meantime and no longer permitted the marriage for one of them.

Moreover, since this 'house' system was directly tied to an agricultural economy and this type of economy usually gives priority, within the sexual division of labour, to activities performed by the men, inheritance usually went through the men and thus created male lines; but these were in no way lineages, since the heir's collaterals – brothers and sisters – were gradually eliminated from the 'house'. This was not the case in the more open world of the medieval European aristocratic 'house', with its broader horizons. The relationship with the land was different, even if agricultural production was still the main source of wealth at the time. 'Feudal' land tenure implied the existence of various forms of relations of servitude between the noble 'houses' and the peasants of the village communities that were tied to them. The peasants did not own the lands they worked, but they could use them upon payment in the form of labour, produce or money. In addition, the aristocracy had a certain number of rights over the land and over the individuals and families that worked it: the right to sit in judgment, to raise troops, to preside over village meetings, to levy taxes on merchandise entering or leaving their domains, and so on.

In this wider world, where rivalries between the noble 'houses' stretched over whole regions and often well beyond, the perpetuation of a 'house', its strategy for maintaining its rank and above all for rising in the aristocratic hierarchy implied that, unlike the strategies deployed between peasant 'houses', the noble 'houses' contracted alliances through marriages between their sons and daughters. These alliance strategies were designed not only to perpetuate the 'house' but to raise it within a political and economic hierarchy that was largely independent of the individual 'houses' that occupied the positions and ranks. There was always one noble 'house' that was 'higher' than the others and against which the lower-ranking 'houses' would abut.

This was just as true of tribal-aristocratic societies and of state-free chiefdoms as it was of aristocratic societies, at the centre of which one 'house' would exercise some form of state power, most often in the form of a 'royal' power exerted more or less strongly over a territory shared among the other noble 'houses'.

We thus find, as Lévi-Strauss pointed out in his Marc Bloch Lecture, 'house' societies on either side of the emergence of the State: before its appearance, in tribal societies with chiefdoms; and during its formation, with the development of castes, orders or classes that called for a more or less centralized form of power.

> Accustomed to observing societies whose armature was provided by kinship relations, anthropologists often wondered what became of descent-based groups when rudimentary forms of the state appear – the state can appear in several ways and at several levels. Furthermore, among the so-called societies 'without a state' and those in which the state is emergent, there is room for numerous different societies, in which descent groups subsist alongside centralized political and administrative bodies.[16]

And he went on, reiterating his praise of Marx and Engels: 'Despite these reservations, we have gained a slightly better understanding of how and in what ways the "old blood ties", as Marx and Engels would say, come to be altered.'[17]

What does this alteration of the 'old blood ties' of kinship relations consist in for Lévi-Strauss? Most likely in the fact that kinship relations ceased to constitute the armature of the society. On this specific point, which is of crucial theoretical importance since it entails a global view of the nature of kinship and its role in the production of societies, I do not concur with Lévi-Strauss. In no society, 'primitive' or otherwise, have kinship relations ever been sufficient to constitute the armature of society. The armature of a society is provided by the combining, each time in a different way, of two sets of social relations: kinship relations, on the one hand, and political-religious relations, on the other. The first generate and structure, through the interplay of descent principles and marriage rules, social groups, kin groups made up in a variety of ways. The second intervene at other levels and have the capacity to gather the kin groups into a whole that exercises a form of sovereignty on a territory, its resources and its inhabitants; this whole forms a society.

---

16  C. Lévi-Strauss, 'Histoire et ethnologie', *Annales ESC* 38, n° 6 (1983), p. 1224.
17  Ibid.

Kinship relations and the network of ties they weave between the groups they create cannot alone unite these groups into a whole that forms a society. Yet the kin groups, whatever they may be (clans, lineages, demes, extended or nuclear families), must reproduce this whole that is their shared condition of existence and the medium in which they act at the same time as they reproduce themselves. Their rivalries and conflicts must be contained within certain bounds. They therefore cannot extend their own life without helping, on other levels than that of matrimonial alliances, to perpetuate the existence of the society as well.

Here are a few of the domains that come under the political-religious relations in which all kin groups that compose a society must participate. In some societies, such as the Baruya of New Guinea, these are the system of male and female initiations and the establishment of age groups into which all members of the tribe – men and women, regardless of their lineage and village – must be distributed; each person must, over their lifetime, go through all stages of these institutions, to which are attached different rights and obligations. In other societies, it is mainly the participation of all (often all the men) in warfare, or in cycles of worship and rituals addressed to the gods and the powers of nature that make up the invisible world, in which everyone believes, whatever their clan, and to which everyone looks for protection and prosperity. For we must be careful to distinguish worship of the ancestors and worship of the gods and goddesses – and other supernatural beings – in which all believe. Everywhere, social relations that do not fall into the domain of kinship, and which are not produced to resolve problems of kinship, overspill and traverse the kinship relations, recruiting them for their own reproduction. Functions that do not fall within the purview of kinship thus become attributes of kinship relations and attach themselves to one or another member of the kin group, according to sex, age and the position occupied.

This analysis of the relationship between kinship and political and religious power points up the existence of an invariable structure, which concerns 'house' societies as well as all societies in which kin groups exist, in the form of clans, demes, family lines and extended or nuclear families alike. Furthermore, all societies have several languages with which to express their social relations. The language of kinship is not alone in allowing us to conceive the universe and society, even when kinship relations play a central role from the standpoint of the society's armature.

For these reasons, even if in 'house' societies kinship is increasingly recruited to serve socio-political interests that have formed and diversified outside this domain, I do not think that these relations had no other language than kinship in which to express themselves (for example, a religious language), nor that, in expressing themselves in the language of kinship, they would necessarily subvert it.

The recurring presence of 'house' systems, Lévi-Strauss writes, 'among peoples far distant in both time and space' originated in 'a structural state where political and economic interests tending to invade the social field did not yet have distinct languages at their disposal and, being obliged to express themselves in the only language available, which is that of kinship, inevitably subverted it'.[18] Such formulations suggest that, at one time in human history, or in so-called primitive societies, kinship relations ensured all functions – social, economic, political and religious – and that, in certain circumstances, these functions broke free of kinship and became embodied in social relations distinct from kinship – something that is by no means substantiated by the available information on the social organization of hunter-gather groups.

For Lévi-Strauss, 'the Kwakiutl, the Nootka, and the Bella Bella . . . fully exploit . . . the flexibility of their cognatic system, and can thus disguise all sorts of socio-political maneuvers under the veneer of kinship'.[19] The image conjures up a certain form of Marxism, which saw the economic interests of a rising social class as advancing dressed up as religious issues. In this, Max Weber is not far from Marx.[20]

Of course, kinship often provides the representations, values and schemata for thinking certain aspects of political and religious relations. Do we not speak of the pope as the 'Holy Father', and of Christ as the 'Son' of God? The paramount chief in Tonga, the Tu'i Tonga, of divine essence, was called the *Tamai*, the 'Father' of his subjects. More recently, Soviet propaganda christened Stalin 'the Little Father of the peoples' of

---

18  *The Way of the Masks*, p. 152.

19  Ibid., p. 171.

20  'Histoire et ethnologie', p. 1224. 'In so-called complex or semi-complex societies, the ideology departs more markedly from the infrastructure.'

the Soviet Union. These words, borrowed from the domain of kinship relations and transferred to other relations, are designed to confer on the figures occupying such exalted positions the virtues of benevolence and protectiveness, but also the authority and responsibility that one expects of a father. The Chinese emperor encouraged (and imposed) filial piety in families and clans so that his subjects would learn, from childhood, to respect their father and their mother and to serve them even beyond death (the degrees of mourning). Filial piety was a means of learning the obedience subjects owed to the emperor and his representatives.

In seeking to define 'house' societies, Lévi-Strauss wanted to illuminate certain complex structures of kinship, 'which limit themselves to defining the circle of relatives and leave the determination of the spouse to other mechanisms'.[21] But, by 1983, he was no longer talking about the Omaha systems. In the courses he gave on New Guinea in 1978–79, he had signalled the existence of numerous Iroquois-type systems with Omaha features (Dani, Iatmul, Manus, etc.), and in 1979–80, he had replied to the criticisms raised by Alfred Gell, in his 1975 book *Metamorphosis of the Cassowaries*, concerning his conception of Crow-Omaha systems as lying midway between elementary and complex structures.[22] In 1979, for Lévi-Strauss the Crow-Omaha systems had become 'the lower limit of complex systems'.[23] But, in his subsequent courses on 'house' systems, which he gave until 1982, and in his Marc Bloch Lecture, there is no more reference to the Omaha systems. Undifferentiated cognatic systems had now moved to the fore. Lévi-Strauss had called for their study as early as 1967, in the Preface to the second edition of *The Elementary Structures of Kinship*. He had thus remained faithful to himself and to his theoretical goals.

Another important aspect of this new research on 'house' systems, for Lévi-Strauss, was their existence in societies with chiefs but without a state (Polynesia) as well as in societies with both a state and 'kings' (Africa, Madagascar) or even an emperor (Japan). In his opinion this clearly showed that 'there is less distance than was once believed between

21  C. Lévi-Strauss, *The Elementary Structures of Kinship*, trans. J. H. Bell and J. R. von Sturmer and R. Needham, ed. (Boston, Beacon Press, 1969), p. xxiii.

22  A. Gell, *Metamorphosis of the Cassowaries: Umeda Society, Language and Ritual* (London, Athlone Press, 1975).

23  *Anthropology and Myth*, p. 170.

so-called 'complex' or 'developed' societies and those incorrectly called 'primitive' or 'archaic'. To close the gap, anthropology needs to learn to seek the help of history, just as history can be helped by anthropology.'[24]

In the spirit of this appeal, he would go as far as to call for historians and anthropologists to work more closely with each other in order to 'edify the sciences of man together', a call that culminated in his final course at the Collège de France (1982):

> It would have been impossible, or at any rate difficult, to discover the distinctive characteristics of the 'house' on evidence drawn solely from non-literate societies. These characteristics become more perceptible in archival documents and literary works produced in the European Middle Ages, as well as in the corresponding or later periods in the East and Far East. Nearer home, the problematic of the 'house' remains alive in . . . Saint-Simon . . . and in the inheritance customs of the peasantry in several regions.[25]

But Lévi-Strauss was advocating more than just collaboration between historians and anthropologists. It was the encounter of structural analysis with history that seemed to him the strategic element in this (future) collaboration. 'Structural analysis joins hands with history when, delving below the level of empirical data, it attains the deep structures that, because they are deeply implanted, can also have been shared in the past.'[26]

Briefly put, structural analysis had the ability to attain hidden structures because it looked for 'the similarities beneath the differences', in other words, it sought to discover 'invariants' and to analyse their possible transformations (even if these had not actually occurred). 'Far from turning its back on history, structural analysis hands it a list of conceivable paths among which history alone will be able to determine that or those that were effectively followed.'[27]

Let us review the specific features of 'house' systems. A 'house' is a social group; it is neither a clan nor a lineage, but a kin group designated

---

24 'Histoire et ethnologie', p. 1226.
25 *Anthropology and Myth*, pp. 193–4.
26 'Histoire et ethnologie', p. 1227.
27 Ibid., p. 1229.

by a name which is not that of the families and individuals that embody and reproduce it. With this name go material and immaterial assets, a particular rank and status that the members of the house are collectively responsible for perpetuating and transmitting within a society characterized by a hierarchy of rival houses. What, then, among the kinship structures necessary for the functioning of 'house' societies, are the invariant components?

Basically, they are cognatic structures, and therefore one becomes a member of a house through one's male or female ascendants. Within a 'house', paternal and maternal lines tend to carry an important, if not equal, weight.[28] Such systems are neither patrilineal nor matrilineal, since both descent rules can be invoked when the need arises. Furthermore, 'houses' include individuals who are not kin or affines but who are counted in because they reside there and contribute to its reproduction. The criterion of (shared) residence thus becomes a criterion of (fictitious) descent.

Like any 'kin' group, a 'house' can reproduce itself only by means of matrimonial alliances, which stand alongside political alliances, military alliances, and so on, which do not necessarily require the exchange of women. On the other hand, matrimonial alliances within a 'house' society characterized by ranks, statuses and unequal wealth are obliged to call on strategies that allow the 'houses' to preserve their rank and even rise in the hierarchy. To this end, a 'house' must know how to take advantage of the marriages of its men as well as its women, and to diversify its alliances by contracting marriages both nearby and far away.[29] Since each group is at the same time a giver and a taker of women and men, each 'house' must have a dual strategy, a necessity in a world where differences of rank often impose hypogamic or hypergamic unions. In the noble families of medieval Europe, women, depending on whether they were given or received, took or brought with them titles, fiefs and other prestigious elements comprising power and wealth; and alliance strategies among the aristocracy entailed complicated, long-range calculations.

On this crucial point, I do not agree with Lévi-Strauss when, concerning 'house' systems, he writes: 'The descent rule, even when one exists,

---

28  Ibid., p. 1222. 'Recruited for political purposes, the language of kinship partially erases the distinction between the paternal and the maternal lines.'

29  Ibid. 'These systems sidestep the distinction between exogamy and endogamy.'

is not the relevant factor. It is the primacy of the exchange relationship over the unilineal criterion that explains that the groups involved in the exchanges at their discretion practice, either simultaneously or successively, exogamy or endogamy.'[30]

Once again, we find the thesis, already exposed in *The Elementary Structures of Kinship*, of the primacy of exchange over descent, the latter being described as a 'secondary feature' of all kinship systems. I have expressed my disagreement and will not repeat it here. In reality, alliances, whether proximate or remote, are always contracted between 'houses' in view of the reproduction of each 'house' and its maintenance (or elevation) in the hierarchy of houses. From this standpoint, descent is just as 'relevant' as alliance, and therefore alliance can never completely substitute for descent, except in the event that the 'house' becomes extinct and another can, in the name of proximate or remote alliances, step in and perpetuate it in turn. Failing this, the house disappears.[31] The inherent flexibility of cognatic kinship systems, whose structure underlies most 'house' systems, means that descent and alliance, which could 'pull' in opposite directions, are manipulated so as to 'pull' in the same direction – in view of perpetuating, come what may, a social unit that is both concrete and abstract, which transcends time and the times, and to which its residents belong more than it belongs to them.

This is, in my view, the deep structure of 'house' systems, in their twofold aspect of social system and kinship structure. The same structure can crop up in different historical and social contexts, which, according to Lévi-Strauss, 'open themselves to history'. How are we to understand the idea that societies located 'in history' can open or close themselves 'to history'? Lévi-Strauss is clear: 'All societies are equally historical, but some admit this frankly, while others are loath to do so and prefer to ignore the fact ... Societies differ from each other less by objective features than by the subjective image they have of themselves.'[32]

Which raises the question: why and how, instead of viewing history as a source of disorder and a threat, did collective and individual thought see it as an instrument for acting on the present and transforming it? We

---

30 Ibid.

31 See the Bourbon family tree and its different branches, from the time this house was founded in the thirteenth century by Robert de Clermont, sixth son of Louis XI (Saint Louis).

32 'Histoire et ethnologie', p. 1218.

can only agree with this approach to the question of history, and numerous cases can be advanced by way of illustration: for example, the Aztecs, who lived with the anxiety that the Sun would cease to shine on the world if they failed to make yearly offerings of the blood of prisoners of war, by tearing out and presenting their hearts to the god. Rome, on the other hand, believed in its destiny and gave itself 800 years to grow and eventually disappear. But, between a deadly threat and the promise of a future, what are the events, the facts that can be interpreted in one sense or the other? These cannot be the recurring events of people's daily life; they are facts that, when they arise, exert a pressure to change something that touches on the organization of the society, on its structure as well as on its way of thinking. Such facts can come from either inside or outside the society. This outside can be either other societies seeking expansion to the detriment of their neighbours, or elements in the environment of these societies that modify the climate, etc.

It is therefore not just any event that 'forces' societies to 'open themselves' to history. When the changes confronting them have matured within the societies, to open themselves to history is the same thing as opening themselves to themselves, and acting either to accept these changes, or to combat them and attempt to return to the (social and/or cosmic) order that formerly prevailed.

History is therefore not a succession of contingent events, contrary to Lévi-Strauss's assertion at the end of the second volume of his Mythology series, in 1967: 'In stating the claims of structural analysis . . . I am not therefore rejecting history. On the contrary, structural analysis accords history a paramount place, the place that rightfully belongs to that irreducible contingency without which necessity would be inconceivable.'[33]

In point of fact, not all historical events are equally contingent, and not all have the capacity to affect the underlying structures of social organization. Only some, which arise in the course of this society's development (such as the French Revolution) or which arrive from outside (like the European invasion of America), have this capacity. Among all the events that found the life of a society and of its members, there are therefore actions that have a structuring power, in other

---

33 C. Lévi-Strauss, *From Honey to Ashes: Introduction to a Science of Mythology 2*, trans. J. and D. Weightman (Chicago, University of Chicago Press, 1973), p. 475.

words, they have the capacity to affect the structures of a society and its internal reproductive mechanisms. This capacity to act on structures can take centuries to build up, like the millennia it took humankind to domesticate plants and animals, and to invent various forms of agriculture and animal husbandry. More rapid were the effects of the development of industrial production and capitalism in nineteenth-century Western Europe, not to mention the effects, at another level, of the English, American and French revolutions. All these historical 'events' brought about irreversible changes within societies as well as between them. To be sure, throughout history, there have always been some societies that have resisted change; but to resist is already to change. And many forms of resistance have not managed to prevent change – such as the Sun dance which spread among the Plains Indians of North America, designed to stem the disappearance of the bison herds systematically slaughtered by the European settlers as they moved westward.

Even if, in 1983, appealing to historians and suggesting they collaborate with structural anthropologists, Lévi-Strauss was no longer opposing structure and event as he did in 1966, he continued to think in 1988 that historical events are contingent occurrences: 'The event in its contingency seems to me an irreducible given. Structural analysis must work with it.'[34]

There is, undeniably, a contingent dimension to every event. But an event also contains aspects that connect it to the structures of the society, that are rooted in it. Every event is a mixture of contingency and necessity; and it is because of the relationship between these two integral parts that the event is, or is not, likely to affect the structures of the society, that it has a structural impact or not. The introduction of the potato into Europe from Indian America in the seventeenth century clearly modified the agricultural and dietary economy of Europeans, but it had no direct effect on the political and social structures of the *ancien régime* monarchies. Lévi-Strauss never analysed the diversity of events that continually cross paths in a society: daily and recurring events, non-recurring but predictable events, unpredictable events, events that affect individuals or those that act on social structures, etc. We need to

---

34  C. Lévi-Strauss and D. Eribon, ed., *Conversations with Claude Lévi-Strauss*, trans. P. Wissing (Chicago and London, University of Chicago Press, 1991), p. 125.

construct this kind of typology, and anthropologists have as much to gain from doing this as sociologists and historians.

We must also remember that events having the capacity to affect the social and mental structures of a society often produce changes that are irreversible. There are two types of irreversible changes: changes occurring *within* the structures of a society, and changes *of* the structures that organize the society. Highly effective structuring events act on societies and cause them to 'evolve', often irreversibly; but these evolutions do not mean that there are 'laws of evolution' or 'development' for societies that would drive them all in the same direction and toward the same outcome, merely at different rates. (Here we recognize the nineteenth-century evolutionist theses, but also the Marxist dogma that flourished in the era of the 'triumph' of socialism in Russia, China and other countries in the communist bloc.)

The irreversible nature of certain historical transformations means they are followed by the beginnings of a new history and evolution. But a transformation with irreversible effects does not open onto a single possible future; it always opens onto several possibilities. To say several, though, is not to say an infinity or even a considerable number of possible outcomes, insofar as the new possibilities in question are rooted in the new social structure that has replaced the old one and transcend the interpretations and actions of individuals and groups. In any case, some events have the effect of eliminating certain components of certain structures and forcing their replacement by other social relations, which means that new possibilities open up. Since structures do not change of their own accord, it must be humans that transform and replace them. I therefore fully agree with Lévi-Strauss when he criticizes those who 'in place of history, set up grand developmental laws that exist only in [their] minds.'[35] But this criticism is aimed at those who turn history into a myth in the service of their own ideals or interests. This is not the way historians use history. For historians, as for anthropologists, coming to know past or present societies requires stepping back and taking a critical look at all the assumptions their own society holds about itself, as well as about the past and present of other societies. Without this work, history and anthropology have no chance of achieving what historians and anthropologists hope, namely, to assert themselves as human sciences.

---

35  Ibid.

The foregoing allows us to measure the vagueness and inadequacy of the notion that certain societies 'open themselves' to history while others refuse to do so. At all events, having stated in 1965 that societies with Crow-Omaha or Iroquois kinship systems were societies that 'opened themselves' to history, Lévi-Strauss then turned to the case of 'house' systems.

In his search for 'house' societies, Lévi-Strauss had set out on a world tour that took him from Indonesia to Africa via Melanesia, Polynesia, Micronesia and Madagascar. He identified 'house' societies in many places where they were already known: in Polynesia and Madagascar, for example, in other words throughout the expansion zone of the so-called Austronesian populations that had left southern China and Taiwan around 3000 BCE on the biggest migration of all time, which took some groups as far as Easter Island and others to Madagascar. These Austronesians had taken with them kinship systems that, as we now know, made the distinction between cross and parallel cousins, and were probably of the Dravidian type. In the course of their migrations, their kinship systems probably gradually morphed into cognatic systems by making cross cousins into siblings, among whom marriage therefore became forbidden, and by eliminating the difference between direct and collateral lines in the ascending and descending generations.

The Austronesian populations had also taken with them their political systems, based on 'chiefdoms', where power was exercised by men regarded as the 'fathers' of the local groups and believed to possess an inborn divine essence, their *mana*, transmitted through the women. In many Polynesian societies, therefore, like Samoa or Tonga, women are represented as being closer to the ancestors and the gods in the religious domain, outranking the men, their brothers. This explains the importance of the maternal kin within the now-cognatic systems, whereas political power is the purview of the men. Lévi-Strauss had thus extracted from all this ethnographic data the indication of the importance of the relationship between paternal and maternal kin in structuring 'house' societies and in the conflicts found there.

But, as we have seen, one criterion on its own is not enough to transform societies with patrilineal or matrilineal clans into, if not fully fledged 'house' societies, at least ones in which a form of 'houses' is taking shape.[36] Not to mention that Lévi-Strauss does not take into account the fact that most of the populations in the interior of New Guinea, where he thought he had detected embryonic 'houses', are of non-Austronesian origin; they are the oldest populations in this region, whose arrival preceded that of the Austronesian populations by some 10,000 years. It so happens that the kinship systems of these non-Austronesian societies were transformations of Dravidian-type systems, which had become variants of Iroquois-type systems. They therefore contained the distinction between cross and parallel kin, which in turn authorized the direct exchange of women, but, in most cases, forbade renewal of the alliance before two, three or even four generations (the Yafar and Umeda systems[37]). But it should be remembered that, for Lévi-Strauss, Iroquois systems fall into the category of semi-complex systems,[38] with which, as he wrote in 1967 in 'The Future of Kinship Studies', 'history comes to the foreground in the life of simple societies'.[39] The Umeda or the Yafar of New Guinea, however, were not at all 'open to history' when Alfred Gell and Bernard Juillerat studied them.

At the time, though, Lévi-Strauss could not know that Melanesian societies can be divided into two groups: those in which power is exercised by 'great men' – great warriors and masters of the initiation rituals – and 'big-men' societies, where power rests on the accumulation of material wealth (pigs, seashells, bird-of-paradise plumes, ceremonial axes, etc.) and women by the headmen of certain lineages in their clans.

But whether they are great-men or big-men societies, all have Iroquois-type kinship systems, most of them patrilineal, though some

---

36 Lévi-Strauss would advance this suggestion several times in his conversation with Lamaison, 'La notion de maison': 'Something that would be very close to existing, the embryo of that, something that falls outside traditional categories without yet having acquired this clearly definable structure' (p. 34, my translation).

37 B. Juillerat, 'Terminologie de parenté yafar. Étude formelle d'un système dakota-iroquois', *L'Homme* 17, n° 4 (1977), pp. 71–81.

38 Lévi-Strauss, in *Anthropology and Myth,* is citing A. Gell's *Metamorphosis of the Cassowaries,* when he describes the Umeda system as a rudimentary form of Omaha system with a generational nomenclature. In reality it is an Iroquois system with Omaha features, of which there are many in New Guinea, but it is one that allows direct exchange with non-kin in Ego's generation and permits the repetition of these alliances after four generations (and not two, as Lévi-Strauss wrote). We are therefore not in the presence of a rudimentary Omaha system, since the direct exchange of women is still the basic rule.

39 C. Lévi-Strauss, 'The Future of Kinship Studies. Huxley Memorial Lecture', in *Proceedings of the Royal Institute of Great Britain and Ireland,* 1965, p. 20.

(like the Telefomin) have a cognatic structure. It has been observed that the marriage, or alliance, rules were different and even the opposite in great-men and big-men societies. In the first case, direct exchange of women was the rule in Ego's generation, but repetition of this alliance was forbidden before two or more generations. In big-men societies, the direct exchange of women was forbidden in order to marry further from home and to multiply the partners and allies within the intertribal network of potlatch-type competitive ceremonial exchanges, which involved all the tribes in a vast area, most of whom did not even know all the others. These societies were thus open to numerous exchanges, which were periodically repeated, and which did not prevent them from making war on each other. But in none of these were 'houses' found – let alone in great-men societies.

The research by anthropologists working in New Guinea since 1982 has thus led to a resolution of the problems Lévi-Strauss raised in 1978–79 without being able to find answers at the time.[40] Following the important observation that 'the notion of ceremonial exchange in these societies enjoys a sort of priority over that of descent', he went on to list the problems he continued to experience: 'The first of these problems concerns the definition of kinship terminologies. Those of New Guinea are not easy to place in the accepted categories. It is often difficult to decide whether a given system is of "Hawaiian" or "Iroquois" type.'[41]

What at this time made a kinship system 'Hawaiian' was that the difference between cross and parallel cousins is cancelled in $G^0$ (as in true Hawaiian-type systems), which obliges marriage with the second- or third-degree cross cousin. In fact, the systems in question were Iroquois rather than Hawaiian, but they had a marriage rule that forbade repeating the same alliances in the following generation, as is the case with kinship systems characterized by true elementary structures. Therein lay the answer to Lévi-Strauss's second question about New Guinea:

> Another problem concerns the disharmony observed in New Guinea between the terminologies and the marriage rules. At the risk of oversimplification, one could almost say that there are 'Omaha' systems

40 M. Godelier and M. Strathern, *Big Men and Great Men: Personifications of Power in Melanesia* (Cambridge, Cambridge University Press, 1991).

41 *Anthropology and Myth*, p. 164.

accompanied by 'Iroquois' preferences, and 'Iroquois' systems with 'Omaha' prohibitions.[42]

With this second hypothesis, Lévi-Strauss was not far from the conclusions today's Melanesian specialists draw from their material.[43] But to conclude, as he did, that these were Iroquois systems with an 'Omaha' prohibition was tantamount to claiming that there were 'Omaha' features in non-Omaha systems. Lévi-Strauss would not continue to explore this problem, which Thomas Trautmann, Peter Whiteley, Robert Barnes and others, including myself, have raised and in part resolved.[44]

Let us take a final example, which shows how cooperation with historians, and the reconstruction of the history of these societies with the help of such members as preserve its memory (very much what Lévi-Strauss had called for in 1983), shed fresh light on an unusual problem raised by the existence in Tonga of two theories about how children are made, which had been revealed in an important article by Garth Rogers.[45]

The Kingdom of Tonga, which takes in over 170 islands in the South Pacific, was, together with Hawaii and Tahiti, one of the most stratified societies in Polynesia. There was an absolute separation between the mass of commoners (the *tua*) and the nobles (*eiki*), endowed with ranks and titles, and at the head of which were the *sino'i eiki*, 'chiefs in their body', who possessed an inborn divine essence and owed their rank to their genealogical proximity to the Tu'i Tonga, the paramount chief of Tonga. The society fulfilled all Lévi-Strauss's criteria for a 'house' society. The nobles were at the head of a *Kainga*, a cognatic kin group that also included clients, protégés residing on the same land, exploiting its resources and being subject to the chief's authority. The chief, called *tamai*, or 'father', had quasi-absolute power over the life and property of the members of his *Kainga*.

There co-existed two theories in Tonga to explain how children are made. One, corresponding to the cognatic kinship system, held that the

---

42 *Anthropology and Myth*, pp. 164–5.

43 Cf. Godelier and Strathern, *Big Men and Great Men*.

44 T. R. Trautmann and P. M. Whiteley, eds, *Crow-Omaha: New Light on a Classic Problem of Kinship Analysis* (Tucson, University of Arizona Press, 2012).

45 G. Rogers, 'The Father's Sister Futa-Helu Is Black. A Consideration of Female Rank and Power in Tonga', *Journal of the Polynesian Society* 86 (1977), pp. 157–82.

man made his child's bones with his semen, while the woman made its flesh and blood with her (menstrual) blood, the child's soul being a gift from the ancestors. The other theory explained that the child's whole body – its bones, flesh, blood and skin – came from the mother. The father's semen had nothing to do with making the child. His role was to keep the menstrual blood inside the woman's body through repeated acts of sexual intercourse. A clot would then form and become an embryo thanks to the intervention of the Tu'i Tonga (who himself descended from the union of Tangaloa, the Polynesian paramount god, and a Tongan noblewoman) or of a god. In this version, the husband disappears as genitor. In his stead, it is the Tu'i Tonga, who, with his divine breath – a veritable *sperma pneumatikos*, as Françoise Douaire-Marsaudon has it – fecundates all the women in his kingdom.[46]

The second model is clearly a transformation of the first. It completely excludes (ordinary) men from the act of engendering offspring, and extols the creative capacity of women even more than the first model. In so doing it enhances the importance of wife-givers with respect to that of wife-takers, and thus the maternal lines. Lévi-Strauss, who was aware of these facts, interpreted them as follows:

> It is evident that in this [last] case, each individual receives his organic substance exclusively from his maternal line, but it emerges also from indigenous testimony that, by way of exchange, the paternal kin hold familial authority, political power and social control. The natural is therefore all on one side, the cultural all on the other.[47]

Yet it has now been clearly established, in particular by the work of the Tongan historian Futa Helu-Aité, that the second version is the more recent. It appeared in the course of the social and ideological transformations that occurred in the Tongan political system when, following several partially successful attempts and then challenges by other noble houses, one chiefly line definitively raised itself above the others and took the name-title of Tu'i Tonga. It was then that, in this family line, the

---

46  F. Douaire-Marsaudon, 'Le Bain mystérieux de la Tu'i Tonga Fefine. Germanité, inceste et mariage sacré en Polynésie occidentale (Tonga)', *Anthropos* 97, n° 2 (2002), pp. 147–62, 519–28.

47  *Anthropology and Myth*, p. 176.

title, formerly handed from brother to brother, henceforth passed directly from father to son. At the same time, commoners began less to be regarded as distant relatives of the noble families and increasingly as subjects over whom the nobles had right of life and death, and from whom they exacted tribute in the form of produce and labour. The process by which a caste-class, once formed, closed in upon itself had taken a big step forward.[48]

In raising himself definitively above the other noble *Kainga*, the Tuʻi Tonga became a near-god, capable of impregnating with his spermatic breath all the women in his kingdom and of being the (imaginary) father of all the children that emerged from their wombs. Likewise, through the rites he celebrated, he ensured the fertility of the land his subjects cultivated and of the sea in which they fished each day. Nothing to do, then, with Lévi-Strauss's structural pseudo-explanation supposing the interplay of oppositions and correlations between nature (women) and culture (men), between wife-givers and wife-takers, and so on. Once again, we see that it is the transformations of political-religious relations that redirect the exercise of kinship and impose transformations on the structures and ideologies characteristic of the kinship system.

But to acknowledge this means coming back to the global vision Lévi-Strauss had of kinship, including the results of his analyses of the Crow-Omaha and 'house' systems. At the same time, it amounts to understanding why political-religious relations make use of images and values associated with the exercise of kinship in order to garner legitimacy. Is not the Tuʻi Tonga the *tamai*, the father, of all Tongans, and the supreme political chief endowed with nearly absolute power? This does not mean, as Lévi-Strauss wrote in 'The Future of Kinship Studies', that the Tongan political sphere lacked a language of its own and so was obliged to borrow that of kinship, while subverting it. Nowhere do political-religious relations entirely coincide with those of kinship. The political-religious sphere subordinates the sphere of kinship to its exercise and often borrows its language and values,

48  F. Douaire-Marsaudon, 'Le Meurtre cannibale ou la production d'un Homme-Dieu', in M. Godelier and M. Panoff, eds, *Le Corps humain. Supplicié, possédé, canniba-lisé* (Amsterdam, Archives contemporaines, 1998), pp. 137–67; new edition, Paris, CNRS Éditions, 2009.

using them as so many metaphors of realities that have nothing to do with kinship.

But now we must conclude. The notion of 'house', too, had opened up new areas of investigation. But they still had to be explored in order to take the measure of the task and pursue it.

After 1983, in the wake of the publication of Lévi-Strauss's text, anthropologists, historians and even archaeologists set about reinterpreting their own data with the help of the concept of 'house'. In France, Cécile Barraud was one of the first to try her hand, publishing her book on the Tanebar-Evav of Kei Island, in the Moluccas.[49] Next, Jean-Pierre Digard applied the concept of 'house' in his analysis of the Bakhtiari of Iran.[50] Lévi-Strauss would allude to this in his interview with Pierre Lamaison in 1987. In the Anglo-Saxon world, Janet Carsten and Stephen Hugh-Jones organized a conference in 1995 that resulted in the publication of a book.[51] In 1996 the American Anthropological Association organized a major symposium on the subject, which also resulted in a publication.[52] In France, the historian Philippe Maurice published a book in 1988 on *La Famille en Gévaudan*, which I have already mentioned, then in 1990 Christiane Klapisch-Zuber brought out *La Maison et le nom*, which took a fresh look at kinship in the Middle Ages.[53]

The intellectual stimulation prompted by the notion of 'house' needed no further demonstration.

49  C. Barraud, *Tanebar-Evav: une société de maisons tournée vers le large* (Cambridge, Cambridge University Press; Paris, Éditions de la Maison des sciences de l'homme, 1979).

50  J.-P. Digard, 'Jeux de structures, segmentarité et pouvoir chez les nomades Baxtyâri d'Iran', *L'Homme*, n° 102 (1987), pp. 12–53.

51  J. Carsten and S. Hugh-Jones, *About the House: Lévi-Strauss and Beyond* (Cambridge, Cambridge University Press, 1995).

52  R. A. Joyce and S. D. Gillespie, eds, *Beyond Kinship: Social and Material Reproduction in House Societies* (Philadelphia, University of Pennsylvania Press, 2000).

53  C. Klapisch-Zuber, *La Maison et le nom. Stratégies et rituels dans l'Italie de la Renaissance* (Paris, Éditions de l'EHESS, 1990).

# 6

## Final Texts (1983–2000)

### 'Cross-Readings' (1983)

'Cross-Readings' is a text in keeping with Lévi-Strauss's Marc Bloch Lecture. In it, he analyses historical and ethnographic data on four aristocratic societies at different times and in different parts of the world: imperial Japan in the Middle Ages, the important nineteenth-century Fijian chiefdoms, the united kingdom established in Madagascar by the Imerina king, Andrianampoinimerina, at the end of the eighteenth century, and the Lovedu kingdom in South Africa, which in the same period saw succession to the throne pass from woman to woman, whereas, until that time, it had been transmitted from father to son.

Lévi-Strauss's goal was to identify, in all this material, 'an underlying pattern that was common to several archaic royal lines and reveals how kinship structures are organized or reorganized when rudimentary forms of a political state emerge in their midst.'[1]

We will not dwell on the use of the term 'archaic' to designate ninth-century Japan or the eighteenth-century Imerina kingdom.[2] What matters is to isolate this underlying pattern. Lévi-Strauss defines it by

---

1 C. Lévi-Strauss, 'Cross-Readings', in *The View from Afar*, trans. J. Neugroschel and P. Hoss (Chicago, University of Chicago Press, 1985), p. 85.

2 *The View from Afar*. In the same text, he had already written that 'an abyss separates the Japan of the Heian period, with an élite that had been literate for several centuries, from an unlettered society like the Fijian' (p. 76).

two features. The first is the existence of marriage strategies in the reign-
ing families that play on the two forms of matrimonial alliance: marriages
with close cross cousins, and marriages with remote kin. In *Genji
Monogatari*, a novel written in the eleventh century, and in the *Eiga
Monogatari*, a historical chronicle of the same period, the characters
weigh the advantages of these different unions in the clearest possible
terms. But their discussions also include the second component of the
shared structure that Lévi-Strauss believed he had identified: the
fundamental role of the givers of sisters and daughters, in other words
the maternal kin, in the succession process but also in the manipulation
of royal power.

In late-eighteenth-century Madagascar, having extended his
hegemony over a large portion of the island and reunified the four
kingdoms his great-great-grandfather had divided among his four sons,
following the principle of agnatic succession, Andrianampoinimerina
reformed the succession process in order to reserve the throne for his
sisters' descendants. The same kind of reform was introduced at the
same period in the South African kingdom of Lovedu. In both cases,
behind the women who occupied the throne stood, according to Lévi-
Strauss, their brothers, their maternal uncles or the men of the noble
house who provided husbands for these politically powerful queens.
Lévi-Strauss thus felt justified in asserting that the brand of comparatism
he practiced took the analysis far enough to reveal the recurring
structures within different cultures that, at some levels, were not
comparable.

In the same year, 1983, on the occasion of a homage to Louis
Dumont,[3] he returned to his analysis of one of the aspects of the
structure he had identified, the so-called strategy of marriage
between close kin.


## 'On Marriage between Close Kin' (1983)

The author explains that this text was written after he had read a 'fine
book' by Nicole Loraux, *Les Enfants d'Athéna (1981)*. Loraux had asked
the following question: 'If paternal heritage alone matters, how is one to

---

3  Ibid., pp. 88–97.

explain that Athens had a law forbidding all unions between children born of the same mother but of different fathers?'[4]

Lévi-Strauss tries to answer this question by, first, looking through the ethnographic literature for other examples of the same phenomenon. In the space of two pages, he cites eighteen societies in Africa, Polynesia, Timor and New Guinea, and in each case he claims to have found, in one form or another, the same principle being applied: the incest taboo is stricter on the maternal than on the paternal side, including in societies governed by 'paternal law'. Since we have no way of following him step by step, we must take his word for it.

Lévi-Strauss finally arrives at theoretical explanations able to account for the marriages with close, and even very close, kin that could be found in certain tribes of New Guinea as well as in several African or Polynesian kingdoms, such as the marriage between the Tuʻi Tonga and his sister, mentioned in the annals of the kingdom of Tonga.

His initial hypothesis is that we are dealing with societies that 'reject long cycles – in preference either to short cycles (from marriage by exchange through marriage with a patrilateral female cross cousin, to royal incest with an agnate half-sister) or to entirely new alliances, which may therefore be considered as limited instances of such long cycles as to exceed the very notion of cycle'.[5]

Yet it is difficult to consider an entirely new analysis, which may or may not be the beginning of a short or long cycle, as a limiting instance of the long cycle. In the end, the explanation he proposes lies elsewhere, 'in the respective power . . . of the paternal and the maternal kin or, more precisely, of the wife-takers and the wife-givers . . . As a taker, a group uses its men to strengthen its position; as a giver, it uses its women, whatever its mode of filiation may be.'[6]

Having advanced this claim ('whatever its mode of filiation may be'), he adds another, more general assertion, which calls for a few reservations:

The societies in question are not distinguished from one another by intrinsic modes of filiation or descent. In varying degrees, these

4  N. Loraux, *Les Enfants d'Athéna* (Paris, Maspero, 1981), p. 130.
5  *The View from Afar*, p. 92.
6  Ibid., p. 94.

societies follow what ... I have repeatedly suggested calling 'undifferentiated systems': that is, a system where the elements of personal
status and hereditary rights and obligations are handed down indifferently in either line or both, which does not prevent people from
thinking of them as distinct.[7]

In short, all these systems would be intrinsically cognatic or, if they were
not so in the beginning, became cognatic through the unstable relationship that grew up between takers and givers of women and through
their opposing interests. The patrilineal or matrilineal features of the
systems would be merely surface phenomena, 'pseudomorphs ...
because even if the rule of filiation or descent exists, it is not the operative factor.'

Once again, Lévi-Strauss reiterated the thesis he had been affirming
since *The Elementary Structures of Kinship*, that of the primacy of alliance
over descent. This would explain how the same groups could practice
endogamy in the case of marriages with close kin (in view of consolidating
their position) and exogamy in marriages farther from home (to win
new advantages), which results in a twofold game of opening and
closing: 'by means of the one, a group opens itself to history and exploits
the resources of chance; while the other assures the preservation or the
regular recovery of patrimonies, ranks, and titles.'[8]

He had thus found the answer to Nicole Loraux's question. In all
societies, the relationship between takers and givers of women, between
paternal and maternal kin, is unstable. It is in the interest of all groups
to marry both close to home and far away. Marriage with one's half-
sister is the closest degree. Where paternal kin outweigh maternal kin,
marriage with a half-sister of the same father is forbidden. Where
maternal kin outweigh paternal kin, marriage between children of the
same mother but different fathers is allowed. This was the case in Sparta,
according to Philo. And Lévi-Strauss evokes what Athenians saw as the
privileged position of women in Sparta, their moral freedom.

Here, Lévi-Strauss seizes the opportunity to launch an attack on his
Anglo-Saxon colleagues, whom he accuses of having 'gone to great
pains' to multiply descent rules – unilineal, bilineal, ambilineal, etc. For

---

7  Ibid., p. 93.
8  Ibid., pp. 94–5.

to his mind, these are only surface phenomena. At bottom, all systems are undifferentiated. The heart of all systems is exchange, the relationship between givers and takers of women. Here descent principles are definitively relegated to last place, since they are produced by power relations within the matrimonial exchanges and are thus by-products, pseudomorphs.[9]

I am unable to agree with these analyses and conclusions, for several reasons. To be sure, there are tensions between givers and takers in all kinship systems. Nevertheless, what matters most is not whether alliances are repeated, it is the appropriation of the children born of these alliances. What matters is to whom they will belong, that is, to whom will be handed down the material and immaterial social realities indispensable for the continuation of the groups that appropriate these children. Except in a minority of strongly cognatic systems, hereditary rights and obligations are never passed on 'indifferently' in one line or the other, in the paternal or the maternal line.

But, in the final analysis, that is not the issue either. Lévi-Strauss's explanation that marriages with close kin are due to power relations between givers and takers is refuted by the example of marriages between full brothers and sisters in ancient Egypt or Persia. In these societies, the parents did not forbid their sons and daughters to marry each other. On the contrary, brother–sister marriages, as we have said, were the form most valued in these societies insofar as they reproduced on the human level the unions practiced by the gods among themselves, which produced the first humans. The existence of such unions had always posed a serious problem for Lévi-Strauss. If this most endogamous of possible unions is also the one that is most valued by society, then the theory that kinship is based on the exchange of women by men (and not vice versa), that 'consanguineous' unions threaten and destroy society, close each family in on itself, etc., no longer has universal value: it is

---

9 In a paragraph that could slip by unnoticed, Lévi-Strauss mentions the existence, in New Guinea and in Africa, of kinship terminologies christened 'partial Omaha systems', because the skewing found in the Crow-Omaha systems is present only on one side, authorizing marriage with the matrilateral cross cousin. That is what I tried to show earlier. But in 1967, in his Huxley Memorial Lecture, these systems with some Omaha features are excluded from the category of Crow-Omaha systems insofar as they are 'as widely dissimilar as, say, fish and a whale'. In 1983, this opposition no longer had a particular status. Cf. *The View from Afar*, p. 91.

relative, and confronts facts that it cannot account for. Hence the pseudo-explanation that such unions mark the outer limit of endogamy, which, so the theory goes, makes it possible to consolidate acquired advantages; or that it is not the elder sister but the younger who is taken as a wife, which would be an extreme figure of relations between the eldest and the youngest, etc.

In reality, brother–sister marriages challenge the hypothesis that, even when kinship rests universally on the exchange of women among men, it does not alter the universal fact of the prohibition of incest, which Lévi-Strauss made the lynchpin of his entire interpretation of human kinship and on the basis of which he argued that exchange (of women) was the essential principle of kinship systems, while descent was secondary. By virtue of these systems, father–daughter and mother–son incest are forbidden, but the union between a brother and a sister is seen as bringing humans closer to the gods.

Such marriages are rooted in the religious perception these societies have of the universe, of the gods and of humans. There is nothing 'aberrant', there is no 'consanguineous egoism' in these unions; on the contrary, they are the expression of a desire to partake of the divine, to contribute to the reproduction of the cosmic and social order, an order that is at once thoroughly supernatural, imaginary and concrete.

All in all, in coming back to the problem of the nature and origin of marriages with close kin, Lévi-Strauss once again sparked a series of studies that are still ongoing today, and have given rise to several important publications.[10] But in this short text on marriages with close kin, he once again overlooked the role played by religious beliefs in structuring kinship relations. Without the caste system and the practice of endogamy that are associated with Hinduism, would the Dravidian systems of South India have the same structure, which has endured until now? Without Christianity and the value it assigns to monogamy and marriage as the union of two beings before God, who become 'one flesh', would the nuclear family have become the paradigm for the Western family?

---

10  For example, see P. Bonte, ed., *Épouser au plus proche. Inceste, prohibition et stratégies matrimoniales autour de la Méditerranée* (Paris, Éditions de l'EHESS, 1994).

## The Second of the Three Tokyo Lectures (1986)

In the spring of 1986, Lévi-Strauss was invited to Japan by the Ishizaka Foundation. There he gave three lectures, the second of which dealt in part with kinship issues. The first was entitled 'The End of the West's Cultural Supremacy', an affirmation that must have pleased the Japanese. The second addressed 'Three Great Contemporary Problems: Sexuality, Economic development, and Mythical Thought'. The third was devoted to 'Recognizing Cultural Diversity: What We Can Learn From Japanese Civilization'.

These lectures were not published in France in the author's lifetime. They only appeared posthumously, under the title *Anthropologie face aux problèmes du monde moderne* (2011), and in English in 2013, as *Anthropology Confronts the Problems of the Modern World*. In the second lecture, in the subsection 'Sexuality', Lévi-Strauss addresses the issues raised in the West by the introduction of technologies enabling infertile couples to have children with the aid of a 'surrogate mother', and also the claim of homosexual couples to the right to satisfy their desire for a child by demanding a legal status for their prospective family.

In 1986, these problems, whose solution relied on an evolution in the law and in mental attitudes, were already attracting public attention as the subject of lively debate and political and ideological controversy. Some countries, the Netherlands and Canada for instance, had rapidly taken a position and passed laws in response to these problems. This was not the case of others, France in particular.

Had Lévi-Strauss's positions, critical of Western fears and prejudices in these domains, been known to the French public at the time, they would surely have propelled him into the eye of the storm. His internationally recognized competence in matters of kinship and his status as a scientist would have weighed heavily in favour of recognition of these new rights.[11]

In the first pages of his text, Lévi-Strauss recalls the role played by kinship relations in numerous human societies and the importance of

11 When I read Lévi-Strauss's text upon its publication in 2011, I discovered his analyses and positions were in line with those I had advanced, without being aware of his text, in my book *Metamorphoses of Kinship*, trans. N. Scott (London and New York, Verso, 2012; first published in French in 2004). See the chapter 'What Future for What Kin Ties?' pp. 521–53.

anthropology in the study of kinship. He stresses that, to reproduce itself, every society must have rules allowing it to determine to whom the children born in the society belong. These rules define the forms of alliance permitted in this society, which in turn supposes rules for classifying kin into consanguines and affines. He goes on to assert: 'Every society must also possess mechanisms to remedy sterility. It is the problem of remedying sterility that has become a pressing issue in Western societies, ever since the invention of artificial methods to assist in reproduction.'[12]

From the start, Lévi-Strauss gives these problems a universal character. How to have children when one cannot have them is not a problem limited to the West, or to our era. Humankind has already invented solutions. A comparative analysis of these is necessary and can be useful, he writes, now that it is possible 'for a couple, one or both of whose members are infertile, to have children through the use of various methods': artificial insemination, egg donation, *in vitro* fertilization with sperm from a man or an egg from a woman who may or may not be part of the couple, etc.[13]

Instead of one father and one mother, a child can now have two fathers (a social father and a father who donated his sperm) and a mother; or one father and two mothers, if the social mother has recourse to a surrogate mother. The child can even have two fathers and two mothers, and so on. One could imagine a couple in which only the woman is infertile: in this case, three women can get together to make a child, one donating an egg that the man fertilizes, the other carrying and giving birth to the child and the third, the infertile woman, becoming the child's social and legal mother. Two lesbians can have a child together if the egg produced by one is fertilized by an (anonymous or not) sperm donor and implanted in the uterus of the other. Yet more possibilities are opened up by recently developed techniques for freezing sperm or embryos. Or a woman can ask to be inseminated with the sperm of her deceased husband in order to bear his children. Lévi-Strauss even evokes the possibility of a woman deciding to be inseminated with the frozen

---

12  C. Lévi-Strauss, *Anthropology Confronts the Problems of the Modern World*, foreword M. Olender, trans. J. M. Todd (Cambridge, MA and London, The Belknap Press of Harvard University Press, 2013), p. 47.

13  Ibid., p. 48.

sperm of her great-grandfather: in this case, the child would be both her son and her great-uncle, the fruit of an unwitting incest on the part of the deceased ancestor by wish of his great-granddaughter.

Lévi-Strauss rightly reminds us that some of the problems that have arisen in the West stem from the fact that, when it comes to defining parenthood, the biological ties between a child and its parents often prevail over social ties. We should add that this emphasis on biological filiation does not stem from any more accurate knowledge Western peoples might have of the biological, genetic and physiological process of making children, but from the fact that the Western family has been shaped for centuries, structured in depth, by the monogamous union imposed by the Christian churches. This history means that from birth children are ascribed to one man and one woman who are (supposed to be) the child's biological and social parents at once. In a great many societies, social and biological paternity do not match at every point. Among the Baruya people of New Guinea, for example, all of a man's brothers are also considered fathers of his children, and all of a woman's sisters are as her children's mothers. Moreover, this social paternity and maternity provide the child with more extensive protection than the restricted paternity and maternity of the Christian or post-Christian West. The question therefore arises in the West of determining 'the respective rights and duties of the social and the biological parents . . . now that they are different people'.[14] The other question that presents itself is: should everything that becomes possible be allowed? And if not, what should be forbidden, and who, if not the State, has the authority to forbid?

Lévi-Strauss tackles the question of the anonymity of egg and sperm donors. Which is preferable: silence or transparency? As early as 1986, Sweden opted against anonymity, while France did not. Yet in many societies, as Lévi-Strauss reminds us, the genitor and the social father are not the same person. In some places a woman can marry another woman and become the legal 'father' of the children that will be born with the help of lovers chosen by the 'husband'. Such was the case among the Yoruba of Nigeria. The children knew who their genitor was. Since this situation was accepted and codified by their society, these children did not go mad or become perverts. Lévi-Strauss also cites the case of

---

14  Ibid., pp. 49–50.

the ancient Hebrews, among whom the practice of levirate stipulated that, if a man should die without issue, one of his brothers must marry the widow and engender children with her who would be attributed to the deceased brother. In modern-day Tibet, polyandry is still widespread. Several brothers marry the same woman, and the children born from these unions are attributed exclusively to the eldest of the brothers, who will inherit the family land.[15] There is no conflict between biological and social parenthood in these societies, which always give priority to social parenthood. And when it comes to using the frozen sperm of a deceased husband to make a child, Lévi-Strauss reminds us that, in many societies, a child is the reincarnation of one of its ancestors, who has chosen to be reborn in this body. One example is the Trobriand Islanders made famous by Malinowski.[16]

Finally, of course, Lévi-Strauss was not urging us to adopt the customs of the Yoruba or the Nuer, but first of all to 'remove our blinkers', to understand that 'what we consider "natural", founded on the order of things, actually amounts to constraints and mental habits specific to our own culture'. It is our moral, philosophical and religious beliefs, he explains, that make it hard to find answers to these new situations. And he stresses the importance of reporting the responses dozens of societies have found to complicated situations, because 'uncertain changes will come about [that] we would be wrong to denounce in advance as deviations or perversions'. In the end, Lévi-Strauss asks our societies not to be too quick to make new laws in this area, for 'even the practices and aspirations that most shock public opinion . . . have their equivalents in other societies, which are none the worse for it.'[17] He therefore counsels waiting until the society has produced its own family structures, some of which will turn out to be viable, while others will be eliminated. Only their development will tell us whether the contradictions to which they give rise can be overcome or not.

In 1986 Lévi-Strauss did not take his Japanese audience any farther. But let us note that even then he pointed out, uncritically, that the new

15 Cf. N. Levine, 'Fathers and Sons: Kinship Value and Validation in Tibetan Polyandry', *Man* 22, n° 2 (1987), pp. 267–86.

16 B. Malinowski, *The Father in Primitive Psychology* (New York, Norton Library, 1928). See also T. Montberg, 'Fathers Were Not Genitors', *Man* 10, n° 1 (1975), pp. 81–113; Godelier, *Metamorphoses of Kinship*, chapters 7 and 8.

17 *Anthropology Confronts the Problems of the Modern World*, pp. 58–9.

technologies can also be made available to homosexual couples. No negative judgment about homosexuality, then.

We can see that these positions, at once 'liberal and cautious' as he said himself, would have strongly influenced the public debate before the state adopted legislation in this area.

It has now been over twenty years since Western societies were called to take a position on these new forms of parenthood. Some have already authorized and provided a legal framework for the practice of 'mother-hood on behalf of another', and the possibility for homosexual couples to start a family if they so desire. These societies have not created insurmount-able contradictions; in fact, in the Western world they are acting as a labo-ratory for others. Henceforth, homosexuality increasingly appears as a sexual orientation that is different, no doubt, but normal; it is indisputable that homosexuals can experience the desire to have children. Likewise, infertile men who accept that their wife or partner be fertilized by the sperm of another man, in order to raise the child together as their own, are no less 'manly' for being infertile. Whole walls of prejudices, value judg-ments, beliefs and old representations are cracking, resisting, crumbling and rising again, only perhaps to disappear completely tomorrow.

But these walls should not be held in contempt. For centuries, they were perceived and experienced as existential truths. And they will not be abolished by dint of legislation. Nevertheless, only the state can impose new obligations, which individuals will then be able to use to construct their way of life.

## 'La Sexualité féminine et l'origine de la société' (1995)

Lévi-Strauss first analyses and criticizes – and with what verve! – certain ideas fashionable in the United States and Great Britain according to which one condition, if not *the* condition, for the passage from the animal to the human state, from nature to culture, was the loss of oestrus in the human female and the fact that, since they did not come into heat like females of the other primate species, they became, like men, capable of sex at any time.[18] He does not cite authors, but he is clearly alluding

18 C. Lévi-Strauss, 'La Sexualité féminine et l'origine de la société', *Les Temps modernes*, n° 598 (1998), pp. 78–84 (first published in *La Repubblica*, 3 November 1995, under the title 'Quell'intenso profumo di donna').

to the influence of feminist movements and what is known in the United States as 'gender studies'.

Lévi-Strauss saw in such notions the unexpected resurgence at the end of the twentieth century of the old story of matriarchal societies, the idea that in the beginning, power in society belonged to women. The explanation advanced this time was that, being able to dissimulate ovulation and to exert sexual attraction on men at all times, women gained two things: the capacity to trade sexual favours for the products of the men's hunt, in other words 'food for sex'; and the capacity to attach men to themselves over a long period, so as to ensure their children's protection until they were grown. As Lévi-Strauss summed it up: 'oestrus thus had to disappear in order for society to come into being.'[19]

Starting from the same premise, the loss of oestrus, other authors imagined – reasoning from the theses set out by neo-Darwinian sociobiologists – that, thanks to the absence of external signs of oestrus (odours, tumescence, etc.), women had been on the contrary able to avoid the control of a single male, and thus to have multiple sexual partners so as to ensure the reproductive success of their genes and thus the species.

We will cite only these examples, which led Lévi-Strauss to conclude that 'one is staggered by these contradictory interpretations which cancel each other out', dubbing them 'robinsonnades génitales' (a sort of genital exoticism).[20] We can only agree with him and, why not, even go a step farther . . .

Lévi-Strauss's second accusation was aimed at those anthropologists and paleo-anthropologists who had erected a wall between our species, *Homo sapiens sapiens*, and Neanderthal man, with whom we coexisted for millennia, on the grounds that Neanderthal man, because of the form of his larynx and pharynx, could not have had an articulated language, which is proof of symbolic thought. Once again, and rightly so, Lévi-Strauss criticizes these hypotheses because 'the origin of language is not tied to the conformation of the speech organs. It must be sought in the neurology of the brain. But this demonstrates that language can already have existed in a very remote era, well before the appearance

19  Ibid., p. 81.
20  Ibid., p. 84.

of *Homo sapiens* some one hundred thousand years ago.'[21] Broca's Area, which is the language centre, and the frontal lobes were already present over two million years ago, in *Homo habilis* and then *Homo erectus*, who had domesticated fire and made already very complex tools. *H. erectus* must have possessed some sort of language, over 500,000 years ago, in order to transmit these skills.

What strikes me in this passage is that Lévi-Strauss no longer sees the appearance of language, and therefore of symbolic thought, as a 'big bang', as he did some fifty years earlier (in 1950), when he wrote in his *Introduction to the Work of Marcel Mauss*, as an extension of his *Elementary Structures*: 'Whatever may have been the moment and the circumstances of its appearance in the ascent of animal life, language can only have arisen all at once. Things cannot have begun to signify gradually.'[22] The biological and social evolution of protohumans and humans has been taken into account by the theory, which does not mean one must adhere to a particular 'evolutionist' version.

I do not think, as Lévi-Strauss suggested, that the 'robinsonnades génitales' and these simplistic theories are down to feminism or to the development of gender studies. Erroneous theories, like erroneous ideas, must be ascribed to their authors and to the way they have understood certain issues or ideas. Furthermore, these erroneous theories grew up around facts that deserve examination. First of all, the idea that women could have – deliberately – hidden the signs of oestrus literally does not make sense, it has no meaning. In all mammals, the physiological process of ovulation is hidden. What may have been lost in the course of evolution are the physical signs that in many species accompany the time of ovulation – bodily odours and signs such as the colours that appear on the skin in certain places, etc. Alternatively, certain anatomical and physical changes in the human female body made women permanently more attractive, independently of the ovarian cycle and periods of ovulation. The breasts, for instance, form at puberty and continue to be present whether or not a woman gives birth, whereas in the female chimpanzee or bonobo, the breasts appear only when lactating.

---

21  Ibid.
22  C. Lévi-Strauss, *Introduction to the Work of Marcel Mauss*, trans. F. Baker, (London, Routledge & Kegan Paul, 1987), p. 59.

I will stop here. The important point is that sexuality in the human species takes the difference between sexuality-as-desire and sexuality-for-reproduction farther than in any other species. In humans, sexuality is polymorphous; it is expressed in several forms – hetero-, homo- and auto-sexuality (masturbation); it reacts more to internal representations than to external stimulation, and is therefore strongly 'cerebralized'.[23] These features specific to human sexuality, above all its asocial character, are why it must be 'domesticated' and subordinated to the production and reproduction of society. All these facts illuminate the prohibition of incest without sufficing, as we have seen, to explain it, for what still needs to be explained is the necessity to exchange, that is, the necessity to forbid in order to give and to give in order to receive.

Another problem addressed in these naïve and sometimes burlesque theories is that of the presence of men in human families. Males are not present in chimpanzee and bonobo families, except on a temporary basis, when a female accepts to 'pair with a male' for a few hours or days, and then breaks the tie by attracting other males.

Yet the presence of men, either as 'husbands', as in most societies, or as 'uncles', women's brothers, as among the Na or the Nayar, cannot be explained by the sexual division of labour alone, which obliges men and women to cooperate in order to survive and to ensure the survival of offspring. And it is explained even less by the love for the children that is supposedly shared by the women's brothers, husband, etc. The main reason lies elsewhere. Children are in fact a fundamental stake in society. It is through children that the kin groups and kinship relations are extended, and material and immaterial goods transmitted. It is on children that future descendants *and* alliances depend, for descent and alliance are not interchangeable. Here I am in agreement with Lévi-Strauss. Since it is the men who usually possess the political and social power, they exercise this power over the women and over the children born of their unions in the kin groups that make up their society, and of course they also wield this power beyond the field of kinship.

---

23 Cf. Godelier, *Metamorphoses of Kinship*, pp. 446–56.

## 'Le Retour de l'oncle maternel' (1997)

Lévi-Strauss's article on the 'return of the maternal uncle' was prompted by the remarks of Earl Spencer, brother of Princess Diana, at the funeral of his sister, who died on 31 August 1997 in a car accident that rocked the world. Charles Spencer had condemned Prince Charles and the royal family for his sister's misfortunes, and demanded a say in his nephews' upbringing.

Lévi-Strauss saw this as reviving the social role of the woman's brother, a wife-giver, a relative who played an important role in family relations in the Middle Ages, at least among the nobility. Roland was Charlemagne's uterine nephew, Gawain, that of King Arthur, and so on. Epics are full of descriptions of the strong, affectionate ties between maternal uncle and nephew. In patrilineal systems, where the father has authority over his sons, the maternal uncle can be seen to reinforce the mother's affection for her children.

Here Lévi-Strauss found the opportunity to recall, first of all, that kinship is not founded on blood ties. Therefore 'there is no need to explain how the maternal uncle comes to feature in the kinship edifice. He does not feature in this structure, he is the condition of its existence.'[24] But any role the maternal uncle might have played in the Middle Ages has long since vanished. 'This structure disintegrated under the effect of the demographic, social, economic and political changes that accompanied – sometime as its causes, sometimes as its effects – the industrial revolution.' Lévi-Strauss thus saw the tragedy of Princess Diana as once more illuminating a kinship structure that was believed to have disappeared.

The reappearance of the role of the maternal uncle provided Lévi-Strauss with an unexpected opportunity to analyse the kinship system of the Na, a Tibeto-Burman–speaking group in the Himalayas. It had been made famous by Cai Hua's book, *A Society without Fathers or Husbands*,[25] which challenged some of Lévi-Strauss's theses, particularly those

---

24 C. Lévi-Strauss, 'Le Retour de l'oncle maternel', *Cahiers de L'Herne*, n° 24, devoted to Lévi-Strauss (2004), pp. 37–9. First published in *La Repubblica*, 24 December 1997, under the title: 'I legami di sangue'; reprinted in *Nous sommes tous des cannibales* (Paris, Seuil, 2013).

25 C. Hua, *Une Société sans père ni mari. Les Na de Chine* (Paris, Presses Universitaires de France, 1997).

concerning the exchange of women. The Na society did not have marriage; their terminology contained no words for 'husband' or 'father'. The society was divided into large matrilineal groups headed by the eldest woman and one of her brothers, also the eldest. The woman managed the activities within the matriline. The man took care of relations with the authorities, trade, etc. Each matriline contained several generations of brothers and sisters, and the children born to the women. Each night, the brothers would leave their sister's house and go to visit women in the other houses, if they accepted them, for the night. All sexual relations or even allusions to sex within the matriline were severely punished, including by banishment. The union between a mother and a son, an aunt and a nephew, an uncle and a niece or a brother and a sister was literally 'unthinkable' and would have been harshly punished.

Children were born as a result of these nocturnal visits, but no one sought to discover who the father might be.[26] There was no father figure, and his function was entirely taken over by the mother's brother, the maternal uncle. Lévi-Strauss considered that, just as our system had jettisoned the maternal uncle and functioned normally, so the Na system had jettisoned the father (and the husband) and functioned normally. There 'should therefore be nothing surprising' about a family with no husband, as we see in the West. In this case, it would be the near (the West) that shed light on the far (the East), just the opposite of what is usually the case in anthropology. But we are surprised that Lévi-Strauss did not reply to Cai Hua that his theories, far from being contradicted by the Na case, were once again confirmed.

First of all, because in this society without husbands the incest taboo was just as strong, if not stronger, than in many others. Secondly, because these matrilines did not reproduce themselves by means of sexual unions within the line, but by exchanges between matrilines – exchanges of semen, the indispensable 'rain' that causes the embryos the women carry in their wombs to grow. There was indeed exchange, then, even if this exchange between matrilines did not create alliances between them: the reciprocal gifts of semen did not make the donors partners. From

---

26 Semen was not thought of as making the child but as a rain that ensured the growth of the embryos of the girls and boys that the goddess Abaogdu, out of benevolence toward human beings, deposited regularly.

this standpoint, the theory of Lévi-Strauss – for whom exchange meant alliance – was contradicted. In a way, the Na made all men anonymous sperm donors by transporting their life-giving water from one matriline to another, thus enabling their sisters and themselves to have and raise together the children their women brought into the world and to fully ensure the paternal and maternal functions in a society without either fathers or husbands. Furthermore, it seems that the children born in this society were as normal as those born in a society where marriage is the rule and the descent rule is patrilineal.

## 'Apologue des amibes' (2000)

This short text is very interesting and very important.[27] In it, besides offering new ways of viewing the sociability and violence lodged in the depths of the structures that gave rise to society, Lévi-Strauss reasserts certain theses he defended fifty years earlier, in *The Elementary Structures of Kinship*. But now the origin of human society and that of articulated speech have clearly been resituated in the evolution of nature – a process that stretches over hundreds of thousands, if not millions, of years.

Lévi-Strauss first reminds us that Freud and Tylor, each in his own way, concurred in placing murder and violence at the origin of the incest taboo and of exogamy, and therefore of life in society. In *Totem and Taboo*, Freud recounted how the sons rose up against their despotic father and, together in the midst of the primal horde, murdered and devoured him.[28] Tylor, for his part, imagined that 'savage' peoples had always been confronted by the choice 'between marrying out and being killed out'.[29] Lévi-Strauss had cited both in *The Elementary Structures of Kinship*, regarding Freud's hypothesis as a myth and Tylor's as a positive suggestion. By the year 2000, both hypotheses had become myths, and the murder of the father in *Totem and Taboo* was once again described

---

27 C. Lévi-Strauss, 'Apologue des amibes', in J.-L. Jamard, M. Xanthakou and E. Terray, eds, *En substances: Textes pour Françoise Héritier* (Paris, Fayard, 2000), pp. 493–6.

28 S. Freud, *Totem and Taboo*, trans. and intro. A. A. Brill (London, George Routledge & Sons, 1919).

29 E. B. Tylor, 'On a Method of Investigating the Development of Institutions, Applied to Laws of Marriage and Descent', *Journal of the Royal Anthropological Institute*, n° 18 (1889), p. 267.

as the 'expression of an enduring ancient dream that has haunted men's minds down through the generations'. And what does this dream consist of? To find out, we must reread the final lines of *The Elementary Structures*, in which he writes: 'To this very day, mankind has always dreamed of seizing and fixing that fleeting moment when it was permissible to believe that the law of exchange could be evaded, that one could gain without losing, enjoy without sharing . . . a world in which one might keep to oneself.'[30]

This dream, it should be noted, this mirage that Lévi-Strauss had not ceased to attribute to the human mind, is every bit as imaginary as the murder of the father invented by Freud.

The surprise comes when we read what Lévi-Strauss has made of the 'vigorous and untranslatable expression' of Tylor,[31] who presented it as being almost self-evident, which 'conveys, in the form of a myth, the retrospective view that biological families must hold of an imaginary past in order to understand that society forbids them to lead separate lives. No one will claim he is stating a historical truth.'[32] Undeniably, but why imagine then that biological families – which do not exist in a pure state, since all human families are at the same time biological and social creations – needed to hold up an imaginary past in order to justify in their own eyes the fact that they cannot reproduce within themselves, but must contract alliances and exchange certain members with others? The paralogism of the incest taboo as being simultaneously the cause and the consequence of the existence of kinship relations – which I criticized when analysing *The Elementary Structures* – is now acknowledged to be a myth.

Lévi-Strauss goes on to evoke the hundreds of thousands of years we would need to pass in review if we wanted to discover the origin of society, but paradoxically, he does not consider the fact that we, like chimpanzees and bonobos – the two primate species which descend together with us from a common ancestor – are a naturally social species. It was therefore not the establishment of the incest taboo and the exchange of women that brought society into being. These probably

---

30  C. Lévi-Strauss, *The Elementary Structures of Kinship*, trans. J. H. Bell and J.R. von Sturmer and R. Needham, ed., (Boston, Beacon Press, 1969), pp. 496–7.

31  Ibid., p. 42.

32  'Apologue des amibes', p. 493.

worked to transform the mode of social life our very remote ancestors had inherited from nature as it evolved. And together with this mode of existence, they probably received the capacity to produce other modes of social existence, other forms of society in order to go on existing.

The capacity to produce new forms of social life, restricted to the *Homo sapiens sapiens* that we are, became possible, according to Lévi-Strauss, with the appearance of 'gestures of reciprocity, not through rational calculation but through the effect of symbolic thought alone'.[33] Here we find ourselves back at the beginning of *The Elementary Structures*. To be sure, gestures of reciprocity have been observed in chimpanzees and bonobos, which moreover are not devoid of a symbolic dimension. These gestures of reciprocity take the form of mutual grooming, sharing meat, helping a 'friend' in difficulties with an adversary, etc. But no one has ever observed individuals of these species exchanging others with members of their own or a neighbouring band. There does exist a biological mechanism, which, activated in all females at puberty whatever band they may belong to, produces transfers between bands. But these reciprocal transfers are not exchanges, because they do not involve a conscious intention. The individuals that disperse, like those that accept them and include them in their own band, are not pursuing any social aim.

The prohibition of incest thus introduces a radically new element into humans' mode of existence, since it applies in advance to all the families that make up a human society and which structures them in such a way that none of them can – without violating this prohibition – close upon itself. 'In this sense,' Lévi-Strauss writes, 'one can say that exchange existed before those enacting it did.' And he goes on to conclude, but this time fifty years later: 'One would therefore be mistaken to think that matrimonial exchange is of the same nature as the contract. It takes only a single prohibited degree for the mechanism of exchange to be set in motion in the group as a whole, outside the conscious awareness of the subjects. Exchange is a property of the social structure.'[34]

---

33  Ibid., p. 494.

34  Ibid. In 1949 in *The Elementary Structures of Kinship*, Lévi-Strauss wrote: 'The total relationship of exchange which constitutes marriage is not established between a man and a woman . . . but between two groups of men, and the woman figures only as one of the objects in the exchange . . . This view must be kept in all strictness, even with regard to our own society, where marriage appears to be a contract between persons' (p. 115).

This calls for a remark, for it is impossible to prohibit one, two or three degrees of kinship without this prohibition being a conscious act, and it would be impossible to apply within all kin groups unless it were consciously shared by all. Every prohibition leads to a mechanism of exchange, but this mechanism can be neither diffused nor reproduced 'outside conscious awareness'. And, of course, once the prohibition of one or two degrees is established, exchange becomes 'a property of the social structure'.

Lévi-Strauss next responds, without naming names and by a pirouette, to a criticism I raised in 1996 in my book *The Enigma of the Gift*, when I showed that, alongside things one sells or gives, there are things that can neither be sold nor given, but must be kept for transmission.[35] These (material or immaterial) 'things' are among those that are the most important and the most sacred, not because they necessarily have to do with religions and their celebrations, but because they embody down through time elements crucial to the identity of a group or a person.

However, in 1952, Lévi-Strauss asserted that social life rests on the circulation of three things: women (kinship), goods (economy) and signs and representations (culture).[36] There was no talk of a sector of life that might be withheld from the sphere of exchange. Marcel Mauss had indeed mentioned the existence of '*sacra*', those sacred objects that never circulated in potlatches and formed part of the treasure of each clan and each tribe. Mauss had not seen this fact as a problem.[37] Nor had Lévi-Strauss. But in 2000, he wrote: 'Not that in society everything can be exchanged (Boas had already demonstrated this), but if there were no exchange, there would be no society.'[38] So, if not everything can be exchanged, one must ask: what are those things that cannot be exchanged, and why not?

---

35 M. Godelier, *The Enigma of the Gift*, trans. N. Scott (Chicago, University of Chicago Press; Cambridge, Polity Press, 1998).

36 In 'Social Structure', in *Structural Anthropology* (written in 1942 in English): 'A society consists of individuals and groups which communicate with one another . . . In any society communication operates on three different levels: communication of women, communication of foods and services, communication of messages' (p. 296).

37 M. Mauss, *The Gift: The Form and Reason for Exchange in Archaic Societies*, trans. W. D. Halls, foreword M. Douglas (New York and London, W. W. Norton, 1990), pp. 65ff.

38 'Apologue des amibes', p. 494.

From this we must conclude that life in society rests on two opposing but complementary principles: exchange, circulate; or, keep for oneself and/or transmit. But in 1949, Lévi-Strauss, who wanted to establish the paramount importance of alliance, and therefore of exchange, in the workings of kinship, had played down the importance of the second pillar of kinship, namely, descent – the domain in which as a rule things are kept to be transmitted.

At last, Lévi-Strauss comes to the amoeba. He chooses amoeba in the hope of finding a natural basis for social life which rests on structures that go deeper than the family. He does this also to see if violence and predation are present in those deep structures. The question then arises of the forms of 'sociability' to be found in living beings, and he chooses for his enquiry the lowliest among these, the single-celled amoeba. Summing up the work of certain biologists, he tells us that one species of amoeba lives two distinct and alternating kinds of life: they live as solitary individuals when the bacteria on which they feed are in plentiful supply; but, when these bacteria become scarce, the amoeba congregate to form a single body. The stimulus for this change is a substance they secrete in these circumstances known as cyclic adenosine monophosphate (cAMP). As a single body, they can then move toward sources of heat and moisture. Cyclic AMP sends out chemical messages that do the work of communication between the cells, in both plants and animals, and therefore of course in human beings.

Lévi-Strauss then suggests that social life in cluster groups of animals is perhaps 'the result of attraction between the individual cells that is strong enough to make them seek each other out, but not so strong that the attraction compels them to eat each other'.[39] 'Without laws', wrote a disciple of Epicurus in the third century BCE, quoted by Lévi-Strauss, 'we would live like wild animals and each would eat his fellow, the first one to come along.'

It is in the last paragraph of this article that the topic of violence reappears. Lévi-Strauss states that he places 'violence at the origin of life in society and . . . on foundations deeper than those who, with the sacrifice or the murder of the scapegoat, suppose society to be born from the customs that already suppose its existence'.[40] He is here alluding to the work of Arthur Hocart, a respected anthropologist who had studied the

---

39  Ibid., p. 495.
40  Ibid.

sacrifice of the scapegoat in Jewish and Greek Antiquity,[41] and to René Girard.[42]

In giving priority to communication as the basis of sociability and by using sociability to limit predation, Lévi-Strauss is maintaining the conclusion he reached in *The Elementary Structures* and even in the article he published in 1945 in the journal *Word*. But it would therefore seem that the fact that men exchange women, rather than the reverse, is not explained only by the appearance of symbolic thought, but also by the continuation of the violence presiding at the birth of the social order in the form of male domination.[43]

## Postface to 'Question de parenté' (2000)

This is, to the best of my knowledge, the last text in which Lévi-Strauss talked about kinship. It was written for a special issue of the journal *L'Homme* entitled 'Question de parenté', edited by Laurent Barry and which turned out to be a huge volume of 791 pages. Contrary to the dominant trend in Britain and the United States since the development of 'postmodernism', kinship studies are alive and well in France and continue to shed light on a number of questions, as the richness and diversity of the contributions to this volume show.

This collection of articles strongly challenges the thesis that kinship is founded on the exchange of women by men; certain authors, mimicking the deconstruction exercises practised in the Anglo-Saxon social sciences, even ask: 'Kinship . . . what is it good for?' Lévi-Strauss, invited to write the postface, graciously accepted. His is a short text (eight pages), which aims to do two things: on the one hand, to clear up misunderstandings about his work and respond to certain criticisms; and on the other, to indicate what he felt to be the importance of some of the studies presented in the volume which struck him as promising.

---

41  A. M. Hocart, *Social Origins* (London, Watts, 1954).

42  R. Girard, *La Violence et le sacré* (Paris, Grasset, 1972).

43  I must point out another, significant dimension of this text. Lévi-Strauss once more desists from presenting articulated language as having suddenly appeared once and for all. Now he suggests that articulated language modelled itself on another language that pre-formed it, and whose origin raises problems that are no longer the exclusive concern of psychologists and linguists. Cf. 'Apologue des amibes', p. 494.

In the first part of the text, we sense the author's irritation at the criticisms and his concern to set right what seemed to him to be misunderstandings. He often taxes his interlocutors with having too narrow a conception of exchange. Exchange is actually a very complex reality, he writes, in which three levels must be distinguished. The first level is the most general. All it takes is a single obstacle to the marriage for the exchange mechanism to be set in motion 'outside the conscious awareness' of the subjects. Here we encounter once more the affirmation found in the 'Apologue des amibes', which we have already commented on. How can the mechanism of exchange be set in motion 'outside conscious awareness', whereas, for an exchange to be carried out and repeated, the governing principle must be known, and its execution consciously implemented? The second, less general level corresponds to societies that define these prohibited degrees more clearly, either by linking them to degrees of kinship or by defining them between the exchanging units. Finally, any specific case of these generalized exchanges constitutes the last level, in which the exchange is restricted to the two units involved, in short, to the repeated exchange between two moieties or two clans. What has changed since *The Elementary Structures* (1949) is that exchange restricted to two exchanging units becomes a special case of generalized exchange, its 'lower limit'. Systems of the Kariera and Aranda types thus find themselves reclassified in the category of 'oriented generalized exchange'. Lévi-Strauss had already suggested this reclassification in the 1960s, when trying to show that South American dual organizations were pseudo-dual organizations structured by at least three dimensions (the third of which did not appear 'on the surface').

Lévi-Strauss then responds to the frequent accusation that he credited himself with having discovered the formula for generalized exchange, whereas it had already been identified by a pair of Dutch researchers in Indonesia and described under the name of 'circular *connubium*'. Lévi-Strauss had first answered this charge in 1967, in his Preface to the second edition of *The Elementary Structures*, where he explained that he had been unaware of the books of van Wouden and Josselin de Jong at the time he was writing his own.[44] But he also

---

44 F. A. E. van Wouden, *Sociale Structuurtypen in de Groote Oost* (Leiden, J. Ginsberg, 1935).

insinuated, without proof it seems, that Granet himself must at least have known about van Wouden's work, and had drawn on it for the analyses of the Kachin and Chinese he presented in *Catégories matrimoniales*.

Lévi-Strauss then goes on to the problem of the Na,[45] whom Chantal Collard had held up as an example of a kinship system without the exchange of women. Lévi-Strauss answered her with the same arguments as in 'Le Retour de l'oncle maternel', going back to the anecdote concerning Princess Diana's brother. Oddly he deduces that, if it no longer surprises anyone that the position of the maternal uncle is not what it was in the medieval European kinship system, given the 'disintegration of kinship structures' produced by the industrial revolution (not mentioned here), the inexistence of the husband or the father in the Na matrilineal system should not come as any more of a surprise. To this end, he cites information on the Na coming from other Chinese anthropologists than Cai Hua, who suggest another explanation for this system *sans* fathers or husbands: the aristocratic families of a patrilineal ethnic group would have forbidden marriage and imposed the rule of descent through the women on commoners. In short, the problems raised by the case of the Na are effectively dodged.

Next come the praise, the positive comments and the encouragements to pursue further research, addressed in the first place to those working on the controversial problem of Arab marriage, that is to say, union within the same lineage between a man and his father's brother's daughter. Where is the exogamy in this close endogamous marriage? Alongside the work of Laurent Barry,[46] Pierre Bonte[47] and Édouard Conte, Lévi-Strauss highlights the studies by Sophie Caratini[48] and Sophie Ferchiou, who independently of each other discovered (as I noted in a previous chapter) the existence of a hierarchy between givers and takers within a same lineage practicing 'marriage with the patrilateral cross cousin'. This

---

45  Hua, *Une Société sans père ni mari*.

46  L. S. Barry, 'Les Modes de composition de l'alliance. Le mariage arabe', *L'Homme*, n° 147 (1998), pp. 17–50; 'L'Union endogame en Afrique et à Madagascar', *L'Homme*, special issue 'Question de parenté', nos 154–155 (2000), pp. 67–100.

47  Bonte, ed., *Épouser au plus proche*.

48  S. Caratini, 'Système de parenté Sahraoui. L'impact de la révolution', *L'Homme*, special issue 'Question de parenté', pp. 431–56.

hierarchy, unnoticed until then by most anthropologists, was a sort of pseudo-relationship of internal exogamy at work within endogamous lineages. Lévi-Strauss points out this theoretically fruitful path. Then he exclaims:

> How many times must I repeat that it is indifferent from the theoretical standpoint whether men exchange women or vice versa – it suffices to reverse the signs and the system of relations remains unchanged. And supposing that the two sexes were held to be equal, one could say, which also comes down to the same thing, that groups of men and of women exchange kinship relations among themselves.[49]

As he sees it, it is well known that, in the majority of societies, people 'do or see things this way and, because it is so widespread, this disparity appears to be fundamental'.[50] And, for this reason, that is not where the problem lies. It lies in the argument Lévi-Strauss put forward in *The Elementary Structures* to explain why it is men who exchange women and not vice versa. Here again is his conclusion:

> The emergence of symbolic thought must have required that women, like words, should be things that were exchanged.
> [The exchange of women] is a primitive and indivisible act of awareness which sees the daughter or sister as a valuable which is offered, and vice versa the daughter and sister of someone else as a valuable which may be demanded.[51]

It was this explanation of why women are exchanged by men and not vice versa that immediately created a problem. The objection was not to male domination, it was to the explanation Lévi-Strauss proposed. For, if humans were endowed with the capacity for symbolic thought by nature, both women and men were equally endowed. Other reasons must therefore be sought. Lévi-Strauss did not look for these. Nothing in the rules of structural analysis justifies his explanation. And it is

49  C. Lévi-Strauss, 'Postface', *L'Homme*, special issue 'Question de parenté', p. 717.
50  Ibid., p. 718.
51  *The Elementary Structures of Kinship*, pp. 496, 139–40.

understandable if some felt insulted by his declaration, repeated on three occasions since 1949, that if women were shocked by his theory, they could always console themselves with the knowledge that nothing, from a theoretical standpoint, would change if it were they who exchanged the men and not vice versa.

Indeed, if male domination is explained by the appearance of symbolic thought, nothing can change women's condition. Their struggles, their demands, their resistance are useless. What more is there to say?

Likewise, it is no longer necessary to criticize the opposition, reiterated in the postface, between the 'natural' process of descent and the 'social' process of alliance. As we have shown, the rules societies develop to define which adults in their birth group the children belong to – descent principles – are thoroughly cultural and just as 'artificial' as alliance rules, be they positive or negative, prescriptive or merely preferential, etc. Yet on this fundamental point, as well as on that of the exchange of women, Lévi-Strauss's positions never wavered.

At the end of his postface, he adds a few words to underscore the growing interest presented by the study of cognatic systems. Already in 1967, the work of R. Firth, W. Goodenough and others in Polynesia had called his attention to these formerly little-known systems. And, when working on 'house' systems, he himself had tended to see cognatic systems as the structural background of all the systems he looked at, from Indonesia to Madagascar – systems that were ostensibly patrilineal or matrilineal and which appeared increasingly, as we have said, as pseudomorphs, the surface effects of power relations between paternal and maternal lines. Furthermore, he reminded his readers that, for him, cognatic systems more than any other showed how kinship relations were entangled with political or economic relations.

Yet he considered that the essential steps in these domains were the result of opening the formerly unknown world of Highland New Guinea to anthropological research. In second place, he cited the work on kinship in Amazonia, which dozens of years later had picked up again. However, he asked specialists of this region to beware the pitfalls of hermeneutics, due to the risk of attributing to the societies under study thoughts that were not theirs. The allusion to the work of Viveiros de

Castro is clear.[52] Lévi-Strauss's final words on kinship amount to a positive verdict: 'The treatment of kinship systems as a separate category, susceptible to be a specific area of study, no longer appears to be a simplification that is justified, from a methodological standpoint, by the needs of formalization.'[53]

52 Cf. E. Viveiros de Castro, *Métaphysiques cannibales* (Paris, Presses Universitaires de France, 2009).

53 'Postface', p. 719.

# 7

# Taking Stock – I

It is now time to take stock of Lévi-Strauss's work on kinship. I have attempted to analyse, step by step, all the significant texts, books and articles he published on this topic. Then they had to be put back, broadly, in the scientific context in which they appeared, together with who and what they opposed or agreed with. Finally, I needed to explain where I stand today on a number of issues that Lévi-Strauss had addressed. These are the three constraints I imposed on myself in the preceding pages, and I am well aware that I have all too quickly passed over one point or another.

If I had to sum up in one sentence the importance of his work in this area, without mentioning his contributions to other fields, the study of myths and mythical thought, for instance, I would say that, a century after Lewis H. Morgan, the original founder of this field, Lévi-Strauss set the scientific study of kinship on new foundations. And given the strategic position this study occupied in the birth and development of anthropology, Lévi-Strauss's writings on the subject inevitably had repercussions on the discipline as a whole.

Let us look back on this career from three angles: ambition, method and results. The ambition was clear at the outset: to develop a general theory of kinship, in three stages and three books.

The first part of the programme was fulfilled with *The Elementary Structures of Kinship*. The other two were partially realized in the form of articles and books spanning the duration of his career. We now know what criteria led Lévi-Strauss to classify all kinship systems, at the time, in two categories: elementary and complex. Elementary systems are those that prescribe marriage between certain types of kin, and therefore divide relatives into possible and forbidden spouses. This prescription is inscribed in the kinship terminology of the society concerned. Complex systems are those in which the choice of spouse is neither prescribed nor inscribed in the kinship nomenclature, but instead is determined by other criteria – political, economic, religious or other.

Suddenly, all known kinship systems found themselves classified, compared and distinguished on the basis of a single criterion: the alliance principle. But the originality of Lévi-Strauss's approach went much further. To conduct the analysis of these two great categories of systems, he started with a universal fact present in all systems, whatever their differences: the prohibition of incest. Leaving aside the many variants of this prohibition, Lévi-Strauss would draw a number of sociological conclusions in keeping with the empirical data typical of each of the known societies.

But Lévi-Strauss set his point of departure at an even more basic level, that of a reflection on the conditions and the forms of the passage from nature to culture, from the animal state of our remote ancestors to the human state of present-day *Homo sapiens*. He presented the prohibition of incest – the subordination of sexuality to social rules – as the site and condition of this passage. But its exploration required the mobilization of all the sciences, the natural sciences as well as the social sciences.

Such a theoretical horizon, taking in all the sciences, and the choice of a universal fact as the starting point of a series of sociological deductions, marked a radical break with the methods generally applied in anthropology and in the social sciences as a whole. And they endowed his approach with a universal dimension that appeared to be philosophical, but in fact had nothing to do with philosophy.

A chain of deductions ensued. If marriage is forbidden with certain relatives, and if this prohibition applies to all individuals and to all groups in a society, obviously these forbidden persons are available to others. Exchange thus becomes possible and necessary. And to exchange is to establish a reciprocal relationship, which implies that humans were conscious of the notion and the advantages of reciprocity. Lastly, owing to the incest prohibition, no kinship system can exist that does not entail the existence of some form of exchange, whether direct or indirect, immediate or deferred. Because of this, all systems involve some form of exogamy. Prohibition of incest/exchange/endogamy–exogamy are therefore the components of a 'structure' present in all kinship systems.

The key question then becomes: if the prohibition of incest implies renouncing unions within the immediate family and exchanging forbidden kin for authorized spouses, who exchanges what? The answer Lévi-Strauss gave in 1949 was clear. The men exchange the women, and not the other way around; and the primary reason for this is that, everywhere, it is men who have the monopoly of political and social power. To this factual explanation, Lévi-Strauss adds a second, 'structural', explanation, which in his eyes lies deeper and which, according to his hypothesis, is the basis for men's monopoly of power, and that is the emergence of symbolic thought and articulated language. For Lévi-Strauss, the appearance of symbolic thought immediately meant that women were perceived by men as values and signs, as the supreme asset that could be given or exchanged. He held fast to this idea throughout his life, despite a constant barrage of criticism.

Building on this series of sociological deductions, all presented as flowing from the prohibition of incest, Lévi-Strauss went on to mobilize the concepts he had deduced and defined in a specific theoretical perspective, with a view to analysing existing kinship systems. The first deduction concerned the difference of nature between cross and parallel female cousins, the former being possible spouses and the latter prohibited.

Armed with this array of concepts, already present in anthropology but which he had redefined, Lévi-Strauss embarked upon a successive examination of Australian systems, which were based on direct forms of exchange of women within a closed universe involving from four and up to eight groups, known as moieties, sections and subsections. He posited an equivalence between prohibitions formulated in ego-centred terms; prohibitions bearing on kin situated at a certain genealogical distance from Ego, in other words prohibitions formulated in terms of kinship relations; and prohibitions formulated in sociocentric terms, according to whether or not the individuals belonged to different sections or subsections. At the time, Lévi-Strauss could not have known – although Radcliffe-Brown had advanced the idea – that the sections and subsections were a relatively recent sociological and historical fact in Australia, and had not been invented to structure or resolve issues of kinship, since before their appearance Australians already had perfectly well-structured kinship systems. Today we know that these systems – except for the Murngin systems – were of the Dravidian type, which forbids marriage with the bilateral or patrilateral female cross cousin.

Based on this material, Lévi-Strauss showed the existence of two different structures underlying matrimonial exchanges: those relying on what he called restricted exchange, in which A gives to B and B gives to A, in a simple formula that can assume more complex forms; and generalized exchange, in which A gives to B who gives to C who gives to $n$, who gives to A. The distinction between the two exchange formulae made it possible to greatly simplify the comparison of kinship systems, and shed new light on the way they worked. In passing, Lévi-Strauss indulged in the pleasure of proposing a new interpretation of certain Australian systems that were the object of lively controversies. These were the so-called Murngin systems, whose deep structure he showed to be based on generalized exchange ($A \rightarrow B \rightarrow C \rightarrow A$) but which, with the arrival of sections, had been deformed by the Aboriginal peoples into a system of restricted exchange of the Aranda type, with eight subsections. Later studies were to prove him right.

We can now understand the tremendous shifts and changes of perspective induced by *The Elementary Structures of Kinship*. The effect was all the greater because its analyses were based on an immense store of erudition – the author's familiarity with the empirical data and debates amassed over more than half a century by anthropologists in the United States, Britain and Australia. Nothing comparable existed in France, or in Europe for that matter. It was Lévi-Strauss who constructed the necessary basis for the work of those to follow.

At the heart of these analyses lay a fundamental theoretical position that placed them beyond the conflicts between idealist and materialist approaches, deductive and inductive approaches, and so on. This was the affirmation that the production of kinship relations, like that of all other social relations, is an act that is at once mental *and* social, a synthesis of the two. Hence Lévi-Strauss's insistence on three intellectual conditions involved in the production of every possible form of matrimonial union. The first condition is the production and understanding of rules, norms that organize the behaviour of the individuals concerned and are imposed on all members of a society. The second is the understanding and implementation of reciprocal relations. The third is the understanding that the act of giving adds social value to the inherent value of the object given, since the act of giving transforms the relation between giver and receiver by binding them together in an alliance.

In pointing up these three – mental, intellectual – preconditions for any matrimonial alliance, Lévi-Strauss was highlighting operations whose source could only lie in the structures of the human mind, which is to say in the brain. And, for Lévi-Strauss, the structures of the human mind are universal and therefore are shared by all members of the human species, whatever the period in history and whatever the society. The universal nature of the deep structures of the human mind forbids the social sciences to conclude that the modes of thought and existence invented by humankind are always and absolutely relative. The relativity of human customs and institutions is real, but it is always limited and partial, not absolute.

Kinship systems can exist and be reproduced only if they are based on principles that generate and structure them. These structures are not a hidden reality, a substratum of social relations concealed by other components of the same system that appear on the surface:[1] they are nothing less than the logic behind the workings of the system as a whole, the logic of the principles that make up its deep structure, which is invariant. What is known as the structural analysis of kinship systems, as of any other system, consists therefore in looking for the principles that generate their structures and the logic underpinning their workings. And since these principles are not directly observable empirical facts, they must be reconstructed by making possible 'models', some of which will be a good fit for the workings observed. Lévi-Strauss thus posits 'structural' analysis as the only method capable of acceding to the principles that generate social systems, and therefore of acceding to their deep structures, which are not 'things' but logics governing relations between relations.

That is why, with *The Elementary Structures of Kinship*, Lévi-Strauss began to emphasize the importance of formulating the rules governing

---

1 C. Lévi-Strauss, *Structural Anthropology, Volume 2*, trans. M. Layton (Chicago, University of Chicago Press, 1983), 'La Structure et la forme. Réflexions sur un ouvrage de Vladimir Propp'. First published in *Cahiers de l'Institut de science économique appliquée*, n° 9 (1960), pp. 3–36: 'Structure has no content of its own: it is the content, apprehended in a logical organization conceived as a property of the real.' This is a fundamental definition.

the workings of kinship systems, either by dealing with them in the framework of an algebra or by using other logical-mathematical instruments. To this end he called on the mathematician, André Weil, whose algebraic study of Murngin marriage rules Lévi-Strauss had included in the book in the form of an appendix to the first part, in which he had defined and analysed the systems practicing restricted exchange.[2] Despite criticism from Malinowski, who condemned this 'algebraization' of kinship – a method he felt deprived kinship of its private, affective, emotional, content – the path opened by Lévi-Strauss proved fertile, and many anthropologists followed it with remarkable results. Among the many names deserving of mention, I will cite only two here: Floyd Lounsbury and Franklin Tjon Sie Fat. It can therefore be claimed that, even if Lévi-Strauss had published nothing but *The Elementary Structures of Kinship*, that book would have sufficed to shake up the field of kinship studies. But he did not stop there. He never ceased raising new issues, or proposing new takes on old problems.

The second wave of fundamental innovations was set off by the Huxley Memorial Lecture, given in 1965 before a select audience of English and American anthropologists. 'Semi-complex structures' was the new name Lévi-Strauss gave to the so-called Crow-Omaha systems, which he had promised, in *The Elementary Structures*, to tackle. He therefore removed from among the systems previously classified as Crow-Omaha all those that prescribed marriage with only one of the female cross cousins, the matrilateral cross cousin. Systems of this type were sent back to the category of systems with elementary structures. 'True' Crow-Omaha systems were those that multiplied the prohibitions on marriage between several lineages or clans having already contracted alliances in the generations preceding Ego's, but which did not prescribe whom to marry. For Lévi-Strauss, by their structure these systems marked the transition between elementary and complex structures. He also designated the Iroquois and Hawaiian systems as semi-complex structures, but he never analysed them.

The lecture made strong waves among anthropologists and, for some, opened new paths to explore. What was to be done with those systems having Crow-Omaha features that had been pruned from the 'true'

---

2  C. Lévi-Strauss, *The Elementary Structures of Kinship*, trans. J. H. Bell and J. R. von Sturmer and R. Needham, ed. (Boston, Beacon Press, 1969), chapter XIV, pp. 221–9.

Crow-Omaha tree? Asymmetric prescriptive systems, too, would have to be re-examined. Lévi-Strauss left this task to others.

But when he was writing *The Way of the Masks* (1975), Lévi-Strauss found himself before the same difficulties Boas had encountered in his attempt to characterize the kinship system of the Kwakiutl, notwithstanding decades of remarkable observation of these creators of the magnificent masks he so admired. Lévi-Strauss therefore undertook to solve the problem, which gave rise to a third series of innovations in the field of kinship theory. In 1979, in the second edition of *The Way of the Masks*, he showed that the Kwakiutl kinship system exemplified a family of systems familiar to historians of Medieval Europe, but never yet clearly identified by anthropologists. These were the 'house' systems.

In 1965, Lévi-Strauss had declared that it would not be possible to understand how complex structures worked until the problem of the Crow-Omaha systems had been resolved. But he now leapt over these in a single bound and began to analyse a species of 'complex' kinship systems that certainly did not feature in the catalogue of complex structures he had had in mind in 1949.

Lévi-Strauss was now confronted with a vast set of systems whose structural underpinnings fell into the category of so-called undifferentiated systems, in other words cognatic systems. From 1967, date of the second edition of *The Elementary Structures*, his attention had been drawn to these systems by the work of Ward Goodenough, and more particularly by that of Raymond Firth on the kinship systems of Polynesia. The internal flexibility that made it possible to determine which kin groups people belonged to, in a context in which these groups were neither truly patri- nor matrilineal but used one or the other principle in the service of political and economic interests, apparently placed them in the category of complex structures because of their general erasure of the oppositions other systems made between descent and alliance, and endogamy and exogamy. But such complex structures were usually found in tribal societies with ranked chiefdoms, or in political states where power resided in noble houses subordinated in varying degrees to a supreme house.

And so Lévi-Strauss set off on a journey around the world, via dozens of anthropological and historical monographs, in search of examples of 'house' societies. As he travelled from Indonesia to Madagascar, by way of Melanesia and Polynesia, he found many such societies – as well as imagining a few more. An important aspect of this journey is that it was also a voyage through time, meaning it was the historians of the European and Japanese Middle Ages who showed him the way. A new dialogue, a new collaboration between historians and anthropologists had become possible.

The last rebound unfortunately did not become known to his colleagues or to the broader public until after his death. In 1986, Lévi-Strauss had begun examining, with a Japanese audience in mind, the new forms of parenthood that had recently appeared in Western societies, some of which raised complex legal, political and ethical questions: surrogate mothers and same-sex parents, for instance, called definitions of filiation and alliance into question. Lévi-Strauss kept an open mind on all such topics, much more than many of his closest disciples, who continued to repeat that kinship rests on the exchange of women by men and for men.

Nor should we forget that Lévi-Strauss had published, at irregular intervals, three articles demonstrating the existence, in one or another kinship system, of what in 1945 he had christened the 'atom of kinship'. These articles are fragments, as it were, of the third book he had originally planned. It would have analysed the attitudes and behaviours exhibited by individuals occupying particular positions in the three kinship relations which, taken together, formed in his view the 'atom' of all kinship systems.

This is obviously a considerable achievement. When it comes to kinship studies, no other anthropologist in the second half of the twentieth century made so many new contributions to kinship theory, challenged so many accepted truths, aroused so much admiration and invited so much resistance, indeed rejection. To this creativity on the theoretical level must be added his immense erudition, informed by everything of significance that was published, his extremely rigorous demonstrations, his clear and exceptionally precise style – and finally his gift for polemics, in which he could be scathing and confident of his own worth.

Taken together, these merits and theoretical feats point to the conclusion that, with Lévi-Strauss, anthropology and its kinship studies had indeed been set on new foundations.

⤻

But however great a work may be, there are bound to be some flaws and limits. In the case of Lévi-Strauss, these were not always his fault but were often the effect of the era. No one, for instance, could blame him for not having seen that the sections he considered to be a key structure of the Australian kinship system were a historically recent invention, whose primary purpose had not been to transform the previous Dravidian-type systems. At the time, the distinction between Dravidian and Iroquois systems was not yet clear; but it is also true that, when Lounsbury's article later clarified their difference, Lévi-Strauss showed no particular interest in Dravidian systems, whereas studying them might have led him to a different analysis of the emergence and role of sections in Australia.

Even stranger is that having scrutinized dozens of kinship systems and societies in which the distinction between cross and parallel kin played a crucial role, and having long distinguished between marriages with the female bilateral cross cousin and those with the female matrilateral cross cousin, to the exclusion of the patrilateral cross cousin, or vice versa, Lévi-Strauss had not paid more attention to the discovery of the Dravidian systems in question, following Lounsbury and especially Buchler. It now appears that Dravidian-type systems were probably the most widespread of all, or at any rate, were those from which other systems clearly derived. But the existence of transformations at work in the structures of a system to engender another type of system – as can be seen or imagined in the case of the mutation of Dravidian systems into Iroquois systems – is the kind of problem, albeit fundamental to understanding the place of kinship in the evolution of societies, that never really interested Lévi-Strauss, except perhaps during his search for 'house' systems. But there, too, by making these a derivative of cognatic structures and undifferentiated systems, he never asked himself whether such systems were not themselves transformations of something earlier.

When it comes to Polynesia, the classic land of undifferentiated systems, it is now all but proven that these are transformations of Austronesian systems that contained the cross/parallel distinction. But that is not the essential weakness. The essential flaw lies in his repeated refusal to recognize that descent is just as crucial as alliance in the production and structuring of kinship relations within human societies. Lévi-Strauss, I must repeat, stubbornly ascribed to those principles that

defined descent, and thus determined who the children born of matrimonial unions belonged to, a 'secondary', 'nonessential' role in the way
kinship worked. He also always placed descent (he used the French
word *filiation*) on the side of nature (the biological process of making
children), and alliance on the side of culture.

Yet, as I have shown, rules determining descent  are every bit as
cultural and 'artificial' as alliance rules. There is no logic behind
whether one descends through men or through women, whether it is
the man's semen or the woman's clotted menstrual blood that makes
the foetus, or whether for these reasons the children belong to their
father's or their mother's clan, or to both but for different reasons.
These are merely cultural constructions, imaginary representations of
the life processes. Furthermore, it is mainly along the descent axis that
groups transmit what they have kept for future generations. And even
when marriage detaches and disperses pieces of an inheritance, the
strategies for repeating alliances after a certain number of generations
bring that which had been separated, or an updated equivalent, back
to the descent axis.

Descent principles are therefore the second invariant structure of any
kinship system. They are just as necessary, but for other reasons, as
alliance principles. Descent principles are few in number: the rule can
be unilineal, ambilineal, bilineal or undifferentiated. But all reflect the
role these societies ascribe to men and women when it comes to
appropriating children, and the responsibilities each sex is supposed to
exercise with regard to the children born of these unions. Four descent
principles are not a lot; and yet this number suffices to cover all the ways
a future child can be attached to one or the other, or one and the other,
of those who caused it to be born.

In fact, looking at the evolution of kinship relations in the West since
approximately the 1980s, of the two axes (descent and alliance) which
combine to produce kinship relations, descent has proved the more
stable, together with the concern shown in our societies to ensure that
children do not depend entirely on the vagaries of their parents'
relationship. Parents can separate, divorce, remarry, alternate custody of
the children; but their responsibility for the children they have produced
remains the same in the eyes of society – personified by the state –
whatever conflicts may oppose them, whatever the conditions of their
separation. Of course, what is at stake – except in certain social classes

– is not primarily, as it was in earlier centuries, the transmission of a name and a heritage. Today, children and childhood have taken on new significance and new value, linked to the defence of human rights in a democratic society. Children have rights vis-à-vis their parents. At a time when new forms of alliance are rife – free unions, cohabitation, etc. – and no longer have much to do with those of a Europe where marriage was a sacrament that could be broken only by one spouse's death, the descent axis remains the social bond in which the interplay of reciprocal rights and obligations between parents and children is the most constant, in most social classes. The future of kinship studies thus demands that we pay as much attention to descent as to alliance.

Another possible shortcoming of Lévi-Strauss's work is that he maintained to the end, without critical examination, the old idea that 'primitive' societies were 'kin-based societies' – even though he often said that kinship systems change when societies 'open themselves' more or less to history, and though this 'opening' may be due, as he said, to transformations in political and economic relations (he almost never mentions religion). But he would go no further.

What did not change for Lévi-Strauss was the idea that, at least in so-called 'primitive' societies – characterized by a kinship system with elementary structures prescribing a given form of marriage – kinship relations determine the overall configuration of the society. However, even if the role and weight of kinship relations change with the global structure of the society – with or without castes or classes, with chief-doms, a state, etc. – nowhere do kinship relations suffice to make a society and serve as its foundation. I repeat, this capacity belongs to what in the West we call political-religious relations.

There are other points awaiting debate; most prominently, the opposition Lévi-Strauss makes between structure and event, between necessity and contingency, between the analysis of structures and the analysis of the succession of facts and historical events. The Marc Bloch Lecture gave him an opportunity to advance along this path by allowing the assembled historians and anthropologists to show that the same structures, 'house' systems, existed in American Indian societies, in medieval Europe and in ninth-century Japan. But things went no further.

Another point, too, remained unanalysed: the respective roles of conscious and unconscious processes in the appearance of the principles and rules that make up a kinship system. We know that the structure of the so-called Iroquois systems is found in many societies the world over, all of which speak different languages and have never been in geographical or historical contact. Except that, for instance, the Iroquois Indians of North America follow a matrilineal descent principle, and the Baruya of New Guinea a patrilineal principle. This shows, contrary to what Lévi-Strauss thought, that descent principles are independent from alliance principles – and 'independent' does not mean that they play a secondary role. Their independence means that a system exists only through the necessary, and always particular, combination of a form of descent and a form of alliance. Furthermore, there is no negative (as in the prohibition of incest) or positive alliance rule that is not conscious. Were the contrary true, they could not be transmitted to following generations. And the fact that there are only a few logical ways of attaching the children born to a heterosexual couple means that the human mind easily reinvents these rules: it lights on them with no need to copy another group.

To conclude, I will mention two weak points in Lévi-Strauss's work. One is the proposition to classify all kinship systems into one of two regimes – harmonic and disharmonic – depending on whether residence and descent rules converge or differ and diverge. Harmonic regimes would, for instance, be those in which the descent rule is matrilineal and residence uxorilocal. Disharmonic regimes would be those in which descent is, say, patrilineal and residence uxorilocal. Lévi-Strauss believed he had found here a criterion for distinguishing restricted exchange systems, which he posited to be disharmonic, from generalized exchanges, which would be harmonic regimes. But this correlation failed to apply in too many cases for the hypothesis to be retained in its general form.

Finally, the last criticism, which I have already addressed at length: the explanation advanced by Lévi-Strauss for why it is the men who exchange the women and not the other way around. Lévi-Strauss always argued in his defence that male domination is a universal fact and not something he invented. The fact is undeniable, but not the explanation. And it is not this aspect of his work that will be retained by history; but neither will it diminish its stature.

# PART TWO
# Myths and Mythical Thought

When it comes to myths and mythical thought, analysing and assessing the work of Lévi-Strauss requires a change of method.

He inaugurated his work in 1951–52, during his first year of teaching at the École Pratique des Hautes Études. In 1951, Lévi-Strauss, whose *Elementary Structures of Kinship* had appeared at the Presses Universitaires de France two years earlier, and who had become a *maître de recherches* at the Centre National de la Recherche Scientifique, was made a *directeur d'études* at the École Pratique, succeeding Maurice Leenhardt, who had occupied the chair of 'Religions of Non-Civilized Peoples' (*sic*) from December 1901 to October 1940. Lévi-Strauss would change the name of the chair, which from 1954 was called 'Comparative Religions of Nonliterate Peoples'.[1] In 1959 Lévi-Strauss was elected to the Collège de France, to a chair created for him and entitled 'Social Anthropology', where he delivered his inaugural lecture on 5 January 1960.

Between 1951 and 2002, the date of his last article, 'De Grées ou de force?'[2] (devoted to the analysis of several Greek myths, which he

---

1 C. Lévi-Strauss, *Structural Anthropology, Volume 2*, trans. M. Layton (Chicago, University of Chicago Press, 1983), pp. 60–7.

2 C. Lévi-Strauss, 'De Grées ou de force ?' *L'Homme*, n°163 (2002), pp. 7–18.

compared with others collected from North American Indian groups), Lévi-Strauss published over forty articles devoted entirely to the study of several thousand myths, the bulk of which came from North and South American Indian societies. However, his first two books, *Totemism* and *The Savage Mind*, were based primarily on Australian material.

Nine further books would appear (by date of publication in France):

*Totemism* and *The Savage Mind* (1962)
*The Raw and the Cooked*, volume one in the Mythology series (1964)
*From Honey to Ashes*, volume two in the Mythology series (1966)
*The Origin of Table Manners*, volume three in the Mythology series
　　(1968)
*The Naked Man*, volume four in the Mythology series (1971)
*The Way of the Masks* (a second, augmented edition) (1975)
*The Jealous Potter* (1985)
*The Story of Lynx* (1991)

To these nine titles must be added four other books, which gather some ninety-four articles or summaries of courses given at the École Pratique des Hautes Études and then at the Collège de France. Of these, forty-four concern the analysis of various myths and rites, or are outlines or condensed versions of the above-cited works. The four collections are (by date of their French edition):

*Structural Anthropology* (1968)
*Structural Anthropology, Volume two* (1973)
*The View from Afar* (1983)
*Anthropology and Myth* (1984)

Lévi-Strauss retired at the end of 1982, and two years later the summaries of the courses he gave between 1951 and 1982 were collected and published in *Paroles données*, which appeared in English as *Anthropology and Myth*. These summaries throw a valuable light on the stages of his work in the two areas of kinship and myth, which, as we know, were to constitute the double axis of his research for over half a century. But, after the French publication of *The Elementary Structures of Kinship*, in 1949, it became clear that he was going to devote the bulk of his time and effort to the second, myths. I will let the reader judge. Between 1949, when he published his first two important articles on myths and rites, 'L'Éfficacité symbolique' and 'Le Sorcier et sa magie', and 2002, when he wrote 'De Grées ou de force?', Lévi-Strauss published forty articles on myths and mythical thought, in addition to the nine books already mentioned. By way of comparison, in those fifty years he would never publish another book on kinship, and of thirteen articles only two would, as I have shown, mark advances in this area. In view of these figures and bearing in mind the number and richness of the texts dealing with myths and mythical thought, it is clear that this became his foremost domain of scientific interest. However, he never lost interest in the area of art, since his final book, *Look, Listen, Read* (French edition in 1993), deals with painting (Poussin), literature (Diderot) and music (Rameau), and ends with two chapters on indigenous American arts. One is devoted to basketry, considered as a minor art in the West, but regarded as a noble art by the Plains Indians – Lévi-Strauss's last occasion to analyse American myths telling how once upon a time, baskets were humans. The other concerns the mystical character of the art of embroidery using porcupine quills, practised by the women of the Plains tribes, as well as the masks and sculptures produced by artists from the aristocratic lines of Northwest American and Canadian tribes, to which he devoted *The Way of the Masks*. Definitively repudiated are the non-figurative painting of Picasso, serial music and the like, which he had already condemned in the first and last volumes of his Mythology series.

It should be remembered that between 1947 and 1949, just as he was planning to devote his life to the study of kinship and myths, Lévi-Strauss would definitively renounce any interest in politics, as an actor and even more decisively as an activist.

The quality and the quantity of the publications Lévi-Strauss devoted to myths and mythical thinking make it difficult to take the same approach as I did when analysing his writings on kinship. A systematic treatment by chronological order of publication is impracticable for two reasons. Firstly, it is not possible to analyse in detail such an enormous mass of texts, for that would suppose summarizing all over again the 2,000 or so myths that make up the raw material. And secondly, because one monument overshadows all the rest: the four volumes of the Mythology series (variously termed 'Mythologiques' or 'Introduction to a science of mythology', neither of which titles he liked), to which Lévi-Strauss dedicated nearly ten years of his life.

He had begun research on this project in 1961, even before the publication of *Totemism* and *The Savage Mind*. At the time, he was fully in possession of the method and the hypotheses he would use to tackle the huge body of Amerindian myths. Three years later, in 1964, the first volume would appear in French, *The Raw and the Cooked*. It would be followed two years later by the second volume, *From Honey to Ashes* (1966) and then by *The Origin of Table Manners* (1968). Finally, after a three-year pause, the last and thickest volume of the tetralogy, *The Naked Man* (1971), appeared. In effect, if we are to believe what he confided to Didier Eribon, exhausted by ten years of intense labour, he was anxious to finish and decided to wind up the book at a moment when he was discovering new cycles of myths concerning the origin of potting clay and that of wind and fog. He decided to cut short the project and close an analysis that promised to be interminable.[3]

But his resolve did not last long. After another decade, in which he would publish several collections of articles – *Structural Anthropology, Volume two* (1973), *The View from Afar* (1983), *Anthropology and Myth* (1984) – in addition to a book on art that would lead him to discover a new component of kinship theory, the concept of 'house', *The Way of the Masks* (1975, 1979), he brought out *The Jealous Potter* (1985). In it, he returned to and developed the analysis of a group of myths that first appeared in the final pages of *The Naked Man*, which explain the origin of potting clay and the firing techniques used in the art of ceramics.[4] Six years later, in 1991, the French edition of *The Story of Lynx* came out, which was to be his last book devoted to mythology. Here he developed a theme also present in *The Naked Man*, namely: the correlation and opposition between Fog and Wind as natural agents and supernatural actors. His very last text on myths would be, as I have said, the article entitled 'De Grées ou de force', published in the journal *L'Homme* in 2002.

From all the texts published after the Mythology books, with which I am acquainted in detail, I will excerpt useful quotations without pausing

---

3 C. Lévi-Strauss and D. Eribon, ed., *Conversations with Claude Lévi-Strauss*, trans. P. Wissing (Chicago and London, University of Chicago Press, 1991). Didier Eribon, commenting on the Mythology series: 'The result is vast; several hundred pages a volume, almost two thousand pages in all.' Claude Lévi-Strauss: 'Mostly I remember the trouble those books gave me. That's even more than the result!' (p. 90).

4 C. Lévi-Strauss, *The Naked Man*, trans. J. and D. Weightman, *Mythologiques, Volume 4* (Chicago, University of Chicago Press, 1981), pp. 610, 615–16, 619–20, 624.

further. There is a simple reason for this. When Lévi-Strauss tackled the planning and writing of his Mythology series, he had fully mastered his hypotheses and his method: the structural analysis of myths. After the four volumes, he continued to apply the same method to other myths. Nothing was different except for one point. In the nearly 2,000 pages of the Mythology series, there are only three allusions to what he had called, in 1955, the 'canonical formula of myth transformation'.[5] This formula designated at the time a 'double inverted group of transformations'.[6] But I will return to this later. In contrast, after the Mythology series, references to the 'canonical formula' began to crop up incessantly and even multiply. The expression occurs three times in *Anthropology and Myth*,[7] five times in *The Jealous Potter*,[8] six times in *The Story of Lynx*.[9] Rarely did Lévi-Strauss expand on this formula: sometimes he merely alluded to it in passing, leaving its reconstruction to the reader, and yet he had never really explained how he had originally gone about constructing it. Which explains the objections advanced by many anthropologists, who deemed 'the canonical formula of myth transformations' not only unintelligible but of no use for understanding Lévi-Strauss's analyses. I will return to this problem, but let me indicate here the important book by Lucien Scubla, exploring Lévi-Strauss's usages of this mysterious formula as well as the different reactions it aroused – sceptical, frankly negative or positive to the point of enthusiasm.[10]

In addition to this new emphasis on putting the famous 'canonical formula' to work, a second difference sets *The Story of Lynx* apart from the preceding works. In the penultimate chapter, vaguely connected

---

5 In *Structural Anthropology*, trans. C. Jacobson and B. Grundfest Schoepf (New York, Basic Books, 1963), pp. 228–9.

6 C. Lévi-Strauss, *The Raw and the Cooked: Introduction to a Science of Mythology* 1, trans. J. and D. Weightman (Harmondsworth, Penguin, 1986), pp. 216ff.

7 C. Lévi-Strauss, *Anthropology and Myth: Lectures, 1951–1982*, trans. R. Willis (London, Blackwell, 1987), Preface, Part 3, chapter VII and Part 5, chapter VI, pp. 4, 114 (a simple reference without the exact term).

8 C. Lévi-Strauss, *The Jealous Potter*, trans. B. Chorier (Chicago, University of Chicago Press, 1988), pp. 57, 126, 156, 170.

9 C. Lévi-Strauss, *The Story of Lynx*, trans. C. Tihanyi (Chicago, University of Chicago Press, 1995), pp. 104, note, 146, 179, 188–9, 208–9.

10 L. Scubla, *Lire Lévi-Strauss* (Paris, Odile Jacob, 1998), pp. 125–97. The last product of such enthusiasm to my knowledge was M. S. Mosko and F. H. Damon, eds, *On the Order of Chaos: Social Anthropology and the Science of Chaos* (New York, Berghahn Books, 2005).

with the analysis of the twins theme in Amerindian mythology and devoted to the sixteenth-century French author Michel de Montaigne, Lévi-Strauss offers us a very personal piece of philosophy, his vision of humankind and of himself, espousing the lesson of Montaigne's 'Apology for Raymond Sebond', namely: that one must content oneself with living 'as if [life] had a meaning, even though intellectual honesty assures that this is not so'.[11] And it is not so because, in the order of nature as in that of knowledge, 'we have no communication with Being'. The formula – expressing a radical doubt – is not that of Lévi-Strauss but of Montaigne. But he seems to have adopted it wholeheartedly, as he would confirm, in 2004, in his correspondence with Victor Stoczkowski.[12]

Although it is not the purpose of the present book, I will say a few concluding words about the man behind the work, who is also often present at its heart. We perceived this presence in Part One, when, for example, Lévi-Strauss was trying to explain why – if kinship comes down to exchange – it is the women who must be exchanged by the men, and not vice versa. This intrusion of a subjective judgment could not be justified by any kind of analysis, structural or other. But, on a deeper level, we discern an overall attitude in the face of life events, the events of his own life, a mixture of misanthropy and wisdom, which compelled the man to 'act as if' life and knowledge had meaning without ever referring to something 'beyond' that might contain a promise of 'salvation', a word he found repellent.

I will devote a first section to Lévi-Strauss's path, from his early research on Amerindian mythology (1951–53) to the publication of the first volume in the Mythology series, *The Raw and the Cooked* (1964). During this period, Lévi-Strauss developed his method step by step and formulated his first hypothesis on the nature of 'mythical thought'. The pivotal text is his 1955 article, 'The Structural Study of Myth', published in the *Journal of American Folklore* in a special issue devoted to the papers presented at a symposium on myth.[13] Several other texts marked

---

11 *The Story of Lynx*, chapter XVIII, 'Rereading Montaigne', p. 216.

12 Lévi-Strauss's letters to the author, dated 9 and 22 November 2006, in V. Stoczkowski, *Anthropologies rédemptrices* (Paris, L'Harmattan, 2008), pp. 332–5, 'Le monde selon Lévi-Strauss'.

13 C. Lévi-Strauss, 'The Structural Study of Myth', in 'Myth, A Symposium', *Journal of American Folklore* 78, n° 270 (October–December 1955), pp. 428–44. Translation with complements in *Structural Anthropology*, pp. 206–31.

this period as well: a long article first published in the 1958–59 *Annuaire* of the École Pratique des Hautes Études, fifth section, pp. 3–43, entitled 'La Geste d'Asdiwal', and, of course, the two books published in rapid succession in French in 1962. Of these, *Totemism* preceded and introduced *The Savage Mind*.

I will single out in each of these texts the elements of method and hypotheses that were appearing for the first time, and would serve the elaboration of the Mythology books. My primary goal is to reconstruct the toolkit used in the structural analysis of myths, for the same tools and the same methods are used in analysing the 2,000 myths of the Mythology series and the hundreds of others presented later in *The Jealous Potter* and *The Story of Lynx*, as well as in the score of articles published after *The Naked Man*.

Among others, allow me to cite: 'Le Temps du mythe' (Mythical time, 1971), 'Comment meurent les mythes' (How myths die, 1971), 'Mythe et oubli' (Myth and forgetting, 1975), 'Quand le mythe devient histoire' (When myth becomes history, 1985), 'Mythe et musique' (Myth and music, 1993): titles that each time show Lévi-Strauss using mythic material to elucidate the relations entertained by mythical thought with history, certain modes of existence, etc. Other texts, such as 'Le Sexe des astres' (The sex of stars, 1967), 'Pythagore en Amérique' (Pythagoras in America, 1979), 'Hérodote en mer de Chine' (Herodotus in the China Sea, 1987), 'Exode sur *Exode*' (Exodus on *Exodus*, 1988), 'De Grées ou de force?' (a pun on 'de gré ou de force', or willy-nilly, 2002), were written in homage to certain colleagues – Jakobson, Dumézil, Aron, Vernant, etc. In these, Lévi-Strauss takes pleasure in surprising his readers and keeping them in suspense, leading them in the space of a few pages of rigorous and brilliant exposition to the solution of an 'impossible' problem set out at the beginning. Many of these are intellectual gems.

After this first section, I will tackle the Mythology series. As I have said, to try to summarize the 818 myths and as many variants analysed step-by-step by Lévi-Strauss over the span of the four volumes of his tetralogy would be senseless. I leave it to the reader to peruse them, and that will take time – several months – and patience, if not a good dose of stubbornness. The reading is made difficult by the fact that, on nearly every page, the author introduces one or two new myths, tying them into several others analysed in the same volume or in one of the preceding volumes, and it is hard for the reader to keep them all in mind.

For the present, and to simplify, let me say that Lévi-Strauss's undertaking is anchored in a reference myth which relates the misadventures of a bird-nester. This tale is found in the mythology of the Bororo, an indigenous group in central Brazil. He goes on to show that this myth reverses several myths from another ethnic group that are the Bororo's neighbours to the north, the large linguistic group of Ge tribes. Then, proceeding from one permutation to the next, Lévi-Strauss finds and follows the same theme all the way to the myths of the Salish Indians on the Northwest coast of the United States, thousands of miles from the central Brazilian home of the Bororo and the Ge.

I will, of course, summarize the key myth and one of the final myths, as well as three others that act as links between the mythology of the South American Indian groups and those of North America. This is the case of a certain Tukuna myth (M354, vol. 3),[14] which belongs to a South American culture in the sub-Andean region. This myth plays a very important role because, according to Lévi-Strauss, it does not refer to any other South American myth but is illuminated as soon as it is compared with myths from some North American Indian groups, which, to be sure, have never had any contact with the Tukuna. This realization opened a two-way trail of myths running between South and North America, each step along which further demonstrated the respective identities of Amerindian societies 'within the framework of a common conception of the world'.[15]

I have included a map so that the reader may locate a few of the main groups cited. I have also drawn up a table of the natural elements and the aspects of society whose nature and origin the myths purport to explain – that being their etiological function. These explanations compose a universe that is a blend of metaphysics and fantasy, which I will describe briefly. Of course, they were true for those who listened to such stories and 'believed' them. But beneath their explicit sense the myths concealed other meanings, implied in the construction of the myth, which only structural analysis could expose. To discover these

---

14 C. Lévi-Strauss, *The Origin of Table Manners*, trans. J. and D. Weightman (Chicago, University of Chicago Press, 1978), pp. 25–8.

15 *The Raw and the Cooked*, p. 8.

meanings is to reveal the semantic function of myths, a function both mobilized and concealed by the mythical discourse and the problem it seeks to express, if not to resolve. The two functions of myths, etiological and semantic, are separate. They do not exclude but rather complete each other. However, one is manifest and the other is not.

When we have made our way through the Mythology series, I will address my principal objective, which is to inventory and define the hypotheses and methods used by Lévi-Strauss in practicing structural analysis on a corpus of myths. I will conclude Part Two of this book by taking stock of the power, but also the limits, of Lévi-Strauss's endeavour.

# 8

## The Major Steps in Lévi-Strauss's Elaboration of His Concepts, Method and Hypotheses (1952–1962)

In Part Two, we will follow Lévi-Strauss as he develops what he called the structural analysis of myths and mythical thought. We will see certain concepts or definitions emerge that will be found in later texts. The initial stage began in 1952–54, with the courses he gave at the École Pratique des Hautes Études, and ended in 1962, with the publication of *Totemism*, which served as an introduction to *The Savage Mind*, published shortly after. In 1962, he defined mythical thought as 'thought in its savage state', meaning not yet domesticated for the purpose of yielding a return, rather than as the thought of savages or primitive humans. *The Savage Mind* ends with a polemical chapter aimed at Sartre and all those who assign a special value to history as the succession of events and facts, and as a discipline. He would return to this theme in the final pages of *From Honey to Ashes* and in the conclusion to *The Naked Man*.

Upon arriving at the École Pratique des Hautes Études, Lévi-Strauss threw himself into the study of Amerindian mythology and embarked on an analysis of the relations between myth and ritual. Prior to 1962, he had published four texts, two of which are fundamental theoretical works, while the other two enabled him to test his method for the first time.

The two theoretical texts were 'The Structural Study of Myth', published at the end of 1955 in the *Journal of American Folklore*, and 'Structure and Form', published in early 1960 in the *Cahiers de l'Institut de science économique appliquée*.

The two texts in which he tried out his method are 'The Story of Asdiwal', published in 1958 in the EPHE yearbook, and 'Four Winnebago Myths', written in 1959 in honour of Paul Radin but published only in 1960, after the latter's death.

The venture began therefore in 1952, when Lévi-Strauss decided to devote his courses to Research in American Mythology. In 1952–53, he studied the emergence myth found among the Hopi, Zuni and Acoma Indians, of the Pueblo group. At this time, he developed his first hypotheses, namely: that a myth is comprised of *all its versions* and that the myth's structure is reproduced within each version. Myth is language, and mythological language is a sort of *metalanguage* whose constituent units, themes or sequences acquire meaning only when articulated into a system. Ways must therefore be found to isolate these components, but not as folklorists do, arbitrarily singling out such and such a theme or word in the myths. Furthermore, the components of a myth must be examined to see whether they are *permutable*, and whether the variations in the structure *correspond* to the economic and sociological conditions in which each Indian group lived. The concepts of metalanguage, permutability, constituent units and correspondence with socio-economic conditions can be found throughout the rest of his work.

In 1953–54, he continued his research into the emergence myth, this time among the eastern Pueblo peoples – the Keres, Tiwa and Tewa – outlining a comparison with Western mythology and the work of Dumézil. Lévi-Strauss advanced the idea that myths often have the function of mediating between opposing extremes: *qualitative* logic and *mediation* between *opposing extremes* became accepted as new concepts.

In 1954–55, Lévi-Strauss tackled a classic problem: that of the relationship between myth and ritual. In that year's course he analysed in detail a complex Pawnee Indian ritual, using a work by Alice Fletcher published in 1904, *The Hako: A Pawnee Ceremony*, which had influenced Hocart. After detailing the symbols, behaviours and ideas involved in this ceremony, Lévi-Strauss concluded, first, that the Pawnee did not have a myth that founded the ritual as a whole and, second, that the myth and the rite completed each other, but their structures were inverted.

Lévi-Strauss refused to accept the trivial thesis that a ritual was an 'enacted' myth. Rituals have specific functions, and their signifying value is contained entirely in the gestures and instruments involved. While myths are a metalanguage, rituals are a *'paralanguage'*. Lévi-Strauss would go on to develop his thesis of the *opposition between myth and ritual* in the conclusion to *The Naked Man*. The term *'paralanguage'* appeared together with the idea that the meaning of a ritual resides above all in the gestures performed and the objects handled, and not in an implicit myth.

In 1954, in a review of a group of books for *Diogène*, Lévi-Strauss advanced the idea that myths could make do with any linguistic support without losing their communicability, which shed some light on his idea of myth as metalanguage. In 1955, in a lecture given in Rome on 'Cosmic Symbolism in Social Structure and the Ceremonial Organization of Several North and South American Peoples', published in 1957, he began by recalling the symbolism of the Sun temple and the Sun garden in Cuzco. He went on to suggest that when it comes to studying myths and rituals, 'it is perhaps preferable to envisage more primitive societies', since unlike the Inca and the Aztecs, they have been observed up to recent times; and also because cosmic symbolism can be found in socie-ties that have no temples or religious monuments. To demonstrate this, he took examples from the Pueblo Indians, then the nomadic Navajo and finally the Pawnee, all in North America, and from the Apinaye, the Ge, the Sherente and the Bororo in South America. He showed how the rituals incorporated this symbolism in the social structure and residen-tial patterns of these groups, and that this symbolism always presented itself as a vast system of correspondences between cardinal points, meteorological phenomena, animal and plant species, colours, gods, etc., following a veritable *qualitative logic*, the rules of which needed to be uncovered.

## 'The Structural Study of Myth' (1955)

In 1955 'The Structural Study of Myth' was published. A veritable mani-festo for the structural analysis of myths, it was initially addressed to Anglo-Saxon specialists. In it, Lévi-Strauss set out the following theses: a myth is made up of all its variants; there is no true version of a myth; the substance of the myth resides in the story it tells; a myth is composed of constituent units, or 'mythemes', which are 'clusters of relations'.

What operations need to be performed in order to identify the 'structural law' of the myth, its 'genetic law'? Lévi-Strauss demonstrates the procedure, using three examples: the Oedipus myth, a Zuni myth and a Plains Indian myth. All known variants of the myth must be laid out in a series. Any mythemes present must be arranged, by theme, into columns. When this is done, we see that a myth, taken as all the variants the analyst has been able to arrange into a complete series, presents itself as a 'permutation group' and possesses a layered structure, in which 'the two variants placed at the far ends [are] in a symmetrical, though inverted, relationship to each other'.[1]

This method reveals the logical operations underpinning mythical thought. Mythical thinking begins with a number of oppositions, and tends toward their progressive mediation. As early as 1955, Lévi-Strauss practically took it for granted that every myth, taken as the totality of its variants, could be reduced to a canonical relation, for which he proposed a mathematical formula:

$$F_x(a) : F_y(b) : : F_x(b) : F_{a1}(y)$$

where $a$ and $b$ are two terms being given simultaneously, together with the functions $x$ and $y$, a relation of equivalence is posited between two situations defined by an inversion of the terms ($a$ is replaced by $a$-1, its opposite) and by an inversion between the function value of one element ($F_y$) and the term value of another element ($a$); $Fy$ becomes a term ($y$) and the inverse of the term ($a$) becomes a function ($F_{a1}$). Many anthropologists have deemed this formula incomprehensible and/or useless. On the other hand, a minority has seen it as the key to understanding the deep structure of myths. I will discuss the formula itself when I come to reconstruct the toolkit Lévi-Strauss put together for the analysis of myths. But allow me to point out as of now that, having arrived at this formula in 1955, Lévi-Strauss would allude to it once again, with no further development, in his 1956 article 'Structure and Dialectic', and just three times in his Mythology series (1964–71); but it would subsequently be very present in the *Anthropology and Myth* lectures (1984) and even more frequent in *The Jealous Potter* (1985) and *The Story of Lynx* (1991).

1 C. Lévi-Strauss, *Structural Anthropology*, trans. C. Jacobson and B. Grundfest Schoepf (New York, Basic Books, 1963), p. 223.

Ultimately, according to this first article, for Lévi-Strauss a myth is an 'absolute object' insofar as it exists both in language and above the linguistic level, both diachronically (what it tells, a series of events) and synchronically (its deep structure). Mythical time is therefore both non-reversible (it is the time in which events unfold until the end of the tale) and reversible (the underlying structure of the myth is timeless). But that still does not imply the existence of Jungian archetypes in mythical thinking. Finally, mythical thinking is logical, not apparently very dissimilar from scientific thinking – and every bit as rigorous. The difference between the two, again according to Lévi-Strauss, resides in the different nature of the things to which they are applied. Humans have always thought equally well. Lévi-Strauss concludes that structural analysis has made it possible to shine new light on the mythology of the North American Indians, even as certain logical operations of mythical thinking in general have begun to be identified.

This is a truly founding text. In it are defined for the first time: the notion of 'mytheme' as a constituent unit of myths; the notion of 'permutation groups' to define the myth under study as the totality of its variants; the idea that the group is closed and that the first and last variants in the group are related symmetrically and inversely; and the idea that there is a canonical formula that expresses the structural law of myths, which can be represented by algebraic symbols and relations. Lastly, the reader will note the author's insistence that mythical thinking and positivist (scientific) thinking are not, or not very, different. This would be a recurring leitmotif throughout his life. Meanwhile, save for the work of Dumézil, Lévi-Strauss deems that little progress has been made in the anthropology of religion, which 'remains the same as it was fifty years ago, namely, chaotic':

Myths are still widely interpreted in conflicting ways: as collective dreams, as the outcome of a kind of esthetic play, or as a basis of ritual. Mythological figures are considered as personified abstractions, divinized heroes or fallen gods. Whatever the hypothesis, the choice amounts to reducing mythology either to idle play or to a crude kind of philosophic speculation.[2]

---

2 *Structural Anthropology*, p. 207.

In the wake of this founding text, Lévi-Strauss undertook to test his concepts and method by analysing two sets of myths. This resulted in three publications: 'Structure and Dialectic' (1956), 'The Story of Asdiwal' (1958) and 'Four Winnebago Myths: A Structural Sketch'[3] (written in 1958 and published in 1960).

## 'Structure and Dialectic' (1956)

This text, written in homage to Roman Jakobson, develops the theme of the relations between mythology and ritual that had been the subject of a course given by Lévi-Strauss in 1954–55.[4] Here he returns to the analysis of a myth told by the Pawnee Indians of the North American plains, the myth of the 'pregnant boy', which explains the origin of certain shamanic powers – those that are inborn, not acquired. He demonstrates that the Pawnee myth does not correspond to one of their own rituals but to one performed by their neighbours, the Mandan, the Hidatsa and other Plains groups, which is the symmetrical opposite of the Pawnee myth. Lévi-Strauss then goes on to refute two theories that had prevailed among anthropologists and sociologists since Malinowski and Durkheim, or Lévy-Bruhl and Van der Leeuw. For the first, each myth was 'the ideological projection of a rite, the purpose of the myth being to provide a foundation'; for the second, it was 'a kind of dramatized illustration of the myth' in the form of moving pictures, as it were.

> Regardless of whether the myth or the ritual is the original, they replicate each other; the myth exists on the conceptual level and the ritual on the level of action. In both cases, one assumes an orderly correspondence between the two – in other words, a homology.[5]

Using the Pawnee and Hidatsa examples, Lévi-Strauss goes on to show that this is not a general homology and that if there are some correspondences between myth and ritual, these are only rarely homologies. They entertain a more complex dialectic, which is

---

3 Ibid.
4 Lévi-Strauss, 'Structure and Dialectic', *Structural Anthropology*, pp. 232–41.
5 Ibid., p. 232.

accessible only once the myth and the ritual have been broken down into their structural elements. He then outlines the structural analysis of several versions of the myth of the pregnant boy, pointing out in passing that, were he to go further, he could uncover the 'rules of transformation which enable us to shift from one variant to another using operations similar to those of algebra'. But he does not do this. Then he analyses the relations between this Pawnee myth and a ritual that is not specific to the Pawnee but is also shared by the Mandan and the Hidatsa, showing that they represent 'so many groups of permutations whose formula is an equivalence between the opposition father/son and the opposition man/woman'. This is also suggested by the canonical formula for myths that appeared in 'The Structural Study of Myth', to which Lévi-Strauss refers explicitly here, without further discussion.[6]

The relation between myth and ritual is therefore dialectical, and is more complex than a relation of homology. To analyse this relation, it is not enough to compare the myths with the ritual practices found in a given society. They must also be compared with 'the beliefs and practices of neighbouring societies'. Which leads him to conclude:

> One cannot rest content with a purely formal analysis. Such an analysis constitutes a preliminary stage of research, which is fruitful to the extent that it permits the formulation of geographical and historical problems in more rigorous terms than is customary. Structural dialectics does not contradict historical determinism, but rather promotes it by giving it a new tool.[7]

This text is a step forward for his theory from several standpoints. The problem of the relations between myth and ritual is set on new foundations. The operations involved in mythical thinking are explicitly compared with those of algebra. Finally, the formal analysis of myths is considered as a prerequisite whose outcome – if we look not merely at the myths in a single society but also at those present within a group of geographically close and historically connected societies – can shed a penetrating light on their real connections and the causes

---

6  Ibid., pp. 235–9.
7  Ibid., p. 240.

that have made them what they are (historical determinism). When this is done, the deep meaning of these myths begins to appear.

It is noteworthy that this was the first time Lévi-Strauss refuted the earlier accusation that his method was a purely formal procedure, reducing myths to abstractions devoid of any real sociological or historical content. He responded vigorously to this criticism in an article entitled 'Structure and Form', published in 1960 and devoted to the work of the eminent Russian folklorist, Vladimir Propp, *Morphology of the Folktale*. But it was not until the Mythology series[8] that he explicitly formulated the three phases of the analysis of a body of myths: formal analysis, ethnographic and historical analysis, and semantic analysis.

In the meantime, and before acquainting himself with Propp's work – published for the first time in English in 1958 – Lévi-Strauss would twice test his method on two groups of myths having several variants, one of which apparently did not jibe with the others. This produced 'The story of Asdiwal', in 1958, and then 'Four Winnebago Myths', published in 1960 but written, as I have said, in 1959.

## 'The Story of Asdiwal' (1958)

'The Story of Asdiwal' analyses four versions of a myth collected by Franz Boas at the end of the nineteenth century from the Tsimshian Indians on the Northwest coast of the United States. The Tsimshian were divided into four nonlocalized exogamous matrilineal clans, which were themselves divided into lineages and houses. The society was organized into chiefdoms ruled by a tribal aristocracy. In the story, a young widow is visited by a mysterious figure one night she and her own mother, also a widow, are about to die from hunger near the bank of a frozen river. The visitor marries the younger woman and subsequently provides the two women with food in abundance. A son is born, Asdiwal, whom his father makes grow through a magical process before disappearing, after having given him some magic objects: a bow, arrows that always hit their target, snowshoes, an invisibility cloak, etc. This is the beginning for Asdiwal of a series of travels, marriages in remote groups and

---

8 Often referred to by the title chosen by the publishers, *Mythologiques*, which Lévi-Strauss did not particularly like.

adventures. When he at last returns to his family, he goes hunting, leaving his snowshoes behind. After a successful hunt, he finds himself stuck halfway up a mountain, unable to go either up or down. He turns into a rock that has been contemplated by the Indians ever since.

From a logical point of view, Asdiwal's adventures take the form of 'a series of impossible mediations between oppositions which are ordered in a descending scale: high and low, water and earth, sea hunting and mountain hunting, and so forth'.[9]

As Lévi-Strauss himself explains, his study has two aims: (1) to compare the different versions and interpret the discrepancies between them; and (2) to isolate and compare the different levels on which the myth evolves: geographical (hence a map of the places visited by Asdiwal and of his travels), economic (fishing for salmon and candlefish, hunting), sociological (though here the picture does not correspond to reality on all points: the hero's marriages are most often matrilocal, not patrilocal as marriage actually was), and cosmological (the hero's two imaginary voyages, one to heaven and the home of the Sun, who brings him back to life, the other to the subterranean realm of the sea lions he has wounded but which he heals). The native mind does not differentiate among the four levels of the myth: the real (levels 1 and 2) and the imaginary (level 4) via a mixture of the two (level 3).

> It is rather that everything happens as if the levels were provided with different codes, each being used according to its particular capacity, to transmit the same message.[10]

Comparing the beginning of the narrative with the end, Lévi-Strauss shows that, having begun by 'the story of the reunion of a mother and her daughter, freed from their affines or paternal kin [the Tsimshian are matrilineal and the father is an affine], the myth ends with the story of the *reunion of a father and his son*, freed from their affines *or maternal kin*'.[11]

This would confirm the hypothesis, presented in the 1955 article, that the first and last versions of a myth stand in a relation of symmetry and

9 C. Lévi-Strauss, *Structural Anthropology, Volume 2*, trans. M. Layton (Chicago, University of Chicago Press, 1976), p. 160.

10 Ibid., p. 158; emphasis added.

11 Ibid., p. 156.

inversion with respect to each other. Lévi-Strauss goes on to draw a theoretical conclusion from his analysis that leads him to distinguish, in the construction of a myth, what he calls sequences and schemata.

> The sequences form the apparent content of the myth, the chronological order in which things happen: the meeting of the two women, the intervention of the supernatural protector ... his successive marriages, his hunting and fishing expeditions, his quarrels with his brothers-in-law, and so forth.
>
> But these sequences are organized on planes at different levels of abstraction in accordance with schemata, which exist simultaneously, superimposed one upon the other; just as a melody composed for several voices is held within bounds by two-dimensional constraints: first by its own melodic line, which is horizontal, and second by the contrapuntal schemata, which are vertical.[12]

The method advocated in 1955 of breaking down the myth and organizing the elements into a diachronic sequence in columns or into synchronic rows is thus confirmed. In fact, Lévi-Strauss would soon call them simply syntagmatic chains and paradigmatic columns.

He then reduces the myth to the opposition between its first and last versions, and builds a simplified table, which lays out the oppositions along two axes (a new term)[13]:

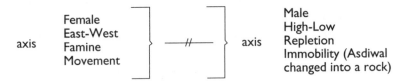

The transformation of the terms into their opposites, their inversion and the passage from one axis to another make up the both logical and formal structure of the message. The meaning remains to be decoded. For Lévi-Strauss, as we know, the meaning of a myth is not to be confused with its 'apparent content'. Finally, after pursuing the analysis for another few pages, he concludes that:

12  Ibid., p. 161.
13  Ibid., p. 164.

All the antinomies conceived by the native mind, on the most diverse planes – geographic, economic, sociological, and even cosmological – are, when all is said and done, assimilated to that less obvious yet so real antinomy, the dilemma which marriage with the matrilateral cousin attempts but fails to solve. But the failure is admitted in our myths, and there precisely lies their function.[14]

This function, which is not the same thing as the 'apparent' content of the myth and is revealed by the structural analysis, corresponds to what Lévi-Strauss would later call the semantic function of myths. Here we see the beginnings of a theme that would be developed in his Mythology series. The substance of myths consists in contradictions that must be either veiled or dissimulated.

'The Story of Asdiwal' contains two other theoretical advances. Lévi-Strauss proceeds by a deductive process, which represents the outline of what he would call, in the Mythology series, 'transcendental deduction' and 'empirical deduction'.[15] He also proceeds by analysing the transformations undergone by the myth in its fourth version, that collected by Boas from the Nisqa, who lived on the Nass River north of the other Tsimshian groups, themselves based on the Skeena River. In moving from the Skeena to the Nass, the myth 'becomes distorted in two ways, which are structurally connected':[16] the oppositions are weakened, and the correlations are reversed.

Let us return to the first theoretical innovation. Lévi-Strauss seeks to understand what the West–East direction represents in native thinking; for this is the direction taken by salmon and candlefish when they arrive each year from the ocean and swim upriver. Lévi-Strauss posits that this orientation is linked to the fact that the Tsimshian put themselves in the place of the fish, and more to the point, 'put the fish in their place'.[17]

The deduction is confirmed by the myths and by the rituals associated with fishing and the preparation of fish. The rituals imply a mythical identification between fish and humans, and are mandatory, since we

---

14  Ibid., p. 170.

15  C. Lévi-Strauss, *The Naked Man*, trans. J. and D. Weightman, *Mythologiques*, vol. 4 (Chicago, University of Chicago Press, 1981), pp. 233, 416, 549, 557, 559.

16  *Structural Anthropology, Volume 2*, p. 183.

17  Ibid., p. 174.

must eat fish, even though they are like men. (The fishbones were carefully gathered up and then immersed, enabling the fish to be reborn.)

The second theoretical innovation comes in the form of a general proposition concerning the properties of mythical thinking, which Lévi-Strauss derives from the fact that the myth undergoes a deformation as it passes from the Skeena to the Nass River:

> When a mythical schema is transmitted from one population to another, and there exist differences of language, social organization or way of life that make the myth difficult to communicate, it begins to become impoverished and confused. But one can find a limiting situation in which, instead of being fully obliterated by losing all its outlines, the myth is inverted and regains part of its precision.[18]

Later on, Lévi-Strauss would analyse how myths die, not over time but when they are transmitted from one society to another, from one culture to another, from one language to another over space.[19]

Lastly, after having shown that the opposition between earth and water, which is 'the one most closely linked with methods of production and the objective relationships between men and the world', Lévi-Strauss advances his fundamental thesis, which will be repeated in *The Savage Mind*, the Mythology series and throughout his work: that, 'formal though it be, analysis of a society's myths verifies the primacy of infrastructures.'[20] He would never abandon the thesis of the 'primacy of infrastructures', borrowed, as he never denied, from Marx. Later, I will analyse just what this theory covers for Lévi-Strauss and what it covered for Marx.

'The Story of Asdiwal', which Lévi-Strauss presents as a kind of 'experiment', a test of structural analysis, is therefore a complete success and constitutes a new step forward. The notions of code, message, schema and axis have appeared and will become part of the vocabulary

---

18 Ibid., p. 184.

19 C. Lévi-Strauss, 'Comment meurent les mythes', *Esprit*, n° 39 (1971), pp. 684–706. Published the same year was 'Rapports de symétrie entre rites et mythes de peuples voisins', in T. Beidelman, ed., *The Translation of Culture: Essays to E. E. Evans-Pritchard* (London, Tavistock, 1971), pp. 161–78.

20 *Structural Anthropology, Volume 2*, p. 196, n. 19. See also *The Savage Mind* (no translator mentioned) (Chicago, University of Chicago Press, 1966), pp. 93, 130.

of the Mythology series. The distinction has been made between the 'apparent content' of the myth and its 'latent meaning'. Also used are the notions of linguistic, cultural and sociological thresholds, which the myths circulating between societies can or cannot cross – and when they do, it is at the cost of transformations that affect their structure and message. All these concepts and hypotheses are now developed. The third and shortest test Lévi-Strauss will carry out will result in a new article, 'Four Winnebago Myths: A Structural Sketch'.

## 'Four Winnebago Myths: A Structural Sketch' (1960)

Here Lévi-Strauss takes on four myths published by Paul Radin, who had pointed out that the fourth was very different from the others without clearly seeing the reason for this.[21] Lévi-Strauss applies his method to show that all four 'are of the same genre and their meanings logically complement each other'.[22] Little by little, he unpicks the armature of the myth, which comes down to 'a polar system bringing together – and at the same time opposing – two individuals, one male, the other female, and both exceptional insofar as each of them is overgifted in one way (+) and undergifted in the other (-)'.[23] The message of the four myths, taken together is that, 'in order to be overcome, the opposition between life and death should be first acknowledged.'[24]

I will say no more about the plot, but will indicate two developments that mark yet another step forward. Radin had wondered to what extent these myths contained elements of Winnebago culture and society. The myth depicted a highly stratified society in which women held high rank, perhaps associated with a matrilineal descent rule. None of this corresponded in any way to the reality of Winnebago society. Did it correspond to some ancient period of their history? No historical tradition, no archaeological findings prove this. Lévi-Strauss tackles the problem from another angle:

---

21  C. Lévi-Strauss, 'Four Winnebago Myths: A Structural Sketch', in *Structural Anthropology, Volume 2*, pp. 198–210.

22  Ibid., p. 199.

23  Ibid., p. 206.

24  Ibid., p. 208.

There must be, and there is, a correspondence between the unconscious meaning of a myth – the problem it tries to solve – and the
conscious content it makes use of to reach that end, the plot. However,
this correspondence is not necessarily an exact reproduction; it can
also appear as a logical transformation. If the problem is presented in
straight terms – that is, in the way the social life of the group expresses
and tries to solve it – the overt content of the myth, the plot, can
borrow its elements from social life itself. But should the problem be
formulated upside down, and its solution sought for *ad absurdo,* then
the overt content can be expected to become modified accordingly to
form an inverted image of the social pattern actually present in the
consciousness of the natives.[25]

The hypothesis that a myth may present a problem in a direct fashion
or seek to resolve it *ad absurdo* is important, for it warns the reader
against any spontaneous attempt to look for a direct correspondence
between the society's real organization and the ideal universe of its
myths, which is an imaginary world, the product of the speculations
of mythic thinking. This type of mindset elaborates representations of
societies that have never existed, and it is therefore unnecessary to
suppose, as Radin did, that these representations might correspond to
an earlier state of the society whose traces must be sought in oral
tradition, or through archaeological research, to verify this
hypothesis.

But, as the fourth Winnebago myth differs from the other three and
opposes them by its plot, which unfolds in a society that did not exist in
reality, Lévi-Strauss advances a second hypothesis, which he will
subsequently apply in all the studies he conducts on groups of myths,
namely:

A plot and [each of] its component parts should neither be interpreted by themselves nor relative to something outside the realm of
the myth proper, but as substitutions given in and understandable
only with reference to a group of myths.[26]

---

25  Ibid., p. 204.
26  Ibid., p. 208.

Both of these quotations confront us with the complexity and difficulty of determining to what degree myths (to which we will add: religions) correspond to the reality of the societies that have developed
them and to that of the surrounding natural environment. Myths are
ideological constructions, grounded in imaginary speculations that
have their own logic. According to Lévi-Strauss, myths seek to resolve,
in the imagination, the contradictions societies must deal with and
which 'in some way' tie in with reality. Furthermore, since a myth is
the totality of its versions and these constitute a permutation group –
in other words, certain of these versions are the product of logical
transformations that turn them into symmetrical but inverted forms
of certain other myths – it necessarily ensues that certain versions, if
they are the symmetrical inversion of other versions that correspond
to elements of a real society and its natural environment, no longer
correspond to real elements of this society and this natural environment. These versions can describe a purely imaginary and unreal society, or one that is virtually possible but is not the one from which the
group of myths comes. It can be a neighbouring society in which this
possibility has been realized and which is known to the authors of the
myth, or other real societies but which are unknown to the authors.
But then how are we to interpret the fact that Lévi-Strauss advises
analysing the infrastructures of the different societies between which
the same myth circulates, in order to understand the transformations
it has undergone in its passage from these to those? What does he
really mean by 'the primacy of infrastructures', which he affirms categorically in 'The Story of Asdiwal' and even more strongly in *The
Savage Mind* (1962)? We will have to wait for the Mythology series to
find out.

## 'Structure and Form: Reflections on a Work by Vladimir Propp' (1960)

In October 1958, a book written thirty years earlier by Vladimir Propp,
the major Russian folklorist, was published in the United States under
the title *Morphology of the Folktale*. Lévi-Strauss read it and discovered,
much to his surprise (and his great admiration), that Propp had already
developed some of the key concepts and methodological principles for

analysing popular Russian tales and fairy stories that he himself had just defined for the structural analysis of myths. He proceeded to write a long article in homage to Propp, listing everything he had found to be prophetic in his book.[27] Nevertheless, he objected to Propp's overly 'formalistic' treatment of the tales, which he felt led him to neglect their content. In criticizing Propp's formalism, Lévi-Strauss clearly wanted to settle his accounts with those who, in Britain, America and France, had taxed him with doing the same thing as the Russian scholar: giving priority to the form of the myths, neglecting their content and turning his back on history. The tone of his criticisms was harsh, not to say rude, and Propp took them badly, even seeing them as a perfidious attack on him by a philosopher who knew nothing about folklore and linguistics. In 1966 Lévi-Strauss replied, in Italian, on the occasion of the publication of his book by the Turin publisher, Einaudi.[28] There the matter rested – with a certain regret on Lévi-Strauss's part, if we believe the postscript he appended to his article in 1973 when it was republished in *Structural Anthropology, Volume 2*.[29]

The opposition Lévi-Strauss drew between formalism and structuralism when he decided to review Propp's work can be summed up as follows:

[Inversely] to formalism, structuralism refuses to set the concrete against the abstract and to recognize a privileged value in the latter.[30]

Before formalism, we were certainly unaware of what these tales had in common. Since formalism, we have been deprived of any means of understanding how they differ. One has passed from

27  C. Lévi-Strauss, 'Structure and Form: Reflections on a Work by Vladimir Propp', *Cahiers de l'ESEA*, n° 9 (1960), pp. 3–36; reproduced in *Structural Anthropology, Volume 2*, pp. 115–45.

28  Ibid., pp. 144–5.

29  In 1983 Gallimard published Propp's even more remarkable book, *The Historical Roots of the Fairy Tale* (published in English by North Holland Publishing Company, 1982, in their Russian Literature series), which had first appeared in Russian in 1946. In a very interesting article, 'Du mythe au conte. Du côté d'*Histoire de Lynx*', published in a special issue of the *Cahiers de l'Herne* devoted to Lévi-Strauss (2004), Nicole Belmont, a specialist of European folktales and a life-long member of the Laboratoire d'Anthropologie Sociale founded by Lévi-Strauss, showed just how regrettable, from a theoretical standpoint, the break between Propp and Lévi-Strauss had been, particularly given the richness of Propp's second book.

30  *Structural Anthropology, Volume 2*, p. 115.

concrete to abstract, but can no longer come down from the abstract to the concrete.[31]

Refining his criticism, Lévi-Strauss laid out his own definitions of the notions of form and structure, which seem clearer to me and which we find time and again in his work.

> Form is defined by opposition to material other than itself. But structure has no distinct content; it is content itself, apprehended in a logical organization conceived as a property of the real.[32]

For formalism, 'only the form of the tale is intelligible', the content is merely a residue devoid of meaningful value:

> For structuralism, this opposition does not exist. There is not something abstract on one side and something concrete on the other . . . Content draws its reality from its structure and what is called form is the 'structural formation' of the local structure forming the content.[33]

If the formal analysis is carried to ever-higher degrees of abstraction, the form ceases to signify and no longer has heuristic value. Formalism carried to such an extreme 'destroys its object'.[34] Lévi-Strauss nevertheless stresses that Propp was aware of this risk, and took pains to reintegrate the content of the tales into his analysis and to discover the 'transformation laws' that applied. The intention was to illuminate the reasons for the attributes of the mythical figures – the hero, the traitor, the usurper, etc. – and the functions they fulfilled – combat, hero's pursuit, unmasking of the usurper, recognition of the hero, etc. The arbitrary character of mythical content, asserted by Propp at the beginning of his analysis, duly faded as these functions appeared and their permutability was recognized. For Lévi-Strauss, this was not the only aspect of Propp's work that deserved praise. He went on to add:

---

31  Ibid., p. 133.
32  Ibid., p. 115.
33  Ibid., p. 131.
34  Ibid., p. 132.

1) the comparison of the mythological matrix with the rules of musical composition, a theme Lévi-Strauss would develop in his introduction to *The Raw and the Cooked* and at the end of *The Naked Man*;

2) the necessity of a simultaneously horizontal and vertical reading of the myths – Lévi-Strauss had formulated the precept for the first time in 1955;

3) the use of the notions of transformation and group of substitutions to explain both the variability of the myths' content and the constancy of their form;

4) the effort to associate different functions with pairs of opposites;

5) the idea that each character in a tale could fulfil several functions in the sphere of action ascribed to them;

6) the hypothesis that there existed a 'canonical formula' for folktales;

7) the hypothesis that all known folktales could be treated as variants of a single tale – which would be Lévi-Strauss's own conclusion at the end of his four volumes of the Mythology series, with its examination of 813 myths together with an even greater number of variants;

8) the hypothesis that the unknown variants could be arrived at through calculation, just as astronomers are able to infer the existence of invisible stars;

9) finally, the idea that the folktale can be assimilated to a myth.

Lévi-Strauss would also say of tales that they are 'myths in miniature', constructed on 'weaker' oppositions than those found in myths – these oppositions being social or moral, rather than cosmological or metaphysical as in myths. Myths and folk tales are for him complementary, distinguished by the fact that the myth often has a sacred character, while the tale is profane. But the tale is not the form in which a myth survives. Both draw on the same sources in the human mind. For Lévi-Strauss, myths and tales 'form a "metalanguage" in which structure operates at all levels'.[35] And that is why they are immediately perceived as tales or as myths, and not as historical accounts or as novels.

Lévi-Strauss ends his analysis of Propp by enriching it with several concepts he had developed between 1952 and 1955. This time he defines mythemes as 'words of words', words with a double meaning: the one they possess in ordinary language, as in the words 'coyote', 'jaguar', 'crow', and the one they acquire in their function as a constituent unit of a

---

35 Ibid., pp. 141–2.

myth. In the second case, they take on a 'supersignification',[36] which one discovers when one has changed the term 'in all its contexts. In the case of oral literature, these contexts are at first provided by the totality of the variants, that is, by the system of compatibilities and incompatibilities that characterize the permutable totality.'[37]

An element of the physical world acting as a mytheme in the metalanguage of a myth (fire, for example) has nothing in common with Jung's archetypes, which he believed to be present in the collective consciousness. That is because the 'supersignification' of a mytheme is given by its 'position', and has no existence outside its mythological contexts. Each protagonist in the myths or the tales results from a 'play of binary or ternary oppositions' combined in different ways. If mythemes are words that designate realities in the physical world, the functions played by these realities once they have been made into mythemes are, so to speak, 'mythemes to the power of two', 'with a double meaning of *words of words*'. Such that 'as opposed to language, where the problem of vocabulary still exists, metalanguage has no level where elements do not result from well-determined operations, effected according to the rules.'[38]

It must be noted that this is the second time (the first was in 1955) Lévi-Strauss mentions the play of 'binary or ternary oppositions' and of correlations. Throughout his work he would lay heavy emphasis on the role of binary operations and operators in myths, something that earned him a reprimand from Leach. As this text and that of 1955 show, Lévi-Strauss was by no means unaware of the existence of more complex forms of correlation and opposition. Further evidence of this was the publication of 'The Culinary Triangle' in the journal *L'Arc* (1965), opposing the raw, the cooked and the rotten, based of course on the analyses contained in *The Raw and the Cooked*, which had appeared the year before.

The last point to which Lévi-Strauss chose to return in his article on Propp was the question of the mythical treatment of time. He concluded that, in any mythical system, the representation of time has a double character:

---

36  Ibid., p. 143.
37  Ibid., p. 135.
38  Ibid., pp. 143–4.

The narrative is both 'in time' (it consists of a succession of events) and 'out of time' (its significant value is always current) . . . the order of chronological succession is reabsorbed into an atemporal matrix structure, the form of which is indeed constant. The shifting of functions is then no more than one of their modes of permutation (by vertical columns or fractions of columns).[39]

Once again, reference is made to the method used to analyse myths, which for Lévi-Strauss consists in discovering the succession of paradigms in a text and organizing them by columns when they share certain content.

By 1960, the theoretical ground was prepared to begin the systematic study of Amerindian mythology, of which he had already analysed and published a certain number of myths (1952–53, 1953–54, 1958, 1960). In reality, one more step remained: *Totemism*, published in French in 1962, was an exercise in deconstructing a notion that had haunted anthropologists since the end of the nineteenth century. But why was it necessary to deconstruct this notion of totemism in order to reveal the nature of human thought 'in its savage state'?

## Totemism (1962)[40]

In 1910, Frazer had published, in London, four volumes entitled *Totemism and Exogamy*.[41] In this monumental 2,200-page work, the author claimed to have assembled all that was then known about totemism, in order to present a synthetic view of this concept and to establish it as a system.

The same year, in a little over 100 pages, Goldenweiser contested the superposition of three social phenomena that were not of the same nature: the division of society into clans, the attribution of animals and plants as clan names, and finally the belief in kinship, or descent ties, between the members of a clan and their totem.[42] It was this last point

---

39 Ibid., p. 138.

40 C. Lévi-Strauss, *Totemism*, trans. R. Needham (Boston, Beacon Press, 1963).

41 J. G. Frazer, *Totemism and Exogamy* (London, Macmillan, 1910), 4 vols.

42 A. A. Goldenweiser, 'Totemism: An Analytical Study', *Journal of American Folklore* 23 (1910).

that Freud retained when writing *Totem and Taboo*.[43] In the United States, the place assigned in textbooks to totemism was so diminishing that the notion did not even feature in G. P. Murdock's *Social Structure* (1949)[44] – a book that was to have a similar impact in the Anglo-Saxon world as *The Elementary Structures* in France, where van Gennep had already published a book on 'the present state of the problem of totemism' (not translated in English) in 1920.[45] This was in fact to be a swan song.

In his own book on totemism,[46] Lévi-Strauss would come to grips with what he christened the 'totemic illusion'.[47] Returning to a distinction made by Boas,[48] he began by showing that the discussion of totemism had constantly confused two different types of problem: on the one hand, the naming of kin-based groups (clans), which can be done in a number of ways, some of which use the names of animals or plants; and on the other hand, the recurring problem of the identification of human beings with plants and animals. In effect, such identification supposes specific representations of humans' relations with nature, which are at the root not only of religious representations and magical practices but also of forms of art.

After recapitulating the stages in the discussion of the notion since Frazer, Lévi-Strauss sums up at length the case of totemism in Australia, which A. P. Elkin had meticulously reconstructed in 1932–34.[49] Elkin

---

43  S. Freud, *Totem and Taboo* (Boston, Beacon Press, 1913).

44  G. P. Murdock, *Social Structure* (New York, Macmillan, 1949).

45  A. van Gennep, *L'État actuel du problème totémique* (Paris, Leroux, 1920).

46  Lévi-Strauss summed up his research in two texts: the abstracts of his courses at the Collège de France for the 1960-61 academic year, the year he wrote *Totemism* and *The Savage Mind*, and in the article 'The Bear and the Barber', text of the 1960 Henry Meyers Memorial Lecture, published in 1963 in the *Journal of the Royal Anthropological Institute of Great Britain and Ireland* 93, n° 1, pp. 1–11.

47  The word 'totem' comes from the language of the Ojibwa, an Algonquin group living in North America north of the Great Lakes. Their clans are named after animals. At the end of the eighteenth century, an English merchant, J. L. Long, described 'totemism' as practiced by the Ojibwa in his *Voyages and Travels of an Indian Interpreter and Trader* (A. H. Clark, 1791; reprinted in 1922). According to Lévi-Strauss, research among the Ojibwa showed that Long had confused the system of clan names, which were not tied to prohibitions, with a system of individual guardian spirits invoked by the Ojibwa.

48  F. Boas, 'The Origin of Totemism', *American Anthropologist* 18 (1916), pp. 319–26.

49  A. P. Elkin, 'Studies in Australian Totemism', *Oceania* 4, n° 1–2 (1933–34).

had analysed the forms of totemism connected with social groups (moieties, sections and subsections) as well as those linked to individuals (sexual, conceptional, local, child's birthplace) and to dreams (the mother's during pregnancy). He concluded there was no unity to be found among all the different forms of totemism, and there were therefore not one but several heterogeneous and irreducible types. Lévi-Strauss would draw an even more radical conclusion: if the different forms of totemism were heterogeneous and irreducible, and if there was really no unity among them, then so-called totemism did not exist.

One of the points in his analysis of Elkin brings us back to our own analysis, at the beginning of the present book, of the chapters of *The Elementary Structures of Kinship* dealing with Australian kinship systems. The time was 1945–46, and though he knew that the section and subsection systems continued to spread in certain Australian groups – some adopting them, others trying and rejecting them – Lévi-Strauss had considered that sections and subsections served primarily to organize the exchange of women between local groups. By 1961–62, doubts had grown, and Elkin, like Radcliffe-Brown before him, no longer thought that sections and subsections had been invented to regulate marriage exchanges. For Elkin, they were a sort of abbreviated method for classifying individuals, on the occasion of large-scale intertribal ceremonies, into kinship categories fitting the needs of the ritual. Even if this were the case, Lévi-Strauss declared, the section system could not and must not run counter to each group's kinship system – yet this is precisely the analysis made by linguists and anthropologists specializing in Australia today. But Lévi-Strauss would reject this interpretation once again in 1962, firmly reiterating his positions:

> Let us suppose, therefore, that each time the sections or sub-sections were invented, copied, or intelligently borrowed, their function was firstly sociological, i.e., they served – and still serve – to encode, in a relatively simple form applicable beyond the tribal borders, the kinship system and that of marital exchange. But once these institutions were given, they began to lead an independent existence ... Their mode of existence remains ideological.[50]

---

50 *Totemism*, pp. 52–3.

Why does totemism attach the names of animals and plants to human groups or individuals? Malinowski explained this by the fact that primitive humans derived their subsistence from plants and animals, and thought they could control their growth and multiplication through ritual and magic. Ultimately, he argued, totemism can be explained by the fact that these plants and animals were good to eat (or to avoid). However, Lévi-Strauss shows that many plants, animals or other features of reality chosen as totems are of no practical use, economic or other. Malinowski's 'functionalist' explanation collapsed.

Lévi-Strauss goes on to examine successively what he calls Radcliffe-Brown's two theories of totemism. The first (1952) was 'functionalist', in line with Malinowski's theory.[51] Radcliffe-Brown began by positing as a universal fact that, for the majority of peoples we call primitive, 'every thing and every event which exercises an important influence on the well-being of society tends to become an object of a ritual attitude', and totemism is merely one aspect of this generalized attitude.[52] But, Lévi-Strauss objects, many peoples, like the Eskimo, the Andaman Islanders, the Indians of California, etc., have ritual practices concerning various animal species without making totems of them.[53] Furthermore, as Raymond Firth had already pointed out in his article 'Totemism in Polynesia': 'As far as the majority of animal totem species is concerned, the economic interest in them is not of a pronounced type'.[54] The reasons for totemism must lie elsewhere.

In 1951, in his Huxley Memorial Lecture entitled 'The Comparative Method in Social Anthropology',[55] Radcliffe-Brown had therefore posed the problem anew:

> What is the principle by which such pairs as eaglehawk and crow, eagle and raven, coyote and wild cat are chosen as representing the moieties of the dual division?[56]

51 A. R. Radcliffe-Brown, 'The Sociological Theory of Totemism', Structure and Function in Primitive Society. Essays and Addresses (Glencoe, Free Press, 1952).

52 Totemism, p. 61.

53 Ibid., p. 65.

54 R. Firth, 'Totemism in Polynesia', Oceania 1, n° 3 (1930), pp. 291–321; 297.

55 A. R. Radcliffe-Brown, 'The Comparative Method in Social Anthropology', Huxley Memorial Lecture for 1951, Journal of the Royal Anthropological Institute 81, nos 1–2, parts I and II, pp. 15–22.

56 Quoted in Totemism, p. 86.

After examination of several myths whose protagonists are the eagle-hawk and the crow, Radcliffe-Brown concluded:

> The resemblances and differences of animal species are translated into terms of friendship and conflict, solidarity and opposition. In other words, the world of animal life is represented in terms of social relations similar to those of human society.[57]

The eaglehawk–crow pair featured two species that share a common trait which allows their comparison – both are meat-eaters – while another trait opposes them: the eaglehawk is a hunter, a predator, while the crow is a scavenger. In sum the choice bore on a particular case of 'the application of a structural principle',[58] that of the union of opposites. Seen in this light, totemism is a way of establishing correlations and oppositions using various codes – animals, plants – which other societies express by opposing two colours – red/white – or two spatial dimensions – above/below, heaven/earth, etc.; the most systematic and widespread model for oppositions of this type is the Chinese Yin and Yang. To be sure, Lévi-Strauss expresses his wholehearted agreement with Radcliffe-Brown's conclusion, but he does not stop there.

Natural species are not chosen for totems because they are 'good to eat', but because they are 'good to think'. 'Their perceptive reality permits the embodiment of ideas and relations conceived by speculative thought on the basis of empirical observations.' These relations and notions manifest a kind of logic, a logic of oppositions and correlations, of compatibilities and incompatibilities, of inclusions and exclusions, that is 'an original logic, a direct expression of the structure of the mind (and behind the mind, probably of the brain)'.[59]

This famous formula places us in the presence of two fundamental aspects of Lévi-Strauss's thought: his materialism, which posits that the structure of the human mind is an expression of the structure of our brain, and the idea that the spontaneous working of the mind follows a logic of oppositions and correlations, of incompatibilities and

---

57 Quoted in ibid., p. 87.
58 Ibid., p. 88.
59 Ibid., pp. 89–90.

compatibilities, which applies in the first place to experience through the senses. It is this original logic that, in the same year, Lévi-Strauss would call 'the savage mind', that is, the mind in its non-domesticated state, not subject to the constraint of yielding a return. He would come back to his theses and even harp on them in *The Raw and the Cooked*. The conclusion of *Totemism* is clear:

> The alleged totemism pertains to the understanding, and the demands to which it responds and the way in which it tries to meet them are primarily of an intellectual kind. In this sense, there is nothing archaic or remote about it . . . Sentiments are also involved, admittedly, but in a subsidiary fashion, as responses of a body of ideas to gaps and lesions which it can never succeed in closing.[60]

Let us pause for a moment and consider this last sentence, for it sums up the way Lévi-Strauss conceives of the nature of emotions and feelings, and their role in the life of the mind as well as in the production of customs and institutions:

> Actually, impulses and emotions explain nothing: they are always results, either of the power of the body or of the impotence of the mind. In both cases they are consequences, never causes. The latter can be sought only in the organism, which is the exclusive concern of biology, or in the intellect, which is the sole way offered to psychology, and to [ethnology] as well.[61]

His darts are aimed at two men: Malinowski and Freud. Malinowski, who explained the origin of magic by humans' need to quell their anxiety when engaging in actions whose outcome is uncertain. And Freud, for having imagined the origin of totemism to lie with the murder of a father behaving despotically toward his women and children within the primal horde, a murder for which the impulse and the guilt would continue to haunt humankind for millennia. In 1962, then, Lévi-Strauss is much more critical of the Freud of *Totem and Taboo* than he was when writing *The Elementary Structures of Kinship* (1945–47).

60  Ibid., p. 104.
61  Ibid., p. 71.

Yet Lévi-Strauss singles out from among the emotions a psychological state that, according to Rousseau, was 'indissociably affective and intellectual', of which it sufficed to become aware to move from one level to the next. This emotion, he suggests, is the spontaneous human disposition to identify with their fellow beings, among which Rousseau placed animals. Oddly enough, Rousseau called this emotion that he believed to accompany the passage from the animal to the human state, from a life governed by the emotions to one governed by the intellect, 'pity'.

Clearly, Lévi-Strauss found in the Rousseau of the *Discourse on the Origin of Inequality* (1755) ideas that he had worked out by himself through his analyses of Amerindian myths. The central idea was this:

> The total apprehension of men and animals as sentient beings, in which identification consists, both governs and precedes the consciousness of oppositions between, firstly, logical properties conceived as integral parts of the field, and then within the field itself, between 'human' and 'non-human'.[62]

To sum up, when the savage mind functions spontaneously according to a logic of oppositions and correlations whose object is the physical world, in which all humans spontaneously identify both emotionally and intellectually with animals and other living organisms, the objective conditions are present for the emergence of mythical and symbolic thought. People can draw on the stock of differences between certain of these species and from these build their model for expressing and conceptualizing differences they have established among themselves, which are social differences. There is therefore no need to think people imagine themselves to be descended from the animal species they have chosen as clan or personal totems. The resemblance posited between humans and animals resides in the comparison between two systems of differences, in 'the resemblances between the differences'.[63] We will see that Lévi-Strauss cried victory a little too soon and that in, for instance, the Aborigines' conception, totems imply a profound, essential identification between humans and other life forms.

---

62  Ibid., pp. 101–2.
63  Ibid., p. 101.

In the end, Lévi-Strauss advances a sociological and cultural explanation for the overwhelming success enjoyed by totemism for over a century before it disintegrated and, according to him, rapidly disappeared from the anthropological scene. According to this explanation, Western scholars unconsciously used the theory to make so-called primitive peoples even 'more different' than they were. They cobbled together a hodgepodge of beliefs and heterogeneous customs under the term totemism, because these showed the existence of attitudes toward nature that were 'incompatible with the exigency of a discontinuity between man and nature which Christian thought has held to be essential'.[64] Totemism having been established as the heart of the religion of primitive peoples, it created a gulf between such religions and those of civilized peoples. By applying to the study of religions those methods and principles used by structural analysis to study other conceptual systems, the anthropology of religions would become a more rigorous discipline, but at the cost of renouncing its purported autonomy. These views are already a foretaste of the conclusion to his final volume in the Mythology series, *The Naked Man* (1971), published ten years later. So what did *The Savage Mind*, appearing a few months after *Totemism*, have to add?

## The Savage Mind (1962)

*Totemism* ended with the affirmation that 'the alleged totemism pertains to the understanding, and the demands to which it responds and the way in which it tries to meet them are primarily of an intellectual kind. In this sense, there is nothing archaic or remote about it.'[65]

The Savage Mind begins by once again analysing totemic classifications and their underlying intellectual operations – relations of opposition and correlation, placed in a relation of correspondence on the basis of perception of a resemblance between their differences, etc. All intellectual operations proceed from humans' previous intellectual and emotional identification with animals and other life forms. Lévi-Strauss coins the term 'science of the concrete' for this familiar relation with

---

64  Ibid., p. 3.
65  Ibid., p. 104.

nature, the attention paid to it and the precise knowledge connected with it that is a response to more than practical needs. He observes that societies everywhere have done more than simply accumulate knowledge. They have systematized it. Mythical and magical thought have grown up, he writes, on the basis of these discoveries and of the 'speculative organization and exploitation of the sensible world in sensible terms'.

> This science of the concrete was necessarily restricted by its essence to results other than those destined to be achieved by the exact natural sciences, but it was no less scientific and its results no less genuine. They were secured ten thousand years earlier and still remain at the basis of our own civilization.[66]

Down to our own time, myth and ritual have preserved modes of observation and thought associated with practical, concrete discoveries. These affirmations nevertheless raise a problem. Lévi-Strauss traces this early knowledge of nature back to the very long period of time that preceded protohistory and the Neolithic era.[67] For tens of thousands of years, man hunted, fished and gathered, and it was thanks to his knowledge of nature that wild plants and animals were eventually domesticated, while pottery and other uses of fire, basketry and other crafts, came to be invented. New forms of thought aimed at increased 'yield', and therefore 'domesticated' by the mental processes deployed to these ends, partially replaced the mind's functioning in its 'savage state'. Nevertheless, it is hard not to think that the techniques and skills entailed in the various forms of hunting, fishing, manufacture of weapons and tools, and so forth did not also represent forms of 'domesticated' thought, the borderline between productions of the savage mind and those of the domesticated mind not being all that clear. Both probably existed side by side for thousands of years, down to our time, and Lévi-Strauss sometimes compares the forms of thought involved in the creation of artworks to the workings of the savage mind.

---

66  C. Lévi-Strauss, *The Savage Mind* (no translator mentioned) (Chicago, University of Chicago Press, 1969), p. 16.

67  Ibid., p. 15.

These, he believes, are the source of fundamental knowledge and representations connected with intuition of the senses, perception and imagination. Scientific knowledge, on the other hand, stems from the observation and experimentation that enable the discovery of connections between phenomena distinct from the data provided by perception or physical experience. Lévi-Strauss stresses that, in his opinion, the 'science of the concrete' and scientific knowledge of nature are not two unequal stages in the development of the human mind, but 'two strategic levels at which nature is accessible to scientific enquiry'; the science of the concrete and modern science are, for him, 'two distinct modes of scientific thought'.[68] From that point on and until his death, Lévi-Strauss would continue to affirm that the workings of the savage mind and the workings of the scientific mind are basically identical. What differentiates them is not a matter of mental operations, but the nature of the objects and the level of the 'reality of the natural entities to which each applies itself'.

> Man began by applying himself to the most difficult task, that of systematizing what is immediately presented to the senses, on which science for a long time turned its back and which it is only beginning to bring back into its purview.[69]

But what is the relationship between mythical thinking and the science of the concrete? What place does it occupy and what role does it play? According to Lévi-Strauss, the science of the concrete systematically organizes data gathered from the visible world and uses this systematized information to construct imaginary, speculative interpretations of nature and society. Mythical thought works on signs that it has itself helped create and which it uses to construct a narrative in which, at the close of a series of events, an explanation is offered, for example, of the origin of the spots on the moon, or the fact that the salmon will not swim up past a given obstacle so that the tribes living upstream are deprived of this resource.

Lévi-Strauss thus has come back to an idea he had advanced in 1955, in 'The Structural Study of Myth'. Mythical thought works with the help

---

68  Ibid.
69  Ibid., p. 11.

not of concepts but of signs that are elements of thought; 'the elements of mythical thought . . . lie half-way between percepts and concepts'.[70] Signs are images that become signs when they serve to support an idea or a concept. The sign thus links an image (that of the coyote, for instance) and a concept (playing the role of deceiver); owing to this union, the image acts as the signifier and the concept as the signified.

> Signs resemble images in being concrete entities, but they resemble concepts in their powers of reference. Neither concepts nor signs relate exclusively to themselves; either may be substituted for something else.[71]

And if they can stand for something other than themselves, they are therefore permutable. Since signs are the substance of myths, the myths that combine them constitute 'permutation groups'. Unlike concepts that open vast fields of transformation in the domains in which they operate, 'signification . . . neither extends nor renews [the sign] and limits itself to obtaining the group of its transformations.'

> Signs and images which have acquired significance may still lack comprehension; unlike concepts . . . They are however already permutable, that is, capable of standing in successive relations with other entities – although with only a limited number and . . . only on the condition that they always form a system in which an alteration which affects one element automatically affects all the others. On this plane logicians' 'extension' and 'intension' are . . . one and the same thing. One understands then how mythical thought can be capable of generalizing and so be scientific, even though it is still entangled in imagery. It too works by analogies and comparisons . . .[72]

In this passage, Lévi-Strauss advances his theory yet another step. We knew that the words of myths belong at one and the same time to the language that enunciates them and in which they possess a specific meaning, and to the metalanguage of myths in which they acquire

---

70 Ibid., p. 18.
71 Ibid.
72 Ibid., p. 20.

another signification, a 'supersignification', as he wrote in 1955. In this case, they designate concrete entities such as the eaglehawk and the crow, which are words in the myths at the same time as they are images located halfway between perceived realities (percepts) and the same things conceived in the mind (concepts). They thus become constituent units of the fabric of myths, mythemes, bearers of relations that will connect them with other mythemes. The eaglehawk and the crow are linked to each other through the fact that both are birds (relation of correlation), but they are opposed to each other as bird of prey (eagle-hawk) and carrion bird (crow). This pair of birds can therefore permute with other birds linked by the same relation of opposition (predator/scavenger) like the eagle and the vulture, but the number of these permutations is necessarily limited.

Indeed, just as myths endlessly combine and recombine the same material to tell their stories, the mind's production of myths looks much like what the French call 'bricolage', the use of whatever is at hand to make what one needs. In myths, the outcome, the end of one myth, can serve as a means in another, and thereby 'the signified changes into the signifying and vice versa'.[73] This is another important advance in Lévi-Strauss's theory of myths.

From this union of percepts and concepts, which constitutes the substance of myths, Lévi-Strauss concludes that 'we are inclined to think of myths both as systems of abstract relations and as objects of aesthetic contemplation'. Even more than tales and fables, myths have the power to 'enchant' us. The myth begins with a structure, which it uses 'to produce what is itself an [absolute] object consisting of a set of events (for all myths tell a story)'. Here the idea of myths as 'absolute objects' appears once again but enriched with a new, aesthetic, dimension. Pursuing this line of thought further, Lévi-Strauss advances the idea that myths are imbued with 'emotional tones', which 'show that the concrete relations between man and other living creatures . . . colour the entire universe of scientific knowledge with their own emotional tone, which is itself the result of this primitive identification and, as Rousseau saw with his profound insight, responsible for all thought and society'.[74]

---

73  Ibid., p. 21.
74  Ibid., pp. 25–6, 38.

Lévi-Strauss thus concurs with Rousseau's idea of the identification between man and other living beings, which he sees as the existential presupposition of all forms of (mythical and scientific) thought in every society. We should not forget that, for Lévi-Strauss, this existential presupposition designates a mixed emotion that mingles and unites affect, percept and (implicitly) concept. For several decades, this thesis would go, if not unnoticed, at least rarely commented on by most students of his work, who saw it primarily as the product of an 'intellectualist' mind.

Having developed these new views on the notions of sign and signifying image, Lévi-Strauss returns to the analysis of totemic classifications and natural elements present in myths, and formulates a methodological principle that he will henceforth apply in all his work – articles and books – on the topic:

> Indeed, it becomes increasingly apparent as time goes by that it is not possible to interpret myths and rites correctly, even if the interpretation is a structural one (not to be confused with just a formal analysis), without an exact identification of the plants and animals which are referred to.[75]

Hence the arduous research Lévi-Strauss would impose on himself for the rest of his life, seeking to identify not only the animals and plants mentioned in the myths, but also all the astronomical, ecological, technological and other references they contain.

> The accurate identification of every animal, plant, stone, heavenly body or natural phenomenon mentioned in myths and rituals is however not enough. It is also necessary to know the role which each culture gives them in its own system of significances . . . only a few [of these details] are however actually employed for giving animals or plants a significant function in the system. And it is necessary to know which . . . The terms never have any intrinsic significance. Their meaning is one of 'position' – a function of the history and cultural context on the one hand and of the structural system in which they are called upon to appear on the other.[76]

---

75 Ibid., p. 46.
76 Ibid., pp. 54–5.

Since the signification of the animals, plants, heavenly bodies, and so on is 'one of position', Lévi-Strauss once more rejects those 'theories making use of the concepts of "archetypes" or a "collective unconscious". It is only forms and not contents which can be common'.[77] Carl Jung and Sigmund Freud are again refuted.

And, since the significations of the entities figuring in the myths are merely 'of position', like the entities that have the property of being permutable with others within certain limits, we understand that the elements combined in myths are not constants, only the relations they entertain in the myth, and we are led to the conclusion that 'analogous logical structures can be constructed by means of different lexical resources'.[78] Lévi-Strauss calls these logical structures the 'armature' of the myths.

Lévi-Strauss mentions one final dimension of the classification systems so-called primitive societies have developed for animals, plants and other species. These systems are 'not only thought but lived'.[79] They never come down to representations. They are lived because they are 'enacted', because they engender norms of behaviour and forms of action. Among these normative extensions, we could cite the prescriptions and prohibitions bearing on foods that often go with them, and, more rarely, certain rules of exogamy. The life and thought of these so-called primitive societies are shaped by what Lévi-Strauss calls 'practico-theoretical logics', whose guiding principle is always to be able to oppose terms 'conceived as being distinct'.[80]

But, he goes on, these terms can only be conceived as being distinct and evincing, by their differences and the distance separating them, 'the formal conditions necessary for a significant message to be conveyed', if their empirical totality has undergone an 'impoverishment'.[81] Lévi-Strauss thinks of the empirical totality provided to the human mind as an indistinct and unintelligible flow. The mind must therefore introduce breaks, contrasts, differential gaps for this totality to become intelligible and the object of a signifying discourse. That is expressed by the notion of necessary 'impoverishment', which must precede the elaboration of

---

77  Ibid., p. 65.
78  Ibid., p. 53.
79  Ibid., p. 66.
80  Ibid., p. 75.
81  Ibid.

the practico-theoretical logics Lévi-Strauss spoke of. The human mind thus inserts discontinuity into this continuous flow of original sensible experience. For my part, this thesis does not stand up to examination.

It is true that the infant is not yet able to distinguish the things in its environment and lives in a fusional relationship with its mother's body. But as the months and years go by, the child comes to perceive and identify the differences *between* things and *between* people, and to perceive *itself* as different from these things and these people, which it will also learn to call by different names. But it is not through these perceptive discoveries, nor through learning the words that designate them in the 'mother' tongue, that these things and these people become distinct and begin to oppose each other. Their distinction and their differences are '*objective*' realities, and it is by selecting some among these, and therefore by omitting others, that the mind will be able to hold a signifying discourse on the world. This idea of a work of impoverishment, of subtractions, of creation of discontinuity will be a recurring theme in the Mythology series. Myths will be on the side of discontinuity, and rituals on the side of continuity.

But let us return to the systems of classification and denomination that characterize mythical and magical thought. It is precisely their formal character that gives them operational value:

> They are codes suitable for conveying messages which can be trans-posed into other codes, and for expressing messages received by means of different codes in terms of their own system.[82]

This is a formula of fundamental importance for the theory of myth. Not only have the terms code and message entered common usage, but above all the idea of 'the [ideal convertibility] between different levels of social reality' has just been advanced.[83] The same message can be deliv-ered in several ways depending on the codes used – sexual, cosmic, culi-nary, etc. – but since all these codes are convertible into one another, it is ultimately always the same message that is delivered by the myth and/ or the ritual. Totemism corresponds to certain modalities of these signi-fying devices.

---

82  Ibid., pp. 75–6.
83  Ibid., p. 76.

How does thought select, in nature or social life, the material that will be incorporated into myths? Lévi-Strauss takes on a twofold task here: first, to refute the hypothesis of a mechanical geographical and ecological determinism and, second, to reassert the primacy of infrastructures, a formula inspired by Marx which Lévi-Strauss would use in the rest of his work, including his very last books, as I have said.

> The first point is that natural conditions are not just passively accepted . . . they are a function of the techniques and way of life of the people who define them and give them a meaning . . . Even when it is raised to that human level which alone can make them intelligible, man's relations with his natural environment remain objects of thought . . . The mistake of the Naturalist School was to think that natural phenomena are what myths seek to explain, when they are rather the medium through which myths try to explain facts which are themselves not of a natural but a logical order.[84]

Why assert the 'primacy of infrastructures'? And what does the notion of infrastructure mean here? In most of his texts Lévi-Strauss defines the infrastructure of a society in vague terms, as all its techno-economic activities taken together. Yet this definition coincides only partially with that proposed by Marx, since the (essential) notion of social relations or relations of production is missing. For Lévi-Strauss, infrastructure boils down to the inventory of the techniques and domains of material activity – hunting, fishing, agriculture, etc. – practiced in a society.

At bottom, too, the notion of infrastructure enables us to grasp the contradictions of life forms in society and in man's representations of the universe and society. But 'nature itself is not contradictory. It can be so only in terms of the particular human activity being exercised.' Here Lévi-Strauss couples the notion of infrastructure with that of contradiction, and then advances this principle:

> The substance of contradictions is much less important than the fact that they exist . . . Now, the form contradictions take varies very much less than their empirical content. It accounts for the fact that men have so often had recourse to the same means for solving problems

---

84  Ibid., pp. 94–5.

whose concrete elements may be very different, but which share the feature of all belonging to 'structures of contradiction'.[85]

He has thus passed (without justification, it must be said) from the notion of the technical, economic and historical infrastructure of societies to that of 'structures of contradiction', which can be present in all areas, and on all levels of life and thought. This shift and this change of meaning explain why, according to Lévi-Strauss, myths do not really seek to explain the natural or social phenomena they talk about, but serve instead to resolve or reduce in the human imagination contradictions that are themselves real or imaginary. But, of course, myths can by no means 'resolve' these real contradictions. In his Mythology series, Lévi-Strauss would assert, much like Marx, that in this case we are dealing with ideological constructions that seek, on the contrary, to veil or mask certain real irresolvable contradictions, or to legitimize them. This leads him to a conclusion that contrasts sharply with his usual praise for the richness of mythical thought: 'The poverty of religious thought can never be overestimated'.[86] We are never far from the famous: 'Religion is the opium of the people.' But this is perhaps because Lévi-Strauss, as he was wont to say, found mythical thought and myths to be far richer than any religions and their rituals, even as they contained and inspired them.

He then sets about showing how the structuralist approach allows him to consider the relations between totemic groups and castes from a new angle. He reminds his reader that 'nothing could be more different than these two forms of institution'.[87] Indeed, totemic groups are usually associated with the most 'primitive' civilizations, and castes with 'highly evolved' societies, those of India in particular. Furthermore, castes are usually endogamous, while totemic groups are often exogamous. How can the two be compared? First of all, he points out that the function of both totemic groups and castes is to produce goods and/or services for the benefit of other groups. Each totemic group, for instance, performs for other groups, who do not possess a particular totem, rites for the multiplication of the plants and animals for which it is responsible. Each caste provides the other castes with the manufactured goods or services in which it specializes.

---

85  Ibid., p. 95.
86  Ibid.
87  Ibid., p. 113.

To bring out the relations of logical transformation that make it possible to connect and oppose totemic groups and castes, Lévi-Strauss goes back to the analyses he developed in *Totemism*. Totemic groups were based on the postulate of a homology between two systems of differences, one between natural species, the other between social groups. One occurs in nature, the other between men, and therefore in culture. This correspondence would begin to undergo profound changes 'if to the homologies between relations were added homologies between the terms of these relations' – between a particular natural species (an animal) and a particular human group (a clan).

Finally, he sees the possibility of a third case: a system in which the homologies were between the terms only. In this case, the structure would no longer mean that clan *a* differs from clan *b* in the same way as the eagle differs from the bear, but only that clan *a* is like the eagle and clan *b* is like the bear. Here, it is the intimate nature of each clan, its individual essence, that is associated with the species eagle or bear. In this case, each human group closes in on itself, is different from the others in its very essence; the conditions are now created for the group to reproduce itself without exchanging with the other groups, and so it becomes endogamous. Instead of the two systems of differences that resemble each other, we now have two systems of resemblances that differ from each other.

| | | | |
|---|---|---|---|
| Schema I | Nature = | species I ≠ species 2 ≠ ... species n | |
| | Culture = | group I ≠ group 2 ≠ ... group n | |

| | | | |
|---|---|---|---|
| Schema 2 | Nature = | species I ≠ species 2 ≠ ... species n | |
| | Culture = | group I ≠ group 2 ≠ ... group n | |

| | | | |
|---|---|---|---|
| Schema 3 | Nature = | species (a) \| species (b) \| ... \| species (n) | |
| | Culture = | group (a) \| group (b) \| ... \| group (n) | |

We immediately see that the third transformation would dissolve the society into various groups closed in upon their identity, which they share with a natural species and, at the end of this process, the society as a totality would have disappeared. Castes, as a structure, would partly correspond to the transformation illustrated in Schema 2. They entertain reciprocal and complementary relations with the other castes, owing to the goods and services each caste provides to the others. Each caste being different in nature from the others, however, each would keep its women for itself and exchange them within the caste, unlike totemic groups, which are usually exogamous. But since castes are rarely associated with natural species but instead with manufactured objects that explain the differential distances between them, Schema 2 does not really correspond to the caste system, and another schema must be created in order to associate, within the same transformation group, both totemic groups and castes. Lévi-Strauss advances the hypothesis that castes regard women as heterogeneous as far as nature is concerned, while totemic groups declare them to be heterogeneous from the point of view of culture. It follows that the women of the different castes can no more be exchanged than the natural species can interbreed. On the other hand, for totemic groups, whereas women are homogenous as far as nature is concerned, they are heterogeneous when it comes to culture.[88]

The two forms of social organization, according to Lévi-Strauss, thus entertain inversely symmetrical relations. Yet this symmetry has its limits.[89] Castes are functionally heterogeneous and produce real objects and services, whereas the function of totemic groups is to control and increase important natural species from the cultural and social standpoints. But

[their function] makes no real yield and amounts to no more than a repetition of the same illusion for all the groups . . . [For] each group similarly imagines itself to have magical powers over a species, but as this illusion has no foundation it is in fact no more than an empty form and as such identical to the other forms.[90]

88  Ibid., p. 125.
89  Ibid., p. 126.
90  Ibid., p. 125.

And he adds the following observation, which, oddly enough, denies the ritual services of the totemic groups their cultural nature:

> Totemic groups certainly [mimic functional prestations]. But apart from the fact that it remains imaginary, it is not cultural either since it must be classed, not among the arts of civilization, but as a fake usurpation of natural capacities which man as a biological species lacks.[91]

To see totemic rituals as services that are not of a cultural nature but are a 'fake usurpation of natural capacities which man lacks' is tantamount to saying that the whole religious domain, its founding myths and rituals are not only imaginary realities but illusions and lies that men tell themselves.

> The notion of a supernature exists only for a humanity which attributes supernatural powers to itself and in return ascribes the powers of its superhumanity to nature.[92]

This leads him to the following conclusion, the final step in his bid to dismantle the idea that totemic groups and castes belong to the same group of sociological transformations:

> Castes naturalize a true culture falsely, totemic groups culturalize a false nature truly.[93]

It is a brilliant formula. But to criticize totemic myths and rites as 'fake' seems inadequate. At any rate, it is hard to claim on the basis of this critique, as Lévi-Strauss would do at every opportunity, that mythical (and therefore religious) thought and scientific thought are not opposed by the nature of their logico-intellectual approaches but by their object, by the level at which each attempts to gain knowledge about the real world. Religious beliefs and their founding myths are conceived and experienced as intellectual and existential truths. And it is this key point,

---

91  Ibid., p. 126.
92  Ibid., p. 221.
93  Ibid., p. 127.

the fact of *believing* in events that never happened, in imaginary stories, as though they contained truths that gave a meaning to existence – it is the very fact of believing, then, that Lévi-Strauss never analyses. He identifies the logical structure of mythological narratives, but never really asks why these mythological stories exist, these purported 'lies' men tell themselves, these pure 'illusions' about their capacity to act on the world around them and on themselves. But in *The Savage Mind*, driven by his argument with Sartre, which is cut short throughout the book the better to burst forth in the final chapter, Lévi-Strauss takes a stand and explains himself:

> It is of course only for purposes of exposition and because they form the subject of this book that I am apparently giving a sort of priority to ideology and superstructures. I do not at all mean to suggest that ideological transformations give rise to social ones. Only the reverse is in fact true. Men's conception of the relations between nature and culture is a function of modifications of their own social relations. But, since my aim here is to outline a theory of superstructures, reasons of method require that they should be singled out for attention . . . we are however merely studying the shadows on the wall of the Cave without forgetting that it is only the attention we give them which lends them a semblance of reality.[94]

As we can read, not only does Lévi-Strauss accept without questioning the 'undoubted primacy of infrastructures',[95] he also considers that his work completes (and perhaps even corrects) the theory of superstructures 'scarcely touched on by Marx'. Here is a Lévi-Strauss more Marxist than Sartre and even, as we shall see, more Marxist than Marx, as *The Savage Mind* and the Mythology series fall into line to complete *Capital*.

It is therefore important to understand what he meant by making 'a contribution [to the theory of superstructures scarcely touched on by Marx]'. Returning to his analysis of the relationship between totemic groups and castes, he emphasizes that, behind what have traditionally been regarded as distinct and opposed social structures, he had shown

---

94  Ibid., p. 117.
95  Ibid., p. 130.

that a single conceptual schema was at work, intervening to create differential gaps between certain terms and to identify each of them in all the empirically observed states that had appeared to be heterogeneous. Yet this conceptual schema dictates the distinctive practices of different ways of life and forms of society, and operates in such a way that 'matter and form, neither with any independent existence, are realized as structures, that is as entities which are both empirical and intelligible'.[96]

The abstract general character of this definition means that it could apply equally to the production of an artwork or technical object and to a social institution. Put back into its original context, it refers to the observable empirical fact that the Aboriginal societies of Australia, for example, used the differences observed between natural species to characterize differences between human groups. It is hard to claim that these distinct species and social groups were 'neither with any independent existence' before they were subjected to a conceptual schema and linked together in a way that gave a (culturally) intelligible meaning to their relations.

Lévi-Strauss then turns to the concept of 'praxis' to designate the totality of the social activity of several human groups that make up a society. He does not define the term, but refers his reader to Sartre's *Critique of Dialectical Reason*,[97] and affirms that 'Marxism, if not Marx himself, has too commonly reasoned as though practices followed directly from praxis'.[98] Once again, Lévi-Strauss fails to give an example and does not define his terms. Praxis appears to be a sort of global view of the world and the men in it that demands, if it is to be translated into practices and the concrete institutions that bring it about, that conceptual schemata operate as mediators between the global view and the distinct domains of people's concrete life. Developing the theory of superstructures would thus consist in isolating these conceptual schemata and discovering how they perform their task of mediation in different sociological and historical contexts. That would be the job of anthropology, which is, therefore, 'first of all psychology'.[99] Much has

---

96 Ibid.

97 J.-P. Sartre, *Critique of Dialectical Reason*, trans. A. Sheridan-Smith (London and New York, Verso, 2009; originally published in French in 1960).

98 *The Savage Mind*, p. 130.

99 Ibid., p. 131.

been written about this formula, which is a provocative way of recalling what Lévi-Strauss had already demonstrated in his study of kinship systems, namely: that social relations cannot exist without the intervention of operations of the human mind or of conceptual schemata to produce and reproduce them. Which brings us to his definition of the dialectic of superstructures.

> The dialectic of superstructures, like that of language, consists in:
>
> (1) setting up *constituent* units (which for this purpose have to be defined unequivocally, that is by contrasting them in pairs)
>
> (2) so as to be able by means of them to elaborate a system
>
> (3) which plays the part of a synthesizing operator between ideas and facts, thereby turning the latter into signs. The mind thus passes from empirical diversity to conceptual simplicity and then from conceptual simplicity to meaningful synthesis.[100]

This description of the dialectic of superstructures (the nature and number of which are not given) sums up everything Lévi-Strauss had worked out since 1955 to describe and define the nature of myths and the operations of mythical thinking: mythemes as constituent units of mythological discourse; transformation of words and images into signs, whose meaning is given by the position they occupy and the function they ensure in the transformations-permutations group that constitutes a mythical system; etc. It is hard to see how this can be used to explain other domains of social life, for example political relations and forms of government. Besides, where does Lévi-Strauss place political relations? On the side of superstructures? If so, he does not say. And when it comes to infrastructures (vaguely defined as techno-economic structures), which of the sciences is responsible for these if anthropology (providing it is inspired by structuralism) and psychology (ditto) are devoted to superstructures? The answer is unclear. Indeed, for Lévi-Strauss, 'the development of the study of infrastructures proper is a task which must be left to history – with the aid of demography, technology, historical geography and ethnography. It is not principally the ethnologist's concern, for ethnology is first of all psychology.'[101]

---

100 Ibid.
101 Ibid., pp. 130–1.

Why is history assigned the study of infrastructures and not that of superstructures? He does not say. And what profit for science can be drawn from the metaphorical use of the terms 'infrastructure' and 'superstructure', which in fact are poor translations of the German terms *Grundlage* and *Überbau* used by Marx? *Grundlage* designates the foundations of a building, and *Überbau* the building resting on these foundations. Marx used these images borrowed from architecture to make it easier to understand his theoretical postulate of the 'primacy' of social relations – which organize and control the production of the material conditions of the existence of societies, and therefore the existence of their members – over the other kinds of social relations with which they compose a given form of society.

But what did this notion of 'primacy' mean? It implied the idea that 'economic' relations alone had the capacity to act on all other social relations, such that the latter would be forced to modify their structures in order to 'correspond' to the conditions of functioning and reproduction of the economic structures. In these terms, Marx postulated the existence of 'correspondence laws' (*Entsprechungsgesetze*) between modes of production, kinship systems, political and religious systems, and so on. It was the discovery of these correspondences, which explain the reason for social facts and changes in history, that was for him the primary task of the social sciences.

*The Savage Mind* was written in Paris in the 1960s, when Marxism dominated the ideological stage alongside structuralism, but to a greater extent. Lévi-Strauss, who claimed to be a materialist and was anxious to refute the accusations of idealism, formalism and intellectualism that his earlier writings had earned him, hence espoused the Marxist thesis of the primacy of infrastructures.

The problem is that, even when used metaphorically, the notions of infrastructure and superstructure are not tools adapted to the scientific analysis of social facts. Within a society, kinship relations, for instance, form a system; they are not a 'superstructure' resting on a mode of production and in a relation of 'correspondence' with it. They have their own reasons for existing and their own capacities to reproduce themselves, even when other social relations that make up the same society change or disappear. Today's Christianity is not that of the early Church; in Europe it changed with the emergence and later the disappearance of feudalism, followed by the development of the capitalist world economic system. But a core constant has survived, namely, the content of the Gospels and the image of a God believed to have died to redeem the sins of mankind and bring the promise of salvation in the next world. The different domains of social life thus function in a largely autonomous fashion, which does not support the hypothesis of the 'ultimate causality' of economic relations. Yet it is this hypothesis that Lévi-Strauss would return to in order to explain the differences between variants of a same Amerindian myth, based on differences between the infrastructures of the societies in which these variants were found.

Following his bold comparison between totemic groups and castes, Lévi-Strauss poses the general problem of classifications, whether totemic or other, as they appear in myths and rituals. And he would underscore another, altogether fundamental, characteristic of these classificatory schemes: they aim to grasp 'the natural and social universe . . . as an organized whole'. Indeed it is typical of mythical thinking and religions to seek to encompass in their discourse the entire universe and to establish man's place within it. But that runs entirely counter to the positive sciences. These are constantly faced with the fact that, just when they have explained one thing, something else pops up demanding to be analysed and explained. Modern scientific thought is thus an open system of provisional knowledge. Mythical and religious thought, on the other hand, is a totalizing thought, which in principle is closed around definitive explanations. In order to attain its goal, the kind of thought that produces myths needs to proceed on the principle that all levels of the universe ideally can be converted into one another. This convertibility supposes a homology among these levels, in other words posits the equivalence between the terms and relations found on one level and the terms and relations found on other levels. Lévi-Strauss would call on the notion of natural species to show that mythical thought made this notion the preferred operator for 'the passage from the unity of a multiplicity to the diversity of a unity'.[102]

Before going any further, let us pause and examine the way Lévi-Strauss presented the caste system of India. In effect, his analysis left to one side (or ignored) one aspect of the system whose crucial importance

---

102 Ibid., pp. 135–6.

would be demonstrated four years later, in 1966, by Louis Dumont, in a masterful book, *Homo Hierarchicus: The Caste System and Its Implications*.[103] This element was the religious, metaphysical basis of the caste system. For the separation between the castes and their hierarchy is not based on the economic principle of the division of labour and the specialization of functions, but on the degree of purity and impurity attaching to each function and task, and of course to the person performing them. The function castes, or *jati*, are, as we know, subdivisions of the four major categories, or *varna*, which divide society and establish its hierarchy.

At the top are the priests, the Brahmins, whose task is to perform sacrifices for the rest of the population. Then come the Kshatriyas, the warriors, who are allowed to spill human blood; then the Vaishyas, the farmers and craftsmen; and, finally, the Shudras, the lowest status, whose members do not have the right to be initiated, to be 'twice born' like the members of the other *varna*. Of course, because all these castes produced goods and services useful to everyone, their functions and activities were at once complementary and mutually exclusive.

Rooted in the religious cosmology of the great Vedic texts, dating from 2000 years BCE and formalized between the second and the seventh century CE at the time of the composition of the Mahabharata and the Ramayana, the caste system gradually organized and restructured all the local groups, with the exception of some that resisted and have preserved their tribal organization down to the present. By ensuring that everyone had a place in their caste, fulfilled their *dharma* and contributed, through their different functions, to the reproduction of society and the universe, the caste system indeed illustrated the *illusion* that Lévi-Strauss spoke of with regard to the Australian Aboriginal totemic groups, and their claim to control through rituals the growth and increase of the animal and plant species that were their totems. Castes therefore do not 'falsely' ground their social and cultural differences in nature, as Lévi-Strauss wrote. They ground them 'really' in an imaginary religious universe that encompasses, in the same way myths do, the cosmos and the society in the form of 'an organized totality'.

---

103  L. Dumont, *Homo Hierarchicus: The Caste System and Its Implications*, complete revised English edition, trans. M. Sainsbury, L. Dumont and B. Gulati (Chicago, University of Chicago Press, 1970).

To be sure, this criticism of his analysis of the Indian caste system takes nothing away from the interest of the comparison Lévi-Strauss had attempted to draw between exogamous totemic groups and endogamous castes. But it does highlight his lack of interest in and frequent blindness to the religious dimension of social facts. Beliefs interested him; the fact of believing did not.

We shall now resume our examination of classification systems and the different levels at which they operate. Several systems exist, ranging from the most abstract and general to the most concrete and particular. In order these are: the level of categories, that of elements, that of species and finally that of names. When it wants to send a message, a society can therefore encode it in different vocabularies. It can use *categories* such as above and below, strong and weak, big and little, which offer 'the greatest rigour and logical simplicity'.[104] But it can also encode the same relations in a different way, and translate the opposition of the categories of above and below by an opposition between two *elements*: heaven and earth. Or by an opposition between two *species*, for instance a celestial animal, the eagle, and a terrestrial animal, the bear. Finally, it can descend the ladder and attach *names* to the individuals belonging to a social group, by reference to a given part of the body of the eponymous species chosen by the group. The final classificatory level is that of *proper names*, which represent 'the *quanta of signification* below which one no longer does anything but point'.[105]

Of these four levels, that of *species* is particularly important for constructing what are known as 'totemic' classifications. First, because, according to Lévi-Strauss, 'the diversity of species furnishes man with the most intuitive picture at his disposal and constitutes the most direct manifestation he can perceive of the ultimate discontinuity of reality. It is the sensible expression of an objective coding'.[106] The human mind borrows this coding to create other taxonomies. But a second aspect of the notion of species makes it a preferential operator:

---

104 C. Lévi-Strauss, *Anthropology and Myth: Lectures, 1951–1982*, trans. R. Willis (Oxford, Basil Blackwell, 1987), p. 35.

105 *The Savage Mind*, p. 215, original emphasis; see also p. 176: 'proper names are formed by detotalizing species and by deducting a partial aspect of them.'

106 Ibid., p. 137.

As a medial classifier (and therefore the one with the greatest yield and the most frequently employed) the species level can widen its net upwards, that is in the direction of elements, categories, and numbers, or contract downwards, in the direction of proper names . . . The network to which this twofold movement gives rise is itself cross-cut at every level, for there are a great many different manners in which these levels and their ramifications can be signified . . . Each system is therefore defined with reference to two axes, one horizontal and one vertical.[107]

These networks of meanings are constructed along both a horizontal syntagmatic axis and a vertical paradigmatic axis. An animal can thus be considered either as representative of a species or as an individual member of its species. It appears as 'a conceptual tool with multiple possibilities for detotalizing or retotalizing any domain, synchronic or diachronic, concrete or abstract, natural or cultural.'[108]

Already this text sheds some light, from a theoretical standpoint, on the nature and conceptual function of the 'animal figures' that will populate the four volumes of the Mythology series: jaguar, nightjar, coyote, Loon Woman and so on.

Having come to this point in his analyses, Lévi-Strauss defines what he will thereafter call 'la pensée sauvage', the book's title (rendered in English as 'the savage mind'), literally 'savage thought', revisiting Auguste Comte's expression 'spontaneous thought':

In this book [The Savage Mind] it is neither the mind of savages nor that of primitive or archaic humanity, but rather mind in its untamed state as distinctive from mind cultivated or domesticated for the purpose of yielding a return. This latter has appeared at certain points of the globe and at certain moments in history . . . We are better able

---

107 Ibid., p. 149.

108 Ibid. In *Anthropology and Myth*, Lévi-Strauss goes on to say: 'But most importantly, the notion of species contains remarkable logical properties, since the two dimensions of extension and intelligibility reach equilibrium at this level: the species is a collection of individuals who are similar in certain respects, and each individual is an organism consisting of different parts. It is thus possible, through the idea of species, to pass from one type of unity to another type, which is complementary and opposed: either the unity of a multiplicity, or the diversity of a unity' (p. 36).

to understand today that it is possible for the two to co-exist and interpenetrate.[109]

If his analyses of totemic systems give the reader an increasingly clear idea of 'mind in its untamed state', alternatively, 'mind domesticated for the purpose of yielding a return' is never defined. Does the expression refer to the long process of observation, reflection and invention that prepared certain human groups, over the course of the five or ten thousand years that constituted what is known as the Neolithic era, to produce the first canoes enabling them to cross lakes and travel on rivers? But was the same concern with 'yield', in other words efficiency, not already at work in the invention of bows and arrows, fishing nets, big-game traps and so on in the Mesolithic era? Must we date the appearance of domesticated thought to the appearance of cities, city-states and empires, in Sumer, Egypt, ancient China, pre-Columbian America, with their temples, palaces, fortresses, but also with their subject populations? It seems that Lévi-Strauss leaned in this direction, but nowhere does he spell it out.

For what reasons did certain 'cold' societies become 'hot'?[110] On this point, again, Lévi-Strauss sticks to generalities. He mentions the incidence of demographic factors, 'smoothing down antagonisms which manifest themselves within the group or between groups' and 'economic and social upheavals'[111] whose formation they were unable to prevent. And we do not know if by 'group' he meant here a society, a local group, a tribe, or one of the 'groups' that make up a society, a clan for example. Nor do we learn what causes the demographic expansion of a society, and at what level this expansion threatens the society's reproduction. Or why the antagonisms within a cold society arise, and why they compromise the continuity of the society in question. Do they stem from rivalry over access to arable land or to fishing and hunting

---

109 *The Savage Mind*, p. 219.

110 It is in his 'Conversations' with Georges Charbonnier (October–December 1959) that Lévi-Strauss drops the distinction between 'societies without history' and 'societies with history' and adopts a distinction between cold and hot societies, speaking of their 'more or less elevated historical temperature'. G. Charbonnier, ed., *Conversations with Claude Lévi-Strauss*, trans. J. and D. Weightman (London, Jonathan Cape, 1969), p. 33.

111 *The Savage Mind*, pp. 234–5.

territories? Or, at another level, from a struggle to appropriate control of the rituals essential to the society's survival? But would such a struggle suffice to turn a 'cold' society into a 'hot' one?

Furthermore, if it is true, as Lévi-Strauss writes, that it 'is tedious as well as useless, in this connection, to amass arguments to prove that all societies are in history and change; that this is so is patent',[112] it is just as patent that societies practise two types of change when faced with accumulations of events that threaten their reproduction: changes the society finds itself forced to implement so as not to alter its structure, its internal organization or its ideology; and changes that engage the society's very structure. It is in these contexts that certain cold societies can turn into 'hot' societies, but also into other forms of 'cold' societies.

Can it be said, as Lévi-Strauss does, that societies compelled to change by antagonisms arising internally or by upheavals imposed from without – wars, prolonged drought, etc. – have 'sided with history', have 'elected to explain themselves by history', have 'resolutely internaliz[ed] the historical process and [made] it the moving power of their development'? These are fine expressions – but what does it mean for a society to 'side with history'? Does it mean to resign itself to change, to no longer doing what 'the ancestors taught us', or on the contrary to desire change ardently?[113] In what sense did 'hot' societies, like those of the Maya or the Aztecs, who believed in the existence of great cosmic cycles culminating in the destruction of a certain form of humanity, choose to explain themselves to themselves *by means* of history and to resolutely *internalize* their historical development? For that to happen, the development had to have been conceived and experienced as devoid of any supernatural dimension or cosmic meaning. That was clearly impossible. Whatever the nature of the changes that occur in the development of a society, whether endured or desired, and however they may have been conceived, we know that any significant change entails unexpected consequences not desired by those who initiated the changes or endured them.

Humans are always faced with the unintended consequences of their acts, of their *praxis*, to use the word proposed by Marx and

112  Ibid., p. 234.
113  Ibid., pp. 232–4, 236.

adopted by Lévi-Strauss and Sartre in their time (1960 for Sartre, 1962 for Lévi-Strauss). In fact, Sartre had invented the term 'practico-inert' to designate the unintended results of an intentional action.[114] Any society, whether cold or hot, must therefore deal with the unexpected consequences of the changes it has desired or endured. It has no choice but 'to side with history', to 'internalize its historical development'.

But Lévi-Strauss does not limit the exercise of mind in its non-domesticated state to cold societies. He maintains that this form of 'savage' thought continued to exist side by side, and to interpenetrate thought in its domesticated state as soon as the latter appeared and began to develop.

> There are still zones in which savage thought, like savage species, is relatively protected. This is the case of art . . . and it is particularly the case of so many as yet 'uncleared' sectors of social life, where, through indifference or inability ... primitive thought continues to flourish.[115]

In what sectors of social life does non-domesticated thought continue to flourish through the indifference or the incapacity of those who would or could domesticate it?[116] And who precisely is indifferent or incapable, and with respect to what? We will never get an answer. And in what sense might painting, sculpture, production of the bronze ritual vessels of ancient China, the Pygmies' polyphonic singing, etc., reflect the savage mind rather than a domesticated mind? Finally, one's best guess is that the mind in its 'savage state' would seem to correspond to the mental activity involved in producing imaginary worlds, myths, religious systems, works of art.

> The exceptional features of this mind which we call savage . . . relate principally to the extensive nature of the ends it assigns itself. It claims at once to analyse and to synthesize, to go to its furthest limits in both

---

114  Ibid., p. 234. For Lévi-Strauss, 'the analysis of the practico-inert quite simply revives the language of animism' (p. 249).

115  Ibid., p. 219.

116  In addition to the artist's activity, Lévi-Strauss refers to that of the 'bricoleur'. Cf. Charbonnier, ed., *Conversations with Claude Lévi-Strauss*, p. 110.

directions, while at the same time remaining capable of mediating between the two poles.[117]

But modern scientific thought, too, is analytical and synthetic at once, and it does not differ from mythical thought, as Lévi-Strauss claims, only because it addresses other aspects of reality than the domain of sensible qualities. The difference goes deeper, and it is intractable. It lies in the fact that myth, as well as religion and ritual, are intended to offer a totalizing – if not total – explanation of the nature of the universe and humankind.[118] For believers, everything is already contained in the Bible or the Rig Veda. Science, on the other hand, does not claim to provide a definitive explanation of the phenomena it studies. Scientific knowledge of one aspect of the way the universe or man functions always opens onto other aspects and other domains needing to be studied and understood. The analytical-synthetic movement of the sciences is and must be unceasing.

But how, according to Lévi-Strauss, can mythical thought encompass the universe and close in on itself? By means of abstract operations that invent imaginary equivalents authorizing 'the convertibility of categories into elements, of elements into species, of species into proper names and vice versa'.[119] Science cannot turn above and below into heaven and earth, then heaven and earth into the relation between the eagle and the bear, etc., and it cannot discover in these conversions a single message emitted through these codes. Scientific explanation, as Lévi-Strauss rightly says, consists 'not in moving from the complex to the simple but in the replacement of a less intelligible complexity by one which is more so'.[120] Mythical thought proceeds in the same manner, except that in this case, *everything* becomes intelligible, whereas no 'experimental' verification is capable of proof. Only the act of believing can attest to the truth. But, as we have said, Lévi-Strauss always leaves believing in the shadows, attending only to the structures of the forms of thought and narrative that express what is believed in.

---

117 *The Savage Mind*, p. 219.

118 Ibid., p. 245. Lévi-Strauss refers to 'this intransigent refusal on the part of the savage mind to allow anything human (or even living) to remain alien to it', and sees in this the same ambition as that pursued by 'dialectical reason'.

119 *Anthropology and Myth*, p. 50.

120 *The Savage Mind*, p. 248.

In short, on the basis of this twofold distinction between the savage mind and the domesticated mind, on the one hand, and between 'cold' and 'hot' societies, on the other, Lévi-Strauss prepares to do battle with Sartre in the final chapter of *The Savage Mind*, proclaiming himself more faithful to Marx than Sartre (when it comes to dialectic) and more materialist (when it comes to philosophy) as well. This stance leads him to launch a violent attack on the privileged position of history among the sciences of man in any attempt to account for humankind. For, to account for humanity, one must 'venture to undertake the resolution of the human into the non-human . . . in so far as I believe the ultimate goal of the human sciences to be not to constitute, but to dissolve man.'[121]

To dissolve man means 'to arrive at invariants beyond the empirical diversity of human societies'. Such should be the task of anthropology, in his eyes, by means of which we may ultimately 'reabsorb particular humanities into a general one . . . [But] the idea of some general humanity to which ethnographic reduction leads will bear no relation to any one may have formed in advance.' It is therefore necessary to go further, toward 'the reintegration of culture in nature and finally of life within the whole of its physico-chemical conditions . . . And when we do finally succeed in understanding life as a function of inert matter, it will be to discover that the latter has properties very different from those previously attributed to it.'[122]

In these lines, Lévi-Strauss lays claim to a materialism that only remotely resembles the nineteenth-century version developed by Friedrich Engels in his *Dialectics of Nature*. In the process of reduction and the passage from one level to another, the richness and complexity of a supposedly higher level will be explained by the properties of the lower level to which the analysis has reduced it. Thereupon, Lévi-Strauss advances a provocative thesis that Engels would probably not have endorsed, due to the choice of the word 'thing' to designate the human mind: 'As the mind too is a thing, the functioning of this thing teaches us something about the nature of things: even pure reflection is in the last analysis an internalization of the cosmos. It illustrates the structure of what lies outside in a symbolic form.'[123]

---

121  Ibid., pp. 246–7.
122  Ibid., pp. 247–8.
123  Ibid., p. 248, footnote.

Clearly this materialist and 'monist' view of the world and man does not allow us to trace as clear a line between nature and man as that proposed by Lévi-Strauss in 1949, in the first two chapters of *The Elementary Structures of Kinship*. Lévi-Strauss acknowledged as much, hence this footnote which anticipates what he would write five years later in the Preface to the book's second edition: 'The opposition between nature and culture to which I attached much importance at one time now seems to be [mainly of] methodological importance.'[124]

He is much less prudent when it comes to philosophical theses – such as his reductionist view of materialism – than when he advances his anthropological conclusions. He does not hesitate, for example, to accept responsibility for a totalizing view of the world and man which is by no means proven. He even justifies his position by declaring that 'this seems to me just the attitude of any scientist who is an agnostic, [and] there is nothing very compromising about it, for ants with their . . . social life and their chemical messages, already present a sufficiently tough resistance to the enterprises of analytical reason.'[125] Indeed, Sartre had accused Lévi-Strauss of behaving like an 'esthete', who 'purports to study men as if they were ants'.[126] This materialist philosophy, which Lévi-Strauss would describe as 'a few homely convictions' in his Mythology series, would be strongly reiterated in his conclusion to *The Naked Man*,[127] again in opposition to Sartre and the philosophers of the Subject, the Self.

The second battlefield on which Lévi-Strauss confronts Sartre is the criticism of his ethnocentrism and, beyond this, a rebuttal of Sartre's accusation of ignoring history as the collecting of facts and as a scientific discipline that supposedly occupies a privileged position among the human sciences for gaining knowledge about mankind: 'He who begins by steeping himself in the allegedly self-evident truths of introspection never emerges from them.'[128]

---

124  Ibid., p. 247, footnote.
125  Ibid., pp. 246–7.
126  Sartre, *Critique of Dialectical Reason*, and Lévi-Strauss *The Savage Mind*, p. 246.
127  'I have no philosophy of my own worth bothering about, aside from a few homely convictions that I have come back to, less through the development of my own thought than through regressive erosion of the philosophy I was taught, and that I myself once taught' (*The Naked Man*, p. 638).
128  *The Savage Mind*, p. 249.

Egocentrism and ethnocentrism go hand in hand, encouraging the belief that 'man has taken refuge in a single one of the historical or geographical modes of his existence, when the truth about man resides in the system of their differences and common properties'.[129] Yet is it not the job of history, with the aid of geography, to study and explain these differences and common properties? This is where the assault begins: 'The anthropologist respects history but he does not accord it a special value. He conceives it as a study complementary to his own.'[130]

Here Lévi-Strauss is talking about history as a human science. However, 'a historical fact is what really took place, but where did anything take place? . . . historical facts are no more given than any other. It is the historian, or the agent of history, who constitutes them by abstraction and as though under the threat of an infinite regress.'[131]

> History is therefore never history, but history-for. It is partial in the sense of being biased even when it claims not to be, for it inevitably remains partial – that is, incomplete – and this is itself a form of partiality. [The history of the French Revolution] cannot simultaneously and under the same heading, be that of the Jacobin and that of the aristocrat. One must therefore choose between two alternatives . . . or a third . . . and give up the attempt to find in history a totalization of the set of all partial totalizations.[132]

> History is a discontinuous set composed of domains of history, each of which is defined by a [specific] frequency.[133]

> The historian's relative choice . . . is always confined to the choice between history which teaches us more and explains less, and history which explains more and teaches less.[134]

---

129 Ibid.
130 Ibid., p. 256.
131 Ibid., p. 257.
132 Ibid., pp. 257–8. See also p. 245: 'The so-called men of the Left still cling to a period of contemporary history [the French Revolution] which bestowed the blessing of a congruence between practical imperatives and schemes of interpretation.'
133 Ibid., pp. 259–60.
134 Ibid., p. 262.

To avoid getting caught up in such a dilemma, we would therefore

> need only recognize that history is a method with no distinct object corresponding to it to reject the equivalence between the notion of history and the notion of humanity which some have tried to foist on us ... [History] consists wholly in its method, which experience proves to be indispensable for cataloguing the elements of any struc-ture whatever, human or non-human, in their entirety ... history may lead to anything, provided you get out of it.[135]

After the analysis of history as historical facts, then history as the activity of historians, there remained history as seen by philosophers: the interpretation by means of philosophy of the history of men or the history of historians. Concerning Sartre's history, Lévi-Strauss's judgment is final: 'In Sartre's system, history plays exactly the part of a myth.'[136]

But let us come back to the criticism of history and historians. With the exception of one point – the distinction between societies that strive to reproduce themselves identically and those that foster change within them-selves – there is nothing original about Lévi-Strauss's criticisms, which remain general. No specific historian is cited, and yet Lévi-Strauss could have mentioned, in France, Marc Bloch and Lucien Febvre. While at the Collège de France, he had as colleagues, among other historians, Fernand Braudel and Georges Duby. Every historian knows that the history of the French Revolution as experienced and told by the Jacobins was not and could not have been the history told by the aristocrats on the receiving end. Historians and anthropologists alike must work to decentre themselves, to bracket off the prejudices of their time and their education that bear on the times and the societies of the past under study. Anachronism and ethno-centrism are the two temptations they must continuously fight, the two primary epistemological obstacles to overcome.

Even without reading Marx or Augustin Thierry, historians know that, in societies divided into castes or classes with forms of state, the relations of subordination binding the different social groups together are relations of both interest and power, and therefore contain the seeds

---

135  Ibid.
136  Ibid., p. 254.

of potential conflicts and antagonisms. They also know that, in any society, including those without castes or classes and without a State, social relations harbour contradictions and oppositions that must be either legitimized, or veiled and transfigured. That can only be done by means of thought and in the mind, and engenders systems of representations and symbolic practices that can, in principle, neither completely coincide with the reality of the facts nor erase them. In short, because it is subjected to the same epistemological constraints, the activity of the historian has much in common with that of the anthropologist. In the end, the criticisms Lévi-Strauss addresses in 1962 to history-as-facts and history-as-discipline are not aimed at historians in general, as an overly hasty reading might suggest, but at bad historians. Two points should be distinguished in his analyses: one is a positive contribution; the other, one of his more debatable theories.

The positive point is his insistence on the need to take into account the way a society thinks and experiences its 'historical development' and how it acts on itself as a function of its representations of the world and of itself. That is what the historian François Hartog has since dubbed 'regimes of historicity', which characterize societies according to their nature and their time.[137] Hartog was preceded in this line of thought, in the anthropological field, by the work of Marshall Sahlins on the circumstances of the death of Captain Cook when he returned unexpectedly (for the islanders) to Hawaii soon after having left.[138] Sahlins describes how this return must have been thought and experienced by the Hawaiians, who had received Cook on his first visit as the personification of one of their gods, arriving from the sea, but who should not have returned before the end of a cosmic cycle. Sahlins thus brought out what he called the 'structure of the conjuncture' that Cook's arrival and return had signified for the population of Hawaii. The expression could apply to the study of other conjunctures: the way Cortés's arrival was perceived and experienced in his first days by the Aztecs and their emperor, as well as many other encounters between different societies and cultures, for example the Greeks and the Persians, or the Romans and the Gauls.

---

137  F. Hartog, *Les Régimes d'historicité. Présentisme et expériences du temps* (Paris, Seuil, 2003).

138  M. Sahlins, *Islands of History* (Chicago, University of Chicago Press, 1984).

The other – highly debatable – point is the opposition Lévi-Strauss establishes between savage thought and domesticated thought ('of which historical knowledge is one aspect'), based on the relationship between discontinuity and continuity in history and in the universe. If he is to be believed, historians were seeking to 'transcend an original discontinuity' by producing knowledge that was not 'discontinuous and analogical', like that produced by the savage mind, but 'interstitial and unifying', intent on reducing gaps and 'dissolving differences'.[139] What does he mean by this description of the historian's work as striving to construct an artificial continuity by dint of reducing gaps and dissolving differences? What differences, what gaps, between what and what? What is this 'original discontinuity' they are seeking to overcome? This is something we are never told.

In reality, whether or not one is a historian, life shows that continuity and discontinuity are present from the start and unfailingly associated in both nature and society. The king dies but the monarchy lives on, light is both a wave and a particle; as we age, each of us feels at once the same and different. The continuity constructed by the historian is not an 'analytical and abstract reality' obtained 'by dint of fraudulent [lines]'.[140] It is synthetic and concrete. Furthermore, historians know that, to understand and explain a bygone era, it is not enough to know what happened afterwards (something the actors of the time could not know); they must rethink each moment of the past as a possible that came to pass among all the other possibles that did not. And among the possibles that came to pass, not all worked out in the same way. Why?

To put the past into the present and discover in this present several possible futures are the difficult tasks the historian must perform for his narrative to come closer to the historical facts than that of the Jacobin or the aristocrat, while at the same time being capable of accounting for their narratives and the role they played in the thick of these facts. Historians strive to restore their twofold nature to historical events, which are both necessary and contingent. But at the time Lévi-Strauss was writing *The Savage Mind* (1962) and until *The Way of the Masks* (1979), if history occupied 'a

---

139  *The Savage Mind*, p. 263.
140  Ibid., p. 261.

paramount place', it was 'the place that rightfully belong[ed] to that irreducible contingency'.[141]

To the historian, contingency; to the anthropologist, assisted by structural anthropology, necessity. I will come back to this debate when I analyse the Mythology series. As of now, though, I would like to mention two sets of facts that contradict the thesis of the irreducible contingency of human history. These are, on the one hand, the appearance, in the fifth millennium before our era, of cities and states at different points on the globe – Sumer, Egypt, China, India, and later, South and Central America; and on the other hand, the emergence of religions looking beyond death, driven by desire for and anxiety about immortality and salvation. Each of these two sets of facts, which appeared at different times and in different places, suggests the existence of sociological and historical processes which gave rise to social institutions and structures that were comparable both in their similarities and in their differences. Each time, depending on the context, the local traditions and the people, similar problems met with responses that were both comparable, because they took societies down parallel paths running in the same direction, and different, because they reflected the particular forms and contents adopted in each instance by the sociological process of state formation or the appearance of religions of salvation.

As we have seen, it was not until 1979 and the second edition of *The Way of the Masks* that Lévi-Strauss would explain that historians of the European Middle Ages had managed to identify the principal features of the kinship systems known as 'house' systems, and that observers like Saint-Simon had shared with us such systems' intrigues and strategies. It was in his 1983 Marc Bloch Lecture that he would propose to historians a scientific collaboration defined in less unequal terms than in 1962, in *The Savage Mind*.[142]

The book ends on a new apology of the 'positive', if not scientific, character of savage thought and therefore of mythical thought, which is, it seems, the spontaneous expression of the former. Lévi-Strauss

141 C. Lévi-Strauss, *From Honey to Ashes: Introduction to a Science of Mythology 2*, trans. J. and D. Weightman (Chicago, University of Chicago Press, 1973), p. 475.

142 C. Lévi-Strauss, 'Histoire et ethnologie', *Annales ESC* 38, n° 6 (1983), pp. 1217–31.

reminds us that the savage mind is 'logical', that 'it proceeds through understanding, not affectivity, with the aid of distinctions and oppositions, not by confusion and participation' (contrary to Lévy-Bruhl's theory of the pre-logical, participative mentality of primitive peoples).[143] He credits the savage mind with having discerned 'as through a glass darkly' the role of information in the natural world, thus anticipating the most recent discoveries of information theory, which now 'extends to phenomena not intrinsically possessing the character of messages'.

> In treating the sensible properties of the animal and plant kingdoms as if they were the elements of a message, and in discovering 'signatures' – and so signs – in them, men have made mistakes of identification: the meaningful element was not always the one they supposed . . . and even though they interpreted them as if they were messages, men were nevertheless able to arrive at some of their properties.[144]

Despite the restrictive 'not always', Lévi-Strauss nevertheless goes on to conclude with what in the end appears as a radical affirmation:

> Certainly the properties to which the savage mind has access are not the same as those which have commanded the attention of scientists . . . The physical world is approached from opposite ends in the two cases: . . . one proceeds from the angle of sensible qualities and the other from that of formal properties . . . [That would explain] why both [approaches], independently of each other in time and space, should have led to two distinct though equally positive sciences . . . We have had to wait until the middle of this century for the crossing of long-separated paths . . . The entire process of human knowledge thus assumes the character of a closed system.[145]

Yet beneath the shiny veneer of the formulas and the confidence with which they are advanced, we perceive a flaw. If it is self-evident that millennia of observation and analysis of nature have allowed men to

---

143 *The Savage Mind*, p. 268.
144 Ibid., pp. 268–9.
145 Ibid., p. 269.

amass a treasure of positive concrete knowledge about the animal and plant species in their environment, and even about the countless species that had no practical use but were 'good to think'; and if, in order to think, men proceeded by logical operations common to men of all times, if then the two forms of thought can be complementary at one level (that of the observation of nature, which nothing can replace), they are mutually exclusive at another. The eaglehawk and the raven are indeed two birds with different 'lifestyles': one hunts its prey, the other eats carrion; but neither emits a 'message'. They are used by men to send messages to themselves, which find a place in their interpretations of the world and of themselves. By contrast, the chemicals secreted by body cells in certain circumstances are not imaginary 'messages' emitted by things and beings distinct from humans and belonging to their natural environment. It is therefore 'as if' these chemical secretions carried information to certain cells along with the order to react. Information in this case designates a property implied by the functioning of finalized living organisms that could only be discovered by modern science.

There is therefore nothing in common between the finality devoid of human intention of biological mechanisms, and the intentional anthropomorphic finality the savage mind attributes to natural species and which is used to emit messages addressed by humans to themselves. One is discovered by hypotheses and the experiments that verify them; the other is imaginary, and convinces only those already willing to believe. Primitive thought is based on concrete knowledge but does not broaden it, instead transforming it into fantasised realities.

In the conclusion to *The Elementary Structures of Kinship*,[146] we had already learned that women were both signs and producers of signs and that, as such, they were used by men to communicate among themselves, since they exchanged women as one exchanges words. In 1962

146 C. Lévi-Strauss, *The Elementary Structures of Kinship*, trans. J. H. Bell and J. R. von Sturmer and R. Needham, ed., (Boston, Beacon Press, 1969), p. 496. See also: 'Social Structure', a paper published in 1952 in A. L. Kroeber, ed., *Anthropology Today* (Chicago, University of Chicago Press, 1953), translated in *Structural Anthropology*, pp. 277–323, see p. 296. In 1952, Lévi-Strauss presented before the International Conference of Linguists and Anthropologists, at Bloomington, Indiana, a paper entitled 'Toward a General Theory of Communication'.

Lévi-Strauss still thought he would develop the elements of a 'general theory of communication'.[147]

At the end of that year, he had thus finished working out the concepts and the method that were to enable him to tackle the huge corpus of Amerindian myths. His demonstration would stretch over more than eight years, at the end of which he thought he had finally set anthropology on new foundations.

---

147 Cf. C. Lévi-Strauss, 'Language and the Analysis of Social Laws', *American Anthropologist* 53, n° 2 (1951), pp. 155–63. Reprinted in *Structural Anthropology*, pp. 55–66.

# 9
## The Mythology Series (1964–1971)

After his election to the Collège de France in 1959, Lévi-Strauss devoted one of the two seminars he gave in 1960–61 to his research on totemism and on the savage mind, which prepared the two books that would appear in 1962. But, in 1961–62, he had already begun the research that would allow him to write *The Raw and the Cooked*, published in 1964. He spent 1962–63 analysing the myths that would provide the material of *From Honey to Ashes*, published in 1967. The academic year 1963–64 was devoted to the myths dealing with the origin of table manners, to which he would return in 1966–67, the book of the same title appearing in 1968. We thus see a gap of several years between the research, the presentation of his findings in his courses – a time corresponding to the writing of the manuscript – and finally the publication of a book.

The final book in the Mythology series, *The Naked Man*, took four years, divided between research and teaching: a first sequence in 1965–66, a second in 1967–68, a third in 1969–70 and a final sequence in 1970–71. *The Naked Man* would appear in 1971, in a single volume that was much longer than the three others: Lévi-Strauss knew he could have written several more, but, exhausted, he wanted to be done with it.

> After writing the third volume I told myself that I would never be able to finish because several more were still required. So I decided that I would do only one more, the fourth, and that I would have to put into

it, in the form of allusions or invitations to future work, everything else I had to say.[1]

Subsequently, *The Jealous Potter*, which would appear in 1985, or six years before the publication of *The Story of Lynx*, returned to and developed the analysis of several myths dealt with in volumes three and four of the Mythology series.

Lévi-Strauss would have devoted ten years of his life – from 1961 to 1971 – to the research for and the writing of the Mythology series. Two of the four volumes demanded more effort and time than the others: *The Origin of Table Manners* (two years) and especially *The Naked Man* (four years). Four more volumes were in gestation, and in 1971 Lévi-Strauss imagined leaving further research to others. But after retiring in 1982, he quickly returned to this labour. In the meantime, he would publish abstracts of all his courses on mythology and kinship, given first at the École Pratique des Hautes Études (1951–60) and then at the Collège de France (1960–82).

| Research and courses at the Collège de France | Books (dates of French edition) |
|---|---|
| 1961–62 The Raw and the Cooked | 1962 *Totemism* and *The Savage Mind* |
| 1962–63 From Honey to Ashes | 1964 *The Raw and the Cooked* |
| 1963–64 The Origin of Table Manners | |
| 1964–65 Sketches for an American Bestiary | |
| 1965–66 The Naked Man | |
| 1966–67 The Origin of Table Manners | 1967 *From Honey to Ashes* |
| 1967–68 The Naked Man | 1968 *The Origin of Table Manners* |
| 1968–69 Wind and Fog | |
| 1969–70 The Naked Man | |
| 1970–71 The Naked Man | 1971 *The Naked Man* |
| | 1984 *Anthropology and Myth: Lectures, 1951–1982* |
| | 1985 *The Jealous Potter* |
| | 1991 *The Story of Lynx* |

Let us consider for the moment the four volumes of the Mythology series from the outside, before diving in and following the paths broken by the author. The full work comes to 2,000 pages. In it he summarizes and analyses 813 myths and as many variants from North and South American Indian societies and cultures, to which must be added some fifty myths

---

1 C. Lévi-Strauss and D. Eribon, ed., *Conversations with Claude Lévi-Strauss*, trans. P. Wissing (Chicago, University of Chicago Press, 1991), p. 132.

from China, Japan and Polynesia, together with a few from ancient Greece and Rome and from the peasant societies of Christian Europe. The number of tribes and ethnic groups from which the Amerindian myths are taken comes to over 350, which supposes the daunting task of reading hundreds of books and articles published in several languages. To this ethnographic material must be added the archaeological and historical data on those societies for which it was available.

But, above all, the four volumes contain the results of a study never before undertaken by an anthropologist or a mythographer: one that aspires to make an inventory of all the animal and plant species, all the techniques, and every piece of ecological, astronomical and meteorological information present in the myths. This colossal effort to reconstruct the Indians' concrete knowledge about nature and the living beings in their environment derived from the methodological imperative Lévi-Strauss had set himself, since 'the tiniest details acquire both meaning and function'.[2]

To this rich content must be added the maps enabling readers to find their way from the heart of Brazil to the northwest coast of North America, by way of the Guianas, the Plains Indian groups, the Great Lakes Indians, and including a side-trip to the Inuit in the far North. We also find dozens of diagrams setting out series of oppositions spread along several axes, summaries by Lévi-Strauss himself of the itineraries followed in each volume and results achieved in terms of theory. Finally, thirty or so plates of old engravings illustrate the bestiary of birds and animals elevated to the rank of supernatural figures and significant actors of the mythical discourse. Remarkable, detailed indexes, a bibliography of several hundred books as well as articles drawn from nineteen international and national scientific journals contribute to making this four-volume study of mythology an exceptional achievement from every point of view.

## At the Outset, the Misadventures of a Bird-Nester Threatened with Death

It all begins in the southern part of central Brazil, among the Bororo people, a group of tribes living in the high Paraguay River Valley, whose

---

2 C. Lévi-Strauss, *The Naked Man*, trans. J. and D. Weightman (Chicago, University of Chicago Press, 1981) (Mythology series, vol. 4), p. 562.

neighbours to the north are the Ge, a large linguistic group whose tribes had formerly appropriated part of the Bororo's territory. The story continues among the Ge, then takes us southward to the Chaco region before leading us back to the French Guianas, to the Arawak, and a 'strange' group, the Warao, amid frequent forays westward as far as the Tikuna and the Jivaro. The circulation of the myths of all these groups in overlapping circuits radiating out from one central myth, in what Lévi-Strauss called 'rose curves' or '*parcours en rosaces*', constitutes the matter of the first two volumes in the series. We do not leave South America for the moment.

But myth number 354 – a Tikuna myth, therefore South American – which opens the third volume, obliges Lévi-Strauss to cross the Panama Canal and venture northward to the Indians of the North American Plains and Great Lakes, because there he finds myths that shed light on the Tikuna myth; whereas he had found none in the South American societies he had 'visited'. But this sojourn with the Plains Indians would take him even further, westward and northward, along a strip of land between the Rockies and the Pacific Ocean, which forms the Oregon northwest.

It was here, in this region populated by many small tribal groups speaking different languages, that Lévi-Strauss unexpectedly found all the mythical schemata he had discovered in South America and reconstructed. At a distance of at least 10,000 kilometres, the story of the Bird-Nester reappeared, but with some differences. The messages were inverted, for this was the Northern rather than the Southern hemisphere, and the Indians did not have the same plant and animal species to hand for telling the same story. Nevertheless, the operations and the schemata of the Indians' mythical thought were the same. Finally, it became obvious that two sets of myths, found respectively among the Ge tribes of South America and the Salish and Sahaptin groups in North America, formed the backbone of these hundreds of myths, which converged or diverged along this axis. Ultimately, he wrote, it could be suggested that all these myths embroider upon a single theme: the conquest of fire, and thus serve as an introduction to the forms taken by the passage from nature to culture, or from animality to humanity.

So, what is this world where mythological characters are spawned and evolve, and who are they?

To define the South American Indian myths, Lévi-Strauss wrote in 1988 that these were stories 'of the time before men and animals became distinct beings'.[3] Indeed, many myths begin with the formula: 'At the time when animals and humans were indistinguishable from each other'.[4] The mythological world is thus entirely focused on an imaginary time, a remote past where gods, humans, animals and plants all lived together, could communicate with each other and change into one another. It was at the close of this time that the world became what it is today, when animals ceased being people, and people ceased being animals. Mythical time is the time of origins: the origin of the Sun, the Moon, the stars and other heavenly bodies, the animal and plant species, humans, the different peoples, cooking, hunting poison, tobacco, rivers, salmon, the woman's vagina, death, water, fire, corn, one-eyed wives, etc. Of 813 myths, more than 250 are explanations of the origin of something. I have drawn up a table, which is by no means complete but which should suffice to give the reader an idea of the world as the Indians imagined and experienced it (see appendixes).

---

Indians turn into animals in order to steal fire, I-76.

A man marries a monkey-woman, I-129.

A woman is unwittingly married to a bat-man, I-130.

A woman has a snake-child, I-132.

A jaguar removes its skin and appears in human form, I-133.

Vultures take off their feather tunics and appear as humans, I-150.

A woman has a snake-lover, I-165.

At that time, birds were people, I-312.

A palm frond turns into a man, II-152.

An exasperated Indian turns into a thorny skate, II-264.

In those times plants were personal beings, II-276.

The grandmother turns into a jaguar and devours her grandson, II-313.

Some people turn into wild pigs, II-381.

A girl marries the wild-pig master spirit, II-381.

A jealous woman turns into a water spirit, III-62.

A man turns into a moon, III-172.

A girl proposes marriage to a porcupine, III-203.

A man turns into a jaguar, III-266.

---

3 Lévi-Strauss and Eribon, *Conversations with Claude Lévi-Strauss*, p. 139.

4 *The Naked Man*, p. 56, M539, Modoc.

In bygone times, the dog shared the human condition, III-353.

A man marries first a grizzly and then a female bear, IV-232.

Grizzly-Woman and Bear-Woman then definitively turn back into
animals, IV-254.

Coyote, before taking on his definitive animal form, sets all the fish
free for man's future use, IV-306.

Geese, which at that time could talk, show the way, IV-366.

A woman marries a root and gives birth to the demiurge, IV-396.

A man marries a muskrat-woman and is the ancestor of the
Montagnais Indians, IV-473.

And so on . . .

> Key: I = *The Raw and the Cooked*; II = *From Honey to Ashes*;
> III = *The Origin of Table Manners*; IV = *The Naked Man*

But animals are not always humans in myths. Some are the incarnation
of gods, nature spirits of various sorts, ogres and demons. In fact, divine
beings sometimes appear as humans or animals, and even sometimes as a
plant such as tobacco, which goes from being a sacred plant to becoming
the hypostasis of a god, according to the Cariri Indians (M25).[5] While the
Cashinahua tell that a girl who had refused to marry men transformed into
wild pigs discovered the tobacco spirit. She raised it and then married it,
and it is from their union that the Cashinahua say they descend.

The supernatural world of myths is at once diversified, multiple and
hierarchical. Among the supernatural beings, demiurges are endowed
with greater powers than the rest, for they can create things and beings,
and organize them, undo their organization or destroy them. They are
creators or tricksters. Often the creator and the trickster are older and
younger brothers, or twins, such as Dyai and Epi in Tikuna lore. Both
fished the first humans from a river. Dyai created laws, customs and arts
for them. Epi, on the other hand, is a trickster, messy and brazen, who
changes into an opossum when he wants to appear as an animal.[6]

---

5  C. Lévi-Strauss, *The Raw and the Cooked: Introduction to a Science of Mythology* 1,
trans. J. and D. Weightman (Harmondsworth, Penguin, 1986), p. 101.

6  Ibid., p. 167.

At that time, divine beings often lived among men. According to the Sherente, Venus (a male figure) lived among them in human shape (M138).[7] His body was covered with foul-smelling sores and he was refused entry into people's homes. Only the Indian Waikaura took him in, cared for him and healed him. Venus thus decided to punish the Indians. He rose up into the sky, taking Waikaura and his family with him, and then sent a huge mass of water to flood the village and drown everyone.[8] In addition to Venus, the Sherente gods were Moon and Mars, on the one hand, and Sun and Jupiter, on the other. Here we have the traces of a pantheon whose cult was celebrated by different priests, depending on whether they officiated in honour of Jupiter and the Sun or in honour of Mars and Moon.[9] But Lévi-Strauss never seeks to reconstruct the pantheon of the societies he cites. He simply takes a few of their myths before turning to other tribes to find the means of reconstructing 'transformation groups' through a process he has christened 'levers en rosaces' ('rose curves'), or working out from the centre in overlapping loops, that would take him from South America to the American Northwest.

It often happens that supernatural beings marry humans. The Atsina tell that, looking for the best wife, Sun and Moon chose a human woman for Moon and a frog for Sun, because the frog does not screw up her face when she looks at Sun's radiance. According to the Crow Indians, it was Sun who chose the girl and Moon the frog.[10] Demiurges live in family groups. For the Arekuna, Wei, the Sun, has daughters and they travel by canoe. He takes in a man whom the vultures have covered in excrement and, when his daughters have cleaned him up, he suggests that his protégé take one of them for his wife,[11] etc. For the Hidatsa, the demiurge Sun was tricked by Moon, who had promised him a beautiful young Indian woman to make love with, but had persuaded Bison-Woman, one of Sun's former mistresses, to take her place.[12] The

7  Ibid., p. 256.

8  Ibid., pp. 250–1, M138.

9  C. Lévi-Strauss, *From Honey to Ashes: Introduction to a Science of Mythology* 2, trans. J. and D. Weightman (Chicago, University of Chicago Press, 1973), pp. 454–5.

10  C. Lévi-Strauss, *The Origin of Table Manners*, trans. J. and D. Weightman (Chicago: University of Chicago Press, 1990) (Mythology series, vol. 3) (second edition), pp. 283–4, M455 et M429a.

11  Ibid., pp. 139–40, M149a.

12  Ibid., pp. 328–30, M465.

Machiguenga tell that Moon married a girl to whom he would pay secret visits when she was menstruating, and through her gave humans the cultivated plants and taught them how to grow them. Then he caused his wife to be fertilized by a fish, and she gave birth to four sons, among whom were Sun and the planet Venus.[13] Elsewhere, it is an ogress that falls in love with a demiurge when he is still a child.[14] Among the Yurok and other Californian tribes, an irresistible seductress, Lady Skate, trapped the penis of the demiurge between her thighs as they were having intercourse and removed him once and for all from the world of humans. Demiurges, too, die, even if they come back to life afterwards. The Chiriguano tell that a demiurge, Añatunpa, killed all the honey-gatherers to offer them as food to an ogre; then one day a honey-gatherer, on the advice of a toucan, managed to kill the ogre by lighting a fire on the back of his neck.[15]

In addition to demiurges and other major gods, the indigenous world contains many beings endowed with personal powers and who are the male or female masters of something. The Bororo thus have a spirit named Burekoibo, who is master of the maize.[16] For the Hidatsa, the maize spirits were female beings associated with 'Old-Woman-Who-Never-Dies', who herself had mastery over all the water birds.[17] For the Ojibwa, Mudjekiwis is the master of the winds and storms. Among the Menominee, Manabush is the master of maple sap, and the West wind is his enemy.[18]

The hero of the Mythology series, the Bird-Nester, is the master of water for the Bororo (M1), and of fire and cooking for the Ge (M7). With the Tacana, he becomes a master of hunting, with dominion over cooking as well since this requires as its primary raw material meat, the product of hunting.[19] We also come across numerous evil and often cannibalistic spirits. A Tikuna myth tells how men exterminated an entire people of cannibalistic spirits by asphyxiating them with the smoke produced by burning pimentos while they were gathered in a

---

13 *From Honey to Ashes*, pp. 320–1, M299.
14 *The Origin of Table Manners*, p. 67, M377.
15 *From Honey to Ashes*, p. 368.
16 Ibid., p. 311, M293.
17 *The Origin of Table Manners*, pp. 440–1, M503.
18 Ibid., pp. 422 and 360, M479.
19 *From Honey to Ashes*, p. 346.

cave.[20] Ever since, the bark tunics worn by the Tikuna when performing certain rites bear the characteristics of the demons that came out of the cave, and make those wearing them the incarnation of these spirits.

A remark is in order here. Lévi-Strauss often takes the liberty of explaining 'a myth from the Gran Chaco by means of a variant from Guiana, or a Ge myth by a similar one from Colombia'. He does this for two reasons. The first is the fact that comparison of these hundreds of myths makes it clear that 'small but numerous communities . . . express their different originalities by manipulating the resources of a dialectical system of contrasts and correlations within the framework of a common conception of the world'. Reaching beyond the differences of language, customs and forms of social organization, indigenous Americans thus shared a deep-seated vision of humankind and the surrounding worlds, produced at once by universal principles underpinning the workings of the human mind and a thousands-of-years-old cultural 'syncretism', which 'for many centuries had contained at one and the same time centres of advanced civilization and savage peoples, centralizing tendencies and disruptive forces'. The second reason is that the structural analysis of the myths makes it possible to show that myths from very different sources belong to a single transformation group, which allows him to refuse 'to be confined within the frontiers already established by historical investigation'.[21]

As early as 1952, Lévi-Strauss had stressed the existence of this far-flung phenomenon of syncretism, which he believed to have grown out of a no-doubt common source in America and from which sprang the cultures of the savannah and forest, as well as the 'advanced cultures of Mexico and Peru'.[22] Yet, with the exception of a few allusions to the Popol-Vuh and to ancient Mexican myths,[23] as well as the description of the altar of the great Temple of the Sun at Cuzco,[24] he would include no other myths from the great pre-Columbian empires among the 2,000 he analysed.

---

20 Ibid., pp. 388–9, M318.

21 *The Raw and the Cooked*, p. 8.

22 C. Lévi-Strauss, 'The Concept of Archaism in Anthropology', *Structural Anthropology*, trans. C. Jacobson and B. Grundfest Schoepf (New York, Basic Books, 1963), pp. 101–19.

23 *From Honey to Ashes*, pp. 446–50.

24 Ibid., p. 269.

I have deliberately avoided using the myths of the advanced civilizations of central America and Mexico because, having been formulated by [highly cultivated] speakers, they call for prolonged syntagmatic analysis before they can be used as paradigms. I am, however,
not unaware of the fact that in many respects they have their place in
several of the sets I have defined.[25]

The argument advanced to justify this exclusion is surprising. If taken
literally, Georges Dumézil should never have used the Vedic texts and
the Mahabharata to reconstruct the architecture and schemata of Indo-
European mythology. But, in fact, sets of myths illustrating certain
complex forms of pantheon, for which there is no equivalent in the
mythology of the Indians of central Amazonia or the Plains Indians of
North America, are lacking in the material used by Lévi-Strauss.
Nevertheless, he points out, as if by way of exception, the Tacana, some
of whose gods had Quechua names.[26] Lévi-Strauss selects myths from
Tacana mythology that seem to him to come from a much older source,
preceding the influence of the great Andean civilizations, a source from
before the appearance of different forms of state and empire, of cities
and urban lifestyles, and also before the appearance of great 'chiefdoms'
bringing together thousands of individuals – such as the ancient Chibcha
chiefdoms of present-day Colombia. For mythologies undergo changes
in content and structure when they are placed at the service of kings or
great overlords related to the gods, when not living gods themselves, as
in the case of the Inca, son of the Sun, or the supreme Mayan chiefs.

But Lévi-Strauss was not unaware that, before the Europeans arrived,
the societies on the middle and lower Amazon enjoyed 'a much higher
level of religious, social and political organization than anything that
has been observed since', something that is attested by the 'existence of
oral traditions, whose extreme complexity, artificial composition and
mystical tone suggest that they must be attributed to schools of sages
and learned men'.[27] Of these schools of 'sages' we know almost nothing,

25 *The Raw and the Cooked*, p. 177, note 18; my emphasis.
26 *From Honey to Ashes*, pp. 343–5. Another exception is the case of the Warao,
thousands of kilometres from the Andes, near the Atlantic Ocean, where there are
temples, a hierarchy of priests, and complex cultures indicative of Andine influences. Cf.
ibid., pp. 437–8.
27 Ibid., p. 272.

'except that they were graded according to a strict hierarchy, and that relatively esoteric versions of the same myths presumably corresponded to different levels of the hierarchy'.[28]

For the same reasons, Lévi-Strauss would exclude very rich and well-documented mythologies from societies on which we have numerous monographs, such as the Navajo, the Pueblo, the Zuni, the Hopi, and so on: 'The mythology of the Navajo, Athapaskan Indians who moved down from the north less than ten centuries ago, is a body of material I do not intend to broach, not only because of its abundance and complexity but also because successive generations of native thinkers have given it a *theological and liturgical* elaboration which would compel the analyst to adopt a different approach.'[29]

Which leads us to wonder in what way the theological elaboration of myths, that is to say here in the form of a representation of a world of gods organized into a pantheon and worshipped, therefore supposing a liturgy, makes it no longer possible to apply structural analysis to these henceforth 'deeply modified' myths. Besides, modified in what sense, and with respect to what? Might it be with respect to older myths, elaborated by more egalitarian societies deriving their livelihood from hunting, fishing and gathering, and practicing non-intensive forms of agriculture? In short, societies whose thinking was still fairly 'non-domesticated', closer to thought in 'its savage state', to the 'spontaneous' workings of the savage mind?

We cannot but notice that, among the nearly 2,000 myths Lévi-Strauss has gathered together and analysed, there is no mention of ranked forms of political power, with two exceptions. On the one hand, the domination of men over women, so widespread among Indian groups, with the possible exception of the Tacana, as Lévi-Strauss points out; on the other, the simple mention, without any particular comment, of the existence of slaves and slave markets in societies on the northwest coast of the United States such as the Chinook and the Coos, where he would stalk the Bird-Nester myth. With these exceptions, no trace of political power relations or forms of sovereignty among the 350 tribes whose myths Lévi-Strauss collated is to be found in any of the four volumes of the Mythology series. Yet information about hunting, fishing and

---

28  *The Origin of Table Manners*, p. 178.
29  *The Naked Man*, p. 530; my emphasis.

gathering techniques, about the species of beasts and plants hunted or foraged, and about the ecological, astronomical and meteorological context of these activities, is meticulously reconstructed and analysed.

'The substance of the myth', Lévi-Strauss writes, 'is . . . in the story that it tells.'[30] We have just had a glimpse of what myths tell. They describe a world that existed before the world in which the tribes people live their everyday lives, where men no longer change into jaguars or jaguars into men, where women do not marry heavenly bodies that appear to them as a handsome young man or a hideous old one. In this earlier world, the gods still lived for the most part with men and could appear as a human, an animal or even a plant. Some animal-humans could also change into gods and dwell in the sky. A man became Moon, whose face still bears the marks his sister made so as to recognize who was visiting her secretly at night and making love to her. When his crime was discovered, the incestuous brother fled to the sky and turned into a heavenly body we see at night. In short, in this earlier world, all beings had supernatural powers, if only that of being able to communicate with each other and to change into each other. All are the master of something: the Bird-Nester is master of the celestial waters, of rain and storms; the jaguar is master of the cooking fire and eats his food cooked, whereas people still eat theirs raw. Yet it was Jaguar who, after marrying a human wife, would give his human brothers-in-law the fire that would give them access to cooking and cooked meat. Later Jaguar would become what he is today, an animal that eats raw meat and is afraid of fire.

It is clear therefore that the representations of the world we find in Amerindian myths are an anthropomorphic conception of nature, of natural beings and phenomena, a view of nature that transmutes the natural world into a supernatural one. All the beings in it behave like humans, but like humans who possess powers we attribute to the gods.

This primordial world is a world that myths explore even as they describe its disappearance, or at least its partial eclipse. It was following numerous events and incidents that came to pass in that world as a consequence of the actions of a given character that the world became the way it is, a reality the Indians deal with on a daily basis.

This primordial world is the world of all origins: the origin of the heavenly bodies, of war, agriculture, the art of pottery, musical instruments,

---

30  Ibid., p. 645.

scalps, sickness and death; the origin of exogamy, of honey and tobacco, of various tribes, the Cashinahua, the Bororo, the Hidatsa, etc. But this world in which everything originated has never ceased to exist. It vanished from the surface of things and from daily life, but it is still present behind each thing of which it has become the invisible foundation, one revealed by the myths and addressed in ritual and liturgy. Myths are believed explanations. They are truths that oblige humans to act. Myths demand rituals.

This world created by humans, and in which they project themselves without ever being able (or willing) to recognize that they are its authors, is therefore fundamentally imaginary; it is attached to those who created it but seems to exist independently, beyond human actions and thoughts. In short, it is a world where humans are at once present and absent; and when they are present, they adopt appearances and are endowed with powers they do not possess in everyday life. In myths – and in religions, since all regions originate and in and are legitimized by a founding myth – humanity both expresses and loses itself. As Lévi-Strauss wrote in *The Savage Mind*, 'the notion of a supernature exists only for a humanity which attributes supernatural powers to itself and in return ascribes the powers of its super-humanity to nature.'[31]

For Lévi-Strauss, myths are, it seems, a production of the non-domesticated, savage mind: 'The savage mind deepens its knowledge with the help of *imagines mundi*. It builds mental structures which facilitate an understanding of the world in as much as they resemble it.'[32]

Set side by side, these two passages raise a problem. For if it is obvious that myths are constructed with the help of operations of the mind, which projects its own structures into them, it is not at all evident that this is enough to explain why the mind should spontaneously attribute supernatural powers to the people and other beings that populate the myths. But Lévi-Strauss's analyses of mythical thought leave aside, as we have said, the fundamental problem of the fact of believing, of the belief in imaginary realities; or he deliberately ignores it. That the *concrete knowledge* present in myths is a positive knowledge is uncontested, and will remain so after his demonstration that mythical thought is *logical*; but in no way does this twofold acknowledgement explain why humanity should spontaneously have credited itself with a supernature, and endowed the worlds in which it lived and from which it derived its livelihood with one as well. Which shows that while deconstructing myths with the help of structural analyses is a necessary task, it still does not explain religions (or political ideologies).[33] For myths claim to explain the true nature of things and the origin of humankind; and, for this reason, we receive them as fundamental truths, not like Aesop's fables or tall tales. And yet it is precisely because myths are conceived of and experienced as truths that they can in no way provide a positive knowledge comparable to – albeit distinct from – the knowledge produced by scientific thought, based on experimentation, verifiable by all those who have the necessary theoretical capacities, whatever their language and culture, or demonstrable through logical-mathematical deductions that specialists can reproduce and confirm or disprove.

It is therefore not enough to assert, as Lévi-Strauss does in his conclusion to the four volumes, that

> we have to resign ourselves to the fact that the myths tell us nothing instructive about the order of the world, the nature of reality or the origin and destiny of mankind. We cannot expect them to flatter any metaphysical thirst, or to breathe new life into exhausted ideologies. On the other hand, they teach us a great deal about the societies from which they originate, they help to lay bare their inner workings and clarify the *raison d'être* of beliefs, customs and institutions, the organization of which was at first sight incomprehensible; lastly, and most importantly, they make it possible to discover certain operational modes of the human mind, which have remained so constant over the centuries, and are so widespread over immense geographical distances, that we can assume them to be fundamental.[34]

If myths do not teach us anything, they nevertheless claim to do so, and it is this dimension that Lévi-Strauss leaves to one side. Myths convey a

---

33 This is illustrated by Lévi-Strauss's declaration in the 'Finale' of *The Naked Man*: 'I too, of course, look upon the religious field as a stupendous storehouse of images that is far from having been exhausted by objective research; but these images are like any others, and the spirit in which I approach the study of religious data supposes that such data are not credited at the outset with any specific character' (p. 639).

34 *The Naked Man*, p. 639.

number of different philosophies that do not speak to other societies and other cultures; and the fact that they do not speak to others also needs to be explained, for this opacity sheds light on their nature. Nor will we learn what these 'exhausted ideologies' might be which call myths to the rescue, nor from whom or what. We also sense a reproach to those who indulge in the hermeneutics of sacred texts in hopes of discovering buried secrets or esoteric knowledge. But, as is his wont, Lévi-Strauss does not name his targets.

## From the Paraguay River to Oregon, from the Bororo to the Salish

For those who have never read the Mythology series, and especially those who never will, I have chosen to summarize seven myths that mark the trail from the key-myth, the tale of the Bird-Nester (M1),[35] to one of the last variants, which closes the vast circle of this mythical cycle, a tale found among the Alsea of Oregon (M796).[36] For the summary, I will use Myth 7,[37] the first Ge myth analysed by Lévi-Strauss, which presents itself as the symmetrical inversion of Myth 1. Myth 1 explains the origin of the celestial waters, while Myth 7 explains that of fire. In reality, the group of Ge myths (M7–M12) is the true base on which the first two volumes of the Mythology series are erected.

I will present four myths that are extensions of this group: one concerns a girl who is mad about honey (M218),[38] while two bear on the origin of tobacco (M191 and M27).[39] The fourth is a Tikuna myth (M354),[40] which opens Volume Two and cannot be interpreted without the help of myths from North America. For Lévi-Strauss, it therefore became necessary and possible to pass to North America. Both *The Origin of Table Manners* and *The Naked Man* connect several hundreds of myths from North America. Among these, we have chosen to present a Quinault myth

---

35  *The Raw and the Cooked*, pp. 35–7.
36  *The Naked Man*, pp. 571–2.
37  *The Raw and the Cooked*, pp. 66–7.
38  *From Honey to Ashes*, pp. 110–11.
39  M191: *From Honey to Ashes*, p. 61; M27: *The Raw and the Cooked*, pp. 104–5.
40  *The Origin of Table Manners*, pp. 25–8.

(M804),[41] which tells of two sisters who want to marry heavenly bodies; the death of the younger sister, who runs away from her home in the Sky, and that of her elderly husband sparks a war between the Earth People, who want to avenge her death, and the Sky People, who fight them off. The war between these two peoples brings the Mythology series to a close.

---

Myth 1. Bororo – The Bird-Nester, 'The Macaws and Their Nest'
In olden times, it happened that, when the women had gone to the forest to gather palm fronds to make penis shields for the adolescents who were to be initiated, a boy secretly followed his mother and raped her. When she got home, her husband noticed feathers caught in her bark-cloth belt, which resembled those worn by the young men. He ordered that a dance should take place so he could discover the culprit. To his stupefaction, the feathers were those worn by his son. He then ordered a second dance, which produced the same result.

Anxious to avenge himself, the father sent his son to the aquatic realm of the 'souls' with instructions to bring back the great dance rattle. The youth's grandmother revealed to him the mortal danger involved and advised him to obtain the help of the hummingbird. When the young man reached the dwelling place of the souls, the humming bird flew ahead and seized the rattle, which fell into the water. The boy recovered it and brought it back.

The father then ordered his son to bring back the small rattle belonging to the souls. The episode was repeated with, this time, the aid of a dove. During a third expedition, the young man, with the help of a large grasshopper, brought back the dancing bells worn on the ankles.

The father was furious and asked his son to come with him to capture the macaws that were nesting in the cliff face. The grandmother gave the boy a magic stick to cling to should he happen to fall. The father leaned a long pole against the cliff. The son climbed up. The father knocked down the pole. The son was saved by thrusting his magic stick into the façade and remained suspended in the void.

Noticing a vine, he climbed to the top of the rock. There he made a bow and some arrows, and killed the lizards that abounded there. He hung them from his belt and around his ankles. The stench of the dead

---

41 *The Naked Man*, pp. 584–5.

lizards caused him to faint. Buzzards swooped down on him, first eating the lizards and then starting on the boy's buttocks. The pain awakened him. The vultures deposited him at the foot of the cliff. The hero was hungry. But without buttocks or an anus, everything he ate passed out of his body. Remembering a story told him by his grandmother, he made himself a bottom from the dough of pounded tubers.

Then he set out in search of his family. He found the village deserted. One day he came upon the footprints of his grandmother. He turned himself into a lizard, which intrigued his younger brother and his grandmother. He revealed himself to them. That night, back in the village, a violent storm extinguished all the fires in the village except his grandmother's. The next day, his father's second wife recognized the son and warned her husband, who believed him to be dead. The father welcomed his son with the customary songs, but the hero was bent on revenge.

One day he told his brother to get his father to organize a collective hunt and to tell him where his father would be lying in wait. He broke off an antler-shaped branch and, changing into a deer, impaled his father, galloped to a lake and threw the body in the water, where it was immediately devoured by carnivorous fish-spirits. The lungs floated to the surface and changed into aquatic plants. When he returned to the village, the hero killed his father's wives, including his mother.

The main mythical schema in this narrative is that of a hero invited to climb a cliff (or a tree, which continues growing and does not let him climb back down). Abandoned, he is saved by different animals and takes revenge. Here the Bird-Nester reveals himself as master of the sky waters, rain and storms, by means of which he drowns the village fires while sparing his grandmother's. In other Bird-Nester myths, other supernatural powers are also attached to him.

Myth 7. Ge (Kayapo) – The Origin of Fire
An Indian took his young brother-in-law, Botoque, to help him capture the young of a couple of macaws that had built their nest at the top of a steep rock. The young man climbed up a makeshift ladder

and, when he got to the nest, said all he saw were two eggs. He threw down the eggs, which turned into stones and injured the other Indian, who, furious, took away the ladder and left.

Stuck on top of the rock, the hero grew thin and, as he was starving, he was forced to eat his own excrement. At last a jaguar came along carrying a bow, arrows and some game. Fear struck Botoque speechless. The jaguar noticed him, put the ladder back and invited him to climb down. The jaguar took him on his back and carried him to its home to eat grilled meat. (In those times, Indians did not know about fire and ate their meat raw.)

At the home of the jaguars, the Indian saw a tree burning and stones to make ovens. The jaguar's wife was an Indian. She did not like the young man, whom she called the 'abandoned one', but the jaguar decided to adopt him. Each day the jaguar would go out hunting. His wife took this occasion to aggravate the boy and when he complained she would scratch his face. In vain the jaguar scolded his wife.

One day the jaguar gave Botoque a bow and arrows and taught him how to use them. He advised him to turn them against the hateful woman if the need arose. Botoque killed her and fled with his weapons and some grilled meat. That night he arrived at his village, revealed his identity, told his story and shared out the meat. The Indians decided to steal some fire.

They came to the jaguar's home, but no one was there. There was some game lying around, uncooked. The Indians roasted it and took away the fire. For the first time, it was possible to keep warm, to have light at night and to eat cooked food. Incensed by the ingratitude of his adopted son who had stolen the fire and the secret of making bows and arrows, the jaguar remained full of hatred for humans. Now jaguars eat their meat raw.

This time the Bird-Nester, once again abandoned on top of a rock as a punishment for having injured his brother-in-law, is saved by a jaguar, who is the master of fire and eats his meat cooked, whereas the Indians eat theirs raw. Furthermore, the jaguar hunts with a bow and arrows, something the Indians do not know how to do. When they stole fire, the Indians passed from the raw to the cooked, which is the theme and title of the first book in the Mythology series. Dispossessed of his supernatural powers, the jaguar becomes the jaguar of today, a hunter and eater of raw meat. Thanks to fire and the bow, the Indians begin a new life, the one they have been living ever since humans became separate from animals, and animals no longer marry Indian women as they do in myths.

---

Myth 218. Matako (Chaco) – The Girl Mad About Honey

In the beginning, animals were men and fed on honey. The youngest daughter of Sun, who was a great chief and lived on the shore of a lake, quarrelled with her father because he did not give her enough bee larvae to eat. Sun advised her to seek out Woodpecker, the best honey-gatherer. Woodpecker's village was a long way away. When the girl got there, she married Woodpecker.

At the beginning of the third moon, Tawkxwax, the demiurge, came to the village on the pretext of taking part in the honey harvest. One day, he deliberately wounded one of his feet with a thorn and asked Sun's daughter to carry him back to the village on her back. On the way, he tried to copulate with her from behind. She dropped him and returned to the house of Sun, her father. Tawkxwax wondered if Woodpecker was going to take revenge and kill him. He took on the appearance of his victim and when Woodpecker came home, he ate the bee larvae in such a way that Woodpecker understood the ploy. Woodpecker asked an ant to check whether this was a man or a woman. Woodpecker killed Tawkxwax, hid the corpse and went off in search of his wife.

He found her at her father's house. The father asked his son-in-law to go and catch an aquatic monster for him. The monster devoured Woodpecker. The young woman pleaded with her father to give her husband back. Sun made the monster vomit, but Woodpecker's soul flew away and changed into a bird. And that is the origin of woodpeckers.

---

Once again, a human-animal is the master of something that humans desire: honey and bee larvae. Sun, master of heat and dryness, feeds on aquatic animals, in this case masters of rain and storms. Woodpecker, a bird that finds its food beneath the bark of trees, lives halfway between above and below. Sun lives above, and the aquatic monsters below. Above is dry, below is wet, and Woodpecker lives halfway between the two, in a 'middle' world where sky and water are united. Whereas Woodpecker was a man at the start of the myth, he turns into a bird at the end of the story. Forever after, there will be no more human master of honey.[42]

---

Myth 191. Irantxe (Tupi language) – The Origin of Tobacco
There was a man who behaved badly toward another. The latter wanted to take revenge. Using a fruit-gathering expedition as a pretext, he got the other man to climb a tall tree and left him there after having removed the climbing pole. Starving and thirsty, the man asked a monkey for help. The monkey brought him some water, but the man said he was too weak to climb down. A foul-smelling vulture helped the man and took him home with him. It was the master of tobacco, of which he possessed two kinds, one good and the other toxic. He presented them to his protégé and taught him to smoke the former and to use the latter as a means of revenge. When he got back, the hero presented the poisonous tobacco to his persecutor, who turned into an anteater. The hero killed him as he was sleeping and invited the vulture to feast on the corpse.

---

But tobacco is first and foremost a plant that makes it possible to communicate with the gods or with supernatural beings. This is what one Bororo myth explains (M27).[43]

---

Myth 27. Bororo – The Origin of Tobacco
Some fishermen had settled down on the shore to grill their fish. One of them opened the belly of a fish and found tobacco inside. He hid it and smoked it alone, at night, without telling anyone. His companions surprised him and he was forced to share. But the Indians swallowed the smoke instead of blowing it out. A spirit appeared to them in the guise of a vampire and told them to blow out the smoke saying: 'Receive the smoke and keep evil away from me. If you don't do this, you will be punished.' But the Indians disobeyed. The next day they were nearly blind and had turned into otters. That is why otters have small eyes.

---

42 *From Honey to Ashes*, p. 119.
43 *The Raw and the Cooked*, pp. 104–5.

For the Bororo (cf. key-myth M1), souls live in an aquatic dwelling. Men will not be completely cut off from the world of the spirits if they make them offerings of tobacco. If not, they will lose their human character and will become, as in this myth, half-blind animals.

The third volume in the Mythology series opens with a Tikuna myth that starts the investigation 'off on a new tack'. The entire book will be devoted to the analysis of this myth.

---

Myth 354. Tikuna – The Hunter Monmaneki and his Wives

In the days of the first people who were fished up by the demiurges Dyai and Epi, the twins, there lived an Indian whose only occupation was hunting. He would often see a frog on his way and would amuse himself by urinating into its hole. One day a beautiful young woman, who was pregnant, appeared there. He took her to live with him, and his mother thought her daughter-in-law very pretty.

The couple would go hunting together, but Monmaneki would eat meat and his wife would eat black beetles, which he caught for her. One day, the old woman came upon the insects, threw them out and replaced them with pimentos. In the evening, the woman heated her meal. The peppers burned her mouth. She ran off, jumped into the water and became a frog. That night she came back and snatched away her son who was crying in his grandmother's arms.

Monmaneki went hunting once more. One day he met a bird perched on a palm tree. 'Give me a gourdful of your drink.' When he returned, a beautiful young woman offered him a gourdful of palm wine. He married her, but she had ugly feet. Her mother-in-law made fun of them. Annoyed, the woman disappeared. Monmaneki went hunting once more.

One day he squatted over a hole to satisfy his needs. An earthworm poked out its head and said: 'Oh, what a fine penis!' The earthworm changed into a beautiful woman. He married her. A child was born. One day Monmaneki told his wife to go hoe the garden and to leave the baby with its grandmother. But the child cried all the time, and the old woman gave it back to its mother before going out to weed, too. Instead of hoeing, the young woman cut the roots of the plants as earthworms do when moving underground. The old woman cut her lips with a sharp shell. That night, the disfigured young woman took her child and ran away.

Monmaneki went hunting again. One day he asked some macaws for a drink of maize beer. When he came back, a macaw-girl offered him some. He married her. Another day, before leaving for the fields, his mother detached some corncobs from the roof and asked the woman to prepare some beer. With a single cob the young woman filled five jars and then went out to bathe. When the old woman came back, she tripped over the unused cobs and accused her daughter-in-law of having done nothing. The young woman climbed up on to the roof, turned back into a macaw and shouted to her husband: 'Follow me if you love me. Find the plant whose shavings turn into fish. Make a canoe and follow me to Mount Vaipi.' And she flew away.

In despair, Monmaneki ran all over in search of the tree. He found one whose shavings turned into fish, and brought back such quantities that his brother-in-law, a good-for-nothing, began to spy on him. The shavings ceased to change into fish. Monmaneki then invited his brother-in-law to help him finish a canoe and put it in the water. He overturned the canoe and the brother-in-law remained trapped in the hull all night. The next day he released him and they descended the Solimoes River toward Mount Vaipi, Monmaneki in the stern and his brother-in-law at the prow. They came to the village where the macaw-woman had taken refuge. She was hiding in the crowd. The brother-in-law changed into a bird and landed on her shoulder. The canoe continued downstream and suddenly stood up on end. Monmaneki changed into a bird and landed on the woman's other shoulder. The canoe changed into an aquatic monster, the master of fish in the Solimoes River.

In the end, Monmaneki married a woman of his people. But each time she would go to the boat landing, her body would divide in two. The head, chest, and arms would go into the water and fish. Abundant numbers of fish were attracted by her flesh. The chest would then return to shore and fit itself onto the lower part from which a piece of spinal cord protruded.

One day, while she was preparing maize beer, the mother-in-law sent her daughter to the river for water. As she was long in returning, the mother-in-law went after her and discovered the lower part of her body on the shore. She tore off the protruding piece of spinal cord. Upon returning to shore, the young woman was unable to reassemble herself. She hoisted herself up onto a tree branch and then dropped onto the back of her husband who had gone looking for her. From then on, she would not let him eat, snatching the food from his mouth and soiling him with her excrement.

The hero thought of a trick to get free. He said he had to inspect his fish weir and described to his wife what the piranhas would do to her if she went into the water with him. She stayed on the bank and he took advantage of this to swim away. She hoisted herself onto a post and after several days turned into a parrot and flew away to the mountains downstream from the Solimoes River.

Let us pause over this myth to which Lévi-Strauss devoted so many pages in *The Origin of Table Manners*. Looking at the sequence of five episodes in which the hero marries five times, we note that the first four marriages are exogamous and the fifth endogamous, since Monmaneki finally marries a woman of his people. The first four marriages are moreover exogamous in a 'hyperbolic' fashion, since they bring together a man and female animals, which are alternatively from above and from below, from the sky and from the earth. The frog is succeeded by the arapaço bird, which is followed by the earthworm and finally by the macaw, also a bird. The first three episodes are constructed from the same two sequences: (a) encounter and marriage, (b) separation of the couple owing to the hero's mother. In the fifth episode, the mother-in-law separates her daughter-in-law from herself, since she prevents her from reforming her body. In the fourth episode, the woman runs away, and the husband follows her. In the fifth, the woman clings to her husband, and it is he who runs away. The fourth wife is a bird who changes into a woman. The fifth is a woman who turns into a bird.

At the beginning of the myth, fish did not exist, nor did canoes for travelling on the rivers. But the fourth wife teaches her husband how to bring forth fish from the shavings of a special tree whose trunk is used to make canoes. And, in the fifth episode, it is the trunk-woman who attracts the newly created fish of which she is now the mistress. Exogamous marriages are occasionally caused by the exercise of either functions of excretion – the man urinates or defecates – or functions of nutrition – a woman offers the man a gourd of palm wine, another some

maize beer. Each time, the man's excretions are associated with copula-
tion, and the wife gives birth to a child that she takes with her when she
runs away. Finally, let us note that the myth shows a succession of four
techno-economic activities characteristic of the Indians' way of life:
hunting, gathering, agriculture (maize) and fishing.

There remains the puzzle of 'the strange notion of a woman capable
at will of cutting herself up into two pieces'.[44] To shed light on this
paradigm, Lévi-Strauss looks some 2,000 kilometres from the Tikuna,
finding a myth from the Kalina people on the northern coast of South
America, which tells that a woman thrown into the water by her son-in-
law and half devoured by carnivorous fish went up into the sky and
became 'Berenice's Hair'. This myth belongs to a large paradigmatic set
of myths that explain the appearance of the constellations Berenice's
Hair, on the one hand, and Orion and the Pleiades, on the other, by the
dismembering of a woman's or a man's body: the head, trunk and arms
become Berenice's hair, while the legs and the viscera give rise to Orion
and the Pleiades.

He still needs to explain why the Tikuna myth (M354) makes it
necessary to pass from South America to North America, acting as a
transition but also as proof that the mythical universe is common to the
two Americas. The answer can be found throughout *The Origin of Table
Manners*, the third volume of the Mythology series, with the analysis of
a group of myths entitled 'The Wives of the Sun and Moon', the richest
versions coming from the Arapaho tribe.[45] These myths tell how one
day the brothers, Sun and Moon, were discussing the respective merits
of the women of the world below. Moon declares that for him, human
women are the most beautiful. But Sun protests for, he says, humans
screw up their face when they look at him, and declares that he prefers
an aquatic creature that looks at him with big eyes and without making
faces. Moon changes into a porcupine and draws a young woman up
high into a tree, which continues growing until it reaches the sky. There
he changes into a handsome young man, and the Indian woman agrees
to marry him. Sun, on the other hand, chooses a frog wife. But his wife
passes urine each time she jumps and drools black saliva when she eats.
Moon makes fun of his sister-in-law. Tired of his sniping, she jumps

44  *The Origin of Table Manners*, p. 37.
45  Ibid., pp. 214–25.

onto Moon's chest and clings there forever. And that is the origin of the dark spots on the face of the Moon.[46]

Monmaneki's trunk-woman clearly belongs to the same family of paradigms as the clinging wife of one of the heavenly bodies for, according to the variants, the offended frog-woman clings forever to the chest of either Moon or Sun as the mocking brother-in-law.

We end our trip across the Americas in the Pacific Northwest, on the Oregon coast, a region that appeared to Lévi-Strauss as a sort of sanctuary where all the mythical schemata he had encountered on his way as he was making his 'rose curves' were conserved (or gathered together).

Here, once again we find our original hero, the Bird-Nester.

---

### Myth 796. Alsea – The Bird-Nester

The demiurge, Seuku, set off on a journey with his son. They stopped in a village, where the young man married two women. Each of them had a child. When his son would go away, Seuku would take on the appearance of a young man and try to seduce his daughters-in-law. Warned by one of the women, the hero subsequently took his father with him whenever he went away.

One day one of the children fancied a bird perched in a tree. The hero climbed the tree, which first grew until it reached the sky and then retracted itself and disappeared. The hero, left in the sky, encountered five Thunderers, who came to his aid and let him down, tied up in a whaleskin, at the end of a rope.

When the young man was reunited with his family, his father immediately resumed the appearance of an old man, but the hero wrapped him up in a whaleskin, which he placed on hot stones. The skin stuck to the old man's body and the entire package was thrown into the sea. Seuku then decided to use the whale to travel and change the world. He travelled southward and then northward, and one day finally landed. He sent the whale on its way but told it that each year it must beach itself on a shore so as to provide the inhabitants with food.

By magical means he created a bow, arrows and a quiver. He wanted to eat berries, but they left his body through holes in his armpits. He blocked up the holes with grass and that is why people have hair

---

46  Ibid., p. 217.

under their arms. Then he caused salmon and sturgeon to appear, made instruments for fishing, and decreed that the salmon would be roasted. He created shellfish and then edible tubers, and placed them where they are found today.

The four-volume series ends with the presentation of a group of myths that explain how humans conquered celestial fire, following a war sparked by the desire to avenge the death of a young woman who wanted to marry a heavenly body and then died, in her attempt to run away and go back down to earth.

Here is a passage from one of the very last of the 813 myths summarized in the series.

Myth 804. Quinault – The Wives of the Sun and Moon
Surprised by nightfall in a prairie where they were digging roots, Crow's two daughters camped where they were. Lying side by side, they gazed at the stars. The younger one wished to be carried up next to a big star, the younger sister next to a small one. In the sky, the younger sister saw that her husband was an old man with runny eyes who wiped the pus with his wife's hair. Her sister's husband, on the other hand, was young and strong.

The younger sister decided to run away. She begged a spider to lower her down to earth. The old woman agreed but not until the rope she was braiding was long enough. The young woman decided to leave immediately, but the cord was still too short and it left her dangling in mid-air. After several days, she died. Her skeleton fell apart and pieces landed in front of her father's house. Crow recognized the bones and called all the animals together: mammals, birds and fish, to go up to the sky with him and avenge his daughter.

To reach the sky, they had to make and hang a chain of arrows. Once they had reached the sky, where it was freezing cold, the animals wanted to get warm. They asked Blackbird, then Dog and then Lynx to steal a firebrand from the sky people. Only Beaver succeeded, and brought back the fire. But the elder of the daughters was still a prisoner in the sky. So, they decided to set her free. The rats and mice gnawed through the bowstrings, and the bindings of the sky people's clothing. At first the sky people retreated. But soon they mounted a counter-attack and put the earth people to flight. So, the latter climbed down their ladder to earth with the woman and the fire. But the ladder broke and the last people were left in the sky, where they became stars.

As Lévi-Strauss wrote at the close of his travels in the two Americas:

This rounds off my analysis of a vast system, the invariant elements of which can consistently be represented in the form of a conflict between the earth and the sky for the possession of fire. Sometimes this conflict involves whole peoples, that is the respective inhabit-ants of the two worlds; or it may take the more modest form of the temporary exile . . . of the hero at the top of a tree or on a rocky cliff, from which he eventually redescends to become the master of fire.[47]

With the tales of climbing up to the sky, we find either a cosmic drama, or a village drama, or a family quarrel. Finally, the path we have followed in pursuit of the Bird-Nester gives the impression, as Lévi-Strauss wrote in the next-to-the-last chapter of *The Naked Man*, that in these 813 myths and as many variants, we are dealing with 'one myth only'.[48]

Yet Lévi-Strauss would temper this affirmation fifteen years later, in his conversations with Didier Eribon, by saying that all the myths analysed in the four volumes were 'variants on a great theme, at least: the passage from nature to culture, which must be paid for with the definitive break-down of communication between the heavenly and earthly realms. And the result for humanity is the problems treated by this mythology.'[49]

But Lévi-Strauss did not travel in a straight line as we have done. He proceeded, as I have said, by working outward from the centre in a

---

47  *The Naked Man*, p. 598. M1, M7–M12.
48  Ibid., p. 561.
49  Lévi-Strauss and Eribon, *Conversations with Claude Lévi-Strauss*, pp. 136–7.

series of what he called 'rose curves' *(levers en rosace)*.[50] He describes this method as consisting of beginning with a myth chosen (almost) at random – we will come back to this point – and 'establish[ing] the semantic field surrounding [it] with the help of ethnography and by means of other myths; and then I repeat the operation in the case of each of these myths. And so we see that the analysis of myths is an endless task . . . Themes can be split up ad infinitum. Just when you think you have disentangled and separated them, you realize that they are knitting together again in response to the operation of unexpected affinities.'[51]

Lévi-Strauss thus proceeded each time by connecting one group of myths to another group, and enclosing a certain number of them within loops that were larger or smaller and longer or shorter when they turned out to belong to the same transformation group. At some point these groups themselves connected with even vaster sets, in which several major myth cycles were knitted together. It is in this sense that, advancing in a spiral movement that gradually joined all these loops together at several levels simultaneously, Lévi-Strauss could suggest that, for all these years, he had been dealing with 'one myth only', which gradually revealed itself to him and in him.

We will now follow in his footsteps and describe some of these loops that channelled and linked together by means of his 'rose curves' the enormous mass of 2,000 myths analysed in the Mythologiques.

## Rose Curves

The first loop, generator of all the others, ties the Bororo myth of the origin of the celestial water that extinguished all the home fires (M1) to the Ge myths on the origin of the fire used to cook with (M7–M12). In reality, the key-myth (M1) appears as an inversion of the myths of the origin of cooking fire. Fire and water are the *means* by which food is cooked, by which raw food is transformed into cooked food. A second group of myths ties into this first group, which no longer deals with the means but with the privileged *substance* of cooking: meat. These are the

---

50  *The Raw and the Cooked*, p. 4; *The Naked Man*, p. 561.
51  *The Raw and the Cooked*, pp. 4–5.

myths relating the origin of wild pigs, meat par excellence (M14, M15, M16, M18, M21). We then move from the Ge myths to Tupi myths. The Tupi myths around the origin of meat themselves refer back to the Bororo myths of the origin of body ornaments and cultural goods. A first cycle is complete.

But it was through honey that finery and ornaments appeared (M20). From these myths in which honey is a *means*, Lévi-Strauss goes on to look for and find myths in which honey is an *end*, an intended goal. And along with honey, the myths about the origin of meat also explain the origin of tobacco. The jaguar, master of fire and cooked meat, the secret of which he reveals to his human brothers-in-law, is ultimately killed and his body burned. It is from his ashes that tobacco is born. Raw meat is thus a natural material that is situated before/on this side of cooking; finery and ornaments are the products of cultural manufacture and are situated after/on the other side of cooking; honey and tobacco are the environs of cooking. The gathering of wild honey draws men back toward nature. The offering of tobacco and the smoking of it take men beyond nature, toward the world of the supernatural.

All these myths connect with others, which this time explain the origin of cultivated plants and, with them, aging, the short duration of life, and death (M87–M92), to which is connected a group of myths about the origin of the differences between animal species – particularly between birds distinguished by the colour of their feathers (M171–M175, M178–M179). The natural order thus echoes the cultural order created by the transition from the raw to the cooked, via cooking and other arts, which separates humans from animals.

Volume Two of the Mythology series, *From Honey to Ashes*, goes back to the Bororo and Toba myths on the origin of wild pigs and tobacco (M21–M27), and articulates them with a group of myths devoted to the origin of tobacco and honey (M188–M191) – and the girl who was mad about honey (M216–M217, M265–M266). The return to the Ge myths about the origin of fire (M7–M12, and M1, the Bird-Nester) is accomplished through a group of Warao, Toba and Tacana myths (M264–M266, M300–M303).

The third volume, *The Origin of Table Manners*, begins with the myth of Monmaneki, the hunter, and his five successive wives, which we summarized and one episode of which – that of the trunk-woman clasped on to her husband and refusing to let go – had incited Lévi-Strauss to turn to the North American Indian myths, where he discovered the same theme, told either directly or in an inverted form. He had found it among the Assiniboine and the Wichita (M369–370), and then among the Arapaho, the Crow and the Hidatsa, in other words among the Plains Indians, where it occurred in numerous variants on the theme of the 'Wives of the Sun and Moon' (M425–M438, M444, M447–M448, M451–M457).

Lastly, in *The Naked Man* all these themes figure either in a literal or in asymmetrically inverted forms. The Bird-Nester reappears, but is called Aishish this time and is the son of a demiurge, Kmukamtch, who covets one of his son's wives and urges the son to climb a tall tree where some eagles are nesting. The tree rises up to the sky, and Aishish is unable to come back down, etc. (M530 a,b). Here we are among the Klamath, south of the Sahaptin, where we find not only the Bird-Nester (M664–M672, M676–M679), but also the theme of the origin of birds' coloured plumage (M643–644), to which are attached new themes that refer to specificities of this coastal region – such as 'the origin of salmon and their freeing' (M606–M607, M694–M699), or the adventures of Lynx and Puma (M645–M649). Finally, after a return in force of the Bird-Nester (M664–M681), we witness the conquest of fire from the sky (M717–M733, M781–M782). We are now among the Quileute. And the last three myths in the book bring us back to the Ge, with the theme of the origin of the earth oven (M812). The Ge had earth ovens but did not make pottery, while the Bororo made pots but did not have earth ovens.

The loops have come full circle, but remain open at some place and onto something. In 1971, Lévi-Strauss, exhausted at the close of nearly ten years of labour, had intended, as I mentioned, to have done with Amerindian myths. But in 1985, fourteen years later, he published *The Jealous Potter*, and twenty years after that, *The Story of Lynx*. Had he not already written in premonitory fashion in the 'Overture' to Volume One, *The Raw and the Cooked*, that 'there is no real end to mythological analysis, no hidden unity to be grasped once the breaking-down process has been completed'?[52]

Nevertheless, a quarter of a century later, he would admit to Didier Eribon:

---

52 Ibid., p. 5.

I began to lean toward mythology in 1950 and I completed my Mythology series in 1970. For twenty years, I would get up at dawn, drunk with myths – truly I lived in another world. The myths filled me up. You have to absorb so much more than you can use . . . I lived with these peoples and their myths as if I were in a fairy tale.[53]

53 Lévi-Strauss and Eribon, *Conversations with Claude Lévi-Strauss*, p. 133.

# 10

## Toolkit for the Structural Analysis of Myths

As we have seen, Lévi-Strauss groped around for several years both to develop his concepts and method for approaching myths, but also to determine the corpus of myths that would best enable him to test these concepts and methods. At last, in 1961, he decided to go back to the Bororo myth of the Bird-Nester, which had already retained his attention a few years earlier.

With what awareness of himself and of the value of his concepts did he address his task? We are obliged to say that Lévi-Strauss's judgments about the mythologists who had gone before were either frankly negative or damned them with faint praise. We will remember that already in 1955 he had declared, in 'The Structural Study of Myth', that when it came to the ethnology of religion, one had the choice 'between platitude and sophism'.[1] He made an exception for Dumézil, having read his *Loki*, and for the Belgian specialist on Greek mythology, Henri Grégoire, without citing his work. He nevertheless stressed that neither 'were ethnologists, properly speaking'.[2]

---

1 C. Lévi-Strauss, *Structural Anthropology*, trans. C. Jacobson and B. Grundfest Schoepf (New York, Basic Books, 1963), p. 207.

2 C. Lévi-Strauss, *Structural Anthropology*; French edition (Paris, Plon, 1958), p. 288; not translated in the English.

Nine years later, in 1964, in the 'Overture' to the first volume of the Mythology series, he calls Richard Wagner the 'undeniable originator of the structural analysis of myths'[3], and admits 'other debts'.[4] Once again he mentions Dumézil and Grégoire, and adds Marcel Granet, to whom he had given a very rough time, as will be recalled, in *The Elementary Structures of Kinship* and to whom he now attributes 'insights of genius'.[5] Once again, he chooses non-mythologists for his homages.

When it comes to experts in mythology, his judgment again ranges from contempt to qualified tribute – such as that explicitly awarded to Max Müller and his school, who, in the nineteenth century, deserve 'great credit for having discovered, and to some extent deciphered, the astronomical code so often used by the myths'. But, 'their mistake, like that of all mythologists of the period and more recent ones too, was to try to understand the myths by means of a single and exclusive code, when in fact several codes are always in operation simultaneously'.[6] We are not told who these early or more recent mythologists are.

Lévi-Strauss also alludes to another group of mythologists (likewise left nameless), who in reaction to Müller had attempted to 'reduce the meaning of myths to a moralizing comment on the situation of mankind and made them into an explanation of love and death or pleasure and suffering, instead of an account of the phases of the moon and seasonal changes'.[7] As he had done in 1955, he rejects Jung, his theory of archetypes and the notion of collective unconscious, which he has been 'careful to leave . . . on one side'.[8]

But what about the specialists of Amerindian mythology, his own area of research? To be sure, this question is not directed at the hundreds of authors he cites – Métraux, Reichel-Dolmatoff, Albisetti and Colbacchini, the authors of the Salesian *Enciclopedia bororo*, Nimuendaju and all the others – who had collected myths in the field

---

3  C. Lévi-Strauss, *The Raw and the Cooked: Introduction to a Science of Mythology* 1, trans. J. and D. Weightman (Harmondsworth, Penguin, 1986), p. 15.

4  Ibid., p. 15, n. 5.

5  Ibid., p. 15, n. 5.

6  C. Lévi-Strauss, *The Naked Man, Mythologiques*, volume 4, trans. J. and D. Weightman, (Chicago, University of Chicago Press, 1981), p. 44.

7  *The Raw and the Cooked*, p. 340.

8  Ibid., p. 187.

and published them. In fact, all Lévi-Strauss sees prior to his own work are the theoreticians from the 'historical method' school, which arose in Finland: Gladys Reichard, Stith Thompson and Dorothy Demetracopoulou. In 1929, Thompson had published an overview of North American Indian myths,[9] while in 1933 Demetracopoulou brought out a collection of all versions of the famous North American Loon Woman myth, which Lévi-Strauss would articulate with the South American Bird-Nester cycle.

Lévi-Strauss acknowledged the immense services rendered by these authors in collecting and grouping all the variants of these major mythic themes, but he criticized the method used in their analysis. What he termed this 'méthode positiviste et empirique' consisted in listing all variants of a myth and then dividing the narrative into episodes and themes, before calculating the frequency with which the themes occurred and drawing a distribution map. By comparing the relative frequency of their occurrence, a relative age was assigned to the myths and an attempt made to determine their place of origin – and therefore the centre from which they spread outward. But, he says, 'all of this is beyond question. The difficulties start with the defining of the facts.'

> The method restricts itself to listing terms without establishing any link between them . . . Little or no attempt is made to effect a reduction that would show how two or more themes, superficially different from each other, stand in a transformational relationship to each other, with the result that the status of scientific fact is not attributable to each particular theme . . . but rather to the schema which gives rise to them, although this schema itself remains latent.[10]

These admonishments were addressed to Thompson, but the same were made to Demetracopoulou. He reproached her for having divided the Loon Woman myth according to subjective criteria and having concluded that 'there [was] nothing intrinsic in the incidents

---

9 S. Thompson, *Tales of the North American Indians* (Bloomington, Indiana University Press, 1929) and 'The Star Husband Tale', *Studia Septentrionalia*, n° 4, Oslo (1953), pp. 93–163; D. Demetracopoulou, 'The Loon Woman Myth: A Study in Synthesis', *Journal of American Folklore*, n° 46 (1933), pp. 101–28.

10 C. Lévi-Strauss, *The Origin of Table Manners*, *Mythologiques*, volume 3, trans. J. and D. Weightman (Chicago, University of Chicago Press, 1978), pp. 227–8.

themselves which could cause them to adhere to one another in a set pattern and thus initiate a myth'. For Lévi-Strauss, 'the real object on which the analysis should centre is the group as a whole, not any one of its particular features', and this group is 'a local or temporary state of a transformation which may give rise to several others, all governed by the same necessity'.[11]

In sum, the mythologists who preceded Lévi-Strauss had not gone beyond the surface of the myths and were therefore incapable of penetrating their nature, since they did not perceive the structure. In the nearly 2,000 pages of the four-volume Mythology series, Lévi-Strauss would refer no more than sixteen times to one or another of his predecessors from 'the old mythography'. For he had initiated 'a new way of apprehending content which, without disregarding or impoverishing it, translates it into structural terms'.[12]

Thanks to structural analysis, myths would finally achieve a rational existence. Their apparent *irrationality* would finally be dispelled, and their true nature and *raison d'être* appear. In the 'Finale' of *The Naked Man*, therefore at the end of over ten years of work, Lévi-Strauss expressed his conviction that 'the structural analysis of myths is preparing the way for a scientific anthropology.'[13] And, gazing even further into the future, he did not hesitate to proclaim that 'structuralism offers the social sciences an epistemological model incomparably more powerful than those they previously had at their disposal.'[14]

Structural analysis, then, ushered in all the human and social sciences, and the promise and warranty that these would at last become true sciences. What does this amount to, and to what extent has Lévi-Strauss's ambition been realized?

*What is a myth for Lévi-Strauss?*
Myths are one way in which human groups talk to themselves. 'The substance of the myth lies neither in the style nor in the form of the narrative, nor in the syntax, but in the story that it tells.'[15] Myths are

---

11 *The Naked Man*, p. 61.
12 C. Lévi-Strauss, *From Honey to Ashes: Introduction to a Science of Mythology 2*, trans. J. and D. Weightman (Chicago, University of Chicago Press, 1973), p. 466.
13 *The Naked Man*, p. 152.
14 Ibid., p. 687.
15 *The Naked Man*, p. 645.

narratives in which events unfold sequentially within a plot. These sequences of events are the 'patent' content of the myth. They obey a chronological order. Lévi-Strauss adds that this 'patent' content is 'apparent', or visible. Which presumes that there is another content, one that is 'latent' and not directly visible, which the analysis will uncover and explore. This latent content is that of the schemata which, at different and unequally deep levels of the narrative, organize the sequences of events: these schemata can be geographical, sociological, techno-economic, and so on; they, too, appear to the analyst as transformations of an underlying logical structure common to all the levels.[16]

*What do the Amerindian myths tell us?*
For Lévi-Strauss, they tell us stories 'of the time before men and animals became distinct beings',[17] and, for the definition to be complete, we must add: stories of the time when the gods, too, could appear as humans or animals, and live among men and animals who were at that time not distinct beings. Myths are therefore the representation of a time and a world that have long since vanished but continue to be present, in the present, because the myths give them meaning and are the *raison d'être* for the rituals the Indians address to the animals they hunt as well as to the plants they cultivate:[18]

> In olden days, goats were of the same nature as the Indians; they took on human or animal appearance at will. The Indians *knew it*, and this is why they continued to observe special rites when they killed a Goat, as well as a Black Bear or a Grizzly, animals who also have this double nature.[19]

---

16 Cf. C. Lévi-Strauss, 'The Story of Asdiwal', in *Structural Anthropology, Volume 2*, pp. 146–97; 146, 161.

17 C. Lévi-Strauss and D. Eribon, ed., *Conversations with Claude Lévi-Strauss*, trans. P. Wissing (Chicago and London, University of Chicago Press, 1991), p. 139.

18 *From Honey to Ashes*, p. 323: 'men could speak to plants . . . at a time when the latter were personal beings'.

19 C. Lévi-Strauss, *The Story of Lynx*, trans. C. Tihanyi (Chicago, University of Chicago Press, 1995), p. 68; my emphasis.

*What is myth for, then?*

> To explain why things, which were different at the beginning, became what they are and why it could not be otherwise.[20]

Let us note first of all that, because of its general character, this definition can apply to the story told in the Book of Genesis, to the Rig Veda or to the countless sacred texts in which religions are grounded. Furthermore, Lévi-Strauss characterized the Amerindian myths as stories that deal with the passage from nature to culture, from the animal state to the human one. But this raises a problem. For modern science, the passage from animality to humanity refers to the process of the separation of prehominids, ancestors of today's *Homo sapiens sapiens*, from the other primates – chimpanzees and bonobos – which descend from the same common ancestor. But his modern representation of the passage from nature to culture obviously does not include the idea that hominids could also be black bears or that protohumans could marry a grizzly, or the idea that the fox could be the animal incarnation of a trickster god.[21] The use of terms like 'nature' and 'culture', and recourse to the notion of a passage from one to the other, thus transfigure the nature of Amerindian myths and give them cultural and mental dimensions they did not have when they were conceived and transmitted by these human groups. But what do the explanations proposed by the myths represent? Lévi-Strauss tells us:

> We have to resign ourselves to the fact that myths *tell us nothing instructive* about the order of the world, the nature of reality or the origin and destiny of mankind. We cannot expect them to flatter any metaphysical thirst . . . On the other hand, they *teach us a great deal about the societies* from which they originate, they help to lay bare their inner workings and clarify the *raison d'être* of beliefs, customs and institutions the organization of which was at first sight incomprehensible; lastly, and most important, they make it possible to discover certain operational modes of the *human mind*, which have remained so constant over the centuries, and are so widespread over immense geographical distances, that we can assume them to be fundamental

---

20 Lévi-Strauss and Eribon, *Conversations with Claude Lévi-Strauss*, p. 140.
21 *From Honey to Ashes*, pp. 91–2.

and can seek to find them in other societies and in other areas of mental life.[22]

To us, then, these myths convey nothing of what they proposed to explain to the Indians, and if myths are a 'parade of fantastic ideas rooted in the understanding',[23] the question arises of the basis of the difference between mythical and scientific thought. Ever since 1955 and 'The Structural Study of Myth', Lévi-Strauss consistently maintained that 'the difference lies, not in the quality of the intellectual process, but in the nature of the things to which it is applied . . . the same logical processes operate in myth as in science.'[24]

Several remarks are called for here. First of all, the fact that, for those who believe in the myths and act on them in their daily life, they provide 'true' explanations, in other words real explanations. The fact of believing in the 'truth' of myths is fundamental. It *precedes* and *underpins* all the processes the human mind brings into play in constructing fantastic stories about the origins of the universe, of man and of society. This fundamental fact is blanked out by Lévi-Strauss, thus attenuating the difference in nature between mythical thought and scientific thought. Instead the resemblances between the two modes of thought – the fact that both apply identical logical operations to forms, judgments and propositions – are pushed to the fore by Lévi-Strauss and used as arguments to affirm that 'the same logical processes operate in myth as in science.'

Not that it is false to say that certain logical operations are present in both cases, and it is clearly to Lévi-Strauss's considerable credit to have shown this; but the likeness does not suffice to erase the differences. And one of the main differences, pointed out by Lévi-Strauss himself, is that mythical thought, unlike 'Cartesian science', is characterized by the fact that 'it refuses to break the difficulty into parts, never accepts a partial answer, and seeks explanations that encompass the totality of phenomena.'[25]

As we have seen, the 'savage mind' 'claims at once to analyse and to synthesize.'[26] It seeks to 'grasp the world as both a synchronic and a

---

22  *The Naked Man,* p. 639; my emphasis.
23  Ibid., p. 684.
24  *Structural Anthropology,* p. 230.
25  Lévi-Strauss and Eribon, *Conversations with Claude Lévi-Strauss,* p. 139.
26  C. Lévi-Strauss, *The Savage Mind* (no translator mentioned) (Chicago, University of Chicago Press, 1969), p. 219.

diachronic totality', and because of this, unlike scientific thinking, which is a historical process open to the production of testable and therefore refutable knowledge, mythical thinking appears as 'time-less'[27] – exactly like religions, revealed or otherwise. It is therefore not because a mode of thought entails logical operations that it is analogous (or complementary) to scientific thinking. But that does not make it any less important to demonstrate the presence of these logical operations in both modes of thought, and Lévi-Strauss did this masterfully.

If the myths tell us nothing about what they purported to explain, they do teach us a lot about two domains they did not claim to elucidate: the workings of the societies in which they originated, their beliefs and their institutions; and the operations the human mind undertakes when it produces myths.

Let us pause for a moment and examine these two points.

If myths bear the mark of the beliefs and institutions of a given society (the Bororo, for instance, are matrilineal, making the Bird-Nester's father, who sends him to his death, an affine and not a consanguine, and the hero's rape of his mother the worst of all crimes of incest), then the members of these societies must have produced or reproduced them after having borrowed them from neighbouring tribes and stamped them with the features of their own society. In *The View from Afar*, Lévi-Strauss writes: 'Societies are not persons. Nothing authorizes us to depict them as customers thumbing through some metaphysical catalogue and obtaining, each for their own use, models different from those other societies would use toward the same ends.'[28] How are these statements to be understood?

If societies are not persons, they are not subjects. Subjects are always specific individuals. It is therefore individuals who create and/or transmit the myths: 'every myth, in the last resort, must have its origin in an individual act of creation. This is no doubt very true but, in order to achieve the status of myth, the created work must cease precisely to be individual.'[29]

---

27  *The Savage Mind*, p. 263.

28  C. Lévi-Strauss, 'From Mythical Possibility to Social Existence', in *The View from Afar*, trans. J. Neugroschel and P. Hoss (Chicago, University of Chicago Press, 1985), p. 157.

29  *The Naked Man*, p. 626.

In order for its mythical character, its 'mythism' to be actualized, the story must be adopted 'collectively'.[30] To be sure. But why would a human group collectively accept a story told by one of its members as being a 'myth', an utterance that is deserving of attention and respect? The group, Lévi-Strauss explains, considers this story to bear fundamental answers to problems it confronts, as stating essential 'truths'. In this way, not only would the creation of a myth be unable to remain an individual act, but it could not be seen as coming from an individual. For the truths or truth told by the story clearly exceed the limits – well understood by the members of the group – of the teller, but also human limits. Lastly, 'myths are anonymous . . . whatever their real origins . . . when a myth is repeated [it is] coming from nowhere'.[31] Or at least it can only have a 'supernatural' origin.

All the more so because myths tell of deeds and invoke reasons that are not part of the everyday, concrete experience of their listeners and believers. Basically, in order to be received and experienced as such, myths must be seen as unconnected to human origins, as having been obtained by humans through 'some mystic revelation'.[32] That is why it can be said that myths are rooted in the sacred, whereas the tales of Aesop or La Fontaine pertain to the secular. The first are communications coming from entities invisible to the human eye, the second are metaphorical tales with a moral, which humans tell each other. In the end, myths are products of the human mind which exist socially and acquire symbolic force and efficacy only if the humans that produced them erase themselves from their source, are hidden and denied.

This concealment, this denial that humans are at the origin of their works are the cognitive and affective preconditions that engender the imaginary places and times in which the different varieties of the sacred arise. Indeed, both written and non-written religions are always perceived to have arisen through the inspiration of invisible entities, superhuman powers. This is as true of the Genesis story that opens the Bible as it is of the Rig Veda texts, which purportedly appeared by fragments to the great 'seers' of ancient times – the Rishis, the 'fathers',

---

30  Ibid., p. 627.
31  *The Raw and the Cooked*, p. 18.
32  *The Origin of Table Manners*, p. 272.

who are held to have first seen, then copied and transmitted them. But before myths and religions (but also other sorts of political and other ideologies) can become established in the human mind, there must already be the belief that the impossible is possible. This prerequisite for mythico-religious thought is at the same time an intellectual and an affective act, an act of faith that does not exclude doubt. What is normally, visibly, commonly impossible is still possible. Once this step has been taken, the mind can construct its palaces of ideas by its rules; but man has amputated a part of himself, which becomes alien to him. Lévi-Strauss did not look any further into the manufacture of the sacred.

But if the Amerindian myths do not explain anything for us, they explain everything for the Indians. So, what do the myths do for them? First, and fundamentally, they explain the origin of the universe, of humans, of society, and the reasons for the order that reigns today and should always reign. That is the *etiological* function of myths. The explanations they propose all flow from the same postulate: in the beginning, humans were not distinct from beasts. This postulate is common to all indigenous tribes of both North and South America, whatever their language and their internal social organization. It is the basis of their shared worldview. But this postulate cannot be deduced from the formal structures of the human mind, which are universal and not cultural. It could arise only because all these tribes shared a common way of life for thousands of years, which entailed continuous close relations with plants and wild animals, and which could therefore suggest the idea that, in the beginning, humans and animals (and even plants) were persons.

But, in addition to this 'gnoseological' function, myths fullfil other functions necessary to the workings of societies.

> What is true of the rules of kinship is also valid for mythic narratives.
> Neither are limited to being simply what they are: they serve a purpose
> – to solve problems which are sociological [kinship] in the one case
> and socio-logical [myths] in the other.[33]

What are these socio-logical functions?

---

33  Ibid., p. 228.

[Myths] should be seen rather as constituting local and temporary answers to the problems raised by feasible adjustments and insoluble contradictions that they are endeavouring to legitimize or conceal.[34]

These socio-logical functions are 'ideological', since they contribute to concealing or legitimizing insurmountable social contradictions or, on the contrary, accompany social transformations that are feasible. To mask or legitimize contradictions, to accompany the workings and reproduction of social systems – such are the very functions Marx attributed to 'ideologies', using a term borrowed from the French philosophers around Destutt de Tracy, known as the 'Idéologues'. But what insurmountable social contradictions – or what feasible adjustments – are the Amerindian myths telling us about?

Apart from discussing men's domination of women, the legitimacy of which is justified by the myths, or on a more abstract level, the impossible access of humans to immortality, the four volumes of the Mythology series have little to say about the contradictions inherent in the societies concerned. We learn that there were flourishing slave markets in the American Northwest. We hear tell of women who marry chiefs, but who are these chiefs? On the other hand, Lévi-Strauss gathers and analyses a wealth of information on the plants that are mentioned, on the ways of the animal protagonists, on constellations and heavenly bodies, hunting and fishing techniques, mountains and streams, the seasons and the cycles of activities those seasons impose on humans depending on whether they are hot or cold, dry or wet, long or short, and so on. All such details form part of what Lévi-Strauss terms the 'techno-economic' infrastructure of societies – another notion borrowed from Marx, but lacking, as I have said, any information on one of the central components of society, namely the social relations of production. The latter are not confined to the division of labour prevalent in hunting, fishing, gathering, weaving, basket making, etc. They also concern ownership of the fishing sites, hunting grounds, etc., as well as the appropriation and redistribution of the products of these activities. Later, we will discuss the role Lévi-Strauss attributed to infrastructures in explaining the differences between the variants of a myth, when he wrote: 'In the last resort, these reasons refer to the techno-economic [infrastructure],

---

34  *The Naked Man*, p. 629.

which is what we must *always* look to *first* if we are to try to understand the differential gaps between ideologies.'[35] Or again:

> The ideological framework of the myths of equatorial America appears to be linked to an infrastructure in which native thought discovers a contradiction: between a temporal axis determined by the equinoxes and a spatial axis where the direction of travel introduces an inequality between distances that are nevertheless identical. Here we can verify the correlation between ideology and infrastructure.[36]

Since the human mind is the same in all humans, and the operations of mythical thought are the same in all humans, but the differences between the infrastructures of societies are alleged to explain the discrepancies between their myths, how is one to construe the relationship between the universality of the formal operations of mythical thought and the always-specific content of the myths? This was a fundamental problem, which Lévi-Strauss took on, and his answers were to deeply transform our understanding of myths and mythical thought.

Before beginning a detailed analysis of his contribution, the following three tables set out our subject matter: the first enumerates the components of a myth, or as Lévi-Strauss says, its 'layered structure'. The second summarizes the main operations of mythical thought. The third presents the conditions and steps involved in the structural analysis of myths.

---

I Components of a Myth
*Armature*
*Axes*
*Mythemes*
*Schemata*
*Message = patent meaning (etiological function)*
             *latent meaning (semantic function)*

---

35  Ibid., p. 107; my emphasis.
36  *The Origin of Table Manners*, p. 174.

II Operations of Mythical Thought
To produce and combine the components of the myth
*Selection of the problem to be solved*
*Logical operations*
*Construction of the myth's armature and of its variants*
*Selection of the mythemes (binary, ternary or analogical operators)*
*Selection of the schemata*
*Creation of the myth as a transformation group by placing mythemes and schemata in a relation of:*
>    *symmetry*
>    *asymmetry*
>    *inversion*
>    *homology*
>    *or in Klein groups*

*Closure of a group of variants of a myth by double or triple twining of the final variant with respect to those preceding (canonical formula)*
*Constitution of a group of myths forming a cycle and closing the cycle*
*Intersections or connections of one myth cycle with others*
*Metalinguistic procedures*
*Use of literal and/or figurative meaning:*
>    *(passage from one to the other and vice versa)*
>    *(confusion of one with the other)*

*Use of metaphor and/or metonymy*
>    *(passage from one to the other and vice versa)*

*Use of contiguity or resemblance*
*Confusion*
>    *of signifier and signified*
>    *of the word and the thing*

III Prerequisites for and Steps in the Structural Analysis of Myths
Prerequisite: *Effacement of the analyst's Self*
Structural analysis: three steps
*1. Compiling the ethnographic material/file*
*2. Formal analysis*
*3. Semantic analysis*

# 11

## The Components of Myths

### The Armature

The *armature* of the myth is a 'combination of properties that remain invariant in two or several myths'.[1]

For example, the armature of a certain group of myths concerning the origin of women – M29 (Sherente), M30 (Chamacoco), M31 (Toba-Pilaga) and M32 (Matako) – consists of three underlying oppositions: male/female, high/low, restrained conduct/unrestrained conduct.[2]

The armature of a myth is thus constituted by a series of oppositions (usually binary), whatever their nature may be. Myths can be juxtaposed and compared precisely because their analysis shows that their armature is based on shared oppositions. For instance, Lévi-Strauss compares a Tikuna myth from South America (myth M354), which relates the hunter Monmaneki's different marriages, with two Arapaho Indian myths from North America (M425 and M426), which tell of the adventures of Sun and Moon when they attempted to choose between a human and an animal wife. Indeed, the three myths share several elements:

---

1 C. Lévi-Strauss, *The Raw and the Cooked: Introduction to a Science of Mythology 1*, trans. J. & D. Weightman (Harmondsworth, Penguin, 1986), p. 199.
2 Ibid., p. 112.

1. Comparison of a human wife with one or several animal wives.
2. Each time, the frog-wife clings to her husband.
3. Each time, the animal wife is discredited by her eating habits.
4. The four elements are connected by an astronomical pair, Sun and Moon, which are also supernatural beings.[3]

Only formal analysis can reveal the myths' logical, internal armature, which is hidden.[4]

## Codes, Vocabularies and Syntaxes

Codes are 'the pattern of functions ascribed by each myth to the armature'.[5] Below is our inventory of the codes used in the hundreds of myths contained in the Mythology series to emit their messages:

1. Sensory: sight (visible/invisible); smell (sweet-smelling/foul-smelling); taste (sweet/bitter); hearing (high-pitched/low-pitched); touch (smooth/rough), etc.
2. Sociological: consanguines/affines; freemen/slaves; partners/rivals; endogamy/exogamy, etc.
3. Technical-economic: hunting/fishing, etc.
4. Culinary: raw/cooked; sweet/salty, etc.
5. Alimentary: eating noisily/in silence, etc.
6. Sexual: man/woman
7. Anatomical: penis/vagina, etc.
8. Vestimentary: naked/clothed, etc.
9. Aesthetic: attractive/ugly, etc.
10. Astronomical: Sun/Moon; celestial/terrestrial, etc.
11. Meteorological: dry season/rainy season, etc.
12. Geological: land/sea; mountain/plain, etc.
13. Botanical: wild plants/cultivated plants, etc.
14. Zoological: grizzly/black bear; coyote/fox, etc.

---

3 C. Lévi-Strauss, *The Origin of Table Manners*, Mythology series, vol. 3, trans. J. & D. Weightman (Chicago, University of Chicago Press, 1978), p. 208.

4 C. Lévi-Strauss, *From Honey to Ashes: Introduction to a Science of Mythology 2*, trans. J. & D. Weightman (Chicago, University of Chicago Press, 1973), p. 157.

5 *The Raw and the Cooked*, p. 199.

15. Ethical: moral/immoral; fair/unfair; virtuous/vicious, etc.

16. Linguistic: literal meaning/figurative meaning, etc.

In total, if we add the five sensory codes individually, we are dealing with twenty codes, which provide as many different vocabularies for the emission of messages. To choose a code is therefore to choose a 'language', which is itself governed by its own syntax. The nature and number of the codes present in myths determines their *semantic field*, and each myth can be defined by the path it takes through the semantic field generated by the codes it uses.[6]

In most cases, myths make use of several codes to emit the same message. This supposes the codes carry messages that can be transposed into other codes and can express, in their own system, messages received by way of other codes.[7] The *mutual convertibility* of the codes is ensured by logical operations, but it is founded on a postulate of mythical thinking that is not of a logical order, but is an essentially philosophical postulate, which posits that all levels of the universe, including those of social life, are ideally mutually convertible. However, this postulate cannot originate in the concrete, practical, effective experience of the universe and of the society in which the individuals live, whatever the period and the society under consideration.

Convertibility of the codes does not imply their strict equivalence. Depending on the story's context, one of the codes may appear as a 'shared language', in which the messages of the other codes are transmitted. In this case, its operational value is greater than that of the other codes. In *The Raw and the Cooked*, Lévi-Strauss shows, for instance, that cooking implies silence, and anti-cooking, noise. Myths about the cooking environment in *From Honey to Ashes* explore this opposition, this time using contrasts contained in the notion of noise: continuous noise/discontinuous noise; modulated noise/non-modulated noise; verbal behaviour/non-verbal behaviour, etc.[8] In other contexts (*The Origin of Table Manners*), an astronomical code – opposing, for example, Sun and Moon – predominates.

--------

6 *The Origin of Table Manners*, p. 168.

7 C. Lévi-Strauss, *The Savage Mind* (no translator mentioned) (Chicago, University of Chicago Press, 1969), pp. 75–6.

8 *From Honey to Ashes*, p. 472.

The fact that myths use several codes at once reveals, as mythical thinking postulates, an (imaginary) homology between certain oppositions found in nature and others found in social life. 'The Story of Asdiwal' offered a demonstration, since Lévi-Strauss showed the existence of a homology between:

| **Oppositions found in nature** and | empyrean sky chthonian world | high low | mountain sea | upstream downstream | winter summer |
|---|---|---|---|---|---|
| **Oppositions found in social life** | descent alliance | endogamy exogamy | hunting/ fishing | abundance shortage | etc. |

A myth using several codes functions as a 'meta-code'.

## Axes

Codes develop their messages along different axes, while along these axes are distributed the transformations enabling the passage from one variant of a myth to another – from a group of Chaco myths to a group of myths from Guyana, for instance. The more axes there are, the harder it is to intuit the architecture.[9] In *The Raw and the Cooked*, the Ge and the Tupi-Guaraní myths concerning the origin of fire operate through a twofold opposition: between the raw and the cooked, on the one hand, and between the fresh and the decayed, on the other.

> The raw/cooked axis is characteristic of culture; the fresh/decayed one of nature, since cooking brings about the cultural transformation of the raw, just as putrefaction is its natural transformation.[10]

Although these oppositions between the raw and the cooked, the fresh and the decayed, etc., correspond to experience, there is a problem with using them to illustrate two inverted transformations within the opposition between nature and culture, posited as the keystone of all Amerindian myths. From one standpoint, placing them under the lamp of the opposition between nature and culture illuminates them with a

9  Ibid., p. 165.
10  *The Raw and the Cooked*, p. 142.

strong meaning, a deep signification; but this meaning, which is clear to
Lévi-Strauss (and more generally to a Western mind), threatens, if not
to replace, at least to deeply alter the way these empirical oppositions
were actually thought and experienced by the Indians themselves.
Twenty years after the publication of the four volumes of the Mythology
series, Lévi-Strauss, in *The Story of Lynx* (1991), distanced himself somewhat from this stance:

> But we have to admit that in the first stages of the research, the selec-
> tion and the definition of the axes on which are located the opposi-
> tions, and the selection and the definition of the codes to which they
> are applicable, *owe much to the analyst's subjectivity*, and thus they
> have an impressionistic character . . . In a domain so new (at least
> from the angle I was using), I proceeded through trials and errors.
> Some oppositions, even real ones, do not always have the form I gave
> them; others *perhaps do not exist*. But I will deem myself satisfied if I
> be granted the recognition that I have been right in a significant
> number of cases.[11]

Willingly granted. The very many oppositions revealed by Lévi-Strauss
have indeed deepened our understanding of Amerindian myths.
Nevertheless, as Philippe Descola has shown, there are several ways of
conceiving the relationship between nature and culture, in the form of
various modes of opposition, or beyond the opposition between nature
and culture.[12]

Lévi-Strauss goes on:

> In the last resort, the differences that can be noted between the myths
> are to be explained by the levels at which the latter select the opposi-
> tions they use, and by the original way in which each myth folds the
> network back upon itself, horizontally, vertically or diagonally, in
> order to make certain pairs coincide and to reveal, in a certain
> perspective, the homology existing between several oppositions.[13]

---

11 C. Lévi-Strauss, *The Story of Lynx*, trans. C. Tihanyi (Chicago, University of
Chicago Press, 1995), p. 186; my emphasis.

12 P. Descola, *Beyond Nature and Culture*, trans. J. Lloyd (Chicago, University of
Chicago Press, 2013).

13 *The Origin of Table Manners*, p. 186.

To illustrate this notion of network of oppositions distributed along several axes, I will reproduce one of the network drawings made by Lévi-Strauss for *The Origin of Table Manners*.

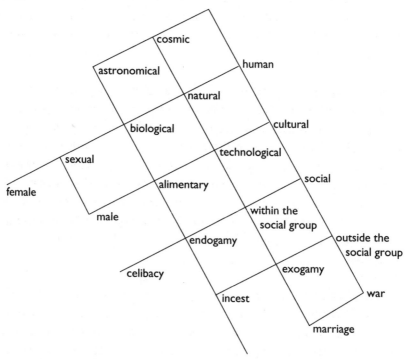

The structural network of a system of mythic oppositions
(from *The Origin of Table Manners*, p. 186)

This network can be enriched and developed in numerous ways. For example, the cosmological axis can be used to think the opposition between a burned world (through conjunction of the sky with the earth) and a decayed world (through disjunction of the sky from the earth). In one case, the Sun is too close to the Earth, in the other it is too far away. The astronomical axis can be spatial and deal with the place of the heavenly bodies and the constellations in the sky, or temporal and deal with the seasonal appearance or disappearance of the stars. The anatomical axis can be used to oppose the man without a penis or with a flaccid penis, who became a Favourite of the Sun (M255, Mundurucu – *From Honey to Ashes*), to the man with a long penis, the Favourite of the Moon (M256, Tacana – *From Honey to Ashes*). But women with a closed vulva can also be opposed to those with a gaping vulva. A whole series of combinations can be developed using the orifices of the human body, according to whether they are in front or in back, at the top or at the bottom: mouth, nose, ears, vagina, anus, and according to the functions each is called upon to fulfil by being open or closed, serving to absorb or eject (for example, food/excrement).[14] And each time, a new semantic field is constructed and enriched.

In the end, myths are narratives that relate series of events brought about through the action of various real and/or imaginary characters, which come to exist in a semantic field determined by different series of oppositions deployed at several levels. Lévi-Strauss christened all these elements that feature in myths and play a role in them, be it Sun or Coyote, an overly long penis or a stopped-up vagina, 'mythemes'. These are constituent units of the language – actually the metalanguage – of the myths, whose combinations are organized by schemata that endow them with meaning and give the myths in question one or several meanings.

## Mythemes and Mythical Schemata

If mythical thinking represents, say, a burned world using the image of the Sky mingled with the Earth, or, by opposition, a decayed world using the image of the Sky and the Earth grown so far apart that the Earth no longer receives the Sun's heat, we must conclude, as Lévi-Strauss did in *The Savage Mind*, that the myth-producing mind 'thinks in terms of concepts', in this case those of conjunction and disjunction, but these are 'imbedded in images'.[15] The image is not a concept, but the image associated with the idea functions as a *sign* that carries a meaning. When this sign is incorporated into the mythical discourse, it becomes a *mytheme*. Anything can be a mytheme: an object (for example, a canoe), an animal (like the jaguar, master of the cooking fire), or a supernatural being (demiurge, creator or trickster) that in the olden days could appear as a human or an animal. Mythemes are thus 'units' characteristic of

---

14 See also C. Lévi-Strauss, *The Jealous Potter*, trans. B. Chorier (Chicago, University of Chicago Press, 1988), p. 163.

15 *The Savage Mind*, p. 265.

myths, within which they acquire a signifying function. Mythical logic is thus a *logic of significations*, which implies concepts; but it is not a logic of concepts.[16]

Among the mythemes are many 'zoemes'. The term designates all living beings that play a role in myths. Zoemes are not only animals. They can also be plants: a palm tree married by a woman; tobacco, which is the hypostasis of a demiurge used to communicate with the gods; cultivated plants, which are persons who can be addressed directly, or when direct communication has been lost, can be addressed through an agrarian god or goddess (corn spirits, for instance).

Among the hundred or so animal characters featuring in the myths are mammals, birds, fish, insects and so on. They usually come in complementary and opposing pairs – coyote and lynx, grizzly or black bear and wolverine, etc. But the same animal can also appear in opposite forms: this is the case of the butterfly or the skate. The butterfly is very broad when it opens its wings; when it closes them and is seen head-on or from the back, it is very narrow. Likewise, the skate in profile is thin, and very broad when seen from above or below. The skate is associated with the female reproductive organs – uterus and placenta, but also with objects that envelop or protect, like the canoe and the house.[17] The skate is also opposed to the serpent, which by its elongated, cylindrical form is reminiscent of a penis.

Lévi-Strauss concludes from this that 'all mythemes of whatever kind must, generally speaking, lend themselves to binary operations . . . it is as if certain animals were more suited than others to fulfil this role . . . because of some striking feature of their make-up or behaviour'. In fact, he adds, 'no feature is significant in itself: it is perceptive analysis, already by definition combinatory and capable of logical operations on the level of the sensibility which, when relayed through or backed up by the understanding, bestows a meaning on phenomena and turns them into articulate statements. We can say, then, that the binary operators are those operators which are already perceptible to empirical deductions as algorithms'.[18]

---

16  *The Origin of Table Manners*, p. 352; C. Lévi-Strauss, *The Naked Man*, Mythology series, volume 4, trans. J. and D. Weightman, (Chicago, University of Chicago Press, 1981), p. 649.

17  *The Naked Man*, p. 551.

18  Ibid., p. 559.

Despite his insistence on mythemes as binary operators, Lévi-Strauss, in response to Leach's criticism that he had ignored other forms of analogy, occasionally referred to ternary series. In certain myths, for example, birds of prey are divided into three categories according to whether they feed on birds, fish or small mammals. They are thus connected with the air, the water and the earth. Finally, in *The Story of Lynx*, Lévi-Strauss would no longer assign binary oppositions the determining role he had ascribed to them in the Mythology series. Instead he writes:

> Mythical thought operates through means of oppositions and codes. However, the notion of binary opposition . . . only intervenes in the analysis of myth as the smallest common denominator of the changing values arising from comparison and analogy.[19]

This turns out to be all the more necessary because the characters in the myths, while conserving something of their empirical reality in the narrative, have been changed into imaginary, symbolic characters endowed with a supernatural nature and attributes. The jaguar in South American mythology is master of the cooking fire and eats his food cooked. He takes a human wife and, as a countergift for the woman they had given him, makes his brothers-in-law a present of fire, whereas they had formerly eaten their food raw. But animals are not only opposed to other animals, like the skate and the snake. They also change into something other than themselves. In the North American Quinault and Quileute myths, the skate is turned into a constellation. In other myths, the spiny skate is the transformation of an exasperated man.[20]

Any mytheme can appear in several forms (or as several objects), which are its 'combinatory variants'. For instance, the vulva and the bladder 'would seem, then, to be two combinatory variants of one and the same mytheme, the relevant function of which transposes, on to the alimentary register, an incestuous connection'.[21] In other myths, a 'magic wampum necklace and [a] severed head . . .

---

19 *The Story of Lynx*, p. 185.
20 *From Honey to Ashes*, M331 and 332, p. 434.
21 *The Naked Man*, p. 168.

constitute combinatory variants of the same mytheme'.[22] This confirms the hypothesis that each mytheme is 'a cluster of differential elements',[23] and that when one mytheme fulfils the same function as another, both are combinatory variants of the same mytheme.[24]

Let us take a closer look at one of the most important mythemes in the Mythology series, the 'canoe' – in this case 'the canoe journey' made by Sun and Moon on a river – which will allow us to hone the notion of mythical schema. Using the analysis of the 'canoe journey' schema, we will be able to define what Lévi-Strauss calls the twofold 'message' of the myth. On the one hand, its patent message, designed to explain something – the origin of thunder or birds, for example – and, on the other hand, its latent message, or semantic function. This latent message is not delivered explicitly, but it could be understood implicitly by an Indian, and is open to elucidation by structural analysis.

A canoe trip requires at least two actors having distinct and complementary functions. The one in the front propels the craft, the one at the back steers it. During the journey, each must remain in place in order not to upset the canoe. They can be neither too close together nor too far apart.

> The limited space in the canoe and the strict navigational rules tend to keep them at the *right distance* in relation to each other, together and separate at one and the same time, as the sun and the moon must be in order to avoid excessive daylight or excessive darkness which would scorch or rot the earth.[25]

The canoe journey thus offers the mind a way to picture a situation that excludes the excessive proximity or distance of two terms. At the cosmic level, the equivalents would be that the conjunction of sky and earth would bring about perpetual day and burn up the world, whereas too much distance between sky and earth would result in perpetual night and decay. On the sociological and sexual levels, the canoe and its two passengers will also be able to signify the prohibition of marriage

---

22  *The Origin of Table Manners,* p. 346.
23  *The Naked Man,* p. 79
24  *The Origin of Table Manners,* p. 346.
25  Ibid., p. 191.

between persons too closely related – incest between brother and sister, or parents and children – as well as the prohibition of marriage between partners that are too distant – between a woman and a serpent, or a man and a grizzly, for example. From the conceptual standpoint, therefore, 'it is the very occurrences of conjunction and disjunction that the canoe is keeping apart.'[26]

This series of equivalences has taken us from the *logical* structure of the 'canoe' mytheme to its present, latent but hidden *semantic* function. Day appears as a temperate conjunction of sky and earth, congruent with the geographical category of near, and night as a temperate disjunction of sky and earth, congruent with far. Extreme conjunction would bring about perpetual day, while extreme disjunction would result in perpetual night. A temperate conjunction and disjunction of Sun and Moon result in the alternation of day and night, thus engendering a form of periodicity that occurs daily, not seasonally like that caused by the appearance and disappearance over the year of the Pleiades, Orion and other constellations.

But a canoe is made for travelling, and the myths that narrate the canoe journey of Sun and Moon make the 'canoe' mytheme the instrument of a mythical schema. A schema is an operation of the mind, the construction of a series of representations through the narrative use of mythemes in the form of binary or ternary operators (or those that carry the possibility of opposing and correlating even more complex, but always analogical, operators). Schemata are thus the products of operations on operators that produce a new meaning, which is added to the meaning of the mythemes. So just what is the mythical schema of the journey by canoe, and what effects does it have on the process of thinking?

At the start of the journey, the canoe leaves its port and the near is very near. Over the course of the trip, the near becomes far and the far draws near. When the destination is reached, the initial values have been inverted: the far has become near, and the near, far. The return trip will involve the same operations with inverse effects. Lévi-Strauss concludes:

---

26  Ibid., p. 190.

The schema of the canoe journey makes it possible, then, to carry out two operations simultaneously: one, which is logical in character, totalizes oppositions selected at various levels, and yields a total product consisting of a system the terms of which, being opposed to each other, form a new opposition. The other, which is semantic in character, totalizes in analogous fashion spatial registers (vertical and horizontal), temporal registers (journey and calendar), sociological registers (celibacy and marriage, endogamy and exogamy, kinship and war) and anatomical registers (mutilations and explosions, openings and closings, physiological deficiencies) and yields a global product, the properties of which are summarized in the sun-moon pair.[27]

Over the course of the journey, the canoe thus brings about the summation of all the values produced by the conjunction (U) and the disjunction (//) of near and far, which Lévi-Strauss represents in the following way:

$$\text{near U far}$$

$$[\text{sky U earth}] \qquad \Sigma \qquad [\text{sky // earth}]$$

$$\text{far // near}$$

It should be noted that this formula elegantly expresses by means of symbols the conclusions of the structural analysis of the canoe journey, but it adds nothing.

Carrying the analysis further, Lévi-Strauss observes that 'the canoe interiorizes the journey within a privileged space, whereas the journey exteriorizes the canoe within an indeterminate period of time. Thus they both act as operators, one spatial and the other temporal, their function being to ensure the arbitration of the near and the far.' Thus, the 'canoe, being *included* within the journey, carries out a topological transformation of the semantic function that the myths attribute to the journey.'[28]

-----

27  Ibid., p. 192.
28  Ibid.

## Mythical Schema, Message and Semantic Function

The schema of the canoe journey not only opposes pairs of terms: sky and earth, high and low, Sun and Moon, burned and rotten. It also opposes 'the various ways in which these terms can be in opposition to each other'. It opposes two forms of opposition. While oppositions of the type 'high and low', 'hot and cold', etc. are governed by a 'logic of sensible qualities', those opposing forms of oppositions 'illustrate the transition from a logic of judgement to a true logic of proposi- tions'.[29] Logic of sensible qualities, logic of judgment, logic of proposi- tions: lacking in this inventory are the logical processes of mythical thought, the logic of 'forms', which no longer opposes high and low, but full and empty, container and contained, etc. I will come back to this later.

The journey of Sun and Moon is an operation performed on two operators – the two heavenly bodies – which engenders a mythical universe that consists of the sum of all the (real and imaginary) rela- tions each heavenly body is held to include. It is these real and imagi- nary relations that Sun and Moon are going to 'symbolize' through their functions in the schema of their canoe journey. Mythemes and schemata thus variously combine the three types of elements, the components of myths: *empirical* components, to which *imaginary* components attach themselves in groups, with their *symbolic* expres- sions; the whole makes up the 'mythical substance', the material of which myths are made.

Myths thus bear a twofold message. On the one hand, there is a patent content, the story itself, often designed to explain why something is (has become) what it is: why there are spots on the moon, why women have periods, etc. This message has an explanatory, 'etiological' function. But the myth's message also, and at a deeper level, consists in the sum of the implicit meanings the mythemes carry with them and which their schemata mobilize in latent fashion. A schema thus possesses both its own logical structure and its own semantic and symbolic efficacy. The logical structure of a schema is its mental (in French: *idéel*) armature. If, in a group of myths, the code is transformed and the armature remains unchanged, it is the (patent) message that is transformed and inverted.

---

29  Ibid., p. 190.

For example, from the key-myth (M1) of the Bird-Nester, which concerns the origin of water from the sky, to the group of Ge myths (M7–M12), the logical armature is the same, but this time the message is the origin of cooking fire and meat. In other myths, it is the socio-logical armature that is transformed. A conflict between a brother and a sister is transformed into a conflict between a husband and his wife, whereas the message does not vary.

In *The Raw and the Cooked* [30] and *From Honey to Ashes*,[31] and then again in *The Story of Lynx*, Lévi-Strauss emphasizes the relations of interdependence between message and armature. He shows that, for an *invariant message* – for example the origin of wild pigs – when the myth passes from the patrilineal Mundurucu to the matrilineal Bororo, the socio-logical armature is transformed:

$$\left[\begin{array}{c} \triangle \quad \bigcirc \end{array} = \triangle \right] \implies \text{Bororo} \left[\begin{array}{c} \bigcirc \neq \triangle \end{array}\right]$$

A conflict between affines is transformed into a conflict between spouses. Alternatively, for an *invariant armature*, for example, $\triangle \ \bigcirc = \triangle$ the message is transformed: Mundurucu, etc. [origin of meat] →Bororo [origin of cultural goods].

From there, we find other transformations between the myths of these different tribes, which are neighbours but have opposite social structures, even though they share the same cultural universe and the same myths. This presents the problem of the relationship between myths and social structures. Clearly, we need to possess extremely detailed ethnological knowledge about the social structures of the societies from which the myths come in order to deal with the problem.

From the moment when, as he progressed in his analysis of the myths, it became progressively clear that certain myths from the North American hemisphere were either identical to or the inverse of myths from South America, Lévi-Strauss formulated the following hypothesis: if the Bororo myth of the origin of finery (M20) transforms a Mundurucu myth (M16) of the origin of meat (the matter of cooking),

30  *The Raw and the Cooked*, pp. 83–90.
31  *From Honey to Ashes*, pp. 20–7.

and if in North America there is a myth of the origin of finery (in this case shells and dentalia) homologous to the Bororo myth (M20), then there *must exist* in North America, in societies nearby to that with the myth of the dentalia thieves,[32] a myth about the origin of meat that is the homologue of the Mundurucu myth, 'subject to an inversion of the armature'.

$$
\text{origin of finery} \quad \triangle \overset{/\!/}{\frown} \bigcirc = \triangle \implies \text{origin of meat} \quad \triangle \frown \bigcirc \neq \triangle
$$

Such a myth exists, and the entire first part of *The Story of Lynx* will successfully be devoted to showing this.

Lévi-Strauss's method thus consists in setting out to discover, for instance, a relation of symmetry or inversion between two myths from South America and positing that the same relation must exist between two myths from North America that present the same thesis. Then he looks for such myths until he finds them. His approach thus combines hypothesis and deduction. Once his method is confirmed by the discovery of a myth corresponding to his hypothesis, Lévi-Strauss can claim to have revealed the myth-producing operations of the human mind, not only *what they say* implicitly without actually saying it, but also *how they say it*. When this happens, we have made headway into the workings of the myth-making function of the human mind.[33] The analyst's hypothetico-deductive method, followed by empirical verification, is the mental reproduction, as Lévi-Strauss sees it, of the operations of mythical thinking in the Indians' mind (and more broadly in that of humankind at large, which produced and continues to produce myths – and to believe in them).

In the end, the mythologist's task is to discover and then reconstruct, at the end of a long, patient process of analysis, 'the mythical patterns fundamental to American Indian thought'.[34] And since his analyses have demonstrated the relationship between South American and North American myths, Lévi-Strauss concludes that

---

32  *The Story of Lynx*, chapter III, 'The Dentalia Thieves', pp. 30–42.
33  *The Naked Man*, p. 684.
34  Ibid., p. 454.

North American myths . . . are absolutely straightforward transformations of South American ones. Those of both North and South must correspond to patterns common to the two hemispheres, and their age should be calculated not in decades but millennia.[35]

The presence of the same mythical schemata in the two Americas cannot be explained by the simple diffusion of the same myths and therefore the same schemata:

> We could not be dealing with myths which had simply been passed by borrowing from tribe to tribe or spread over vast areas during the peopling of America, but with separate formulations generated by the same underlying patterns. What is important for me is, then, generative patterns or schemas. I want first of all to prove their general validity and then to elucidate their mode of operation.[36]

Because Indians have the same brain as all other humans, which endows the human mind with the capacity to spontaneously carry out a certain number of intellectual operations that are the same for everyone, should we not expect to find, in Africa, Asia, Oceania and of course Europe, the same mythical schemata that are elements and proof of the existence of a universal mythology? Lévi-Strauss categorically rejects both the idea and the project.[37] And we will see why. But the fact that the same schemata are found in the myths of Amerindian tribes with different languages and social organizations, in different geographical locations and ecological contexts, poses the further problem of knowing in whose mind the myths reside. Is it mythical thought, activated by a particular individual, that begins thinking in

---

35 *The Origin of Table Manners*, p. 233. In *From Honey to Ashes*, Lévi-Strauss dates them back to the Paleolithic era (p. 304, n. 18).

36 *The Naked Man*, p. 184.

37 *The Story of Lynx*, p. 187. Lévi-Strauss often flaunted his own principles when comparing myths, even if he apologizes. For example, in *From Honey to Ashes*, he expresses his 'deep conviction that Japanese mythology and American mythology, each in its own way, are using sources which go right back to Paleolithic times and which were once the common heritage of Asiatic groups later disseminated throughout the Far East and the New World' (p. 378). But there are equally clear links with the myths of the peoples of Oceania. Cf. S. Dunis, *L'Île aux femmes. 8000 ans d'un seul et même mythe d'origine en Asie-Pacifique-Amérique* (Paris, CNRS Éditions, 2016).

him, or is it the individual who sets about inventing narratives by thinking with the help of categories of mythical thought, and thus reinvents or transforms older myths? To answer this question, we must consider the operations of the human mind when it produces this form of thought we call 'mythical'.

# 12

# The Operations of the Myth-Producing Mind

In the 'Overture' to the first volume of the Mythology series, Lévi-Strauss answers the question we asked at the end of the last chapter. Is it mythical thought, activated by a particular individual, that begins thinking in him, or is it the individual who sets about inventing narratives by thinking with the help of categories of mythical thought, and thus reinvents or transforms older myths? Let's listen:

> It is doubtful, to say the least, whether the natives of central Brazil, over and above the fact that they are fascinated by mythological stories, have any understanding of the systems of interrelations to which we reduce them ... I therefore claim to show, not how men think in myths, but how myths operate in men's minds without their being aware of the fact.[1]

We could object to this that myths are not only enchanting stories, like the tales and legends of old; they are also narratives that explain the universe and society. They are truth-narratives. And more importantly, since it is clearly human beings who produce and think myths, what can he mean by claiming that 'myths operate in men's minds without their being aware of the fact'? He goes on to clarify his proposition:

---

1 C. Lévi-Strauss, *The Raw and the Cooked: Introduction to a Science of Mythology 1*, trans. J. and D. Weightman (Harmondsworth, Penguin, 1986), p. 12.

It would perhaps be better to go further and, disregarding the thinking subject completely, proceed as if the thinking process were taking place *in the myths*, in their reflection upon themselves and their interrelation.[1]

To disregard the subject completely is quite simply to transform myths from objects of thought into thinking subjects in their own right. Having become subjects that reflect upon themselves in men's minds, myths substitute themselves for the latter and delete their existence. For Lévi-Strauss, deleting the subject, placing his original culture in brackets and suspending judgment are fundamental conditions of his own method and necessary to the practice of anthropology and the social sciences. However, here they no longer appear as the conditions of the analyst's transformation from simple individual to knowledge-producing subject, but as the conditions of his necessary abolition as a subject so that the myths can begin to think themselves in his mind, in his stead. In the 'Finale' of the Mythology series, Lévi-Strauss would not hesitate to write that, 'contrary to what might be supposed, it was not so much the case that the Self was the author as that the work, during the process of composition, became the creator of an executant *who lived only by and through it*.'[2] It is as though, as he advanced in his work, Lévi-Strauss gradually turned into a medium or a ventriloquist's dummy for the myths which, owing to the methods used in structural analysis, began to speak inside his mind and to him alone. My conclusion will criticize this requirement of the 'deletion of the subject' in scientific research.

For the time being, let us complete the inventory and analysis of the operations of the human mind as revealed by Lévi-Strauss. First, however, I would point out that all these myths presuppose a philosophical underpinning, a metaphysical a priori, the idea that 'in the beginning, humans and animals were a single family' and that 'the gods could appear as humans or as animals', together with the idea that this original state yielded to the way things are now. Today humans are distinct from animals and can no longer relate to them in the same way.

---

1 Ibid.; my emphasis.

2 C. Lévi-Strauss, *The Naked Man*, trans. J. and D. Weightman, Mythology series, volume 4 (Chicago, University of Chicago Press, 1981), p. 630; my emphasis.

Likewise, direct communication between humans and gods, between Heaven and Earth has disappeared, and humans now deal with the gods and with the masters of the animals and the plants through ritual and prayer.

The universe of Amerindian mythology is thus built on a purely imaginary representation of humanity's past, but it is not conceived or experienced as such by those who produced and transmit it. In *The Story of Lynx*, Lévi-Strauss would write that myths reveal the gap between the Indians' imaginative powers and their positive knowledge of their natural and human environment. But myths do more than reveal this gap, for, he writes, 'they fill it in'. Yet if they were to fill it in, they would abolish it. For this gap can be recognized only by other humans who do not share the same myths and/or do not grant them the same truth-value. All Amerindian myths (and more generally, all myths) combine and unfold on three levels at once. One is imaginary, another symbolic and the third empirical. The characters in the myths are a mixture of these three components. But not all three are of equal importance, and it is the imaginary that predominates and lends meaning to the other two.

The marriage between an Indian and a frog-woman or an earthworm is a creation of the imagination. That this frog changed into a young woman in order to reveal herself to Monmaneki, and that furthermore she was already pregnant because he was accustomed to urinate into the hole she lived in when she was a frog, are equally imaginary sequences of events. The imaginary frog, one of the protagonists of the Tikuna myth (M354), becomes the symbol of the woman a man is forbidden to marry because her ways are too different, too distant from those of the women he is allowed to marry. But Monmaneki is not a real man, either. He can marry a frog, then an earthworm, an arapaço bird, a macaw and finally a woman – a woman whose body splits in two and who catches fish by miraculous means. All these are imaginary characters, whose place and function in the story endow them with a symbolic dimension. They can also have a literal or a figurative meaning. The clinging woman of the Tikuna myth and the torso-woman can represent a real wife who 'sticks' to her husband, as well as an imaginary woman who is 'stuck' to an equally imaginary husband.[3]

---

3 C. Lévi-Strauss, *The Origin of Table Manners*, trans. J. and D. Weightman, Mythology series, volume 3 (Chicago, University of Chicago Press, 1990), p. 84.

Mythical thinking thus does not proceed from the empirical, real world to an imaginary world but the other way around. It starts with an imaginary world and seeks its presence and 'proof' in the empirical world, the world the Indians know through concrete experience. In an article that appeared the same year as *The Naked Man* (1971), entitled 'Relations of Symmetry between Rituals and Myths of Neighboring Peoples', Lévi-Strauss gave an example of this process, involving 'a threefold transformation [which] can thus be traced, from the imaginary level to the empirical level, by way of the symbolic level'.[4]

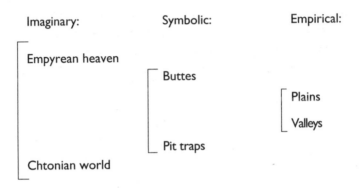

Imaginary:              Symbolic:                Empirical:

Empyrean heaven
                        Buttes
                                                 Plains

                                                 Valleys

                        Pit traps
Chtonian world

In this text, Lévi-Strauss was comparing the myths of the Mandan Indians, focused on a celestial people, with a myth of one of their Hidatsa neighbours, which, on the contrary, focused on an underground world. To avoid being attacked by a bird who is really a celestial ogre, the myth's heroine, with the help of some moles, which are chtonian animals, lies down in a ditch, an analogy of the pit trap used by eagle hunters. The hills play a positive mediating role between the sky and the earth, while the ditch acts as a negative mediator. It is clearly the imaginary core of the Mandan and Hidatsa myths, the tale of the imaginary existence of a celestial people and a chthonian world, that gives a symbolic meaning to the hills and hollows of the plains and river valleys that are home to these tribes. In *The Raw and the Cooked*,

4 First published in 1971 in T. Beidelman, ed., *The Translation of Culture: Essays to E. E. Evans-Pritchard* (London, Tavistock Publications, 1971), pp. 161–78, and then as 'Relations of Symmetry between Rituals and Myths of Neighboring Peoples', *Structural Anthropology, volume 2*, trans. M. Layton (Chicago, University of Chicago Press, 1976), pp. 238–55; p. 253.

Lévi-Strauss further underscores the error committed by mythologists in supposing 'that the natural phenomena which figure so largely in myths for this reason constituted the essential part of what myths are trying to explain'.[5] The criticism was aimed at Max Müller, who thought myths principally served to explain cosmological and astronomical phenomena.

Mythical thought, however, does not restrict itself to borrowing from nature 'only a few of its elements . . . those suitable for the expression of contrasts or forming pairs of opposites . . . The virtually unlimited total-ity of the elements always remains available'.[6] In the course of selecting contrasts to be used in its imaginary constructions, mythical thought plays on three logics, which it combines and manipulates within the same myths: a logic of perceptible qualities, a logic of forms and a logic of propositions (which are the hidden properties of the mythical discourse).

The first form of logic predominates in *The Raw and the Cooked*, since the oppositions mobilize terms almost all of which 'referred to tangible qualities: the raw and the cooked, the fresh and the rotten, the dry and the wet', etc.[7] The second type of logic prevails in *From Honey to Ashes*, since here the opposing terms refer to 'a logic of forms: empty and full, hollow and solid, container and contained, internal and external, included and excluded', etc.[8] This was the logic involved, for example, in the representations of gourds that have a number of functions: ritual, because the gourd is an instrument used to play sacred music; domestic, because it is also a kitchen utensil, a recipient. Similarly, the hollow tree can be made into a drum or a trough.[9]

In *The Origin of Table Manners*, however, when going from myths of the origin of cooking to myths concerning the origin of the alternation of day and night, we are faced with logical oppositions of a much more complex character. In place of simple opposition between the terms, we are dealing with 'different ways in which these terms can be in opposition to each other'. These myths are therefore '*opposing*

---

5 C. Lévi-Strauss, *The Raw and the Cooked*, p. 340.

6 Ibid., p. 341.

7 C. Lévi-Strauss, *From Honey to Ashes: Introduction to a Science of Mythology 2*, trans. J. and D. Weightman (Chicago, University of Chicago Press, 1973), p. 472.

8 Ibid., p. 474.

9 Ibid., p. 472.

*oppositional modalities*, and thus illustrate the transition from a logic of judgement to a true logic of propositions'.[10] The complexity becomes even greater when myths concerning the origin of day and night include the concepts of space and time. 'Thus in mythical thought the category of time appears as the necessary means for revealing relations between other relations already given in space'.[11] On a canoe journey, time is not the same, for instance, when travelling upstream or downstream.[12]

The mechanism of these increasingly complex oppositions applied to tangible experience proceeds by using 'contrasts between tangible qualities, which are thus raised to the point of having a logical existence',[13] with the result that logical properties appear as attributes of things, thereby seeming to 'transcend the contrast between the tangible and the intelligible'.[14] If this is possible, it is because the oppositions drawn from tangible experience are conceptualized as 'signs'. And, these 'secondary qualities' being perceived as signs, they are introduced into 'the operations of truth'.[15]

The correlation and opposition of empirical information, for instance about certain kinds of bee and frog in the South American myths concerning the origin of honey, constitute what Lévi-Strauss calls 'empirical deductions'.[16] For instance, there are bees that live in tree trunks, where they make combs from wax or resin, and certain tree-dwelling frogs that build nests from resin in hollow trees, where they lay their eggs. The indigenous mind has compared these two ways of life and established an empirical relation between the two animal species, one of which is celestial and the other terrestrial. From such 'empirical

---

10 *The Origin of Table Manners*, p. 190; my emphasis.

11 Ibid.

12 *The Naked Man*, p. 330: 'The myths are not simply content, then, to consider straightforward operations such as conjunction and disjunction, and situate them along horizontal or vertical axes, they also distinguish between the *directions* in which these operations occur, and between degrees.'

13 *The Raw and the Cooked*, p. 164.

14 Ibid., p. 14.

15 Ibid.

16 For example, in *The Jealous Potter*, trans. B. Chorier (Chicago, University of Chicago Press, 1988), the ' "jealousy" function of the Goatsucker depends on what I have elsewhere called an empirical deduction: it is an anthropomorphic interpretation of the bird's anatomy and observable habits' (p. 58).

deduction', mythical thinking will go on to deduce other relations, purely imaginary this time, which Lévi-Strauss christens 'transcendental deductions'.[17] The bee will appear in myths as a supernatural character, the master of honey, and the frog as the master of stagnant waters. Products of the imagination, these 'transcendental' deductions found in mythical thinking both flow from 'empirical deductions' and run counter to them. For example, in the myths relating the origin of honey:

> The congruence between man and the macaw in respect of vegetarianism and between man and the jaguar in respect of carnivorousness, are deduced from empirically deduced data. On the other hand, the congruence between the macaw and the jaguar, which can be inferred from the other two instances of congruence, is synthetic in character, since it is not based on experience, and is even contrary to observation.[18]

## Empirical Deduction and Transcendental Deduction

Lévi-Strauss regards these two forms of deduction as 'systems of knowledge'. Empirical deduction clearly corresponds to what, in *The Savage Mind*, he calls the 'science of the concrete'. As an analyst attempting to understand the reasoning behind correlations and oppositions imagined by the Amerindians, he was obliged to imagine and reproduce the 'transcendental' deductions generated by other aspects of the content of their mythology. As he worked his way through the mythical structures and the discovery of their latent and hidden semantic functions, he came to formulate a certain number of hypotheses, such as: if a myth is found in South America that X then a myth must exist in North America that delivers the same message, but in another code, adapted to the Northern hemisphere. And in fact, there are many myths concerning the origin of honey in South America which are also found in North America, but transformed into myths about the origin of maple sugar.

---

17 *From Honey to Ashes*, p. 38, n. 6. See also Lévi-Strauss, 'The Deduction of the Crane', in P. Maranda and E. Köngäs-Maranda, eds, *Structural Analysis of Oral Tradition* (Philadelphia, University of Pennsylvania Press, 1971), pp. 3–21.

18 *From Honey to Ashes*, p. 38, n. 6.

But does it follow that the myths of North and South America deal with sugar and honey in the same way? If the answer were in the affirmative, this would be tantamount to having instituted a genuine experiment, the results of which would validate a posteriori the hypothesis about the semantic function of honey which I put forward on the basis of purely South American data.[19]

Lévi-Strauss goes on to show that there is indeed an Ojibwa myth (M499) which confirms this hypothesis, and that this discovery is tantamount to the experiment he wanted to carry out on his method of structural analysis. The actual existence of the Ojibwa myth offers 'proof' of the validity of his deductions, and therefore of his method.[20] Ultimately, it was by discovering the content of the mythic schemata worked out in Amerindian mythical thinking that Lévi-Strauss was able to reconstruct the transcendental deductions, which were imaginary but subject to rules, from which they sprang.

In moving from empirical to transcendental deductions, mythical thinking transforms the empirical data it uses into one possibility selected from among the sum of all possibles imagined in its 'sovereign independence'. Here is an example:

On the level of the myths, the empirically proved negative connection between otters [otters have a very keen sense of smell] and excrement becomes part of a combinatory system which operates with sovereign independence and exercises the right to effect different interchanges between the terms of an oppositional system which exists experientially in only one state but of which mythical thought gratuitously creates other states.[21]

---

19  *The Origin of Table Manners*, p. 412.

20  See also ibid., p. 349., where he recalls that in *From Honey to Ashes*, 'I made the suggestion that limping symbolized some failure in seasonal periodicity, which at times was desired and at other times feared. We now have *confirmation* of this hypothesis, since a woman experiencing her first monthly periods, i.e. who has been made periodic, is placed by the myths in opposition to, and correlation with, a lame woman, i.e. an aperiodic creature'; my emphasis.

21  *From Honey to Ashes*, p. 202; our emphasis. This formula reiterates and extends what Lévi-Strauss wrote in 1962, in *The Savage Mind* (Chicago, University of Chicago Press, 1969), p. 263: 'The savage mind deepens its knowledge with the help of *imagines mundi*. It builds mental structures which facilitate an understanding of the world in as much as they resemble it.'

The 'transcendental' deductions of mythical thought thus add to the concrete data supplied by empirical deductions 'a whole series of images, which it then *reincorporates* into the real world'.[22] Here we find ourselves at the source of what – in my opinion but not in that of Lévi-Strauss – makes mythical thought a pseudo-knowledge and not a positive science: by embodying the symbols that correspond to them in concrete images, the schema created by mythical thought 'produces a kind of self-evident proof which can rightly be called apodictic, since the image ... gives concrete form to a pattern which was both abstract and concealed',[23] and which can be found in hundreds of societies that do not share the same language, culture or internal organization.

When given concrete form in images that then take on symbolic dimensions and functions, the schemata generating the myths endow them with 'truth-value' since their 'self-evidence' is 'apodictic', undeniable. Mythical thought, like all forms of thought that produce ideologies, whether religious or political, is thus a 'captive' thought, a form of thought whose proofs of truth-value are circular. For those who believe that Jesus of Nazareth, son of Joseph the carpenter, was the Son of God and was God, one proof of his divinity is his resurrection. And the proof that he rose from the dead is that, when the Sabbath was past, Mary the mother of James, Mary Magdalene and Salome went to the tomb with a preparation containing herbs to anoint the body, but they found the tomb empty. The absence of the body proved that he had risen, and that was proof that he was God, since only (a) god can rise from the dead.[24] It would be easy to find this type of circular proof in other religions as well. For instance, for duodecimal Shiite Muslims – who believe that the twelfth Imam did not die, but vanished, and will one day reappear to put an end to the strife that reigns among men and bring about a definitive peace and the triumph of Islam – the fact that neither his body nor his grave was ever found is the proof that he is still living and present, but in an invisible manner.

---

22  *The Naked Man*, p. 557; our emphasis.

23  Ibid., p. 542.

24  The Gospel according to Saint Mark, 16:1–14. But the disciples did not believe Mary Magdalene when she came to tell them that Jesus had risen and that Christ 'showed himself to the Eleven themselves while they were at table. He reproached them for their incredulity and obstinacy, because they had refused to believe those who had seen him after he had risen.' *The Jerusalem Bible*, reader's edition (Garden City, Doubleday & Co., 1968).

According to Lévi-Strauss, then, the Amerindian myths possess this character of circular self-evident truth in the extreme because the world of myths is 'round', and constitutes a sort of closed sphere of ideas and images.

Myths, as we have seen, are narratives that combine two approaches: one, analytical, which makes a distinction between elements and relations belonging to different levels of reality; the other, synthetic, since the homology among these levels posited in the myths confines them in a totalizing discourse. But the institution of relations of equivalence between terms or relations, and of homology between levels, is not enough to make the world of myths round. For that to happen, myths must form groups that come full circle but without closing upon themselves. A group of myths is thus always connected to other groups, which encompass it and which are themselves encompassed, and so on round and round, which produces the 'rose curves' practised by Lévi-Strauss.[25]

Why do the myths and groups of myths come full circle without closing upon themselves? The explanation lies in the fact that myths are 'transformation groups'.

> The notion of transformation is inherent in structural analysis . . . It is impossible to conceive of structure separate from the notion of trans-formation. Structure is not reducible to a system: a group composed of elements and the relations that unite them. In order to be able to speak of structure, it is necessary for there to be invariant relation-ships between elements and relations among several sets, so that one can move from one set to another by means of a transformation.[26]

---

25 C. Lévi-Strauss, 'How Myths Die', *Structural Anthropology, Volume 2*, pp. 256–68.

26 C. Lévi-Strauss and D. Eribon, ed., *Conversations with Claude Lévi-Strauss*, trans. P. Wissing (Chicago, University of Chicago Press, 1991), p. 113. Lévi-Strauss claimed to have borrowed the notion of transition from the illuminating work of the famous Scottish biologist and mathematician, D'Arcy Wentworth Thompson (*On Growth and Form*, 1917). Using geometric transformations, Thompson had reproduced the differences of forms that existed between the animal or plant species of a genus. In *The Naked Man* (p. 677) he had reproduced one of the plates from D'Arcy Thompson's book, showing the transformation of forms in ten species of fish. Nevertheless, it should be noted that the transformations in the form of the fish's body, for example, can be explained by factors that are both external and internal to the body: the depth at which they live, the way they eat, whether they are predators or prey, how fast they can get away, and so on.

We have seen that the logical structure of myths consists of a set of relations of correlation and opposition between components and between
relations, and these relations are themselves in relations of transformation which connect them to each other. A myth never exists as a single
version, but always as several variants.[27] Furthermore, a myth never
exists in isolation. On the one hand it is part of the group of myths
belonging to the society in which it is found, and on the other it takes its
place, by the nature of its schemata and mythemes, in several groups of
myths in which these same schemata are present, in the form of either
inversions or oppositions, etc. These groups of myths bring together
myths that do not belong to either the same society or the same culture,
but to societies that can be close together or thousands of miles apart
and which may differ in their languages, their social organizations, their
cultures.

> Between one variant and another of the same myth, there always
> appear differences expressible, not in the form of small positive or
> negative increments, but of clear-cut relationships such as contrari-
> ness, contradiction, inversion or symmetry.[28]

For example, between the Mandan and the Hidatsa, two neighbouring
tribes, we find 'complex relations of correlation and opposition, of
symmetry and antisymmetry among their respective myths ... From a
patrimony which has become common, each tribe tended to choose
opposite or complementary variants when it came to founding similar
rituals (or rituals fulfilling the same functions).'[29] But myths can correspond to each other and come together to form a group without belonging to the same geographical zone.

----

27 This is why, he says, there is no 'true' form of a myth. C. Lévi-Strauss, 'The
Structural Study of Myth', *Structural Anthropology*, trans. C. Jacobson and B. Grundfest
Schoepf (New York, Basic Books, 1963), pp. 206–31; p. 218. *The Raw and the Cooked*,
pp. 341–2.

28 *The Naked Man*, p. 675. Twenty years later (1991), in *The Story of Lynx*, trans. C.
Tihanyi (Chicago, University of Chicago Press, 1995), Lévi-Strauss, as I have said, gave
less importance to the binary oppositions than he had done in the 'Finale' of *The Naked
Man*.

29 'Relations of Symmetry', p. 254.

The versions of the same myth, forming as such a paradigmatic set, can each taken by itself be inserted into other paradigmatic sets intersecting with the first one at various points.[30]

To describe this abstract, mental universe in which a large number of groups of myths are articulated with and inserted into each other at different levels, through the schemata they share, Lévi-Strauss speaks of a 'hyper-space'.[31] Each of these groups forms a loop in the mythic field that encompasses them. But how are these loops generated? The answer is simple: starting from a myth or a variant of a myth, a series of transformations must produce other myths or variants which lead back to the initial myth.

For example, in *The Raw and the Cooked*, the Bororo myth of the Bird-Nester (M1) is a transformation, by inversion, of several Ge myths (M7–M12) along one axis. The Ge myths are themselves transformed into two Tupi myths (M15, M16) along another axis. And by means of a transformation, M16 brings us back to M20 (once again a Bororo myth). This transformation brings the 'chain full circle'. In terms of their 'messages', the Ge myths concern the origin of cooking fire, and the Bororo myth (M1) is about the origin of celestial water, which, for Lévi-Strauss, represents anti-cooking fire because it extinguishes fire. M1 is a myth of the origin of water as the *anti-means* of cooking as represented by fire.[32] This example gives us an idea of the risks taken by the analyst. There is no risk involved when he qualifies fire as the means of cooking and meat as the privileged cooking substance. There is more risk when he qualifies rain as anti-cooking fire, and even more when ornaments become an 'anti-matter' with respect to cooking, since ornaments are not edible.

Note, too, that, in our example, the series of transformations that made it possible to start with M1 and to return to Bororo myths does not return precisely to M1, but to M20. And from M20, a new series of transformations can start another loop. The loops are thus not completely

30 *The Story of Lynx*, p. 149.

31 *The Origin of Table Manners*, p. 105: 'When defined in terms of a limited number of oppositions . . . several myths can, then, be arranged in a closed set. However . . . when viewed from other angles, they remain spread out over a hyper-space, also occupied by other myths.'

32 *The Raw and the Cooked*, pp. 201–13.

closed. Each continues 'on top' of the next, proceeding in a spiral movement.[33] Furthermore, given that because of these successive transformations, quite dissimilar myths are connected and grouped together
through logical operations that engender their differences, it is not the
apparent resemblances among myths that ground their comparison;
what makes them comparable is the fact that they are different outcomes
of the same logical structure.[34] Or, as Lévi-Strauss put it: 'it is not
comparison that supports generalization, but the other way round'.[35]

## The Canonical Formula of Myths and its Destiny

Lévi-Strauss discovered two formulas to describe the 'looping' effect in
groups of myths: he described the first early on, in his 1955 article on
'The Structural Study of Myth', and used it numerous times and until as
late as *The Story of Lynx*. He called this first formula 'the canonical
formula' of myths. The second appeared in his work after 1966. This one
concerned the groups of four myths that oppose and complete each
other and are analogous in their structure to what in algebra are known
as 'Klein groups'. In 1966 the mathematician, Marc Barbut, published an
article in *Les Temps modernes* on 'the meaning of the word structure in
mathematics'. In it he demonstrated the interest of applying Klein group
theory to the human sciences.[36] Lévi-Strauss seized upon this theory
and, in *The Origin of Table Manners*, used it to analyse the corpus of
Amerindian myths, but he practically stopped using it after the publication of *The Naked Man*. Later, in *The Jealous Potter*, he used a different

---

33  *The Origin of Table Manners*, p. 469: 'By persistently going over and over the same
myths, or through the incorporation of myths that are new (but belong, from the formal
point of view, to the same set, in so far as they can be shown to be transformations of the
preceding ones) structural analysis follows a spiral course.'

34  *The Naked Man*, pp. 37–8: 'I am not trying to discover why these resemblances
occur, but how. The peculiar feature of the myths I am comparing is not their similarity;
in fact, they are often dissimilar. The aim of my analysis is rather to bring out certain
characteristics they have in common, in spite of differences sometimes so great that
myths I include in the same group were formerly considered as being completely separate entities ... I start from the principle that a myth can never be reduced to its
appearance.'

35  *From Honey to Ashes*, p. 466.

36  M. Barbut, 'Sur le sens du mot structure en mathématiques', *Les Temps modernes*
22, n° 246 (1966), pp. 791–814.

mathematical configuration, called 'the Klein bottle', whose properties are similar to the canonical formula.[37]

Let us begin with the analysis of the myths in his 'Klein groups'. These are 'quadripartite groups', structures that combine and oppose four terms present in different myths or different variants of a single myth.

We saw then that myths or variants of myths were arranged like Klein groups including a theme, the contrary of the theme and their opposites. This gave sets of interlocking four-term structures, retaining a relationship of homology with each other.[38]

We can express this structure in the following symbolic form, just as Lévi-Strauss himself did:[39]

$$
\begin{array}{cc}
x \text{ (term)} & -x \text{ (the contrary of the term)} \\
\Downarrow & \Downarrow \\
1/x \text{ (its opposite)} & -1/x \text{ (its opposite)} \\
\end{array}
$$

$$[x - x] \qquad\qquad [1/x - 1/x]$$

In *The Naked Man*, for example, Lévi-Strauss shows that one series of myths opposes youth and old age, fecundity and sterility, short periodicity and long periodicity, reversible evolutions and irreversible ones. The schema that combines these oppositions 'has a logical structure at the same time as it is semantically effective'. The logical structure 'can be reduced to a quadripartite formula, in which the pregnant woman is opposed to the menstruating mother, just as the grandmother who cannot recapture her youth, in spite of her lewdness, is opposed to the sister, who counts on the reversibility of the aging process to ensure her virginity'.[40] Ultimately, the logical structure of these myths can be reduced to the opposition between:

---

37  *The Jealous Potter*, pp. 157–9.

38  *The Naked Man*, p. 649.

39  *The Origin of Table Manners*, p. 403; *The Naked Man*, p. 274. Lucien Scubla showed that the set: [x, -x, 1/x, -1/x] is not a true Klein group but is still in the orbit of a Klein group. Cf. L. Scubla, *Lire Lévi-Strauss* (Paris, Odile Jacob, 1998), p. 82.

40  *The Naked Man*, p. 274.

$$\begin{bmatrix} \text{fertile youth x} & \quad\text{- x barren youth} \\ \\ \text{reversible old age l/x} & \quad\text{- l/x irreversible old age} \end{bmatrix}$$

But Lévi-Strauss emphasizes that these 'Klein groups' do not function independently of each other, as it appears on a purely formal level.

> Actually, the ordered series of the variants does not return to the initial term after running through the first cycle of four . . . The variant-producing cycle thus takes on the appearance of a spiral, whose progressive narrowing disregards the objective discontinuity of the interlocking levels . . .Unlike mathematics, myth subordinates structure to a meaning, of which it becomes the immediate expression.[41]

After having used the Klein group formula three or four times, Lévi-Strauss would not have recourse to it again, finding it too mechanical, too weak to translate the double (or triple) twist entailed in the generative structure of myths, which would be better handled by the canonical formula. Nevertheless, his use of the notion of Klein group – even if he did not follow it up – was an important moment in his search for the structures operating in a corpus of myths.[42] In *The Naked Man*, he stresses that, in a quadripartite system, it is often the case that 'relationships exist between the four terms, but they must be more complex than would be allowed by a quadripartite structure, which would be reminiscent, if only approximately, of that of a Klein group.'[43]

The interest and import of the 'canonical formula' are altogether different. Why did Lévi-Strauss set out in search of such a formula? In his 1955 article, he wondered if, 'when we have succeeded in organizing a whole series of variants into a kind of permutation group, we are in a position to formulate the law of that group.'[44] The goal was thus to set a formula that would both sum up and symbolize the process of generating

---

41  *The Naked Man*, p. 650.
42  Ibid., p. 649.
43  Ibid., p. 270.
44  'The Structural Study of Myth', p. 228.

a set of variants of a same myth, and which would account for the myth's closure. But Lévi-Strauss did not want to limit the field of application to one myth and its variants: he wanted to extend it to sets of myths that, taken together, formed a permutation group. In 1955 he thus wrote:

---

### The Canonical Formula

Whatever clarifications and modifications we will need to add to the following formula, it now seems certain that every myth – considered as the aggregate of all its variants – can be reduced to a canonical relation of the following type:

$$F_x(a) : F_y(b) :: F_x(b) : F_{a-1}(y)$$

in which, two terms, a and b, being given as well as two functions, (x) and (y), of these terms, a relation of equivalence can be said to exist between two situations defined respectively under two conditions:

1. that one term be replaced by its opposite (a by a-1)
2. that a correlative inversion be produced between the function value and the term value of two elements (the function $F_y$ becomes the term y) – and (the term a becomes the function $F_{a-1}$).[45]

---

The formula is proposed, as Lucien Scubla stresses, 'without any specific indications that would allow it to be effectively applied to ethnographic material'.[46] In the same text, Lévi-Strauss indicates that, when one has managed to order all known variants of a myth into a series that forms a sort of permutation group, 'the two variants placed at the far ends [find themselves] in a symmetrical, though inverted, relationship to each other.'[47] In the formula, this corresponds to the relation between $F_x(a)$ and $F_{a-1}(y)$. The term (b), on the other hand, appears twice in the formula: $[F_y(b), F_x(b)]$, that is, once in each equivalence relationship, thus serving as a mediator between the two. For Lévi-Strauss, then, 'mythical thought always progresses from the awareness of oppositions toward their resolution.'[48] And he adds, 'the purpose of myth is to

---

45  Ibid.
46  Scubla, *Lire Lévi-Strauss*, p. 27.
47  'The Structural Study of Myth', p. 223.
48  *Structural Anthropology*, p. 224.

provide a logical model capable of overcoming a contradiction (an impossible achievement if, as it happens, the contradiction is real).[49]

In 1971, in the 'Finale' to *The Naked Man* as well as to the whole Mythology series, Lévi-Strauss would return to this function of 'resolving contradictions' through 'mediation', and would add that these are 'local and temporary answers to the problems raised by feasible adjustments and insoluble contradictions that they are endeavouring to legitimize or conceal'.[50]

Myths have a double function, then, which always unfolds in the imaginary world of the speculations of 'mythical thought', a world built according to the principles of a logic of deductions by analogy, embodied in combinations of mythemes and schemata engendered by counter-intuitive transcendental deductions.

What matters here is the idea that analogical reasoning consists in positing the equivalence between a series of different situations, which gives rise to counter-intuitive deductions. The general substance and mainspring of myths is therefore primarily metaphor. In *The Jealous Potter*, published in 1985, Lévi-Strauss would describe the nature of the solutions myths propose, and which they posit in the following terms:

> Every myth confronts a problem, and it deals with it by showing that it is analogous to other problems, or else it deals with several problems simultaneously and shows that they are analogous to one another. No real object corresponds to this set of images, which mirror each other . . . A solution that is not a real solution to a specific problem is a way of relieving intellectual uneasiness and even existential anxiety when an anomaly, contradiction, or scandal is presented as the manifestation of a structure of order that can be perceived more clearly in aspects of reality that are less disturbing to the mind and the emotions.[51]

This is an important passage, insofar as Lévi-Strauss clearly associates the activity of the myth-producing mind with the need to imagine illusory solutions[52] to real or illusory problems, and to *believe in them*. To

---

49 *Structural Anthropology*, p. 229.
50 *The Naked Man*, p. 629.
51 *The Jealous Potter*, p. 171.
52 *The Naked Man*, p. 659. In the 'Finale' to the Mythology series, Lévi-Strauss compares the role of music to that of mythology: 'myth coded in sounds instead of

*truly* believe in the solutions offered by myths 'relieves' an 'intellectual' uneasiness that is the source of 'existential' anxiety. Mythical thought is thus a response to the need to believe that the impossible is possible. But, as I have said, Lévi-Strauss left the problem of belief to one side, preferring instead to analyse the grammar and vocabulary of the beliefs found in the Amerindian myths.

We saw that, in the formula $[F_x(a) : F_y(b) : : F_x(b) : F_{a-1}(y)]$, the term (b) fulfils two distinct (and opposite) functions in turn: $F_y$ and then $F_x$. Through this transformation, it serves as a mediator between the initial term (a), assigned the function $F_{(x)}$, and the final term (y) assigned the opposite function a-1. The closure of the group of variants of a myth or a group of myths would thus be carried out by the operation of a double twist, one affecting the initial term and the second, the function of the second term. In this case, the variants of the myths in the initial position and in the final position appear, as Lévi-Strauss said in 1955, in a symmetrical but inverted relation, whereas the two situations $[F_x(a) : F_y(b)]$ and $[F_x(b) : F_{a-1}(y)]$ are posited as equivalent. Nevertheless, he adds, in the only mention of the canonical formula in the Mythology series, 'it is impossible that any real parity should appear between the beginning and the end, except for the inversion which generates the group. The group, being in a state of equilibrium along one axis, shows evidence of imbalance along another axis. This obligatory feature, which is inherent in mythical thought, protects its dynamic force while at the same time preventing it from becoming really static.'[53] As the myth moves through a series of equivalences and permutations, from $F_x(a)$ to $F_{a-1}(y)$, it closes upon itself, but, since it switches codes and therefore axes, it does not really come back to its point of departure but passes above it, as it were, and opens onto other myths.

We now need to clarify somewhat the nature of the functions attaching to terms. Indeed, we can define $(F_x)$ as an attribute of (a), in which case we can write (a) is (x). But we can also define $(F_x)$ as an action that (a) can perform, and in that case (a) is an agent, an actor, as Algirdas J. Greimas and Jean Petitot would say, an agent acting on a

---

words, offers an interpretative grid, a matrix of relationships which filters and organizes lived experience, *acts as a substitute for it and provides the comforting illusion* that contradictions can be overcome and difficulties resolved'; my emphasis.

53 *From Honey to Ashes*, pp. 248–9.

patient. This second interpretation of the nature of the functions attaching to terms corresponds perfectly to the way the canonical formula can be used to interpret *rituals*. And this is precisely what Lévi-Strauss did when, in his 1974–75 course at the Collège de France, he analysed the relationship between cannibalism and ritual transvestism.[54]

He had chosen the example of the Naven ceremony performed by the Iatmul people of New Guinea and described in detail by Gregory Bateson.[55] The ceremony was 'intended to honour a uterine nephew, [in which] the maternal uncle disguises himself as an old female gossip and plays the clown, while the women of the paternal side put on warrior's dress and make themselves out to be head-hunters, which the Iatmul indeed were.'[56] Lévi-Strauss used this ceremony to exemplify the rituals he found in many societies in the Americas, Oceania and Africa, namely: women dressing up as men and/or behaving like men while, inversely, the men behave like women. He sums up this 'law of transformations' as follows:

> The function 'woman' among fellow females is to the function 'man' among fellow males, as the function 'woman' among male fellow tribes-men is to the function 'non-fellow' tribesman (= enemy) among men.[57]

What concrete ethnographical data gave this formula meaning for him, and how can it be translated into symbols in the specific case of rituals analogous to the Iatmul Naven ceremonies that he found scattered throughout the world, above all in the Americas and in Oceania?

The ethnographic contexts are those of cannibalism and head-hunting. Women always played an important role in the rituals following the return of the victorious warriors from confronting their enemies. They often received the severed heads, or pretended to seize them. Often, too, a warrior's return with an enemy head (or scalp) opened the way to his

---

54  C. Lévi-Strauss, 'Cannibalism and Ritual Transvestism (1974–75)', in *Anthropology and Myth: Lectures, 1951–1982*, trans. R. Willis (Blackwell, 1987), pp. 111–17.

55  G. Bateson, *Naven: A Survey of the Problems Suggested by a Composite Picture of the Culture of a New Guinea Tribe Drawn from Three Points of View* (Palo Alto, Stanford University Press, 1958).

56  'Cannibalism and Ritual Transvestism', p. 114.

57  Ibid.

marriage; or, if he was already married, the trophy was associated with women's procreation of children. Lévi-Strauss interprets the women's place in cannibal rituals and their dressing up as warriors not as an elevation of their status as women, but as 'the way men think of women, or rather in which men think of masculinity [through] women'.[58] Women provide a way for men to 'symbolize themselves to themselves'. Hence the formula:

$$F_x(a) : F_y(b) : : F_x(b) : F_{a-1} (y)$$

$F_x$ = the function 'woman' of fellow tribeswomen – $F_x(a)$

$F_y$ = the function 'man' of fellow tribesmen – $F_y(b)$

$F_xb$ = the function 'woman' of fellow tribesmen

in which, in the second part of the formula, the men are present twice: as members of the tribe (fellow tribesmen [b] and as men [y] capable of acting as enemies and in opposition to the women [a-1]). It was not until the 1981–82 school year that Lévi-Strauss would again mention the canonical formula, in a course devoted to the ritual killing of the king in certain African societies, which other societies echo by inverse rituals involving the 'murder, by his associates, of the rivals or adversaries of the dead king'.[59]

These two new references to the canonical formula (in 1974 and 1982) would become known in 1984 with the publication of the abstracts of Lévi-Strauss's courses at the Collège de France.[60] The formula would subsequently be repeated several times in *The Jealous Potter* and in *The Story of Lynx* – without ever being truly explained and expressed in symbols.[61]

With the return of the canonical formula came for the first time the image of the 'Klein bottle' (not to be confused with 'Klein groups'), about which I will say a few words. In short, Lévi-Strauss revived his formula in 1984 and, in the preface to his book, now defended it vigorously, writing:

58  Ibid., p. 117.

59  C. Lévi-Strauss, 'On Africa (1981–2)', *Anthropology and Myth*, pp. 185–94; p. 190.

60  They appeared under the title *Paroles données*, and were translated to English as *Anthropology Today*.

61  For example, an article in the journal *L'Homme* (vol. 25, n° 1 [March 1985], pp. 5–12), entitled 'D'un oiseau l'autre: un exemple de transformation mythique', presents a development that we will later find in *The Jealous Potter*.

From various quarters I have been reproached for failing to explain, develop or, according to some, even employ the formula I had set out. Did not this 'failure' implicitly confirm the contentions of those who claimed the formula was meaningless? Therein lies a misunderstanding that several scattered references in the Mythologics have not succeeded in dispelling.

Before continuing the quotation, let us note that the criticisms he was refuting were perfectly founded. He had never really explained his formula, nor provided any specific indications that would authorize its use on ethnographic data, and this vagueness would persist. The rest of the quotation is illuminating:

> Despite its vaguely algebraic appearance, my formula *does not constitute an algorithm according to which calculations can be made.* I put it forward as an image or picture, a graphic design that, I thought, could facilitate the *intuitive grasp of a chain of relations.*[62]

The terms he has chosen are important. The canonical formula is a *graphic design* that is meant to facilitate the *grasp of a chain of relations.* It is not a mathematical formula, despite having the vague appearance of one. But of what chains of relations does it facilitate the *intuition*? He explains that he wanted to bring out that '*the unbalanced configuration* of elements that [he] had thought to have shown to be inherent in *mythical transformations* was more than abundantly illustrated in [his] analyses of hundreds of different myths'.[63] The unbalanced configuration typical of transformations is that which is expressed by replacing a term by its contrary (a by a-1) and the transformation of a function into a term ($F_y$ into y). And it is because this double transformation generates 'transcendental' deductions in the myth-producing mind, whose conclusions are counter-intuitive, that Lévi-Strauss invented a formula to express the passage from empirical data to a counter-intuitive imaginary universe.

In 1984, Lévi-Strauss reiterated the caveats he had made to his readers twenty years earlier in the 'Overture' to *The Raw and the Cooked* on

---

62  *Anthropology and Myth*, p. 4; my emphasis.
63  Ibid., p. 5; my emphasis.

the way they should understand his 'occasional' use of 'apparently logico-mathematical symbols, which should not be taken too seriously':

> There is only a superficial resemblance between my formulas and the equations of the mathematician, because the former are not applications of rigorously employed algorithms, allowing the demonstration of the various points to be interlinked or condensed . . . The formulas I have written with the help of symbols borrowed from mathematics . . . are not intended to prove anything; they are meant rather to suggest in advance the pattern of some discursive account, or to sum up such an account, by bringing within a single purview complex groups of relations and transformations, the detailed description of which may have sorely tried the reader's patience.[64]

However, he did not exclude the possibility that the concepts of symmetry, inversion, equivalence, homology, isomorphism, etc. as well as the canonical formula he had 'diagrammed', and which served as a 'stenogram',[65] might one day be used to 'subject myth to a genuine logico-mathematical analysis' after having been the target of severe criticism.[66]

Six years later, in *The Naked Man*, the final volume of the Mythology series, Lévi-Strauss declared that he had taken a step toward a logico-mathematical treatment of myths:

> The difficulties in the way of a logico-mathematical treatment of myth, which can nevertheless be seen to be desirable and possible, are of a different order. They are linked in the first place with the problem of arriving at an unequivocal definition of the constituent elements of myths either as terms or as relations . . . Secondly, these relations illustrate types of symmetry which are different from each other, and too numerous to be defined in the limited vocabulary of contrariness, contradiction and their opposites.[67]

---

64 *The Raw and the Cooked*, pp. 30–1.
65 *The Naked Man*, pp. 633–4.
66 *The Raw and the Cooked*, p. 31.
67 *The Naked Man*, p. 635.

Klein groups have been abandoned. But Lévi-Strauss writes that 'both in France and the United States, mathematicians have drawn my attention to the fact that a recent development of their subject', known as 'category theory', might be applicable to myths:

> The definition of categories, as systems formed both by a set of terms and by the set of relations between these terms, corresponds closely to that which can be given of myth . . . [I was] convinced that others, helped perhaps by the fact that I had cleared the ground, would shoulder the task of solving these problems by the use of new logico-mathematical instruments more finely tuned than those which have already proved effective in less complex areas.[68]

In 1988, in a series of conversations with Didier Eribon, Lévi-Strauss mentions the existence of another difficulty involved in the mathematical formulation of myths, that of 'substitution groups': 'The problems raised by mythology seem impossible to dissociate from the aesthetic forms in which they appear. Now these forms are both continuous and discontinuous, an antinomy that catastrophe theory offers a new way to overcome.'[69] To the theory of categories is now added catastrophe theory, developed since 1972 by René Thom and presented by Jean Petitot in 1979 in Lévi-Strauss's seminar on identity. In 1988 Jean Petitot published an article in the journal L'Homme entitled 'Approche morpho-dynamique de la formule canonique du mythe' (Morphodynamic approach to the canonical formula).[70] The same year, Lévi-Strauss confided to Eribon that certain mathematicians had told him that the mathematical formalization of myths was now possible, but it was 'too difficult for [him]'.[71]

What conclusions can be drawn from this succession of declarations over nearly half a century? First, that the canonical formula is the expression – imperfect in his eyes, to be sure, but which has ultimately

---

68  Ibid., p. 636. The theory of categories calls on the notion of morphism, which is based on the existence of a relation between two terms whose nature it is not necessary to specify.

69  Lévi-Strauss and Eribon, *Conversations with Claude Lévi-Strauss*, p. 138.

70  J. Petitot, 'Approche morphodynamique de la formule canonique du mythe', *L'Homme*, nos 106–7 (1988), pp. 24–50.

71  Lévi-Strauss and Eribon, *Conversations with Claude Lévi-Strauss*, p. 137.

improved the situation for communicating the intuition that was his as early as 1955 – of an inherent imbalance in the structure of myths that is due to the way they are generated, which he called their 'genetic law'. This imbalance is caused by the 'double twist' stemming from the double permutation by contrariness of a term, and by the inversion of a function among the variants of a myth or a series of myths. This double permutation engenders a fantasized universe that is contrary to concrete experiences, runs counter to intuition, but is endowed with apodictic self-evidence. Secondly, far from regarding the logico-mathematical formulation of myths as an impossibility, Lévi-Strauss considered it possible, but something to be done by others than himself: by true mathematicians armed with new theories.

The future would prove him right on this count: after Petitot's use of catastrophe theory, another mathematician, Jack Morava,[72] turned to chaos theory, related to René Thom's theory on the structural stability of forms.[73] Morava offered a mathematical model that this time seemed to correspond closely to Lévi-Strauss's intuitive formula: $F_x(a) : F_y(b) :: F_x(b) : F a\text{-}1_{(y)}$.

In 2004, in an appendix to an article by Scubla, who had been anxious to make known the importance of Morava's work, Morava described his model as 'calling on homomorphisms of quaternion group Q. This is a group of order eight which is a sort of "twisted" duplication of a group of order four, the Klein group, K, which Lévi-Strauss used in parts of his work.'[74] I do not have the necessary competence to say that, with Morava and quaternion theory, the exact mathematical formulation of the canonical formula had at last been found. But it is important to note here that quaternion group Q is an extension of the Klein group which, Morava writes, 'does not take its truth values from the classic two-value system, namely the group [0,1], nor from a broader commutative group such as the Klein group, but from the non-commutative quaternion group Q'. However,

72 J. Morava, 'From Lévi-Strauss to Chaos and Complexity', in M. S. Mosko and F. H. Damon, eds, *On the Order of Chaos* (Oxford and New York, Berghahn Books, 2005), pp. 47–63.

73 R. Thom, *Structural Stability and Morphogenesis* (Boulder, Westview Press, 1994 [1972]).

74 J. Morava, 'Une interprétation mathématique de la formule canonique de Claude Lévi-Strauss', *Cahiers de L'Herne*, n° 88 (2004), pp. 216–18.

in a non-commutative logical system, the relations between variables are extremely complex. This model corresponded to the stages Lévi-Strauss had gone through in his thinking on the structure of permutation groups as found in myth. He had first looked to Klein groups (K), as suggested by Marc Barbut, but eventually judged these groups to be too narrow to represent the complexity of the logical operations behind the production of groups of myths. Nor did the notions of symmetry, asymmetry, inversion and homology seem to him adequate to describe fully the complex systems of equivalence invented by a mind operating by means of analogical deductions running counter to intuition. An additional argument in favour of the theory of quaternion group Q was that it was associated with category theory, which certain mathematicians had called to Lévi-Strauss's attention.[75]

In short, it is entirely understandable that, after the publication of the Mythology series, Lévi-Strauss, far from renouncing his formula, repeated it time and again in *The Jealous Potter*, *The Story of Lynx* and, lastly, in an article on the hour-glass ($\overline{\text{X}}$) roof configurations found in the architecture of numerous present-day societies in Siberia, China, Japan, Indonesia, Fiji and the Americas.[76] In 1991, in a note to *The Story of Lynx*, he would write with the greatest satisfaction:

> When I proposed this formula for the first time in 1955 ... it was shrugged off, but during these last few years, it has been met with interest and used in various applications ranging from rural architecture to the Cogito.[77]

75 In his commentary on Morava's work, Scubla writes: 'This mathematical model clearly shows the structural specificity of the formula both with respect to the "Klein group", which Lévi-Strauss used to formalize myths, and to the permutation groups used since A. Weil to model systems of kinship and marriage. Alternatively, it leaves the anthropological interpretation of the formula completely open. Jean Petitot's earlier "catastrophic schematization" does not come as close to the literal structure of the formula, but it does provide the beginnings of a mathematical expression of the basic structuralist concepts (binary oppositions, emergence of the discrete from the continuous, etc.) and of the anthropological objects to which these apply, the myths and their transformations' (L. Scubla, 'Structure, transformation et morphogénèse', *Cahiers de L'Herne*, n° 82 (2004), p. 218, n. 8).

76 C. Lévi-Strauss, 'Hourglass Configurations', in P. Maranda, ed., *The Double Twist: From Ethnography to Morphodynamics* (Toronto, University of Toronto Press, 2001), pp. 15–32.

77 *The Story of Lynx*, p. 104, note. Lévi-Strauss cites five articles and a book.

In the Preface to his conversations with Didier Eribon in 1984, Lévi-Strauss tells us why he once again took up the canonical formula. It gave him, he says, a structure for his intuition that myths contain a 'relation of imbalance'. From all that had gone before, it appears that this relation can only be that which is generated by the mind when, through a succession of analogical equivalences, it proceeds from empirical deduction to transcendental deduction. Lévi-Strauss gives us a demonstration of this first in *The Jealous Potter* and then in *The Story of Lynx*.

The example set out in *The Jealous Potter* had been the object that same year (1985) of a remarkable article published in the journal *L'Homme*, entitled 'D'un oiseau l'autre: un exemple de transformation mythique'.[78] It was the epitome of elegance and clarity.

Lévi-Strauss took as his point of departure a myth found among the Jivaro Indians, which recounts the origin of potting clay. In the olden days, Sun and Moon had the same wife, Goatsucker, and lived on the earth. Goatsucker loved Sun but shunned Moon. A quarrel ensued, in the course of which the two husbands climbed up into the sky using a vine that at that time connected the sky and the earth. Goatsucker attempted to follow them, but Moon caused her to fall, along with her basket, which was full of clay. She died and changed into the bird that bears her name. The myth thus explains at the same time the origin of potting clay and of the jealousy between husband and wife. How can the myth establish a relation between potting, jealousy in marriage and the goatsucker?

The Indians often describe potters as having a jealous and suspicious nature. As for the goatsucker, or nightjar, it is believed to have a sorrowful character because of its dismal cry and its solitary nocturnal ways. There would thus seem to be a twofold connection between potters and jealousy, and between the goatsucker and jealousy. What then could be the connection between the goatsucker and ceramics? To discover this relation, Lévi-Strauss would have to 'go through another bird, absent from the myths considered earlier'.[79] This is the ovenbird, whose ways are just the opposite of those of the goatsucker. The goatsucker does not make a nest but lays its eggs directly on the ground. The ovenbird makes an elaborate nest of clay on a tree branch. Both the male and the female

---

78  'D'un oiseau l'autre', pp. 5–12.
79  Ibid., p. 7.

participate in the construction of the nest, providing the 'image of a well-suited couple, the opposite of the goatsucker', etc. In the native mind, then, the ovenbird is in a relation of correlation and opposition with the goatsucker, and is directly associated with clay, the material from which it makes its nest, and by extension with pottery. Lévi-Strauss then allows himself to 'close one transformation cycle using a state (the ovenbird mytheme) that is not directly found in the myths that illustrate the other states'.[80] And he asserts that this approach is legitimate because the Indians could not help thinking of the ovenbird, 'even when they were not talking about it'. The ovenbird thus appears as a 'reversed goatsucker', which confirms the ovenbird myths that present themselves as inverted transformations of goatsucker myths.[81]

The Jivaro myths tell us that humans were unable to procure potting clay because the jealous wife, Goatsucker, lost it when she fell and that, being dead as a (mythic) wife, she turned into the bird that bears her name. Hence the transformation suggested by Lévi-Strauss: the 'jealousy' function of the Goatsucker-wife is to the function 'potter' of the woman as the function 'jealousy' of the woman is to the 'reversed Goatsucker' function of the Potter.

$$F_x(a) : F_y(b) :: F_x(b) : F_{a\text{-}1\ (y)}$$

$F_x(a)$ = function 'jealousy' of the supernatural Goatsucker-wife

$F_y(b)$ = function 'potter' of the Woman

$F_x(b)$ = function 'jealousy' of the Woman

$F_{a\text{-}1\ (y)}$ = function 'ovenbird' of the Potter

$F_{a\text{-}1}$ = function 'ovenbird' opposite of the function 'jealousy' of the Goatsucker.

To establish a relation between a human woman and a bird, on the one hand, and jealousy and pottery, on the other, it was necessary to posit a congruence between the human woman and a bird in the relation of jealousy, as well as a congruence between pottery and another bird. To do this, the ovenbird is introduced into the canonical formula because its ways make it the reversed opposite of the goatsucker.

The establishment of a correlation and an opposition between two kinds of bird on the basis of empirical observation of their ways is what

---

80  Ibid., p. 10.
81  Ibid., p. 11; see also *The Jealous Potter*, pp. 56–7.

Lévi-Strauss calls an 'empirical deduction'. That explains the jealousy function assigned to the goatsucker-supernatural wife. But, in order for the goatsucker to be at the origin of potting clay, which is posited by a transcendental deduction, a series of equivalences and inversions must intervene by means of a mytheme that is not in the original myths. This is the ovenbird. In the end, the supernatural goatsucker has disappeared, and the (supernatural) ovenbird has appeared, this time as the master of ceramics, which associates it with the woman potter: $F_{a-1 (y)}$.

The empirical proof of a transcendental deduction consists therefore, as Lévi-Strauss asserted in his conclusion to *The Naked Man*, 'in [the myths'] embodiment, in concrete images, of what was previously no more than an abstract and rhetorical pattern, produced by pure speculation'.[82]

To complete this claim, we must pause for a moment over the fact that, in *The Jealous Potter*, as we have said, in addition to the canonical formula, Lévi-Strauss called upon another formula, inspired by algebra and topology, the 'Klein bottle', which Lucien Scubla describes in the following terms: 'A Klein bottle is constructed from a tube twisted in such a way that it passes through itself, bringing the two openings to coincide with each other, as it were, from within.'[83]

In *The Jealous Potter*, Lévi-Strauss would apply this topological model to a series of myths in which imaginary beings possess a body with a single opening that serves both as a mouth and an anus. In North America, some of these myths are in effect associated with the origin of potting clay, and it was with reference to them that Lévi-Strauss introduced the model of the 'Klein bottle' to describe another form of coming full circle. As Scubla notes:

Potting clay, having first been extracted, then modelled and finally fired, becomes a container designed to receive a contained, food. The food follows the same path but in reverse: first placed in an earthen container, then placed in the oven, and elaborated inside the body by the process of digestion, it is finally ejected in the form of excrement.[84]

---

82  *The Naked Man*, p. 549.
83  Scubla, *Lire Lévi-Strauss*, p. 301, n. 22; my translation.
84  Ibid., p. 106.

In the end, potting clay is thus comparable to excrement, the human body to a pottery vessel, and cooking to digestion, three equivalences that structure these myths.

Having come this far, we now need to take a position on the question of the theoretical validity and importance – or lack thereof – of Lévi-Strauss's canonical formula for explaining, if not all forms of myth-producing thought, at least those present in Amerindian mythology. To my mind, this formula is the translation in logico-mathematical terms of a remarkable and very early (before 1955) intuition Lévi-Strauss had concerning the nature of the logical structures that underpin mythical narratives, and hence about the nature of the mental operations that generate them. He had understood by then that mythical thought proceeds by establishing a succession of equivalences between relations of correlation and of opposition between beings, between things and actions selected from the real world, which, finally, through a series of twists, transform them into supernatural beings and counter-intuitive actions.

This process, which proceeds by analogical deductions, is indeed expressed in the canonical formula, which posits that A is to B as B is to C (A : B :: B : C). But the formula contains more than this equivalence between two oppositions between two terms. It also contains the process by which the transcendental deduction, which lies at the heart of a myth or a group of myths, can be articulated with an empirical deduction that serves as the starting point and to which it gives a new, imaginary meaning that runs counter to intuition. This transfiguration and this transmutation are obtained through a mental operation that Lévi-Strauss has christened a 'twist'. Twists can be simple, double and even triple, but, in most cases, they are double. They are the means by which the transfiguration-transmutation of the terms (a and b) and the functions ($F_x$ and $F_y$) given at the beginning is effected.

It is now clear to us that, after having familiarized himself with hundreds of South and North American myths, Lévi-Strauss had been struck by an overall intuition concerning the deep structures of mythical narratives and the capacity to string together their narratives in the form of groups of myths tending to close upon themselves, though never completely. The choice of the formula $F_x(a) : F_y(b) :: F_x(b) : F_{a-1(y)}$ to translate these properties increasingly appears to have been fortunate, on the whole, although Lévi-Strauss never explained how it had come to mind. Did he know enough mathematics to formulate it himself? Had it been suggested to him by a mathematician friend? Today we may have the answer.

In a personal communication for which I am most grateful, Lucien Scubla told me that, from the beginning of his mythology course at the École Pratique des Hautes Études, which began in 1951–52, Lévi-Strauss had laid out the initial lines of this canonical formula. From 1951, the great linguist, Émile Benveniste, the mathematician, Georges Guilbaud, who would later found the Centre de Mathématiques Sociales at the EHESS, and sometimes Jacques Lacan would meet regularly with Lévi-Strauss to discuss the problem of formalization in the social sciences.[85] It was in the course of these discussions that Lévi-Strauss reportedly began searching for an equation that would allow him to formalize the structures of myths, and it was then that he probably received suggestions from Guilbaud. This conjecture was recently confirmed by Juan Pablo Lucchelli, who, while going through the Lévi-Strauss manuscripts at the Bibliothèque Nationale, discovered the canonical relation expressed in a different form, which we find Lacan using in 1956.

Whatever the case may be, sixty years after its initial formulation, the canonical formula is still drawing positive reactions. I have suggested some of the reasons for this relatively recent development. And I would add Lévi-Strauss's own point of view, which, through the following quotation, takes on an exceptional theoretical importance. It defines the way the formula should have been – and still should be – understood:

> Mythical beliefs . . . do not accept the limits of observable data. To the results of empirical deduction, that is binarism, they added a transcendental deduction which . . . proceeds to *create a whole series of images, which it then reincorporates into the real world*; e.g., the Grouse's head, which is alive on one side and dead on the other; the supernatural gnomes who give explicit expression to the empirically evident peculiarities of the Squirrel.[86]

This quotation gives us the reason for the 'self-evident' character of the myths. It is at the close of the several twists which a transcendental

---

85 É. Roudinesco, *Jacques Lacan. Esquisse d'une vie, histoire d'un système de pensée* (Paris, Fayard, 1993), p. 469.
86 *The Naked Man*, p. 557; my emphasis.

deduction imposes on the empirical data that the imaginary representations produced by this deduction are 'reincorporated' into the data. The
imaginary content that has been 'deduced' finds itself attached to these
empirical realities, which it penetrates and transforms into symbols of
itself. The imaginary and its counter-intuitive constructions have
become 'self-evident'.

For instance, one Salish myth 'explains' that, following a number of
adventures, Grouse's daughter finds herself blind in one eye. An Indian
informant 'explained' to the anthropologist, Arthur C. Ballard, that,
when the grouse talks to the spirits, it looks with its blind eye, and when
it addresses the living, it looks out of the right side. This is why Indians
never eat the head of the grouse, 'because it is dead on one side'.[87] In
refusing to eat it, the Indians are therefore acting in accordance with
their beliefs. Since their myths tell them that this bird connotes both
death and life, and that the bird's head connotes the intersection of life
and death and the passage from one to the other, they cannot eat it.
These imaginary connotations make up the 'semantic function' attached
through mythical deduction to the grouse 'zoeme', and more generally
to all gallinaceans. Of course, we should not forget that, in the real world,
grouse are not blind in one eye and never have been. But we now know
that the concrete and verifiable knowledge about the anatomy and ways
of this bird cannot stop the Indians from 'seeing' (i.e. believing) it to be
blind in one eye and a bearer of death. When myths make the law, reality
steps aside and is transformed in the human mind into observance of
this law. This law is none other than the necessity and strength of the
desire to believe in the truth of what the myths recount.

What the Indians hear when they listen to their myths is not just the
story that is being told, which explains why women have periods or why
the moon has spots. What they are listening to is the patent discourse of
the myths, but what they hear through the images, ideas and symbolic
figures underpinning the myth is the latent content of this discourse.
This is where a problem arises. In several places, Lévi-Strauss states that
these stories are apparently without rhyme or reason, whereas we know
(as does Lévi-Strauss) that the Indians received and experienced them
as 'existential truths'. That is an important point, which would shed light

---

87 A. C. Ballard, *Mythology of Southern Puget Sound* (Seattle, University of
Washington Publications, 1929), quoted in *The Naked Man*, p. 499.

on the way Lévi-Strauss defines the relationship between myth and ritual. Here we must pause a moment, because my views on this point differ.

The latent content of the myths effectively consists of the implicit meanings that the schemata which generate their myths have for Amerindians. The latent content is therefore not opposed to the patent content, since it is the latent content that endows the actors (= mythemes) featured in these stories, the events that transpire in them and the consequences that flow from them for humans, with their experienced ideological meaning – their force as myth. Through the latent content, the mythical narrative becomes a narrative that does indeed have rhyme and reason for the Indians. For by 'experienced meaning', we must understand the meaning that was culturally thinkable for the Indians and socially enacted by them in the form of institutions and magico-religious practices.

And just as the grammar of a language is present and implicitly encodes the speakers' utterances, so that what they say is mutually understandable, so the latent content of the myths makes them mutually understandable to those who tell or hear them. Of course, that is true only up to a point, since there are cultural (or other) limits to the diffusion of a myth and to its comprehension, and even more to its adoption by other societies. And just as the grammatical rules of a language cannot be laid out each time people say something in that language, on pain of bringing all speech to a halt, so the rules for constructing myths and the latent content of their counter-intuitive schemata cannot be laid out as people are reciting them, listening to them and believing in their truth. But at the same time it is the *presence-absence* of the operations of mythical thought, and the latent content of the counter-intuitive schemata organizing the myths of societies sharing the same cultural universe, that make myths appear to be 'authorless' stories, 'revealed' truths; in other words, that endow them with the attributes of 'sacred' texts which those who tell them, like those who listen to them, can only believe in and accept. Now, we have already pointed out that the notion of 'sacred' is sadly absent in Lévi-Strauss's analysis of the myths and religions he studied – almost all of which were from tribal and polytheistic groups.

But let us return to the way the canonical formula was received. On this question, nothing can supersede the remarkable book Lucien Scubla devoted in 1998 to the analysis, text by text, period by period, of all the passages in Lévi-Strauss's books where he actually used (or sometimes merely mentioned) the formula, each time referring his readers to the texts published in 1955 where it first appeared.[88] Scubla thus reconstructs the winding career of the formula from its first version, followed by its relative eclipse at the time of the Mythology series, and its forceful return with *Anthropology and Myth* and until *The Story of Lynx*.

But Scubla has also analysed the reception of the formula, the debates surrounding it and the research it has sparked. He lists, first, all those who never saw the point of subjecting myths to a structural analysis. The canonical formula was obviously met with irony on their part, dismissed as logico-mathematical window-dressing designed to make a rhetorical undertaking look like 'hard' science, 'real' science. Secondly there were those, myself among them, who immediately welcomed structural analysis as an essential advance for anthropology and, more broadly, for all the social sciences. But to these scholars, it was demonstrably possible to read the four volumes of the Mythology series and benefit greatly from them, without necessarily adopting the canonical formula.[89] That did not prevent the reader from understanding the mythemes and schemata present in the myths, the oppositions, inversions, symmetries, etc. which connected a number of myths and arrayed them in loops and cycles.[90]

---

88 Scubla, *Lire Lévi-Strauss*. In 1998, Scubla could not discuss the latest appearance of the formula, in a text entitled 'Hourglass Configurations', which was published only in 2001; see Maranda, *The Double Twist*.

89 The Mythology series was and remains difficult to read, for two reasons. First, because the publication of the four volumes stretched over eight years with one or several years between each volume, it was difficult when reading the second or third, and then the fourth volume, to remember the myths one had read one or several years earlier, which were once again used to shed light on a new series of myths. After 1971 it became possible to read all four volumes in one go. But few have done this. The second difficulty for readers is that of following Lévi-Strauss as he intertwines and crosses his demonstrations devoted to the existence of relations of symmetry, inversion, contrariness, etc. between myths which at times reappear in several volumes. The memory cannot always hold and totalize them in order to construct the horizon for reading the new myths introduced further on.

90 For example, of the 187 myths presented in the first volume of the Mythology series, Lévi-Strauss gathered 27 into one or several loops; in the second volume, of the 175 new myths and the 56 myths already presented in the first volume and reused in the second, Lévi-Strauss constructed at least 30 into loops. In all, of 813 myths, fewer than a quarter were gathered into loops and cycles by Lévi-Strauss himself.

In short, to my mind and that of many others, the successive volumes in the Mythology series provided a deeper knowledge of the hidden richness of Amerindian myths and the complexity of the mental operations that had generated them. And yet the canonical formula remained opaque, and it did not seem to be necessary to understand it in order to practice the structural analysis of myths. It was opaque because Lévi-Strauss had never specifically indicated how to use it, and also because he had formulated it in three different ways without ever explaining the reasons for these differences – and therefore for his choices.[91] And, finally, it was opaque because Lévi-Strauss himself had stressed on several occasions that his formula was not an algorithm, but a sort of 'stenogram', an abbreviated formulation of a global, synthetic intuition that he had had about the nature of myths and which had never left him. That said, the formula is neither a key to all the doors of mythical content, nor a meaningless rhetorical formula in a logico-mathematical guise that masks its emptiness and gives it the look of a scientific theorem.

But there was a third group: those who immediately accepted the formula as being of scientific interest and greeted it with enthusiasm. This group featured anthropologists, to be sure, but also mathematicians, semioticians, psychologists and 'cognitive' philosophers. All attempted, each according to their discipline, to give the formula a precise, operational content. The movement started with an article by Pierre Maranda and Elli Köngäs, which appeared in 1962,[92] and referred to Lévi-Strauss's 1955 article. Today, after a half-century of debates and the publication of numerous articles and major books,[93] and after

---

91 Lévi-Strauss produced three different versions of his formula:

1) $F_x(a) : F_y(b) :: F_x(b) : F^{a-1}_{(y)}$ – 1955, 'The Structural Study of Myth'.

2) $F_x(a) : F_y(b) :: F_x(b) : F^{b-1}_{(y)}$ – 1984, *Anthropology and Myth* .

3) $F_x(a) : F_y(b) :: F_y(x) : F^{a-1}_{(b)}$ – 1985, *The Jealous Potter*. Alain Côté has shown that the formula can be expressed in 144 different ways, and he produced a table of permutations for generating the 'field of expressions of the canonical formula'. A. Côté, 'Qu'est-ce que la formule canonique?', *L'Homme*, n° 135 (July–September 1995), pp. 35–41.

92 P. Maranda and E. Köngäs, 'Structural Models in Folklore', *Midwest Folklore* XII, Indiana University (1962), pp. 133–92.

93 Among others, the contributions to the special issue of *L'Homme* devoted to the canonical formula (n° 135, July–September 1995); E. Désveaux, *Quadratura Americana. Essai d'anthropologie Lévi-Straussienne* (Geneva, Georg, 2001); Maranda, *The Double Twist*; Scubla, *Lire Lévi-Strauss*; Mosko and Damon, eds, *On the Order of Chaos*.

Lévi-Strauss's own responses to the questions raised by these researchers (notably Maranda, Marcus, Côté, Désveaux, Scubla and Petitot), the formula has begun to take a more precise mathematical form (Morava). It is beginning to be employable by anthropologists who want to analyse, for instance, certain sequences of initiation rituals embedded in a given cosmology; a case in point is Laurent Berger's analysis of the circumcision rituals found among the Imerina of Madagascar.[94]

Berger's analysis shows that it is now possible to combine the cognitive and the social sciences, and to go even further than we previously could in interpreting, in the absence of all reductionism, the domain of religions and ritual. In this case, Lévi-Strauss's canonical formula appears clearly as the intuition of a logic productive of counter-intuitive analogies which explain the permutations of roles, agents and statuses that constitute both the moments and the results of the performance of rituals for the individuals, the groups, and therefore for the societies, that practice them. It is worthwhile looking into this here.

The Imerina rites for the circumcision of boys are performed by the men of their kin group (their deme, a cognatic group) acting in the name of all the ancestors, whose life-force they transmit to their descendants. These rites entail the (counter-intuitive) representation of a boy's circumcision by the men as the equivalent of the women's giving birth to children. Cutting the foreskin is designated by the same term as that for cutting a child's umbilical cord. The man representing the community of all the boy's ascendants (who though dead are still present) swallows the foreskin, just as the earth absorbs the newborn's placenta. Circumcision and parturition are thus equivalents. And circumcision is conceived and experienced as a second birth for the boys, which makes them fully fledged members of their kin group. This second birth entitles them to marry, to enter the ancestors' tombs, to transmit property rights; but above all, the ritual enables the circumcised boy to receive the ancestors' strength and life-force and to transmit these ritually to his own children. But something else happens as well. When the new initiate receives the ancestors' sacred life-force into his body, he

---

94 L. Berger, 'Ritual, History and Cognition: From Analogy to Hegemony in Highland Malagasy Politics', *Anthropological Theory*, n° 12 (2013), pp. 1–36. The author uses another expression of the canonical formula: $F_x(a) : F_y(b) :: F_y(a) : F^{a-1}_{(x)}$, which he personally reconstructed and which appears as the reason for the succession of circumcision rites undergone by Imerina boys.

becomes capable of assimilating the (imaginary) energy that circulates throughout the universe and of subjecting and domesticating any entity that might oppose the ancestors' sacred force. The patient becomes an agent. At the close of these rituals, several aspects of the culture are also legitimized: the power of the men over the women, of the elder men over the younger, of the chiefs over their dependents, of the king over his subjects and of humans over wild nature – plants and animals – in which a non-domesticated life-force circulates. Finally, the boy's social 'birth certificate' in the form of his circumcision is rendered equivalent to the right to exert a force of domination and predation, not only in the social world, but in the cosmos, a universe organized according to a hierarchy that is both real and imaginary. The transformation of a patient into an agent, and the equivalence between birth and predation result from a double twist of both the terms and their functions.

This series of imaginary equivalences, which ends on an inversion of the terms and the functions assumed by agents and patients, can be represented by one of the expressions of the canonical formula:

---

– The women (a) giving birth ($F_x$) to a child = $F_x(a)$
– are to the representatives of the (political) community of the ancestors (b) circumcising ($F_y$) a boy = $F_y(b)$
– as the representatives (b) of the (political) community of the ancestors giving mystical and social birth ($F_x$) to a boy = $F_x(b)$
– are to the action ($F^{b-1}$) performed by the circumcised person (y) on any entity likely to oppose the representatives of the ancestral political community and to himself: = $F^{b-1}(y)$.
– which yields the expression of the canonical formula able to translate and symbolize these equivalences and twists:[95] $F_x(a) : F_y(b) :: F_x(b) : F^{b-1}(y)$

---

By reconstructing this sequence of imaginary equivalents and counter-intuitive twists, Berger was able to isolate the components of the Imerina myths and circumcision rites that have remained invariable

---

95 This is a different expression from that usually employed by Lévi-Strauss: $F_x(a) : F_y(b) :: F_x(b) : F^{a-1}_{(y)}$.

from those that have varied over the last three centuries. The invariants are, on the one hand, the representations of the equivalence between female parturition and male circumcision and, on the other hand, the representations of the opposition between an untamed life-force, not subject to domination (called *hery*), and a life-force characterized by subjection and domination, inherited from the ancestors (called *hasina*), which is supposed to be exercised over everything likely to oppose it.

On the other hand, what varies over the course of time is the nature of the entities that have opposed or seemed to oppose the ancestors' life-force: women, younger kinsmen, fallen aristocrats, rebel chiefs, neighbouring peoples, but also wild animals, terraced hills, etc. In the different eras and contexts of Imerina history, each time new economic and political relations have arisen outside the indigenous mythico-religious field of representations and symbolic ritual practices, a representation has been suggested by the conceptual prism of opposition and conflict between two imaginary categories of life-force: the non-domesticated life-force (*hery*) that the men must always subject to the life-force of their ancestors (*hasina*). Among the possibilities offered by this system of counter-intuitive representations, new social relations became at once intellectually thinkable because they were culturally meaningful, and socially legitimized. The imaginary always – up to a certain point – has the capacity to absorb new realities and to reshape them in its own image.[96] The more counter-intuitive a schema, the more believable it is. That is why mythical thought and religions have a fine future. Laurent Berger's analysis of Imerina circumcision rituals and of the cosmo-sociological myths that give them their meaning clearly shows the methodological and theoretical interest of the canonical formula for penetrating the counter-intuitive world of myth and ritual. At the same time, it enables us to identify one of the weaknesses of Lévi-Strauss's theoretical view, not of myth but of ritual. We are familiar with

---

96 Concerning rituals in Madagascar: M. Bloch, *From Blessing to Violence: History and Ideology in the Circumcision Ritual of the Merina of Madagascar* (Cambridge, Cambridge University Press, 1986); M. Bloch, *Prey into Hunter: The Politics of Religious Experience* (Cambridge, Cambridge University Press, 1992). For reasoning by analogy, see: D. Gentner, K. Holyoak and S. Kokinov, eds, *The Analogical Mind: Perspectives from Cognitive Science* (Cambridge, MA, MIT Press, 2001); H. Whitehouse and R. N. McCauley, eds, *Mind and Religion: The Psychological and Cognitive Foundations of Religiosity* (Walnut Creek, AltaMira Press, 2005).

his theses on the nature of ritual, which he sees as being radically opposed to that of myth. These theses were hammered home in the 'Finale' of *The Naked Man*:

> Ritual, by fragmenting operations and repeating them unwearyingly in infinite detail . . . encourages the illusion that it is possible to run counter to myth, and to move back from the discontinuous to the continuous . . . In this sense, ritual does not reinforce, but runs counter to, mythical thought, which divides up the same continuum into large distinctive units separated by differential gaps . . . On the whole, the opposition between rite and myth is the same as that between living and thinking, and *ritual represents a bastardization of thought, brought about by the constraints of life* . . . This desperate, and inevitably unsuccessful, attempt to re-establish the continuity of lived experience, segmented through the schematism by which mythical speculation has replaced it, is the essence of ritual.[97]

The Imerina's circumcision rituals and the founding myths concerning their power run counter to the thesis positing that ritual seeks to move back from the discontinuous to the continuous of myth, but the effort is doomed. For the Imerina, the rites that prepare, perform and follow the circumcision of a boy establish, on the contrary, a *twofold continuity*. They definitively integrate the boy in his deme (kin group) and endow him with rights over lands, access to ancestral tombs and the power later to circumcise other members of his deme. Secondly, they ensure that (the life-force of) the ancestors of the members of the deme will continue to take part in the management of the society and the surrounding world. In the eyes of the Imerina, rituals therefore do not fail to 're-establish the continuity of lived experience', nor are they in any way a 'bastardization' of their thought. Furthermore, although this goes beyond the problem of ritual, each of us, Amerindian or not, learns that our concrete, lived experience, of nature, society and ourselves, is a combination of continuities and discontinuities. You never bathe in the 'same river' twice, and yet it is always in the same river that you bathe – and that your ancestors bathed before you.

---

97 *The Naked Man*, pp. 674–5; my emphasis.

## Myth and Ritual

We must nevertheless be aware that, in Lévi-Strauss's mind, relations between myth and ritual are more complex than the above clear-cut opposition would suggest. In order to gain a both broader and clearer view, we must look back at the way his work unfolded.

In 1954, in an article entitled 'Relations between Mythology and Ritual',[98] Lévi-Strauss analysed a major Pawnee Indian ritual, the Hako, using material published by Alice Fletcher.[99] In the article, he drew a number of conclusions concerning 'this old and much-debated problem', and would uphold them to the end. He had in effect discovered that, in the vast corpus of Pawnee mythology, there was no myth 'underlying the ritual as a whole'. And yet, if myth and ritual do not 'mirror each other, they often reciprocally complete each other'. The aim of the Hako ritual is to achieve, with the help of sacred objects, a series of mediations between opposites – human/non-human, men/women, members of one's own and of other tribes, allies/enemies, heaven/earth, day/night, etc. Finally, somewhat later Lévi-Strauss thought he had proven that

> the signifying value of the ritual is entirely contained in its instruments and actions. The words – prayers, incantations, formulae – appeared meaningless, or at most endowed with only a slight functional utility. From this point of view, a veritable opposition appeared between the myth and the rite. Whereas the former is language, but draws its meaning from a particular use of that language, the ritual uses language in the ordinary way, and elects to signify at another level. The terms *metalanguage* and *paralanguage* were proposed to render this distinction.[100]

Since the publication of 'The Structural Study of Myth' (1955), we know that myths that produce meaning through the production of mythemes implemented by counter-intuitive schemata are a metalanguage. We now learn that the objects handled and the actions

---

98 'Relations between Mythology and Ritual', *Anthropology and Myth*, pp. 204–6.

99 A. C. Fletcher and J. R. Murie, *The Hako, a Pawnee Ceremony*, 22nd Annual Report of the Bureau of American Ethnology (1900–1901), part II, 1904. See also C. Lévi-Strauss, 'Structure and Dialectics', *Structural Anthropology*, pp. 232–41.

100 *Anthropology and Myth*, p. 205; our emphasis.

performed during these rituals are the only means of endowing the rituals with a signifying value. Then in a slightly later text, 'Structure and Dialectics' (1956), Lévi-Strauss mentions another fact that would exclude postulating a term-for-term correspondence between the myths and rituals of a same society. Indeed, one Pawnee myth 'reveals a ritual system which is the reverse, not of that prevailing among the Pawnee, but of a system which they do not employ and which exists among related tribes whose ritual organization is exactly the opposite of that of the Pawnee'.[101]

In 1956, then, Lévi-Strauss had demonstrated his determination to take serious account of the complexity of relations between myth and ritual. In suggesting that the objects and actions involved in the rituals are a paralanguage endowed with its own signification, irreducible to that of myths, he had made an important observation, but did not go on to say what this signification independent of actions and objects might consist of. At that time, he had not 'accused' rituals of being 'a bastardization of thought ... [an] inevitably unsuccessful attempt to re-establish the continuity of lived experience'. For that, we would have to wait another fifteen years, for the 'Finale' of *The Naked Man*.

Lévi-Strauss devoted numerous pages of the Mythology series, above all in *The Origin of Table Manners*, to a detailed analysis of the sequences of the so-called 'Great Fast' rituals of the South American Sherente.[102] Based on the wealth of ethnographic data gathered by Curt Nimuendajo, Carlos Estevão de Oliveira and many other anthropologists, he shows the close intertwining of mythical representations and ritual performances. He then extends his analysis by comparing (once again via a number of excellent monographs)[103] the Sherente rites with the Sun dance as performed by the Arapaho and other Plains Indians, then with the rituals accompanying the sacred eagle hunt, the summer and winter buffalo hunts, and the agrarian rites of the Mandan and the Hidatsa.[104] In these two groups of societies, from South America and North America respectively, the Sun is seen as a cannibalistic ogre, a threat to

---

101 *Structural Anthropology*, p. 237.

102 See also *The Raw and the Cooked*, pp. 289–91.

103 G. A. Dorsey, *The Arapaho Sun Dance: The Ceremony of the Offerings Lodge* (Chicago, Field Columbian Museum, 1903); G. A. Dorsey and A. L. Kroeber, *Traditions of the Arapaho* (Chicago, Field Columbian Museum, 1903).

104 *The Origin of Table Manners*, p. 412.

human survival.[105] He goes on to show the existence of a remarkable parallel between the rituals in the two societies, in spite of the thousands of kilometres that separate them and the differences between their languages, cultures and social organizations.[106]

In these tribes, the rituals have the double objective of keeping the sun far from the earth and of calling and obtaining rain, the guarantee of abundant harvests. Each year both the Sherente and the Plains Indians performed a major ritual that 'gave the whole group the opportunity to live together again *as an entity*, and to celebrate its new-found unity with a great religious feast'.[107] To live together as an entity: a very important remark that Lévi-Strauss would not develop further, though to have done so would have deepened his understanding of part of what these rituals add to the myths.

Finally, following a series of deft analyses of the complex intertwining of myth and ritual, Lévi-Strauss addresses the question of the true 'signifying value' of ritual. After recalling that 'explicit mythology [which founds a ritual] and implicit mythology [which is present in the ritual] are two different modes of an identical reality: in both cases we are dealing with mythical representations', he asks the question: what is a ritual? The answer comes as a surprise, to say the least:

> If we wish to study ritual *in itself and for itself*, in order to . . . determine its specific characteristics, we should . . . begin by removing from it all the implicit mythology which adheres to it *without really being part of it*.[108]

Once we have removed all the 'implicit mythology' from ritual, we would then find ourselves in the presence, as it were, of 'pure ritual'. But what is ritual in its pure state?

> We can say that it consists of words uttered, gestures performed and objects manipulated, independently of any gloss or commentary . . . which would belong not to the ritual itself but to implicit mythology.[109]

---

105  Ibid., p. 308.

106  Ibid., pp. 213–14.

107  Ibid., p. 211; my emphasis. Lévi-Strauss drew on the rich work by C. Wissler on the Plains Indians' Sun dance.

108  *The Naked Man*, p. 669; my emphasis.

109  Ibid., p. 671.

But what function does ritual assign to gestures and objects?

> They are a substitute for words. Each is a global connotation of a system of ideas and representations; by their use, ritual condenses into a concrete and unitary form procedures which otherwise would have had to be discursive . . . The performance of gestures and the manipulation of objects are devices which allow ritual to avoid speech.[110]

Something is not right in these successive affirmations. For, if ritual adds meaning through the use of gestures and objects that substitute for words but globally connote the system of ideas and representations, exactly what ideas and representations might we be talking about since they cannot belong to the realm of myth, explicit or implicit, from which objects and gestures have been removed? If objects are indeed condensations of representations – which has been shown – the latter cannot be different from the mythico-religious representations the society performing these rituals holds of the universe and itself. They are necessarily connected with them, belong to them.

Another problem. The manipulation of objects is supposed to substitute for speech and even be a means to avoid speech. Is that really the explanation for the presence and handling of objects in ritual? The analysis of a drum used in funeral rituals by the Ankave, a small tribe in Papua New Guinea studied in several publications by the anthropologist Pierre Lemonnier, leads me once more to conclude in the negative, and to suggest an entirely different perspective.[111]

---

110  Ibid., pp. 671–2.

111  P. Lemonnier, *Le Sabbat des lucioles. Sorcellerie, chamanisme et imaginaire cannibale en Nouvelle-Guinée* (Paris, Stock, 2006); 'Mythes et rites chez les Anga', *Journal de la Société des océanistes*, n$^{os}$ 130–1 (2010), pp. 67–77; *Mundane Objects : Materiality and Non-Verbal Communication* (Walnut Creek, Left Coast Press, 2012), pp. 63–76. Lemonnier cites several publications on the same lines as his own: E. Hutchins, 'Material Anchors for Conceptual Blends', *Journal of Pragmatics*, n° 37 (2005), pp. 1555–77; D. Tuzin, 'Art, Ritual and the Crafting of Illusion', *Asia Pacific Journal of Anthropology* 3, n°1 (2002), pp. 1–23; E. Leach, *Culture and Communication* (Cambridge, Cambridge University Press, 1976); N. Munn, 'Symbolism in a Ritual Context', in J. Honigmann (ed.), *Handbook of Social and Cultural Anthropology* (Chicago, Rand McNally, 1973), pp. 579–607; S. J. Tambiah, 'Forms and Meaning of Magical Acts. A Point of View', in: R. Horton and R. Finnegan, *Modes of Thought* (London, Faber & Faber, 1979), pp. 199–229; R. McCauley and T. E. Lawson, *Bringing Ritual to Mind* (Cambridge, Cambridge University Press, 2002).

Here are the facts. During the rites through which the Ankave undertake to drive the spirits of the recently deceased away from their living environment, everyone, men, women and children (even little ones, carried on shoulders), circle around all night, for several nights running, while beating drums. Their round dance reproduces the original whirlpool from which the first drums are supposed to have sprung together with the Ombo, cannibalistic monsters who dance, at the same time as the humans, round and round to the sound of the drums in another world, preparing to devour the innards of the deceased. In reality, among the Ombo the Ankave find the spirits of their maternal kin, who were givers of life when alive and became Ombo after death, and are now eager to devour the corpses of their nephews and nieces. There is an Ankave myth that describes in detail how the drums should be made (kind of wood, membrane, assembly, shape) and how the dancers should use them. Myth, materials, techniques and ritual all constitute an inextricable mixture.

The fact of making and beating the drums necessarily produces in an Ankave, through the involvement of his body and senses and independently of any speech, the intuitive fusion of representations stemming from different domains of social life and the cultural universe (gifts of game to the maternal kin; interventions of the shamans on behalf of victims of the blatant Ombo aggression of entering their body at night and devouring part of their intestines; dispersion of the Ankave in forest camps to protect themselves from these invisible aggressors, etc.). The drums mobilize both body and mind; their beating is not a 'bastardization of thought' nor a 'desperate, and inevitably unsuccessful, attempt to re-establish the continuity of lived experience' through the multiplication of discontinuous and rapidly repeated gestures. They partake of the non-verbal presence in the body and mind of each Ankave of truths verging on the *unspeakable* because they meld, in a form that cannot otherwise be expressed, numerous aspects of the Ankave's way of life and thought. This fusion, which does not transpire through language or the telling of a myth, thus permeates the mind and the body simultaneously. It is quite simply 'experienced'. And this experience becomes an inseparable mixture of (non-explicit) representations, (non-formulated) judgments and (felt) emotions, in short a 'blend' of affect and intellect.

The reason rituals can produce something that myths cannot is that they involve action. Rituals are forms of acting on the world and on oneself in accordance with a society's representations of the world and of the self. Myths interpret the world, but cannot act on it directly. Only rituals can transform mythico-religious thought into actions. Rituals transform the imaginary explanations of the world proffered by myths into experienced, existential truths. And they cause these to be lived in the body, they embody them. Myths are not stories to be read but to be lived, stories to listen to and believe in order to act on oneself, on others and on the universe. Ritual thus adds to myth the power of the materiality of bodies, gestures and manipulated objects, as well as the social and material power to act and live as an entity with those who share the same ideas, values and way of life. Ritual causes everyone to act together in accordance with a shared vision of the world and of themselves. All aspects, all components of their social identity are gathered together and experienced in their bodies, while their society is present, for the duration of the ritual, for everyone to see, as the entity to which all belong.

Mythical thought is therefore not, as Lévi-Strauss claimed, 'understanding as the source of an autonomous activity, which is subject in the first place to its own constraints'. It does not roll out for its own benefit 'a parade of ideas no less fantastic than the indescribably poetic performance that the genius of the species, during the mating season, imposes on bower birds'.[112] Men do not produce myths for the enjoyment of their mind. Or one could say that mythical thought does not, as Lévi-Strauss would put it, produce myths in order to enjoy itself in men's minds. Something wholly different is going on. Since the beginning of time, men, in producing myths, strive by means of thought to explain to themselves the surrounding universe and their existence in this world. And they do this, not for the pleasure of manufacturing theories, but out of the need to act upon the world and on themselves.

Contrary to what Lévi-Strauss claims, then, ritual does not 'run counter to mythical thought'.[113] It reinforces it, for it adds to mythical thought the power to act and, even more, the social, emotional and bodily strength to act together in order to reproduce both the society to which its members belong and their relations with a world whose representation they share with others.

---

112  *The Naked Man*, p. 684.
113  Ibid., p. 674.

The differences between myth and ritual are therefore not founded, as Lévi-Strauss claimed, on an ostensible antinomy between discontinuity (myth) and the impossible restoration of continuity (ritual), and even less on 'the contradiction inherent in the human condition, between two inevitable obligations: living and thinking'.[114] Ritual *does not oppose* living and thinking. It adds acting to thinking. However, the union of thinking with acting means quite simply living. And living fully means transforming mental realities into realities experienced by individuals, and that is possible only if these mental realities have been transformed into social relations, institutions and therefore social practices.

As Victor Turner objected to Lévi-Strauss: 'the whole person and not just the mind . . . is existentially involved in life and death issues'.[115] To which Lévi-Strauss responded with irony: 'This may well be so; but when it has been said, and lip service has been paid to the importance of the emotions, we have not advanced one step nearer an explanation of . . . the strange activities characteristic of ritual, and the symbols relating to them.'[116] In point of fact, the issue is not to contradict Lévi-Strauss by asserting that affectivity, the emotions, anguish in the face of death, etc. are behind the 'operations of the intellect, in relation to which they would have the privilege of priority in time' and that the 'intellectual operations [would be] secondary in relation to emotional experiences'.[117] We can only agree with him that it is not the emotions, fear of death or anguish before the Sun's strength that can 'explain' either the

114  Ibid., p. 681.

115  V. Turner, *The Ritual Process: Structure and Anti-Structure* (Chicago, Aldine, 1969), pp. 42–3; cited in *The Naked Man*, p. 668.

116  *The Naked Man*, p. 668.

117  *The Naked Man*, p. 667–8: 'contrary to what certain critics have said, I do not underestimate the importance of the emotions. I merely refuse to give in to them . . . On the other hand, it is true that I try to discern, behind emotional phenomena, the indirect effect of changes occurring in the normal course of the operations of the intellect' (p. 667). It is hard to see what normal course of the operations of the intellect could prevent a mother being overwhelmed with pain by the death of her son in an accident. Nevertheless, in *Totemism* (trans. R. Needham, Boston, Beacon Press, 1963), Lévi-Strauss had praised Rousseau for having defined 'the natural condition of man, while still retaining the distinctions, by the only psychic state of which the content is indissociably both affective and intellectual, and which the act of consciousness suffices to transform from one level to the other, viz., compassion, or, as Rousseau also writes, identification with another' (p. 101). 'For Rousseau . . . the origin [of language] lies not in needs but in emotions, so that the first language must have been figurative' (p. 102).

appearance of the founding myths of Taoism, Hinduism or Christianity, or the content of the promises each of these religions holds out to mankind. But we still need to understand the *raisons d'être* of the answers offered by founding myths and religious rituals – whether tribal or universal – to a certain number of fundamental existential questions every society, at every period, asks itself; universal questions that connect with each other, intersecting at a number of points. For instance:

– What does it mean to be born? to live? to die? How is one born? Why does one die?

– What are and should be the relations humans entertain with invisible entities: ancestors, spirits, gods, God?

– What forms of power can and should humans exercise over other humans? What forms are illegitimate?

– What is the nature of the universe around us? How can we think about and act on it? And so on.

Myths and rituals offer answers to these questions that are thought out, enacted and experienced. The answers have varied with the society and have often undergone profound changes over their history, which is, always, singular. The need to ask these questions and find answers to them is therefore not specific to any of these societies or times. And the need is not only to ask these questions and find answers to them, but to believe, collectively and individually, *in the truth* of the answers proposed and, because they are true, to *act in accordance* with them *on* oneself, *on* others and *on* the world.

As I have said, Lévi-Strauss never broaches the question of why men and women attach a 'truth-value' to the answers that myth and religion propose to these existential questions, even when these answers take the form of counter-intuitive representations and demonstrations that contradict the concrete experience and practical knowledge these men and women have of the world and of themselves. No one has ever seen a grizzly she-bear turn into an Indian woman or, conversely, an Indian woman turn into a grizzly, and yet . . . Lévi-Strauss's explanation skirts the issue:

For a myth to be engendered by thought and for it in turn to engender other myths, *it is necessary, and sufficient, that an initial opposition*

should be injected into experience and, as a consequence, other oppositions will spring into being.

An arrangement of matching oppositions inbuilt, as it were, in the
human understanding, begins to function whenever recurrent experiences, which may be biological, technological, economic, sociological, etc. in origin, activate the control . . . the social apparatus begins
to operate; from every concrete situation, no matter how complex, it
unflaggingly extracts a meaning, and turns it into an object of thought
by adapting it to the imperatives of formal organization.[118]

Lévi-Strauss describes in these lines how counter-intuitive explanations
of the world and of people are generated when the rules of a logic of
analogical deductions are applied to concrete experiences, presented in
the form of pairs of opposite but correlated realities, resulting in the
attachment of a fantastic meaning to these experiences. But that by no
means explains why these imaginary significations are *thought and
experienced as 'truths'*, rather than as stories told around the fire or fables
for children. In fact, it is because they are conceived as statements of
truth that myths are at the origin of institutions and practices which
provide the mental armature of real social relations. And it is because
these social relations, institutions and rituals are real that their founding
myths can only be true – the self-evident nature and the proofs of the
'truth' of the founding myths of religions, as well as the forms of political-religious sovereignty, come full circle.

   It is therefore neither enough nor even true to say that this sudden
appearance in concrete experience of an opposition (high and low, for
example) is sufficient to cause the mind to begin producing myths. In
order for that to happen, something else is necessary: an a priori
judgment must exist in the mind of the men and women who undergo
this experience. This judgment is clear, simple and universal. It can be
summed up in the formula: 'The impossible is possible.' That which is
clearly impossible, as concrete, daily experience has shown thousands of
times over, is nevertheless possible. And if the impossible is not possible
today, it may have been once upon a time (for example, when men and
animals were not yet distinct from each other), or it may be in the future

---

118 *The Naked Man*, pp. 604, 603; my emphasis.

(for example, at the Last Judgment, when the dead rise again, the virtuous are called to sit at the right hand of God and the evil-doers are cast into eternal hellfire).

But it is not enough to *imagine* that the impossible is possible. It has to be *believed*. It is the fact of believing in them that gives the imaginary deductions of myths their truth-value. If 'mythemes' are binary operators that combine the schemata of mythical thought, and if binary operations 'are an inherent feature of the means invented by nature to make possible the functioning of language and thought',[119] it is not the combinatory machinery of the mind that gives myths their truth-value. Rather it is the belief in the 'possibility of the impossible' that underlies the production of the imaginary equivalences between opposing terms and relations which founds the possibility for the mind to reverse their relations, to twist them once, twice and even three times. Belief in the veracity of the conclusions of this series of 'mental operations' is therefore assured even before they are set in motion.

When Lévi-Strauss tried to show that an initial opposition injected into experience generates a myth that then generates others, he wrote the following:

> [The opposition] between the high and the low admits of three modalities, according to whether the movement from one pole to the other occurs in one direction, in the opposite direction or in both. The axis of reference, which is sometimes kept vertical, sometimes changed to the horizontal, and sometimes partakes of both at once, may have, as its poles, the sky and the earth, the sky and water, or land and water ... Considered in their reciprocal relationships, the sun and the moon themselves may be both male, or both female, or of different sexes; they may also be strangers to each other, friends, blood relations or affines.[120]

Let us put aside the issue of the conversion of the high and the low to the horizontal; what matters here is the apparently possible passage between the high and the low as categories, as an opposition inherent in the concrete experience of every human being, and the opposition between a

119  Ibid., p. 559.
120  Ibid., p. 604.

Sun and Moon changed into brothers, or into enemies, allies, etc.; in short, entities endowed with powers that are at once analogous to human powers and different from these. Different because they are exercised in another world than that of humans (or in another part of the same world), but also because they accomplish things that are impossible for humans.

Between the mind's two uses of the opposition between the high and the low there is therefore a fundamental difference: one lends meaning to everyday, concrete experience of the world (a tree, a house or a bow have an upper and a lower part); the other describes beings and relations that exist in another world, or in another part of the world to which humans do not have access. To shift from one of these uses to the other, the mind must make a leap. This leap is precisely the act of positing that the impossible is (or was or will be) possible.

To believe that the impossible is possible necessarily means postulating at the same time that, somewhere, beyond or in the world where each person lives and performs their actions on others, on nature and on themselves, there exist entities and forces that are normally invisible but which are capable of doing what humans cannot. That being so, humans are bound to want to communicate with these entities and strive to convince them to act in their favour. Among the Pawnee Indians, for example, the (imaginary) thunderbirds are supposed to be masters of rain, so, in the ceremonies designed to keep the Sun – a man-eating monster whose heat produces famines – at a distance, the Pawnee call on these birds to hasten to bring rain and the abundance that comes with it. The invention of the thunderbirds, of the Sun and the Moon as rival brothers, etc., like that of all the figures and events featured in myths (and not only those of the Amerindians), makes it necessary also to invent various forms of communication and action aimed at entities endowed with such powers: invocations, prayers, sacrifices, rituals, etc. Thinking for the pleasure of thinking is therefore not the profound reason for myths. Myths are invented for the purpose of understanding, and understanding provides the means of acting in accordance with what one has understood. To act is to strive to achieve the goals humans pursue: to have fine harvests, to triumph over one's enemies, to avoid illness, to win the gods' favour, to obtain the ancestors' help, etc. The list of human desires is endless. To unite thought to action in order to satisfy one's needs and desires is precisely what myth and ritual combine to do, each mobilizing the intellect as well as the affects.

Let us take a closer look at the proposition that the same oppositions, between high and low, full and empty, etc., are used, on the one hand, to produce mythical interpretations of the universe and man, and, on the other hand, to act in daily life (to obtain concrete, visible and reproducible results) in this world. Take for example the construction of the big outrigger canoes that still today allow the Trobriand Islanders (living to the west of Papua New Guinea, where Malinowski spent many years) to navigate hundreds of miles over the Pacific Ocean, going from island to island practising *kula* and the other forms of exchange for which this circuit provides the opportunity. Building the canoes requires mastering and combining many areas of empirical know-how and practices, involving, for instance, the nature of the woods to be used for the hull, the outrigger and the mast, the height of the mast, the area of the sail and the type of material needed to make it. Then, when the time comes to set out, the navigator must have a perfect knowledge of the currents, the winds and their direction and force according to the seasons, but also the position of the stars in the sky for travelling at night. This concrete knowledge is shared by the other islanders in the Kula ring (the Muyuw, for example), who make the same type of canoe. But what is not shared are the rituals and the magical practices that, on each island, necessarily accompany making, launching and sailing the vessel.

Here we touch on a universal feature of societies and activities that we call, for lack of a better term, non-industrial. In all human groups (in all societies) that hunt, fish, grow crops, navigate, wage war, etc., it was (and still is) inconceivable that concrete knowledge and practical know-how could *in themselves* ensure the success of such enterprises, and therefore the continuity of the existence of those who practiced them. Without the help of the gods and the spirits of the earth and the sea, without the support of the ancestors, none of these undertakings could prosper, and even the best canoe would not hold up at sea. Once again, the example of the Kiriwana Island Trobrianders will serve as an illustration.

In order to choose and work the tree that will be used for the hull, the outrigger or the mast of a canoe, magic and ritual are required. In every canoe, the place where the 'canoe master' will sit and perform the rites that precede any journey is regarded as sacred. The canoe itself is seen as the union of a male part – the hull – and a female part – the outrigger. The carvings on the sides represent wild animals that will lend men the help of their magical powers when the vessel sets sail. Fore and aft, other carvings represent and harbour female spirits that will protect the crew from the attacks of enemy sorcerers during their journeys.

This example suffices to illustrate the fact that in none of these pre-industrial societies are concrete empirical knowledge and mythico-religious representations of the universe and society conceived or experienced as *mutually exclusive*. On the contrary, they are conceived and experienced as complementary, and because of this they intertwine and imbed themselves in each other within individual and social practices. Ritual acts, imaginary and symbolic practices supposed to contribute their power and ensure the success of the material and intellectual enterprises involved, always infiltrate the 'operational sequences' of activities bearing on nature (making tools or weapons, building houses, growing food, fishing) or on humans (assisting in childbirth, caring for the sick, the injured, etc.), to help achieve the proposed aims.

It is as though, ever since *Homo sapiens sapiens* appeared (and probably well before), two forms of thought have existed and combined in the human mind, without either opposing or excluding each other. And thanks to this, humans have invented, developed and transformed their relations with each other and with their environment, some of whose elements enable them to live.

One of these forms of thought is based on the idea that certain things are possible for humans while others are practically impossible. Of course, the nature and extent of the field of the possible vary with the era (Paleolithic, Neolithic, modern times, etc.) and with the society. Icarus dreamed of flying like a bird, but after having made wings for himself and taken off, he tumbled down into the water. His dream of flying has now become a reality. What is more, we have walked on the Moon.

The other form of thought, on the contrary, is based on the idea that the impossible is always possible. That holds true only for beings and powers that dwell in a world other than that of humans, or in the same world but usually hidden from sight. A few humans, however, also possess such powers, either innately or acquired in the course of interaction with these supernatural beings and forces.

This second form of thought, unfettered by the limits of knowledge and empirical practices, is precisely the one from which myth and religion spring. The explanations developed by this form, which are by nature fantasized, counter-intuitive speculations, are for this very reason regarded as undisputed truths. And it is the truth-value attached to them that obliges humans, because they *believe them to be true*, to act on the world and on themselves in accordance with what they have learned (hence rituals, or a certain moral code, or a certain way of governing, etc.). They entrust them with their lives, as it were.

When Lévi-Strauss wrote: 'We have to resign ourselves to the fact that the myths tell us nothing instructive about the world, the nature of reality or the origin and destiny of mankind. We cannot expect them to flatter any metaphysical thirst',[121] he was quite right insofar as we are concerned. But the Amerindian myths were not invented for our sake. They were recited and enacted by Amerindians, who did learn from them the order of the world, the nature of reality, the origin of humans and their fate. The myths had truth-value, and instructed the Indians in their manner of thinking and acting, in short: of living. Lévi-Strauss was also correct when he went on to write:

> On the other hand, they teach us a great deal about the societies from which they originate, they help to lay bare their inner workings and clarify the *raison d'être* of beliefs, customs and institutions, the organization of which was at first sight incomprehensible; lastly, and most importantly, they make it possible to discover certain operational modes of the human mind, which have remained so constant over the centuries and are so widespread over immense geographical distances, that we can assume them to be fundamental.[122]

But if myths could be the *raison d'être* of beliefs, of Amerindian customs and institutions, it is because their explicit (patent) and implicit (latent) contents were believed to be true. And their truthfulness is associated precisely with the counter-intuitive character of the figures and events contained in their narratives, that is, the mythemes and the schemata structuring them.

Of course, there is no question of denying the reality of the mental operations that generate and structure myths, and whose revelation was a major discovery. But are these operations (which the introduction of a single binary opposition of empirical data would suffice to set in motion

---

121 *The Naked Man*, p. 639.
122 Ibid.

and cause myths to appear) *enough* to endow myths with their *character of true explanations* of the world, a sacred character that imposes respect and trust? To my mind, the answer is no. As Propp showed before the Mythology volumes, folk tales entail mental operations that are in many ways similar to those Lévi-Strauss discovered through his analysis of myths. But we take delight in folk tales without feeling obliged to believe in them. That is even more obvious in the case of fables. The fable of the Ant and the Grasshopper is built on a binary opposition, that between two real animals made into imaginary characters symbolizing opposite human behaviours, from which the fable draws a moral at the end. Furthermore, every day we see that myths regarded as sacred by those who believe in them are considered fables by those who do not. Did not, the early Christians refuse to comply with the religious rituals of Rome because to them they were mere 'superstitions', the worship of 'false' gods, whereas they knew that there was only one true God, their own, alone deserving of their prayers and the sacrifice of their life?

It is clear why the operations of the human mind – establishment of correlations between opposing terms, symmetry, inversion, contrariness, contradiction, equivalences, homologies, double or triple twists, etc. – are in themselves not enough to attach truth-value to the narratives of these myths. They help, of course, since they generate the representations of these supernatural fantasy worlds. But they suppose a human need and desire to believe that such worlds exist. And to imagine they exist, allow me to repeat, the mind must posit – in the teeth of all concrete experience – that the impossible is possible. But, as I have said, it makes no sense to believe such a thing unless it is postulated at the same time that, somewhere, beings or powers exist for which the impossible is indeed possible. Without these a priori judgments, without these postulates, there is no way the 'vast combinatory apparatus, which is what any mythical system amounts to',[123] according to the expression used by Lévi-Strauss to designate mythical thought, can be set in motion and produce meaning for humans.[124] It is not enough, then, to introduce a binary opposition. For exceeding the limits of concrete experience is not only a desire imbedded in an intellectual act. It is an existential act.

123  Ibid., p. 559.
124  Ibid., p. 603.

I therefore find it difficult to agree with Lévi-Strauss when he writes:

The truth of the myth does not lie in any special content. It *consists in logical relations* which are devoid of content or, more precisely, whose invariant properties exhaust their operative value, since comparable relations can be established among the elements of a large number of different contents.[125]

For even if some myths explain, in different codes – sexual, culinary, astronomical, etc. – that are in relations of homology with each other, why men must die, it is always the same message and the same truth that the Indians hear. Furthermore, these myths about the origin of the brevity of life explain not only why humans must die, but also why they are not (or are no longer) immortal like the demiurges, and why they can no longer come back to life after death, as they could in olden times.

But, in the end, it is the same postulate: behind those things we see are things we do not see, able to do what men cannot, and constituting the common source of religion and science. With regard to science, religion aims to explain everything, from the origin of the cosmos and humanity down to the fate of men after death. The discourse of religions is totalizing on principle, both analytical and synthetic. They may even, as in the Chinese theory of Yin and Yang, include empirical knowledge from what today we call chemistry, physics and mathematics, while endowing it with symbolic and imaginary meaning in accordance with their view of the world and the people in it. This happened in China and also in India (with its great grammarians, logicians, ayurvedic practitioners, etc.).

For centuries, concrete knowledge, forms of mythico-religious thought and the early stages of the sciences co-existed without conflict, and the constructions of mythico-religious thought often included them in their systems.[126]

But since the advent of the experimental sciences together with modern logic and mathematics, this is no longer the case. A plasma physicist or molecular biologist can be American or Chinese, Protestant or Taoist, and

125  *The Raw and the Cooked*, p. 240; my emphasis.
126  As in the case of the 'arithmetical philosophy' found in the Amerindian myths; cf. *The Origin of Table Manners*, pp. 331–6. According to Lévi-Strauss, we even find an early version of set theory in their myths, ibid., p. 352.

the results of their experiments, if confirmed by their scientific community – having reproduced and verified them – are unaffected by the authors' nationalities, cultures and religions. These features disappear, as it were, behind the universal character of their findings. And, of course, no physicist would receive the Nobel prize if he brought the existence of Lao-Tzu or Jesus Christ into his calculations. From this standpoint, the distance between scientific thought and mythical thought has grown into a yawning abyss. And that is because we can now devise experiments to reproduce complex processes that exist objectively in nature.

It remains to explain how Lévi-Strauss accounted for the differential gaps between myths belonging to neighbouring societies – having the same or different cultures – and the external pressures that might cause these myths to evolve, or even to disappear. In short, we still need to shed more light on the relationship between myth and society.

## Myth and Society

To reconstruct Lévi-Strauss's position on these fundamental theoretical questions, we must start with a number of assertions that appear, up to a point, to contradict each other. In *The Raw and the Cooked*, Lévi-Strauss writes:

> A myth derives its significance not from contemporary or archaic institutions of which it is a reflection, but from its relation to other myths within a transformation group.[127]

Four pages later, discussing relations between myth and the social hierarchy among the four clans of the Tikopia Islanders studied by Firth, he writes:

> I have merely tried . . . to stress the central position occupied by the Bororo myths and the way they conform to the main outlines of social and political organization.[128]

---

127  *The Raw and the Cooked*, p. 51, n. 5.
128  Ibid., p. 55.

In *The Naked Man*, speaking of the elements that 'provide a solid anchorage to which the myths can attach themselves', he writes:

> It is impossible to give an exhaustive analysis of the ideology of any human group without taking into account its concrete relationships with the world; the ideology expresses these relationships, at the same time as the relationships in turn translate the ideology.[129]

And among the 'concrete relationships' a society entertains with the world, some are more important than others:

> *In the last resort, these reasons refer to the techno-economic substructure, which is what we always look to first if we are to try to understand the differential gaps between ideologies.*[130]

We recognize here the thesis of the 'primacy of infrastructures', advanced as early as 1958 in 'The Story of Asdiwal'[131] and reiterated in *The Savage Mind*,[132] ten years before *The Naked Man*. In *The Savage Mind*, Lévi-Strauss asserted that, in studying kinship systems and myths, he was simply contributing to the 'theory of superstructures, scarcely touched on by Marx',[133] and went as far as to affirm: 'I do not at all mean to suggest that ideological transformations give rise to social ones. Only the reverse is in fact true . . . We are however merely studying the shadows on the wall of the Cave'; and he then went on to say, with undue modesty: 'it is only the attention we give them which lends them a semblance of reality.'[134]

But these 'shadows' still have a few functions:

> What is true of the rules of kinship is also valid for mythical narratives. Neither are limited to being simply what they are: they *serve* a

---

129 *The Naked Man*, p. 610.

130 Ibid., p. 107.

131 'The Story of Asdiwal', *Structural Anthropology, volume 2*, pp. 146–97, p. 196, n. 19: 'Formal though it be, analysis of a society's myths verifies the primacy of the infrastructures.'

132 *The Savage Mind*, p. 93: 'The primacy of the infrastructure is thus . . . confirmed.'

133 Ibid., p. 130.

134 Ibid., p. 117.

purpose – to solve problems which are sociological in the one case and socio-logical in the other.[135]

What are these socio-logical problems that myths strive to solve?

[Myths] should be seen ... as constituting local and temporary answers to the problems raised by feasible adjustments and insoluble contradictions that they are endeavouring to legitimize or conceal. The content with which the myth endows itself is not anterior, but posterior, to this initial impulse: far from deriving from one content or other, the myth moves towards a particular content through the attraction of its specific gravity. In each individual case, it alienates, in the process, part of its apparent liberty which, looked at from another angle, is no more than an aspect of its own necessity.[136]

And, in all these cases, whether the oppositions or contradictions dealt with in the myths are surmountable (feasible adjustments) or insurmountable, 'mythical thought always progresses from the awareness of oppositions toward their resolution.'[137] This was already Lévi-Strauss's thesis in his founding text of 1955, 'The Structural Study of Myth'. Thirty-three years later, in his conversations with Didier Eribon, his answer to the question, 'What is myth for?', is clear: 'To explain why things which were different at the beginning became what they are, and why it could not be otherwise.'[138] For Lévi-Strauss, then, mythical thought and myth are under 'the influence of a twofold determinism':

Each version of the myth then, shows the influence of a twofold determinism: one strand links it to a succession of previous versions or to a set of foreign versions, while the other operates as it were transversally, through the constraints arising from the infrastructure which

135 *The Origin of Table Manners*, p. 228; original emphasis. This statement is opposed to his declaration in the 'Overture' to *The Raw and the Cooked* (p. 10): 'Mythology has no obvious practical function ..'

136 *The Naked Man*, p. 629.

137 'The Structural Study of Myth', p. 224. See also, p. 229: 'the purpose of myth is to provide a logical model capable of overcoming a contradiction (an impossible achievement if as it happens, the contradiction is real).'

138 Lévi-Strauss and Eribon, *Conversations with Claude Lévi-Strauss*, p. 140.

necessitate the modification of some particular element, with the result that the system undergoes reorganization in order to adapt these differences to necessities of an external kind.[139]

Let us try to clarify the nature of these two determinisms and show how they are articulated, in the absence of any mechanical correlation between mythical representations and social structures that might be expressed through the same polar opposites: for were this the case, in patrilineal societies the sky should be masculine and the earth feminine, and vice versa in matrilineal societies.[140]

Explaining the origin of things is not the only function of myths. The other, as Lévi-Strauss points out on several occasions, is to legitimize or conceal the real and insurmountable contradictions societies face, due to the ecological contexts in which they live or the conflicts of interest that develop within them (for instance between nobles and commoners, who are not allowed to intermarry, as among the Sahaptin).[141]

Myth does not resolve these problems, but it does give them meaning by explaining them with the help of various codes that transform them, at the end of a series of equivalences and permutations, into a problem that, if not soluble, is at least one that has been explained. We read in his dialogue with Eribon:

> LÉVI-STRAUSS: [A myth] will attempt to show that [the] problem is formally analogous to other problems that men raise concerning heavenly bodies, the alternation of day and night, the succession of seasons, social organization, political relations among neighbouring groups . . .
>
> DIDIER ERIBON: It's explanation by means of successive problems.
>
> LÉVI-STRAUSS: Without ever solving any of them. It is the similarity among all these problems that gives the impression that they can be solved, since one becomes aware that the difficulty perceived in one case isn't a difficulty at all in the others.[142]

---

139 *The Naked Man*, pp. 628–9.
140 *The Raw and the Cooked*, p. 332.
141 *The Naked Man*, p. 282, M610.
142 Lévi-Strauss and Eribon, *Conversations with Claude Lévi-Strauss*, p. 140.

What are the social relations that raised such problems for the Amerindians? Paradoxically, the problems that might be posed by the exercise of power in strongly ranked societies (forms of political-religious hierarchy) are absent in the 2,000 myths reviewed in the Mythology series, with the exception of allusions in *The Naked Man* to chiefdoms among the Klamath, Modoc and Salish Indians.[143] The reason for this, according to Lévi-Strauss, is as follows:

> I have deliberately avoided using the myths of the advanced civilizations of Central America and Mexico because, having been reformulated by educated speakers, they call for prolonged syntagmatic analyses before they can be used as paradigms.[144]

Another example is the mythology of the Navajo, the Pueblo and the Zuni, which has been excluded for the same reason – although the material was available, and did not constitute either the remains of a civilization that had disappeared with the arrival of the Europeans,[145] or fragments of the great pre-Columbian civilizations that had been systematically destroyed by Christian priests and pastors intent on eradicating idol worship, no matter how violently.

> The mythology of the Navajo, Athapaskan Indians who moved down from the north less than ten centuries ago, is a vast body of material that I do not intend to broach, not only because of its abundance and complexity, but also because successive generations of native thinkers have given *it a theological and liturgical elaboration* which would compel the analyst to adopt a different approach.[146]

In what way would the elaboration of myths by native thinkers, in a theological (pantheonic) and liturgical (ritualistic) form alter the conditions in which the structural analysis of the myths would be carried out? We will not get an explanation. How can we try to interpret this, and with what consequences? I will return to this matter later.

---

143 *The Naked Man*, pp. 20–1, 358.
144 *The Raw and the Cooked*, p. 176, n. 18.
145 *From Honey to Ashes*, p. 271; *The Origin of Table Manners*, p. 178.
146 *The Naked Man*, p. 530; my emphasis.

If the political-religious relations characteristic of Amerindian societies are rarely to be found in the myths selected by Lévi-Strauss, and
benefit from little commentary (other than his reference to the 'political
relationship of the men's domination of the women'[147]), kinship relations
are very present, and what Lévi-Strauss calls the 'techno-economic
infrastructure' of societies even more so.

In effect, the myths are inverted when going from the matrilineal
Bororo or Apinaye to the patrilineal, patrilocal Sherente. In the key-myth
(M1), the Bird-Nester's father is an affine for his son, since the Bororo
are matrilineal, and the Bird-Nester's rape of his mother is therefore a
particularly vile crime, as we saw. But in myths, problems of descent are
less present than problems of alliance. Who to marry? We find marriage
close to home, marriage far away, marriage rejected, marriage accepted,
endogamy, exogamy, exchange of women, relations between wife-givers
and wife-takers, behaviour toward wife's brothers, toward wife's parents.
The Girl Mad about Honey is simultaneously a bad wife and a bad
daughter: she takes for herself the honey her husband had harvested and
which he was supposed to give to his wife's parents. Even more present
are the problems posed by incest, especially between brother and sister.
It was when she wanted to find out who had been visiting her nightly
that a woman made a black mark on the visitor's face, and discovered
the next day that it was her brother. The brother was so ashamed that he
fled up into the sky where he changed into Moon. The desire for an
incestuous relation is also at the origin of the eclipses of the moon. In
other myths, a lewd grandmother takes her grandson as a lover, etc.

But the social relations with which Amerindian myths correlate most
closely, according to Lévi-Strauss, are those that constitute the techno-
economic infrastructure of the societies from which they originate. The
term 'infrastructure' is, as we know, borrowed from Marx.

For Marx, the economic infrastructure of a society combines two
kinds of social and material relations. On the one hand, the intellectual
and material relations involved in carrying out various activities required
to produce the material conditions of a collective form of social existence.

---

147 *The Origin of Table Manners*, p. 221: 'the veil lifts to reveal a vast mythological
system common to both South and North America, and in which the subjection of
women is the basis of the social order.' Likewise, *The Elementary Structures of Kinship*,
p. 117: 'political authority, or simply social authority, always belongs to men'. See also
*From Honey to Ashes*, pp. 285–6.

These may be hunting, fishing, gathering, farming, various types of craft, and so on. Such activities entail familiarity with the natural environment, the manufacture of tools, the knowledge and skills needed to use them effectively, etc. The set of relations among people combining immaterial and material components necessary for acting on nature corresponds to what Lévi-Strauss calls the techno-economic infrastructure of a society.

But another set of relations is missing. For Marx, these relations combine with those I have just described and constitute the strategic component of the economic infrastructure of a society: they are relations of production. These are the social relations that determine the rights of the groups or individuals that make up a society to control, exploit or cause to exploit, for their own benefit, the elements of nature that are necessary for their existence and their social reproduction. Relations of production can be a component of what we call kinship relations or religious relations, or they can exist in some other form. At all events, these relations determine why and how the product of the economic activities of the members of a society will be distributed. Yet this type of ethnographic material is lacking in the myths summarized by Lévi-Strauss, if we except the material on the market economy developed in the American Northwest, among the Chinook for instance, in which a wide variety of goods was exchanged, from slaves to subsistence goods to valuables. But even in this case, the information selected by Lévi-Strauss remains laconic.

Alternatively, as soon as it comes to describing the ways of the animal characters in the myths, Lévi-Strauss's descriptions are exceptionally rich and precise. We discover the habits and habitat of over 125 animal species, from the harpy eagle to the spider, from the jaguar to the skate, the bee or the earthworm. The economic life-cycle in the Chaco, too, is meticulously reconstructed. Sky maps tell us the place of the constellations and the stars, and their seasonal appearances. For purposes of comparison, we are even given a map of the sky over Athens in 1000 BCE, courtesy of the astronomer Jean-Claude Pecker, which represents the path of Orion in the Old World compared with that of the Corvus constellation in the New.[148] The techniques of fishing with poison (Timbo) or embroidery with porcupine quills are minutely described, as is the nature of the sounds and calls that appear in the myths – whistled

---

148 *The Raw and the Cooked*, p. 236.

calls, knocking calls, warbling calls. All this enabled Lévi-Strauss to conduct an original reconstruction of the musical organology of the Indians of the Amazon. I will stop here, though, for I simply wished to give a few examples of the correlations Lévi-Strauss had uncovered between certain myths and the techno-economic infrastructures of the societies from which they originated.

In *The Naked Man*, after conducting a detailed analysis of the symmetrical but inverted functions the Bird-Nester myth performs in a group of tribes, Lévi-Strauss concludes:

> We thus arrive at a comprehensive picture of the symmetrical values and functions – each of them linked with the empirical substructure – embodied in the Bird-Nester story in the mythology of the Klamath and the Modoc on the one hand, and in that of the Coast Salish and Sahaptin on the other.[149]

And again:

> In short, the transformation which causes the ideological superstructure to change as we move from the Brazilian plateau to the Guiana-Amazonia area – centring in the latter on the canoe and fishing and in the former on cooking fire and cultivated plants – corresponds all the more closely to the differential characteristics of the infrastructure, in that fishing or agriculture are the technical activities most rigidly subject to seasonal periodicity.[150]

In addition, the relationship between a given technique, such as cooking in an earth oven, and a given ideology can be so tight that altogether similar myths are present in societies using that technique but living thousands of kilometres apart.

> Of all culinary techniques, cooking in the earth oven would appear, then, to be the one which reveals most meaningfully a close and formal homology between infrastructure and ideology.[151]

---

149  *The Naked Man*, p. 352.
150  *The Origin of Table Manners*, p. 182.
151  *The Naked Man*, p. 623.

And further on:

> If we bear in mind that, in the case of South America the Ge myths, and
> in the case of North America the Salish myths, have, as it were, formed
> the backbone of the argument developed in this study [presented in the
> four volumes of the Mythology series], we can attach even greater
> importance to the presence in the two communities of the earth oven,
> associated in both cases with very similar ideological patterns.[152]

Finally, when Lévi-Strauss comes to the myths of the Indians of the
Northwest American coast, where local and international trade fairs
were linked to a market economy, the opposition is no longer between
the raw and the cooked, but between the naked and the clothed:

> The existence of a market economy leads to a transformation on the
> level of the superstructures. Instead of the transition from nature to
> culture being expressed by means of a straightforward opposition
> between the categories of the *raw* and the *cooked*, it resorts to a more
> complex ideology which expresses the relevant opposition in terms of
> contrasting maxims: every man for himself and give and take.[153]

As Marx would say, the techno-economic infrastructure of societies,
in Lévi-Strauss's sense, is constituted by the combination of the
productive forces (intellectual, material and social together) engaged
in the production of the material means of social existence of the
groups and individuals that make up a society, and the ecological
context in which these activities are carried out,[154] and which places on
them specific objective constraints. Of course, the knowledge of the
natural environment amassed by Amerindian societies is far broader
than what was directly useful to their productive activities, which
explains the presence in the myths of multiple explanations of the
origin of the Pleiades, Orion's shield, Berenice's hair or the colour of
the plumage of the different birds, their songs, etc. The Indians' science

---

152  Ibid., p. 612.
153  Ibid., p. 284.
154  Cf. Lévi-Strauss, 'Structuralism and Ecology', Gildersleeve Lecture, Barnard
College, New York, 1972; reprinted in *The View from Afar*, trans. J. Neugroschel and P.
Hoss (Chicago, University of Chicago Press, 1985), pp. 101–20.

of the concrete is always part of a global vision – imaginary to be sure – of their natural environment, which surpasses and contains their concrete experience of the world and of humans and its own utilitarian deals.

Yet, in a number of key societies along the Bird-Nester's trail, Lévi-Strauss has marshalled numerous details to show that the central myths are those that explain the diversity and richness of rituals and religious ceremonies, and adhere to the essential contours of the social and political organization of these societies. These more detailed sociological descriptions concern the Bororo, the Ge, particularly the Sherente and their Great Fast ritual, the Warao and the Tacana in South America; the Mandan,[155] the Hidatsa and the Pawnee for the Plains Indians of North America; the Klamath, the Modoc, the Salish in general and the Sahaptin in particular for the West Coast – in sum, fewer than twenty of the 348 societies mentioned in the four volumes of the Mythology series. Lévi-Strauss could obviously not have described, or even outlined, the social organization of 348 societies. It would have been impossible, and the extreme disparity and unevenness of the information concerning these societies would have been enough to discourage even an attempt. But Lévi-Strauss had other reasons for not proceeding. Not only 'the task of constructing the total system [of the Plains Indians] would be enormous,'[156] but their myths are not explained by the social characteristics and infrastructure of the society they were collected in, since these myths also belong to cycles that go beyond the borders of these societies.

An anthropologist may confine himself for one or more years within a small social unit, group or village, and endeavour to grasp it as a totality, but this is no reason for imagining that the unit, at levels other than the one at which convenience or necessity has placed him,

---

155 Despite his detailed analysis of the rituals and social structures of the Mandan, based on A. W. Bowers's monographic study, Lévi-Strauss emphasizes that his analysis 'is not complete ... Mandan mythology is virtually inexhaustible in its richness and complexity. Here I can do no more than scratch the surface' (*The Origin of Table Manners*, p. 452, n. 1). He would say the same thing about the mythology of the Navajo, the Zuni, etc. See A. W. Bowers, *Mandan Social and Ceremonial Organization* (Chicago, University of Chicago Press, 1950).

156 *The Origin of Table Manners*, p. 312.

does not merge in varying degrees into larger entities, the existence of which remains, more often than not, unsuspected.[157]

It is at these levels where, 'in varying degrees', the singularity, the specificity of local societies and the originality of their myths and institutions dissolve, that Lévi-Strauss places himself; the structural analysis of the myths allows this – and, more importantly, requires it. For if a myth has no meaning taken alone but only by opposition to other myths, or it resembles them but inverts the message, it is the reconstruction of this group of myths that reveals the latent meaning of each of them once the analyst has teased out the logical armature and the semantic functions. That is what Lévi-Strauss did in his articles published in 1971 (the same year as *The Naked Man*): 'How Myths Die'[158] and 'Relations of Symmetry between Rituals and Myths of Neighbouring Peoples'.[159] And he would proceed in the same way in *The Way of the Masks*.

But the level at which Lévi-Strauss placed himself to conduct a structural analysis of the myths meant that he could never account for the totality of the mythico-religious representations that make up the cultural universe of a given society. The Mythology series opens on a Bororo myth, which turns out to be the inverse of some Ge myths, which in turn are the opposite of some Tupi myths, and so on, before coming back to the Bororo, having 'hooked' other myths referring to other societies. Lévi-Strauss thus never conducts an exhaustive analysis of the mythical representations of a particular society.[160] He selects certain myths in several societies that appear to belong to the same transformation group, but he leaves aside, without benefit of analysis, the configuration of the entire set of myths a society tells itself. What his references to the infrastructure, kinship system or other aspects of the social organization of societies will, if not explain, at least shed light on are the variants of a local myth or a group of myths; but not the schemata that generated them, which can be

---

157 *The Naked Man*, p. 609. This text is a critique of 'the illusion gratuitously created by the functionalists', Anglo-Saxon and others, who consider societies to be monads, totalities closed upon themselves.

158 C. Lévi-Strauss, 'How Myths Die', *Structural Anthropology, volume 2*, pp. 256–87.

159 C. Lévi-Strauss, 'Relations of Symmetry between Rituals and Myths of Neighbouring Peoples', *Structural Anthropology, volume 2*, pp. 238–55.

160 *The Naked Man*, p. 500: 'the mass of material is so great that a truly exhaustive study of North American mythology would require a whole lifetime, if not several.'

found in various forms in societies that have never been in historical or geographical contact with each other.

And this brings us to the central problem of the role and extent of unconscious and conscious thought processes in the creation of myths. As we have seen, Lévi-Strauss eliminates from his corpus all myths that have been consciously elaborated, developed or shaped into theologies and liturgies by priestly or scholarly élites. These include the versions of the myths that provide intellectual justifications for the complex pantheons characteristic of the polytheistic religions of numerous Indian societies. And yet the Jaguar was just as much a part of Inca as of tribal Amazonian mythology, but with a different meaning: here he was associated with the Inca ruler, the son of the Sun, who reigned over a multi-ethnic empire, a form of sovereignty that did not exist in central Amazonia.

To explain the differences between the myths from these nearby societies, Lévi-Strauss advanced two interrelated causes, *sociological* reasons that he saw as having an *unconscious* effect on the societies, leading them to formulate different versions of the same myths in order to distinguish themselves from each other while remaining connected. That would show that

> communities living in close proximity to each other need to feel that they are at once similar and different. Reflection, inversion and symmetry, as they occur in the myths, bear witness to an unconscious effort to overcome contradictory urges: on the one hand, those resulting from territorial nearness and the political and economic advantages inherent in collaboration; and, on the other, parochialism and the need for a collective identity . . . the twofold necessity to reconcile and contrast what one knows of the other, and what one believes to be peculiar to oneself.[161]

It would thus be for social reasons, but through unconscious workings of the mind, that the transformations generating the different states of a single myth would come about. And this work of generation is one of both 'imitation and distortion'.[162] The widespread sociological need to differentiate oneself would thus add to the constraints imposed by the

---

161  Ibid., pp. 311–12.
162  Ibid., p. 141.

infrastructure of each society to explain the differential gaps between variants of a same myth. But something of the myth must already be shared before it can be subjected to 'a succession of distortions which preserve the unity of the group, while at the same time allowing each variant to retain its original and specific character'.[163] While it is entirely conceivable that the sociological reasons for generating different versions of a same myth may not be conscious, it is hard to think that the process takes place entirely unbeknownst to the members of these societies, or at least to those who know the myths and recount them in the appropriate contexts. Yet, Lévi-Strauss tells us, 'even if the ancestors of present-day story-tellers imagined they were inventing it, or had obtained it through some mystic revelation, the new version had to respect the already existing constraints.'[164]

In point of fact, any new version would 'allow certain possibilities inherent in the system to be brought into actual existence'.[165] The individuals and societies would only be actualizing the possibilities contained in the schemata of the myths they share, usually unwittingly, with other societies. This view would eliminate the role of those individuals capable of formulating or reformulating imaginary explanations of the world and the events that occur there. It would no longer be men who invent myths to explain the world to themselves, but 'myths operat[ing] in men's minds without their being aware of the fact ... And ... it would perhaps be better to go still further and ... proceed as if the thinking process were taking place in the myths and in their reflection upon themselves and their interrelation.'[166]

Lévi-Strauss's formulas are superb and provocative, but they, literally, make no sense. Myths are thought expressed in different languages, but they are not thinking subjects. They can neither operate 'in men's minds' nor reflect upon themselves. A physicist may as well say that the waves and particles that make up light are operating in his mind and reflecting upon themselves there.

It is therefore reasonable to posit that it is indeed men, and not gods, who invent myths. But not all men invent them. Only some do: those who

---

163  Ibid.
164  *The Origin of Table Manners*, p. 272.
165  Ibid.
166  *The Raw and the Cooked*, p. 12.

seek to explain to themselves and to others why the world and society are the way they are, and what needs to be done so that things may be reproduced for the benefit of humans. These explanations take the form and content of myths when the causes and events they imagine deny or contradict the limits with which men are confronted in the concrete experience they have of themselves and of the world around them.

As soon as it crosses these boundaries, the mind sets about constructing representations of one or several worlds in which things happen differently, or contrary to what happens in the visible world, while seeming to underlie the visible world. The mind constructs these representations by means of a counter-intuitive reasoning that proceeds according to a logic of analogy, whose existence and mechanisms Lévi-Strauss demonstrated and unravelled. And it is because these representations run counter to intuition that mythical speech appears as a series of revelations, which in turn appear as truths that their hearers believe and experience as true. Lévi-Strauss identified and described this mechanism as the passage from empirical to transcendental deductions and their combination, performed by the mind through a series of imaginary and symbolic equivalences and twists between various aspects of man and nature.

Yet, if mythical discourse is to be received as a vehicle of revealed truths, attesting to worlds that are usually invisible to the average person, it is vital that those who imagine and recount them not be perceived as their authors. Failing that, the myth would be received as a story or a fable, a secular discourse. For myths to fulfil their functions, their human authors must disappear and be replaced by gods or imaginary ancestors who, in the olden days, had the power to communicate directly with the gods. Today only shamans and priests preserve this power.

Nothing makes this process by which man absents himself from what he has produced over the course of his history more visible than the myths explaining the origin of cultivated plants and agriculture. According to the Tembe people, of the Tupi group, it was a demiurge, Maira, who showed a man who had spoken courteously to her how to plant manioc.[167] And it was Old-Woman-Who-Never-Dies, a goddess associated with the moon, who, according to a Mandan myth,[168] made

---

167  *From Honey to Ashes*, p. 312.
168  *The Origin of Table Manners*, p. 292.

men the gift of maize. In short, the complex processes involved in the domestication of plants and animals, which are the basis of agriculture and stock-breeding and which suppose a long history of observation, experimentation and error, and therefore time invested by the human groups that were at their origin, are erased and replaced by representations of gifts made to humanity by the gods or by beneficent spirits.

But in order for myths to be received as truths and to travel beyond their society of origin, the schemata they employ to explain certain aspects of the universe or the society must have meaning for those who did not make them but who heard them for the first time and repeated them in turn (if they had the right). The schema of Sun and Moon's canoe journey must allow listeners to think the rules of a proper marriage, neither too close to home (to avoid incest), nor too far away (with strangers or non-human beings). For the myths featuring a similar hero to be found from central Amazonia to the northwest coast of America, the schema of the Bird-Nester – victim of someone who, by magical means, causes the tree or the rock on which the Bird-Nester has climbed to rise higher and higher so that he cannot get down without the help of supernatural creatures – must evoke the conquest of celestial fire and its transformation into domestic fire. Here is evidence that the Amerindians share a cultural world based on the same foundations over and above differences of language, way of life and natural environment. But these schemata are not found in Sumero-Babylonian mythology, or in the tri-functional ideology of the Indo-European peoples. How are the schemata that will be shared over centuries by such different societies formed? This is a difficult question to answer.

But, whether we are dealing with a tribesman who invents a myth or with schools of Brahmins commenting revelations found in the Vedic texts and putting them into theological and liturgical form, the process is the same: in both cases, man disappears into his work, and the gods or other imaginary entities take his place, subsequently commanding worship.

In excluding the myths and rituals of the great pre-Columbian civilizations but also those of the great chiefdoms of South and North America, Lévi-Strauss passed over the complex pantheons of the polytheistic religions that had developed over the thousands of years of the Neolithic era, following the appearance and dissemination of various forms of agriculture and stock-breeding. These new ways of life would bring men increasingly to depend on natural entities (plants and animals), which in turn depended on man for their existence, but did not depend only on man for their reproduction. This double bind introduced new threats and risks with which humans who made their livelihood from hunting, fishing and gathering had not been acquainted. To ward off such threats, men invoked the increasingly numerous ranks of gods. These numbers and hierarchies are clearly illustrated by the pantheons and cultures of the Plains Indians, but also those of the Pueblo, the Zuni and the Hopi. To be sure, in certain village societies, like the Mandan and the Hidatsa, buffalo hunting remained central to their religious ideology. Elsewhere it was ritual eagle hunting that occupied this place. But on the whole, reading the Mythology series, we are left with the impression that Lévi-Strauss presents Amerindian myths as the product of the human mind in its 'savage' state, in touch with a still largely undomesticated nature, whereas today we know that the multiplication of the buffalo, which 'blackened' the plains of North America, was the result of the disappearance, after the arrival of European settlers, of hundreds of Indian villages and groups that had practiced agriculture and carefully managed the wild herds. And we also know that the immense Amazonian forest, once a symbol of pristine nature, was partly the work of humans.

Finally, having shown that the same schemata are found thousands of kilometres apart and attest to the existence of a shared cultural world, Lévi-Strauss describes how mythical thought and myths themselves resist in the face of the disappearance or transformation of their original meaning.[169] Given that each Indian community 'had its own independent and extremely complicated history' (migrations, displacements following war or epidemics, etc.), 'it constantly tried to neutralize [those dramatic events] by reshaping the myths, in so far as this was compatible with the constraints of the traditional moulds into which they always had to fit.'[170]

[The groups that] peopled North and South America in successive migratory waves, moving along the coasts or inland, through rain forests or deserts, over the plains or into the mountains, struggled, consciously or unconsciously, to ensure that the essential elements of

---

169  *The Raw and the Cooked*, p. 245.
170  *The Naked Man*, p. 610.

their system should be neither lost nor scattered . . . to allow the re-establishment of the invariant relationship with entirely new forms of animal and vegetable life, a different distribution of fauna and flora, and the new exploitation of animals and plants made possible by techniques and lifestyles that were also in process of change.[171]

Myths and mythical thought thus function as 'machines for abolishing time', for neutralizing history. That is possible for at least two reasons: because the need to believe that the impossible is possible never goes away, and because the symbols that translate these imaginary processes can take on new meanings, which no longer have anything to do with those they expressed at other times and in other contexts. The Sun–Moon pair, whether they are twin brothers, husband and wife or simply rivals, can signify, if not just anything, at least a great number of very different oppositions.[172] What today's Christianity means is very different from what it meant for the early Church Fathers, even though the idea of a God who died on the cross to redeem men's sins and promises a life of bliss after death is an invariant of this religion and its symbolic strength, the source of its continual appeal for millions of people. Lévi-Strauss's final vision of the capacity of mythological systems to resist the transformations imposed by history proposes

a mythology which may be causally linked to history in each of its parts, but which, taken in its entirety, resists the course of history and constantly readjusts its own mythological grid so that this grid offers the least resistance to the flow of events which, as experience proves, is rarely strong enough to break it up and sweep it away.[173]

Unfortunately, insofar as the mythology and religions of the Amerindians or the peoples of Oceania are concerned, Western domination and Christianity have been strong enough to 'break them

---

171 Ibid., p. 560.

172 *The Origin of Table Manners*, p. 195: 'Provided we stand far enough back, a mythical field which appeared extraordinarily rich and complex when subjected to a close and detailed study will, seen from a distance, seem completely empty: the opposition between the sun and the moon, provided it remains an opposition, can take on any meaning.'

173 *The Naked Man*, p. 610.

up' and sweep away their resistance (and today the same is true of Africa, with the rise and expansion of Islam). But the quasi-total disappearance of the ancient religions of the Americas was not the product of a theological debate. It was the consequence of European conquerors' systematic destruction of tribal organizations and pre-Columbian states and empires built on political-religious hierarchies. It was the outcome, too, of the dogged efforts of priests, monks and pastors to wipe out, often with the utmost violence, all traces of 'idol worship' among the Indians. And we can only agree with Lévi-Strauss when he writes in the Preface to *The Story of Lynx*, concerning the upcoming celebration of the 500th anniversary of the discovery of America (1492): 'rather than the discovery – I would call [it] the invasion of the New World, the destruction of its peoples and its values.'[174] It was this thought that made him regard his work on Amerindian mythology as 'an act of contrition and devotion'.[175] Yet once again, I repeat that I do not share Lévi-Strauss's conception of a history that 'belongs to the irreducible contingency', a domain governed by 'the powerful inanity of events'.[176] If it is true that, at the end of the Paleolithic era and during the eight or ten thousand years of the Neolithic, hundreds of human groups set about selecting and domesticating plant and animal species for their own use, and progressively abandoned hunting and gathering, these changes, which spread throughout the Old World first and later appeared in the New, can by no means be purely accidental. The fact that these transformations were more successful in some places than in others, that city-states appeared, together with kingdoms and empires, cannot have been the outcome of a purely contingent sequence of events. Falling off a horse that rears at the sight of a snake is a matter of pure contingency, but constructing temples, cities, palaces, fortresses, markets and fairs is not.

To assert the foregoing does not assume that these historical transformations all went in the same direction and were irreversible. The extinction of the great Mohenjo-daro and Harappan civilization, which stretched to northwest India, is a prime example. Many important political structures – states, empires – have disappeared, often to be replaced by others. Which means that in those times, the causes or forces that

---

174  *The Story of Lynx*, p. xvii.
175  Ibid., p. xvii.
176  *From Honey to Ashes*, p. 475.

drove the creation of states and empires continued to be active in the local populations. Lévi-Strauss was not unaware of these facts, and yet he chose to ignore – with some exceptions – the material contained in the myths and religions of the pre-Columbian states and empires,[177] as well as the data from the pantheons of the North and South American 'chiefdoms'. This task should therefore be revisited since, for instance, thanks to the deciphering of Mayan writing, we now know much more about the Mayan gods and their relations with the forms of power and social hierarchy prevailing in their city-states.

But elsewhere, for example regarding the ancient Indo-European-speaking peoples, analysis of the myths and religions of these societies already having castes or orders and classes was underway well before Lévi-Strauss tackled the Amerindian myths.[178] Georges Dumézil had already shown, using texts from the Vedic period which saw, it seems, the crystallization and expansion of castes in North India,[179] the existence of a structured Indian pantheon that ranked the highest gods according to the functions they performed. These functions were three in number: sovereignty, physical might and provision of sustenance. He had found this tri-functional ideology again in the pantheon of certain Indo-European societies, from the gods of Scandinavia to those of the Mahabharata.

---

177 Lévi-Strauss and Eribon, *Conversations with Claude Lévi-Strauss*, p. 56: 'America offers the stupefying spectacle of very high cultures next to those of very low technical and economic levels. Furthermore, these high cultures knew only an ephemeral existence: each one was born, developed, and perished during the period of a few centuries. And the cultures that had disappeared before the arrival of the Spaniards were probably more learned and refined than the ones in their decline that the Spaniards saw – and that still astonished them.'

178 Lévi-Strauss had privileged what he called 'cold' societies, those presenting little differentiation between their component groups (with the exception of gender relations), as opposed to 'hot' societies, which appeared in various parts of the world in the wake of the Neolithic revolution, where caste and class differentiations were relentlessly exploited to extract development and energy ('The Scope of Anthropology', *Structural Anthropology, volume 2*, pp. 3–32. First published as *Chaire d'Anthropologie sociale: Leçon inaugurale faite le mardi 5 janvier 1960 par M. Claude Lévi-Strauss, Professeur* (Paris, Collège de France, 1960).

179 In 1952, Lévi-Strauss wrote: 'We can wonder if this *internal diversification* does not tend to increase when the society becomes, in other ways, larger and more homogeneous. Such was perhaps the case of ancient India, with its system of castes which flourished after the establishment of the Aryan hegemony' ('Race and History', *Structural Anthropology, volume 2*, pp. 323–62; p. 327).

In addition, in his remarkable work, *Loki* (1948), Dumézil had shown that the deity known in Scandinavia as Loki was the same as Syrdon in the mythology of the Ossetes, a Caucasian people descended from the Scythians and the Alani, and described in Antiquity by Herodotus. With his comparison of such diverse sociological and historical contexts, Dumézil had thus already demonstrated that mythical accounts were structured by certain invariant relationships. He had, as it were, brought to light a number of Indo-European 'mythemes' (variants of the same character – Loki, Syrdon, etc.) and schemata that generated the discourse of myths and epic poems (the schema of the three functions defining the powers of the gods). It was therefore not by chance that Lévi-Strauss cited Dumézil on several occasions as the predecessor par excellence, to whom he was heavily indebted.

After Georges Dumézil, Jean-Pierre Vernant, explicitly espousing Lévi-Strauss's structural method, would analyse the transformations of the Greek myths and religions that were tied to the formation of the city-state, the polis, and the emergence of a power shared by all citizens (*Homoioi*), who were equal before the law (*Nomos*). In Athens, citizenship was restricted to free males born in Athens of Athenian parents. They alone had the right to enter the temples of the City and worship its gods, to own land and to bear arms. Metics, freemen but citizens of other polises, did not have these rights but did enjoy certain privileges. The bulk of the population, made up of slaves of different origins, lived 'outside' society, while being indispensable to the existence and life of the polis.

In reality, Lévi-Strauss always assigned a special status to the smaller, casteless and classless societies that are 'to a far greater degree than the others, based on personal relationships, on concrete relations between individuals'.[180] In these cases, he writes, we are dealing 'with those forms of social life – of which the so-called primitive societies are merely the most readily identifiable and most developed examples – whose degree of *authenticity* is estimated according to the scope and variety of the concrete relations between individuals'.[181] Simultaneously we find 'a more modern form of existence, from which the first-named type is not

---

180  C. Lévi-Strauss, 'The Place of Anthropology in the Social Sciences and Problems Raised in Teaching It', in *Structural Anthropology*, pp. 346–81; p. 365.

181  Ibid., p. 369; my emphasis.

absent but where groups that are not completely, or are imperfectly, "authentic" are organized within a much larger and specifically "unauthentic" system.'[182] And again: '*Unauthenticity* has become typical of the relationship between the citizen and the public authorities.'[183] He would reiterate these positions nearly word for word thirty years later, in a lecture delivered in Japan in 1986.[184] And again in an interview on 26 June 2000, in which he explained why he had distanced himself from Rousseau in favour of Montesquieu, and the importance of intermediate bodies between individuals and the state:

> What subsequently led me to distance myself from Rousseau was his political philosophy, the version claimed by the Revolution and which had atomized, as it were, the individual with respect to the sovereign, in other words the collectivity. Furthermore, I was aware of the importance, for a well-balanced society – which placed me more in the tradition of Montesquieu than in that of Rousseau – of the existence of intermediate bodies that provided a series of screens, of buffers, between the public authorities and individuals.[185]

Reading these lines, I get the feeling that Lévi-Strauss was absolutely convinced that humanity's entrance into increasingly less 'authentic' forms of social life had begun with the birth of agriculture and stock-breeding, the demographic growth of the societies spawned by these new relations with the natural environment, and the invention of writing.[186] In 1986, addressing a Japanese audience, Lévi-Strauss returned to these themes, with the statement that those peoples 'called "primitive" . . . [who] live primarily on hunting, fishing, and the gathering of wild plants, do not have a gnawing fear of starving to death or anxiety

---

182  Ibid., p 367.

183  Ibid., p. 366; my emphasis.

184  C. Lévi-Strauss, *Anthropology Confronts the Problems of the Modern World*, foreword M. Olender, trans. J. M. Todd (Cambridge, MA and London, The Belknap Press of Harvard University Press, 2013), pp. 41–2.

185  M. Massenzio, ed., *Claude Lévi-Strauss. Un itinéraire* (Paris, L'Échoppe, 2000), pp. 31–2.

186  'The Place of Anthropology', *Structural Anthropology*, p. 366: 'It is essential to realize that writing, while it conferred vast benefits on humanity, did in fact *deprive it of something fundamental*' (my emphasis). This thesis reappears the following year, in 1955, in *Tristes Tropiques*, chapter XXVIII .

about being unable to survive in a hostile environment'. And that is because, he said,

> they enjoy vis-à-vis the environment a much greater independence (owing to their small population and their prodigious knowledge of the natural resources) than farmers and stock breeders. They have more leisure time, which allows them to make a large place for the imagination, to insert between themselves and the external world, as shock absorbers, beliefs, reveries, rites, in a word, all the forms of activity we would call religious and artistic.[187]

And he goes on to warn us that the whole of humankind is now confronted with a grave problem:

> the end of a world that human beings had lived in for hundreds of millennia, perhaps a million or two million years. At that time, they lived in groups long separated from one another [by geographical distance and by linguistic and cultural barriers], each of which had evolved differently at both the biological and cultural level.[188]

This vision of 'primitive' ('archaic', 'traditional') societies seems to me somewhat prettified. Anyone who has spent several years in a tribal society without castes or classes, with a small population whose hunting grounds and agricultural lands are collectively owned, so that the right to exploit these resources is not based on labour; where conflicts frequently flare between individuals or lineages and can lead to murder or expulsion from the group, and where relations with neighbouring tribes alternate between hostility and friendship, will find it hard to award these societies high marks for authenticity.

To argue that this way of life, which allegedly gives individuals more time for dreaming, for rituals and for art than more complex or hierarchical societies, has existed for hundreds of thousands of years (or a couple of million) also seems somewhat 'literary'. Several hundreds of thousands of years would take us back to the appearance of *Homo erectus* (between 700,000 and a million years BCE), in other words to

---

187  *Anthropology Confronts the Problems of the Modern World*, p. 39.
188  Ibid., p. 120.

the time when pre-hominids had not yet, it seems, domesticated fire and were still eating their food raw, in other words, well before Neanderthal man (-300,000) and *Homo sapiens sapiens* (150,000–120,000 BCE). Looking back two million years, we see various pre-hominid species about whose social life and ways of thinking we know nothing. Lévi-Strauss's formulae are thus more attractive than convincing, more visionary than scientific, but they correspond deeply to what he had always thought about the origin and antiquity of myths and customs.

> It cannot, of course, be postulated – neither on the other hand can the possibility be ruled out – that certain myths about the origin of the constellations or subsequently associated with them, came into being during the late Paleolithic or even before; if they did, they could have been carried by waves of immigrants from Asia to America, just as different population shifts, spreading in the opposite direction, would explain why these same myths were disseminated westward as far as the Mediterranean basin.[189]

Finally, by harnessing the power of the structural method to reconstruct the hidden meaning of thousands of Amerindian myths and by discovering the nature of the universal mental operations he believed had generated them, Lévi-Strauss was probably the first to hear and understand 'the great anonymous voice whose utterance comes from the beginning of time and the depths of the mind'.[190] And the first to assert that he had established a dialogue that was richer in meaning than those of previous philosophers, a dialogue 'which has no need of them and to which they have nothing to contribute'.[191] With this, he had evicted the philosophers and sent them back to their tête-à-têtes, to their fascination with the self and to the 'ideological Café du Commerce'.[192]

And yet, once he had identified the myths whose schemata could be found in both the Old and New Worlds, Lévi-Strauss found himself

---

189 *The Naked Man*, pp. 232–3.

190 Ibid., p. 640. The same formula appears in *The Jealous Potter* (p. 206): 'With an authority that cannot be denied, it arises from the depths of time, setting before us a magnifying mirror that reflects, in the massive form of concrete images, certain mechanisms by which the exercise of thought is ruled.'

191 *The Naked Man*, p. 640.

192 Ibid., p. 640.

before a thorny theoretical dilemma. Either the myths were found in both worlds because they had been invented in the Paleolithic era and then transported and spread by human groups migrating in various directions (the favoured hypothesis to explain the diffusion of the tri-functional ideology among Indo-European peoples); or, since the human mind is everywhere the same, faced with analogous material or situations certain human groups made comparable empirical and transcendental deductions. This was the hypothesis of a universal mythology. Lévi-Strauss rejected this possibility, because the meaning of a paradigm, of a schema, is always one of 'position': it has no specific meaning other than the one it takes when it is made to vary in the series of variants of a myth or myths in which it is present. When a schema is isolated from all its contexts, it is reduced to a purely formal abstract structure – like the relation of opposition between the Sun and the Moon – and can then be made to say anything (and its contrary). It is the analyst who, depending on their personal a priori, will 'lend' it a meaning.[193] Lévi-Strauss thus denies any scientific value to Mircea Eliade's hermeneutics, which supposed the existence of universal archetypes present in the minds of men at all periods, from the beginning of time. For Lévi-Strauss, there are to be sure several latent meanings in one myth or another, and structural analysis even claims to be able to uncover these; but there is no hidden meaning behind a hidden meaning behind a hidden meaning, and so on. The 'anagrammatic capacity'[194] of the myths – a notion introduced by Saussure and taken up in a broader sense by Lévi-Strauss – exists, but it is always finite, and its limits can always be attained and unveiled.

His criticism this time was aimed more at Ricœur[195] than at Jung.[196] From the outset, Lévi-Strauss had rejected the temptation to develop a universal mythology:

When I was investigating kinship systems and marriage rules, the literature was full of special explanations. On the contrary, the study of myths remained the object of a comparativist mania that extended

---

193  *The Story of Lynx*, p. 253.
194  *The Naked Man*, p. 650.
195  *The Raw and the Cooked*, p. 11.
196  'The Structural Study of Myth', p. 208; *The Naked Man*, p. 38; *The Raw and the Cooked*, pp. 56, 187.

to the whole world and was inspired by superficial resemblances. I
had to react in opposite ways.[197]

He would go into more detail in *The Story of Lynx*.

Of all the paths undertaken or simply possible, general mythology
can always offer a theory . . . The more the field of analysis is broad-
ened, *the more resemblances are uncovered, but they have less and less
meaning* . . . the more the field is restricted, the more differences are
uncovered. It is to the relations these differences have with one
another that meanings are attached. A comparative study of Indo-
European, American, and African myths is valid; *a mythology with
universal pretensions is not.* Structural analysis demonstrates this *a
contrario* by identifying the level on which myths do say something.
That everyone may find in myths what he or she is looking for simply
proves that nothing of the sort is actually there . . . This is precisely the
case for general mythology . . . Emptied of their content, reduced to
hollow forms, myths then receive as a substitute the content that the
philosopher thinks himself permitted or forced to introduce in
them.[198]

These are wise principles, but Lévi-Strauss did not always stick to them,
since he sometimes ventured to compare certain American myths with
myths from Japan, in particular, but also from ancient China, Polynesia
and Europe.[199] Writing about the instruments of Darkness, Lévi-Strauss
allows himself to compare a Tikuna myth (M310), which opens with a
child who cries all the time, with a Japanese myth (M511), which
recounts that one of the three sons of the god Izanagi, who had married

197  Lévi-Strauss and Eribon, *Conversations with Claude Lévi-Strauss*, pp. 130–1.
198  *The Story of Lynx*, pp. 188–90; my emphasis.
199  China: *From Honey to Ashes*, p. 462, referring to M. Granet, *Danses et légendes
de la Chine ancienne* (Paris, 1926), vol. 3, pp. 315, 334, 557. Japan: *From Honey to Ashes*,
pp. 378–81; *The Origin of Table Manners*, pp. 125, 281. Europe: *From Honey to Ashes*,
p. 465; *The Raw and the Cooked*, pp. 286, 294, 300, 327–38; *The Origin of Table Manners*,
pp. 65, 234, 440, 475, 483, 485, 486, 498. Polynesia: *The Raw and the Cooked*, pp. 230,
242, 298; *The Origin of Table Manners*, p. 396; *The Naked Man*, p. 672. Africa: *The Raw
and the Cooked*, pp. 296, 328; *The Origin of Table Manners*, pp. 495, 500, 504; *The Naked
Man*, pp. 668, 672, 674. Asia: *The Raw and the Cooked*, pp. 202, 335; *From Honey to
Ashes*, pp. 229, 378, 406–7, 413; *The Naked Man*, pp. 14, 37, 232, 674.

his sister, did nothing but cry and moan. And he apologizes, pleading 'extenuating circumstances':

> I shall not try to justify my action, and I admit that it is irreconcilable with a sound use of structural method. I will even refrain from using as an argument, in this very special case, my deep conviction that Japanese mythology and American mythology, each in its own way, are using sources which go right back to Paleolithic times and which were once the common heritage of Asiatic groups later disseminated throughout the Far East and the New World. Without putting forward any such hypothesis, which would in any case be unverifiable in the present state of knowledge, I shall merely plead extenuating circumstances: only very rarely do I allow myself this kind of digression.[200]

We will not complain that Lévi-Strauss took this liberty.

---

200 *From Honey to Ashes*, p. 378.

# 13
# The Three Steps in the Structural Analysis of Myths

I will merely summarize these three steps, since we are now in possession of an overview of the toolkit for the structural analysis of myths. But the condition for realizing this task, Lévi-Strauss tells us, is that, throughout the analysis, the analyst as 'subject' must have withdrawn himself. I will return to this.

## Compiling an Ethnographic and Historical File

The first step is to collect a number of myths from a set of geographically close societies and to compile a solid file on each of them, containing all the ethnographic information available. 'We should give up pursuing the structural analysis of the myths of a society for which we lack an ethnographic context or, at any rate, a context that is independent from the information carried by the myths themselves. Such an analysis would run on empty.'[1] The file will then have to be subjected to ethnographical and historical criticism, so as to discover the connections existing between the myths and the social organization, between the techno-economic infrastructure and the ecological context of the societies in which the myths originate. This first step also prepares the way for

---

1 C. Lévi-*Strauss*, *The Story of Lynx*, trans. C. Tihanyi (Chicago, University of Chicago Press, 1995), p. 189.

an inventory of the facts the myths claim to explain, in other words, their etiological functions. For example, one Yana myth (M546) fulfils a double function. It explains both the origin of the salt springs that attract the deer and make them easier to hunt, and the origin of porcupine-quill ornaments.[2] Or one of myths of Atsugewi people (M550), the Yana's neighbours, explains the origin of the stone arrowheads used for hunting, the origin of the knives for cutting up the meat and the origin of the fire to cook it.[3] The characters (mythemes) of this myth are Loon Woman, Dog, Eagle, Lynx, Butterfly, Spider, etc. My inventory of the 'origin' myths found in the Mythology series lists them in a table according to their different subsets: the universe, animal and plant species, social relations, and so on. Yet it must be remembered that, despite the care he took to identify the myths' etiological functions, Lévi-Strauss noted how 'myths first seem like puzzles. They tell stories without any rhyme or reason, full of absurd incidents.'[4]

This is true for us, no doubt, but not for the Indians. Whatever the case may be, however, the object of the structural analysis of the myths lies beyond their explicit, patent meaning. It resides in the search for their latent, implicit meanings. And to discover these, two types of analysis are needed: a formal analysis, intended to bring out the logical structure of the myths, and a semantic analysis, which strives to understand what mythical thought claims to be saying through the adventures of Loon Woman, Porcupine or the canoe journey of Sun and Moon.

## Undertaking the Formal Analysis

The formal analysis of a myth enables us to reveal the hidden armature of 'seemingly strange and incomprehensible stories'.[5] But for this analysis to be conducted profitably, the analyst must follow two principles.

---

2  C. Lévi-Strauss, *The Naked Man*, trans. J. and D. Weightman, Mythology series, volume 4 (Chicago, University of Chicago Press, 1981), p. 99.

3  Ibid., pp. 117, 130.

4  C. Lévi-Strauss and D. Eribon, ed., *Conversations with Claude Lévi-Strauss*, trans. P. Wissing (Chicago and London, University of Chicago Press, 1991), p. 133.

5  C. Lévi-Strauss, *From Honey to Ashes: Introduction to a Science of Mythology 2*, trans. J. and D. Weightman (Chicago, University of Chicago Press, 1973), p. 157.

First of all, it must be understood that myths are not simply clusters of odds and ends.[6] 'The tiniest details, however gratuitous, bizarre, and even absurd they may have seemed at the beginning, acquire both meaning and function.'[7] The slightest details are 'meaningful',[8] such that 'myths do not admit of discussion, they must always be accepted as they are'.[9] That is the first principle. And the second is that the analysis of a myth must be exhaustive.[10]

The formal analysis begins when the analyst reconstructs the myth's armature and message. The armature is made up of a series of oppositions that form the logical underpinning of the story and remain invariant in one or several myths, such as the threefold opposition (male/female, high/low, moderate conduct/immoderate conduct) that characterizes the group of myths (M29–M32) concerning the origin of women.[11] In this example, the same armature is found in myths from four different societies, which implies that a myth never exists on its own but entertains relations of symmetry, inversion or contrariness with other myths found in one or several societies. These relations determine and delineate the semantic field of this group of myths.[12]

Next the analyst must isolate the codes used by a myth to deliver its message. These codes can be sexual, sociological (father–son, husband–wife, brothers-in-law), astronomical, culinary (raw–cooked), and so on. The relations the myth establishes between these codes must then be brought out as they distribute its material along several axes, each time using a different vocabulary. It is along these axes that the transformations[13] are located which generated the variants of the myth. Each myth

---

6 C. Lévi-Strauss, *The Raw and the Cooked: Introduction to a Science of Mythology 1*, trans. J. and D. Weightman (Harmondsworth, Penguin, 1986), p. 136.

7 *The Naked Man*, p. 562.

8 Ibid., p. 361.

9 *From Honey to Ashes*, pp. 121.

10 *The Raw and the Cooked*, p. 147.

11 Ibid., pp. 112–14. M29: Sherente; M30: Chamacoco; M31: Toba-Pilaga; M32: Matako.

12 *The Story of Lynx*, p. 135.

13 Lévi-Strauss distinguishes transformations by inversion, symmetry, anti-symmetry, contrariness, contradiction, relative values and meta-linguistic procedures that are relatively easy to identify, as well as two other more complex kinds: racemic transformations (a term used in chemistry) and Putiphar transformations. A racemic transformation 'welds' two groups of myths into a single body but neutralizes their opposition (cf. *The Naked Man*, pp. 107–8, 116): for example, a

or group of myths therefore represents a series of paths through the levels of a global semantic field defined by the nature of the codes used. These levels make up a sort of matrix of meanings within which the messages of the myth move about and develop.[14]

## Moving on to the Semantic Analysis

By definition, a semantic field is multidimensional, and it is the presence of certain transformations of a myth or group of myths distributed along certain axes that allows the analyst to move from one group of myths to another. This can be illustrated by the series of transformations that allowed Lévi-Strauss to go from the Chaco myths to those from Guyana: male/female, spouse/affine, honey/game, raw/cooked, dry/wet, high/low, literal sense/figurative sense, diachrony/synchrony, life/death. The complexity of the combinations found in this series of oppositions is such that it cannot be apprehended intuitively or represented by a diagram.[15]

The second condition for passing from one group of myths to another is that some of the paradigms, some of the mythical schemata found in a given group are also present in another. In this case, the two groups intersect at various points and combine into networks and loops.[16] For there to be a loop, transformations of a myth must exist on certain axes which make it possible to return by another path to the initial myth.[17] But the

---

Yana myth (M546) welds the Bird-Nester myth with that of Loon Woman, but inverts them on a different axis from that along which their opposition was located (ibid., p. 108). Alternatively, M661 is the Putiphar transformation of the Bird-Nester myth owing to the fact that, instead of the elder of the two men seeking to seduce his younger brother's wife or wives, it is the wife of the elder – the father or brother – who tries to seduce the younger (ibid., p. 342). And M762 in turn inverts the Putiphar transformation (ibid., p. 508).

14 C. Lévi-Strauss, *The Origin of Table Manners*, trans. J. and D. Weightman, Mythology series, volume 3 (Chicago, University of Chicago Press, 1990), p. 168.

15 *From Honey to Ashes*, p. 165. It should be remembered that oppositions are not always binary. There exist more complex forms – ternary, quaternary, etc. Binary oppositions are in fact 'the smallest common denominator of the changing values arising from comparison and analogy' (*The Story of Lynx*, p. 185).

16 *The Story of Lynx*, p. 140.

17 *From Honey to Ashes*, p. 21.

loop is never closed.[18] The myths that form the 'return' path pass above the myth from which the analyst departed, and other pathways open up in an even wider semantic field, a sort of 'hyper-space', in which these groups of myths circulate and connect in a spiral movement.[19]

Isolating the paradigms brought into play by the myths involves making an inventory of the mythemes present in the myths and of the schemata that use these mythemes to effect diverse deductions. This approach combines and intertwines the semantic analysis of the myths with the analysis of the logic underlying their construction, since a mythical schema possesses both a logical structure and a semantic effectiveness. However, the purely formal analysis of the myths, of their armature, 'tells us nothing about what they say'.[20] For that, it is necessary to analyse the meaning of the operations (deductions) the schemata perform on the mythemes present in the myths.

Take, for example, the mytheme of the canoe and the schema of the canoe journey of Sun and Moon. The canoe is an operator, and the canoe journey is an operation performed on the two heavenly bodies that generates the myth and structures the way it unfolds.[21] The canoe is a mytheme that 'operates' the intersection between two relations – one of conjunction, the other of disjunction – between two elements, and keeps them apart. The schema of the journey performs two operations, one logical and the other semantic. At the end of the journey, the initial values of the terms *near* and *far* are inverted. The return trip performs the same operations in the other direction. In the end, we discover that the canoe journey involves establishing a relation between the mental operations of conjunction, disjunction and inversion;[22] but these are materialized in the form of images rather than concepts.

---

18 *The Raw and the Cooked*, p. 107.

19 *The Naked Man*, p. 650.

20 Ibid., p. 272.

21 *The Origin of Table Manners*, p. 192: 'When it takes the sun and the moon aboard as passengers it forces them to remain at a fixed distance apart. The journey transports this standard of measurement over a course the various points of which are traversed in succession by the canoe. This movement of a segment of discontinuous space over continuous space makes it possible to effect the summation of the unlimited series of inversely proportional values taken on the journey by the distances of both the near and the far.'

22 Ibid., pp. 193–5.

The outcome is the 'embodiment in concrete images of what was previously no more than an abstract and theoretical pattern,'[23] proof that the mind has performed a transcendental deduction based on material from an empirical deduction – in the present case, the opposition and the correlation of two heavenly bodies, Sun and Moon.[24] The relations of correlation and opposition isolated by an empirical deduction 'in no way constitute objective properties, immediately perceptible by the senses. These properties are drawn from experience, through abstraction, in which the understanding is at work. They consist in logical relations that, by reason of their formal nature, can accept a wide variety of different contents.'[25]

The mind uses these empirical deductions as algorithms to effect the operations that come under another form of deduction, which Lévi-Strauss called 'transcendental,'[26] which, through a series of inversions[27] and twists, generates counter-intuitive conclusions that depict a totally fantasized world.[28] To the outcome of empirical deductions, 'mythic beliefs ... added ... a transcendental deduction which ... proceeds to create a whole series of images, which it then reincorporates into the real world; e.g., the Grouse's head, which is alive on one side and dead on the other.'[29] It is the operations entailed in such counter-intuitive deductions that Lévi-Strauss attempted to translate by his famous canonical formula:

$$F_x(a) : F_y(b) :: F_x(b) : F_{a\text{-}1}(y)$$

where the term (a) is replaced by its opposite (a-1), and at the same time an inversion occurs between the function value $F_{(y)}$, which becomes a term (y), and the term value (a), which is transformed into a function value $(F_{a\text{-}1})$.[30] It is these inversions and twists that engender the

---

23 *The Naked Man*, p. 549.

24 *The Origin of Table Manners*, p. 195; also 207–10, 279–80, 291, 423, 449. Empirical deductions are 'anthropomorphic interpretations of nature'. Cf. *The Jealous Potter*, trans. B. Chorier (Chicago, University of Chicago Press, 1988), p. 136.

25 *The Jealous Potter*, p. 149.

26 *The Naked Man*, p. 549.

27 'The last stage of a mythical transformation presents a double twist' (*The Story of Lynx*, p. 132). See also 'De Grées ou de force?', *L'Homme*, n° 163 (2002).

28 Such as the fantasy of rivers that originally flowed in both directions at once. *The Origin of Table Manners*, p. 160.

29 *The Naked Man*, p. 557.

30 C. Lévi-Strauss, 'The Structural Study of Myth', *Structural Anthropology*, trans. C. Jacobson and B. Grundfest Schoepf (New York, Basic Books, 1963), pp. 206–31; pp. 228–9. Cf. *From Honey to Ashes*, p. 249; *The Origin of Table Manners*, p. 405; *The Naked Man*, p. 538. '[The canonical formula] can represent any mythical transformation' (*The Jealous Potter*, p. 57).

(relative) closure of a group of myths and are, in addition, the source of their deep or latent meaning.[31] The analyst, for his part, must reconstruct the nature of and the logic behind the transcendental deductions effected by the Indian mind based on oppositions selected by empirical deductions and transformed into metaphors.[32] At the close of these empirical and transcendental deductions, which build on to each other, a series of thresholds are crossed, from the real to the imaginary and thence to the symbolic. Experience undergoes a deep-seated transformation. The real world becomes only one of the possible worlds available to mythical thought.[33] The production of myths, like the production of artworks, manifests the intrinsic power of the human mind to 'create possibilities and arrange them logically'.[34] The mythical schemata common to the Indians of North and South America are 'absolute objects',[35] as it were, that abolish time in their narrative and perpetuate themselves over centuries despite the pressures imposed on them by the diversity of societies, natural environments and periods.

However, if the mythical schemata are the paradigms that generate and lend meaning to the syntagmatic sequence of the mythical narrative, we cannot content ourselves with interpreting myths in function of the syntagmatic sequence alone. Lévi-Strauss went so far as to assert: 'Considered purely in itself, every syntagmatic sequence must be looked upon as being without meaning: either no meaning is apparent in the first instance; or we think we can perceive a meaning, but without knowing whether it is the right one.'[36]

---

31 '[Scientific thought] works with concepts, [mythical thought] with significations' (*The Origin of Table Manners*, p. 352).

32 *The Raw and the Cooked*, p. 341: 'the [empirical] material is the instrument of meaning, not its object.'

33 *From Honey to Ashes*, p. 202: 'on the level of the myths, the empirically proved negative connection between otters and excrement becomes part of a combinatory system which operates with sovereign independence and exercises the right to effect different interchanges between the terms of an oppositional system which exists *experientially in only one state* but of which mythical thought gratuitously creates other states'; my emphasis.

34 C. Lévi-Strauss, 'From Mythical Possibility to Social Existence', in *The View from Afar*, trans. J. Neugroschel and P. Hoss (Chicago, University of Chicago Press, 1985), p. 174.

35 *The Naked Man*, p. 38. They are absolute objects because they are objects 'from which nothing can be subtracted and to which nothing can be added'.

36 *The Raw and the Cooked*, p. 307.

But, at the outset, the analyst knows nothing of the mythical paradigms he is setting out to explore, and he must look for them in the ethnography of the societies those myths come from.[37] As the analysis proceeds, the syntagmatic sequence will gradually be replaced by groups of paradigms (schemata), that interconnect within a semantic field extending beyond the borders of the societies of origin.[38] And 'as soon as all the available ethnographical information has been assembled and utilized . . . the context of each myth consists more and more of other myths and less and less of the customs, beliefs and rites of the particular population from which the myth in question derives.'[39]

In the end, the mythical schemata and the myths themselves appear to be caught between two determining constraints, one internal (the myths referring to other myths) and one external (the myths adapting to and being transformed by the social organization, techno-economic infrastructure and ecological environment of the societies that use them[40]). That is why, 'however diverse appearances may be, they conceal structures which, although probably less numerous, are also more real.'[41]

The structures of the myths can therefore be defined as 'matrices which, by means of successive deformations, engender types which can be arranged in series and should enable us to determine the most minute shades of meaning in each myth, considered as a concrete, individual entity'.[42] At this stage, the loop appears to have come full circle. The structural analysis has fulfilled the goal it had imposed on itself at the start, since its method 'is legitimate only if it is exhaustive'.[43] The analyst has withdrawn behind his method and principles. His interpretations 'must emerge from the myths themselves or from the ethnographic

---

37  *From Honey to Ashes*, pp. 355–6.

38  Structural analysis ends up recomposing the myths in the form of a 'matrix of meanings which are arranged in lines or columns', or as Lévi-Strauss calls them elsewhere, syntagmatic sequences and paradigm columns (*The Raw and the Cooked*, p. 340).

39  *From Honey to Ashes*, p. 316.

40  *The Naked Man*, pp. 628–9.

41  Ibid., p. 38.

42  Ibid.

43  *The Raw and the Cooked*, p. 147.

context, and as far as possible from both'.[44] The Subject has disappeared completely, it seems, and the results of the structural analysis of the myths possesses a truly 'objective' and therefore 'scientific' character.

## The Triumph of Structural Analysis and the Analyst's Pride

Before coming back to what Lévi-Strauss meant by his own withdrawal as a 'Subject', whose abolition he had proclaimed in order to write a 'work which excluded it throughout',[45] we must pause over the declarations in which he expresses his pride in having conducted 'a lengthy analysis of a whole set of South American myths' whose patterns 'are fundamental to American Indian thought', and in having seen the hypotheses he had formulated on the basis of the South American myths confirmed by finding the same schemata in the Northern hemisphere. 'The parallel I have just drawn has, then, an *experimental value*, in that it confirms the virtues of the method used and corroborates the relevance of its results.'[46]

Through his method, he tells us, we gain access to 'a new way of apprehending content [of the myths] which, without disregarding or impoverishing it, translates it into structural terms'.[47] Elsewhere he writes: 'the analysis of myths is *preparing the way* for a scientific anthropology.'[48] And again:

Structuralism offers the social sciences an epistemological model incomparably more powerful than those they previously had at their disposal . . . By changing the level of observation and looking beyond the empirical facts to the relations between them, it reveals and confirms that these relations are simpler and more intelligible than the things they interconnect, and whose ultimate nature may remain unfathomable, without this provisional or definitive opacity being, as hitherto, an obstacle to their interpretation.[49]

---

44  Ibid., p. 173.
45  *The Naked Man*, p. 630.
46  Ibid., p. 454; my emphasis.
47  *From Honey to Ashes*, p. 466.
48  *The Naked Man*, p. 153; my emphasis.
49  Ibid., p. 687.

It is not 'the great anonymous voice whose utterance comes from the beginning of time and the depths of the mind'[50] that can be heard in this passage, but that of a thinker conscious of having achieved an epistemological breakthrough in the field of anthropology – and more broadly in that of the social and human sciences as a whole – and calling on the rest of the research community to follow.[51] Lévi-Strauss goes on to defend 'genuine structuralism' against all those interpretations claiming to practice the approach which do not share his method and rigour, but are merely the effect of a (Parisian) fad.[52] This is indeed the attitude of a founder, and it was fully justified. His 'Self' was altogether present. So, how were the myths operating in Lévi-Strauss's mind?

What did he mean when he said that 'structuralism [makes] it possible to disregard the subject – that unbearably spoilt child who has occupied the philosophical scene for too long now, and prevented serious research through demanding exclusive attention . . .'?[53] In the 'Finale' to *The Naked Man*, he claims that, over the twenty years he has devoted to the study of myths, he has acquired the intimate experience that 'the solidity of the self, the major preoccupation of the whole of Western philosophy, does not withstand persistent application to the same object, which comes to pervade it through and through and to imbue it with an experiential awareness of its own unreality.' Throughout his endeavour, he explains, he made a conscious effort to reduce his inner subject to 'the insubstantial place or space where anonymous thought can develop, stand back from itself, find and fulfil its true tendencies and achieve

---

50  Ibid., p. 640.

51  On several occasions over the four volumes of the Mythology series, Lévi-Strauss states that he has left it to others to explore in more detail one or another group of myths or one or another theme (the rolling-head myths, for instance).

52  *The Naked Man*, pp. 626–7, 641. This fad was a '"structuralism-fiction", which has recently flourished on the philosophico-literary scene'. See also in *Conversations with Claude Lévi-Strauss*: 'I placed myself in the same intellectual province as Saussure, Trubetzkoy, Jakobson, Benveniste . . . But the vogue for structuralism unleashed all manner of unfortunate results. The term was besmirched; illegitimate, sometimes ridiculous applications were made of it' (p. 68). Eribon: In the 1960s and 1970s, people spoke of 'structuralism' as if it were a worldwide phenomenon, and the same list of names always occurred: Lévi-Strauss, Foucault, Lacan, Barthes . . . LÉVI-STRAUSS: That still bothers me, *as there were no grounds for that combination*. I don't see what these names have in common. Or rather I do see it: it is deceptive' (pp. 71–2); my emphasis.

53  *The Naked Man*, p. 687.

organization, while coming to terms with the constraints inherent in its very nature'. Lévi-Strauss's Self thus deliberately let itself be filled, not only by the thousands of myths he was analysing, but by the anonymous 'mythical thought' that had produced them through all those who had told these myths for the first time in the belief that 'they had invented them'. His self had become, as it were, a place 'in which phenomena are occurring . . . of which it is the place of intersection, [that] originate from other sources, for the most part unknown'.[54] It would seem that over all the years of rising at five or six every morning, seven days a week, Lévi-Strauss had allowed a thinking process that was not his to take possession of his mind and produce in him the myths he had selected for study. By offering himself up to mythical thought, Lévi-Strauss would be in a position to watch it operate 'from the inside' and to discover the secret and the nature of the mental operations it brought into play everywhere, in every era and in all human beings in order to produce myths. Hence his famous declaration at the beginning of the Mythology series:

> I therefore claim to show, not how men think in myths, but how myths operate in men's minds without their being aware of the fact. And . . . it would perhaps be better to go still further and, disregarding the thinking subject completely, proceed as if the thinking process were taking place in the myths, in their *reflection upon themselves and their interrelation.*[55]

Lévi-Strauss is interested here less in what men say in and through myths than in the system of mental operations that structure mythical narratives. He has thus chosen to reduce his role in the writing of his study to the effort of having allowed the myths to speak in his own mind, thereby being able for the first time in human history to witness at first hand the mental operations that generated them. From an active subject, Lévi-Strauss claims to have become a voyeur, writing down the thinking process as it unfolded in his mind, 'since, contrary to what might be supposed, it was not so much the case that the Self was the author as that the work, during the process of composition, became the creator of an executant

54  Ibid., pp. 625–6.
55  *The Raw and the Cooked*, p. 12; original emphasis.

who lived only by and through it.'[56] For 'it would be truer to say that the myths criticize and select themselves, opening up, through the confused mass of the corpus, certain paths which would not have been the same, had one particular myth rather than another been the first to emerge.'[57]

> What structuralism tries to accomplish in the wake of Rousseau, Marx, Durkheim, Saussure and Freud, is to reveal to consciousness *an object other than itself*; and therefore to put it in the same position with regard to human phenomena as that of the natural and physical sciences, and which, as they have demonstrated, alone allows knowledge to develop ... But this assumption of consciousness remains intellectual in character, that is to say it does not substantially differ from the realities to which it is applied; it is these very realities arriving at their own truth.[58]

Thanks to the methods of structural analysis, myths thus operate in men's minds of their own accord – 'there can be no question ... of smuggling the subject in again'[59] – and arrive, in this insubstantial place that Lévi-Strauss has striven to become, at their own truth: 'the structure of the myth, having been revealed to itself, brings to a close the series of its possible developments.'[60]

Mythical thought, which existed 'in itself' in the myths, has thus become 'for itself', conscious of itself in Lévi-Strauss's mind. This resembles not so much Kant without a transcendental subject, as Ricœur wrote,[61] as Hegel inhabited by mythical thought instead of absolute spirit. But Lévi-Strauss is not Hegel, nor is he an 'idealist'. He is a materialist, since for him the human mind (behind which lies the brain) is 'of the nature of a thing among things'.[62] In this respect, structuralism

---

56 *The Naked Man*, p. 630. 'The subject, while deliberately remaining in the background so as to allow free play to this anonymous deployment of discourse, does not renounce consciousness of it, *or rather does not prevent it achieving consciousness of itself through him*' (p. 629); my emphasis.

57 Ibid., p. 632.

58 Ibid., pp. 629–30; original emphasis.

59 Ibid., p. 630.

60 Ibid., p. 628.

61 *The Raw and the Cooked*, p. 11. Cf. P. Ricœur, 'Symbole et temporalité', *Archivio di Filosofia*, nos 1–2 (1963), pp. 9, 10, 24.

62 Ibid., p. 10.

'reintegrates man into nature'.[63] It reveals to the mind the 'processes according to which thought finds itself to be operating, these processes being the same in both areas, since thought, and the world which encompasses it and which it encompasses, are two correlative manifestations of the same reality'.[64] The human mind is one moment and one aspect of the 'dialectics of nature', and it is no accident that Lévi-Strauss cites Friedrich Engels several times in his work.[65]

Structuralism, with its 'anti-idealism' and 'anti-formalism', thus in a single bound transcends the boundaries of anthropology – and more broadly of the human and social sciences, henceforth promoted to the status of 'sciences', thanks to the methods of 'genuine' structuralism. Here we are navigating the waters of materialist philosophy.[66] For Lévi-Strauss asserts that thought is encompassed by the world, and that 'even a form of thought which seems to be highly irrational is thus contained within a kind of external framework of rationality; later, with the development of scientific knowledge, thought interiorizes this rationality so as to become rational in itself.'[67] Marx would no doubt not have argued with this. But to say that encompassed thought is at the same time encompassing, because it 'encompasses' the world that encompasses it, is reminiscent less of dialectical materialism[68] than of certain forms of mythico-religious thought that claim to embrace everything in a single system, a single vision: the origin and nature of the universe as well as that of man. But, Lévi-Strauss declares,

63 *The Naked Man*, p. 687.

64 Ibid., p. 678.

65 Ibid., pp. 535, 622.

66 *The Raw and the Cooked*, p. 27: 'structural thought now defends the cause of materialism . . . Structuralism has only to be confronted with true manifestations of idealism and formalism for its own deterministic and realistic inspiration to become clearly manifest.' Cf. also the critique of Propp, 'Structure and Form: Reflections on a Work by Vladimir Propp', in C. Lévi-Strauss, *Structural Anthropology, Volume 2*, trans. M. Layton (Chicago, University of Chicago Press, 1976), pp. 115–45; pp. 127, 141.

67 *The Naked Man*, p. 687.

68 Ibid., p. 689: 'Structuralism, unlike the kind of philosophy which restricts the dialectic to human history and bans it from the natural order, readily admits that the ideas it formulates in psychological terms may be no more than fumbling approximations to organic or even physical truths.' But, contrary to a dialectic of nature, in which each higher level of complexity contains the lower levels and includes them while adding something irreducible, Lévi-Strauss describes an inverse movement – the reduction of levels of complexity to the earliest stages of organic and even physical nature.

although, from time to time, I take the trouble to indicate briefly in passing the philosophical implications that arise from my work, I attach no importance to this aspect of it. I am more concerned to deny in advance what philosophers might read into my statements . . . I have no philosophy of my own worth bothering about, apart from a few homely convictions . . . I shall do no more than point out that, in my view, my findings can, at best, only lead to the abjuration of what is called philosophy at the present time.[69]

Let me try to clarify some of this. Lévi-Strauss's approach supposes the withdrawal of both his social self and his intimate self, but by no means his 'cognitive' self. In fact, it is precisely his cognitive self that has caused the others to withdraw and has enabled him, for years on end, to explore the considerable mass of mythical material he had gathered and to penetrate it ever further, to the point where connections that had at first gone unnoticed between one myth and another gradually appeared to him and began to proliferate before his eyes. It seemed as though the myths were now linking up with others inside his mind, and through them it was mythical thought that dictated the four volumes of the Mythology series to Lévi-Strauss.

Far from having withdrawn, however, it was a cognitive Subject-Self constructed by Lévi-Strauss, that, over a period of ten years, analysed the thousands of myths he had selected on the strength of his intuition that the story of the Bird-Nester found in a certain South American tribe (the Bororo) could take him far. But Lévi-Strauss preferred to believe that, once the machinery of structural analysis had been set in motion, it was mythical thought itself, come from the beginning of time and the depths of the mind, that began to operate in his own mind, independently of his will.

For the first time in human history, he believed, a human had managed consciously to watch mental operations taking place within himself that normally and necessarily occurred at the unconscious level when producing myths. For the first time, mythical thought gained a *reflective* awareness of itself. From thought in-itself, it became thought-in-itself-thinking-itself, thought in and for itself. Here the Hegel of the 'Greater Logic', basis of the 'phenomenology of Spirit', is not far away.

---

69  Ibid., p. 638.

The Subject has not withdrawn, then, but the social self and the intimate self have – and a Cognitive Self appears, self-made by a Thinking Subject which Lévi-Strauss has endowed with the status of an anonymous, universal thought that he sees as having begun to operate within him once structuralist methods had provided it with an ideal, mental space in which to do so. In sum, in illusorily removing himself as a subject, Lévi-Strauss had brought himself back as the Subject he had always been, but disguised and transformed into anonymous thought come from the beginning of time.[70] Rather like saying that the waves and particles that make up light had begun to reflect on themselves *in* the physicist's mind and caused his discoveries concerning the nature of light. But Lévi-Strauss goes even further:

> Structural analysis, which some critics dismiss as a gratuitous and decadent game, can only appear in the mind because *its model is already present in the body* . . . What we might call the raw material of immediate visual perception already consists of binary oppositions: simple and complex, light and dark, light on a dark background, dark on a light background . . . Structuralist thought . . . rediscovers, then, and brings to the surface of the conscious profound organic truths.[71]

But why – if structuralism is already present 'in the body' – did it take so many thousands of years to manifest itself? The analysis of social and ideological systems in terms of structures did not wait for Lévi-Strauss or the twentieth century to be practised. Must I again cite Marx, for his analysis of the capitalist 'system', or Ernest Renan for that of the ancient City? And this was quite a few years before Saussure imposed structural analysis in the field of linguistics.

The human body offered, as it were, the possibility for Lévi-Strauss to find in living matter the 'natural and objective' model for structuralist thought, before the discovery and unravelling of the genetic code and DNA.

---

70 *The Raw and the Cooked*, p. 6: 'In seeking to imitate the spontaneous movement of mythological thought, this essay, which is also both too brief and too long, has had to conform to the requirements of that thought and to respect its rhythm. It follows that this book on myths is itself a kind of myth.'

71 *The Naked Man*, p. 692; my emphasis.

As can be seen, when Nature, several thousand million years ago, was looking for a model, she borrowed in advance, and without hesitation, from the human sciences: this is the model which, for us, is associated with the names of Trubetzkoy and Jakobson.[72]

It is understandable, then, that Lévi-Strauss could claim that through myths and mythical thought, 'nature can signify itself'.[73] And that he could write:

Only its practitioners [of structural analysis] can know, from inner experience, what a sensation of fulfilment it can bring, through making the mind feel itself to be truly in communion with the body.[74]

It is no longer Hegel who springs to mind, but Spinoza, who described the sense of fulfilment that comes over the thinker when he discovers that his body and his mind are two finite modes of two infinite aspects of God, a God that is at the same time Nature: *Deus sive Natura*. Assert as he might that such reflections are 'free-ranging, intellectual musings, tinged with confusion and error, that the subject indulges in',[75] by the end of the Mythology series the notion had evolved from a rough outline into a full-blown philosophical theory. And this philosophy is that of Western thought, even if the status granted to life and nature are reminiscent of some positions developed by Japanese or Chinese thinkers.

This is no doubt the origin of the battle Lévi-Strauss would wage throughout his life against the opposition (arising in the West with Descartes) between scientific thought and mythical thought. But he was not trying to 'reduce the gap' between the two. He wanted to reinstate mythical thought as a certain level of scientific thought. But on this point, as on others, I cannot follow him.

Indeed, as early as 1955, he wrote in 'The Study of Myth', as I have said:

---

72 Ibid., p. 685. Cf. already in C. Lévi-Strauss, *The Savage Mind* (no translator mentioned) (Chicago, University of Chicago, 1969), p. 247: 'the reintegration of culture in nature and finally of life within the whole of its physico-chemical conditions . . . are incumbent on the exact natural sciences'.

73 *The Raw and the Cooked*, p. 341.

74 *The Naked Man*, p. 692.

75 Ibid., pp. 692–3.

The kind of [logic] in mythical thought is as rigorous as that of modern science, and . . . the difference lies, not in the quality of the intellectual process, but in the nature of the things to which it is applied . . . In the same way, we may be able to show that the *same logical processes* operate in myth as in science, and that man has always been thinking equally well.[76]

Later, in the 'Finale' to *The Naked Man*, he does not beat around the bush, asserting that

scientific knowledge . . . however harmful it may have been, and further threatens to be, in its applications, is nevertheless a mode of knowledge whose absolute superiority cannot be denied . . . Only during the last few years has science taken a different turn. By venturing into areas close to human sensibility, areas which may seem novel but which in fact it is only rediscovering, it is proving that, from now on, knowledge can progress only by broadening out to comprehend other forms of knowledge . . . that it previously considered as being irrational and beyond the pale.[77]

In 2004, at the end of his life, in a special issue of the *Cahiers de l'Herne* devoted to him, Lévi-Strauss published a recent text on the relationship between mythical and scientific thought, in which he wrote:

It is clear: phenomena, large or small, that belong to previously unsuspected orders of magnitude offend common sense in the same way as the most extravagant mythical constructions do. For the non-specialist, and even more for the man in the street, the world that physicists are attempting to describe reproduces a sort of equivalent of what our remote ancestors regarded as a supernatural world, where everything was different from the way it was in the ordinary world and in most cases was the opposite. Attempting to imagine this supernatural world, the Ancients, and closer to us peoples without writing, invented myths . . . In making this comparison, I eschew any kind of mysticism. Nothing permits us to create or entertain a confusion between archaic forms of thought and

---

76  *Structural Anthropology*, p. 230; my emphasis.
77  *The Naked Man*, p. 637.

scientific thought. With respect to experience, one is valid and the other is not ... But it is because they are *already part* of the architecture of the mind that is of the world, that one day or another, the images of the world proposed by the myths will reveal themselves to be relevant to this world and adequate to illustrate aspects of it.[78]

This series of quotations strung out over half a century (1955–2004) shows Lévi-Strauss's obstinacy and the difficulties he encountered in his attempt to reduce the gap and the structural differences between mythical thought and *modern* scientific thought, whose 'absolute superiority' he acknowledged and on which he modelled his own intellectual rigour. But to say that modern physicists are forced to invent a language analogous to that of myths to explain phenomena whose existence goes unnoted by non-specialists, and which they do not have the knowledge to understand, is quite simply to ignore the fundamental difference between the discoveries made in physics and the deductions made in myths. The first are the result of calculations and experiments that all physicists working in the same area, whatever their national origin and their intimate 'self', can disprove or prove, while the results yield information about real properties of the universe. The transcendental deductions of myths, on the other hand, while authorizing conclusions as counter-intuitive as those reached by physicists, describe a world that does not exist – or exists only through and in the mind, but whose existence must be believed to explain that which everyday experience can neither accomplish nor account for.

Even if the theory of the internal combustion engine is incomprehensible for the man in the street who has never studied it, all those who drive a car benefit from the fact that this theory enabled the construction of their car's motor. And it is not because the human mind is 'of the world', or because its operations make it possible to construct both imaginary worlds and representations verifiable by experimentation, that the images proposed by the myths will one day turn out to be

---

78 C. Lévi-Strauss, 'Pensée mythique et pensée scientifique', *Cahiers de l'Herne*, n° 82 (2004), pp. 40–2; my emphasis. See also *The Story of Lynx*, p. xii: 'between the scientist who through calculations gains access to a reality that is unimaginable and the public eager to know something of this reality, which is evidenced mathematically but entirely against the grain of sensible intuitive perception, mythical thought again becomes a mediator, the only means for physicists to communicate with non-physicists.'

'relevant to this world and adequate to illustrate aspects of it'. The atom of the Greek philosophers expressed the idea of the existence of the smallest indivisible (*a-temno*) particle of matter, itself reduced to a philosophical abstraction, whereas, for today's physicists, the real existence of the atom has been demonstrated – and this atom is no longer the smallest, indivisible particle of matter but a complex universe made up of neutrons, protons, and so on. In short, the image of the world proposed by the Greek 'physicists' turned out to be inadequate to explain this world. Yet these 'physicists' were conscious of having broken with the myths of their ancestors and of proposing explanations of a new type, compatible with *logos* and reason. As Aristotle declared in his *Metaphysics*:[79] 'In to the subtleties of the mythologists it is not worth our while to inquire seriously' (*Metaphysics* III, 4, 10).

Of course, myths should be taken seriously and be an object of science. But this is altogether different from wanting to convince people that myths are (already something of) a science. Aristotle was not mistaken. Imagining other possibilities and varying them in the mind is not the sole preserve of mythical thought. It is the source not only of much scientific knowledge but also of the imaginary world of myth and of the arts. Both practical life and theoretical endeavour seek to understand how what exists could have come to be, or to imagine how what seems possible might come to be. But whereas the possible imagined by an artist exists only in the form of an object (a sculpture, painting, song), the possible imagined by myths is of an entirely different order. That is, things considered to be impossible in everyday life become possible in myth; but in myth, the impossible declared possible by the mind continues to exist only in the mind. For it to become manifest, it must be transformed into theology, ritual, temples, priests, masks, sacrifices, etc. In short, into fantasies made real by society, into a fantasized reality. The gap between mythical thought and scientific thought is thus not diminished simply because both rely on the imagination.

But on several occasions Lévi-Strauss advanced other, apparently more convincing, arguments in favour of his thesis that the logic of mythical thought was basically not that different from, and just as

---

79 Cf. M. Godelier, 'Mythe et histoire: réflexions sur les fondements de la pensée sauvage', *Annales* 26, nos 3–4 (1971), p. 541.

rigorous as, scientific thought. These arguments can be divided in two groups.

In the first three volumes of the Mythology series, Lévi-Strauss shows that three kinds of logic, or 'logicalities', are found at work in the Amerindian myths, which accumulate and intertwine to produce the material used by the myths to manufacture their narratives.[80]

By 'logic of sensible qualities', Lévi-Strauss designates the oppositions perceptible by the five senses and worked out by our understanding: high–low, hot–cold, dark–light, hard–soft, sky–earth, and so on. Mythical thought endows these oppositions with a genuine existence in logic, and uses them to construct the codes in which it formulates its messages. Myths are thus based on the hypothesis that there is 'no clear-cut distinction between subjective states and the properties of the cosmos'.[81] However, the sciences emerging in the seventeenth century with Descartes and Locke made a distinction between the primary qualities of objects and their secondary qualities, those that make themselves intelligible through our five senses: hot and cold, dry and wet, silence and noise, etc. But Lévi-Strauss said he had always sought to 'transcend the contrast between the tangible and the intelligible' that had characterized the first stages of Western science. In mythical thought, sensible qualities are regarded as 'attributes of things'.[82] From this, Lévi-Strauss concludes that the distinction between the states of a subject and the properties of the cosmos, as posited by science, 'has corresponded, and to a lesser extent still corresponds, to a particular stage in the development of scientific knowledge – a stage that in theory, if not in actual fact, is doomed to disappear. In this respect, mythological thought is not prescientific; it should be seen rather as an anticipation of the future state of science, whose past development and present trend show that it has always been progressing in the same direction.'[83]

But, if chemistry and physics teach us about the molecular changes to which the heat of a body corresponds, and if biology teaches us the mechanisms of the human body that allow this degree of heat to be felt and the neural circuits through which this sensation is transmitted to

---

80  *The Origin of Table Manners*, p. 469.
81  *The Raw and the Cooked*, p. 240.
82  Ibid., p. 10.
83  Ibid., p. 240.

the brain and understood by the person that feels it, the progress made by the sciences has in no way eliminated the distinction between the state of the world and the state of the human body. The advances of these sciences have therefore in no way 'legitimized' the forms of thought they initially rejected in order move forward.[84]

The second logic Lévi-Strauss discovered in the myths is that of forms, involving oppositions of another kind: empty and full, inside and outside, container and contents, included and excluded, and so on. This logic deals with contrasts that are more complex than simple oppositions, for instance between silence and noise. It can oppose continuous noise and discontinuous noise, modulated and non-modulated noise, etc.[85] The differential gaps that the myths exploit thus appear as 'a body of common properties, expressible in geometrical terms and transformable one into another by means of operations which constitute a sort of algebra'.[86] But for them to be 'already an algebra', these operations must be detached from any empirical, concrete object whose properties they might express, and become attached to 'any object' constructed through the operations that cause it to exist. Mythical thought never crosses this line; it draws its abstractions from the knowledge entailed in concrete human existence, knowledge that contains – independently of mythical thought – abstract, objective knowledge, mobilized and verified in the practices of hunting, agriculture or basketry, in the production and management of kinship relations, and so on; in short, the totality of knowledges and skills from which mythical thought draws its material. But it is not in its capacity as a myth-maker that the mind produces such knowledge from the many areas of concrete, lived experience. However, this abstract knowledge and this pre-scientific know-how can be included and developed in the course of scientific progress – unlike the images and interpretations of the world proposed by forms of mythical and religious thought.

The oppositions present in the myths can be even more complex when time intervenes to modify the spatial relations between here and there, near and far, as in the case of a canoe journey. Lévi-Strauss identified a third logic, a 'logic of propositions', also at work in the myths.

---

84  *The Naked Man*, p. 637.
85  *From Honey to Ashes*, p. 472.
86  Ibid., p. 473.

This logic, first introduced in *The Origin of Table Manners*, no longer opposes polar or mediatory terms, but relations perceived or established between these terms. For example, the terms will be posed as being too close together (incest between a brother and a sister) or too far apart (marriage between a woman and a grizzly bear) or at the right distance (marriage with a woman from one's own tribe), and depending on the case, the conjunction, disjunction or mediation between these terms will take very different forms and values from those that characterize these terms when laid down in the absolute as simply conjoined or disjoined.[87]

Here again, I am led to point out that all these kinds of knowledge deal with sensations, with forms, with relations – and with relations between relations – which do not stem from mythical thought, even if it does mobilize and exploit them to fuel its 'empirical and transcendental deductions' with concrete material, thus transforming empirical realities into a basis for fantasized worlds. And the same remark applies to the second group of abstract relations used in constructing the sequences of events in the myths: relations of symmetry, inversion, contrariness, contradiction, mediation, equivalence, homology, transformation, cancelling, etc., imagined between certain terms or certain relations. All such relations are experienced by humans in the course of their daily, concrete, material and social lives. Namely, for instance, that yesterday's enemies can be today's allies, that some people do the opposite of what they think, that a gift calls for a countergift, that to decrease is not to increase, etc.

All those concrete relations that humans contract with each other and with nature are established by men and women who discover, internalize and manipulate the abstract relations and therefore conduct the mental operations that make it possible to discover and understand them. Such cognitive operations are clearly part of our brain's capacities, of its structure, and can be used to make an outrigger canoe and to tack against the wind as well as to imagine the consequences of incest between a brother and a sister, or a mother and Oedipus, her son. Once again, I repeat, these mental operations, this knowledge and know-how are not exclusive to mythical thought. What operations are, then? They are of two kinds: first, those that consist in positing the equivalence of

87 *The Origin of Table Manners*, p. 469.

beings, relations and situations in accordance with a logic of transformations and *analogical* deductions; and second, the approach that claims to be *at the same time* analytical and synthetic, and which aims to gather up into a single system the totality of a set of representations of the universe, the cosmos and man. But the equivalences invented by mythical thought are based on purely anthropomorphic representations of the things chosen to be the agents – active or passive – of the stories the myths tell.[88] These successions of analogies lead to permutations between the figures and their functions, which transport us to a counter-intuitive universe where things happen and end differently from, or contrary to, the way they do in the real world of human experience, but whose existence and truth are experienced by those who believe as 'apodictic self-evidences'. The impossible was thus possible.

The gap is immense, and cannot be closed by scientific thought. For even though ordinary human beings are incapable of fully understanding the discoveries made in astrophysics, for example that our galaxy is travelling at the speed of 600 kilometres per second in an expanding universe, they still believe in them because they knows that their hypotheses have been confirmed and accepted by all scientists – Chinese, American and Russian alike. But when the myths of hunter-fisher-gatherer peoples describe the world when men were beasts and beasts were men, it is not because their imagination enabled them to anticipate Darwin's future discoveries about the evolution of species and the descent of man, but because, living in the natural environment and relying on its resources, they credited the wild plants and animals around them with a soul and a personality like their own, obliging themselves to establish relations of reciprocity and good conduct with the animals they killed and the wild or domesticated plants they consumed.

The gap with science becomes even greater when we consider the second characteristic of mythico-religious thought (a characteristic that neither the pragmatic thought of concrete experience nor the theoretical thought of the logico-mathematical and experimental sciences possess),

---

88 For example, in *The Jealous Potter*, concerning the Goatsucker representing the 'jealousy' function of women, Lévi-Strauss emphasizes that the 'empirical deduction' that ascribes this function to this bird 'is an anthropomorphic interpretation of the bird's anatomy and observable habits' (p. 58).

and that is the totalizing character of mythico-religious representations and interpretations of the universe and of man. In a few narratives of variable length,[89] the myths thus explain to us the origin of the sun, of the spots on the moon, of the female vulva, of the cry of the owl, and much more. Chinese philosophy, in which Yin and Yang are the two opposing yet complementary components and forces, present and acting in all beings as well as in the whole universe, is another notable example. We find such 'fractal' representations of the universe, of beings and of men in Melanesia, too, among the Trobriand Islanders, on Muyua and other famous islands of the Kula ring.[90] The structure of the whole is found in each of its parts.

We saw above that thought in its savage state aspires to be both analytical and synthetic.[91] Using the differences between animal species to represent the differences between human groups, it employs the animal as 'a conceptual tool for detotalizing or retotalizing any domain, synchronic or diachronic, concrete or abstract, natural or cultural'.[92] Mythical thought 'inserts the pattern of human relations into a cosmological context which seems to extend beyond them on all sides but which as we have proved, is, when taken in its entirety, isomorphic with them and in its way able both to include them and to imitate them'.[93] We could be reading Granet on Chinese philosophy.[94] In this view, mythical thought would be fundamentally anti-Cartesian:

> We learned . . . from Descartes: to divide each difficulty into as many parts as necessary the better to solve it. The way so-called primitive people think challenges this division. An explanation is worthwhile only insofar as it is total.[95]

---

89 Here it is interesting to reread the biblical story of Genesis, the life of Adam and Eve in Paradise, Satan, the fallen angel, etc.

90 Cf. F. H. Damon and M. S. Mosko, eds, *On the Order of Chaos* (New York, Berghahn Books, 2005). Cf. R. Wagner, 'The Practical Person', in M. Godelier and M. Strathern, eds, *Big Men and Great Men: Personifications of Power in Melanesia* (Cambridge, University of Cambridge Press, 1991), pp. 159–73.

91 *The Savage Mind*, p. 219.

92 Ibid., p. 149.

93 *The Raw and the Cooked*, p. 339.

94 M. Granet, *La Pensée chinoise* (Paris, Albin Michel, 1988) (First edition 1934).

95 Lévi-Strauss and Eribon, *Conversations with Claude Lévi-Strauss*, p. 112.

Hence the systematic recourse to metaphor, which is an act of under-standing, 'the primitive apprehension of a global structure of signification'.[96] In fact, there lies precisely the basic difference between mythico-religious thought and modern scientific thought as expressed in the 'hard' sciences that strive to explain the nature of the universe and of life within it. The sciences do not explain the world by dint of meta-phor. They analyse and then produce syntheses that unfailingly open onto new problems at other levels of reality. They are analytical, then synthetic, but never totalizing. Above all, they do not see the relations between natural realities as so many 'signs' engaged in sending them 'messages'. Already in 1962, analysing the workings of 'thought in its savage state', Lévi-Strauss conceded that:

> In treating the sensible properties of the animal and plant kingdoms as
> if they were the elements of a message, and in discovering 'signatures'
> – and so signs – in them, men have made mistakes of identification . . .
> and even though they interpreted them as if they were messages, men
> were nevertheless able to arrive at some of their properties.[97]

But the sciences do not transmit messages they believe are being sent by nature (or the gods, or God). Nature does not tell us anything. Nature simply is, and undergoes transformation. Nor was it by deciphering supernatural messages that men built the vessels that enabled them to sail from island to island in the South Pacific. It was not myths but hundreds of patient observations, with the deductions and concrete experiments derived from these, that enabled them to select the best wood for making canoes, to study the direction of the winds in order to navigate in all seasons, etc. But men have always known as well that acquired knowledge could never guarantee the success of their enter-prises, thus making it necessary to win the good graces or ensure the help of the invisible entities that command the winds, the sharks, etc. In this regard, only myths and rituals seemed likely to allow them to achieve their aims.

The international team of physicists working at CERN on experi-ments to find the Higgs boson is probably made up of Christians,

---

96  *The Jealous Potter*, p. 195.
97  *The Savage Mind*, pp. 268, 269.

Muslims, atheists, and others. But surely none of them thinks that the results of the experiments, when they come, will be messages sent by nature or by God. I cannot therefore endorse or adopt the thesis Lévi-Strauss repeated insistently, from *The Savage Mind* (1962) to his article in *L'Herne* (2004):

> We therefore remain faithful to the inspiration of the savage mind when we recognize that ... the scientific spirit in its most modern form will have contributed to legitimize the principles of savage thought and to re-establish it in its rightful place.[98]

In fact, Lévi-Strauss seems always to have sought, in repeating these declarations, to close the gap between mythical thought and modern scientific thought by dissociating the former as much as possible from rituals, liturgies, theologies, in short from everything entailed in religious thought and practices. When dissecting the mechanisms of the human mind that create mythical explanations of the world, of man and of their origins, he had left aside the reasons that for millennia have driven men to invent and perpetuate them, and then to invent new explanations and again perpetuate those, without ever attributing them to themselves. Thanks to Lévi-Strauss, today we have a much clearer understanding of how men come up with fantasized worlds and counter-intuitive explanations that seem to emanate from somewhere else and which they receive as so many 'apodictic self-evidences'; but he told us nothing about the reasons that lead men to imagine more than they actually know about the world in which they live and what they are able to do there.

Lévi-Strauss richly deserves credit for having 'carried the investigation beyond the limits of consciousness'.[99] Now we must go even further, but in other directions. First, we need to work with cognitive psychologists to continue the inventory and analysis of the mental operations involved in the construction of these counter-intuitive worlds. Second, and above all, we should push forward with the analysis of myths in connection to the content of the social relations in the societies in which they were gathered, and analyse the transformations

---

98  Ibid., p. 269.
99  *Structural Anthropology, Volume 2*, p. 67.

in these societies' specific histories, including the impact of world religions – Christianity, Islam, Buddhism – and their efforts to convert local populations.

From this standpoint, it is essential to be aware that, from 1962 (the year of *Totemism* and *The Savage Mind*) to 2004 (*Cahier de l'Herne*), Lévi-Strauss published eight books and dozens of articles devoted to mythical thought, and yet he did not devote even twenty pages to the analysis of religion and the relationship between myth and religion.

In *The Savage Mind*, Lévi-Strauss, speaking personally, declares that his 'thought is not tormented by transcendence even in a latent form', and stresses that 'the poverty of religious thought can never be overestimated.'[100] He announces that 'magical rites and beliefs appear as so many expressions of an *act of faith in a science* yet to be born.'[101] Finally, he concludes that 'religion consists in a *humanization of natural laws* and magic in a *naturalization of human actions* . . . The notion of a supernature exists only for a humanity which attributes supernatural powers to itself and in return ascribes the powers of its superhumanity to nature.'[102]

It is astonishing to speak of the 'poverty of religious thought' after having analysed, in *Totemism* and *The Savage Mind*, dozens of Australian myths and rituals concerning supernatural beings that left along their imaginary paths hundreds of totemic sites where the Aborigines regularly worship them.

It is less astonishing to read some ten years later (1971), in the final pages of the fourth volume of the Mythology series, that Lévi-Strauss is 'someone who has never felt the slightest twinge of religious anxiety.'[103] In the meantime, in the 1968 summary of his courses at the École Pratique des Hautes Études as occupant of the Chair of Comparative Religions of Peoples without Writing, he stressed that 'one aspect of our attempt consists in stripping [religious facts] of their specificity.'[104] And

---

100  *The Savage Mind*, pp. 255, 99.
101  Ibid., p. 11; my emphasis.
102  Ibid., p. 221; original emphasis.
103  *The Naked Man*, p. 688.
104  *Structural Anthropology, Volume 2*, p. 66. See also *The Naked Man*, p. 639: 'I too, of course, look upon the religious field as a stupendous storehouse of images that is far from having been exhausted by objective research; but these images are like any others, and the spirit in which I approach the study of religious data supposes that such data are not credited at the outset with any specific character.'

in the 'Finale' to *The Naked Man*, he once again asserts that: '[structuralism] feels ... better able to explain and validate the place that religious feeling has held, and still holds, in the history of humanity' because 'finality, after being long banned by a form of scientific thought, has been restored to its true place and again made respectable by structuralism.'[105] So what, for him, is this religious feeling that humanity 'still holds'?

> Religious feeling senses confusedly that the hiatus between the world and the mind, and between causality and finality, does not correspond so much to things as they actually are as to the limit beyond which knowledge strains in vain to reach, since its intellectual and spiritual resources will never be commensurable with the dimensions of the essence of the objects it studies.[106]

For Lévi-Strauss, then, religions come down to feelings, to the domain of emotions and the affects elicited by the intellectual apprehension of the idea, which 'religious feeling senses confusedly', that there is after all no real hiatus between the world and the mind, and that the facts of the universe will always exceed man's efforts to know them. We are not far here from the Montaigne of 'Apology for Raymond Sebond', for which Lévi-Strauss expresses his admiration in *The Story of Lynx*. Lévi-Strauss thus equates 'religions' not only with the affects, but also with rituals and liturgies, which strive in vain 'to move back from the discontinuous to the continuous', by multiplying gestures and words and waving objects in a 'desperate and inevitably unsuccessful attempt to re-establish the continuity of lived experience'.[107] To this end, he cites the work of Dumézil on Ancient Roman religion to suggest that only the key divinities of a pantheon are connected with the myths, while the rituals take care of a great number of minor divinities; but those are Dumézil's ideas. However, Lévi-Strauss did not follow up on Dumézil and the Romans, since nowhere in the Mythology series did he analyse in detail the complex pantheons of the societies from which he had taken a few

---

105 *The Naked Man*, pp. 688, 687.
106 Ibid., p. 688.
107 *The Naked Man*, p. 675, where it is also stated, 'Ritual represents a bastardization of thought, brought about by the [servitudes] of life.'

myths – Mandan, Hidatsa, Pawnee, Tacana, Warao – not to mention the pantheons of the great Amerindian civilizations, excluded from the outset, as we have seen.

In fact, Lévi-Strauss is interested only in the operations of the mind that endow myths with a structure – and on another level with a meaning. But precisely, this meaning draws those listening to the myths and who believe in them into a supernatural, fantasized world where everything happens differently than in the world of human experience. The myths are thus received as truths that can only be believed and which give a meaning – their meaning – to human existence. They are existential truths, but Lévi-Strauss does not broach this aspect.

Myths are not the product of the mind communing with itself, as he repeats over and over.[108] They are thoughts intended to enable men to act on the world around them, and at the same time on themselves and on others. Myths and rituals are a response precisely to this need to understand in order to act. And particular sets of myths and rituals are what constitute the various religions.

For the Aborigines, myths recount the paths taken by the beings that, in the Dreamtime, fashioned the mountains and deserts of Australia and multiplied the species, including the 'spirit children', certain of which come to reincarnate themselves as humans in each generation. The Vedic texts appeared one day to the Rishis, the 'Fathers', who saw them transcribed and written in Sanskrit. The surahs of the Quran were directly transmitted by God to Muhammad, his Prophet, who spoke them aloud before they were collected and written down in Arabic by his disciples; and so on.

Clearly, there is no question of denying that the human mind – in inventing the many gods of the pantheons, in relating their genealogies and their fates, and in assigning them responsibility for one or several functions in order to ensure the universe and society work as they should – takes pleasure in producing and endlessly enriching these imaginary worlds. But the 'leeway' is not infinite. Ultimately, Zeus or Jupiter must be the supreme gods. And while Zeus and Jupiter exercise their dominion in Heaven, they are also associated with the exercise of

---

108 Lévi-Strauss defends his 'conception of the understanding as the source of an autonomous activity, which is subject in the first place to its own constraints' (ibid., p. 684).

power among humans on Earth. Jupiter was the *primus civis*, the first among Roman citizens, and it was first to Jupiter that the laws voted by the Senate were presented, so that they might be accepted 'by Him' before being implemented.[109] Thus, for thousands of years, myths and religions were always associated with different forms of power – either to legitimize or to contest them.

By separating myth and ritual, Lévi-Strauss believed he could narrow the differential gap between mythical thought and scientific thought – but at the cost of neglecting religion. He may have thought it would suffice to show that myths had no transcendental origin (since they were the products of combinatory operations of the mind, which is the same in all humans) for the problem of religion to be all but resolved. But he was mistaken, as I have said.

One last point. In the sole opinion Lévi-Strauss ever expressed on the Judeo-Christian tradition and the myth of Adam and Eve, created by God and then expelled from Paradise in punishment for trying to steal the fruit of the tree of knowledge and thus become as gods, he writes:

> Despite the ink spilled by the Judeo-Christian tradition to conceal it, no situation seems more tragic, more offensive to heart and mind, than that of a humanity coexisting and sharing the joys of a planet with other living species yet being unable to communicate with them.[110]

In the case of the Amerindians, this inability to communicate is believed to date from mythical times, and what the myths tell of 'the event that inaugurated the human condition and its weakness'.[111] The Amerindians would thus have worked out in their myths a philosophical vision of mankind, sensed in part by Rousseau, that went beyond that which the Judeo-Christian West would develop. It is 'because man originally felt himself identical to all those like him (among which, as Rousseau explicitly says, we must include animals) that he came to acquire the capacity to distinguish *himself* as he distinguishes *them*'.[112] Hence Lévi-Strauss's

---

109 G. Dumézil, *La Religion romaine archaïque* (Paris, Payot, 1966); J. Scheid, *Quand faire c'est croire. Les Rites sacrificiels des Romains* (Paris, Aubier, 2005).

110 Lévi-Strauss and Eribon, *Conversations with Claude Lévi-Strauss*, p. 139.

111 Ibid.

112 C. Lévi-Strauss, *Totemism*, trans. R. Needham (Boston, Beacon Press, 1963), p. 101; original emphasis.

profession of faith in favour of a 'sound humanism' which brings *The Origin of Table Manners* to a close:

> In the present century, when man is actively destroying countless living forms, after wiping out so many societies whose wealth and diversity had, from time immemorial, constituted the better part of his inheritance, it has probably never been more necessary to proclaim, as do the myths, that sound humanism does not begin with oneself, but puts the world before life, life before man, and respect for others before [pride].[113]

In espousing this philosophy, which he attributes to the Indians, Lévi-Strauss not only distances himself from those Western philosophies that postulate a radical discontinuity between humans and the other living species,[114] he also addresses a rebuke to the men of his time – the time of capitalism, a word he does not pronounce – who are actively destroying natural resources and who have, by their domination and violence, 'wiped out' hundreds of 'traditional' societies.[115]

---

113    *The Origin of Table Manners*, p. 508. See one of Lévi-Strauss's last articles: 'Le "Sentiment de la Nature", un besoin fondamental', *Ethnies*, nos 29–30 (2003), pp. 88–94.

114    This is why it has been written that this thesis converges with that of Buddhism. See *L'Autre face de la lune* (Paris, Seuil, 2011), pp. 49–56, on the principal differences between Eastern and Western thought: rejection of the subject, rejection of discourse, of the logos.

115    Hence Lévi-Strauss's article on the notion of 'productivity' in *Études rurales* (2001), reprinted in *Anthropology Confronts the Problems of the Modern World*, foreword M. Olender, trans. J. M. Todd (Cambridge, MA and London, The Belknap Press of Harvard University Press, 2013), pp. 59–71.

# 14
## Taking Stock – II

Unlike kinship studies which, in France, had made no further strides during the first half of the twentieth century after Durkheim, the study of myths and religious systems had moved forward with Marcel Mauss, Robert Hertz, Marcel Granet, Louis Gernet and Georges Dumézil.[1]

Both Mauss and Durkheim had inquired into the nature of the classification systems of certain so-called primitive peoples, fifty years before Lévi-Strauss took up the task in *Totemism* and carried the analysis much farther. Mauss also saw myths and the mental categories they entailed as the means these societies used to organize their experience of the world at all levels, which we divide today into economic, religious, artistic and other activities. In two of his books, *Danses et légendes de la Chine ancienne* (1926) and *La Pensée chinoise* (1934),[2] Granet used legends and myths to attempt to reconstruct the mental world of ancient China, structured around the dynamic opposition between the reality principles of Yin and Yang. Less familiar to the general public, Gernet's *Recherches sur le développement de la pensée juridique et morale en Grèce* was a meticulous analysis of the transformation of the terms present in the myths – such as dikē and hubris (Justice, excessive pride) – into legal

---

1 I summarize the stages outlined by Jean-Pierre Vernant in *Raisons du mythe*, II. *Le Mythe aujourd'hui*, in *Œuvres* (Paris, Seuil, 2007), vol. 1, pp. 790–803.

2 M. Granet, *Danses et légendes de la Chine ancienne* (Paris, Presses Universitaires de France, 1926); *La Pensée chinoise* (Paris, La Renaissance du Livre, 1934; Albin Michel, 1988).

concepts associated with new institutions created to judge crimes, but also offences to the gods of the City.[3] Like Mauss, Gernet stressed that mythical and religious thought were present in all the ancient Greeks' activities.

Dumézil was the first to have discovered a fundamental ideological structure that gave meaning to the mythic narratives and to the pantheons of numerous Indo-European-speaking peoples. This structure determined, with reference to three ranked functions – sovereignty, physical force and provision of sustenance – each divinity's position in the pantheon of Indo-European religions. Dumézil had also shown that these representations were ways of conceiving the world and society, without necessarily corresponding to the real social and political structures of the Indo-European societies in question.

But with Lévi-Strauss, the analysis of myths and mythical thought would make a considerable leap forward. With respect to his predecessors, Lévi-Strauss's work would indicate, as Jean-Pierre Vernant emphasized,[4] at once a continuity, a break and a new start.

The continuity with Mauss and Durkheim can be seen in *The Savage Mind*. That with Dumézil, which Lévi-Strauss reasserted several times, began with his 1955 article, 'The Structural Study of Myth',[5] and persisted until 2001, in the last edition of his long interview with Didier Eribon, *Conversations with Claude Lévi-Strauss*.[6] Lévi-Strauss drew on Dumézil's work to show that 'even history can be approached in a

---

3 L. Gernet, *Recherches sur le développement de la pensée juridique et morale en Grèce, étude sémantique* (Paris, Albin Michel, 2001) (first edition, 1917).

4 Jean-Pierre Vernant devoted several books to ancient Greek mythology and religion: *Mythe et pensée chez les Grecs* (1965); *Mythe et société en Grèce ancienne*, (1974); *Mythe et religion en Grèce ancienne* (Paris, Seuil, 1990); *Mythe et tragédie en Grèce ancienne* (with Pierre Vidal-Naquet), vol. 1 (Paris, Maspero, 1972; vol. 2, Paris, La Découverte, 1986). In an interview published in *L'Âne*, he told Judith Miller: 'Seeing that our categories do not coincide with those of ancient Greece, I realized that religion is present at all levels and in all areas of the intellectual activities and social realities of this world . . . Agricultural work is inserted in a conception where the gods intervene. The act of farming is both technical and religious, as is craftwork, but in a different way' (*L'Âne*, January–March, 1987, p. 25).

5 *Structural Anthropology*, pp. 207, 290, 314.

6 Lévi Strauss and Eribon, *Conversations with Claude Lévi-Strauss*, p. 131: 'I don't need to tell you how much I owe to the work of Dumézil. I learned a great deal and found much encouragement there'. See also Lévi-Strauss's speech welcoming Dumézil into the Académie Française, 14 June 1979.

structural way',[7] with reference to *L'Héritage indo-européen à Rome* (1949). In *Loki*, Dumézil had already brilliantly demonstrated that it was indeed the same 'previously enigmatic figure' that was mentioned in documents from Iceland, Ireland, the Caucasus and India, and he had managed to establish a correlation between this figure's role and manifestations and 'certain specific features of social organization'.[8] Lévi-Strauss would again declare his debt to Dumézil in the speech with which, years later, he welcomed Dumézil into the Académie Française.

The break was ultimately induced by Lévi-Strauss's systematic recourse to two new concepts: structure and transformation. The first is always mentioned while the second is often forgotten, not being from the same source. As we know, the concept of structure was borrowed from structural linguistics, inaugurated by Saussure and developed by Trubetzkoy and Jakobson, with whom Lévi-Strauss became friendly in New York. This notion meant, first of all, that 'the components of a system do not have any inherent signification: their meaning results from their position', but also that, in order to understand the deep meaning of a story, one must isolate the paradigms underlying the syntagmatic sequence. In these conditions, Lévi-Strauss quickly realized that 'structure is not reducible to a system: a group composed of elements and the relations that unite them. In order to be able to speak of structure, it is necessary for there to be invariant relationships between elements and relations among several sets, so that one can move from one set to another by means of a transformation'.[9] In fact, it rapidly became apparent to him that the concept of transformation was 'inherent in structural analysis'.[10] However, he had not borrowed this concept from logicians but from the Scottish biologist and mathematician, D'Arcy Wentworth Thompson, who, he says, played a 'decisive role'. Indeed, Thompson had shown that, by varying the geometrical points that describe the outline of representations of different species of animals and plants of the same class, it was possible to generate all the different forms found in the same species.[11] For Lévi-Strauss, this was an 'illumination'. He discovered that a similar approach had inspired Goethe in

---

7  *Structural Anthropology*, p. 290.

8  Ibid., p. 314.

9  Lévi-Strauss and Eribon, *Conversations with Claude Lévi-Strauss*, p. 113.

10  Ibid.

11  *The Naked Man*, p. 677, plate from D'Arcy Thompson's *Zoological Transformations*.

his *Metamorphosis of Plants* and, before him, Albrecht Dürer, in his *Four Books on Human Proportion*. In fact, Lévi-Strauss could also have found the notion of transformation in Marx's *Capital*, where it was used to describe the movement whereby new relations came to replace old ones, building on earlier relations whose function and importance they transformed.[12]

Armed with these two concepts, which were now linked, Lévi-Strauss embarked on the analysis of several thousands of myths from Indian societies in South and North America. The harvest of scientific findings was considerable, as we have seen. First, the revelation of the presence in myths of a logical armature consisting of relations of opposition (binary or other), of different codes used to send messages and the inventory of these codes. To this must be added the definition of the constitutive units of myths, the mythemes, as clusters of differential relations, and their implementation in schemata having a double function – logical and semantic. We must also add the methodological principle that everything in a myth has a meaning and a function, that a myth is not open to discussion and that its analysis must be exhaustive.

Identical or opposing mythemes and schemata, once identified by the analyst, could be found in different societies that were often geographically remote from those in which the myths under study were gathered. Lévi-Strauss thus demonstrated the existence of a cultural world shared by hundreds of tribal societies in North and South America, even if they did not belong to the same linguistic group, like the societies of the Indo-European languages group. Then, comparing all variants of the myths with data on social and religious organization, techno-economic infrastructure, and the plants, animals and environment exploited by these societies, Lévi-Strauss came to explain the different meanings carried by the mythemes and the schemata linked to these variations. The process of transformations could be explained without the presence of an automatic correspondence between the myths and the socio-economic structures. Mythemes and schemata are therefore not universal archetypes that might connect each of us intimately, without the aid of concepts, with the secret of things, the mystery of being, the numinous, etc. They are instruments for

---

12 M. Godelier, 'Les Structures de la méthode du *Capital*', I, II, III, *Économie et Politique*, nos 70, 71, 80 (1960 and 1961).

constructing counter-intuitive representations of the world that possess truth-value. Lévi-Strauss discovered and demonstrated the logic behind the analogical transformations that built these counter-universes endowed with apodictic self-evidence. This transmutation of experiential data into a mixture of the real and the imaginary functions as a symbol, which Lévi-Strauss intuitively expressed in a sort of mathematical formula he christened the 'canonical formula' of myths. We have attempted to show its full interest and importance here.

In short, it is because Lévi-Strauss approached myths in the same way as he had kinship structures – looking for the mental operations involved in the production of social relations and facts (marriage rules, myths and rituals, etc.) and adhering as closely as possible to the ethnographic and historical data – that he advanced the study and understanding of certain fundamental aspects of human life by a quantum leap.

Of course, his endeavours and his findings also have their limits, and to attempt to surpass them is to comply with the wishes of Lévi-Strauss himself. And yet, nothing will be the same after him, and thanks to him we will continue to progress. Allow me to recapitulate a few of the critical issues raised in the preceding pages, which should constitute a number of avenues for future research. We need to:

– Re-examine and rethink the relationship between myth and ritual; while recognizing their differences, not conceiving of them as a manifestation of the opposition between thinking and living, but as the expression of the difference and the bond between thinking and acting, on the world and on oneself, using fantasized representations of the world and of oneself.

– Re-examine and rethink the relationship between the patent, explicit content of the myths and their latent content, their semantic field, once the nature and function of the mythemes and schemata organizing the mythical narrative have been understood; not starkly opposing patent narrative and latent narrative, but understanding them as two narratives subject to different degrees of conscious and unconscious processes.

– Conduct a new analysis of the mythemes and schemata based on the semantic field of the languages in which the myths were gathered, and not only using European-language translations of the myths.

– Reconstruct insofar as possible the variations of the myths over the centuries, and look for connections between these variations and the transformations undergone by the societies in question; compare, as Vernant did for Hesiod's *Theogony* and his *Works and Days*, the historical variations and the variants of myths present in several societies.

– In collaboration with cognitive scientists and logicians specialized in the logic of analogical transformations between terms that imply and oppose one another and can even encompass one another, pursue the analysis of the operations of the mind that engender counter-intuitive worlds endowed with truth-value.[13] For the rationality present in the myths does not mean they are either manifestations of scientific knowledge or anticipations of certain recent discoveries. To be sure, after Lévi-Strauss, myths could no longer be regarded as the fruit of 'pre-logical' forms of thought. It has been proven – as Lévi-Strauss superbly put it – that 'nothing is too abstract for the primitive mind'.[14] Yet we cannot say, as he nevertheless repeated on several occasions, that myths are the product of the human mind 'communing with itself'.[15] The human mind is never left to commune with itself alone. The world – a world – always exists before humans are born and begin to think. Nor is the mind 'a thing among things',[16] and the world, whatever world, into which each human is born and begins to live is never a space where everything that happens is a matter of 'pure contingency'.

As I have said, I do not espouse these theses and I have explained my reasons. Now we must move forward.

---

13  Polysemy and ambiguity are essential characteristics of the symbolic function of the imaginary beings in the myths. Cf. *From Honey to Ashes*, p. 185.

14  Ibid., p. 467.

15  *The Naked Man*, p. 684: 'This conception of the understanding as the source of an autonomous activity, which is subject in the first place to its own constraints, is criticized by all those who imagine that a display of [fine "sentiments"] can be a substitute for the search for truth.'

16  *The Raw and the Cooked*, p. 10: 'When the mind is left to commune with itself . . . it shows itself to be of the nature of a thing among things.'

# By Way of a Conclusion

As I said at the outset, I have deliberately passed over certain aspects of Lévi-Strauss's work. For example, I have not mentioned his very rich developments, in the Mythology series, of the relationship between myth and music. I did not mention the fact that the first volume of the series, *The Raw and the Cooked*, contains sections entitled: 'The "Good Manners" Sonata', 'A Short Symphony', 'Fugue of the Five Senses', 'The Opossum's Cantata', 'Double Inverted Canon', 'Toccata and Fugue', and 'Rustic Symphony in Three Movements'. I also left to one side the six pages of the 'Finale' of the last volume of the series, devoted to Ravel's *Bolero*, and the analysis of the binary and ternary principles that punctuate the movement. This is because Lévi-Strauss's relationship with music has been excellently covered by Jean-Jacques Nattiez, a musicologist who interviewed Lévi-Strauss on several occasions and published a book on 'Lévi-Strauss the musician' in 2008.[1] In particular, he concluded that the homology Lévi-Strauss claimed to have established between learned Western music and myth was baseless.

Furthermore, when, in 1987, Olivier Revault d'Allonnes and Marc Jimenez asked Lévi-Strauss what he felt when he heard African or Melanesian music, so closely bound up with certain rites and myths, Lévi-Strauss made this surprising reply:

---

1 J.-J. Nattiez, *Lévi-Strauss musicien. Essai sur la tentation homologique* (Paris, Actes Sud, 2008).

I am utterly incapable of penetrating what this music is, why it pleases or displeases me. We call it music because we have no better word for it. Let us say that it is what most resembles what we call music without really being the same thing.[2]

Since I myself enjoy the music of Africa and Melanesia, as well as the sacred music of India, but am not a musicologist, I cannot make an informed judgment. Except to say that if one had to be a musician, and an admirer of Richard Wagner's Ring cycle to boot, in order to understand myths in general and Lévi-Strauss's Mythology series in particular, not many readers would pass the test.

Nor will I discuss the fact that Lévi-Strauss did not like Picasso's work, preferring that of Poussin,[3] or that he detested serial music, let alone that he regarded the novel as a weak form of myth and comic strips as the weakest form of the novel. These views were clearly not based on the fundamental principles of structural analysis.

And yet it seemed interesting to collect a number of such affirmations, scattered throughout his books or in the many interviews he gave, as expressions of his subjectivity. It is hard to explain why, for example, commenting on myths giving the reasons for preferring dark-skinned women, Lévi-Strauss adds the note: 'Hence the often treacherous appeal of blondes, who, as we know, function as home-breakers'.[4] Where does this 'as we know' come from? And how many blonde Indian women were there in pre-Columbian America? Likewise, how are we to understand that, having explained in the final chapter of *The Origin of Table Manners*, 'The Moral of Myths', that Indian morality is superior to that of the West (which he identifies with Sartre's idea that 'Hell is other people', while the Indians believe that 'Hell is ourselves'), he can assert that the lesson (some) Amerindian myths teach about women and their sexual organs displays any sort of moral or social superiority: 'If you remove the maternal element from femininity, what is left is stench'?[5] That is why, in the

---

2  C. Lévi-Strauss, 'Musique et identité culturelle', in *Harmoniques*, n° 2 (1987), pp. 8–14.

3  C. Lévi-Strauss, *Look, Listen, Read*, trans. B. Singer (New York, Basic Books, 1997), chapters I–VI and VII–IX.

4  C. Lévi-Strauss, *The Naked Man*, trans. J. and D. Weightman, Mythology series, volume 4 (Chicago, University of Chicago Press, 1981), p. 349, note.

5  C. Lévi-Strauss, *The Raw and the Cooked: Introduction to a Science of Mythology 1*, trans. J. and D. Weightman (Harmondsworth, Penguin, 1986), p. 271.

myths, the opossum and the fox symbolize woman – the opossum for its plentiful, nutritious milk and its stench, the fox for its wiliness and treachery.[6] Of course, I by no means intend to reverse the argument and assert the superiority of Western 'morality' and ethical principles over the 'morality' (there were probably several) of Amerindians living in more 'authentic' societies. The enigma remains.

Countless myths, Lévi-Strauss points out, legitimize the prerogatives and privileges men have awarded themselves and their disablement of women, as if, he suggests, 'in subordinating one sex to the other, they had evolved a blueprint of the genuine, but as yet inconceivable or impracticable solution, such as slavery, which would involve the subjection of certain men to the dominion of other men.'[7]

Of course, it is commonly recognized today that men's dominion over women existed in several parts of the world long before the institution of castes, classes or other forms of servitude. But this quotation calls for two critical remarks. Women's submission to men is not merely 'mystical', in other words ideological and ritual. I observed this in a tribal society in New Guinea, where there were no caste or class relations: the violence shown to women was not merely 'mystical'; it was physical (bodily harm), psychological (insults, denigration, scorn), political and religious. Furthermore, slavery, bondage and other forms of subjugation of man by man were certainly not invented, as Lévi-Strauss claims, as solutions to 'the problems created by the numerical dimensions of society'.[8] To take a concrete example: it was clearly not as an effect of demographic growth in the Vedic era, during the two millennia before our era, that the population was divided into ranked castes under the authority and power of the priests (Brahmins) and warriors (Kshatriyas).

Moreover, to write, as Lévi-Strauss did, that hunter-gatherer-fisher societies were more 'authentic' than societies ordered into hierarchies of dominating or dominated castes or classes because they were based on personal relationships, facilitated by their small size, suggests he

6 C. Lévi-Strauss, *From Honey to Ashes: Introduction to a Science of Mythology 2*, trans. J. and D. Weightman (Chicago, University of Chicago Press, 1973), p. 295: 'Woman, eternally doomed to be opossum and fox, is unable to overcome her self-contradictory nature . . .'. See also *The Naked Man*, pp. 309–10.

7 *From Honey to Ashes*, p. 286.

8 Ibid.

probably did not spend long enough with a tribal society – or even in a French village – to become aware of the vicious rivalries and conflicts of interest (that could lead to murder) over land, women, livestock, inheritances, etc., even when the land was owned collectively by a lineage or a clan.

If demographic expansion had been the main problem humanity had to resolve, its misfortunes would have begun in the Neolithic and gone on to become ungovernable today. Levi-Strauss makes this sugges-tion when, for example, dealing with the invention of agriculture, or of writing.[9] From *Tristes Tropiques* and increasingly until his death half a century later, Lévi-Strauss adopted the stance of the sage handing down lessons to his contemporaries (especially in the West, for the salvation of humanity, if salvation there be, could come only from the East). And so, against a backdrop of scepticism, pessimism and that radical misan-thropy whose source (and reason) was not only his empathy with the suffering, massacres and destruction unleashed on the small Amazonian Indian societies he had visited as a young anthropologist, Lévi-Strauss proclaimed both the end of Western supremacy and the total extinc-tion of humanity when our planet disappears some billions of years hence.

In 1986, speaking before a Japanese audience who must have been delighted by his words, Lévi-Strauss asks: 'Now that Western-style civilization no longer has the resources it needs to regenerate itself on its own and to thrive once again, can it learn something . . . from the humble societies . . . long held in contempt?' He implores 'the people who have achieved independence in the course of the last half century' to not continue to 'champion it'.[10] For the capitalist economic system invented in the West imposes on all nations and all peoples the laws of competition and profit-seeking, which are not apt to perpetuate traditions. Finally, he reiterates his earlier conviction, that 'this kind of helplessness shown by man when faced with human problems is, to a

---

9 C. Lévi-Strauss, *Anthropology Confronts the Problems of the Modern World*, fore-word M. Olender, trans. J. M. Todd (Cambridge, MA, The Belknap Press of Harvard University Press, 2013), pp. 63–4. 'It is essential to realize that writing, while it conferred vast benefits on humanity, did in fact deprive it of something fundamental', *Structural Anthropology*, trans. C. Jacobson and Brooke Grundfest Schoepf (New York, Basic Books, 1963), p. 366; *Tristes Tropiques*, chapter xviii.

10 *Anthropology Confronts the Problems of the Modern World*, pp. 5, 119.

very large extent, the result of the enormous demographic expansion of modern societies.'[11]

And in 1988, in his conversations with Didier Eribon, Lévi-Strauss doubles down on his criticism of humanity's bad behaviour and on his prophesy of the cosmic deflagration that, in any event, will annihilate our species. This should prompt awareness of the derisory character of our existence, and temper our pride: 'I've said it often. If we wish to give a kind of moderate humanism a chance, humanity will have to temper its excessive pride and convince itself that its time on earth, which will come to an end in any case, does not give it all rights.'[12]

Clearly, we can only concur with this conclusion. In the 'Finale' to *The Naked Man*, Lévi-Strauss had already invited man to 'preserve his courage, although he can never at any moment lose sight of the opposite certainty, that he was not present on earth in former times, that he will not always be here in the future and that, with his inevitable disappearance from the surface of a planet which is itself doomed to die, his labors, his sorrows, his joys, his hopes and his works will be as if they had never existed.'[13]

The final word of the Mythology series in French is '*rien*', 'nothing' – just when Lévi-Strauss claimed to have, with his four volumes, laid the foundations of an anthropology that had finally attained the status of a science, and which others were now invited to carry forward.[14] Today astrophysicists tell us that planet Earth should come to an end in a little over seven billion years. And palaeontologists tell us that our species, *Homo sapiens sapiens*, probably appeared, at the earliest, 150,000 years ago. How can we not keep alive the hope that humanity will find solutions to the problems confronting it?

In *The Origin of Table Manners*, Lévi-Strauss calls for a 'sound humanism'.[15] But how might this humanism that shines out of his works

---

11 C. Lévi-Strauss and C. Charbonnier, ed., *Conversations with Claude Lévi-Strauss*, trans. J. and D. Weightman (London, Jonathan Cape, 1969), p. 51.

12 C. Lévi-Strauss et D. Eribon, ed., *Conversations with Claude Lévi-Strauss*, trans. P. Wissing (Chicago, University of Chicago Press, 1991), p. 160.

13 *The Naked Man*, p. 695.

14 Cf. ibid., pp. 153, 634–5, 687.

15 'Sound humanism does not begin with oneself, but puts the world before life, life before man, and respect for others before self-interest' (C. Lévi-Strauss, *The Origin of Table Manners*, trans. J. and D. Weightman, Mythology series, volume 3 (Chicago, University of Chicago Press, 1990, p. 508.)

and the some hundred interviews given to newspapers and magazines become a social force capable of changing the course of events if, as Lévi-Strauss openly maintains, no honest man is an engaged intellectual? Others, like Zola in his article in support of Dreyfus, 'J'accuse', or Jean-Pierre Vernant, leading a local Resistance movement to liberate the city of Toulouse, did not hesitate to commit themselves to a cause and then return to their occupation as writers or scholars. No one is demanding as much, of course. But even so, we cannot but note that the enthusiastic young pre–World War II socialist described himself some fifty years later as an 'old right-wing anarchist . . . faithful to Marx . . . but not when it comes to his political ideas'. And in 1993, in response to a journalist who put it to him that: 'You are criticized for being outdated and conservative', he replied unambiguously: 'Me? But completely.'[16]

There remains his work, immense, inescapable, and which I have attempted to assess.

---

16 *Le Figaro*, 26 July 1993.

# Appendixes

# Toolkit for the Structural Analysis of Myths

Algorithm
Analogy
Analysis, ethnographic
Analysis, formal
Analysis, semantic
Analysis, structural
Analytic / synthetic
Animality / humanity
Armature (of a myth)
Axis
Canonical formula
Codes
Combinatory
Concept
Concrete / abstract
Congruence
Conjunction / disjunction
Consolidation of groups of myths
Continuous / discontinuous
Contradiction and its opposite
Contrariness and its opposite
Correlation / opposition
Correspondence

Correspondences, myths / infrastructure
Cycle of myths
Deduction, empirical / transcendental
Determinism, horizontal / vertical
Diachrony / synchrony
Equivalence
Etymology / meaning
Function, etiological
Function, semantic
Genetic law of a myth
Group of myths
Homology
Hypothesis / verification
Imaginary / real
Imaginary / symbolic
Invariant / variant
Inversion
Isomorphism / heteromorphism
Klein bottle
Klein group

# II

# Principal Empirical Binary Oppositions Present in the Amerindian Myths

Above / below
Active / passive
Aggressive / pacific
Air / water
Benevolent / malevolent
Boiled / roasted
Brother / sister
Burned / rotted
Chromatic / achromatic
Clever / awkward
Complementary / supplementary
Conjugal / non-conjugal
Container / contents
Continence / incontinence
Continuous sound / discontinu-
    ous sound
Creator / deceiver
Dawn / dusk
Day / night
Delicious / poisonous
Destruction / reconstruction
Destruction / repair
Detachable / undetachable

Devouring / devoured
Dry / wet
Earth / sky
Ebb / flow
Edible / inedible
Empty / full
Endogamy / exogamy
Famine / abundance
Father / son
Fertile / infertile
Full / empty
Food / excreta
Food / seasoning
Fresh / fermented
Fresh / rotten
Friendly / hostile
Front / back
Give / keep
Give / steal
Give / take
Handsome / ugly
Hard / soft
Healthy / toxic

Hearing / deafness
Heavenly / earthly
Heavy / light
Here / there
High water / low water
Honey / wax
Horizontal / vertical
Hot / cold
Human / non-human
Hunting / farming
Hunting / fishing
Husband / wife
In front / behind
Included / excluded
Inside / outside
Intelligent / stupid
Joined / disjoined
Kin / affines
Knocking call / whistled call
Land / water
Life / death
Lifeless / teeming
Little / big
Long / round
Male / female
Man / woman
Marked / unmarked
Marriage, close / far away
Married / unmarried
Masculine / feminine
Modulated sound / non-modu-
    lated sound
Morning / evening
Naked / clothed
Near / far
Noise / silence
North / south
Open / closed

Oral / anal
Ornaments / wounds
Parallel / perpendicular
Partners / adversaries
Partners / rivals
Periodic / aperiodic
Perishable / non-perishable
Persecutor / helper
Plugged / pierced
Raw / cooked
Raw / fermented
Reversible / irreversible
Rotten / cooked
Sacred / profane
Saviour / destroyer
Sea / mountain
Sick / well
Sighted / blind
Skilled / clumsy
Sky, heaven / earth
Smooth / lumpy
Spatial / temporal
Surplus / lack
Sweet / unpalatable
Sweet / salty
Sweet / sour
Symmetric / asymmetric
Thin / thick
Timid / confident
Upstream / downstream
Virtue / vice
War / peace
Water / fire
Water, celestial / terrestrial
Water, flowing / standing
West / east
White / black
Whole / fragmented

Wide / narrow                                    Wise / foolish
Wild / cultivated                                Young / old
Wind / fog

# III

# Table of Origin Myths Present in the Mythology Series

---

| Volume 1<br>**Universe** | Volume 2<br>**Species** | Volume 3<br>**Humanity** | Volume 4<br>**Cultures and Societies** |
|---|---|---|---|
| Sun and Moon | The different species | Humanity | Civilization |
| Spots on Moon | Differentiation of species, and of the blackbird, wood-pecker, red-winged blackbird | Men | Different peoples |
| Sun of the inner world | Animals | Women | Cooking |
| Nocturnal Sun | Wild animals | Two distinct species: men and women | Cooking fire |
| Phases of the Moon | Jaguar | Winter woman | Heating stones, oven |
| Sun, summer and winter | Wild pigs | Clinging woman | Cooking fire and wives of heavenly bodies |
| Moon's halo | Bison as game | | Earth oven |
| Stars | The capybara | Gourds and humanity | Stones for earth oven |
| Certain stars | | Palm nuts and humanity | Wood for making fire by friction |

| | | | |
|---|---|---|---|
| Wives of heavenly bodies | The opossum | | Making fire by striking |
| Pleiades | The flying squirrel | Stench | |
| Pleiades and Orion | | Menstruation | Boiling and roasting |
| | The anthill | The stench of women's sexual organ | Foods |
| Names of the constellations | The paca (rodent) | Women's periods and length of pregnancy | Winter famine and hydromel |
| Venus | Dogs | Women's vagina | Fermented beverages |
| The star Antares in Scorpius | Frogs and toads | Penis, piece of the Great Serpent | Maize and the distribution of populations |
| The Pleiades | | The penis and the first intercourse | Scarcity of honey |
| The Pleiades and Orion | Venomous snakes | | Sweet drinks and the scarcity of honey |
| Quarrel of heavenly bodies | Bats | Women's suicide | Honey feast |
| Stars and anthills | | The conquest of women | |
| The rolling head and the origin of Moon and menstruation | The colours of bird plumage | | |
| Moon, stars, rainbow and women's periods | Ducks | Racial differences | |
| | Bird that eats castor-oil seeds | | |
| The drink of immortality | The goatsucker | | Hydromel and the first drum |
| Orion's chest band, Venus, Sirius | The crow | The story of Wet-the-Bed (dandelion): origin of sibling incest taboo | Agriculture |
| The constellations | Tits | Fishing apparatus | |
| Southern Cross | Woodpeckers | Digestion | Curare |
| Meteors | | Baldness | Hunting and fishing poison |

| | | | |
|---|---|---|---|
| Pleiades, springs and respect toward dogs | | Armpit hair | Fishing poison and diseases |
| Sun spots and moon spots, the thin waist of wasps and hornets | The loon | Disease | Prescriptions and prohibitions associated with hunting and fishing |
| Stars and anthills | | Trances and the art of healing | Canoes and the fact that ducks can swim |
| Berenice's Hair | The loon's spots | Old age, aging | Canoes, making fire by striking, rapids and rain |
| War against the Sky people | The tayra's yellow spot | Long life | Dwellings |
| Comets and aeroliths | Macaws | Short life | Overland portaging |
| The rainbow | The blackbird | Irreversibility of death | Painted pottery |
| The rainbow and short life | | Death | Ornaments |
| Clouds | | Immortality | Ornaments and parures |
| Storms | Termites and termite mounds | Incest and death | Anti-parures |
| Rain | | Prohibitions concerning marriage | Bark masks |
| Gentle rain | Otters | Marriage | Polychrome painting |
| Storms and rain | | Bigamy | Cultural goods |
| War and wind | Fish and fishing | Marriage transactions | Fire and basketry |
| Day | Whales | Polygamy | Cultural goods, birds and cotton gourds, urucu |
| Daylight | Sea lions | Exogamy | Porcupine-quill embroidery |
| Night | Distribution of fish | Bigamy, agriculture, arts of civilization | Spinning and weaving, clothes making, potting |
| The first night | Dolphins | Conjugal jealousy | Sorcery |
| Day and night | Piranhas | Men's infidelity | Shamanic powers |
| Alternation of day and night | The skate | Marriage rites | Sacred weapons |

| | Electricl eel | Impossible marriages, love marriages | Scalping knive |
|---|---|---|---|
| The seasons | Salmon | | Scalps |
| Alternation of days and seasons | Liberation of the salmon | | The bow, the various types of arrows |
| | Salmon and hot springs | Widowhood | Stone arrowheads and fire |
| | The spiny skate | | |
| Tides | Seashells | | |
| Lakes | | | |
| Water released | The beluga | | Salmon rites |
| Liberation of drinkable water and salmon, sparrowhawk, master of the flood | | Decline of morality | Cult of Jurupari |
| The flood | Vermin | Initiation rites of young men | Cult of Bokan or Izy |
| Rivers, waterfalls, fishing sites, species of salmon and exchanges | Ants | Education of boys and girls | Funeral rites and sacred flutes |
| Mountains and rivers | | Wicked stepfathers and stepmothers | |
| Water and fire | The butterfly | | The flutes |
| Springs | The sloth | | The rattle |
| Hot springs | The badger | | Prohibition on musical instruments |
| Salt springs | Burdock | Self-cannibalism | |
| High water | Climbing vines | | |
| Waterfalls | The tree of life | Language | The Apapocuya and the opossum's pouch |
| Water, finery and funeral rites | The first tree | Laughter | Religious ceremonies |
| | The maple | | The Mandan |
| Fire | Maple sugar | | The Hidatsa |
| Fire lost and found | Honey | | The Hidatsa and descent from the sky |
| Liberated fire | Wild plants | | The Hidatsa, their emergence and the flood |

| | |
|---|---|
| Celestial fire | Marsh plants |
| Terrestrial fire | Aquatic plants |
| Conquest of fire in the sky | Wild berries |
| | Tobacco |
| Savannah and forest | Tobacco, maize, cotton, urucu fruits, resinous trees |
| Fire and culti-vated plants | Tobacco and otters |
| | Macerated tobacco |
| | Tobacco and other magical drugs |
| | Tobacco and the shaman's powers |
| | Tobacco and the rattle |
| | Cultivated plants |
| | Edible bulbs |
| | Wild rice |
| | Manioc, its slow growth |
| | Maize |
| | Colour of maize and beans |
| | Small cobs of maize |
| | Maize, beans, squashes, the sunflower, and the arts of civilization and sacred song |

# IV

# Myths with Human–Animal–Plant Transformations

*From Honey to Ashes*

| | |
|---|---|
| 42 | Animal seducers: tapir, jaguar, caiman, otter |
| 65 | In the beginning beasts were human |
| 72 | Mythic time when animals were not distinct from humans, before the nature / culture distinction: state of nature |
| 132–3 | Transformation of humans into various animals |
| 155 | The wife turns into an animal |
| 161 | The bee Simo |
| 166–7 | The frog Adaba |
| 171–5 | The frog Wau-uta |
| 173 | The jaguar is an ogre |
| 180–4 | A palm tree changes into a man |
| 189–90 | Exchange of sisters between men and water spirits |
| 213 | Women were once fish |
| 281, n. 8 | A woman turns into a monkey |
| 311 | An exasperated man turns into a spiny skate |
| 320–1 | A woman fertilized by a fish becomes the Sun's mother |
| 323 | At that time plants were persons. Plants as daughters of a god |
| 340–1 | A deer was a transformed man |
| 363–4 | The grandmother turns into a jaguar and devours her son |
| 396 | The agouti, master of the fruits and the primordial tree |
| 423, 430 | The island of the women guardians of tobacco |
| 434 | The Jivaro and the Ipurima descend from the sloth |
| 438 | Birds turned into humans |
| 443 | Men turned into wild pigs |
| | A young woman married to a water spirit |
| | A young woman married to the spirit master of wild pigs |

*The Origin of Table Manners*

| | |
|---|---|
| 57 | The time when humans were not distinct from animals |
| 77, n. | A jealous woman turns into a water spirit |
| 115 | At night the monkeys take on human form |
| | The leader: a jaguar in human form |
| 169 | Birds turned into sacred flutes |
| 173 | Sun and Moon used to be humans |

*The Naked Man*

# V

# Itinerary of the Bird-Nester myth (from the Bororo to the Salish)

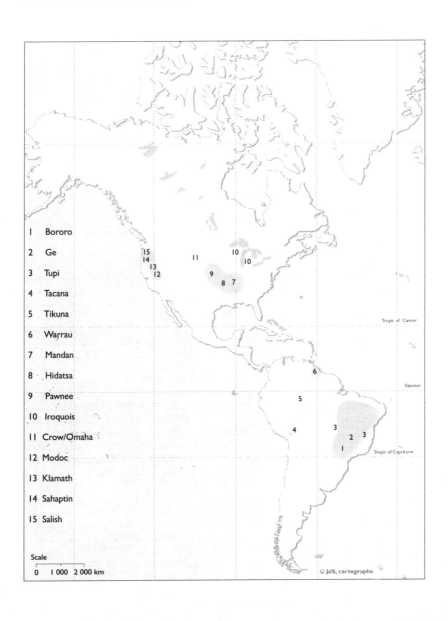

| | |
|---|---|
| 1 | Bororo |
| 2 | Ge |
| 3 | Tupi |
| 4 | Tacana |
| 5 | Tikuna |
| 6 | Warrau |
| 7 | Mandan |
| 8 | Hidatsa |
| 9 | Pawnee |
| 10 | Iroquois |
| 11 | Crow/Omaha |
| 12 | Modoc |
| 13 | Klamath |
| 14 | Sahaptin |
| 15 | Salish |

Scale

0    1 000    2 000 km

Tropic of Cancer

Equator

Tropic of Capricorn

© JdS, cartographe

# VI

# Location of Tribes and Ethnic Groups

| Central America | North America | South America | Africa | Asia | Oceania | Europe / Caucasus |
|---|---|---|---|---|---|---|
| Aztec | Acoma | Aguaruna | Akan | Byansi | Aluridja | Alani |
| Maya | Algonquin | Apinaye | Ashanti | Han | Aranda | Ossetes |
| | Alsea | Arekuna | Bantu | Hmong-Gar | Kariera | Scythians |
| | Apache | Bororo | Bedouin | Hmong-Khmer | Murinbata | |
| | Arapaho | Cariri | Fanti | Kachin | Murngin | |
| | Assiniboine | Cashinahua | Herero | Lolo | Ngaanyatjarra | |
| | Athapaskan | Chamacoco | Kasai | Lushai | Pintupi | |
| | Atsina | Chibcha | Lele | Manchu | Yolngu | |
| | Atsugewi | Chiriguano | Lovedu | Na | | |
| | Bella Bella | Ge | Mkako | Naga | **Melanesia** | |
| | Bella Coola | Guaraní | Mossi | Nasupo | Ambrym | |
| | Cherokee | Inca | Nuer | Rhades | Lambumbu | |
| | Cheyenne | Iparina | Samo | Sherpa | Muyuw | |
| | Chinook | Iranxe | Shilluk | Swat-Pathan | Nagovisi | |
| | Choctaw | Jivaro | Yako | | | |
| | Coos | Kayapo | Zulu | Dravidians | **New Guinea** | |
| | Fox | Matako | | Munda | Ankave | |
| | Haida | Machiguenga | **Madagascar** | Nayar | Arapesh | |
| | Hidatsa | Mundurucu | Imerina | | Banaro | |
| | Hopi | Nambikwara | | **Indonesia** | Baruya | |
| | Inuit | Sherente | | Iban | Chimbu | |
| | Iroquois | Tacana | | Tanebar-Evav | Dani | |
| | Kalina | Tikuna | | Tetum | Garia | |
| | Kaw | Toba | | | Iatmul | |
| | Keres | Tupi | | **Siberia** | Melpa | |
| | Klamath | Tupi-Kawahiva | | Gilyak | Mundugumor | |
| | Kwakiutl | Warao | | Tungus | Omarakana | |
| | Lillooet | | | | Telefomin | |

| | Mandan | | | **Iran** | Trobriander | |
|---|---|---|---|---|---|---|
| | Mascouten | | | Bakhtiari | Umeda | |
| | Menomini | | | | Yafar | |
| | Miwok | | | | | |
| | Modoc | | | | **Polynesia** | |
| | Navajo | | | | Hawaii | |
| | Nisqua | | | | Maori | |
| | Nootka | | | | Samoa | |
| | Ojibwa | | | | Tonga | |
| | Omaha | | | | | |
| | Osage | | | | | |
| | Otoe | | | | | |
| | Pawnee | | | | | |
| | Pueblo | | | | | |
| | Quileute | | | | | |
| | Quinault | | | | | |
| | Red-Knife | | | | | |
| | Sahaptin | | | | | |
| | Salish | | | | | |
| | Squamish | | | | | |
| | Tewa | | | | | |
| | Tiwa | | | | | |
| | Tlingit | | | | | |
| | Tsimshian | | | | | |
| | Wichita | | | | | |
| | Winnebago | | | | | |
| | Yana | | | | | |
| | Yurok | | | | | |
| | Zuni | | | | | |

# Bibliography

Allen, N., 'Sherpa Kinship Terminology in Diachronic Perspective', *Man* 11 (1976), pp. 569–97.

Augustins, G., *Comment se perpétuer? Devenir des lignées et destins des patrimoines dans les paysanneries européennes* (Nanterre, Société d'ethnologie, 1989).

Ballard, A. C., *Mythology of Southern Puget Sound* (Seattle, University of Washington Publications, 1929).

Barbut, M., 'Sur le sens du mot "structure" en mathématiques', *Les Temps modernes* 22, n° 246 (1966), pp. 791–814.

Barnes, R., 'Omaha and "Omaha"', in T. Trautmann and P. Whiteley, eds, *Crow-Omaha: New Light on a Classic Problem of Kinship Analysis* (Tucson, University of Arizona Press, 2012), pp. 69–82.

Barraud, C., *Tanebar-Evav, une société de maisons tournée vers le large* (Cambridge, Cambridge University Press; Paris, Éditions de la Maison des Sciences de l'Homme, 1979).

Barry, L. S., 'L'Union endogame en Afrique et à Madagascar', *L'Homme*, nos 154–155 (2000), pp. 67–100.

———, 'Les Modes de composition de l'alliance: Le mariage arabe', *L'Homme* 38, n° 147 (1998), pp. 17–50.

Bateson, G., *Naven: A Survey of the Problems Suggested by a Composite Picture of the Culture of a New Guinea Tribe Drawn from Three Points of View* (Palo Alto, Stanford University Press, 1958).

Beidelman, T., ed., *The Translation of Culture: Essays to E. E. Evans-Pritchard* (London, Tavistock Publications, 1971).

Belmont, N., 'Du mythe au conte. Du côté d'*Histoire de Lynx*', *Cahiers de l'Herne*, n° 82 (2004), special issue devoted to Lévi-Strauss.

Berger, L., 'Ritual, History and Cognition: From Analogy to Hegemony in Highland Malagasy Politics', *Anthropological Theory*, n° 12 (2013), pp. 1–36.

Bloch, M., *From Blessing to Violence: History and Ideology in the Circumcision Ritual of the Merina of Madagascar* (Cambridge, Cambridge University Press, 1986).

——, 'Lévi-Strauss chez les Britanniques', *Cahiers de L'Herne*, n° 82 (2004), pp. 349–56.

——, *Prey into Hunter: The Politics of Religious Experience* (Cambridge, Cambridge University Press, 1992).

Boas, F., *Kwakiutl Ethnography*. (Chicago, University of Chicago Press, 1967).

——, 'The Origin of Totemism', *American Anthropologist* 18 (1916), pp. 319–26.

Bonte, P., ed., *Épouser au plus proche. Inceste, prohibition et stratégies matrimoniales autour de la Méditerranée* (Paris, Éditions de l'EHESS, 1994).

Bourdieu, P., *Outline of a Theory of Practice*, trans. R. Nice (Cambridge, Cambridge University Press, 1977); translated from the French, *Esquisse d'une théorie de la pratique* (Paris, Minuit, 1980) (1st ed., 1972).

Bowers, A. W., *Mandan Social and Ceremonial Organization* (Chicago, University of Chicago Press, 1950).

Caratini, C., 'Système de parenté Sahraoui. L'Impact de la révolution', *L'Homme*, special issue, *Question de parenté*, nos 154–5 (2000), pp. 431–56.

——, 'À propos du mariage "arabe". Discours endogames et pratiques exogames: l'exemple des Rgayb'at du Nord-Ouest saharien', *L'Homme* 29, n° 110 (1989), pp. 30–49.

Carsten, J. and S. Hugh-Jones, *About the House: Lévi-Strauss and Beyond* (Cambridge, Cambridge University Press, 1995).

Copet-Rougier, É., 'Mariage et inceste. L'Endogamie dans une société à fortes prohibitions matrimoniales', *Bulletin de la Société d'anthropologie du Sud-Ouest* 15, n° 1 (1980), pp. 13–53.

Côté, A., 'Qu'est-ce que la formule canonique?' *L'Homme*, n° 135 (July–September, 1995), pp. 35–41.

Cuisenier, J., 'Endogamie et exogamie dans le mariage arabe', *L'Homme* 2, n° 2 (1962), pp. 80–105.

Deacon, A. B., 'The Regulation of Marriage in Ambrym', *Journal of the Royal Anthropological Institute* 57 (1927), p. 329.

Demetracopoulou, D., 'The Loon Woman Myth: A Study in Synthesis', *Journal of American Folklore*, n° 46 (1933), pp. 101–28.

Deputte, B., 'L'évitement de l'inceste chez les primates non humains', *Nouvelle Revue d'ethnopsychiatrie*, n° 3 (1985), pp. 41–72.

Descola, P., *Beyond Nature and Culture*, trans. J. Lloyd (Chicago, University of Chicago Press, 2013); translated from the French, *Par-delà nature et culture* (Paris, Gallimard, 2005).

Desveaux, E., *Quadratura Americana. Essai d'anthropologie Lévi-Straussienne* (Geneva, Georg, 2001).

Digard, J.-P., 'Jeux de structures, segmentarité et pouvoir chez les nomades Baxtyâri d'Iran', *L'Homme*, n° 102 (1987), pp. 12–53.

Dorsey, G. A., *The Arapaho Sun Dance: The Ceremony of the Offerings Lodge* (Chicago, Field Columbian Museum, 1903) (Anthropological series 4, publication 75).

——, *The Arapaho Sun Dance: The Ceremony of the Offerings* (Kessinger Publishing, 2006 [1930]).

——, and A. L. Kroeber, *Traditions of the Arapaho* (Chicago, Chicago Field Columbian Museum, 1903).

Douaire-Marsaudon, F., 'Le Bain mystérieux de la Tu'i Tonga Fefine. Germanité, inceste et mariage sacré en Polynésie occidentale (Tonga)', *Anthropos* 97, n° 2 (2002), pp. 147–62, 519–28.

——, 'Le Meurtre cannibale ou la production d'un Homme-Dieu', in M. Godelier and M. Panoff, eds, *Le Corps humain. Supplicié, possédé, cannibalisé* (Amsterdam, Archives contemporaines, 1998), pp. 137–67 (new ed. Paris, CNRS Éditions, 2009).

Dousset, L., *Assimilating Identities: Social Networks and the Diffusion of Sections* (Sydney, University of Sydney, 2005) (Oceania Monograph, n° 57).

——, *Australian Aboriginal Kinship*. Marseille, Pacific-Credo Publications, 2011.

——, '"Horizontal" and "Vertical" Skewing: Similar Objectives, Two Solutions?' in T. Trautmann and P. M. Whiteley, eds, *Crow-Omaha: New Light on a Classic Problem of Kinship Analysis* (Tucson, University of Arizona Press, 2012), chapter XIII.

——, 'On the Misinterpretation of the Aluridja Kinship System Type', *Social Anthropology* 11, n° 1 (2003), pp. 43–61.

——, 'Production et reproduction en Australie. Pour un tableau de l'unité des tribus aborigènes', *Social Anthropology* 4, n° 3 (1996).

Dumézil, G., *La Religion romaine archaïque* (Paris, Payot, 1966).

———, *Mariages indo-européens* (Paris, Payot, 1979).

———, *Naissance d'échanges* (Paris, Gallimard, 1945).

Dumont, L., *Dravidien et Kariera. L'Alliance de mariage dans l'Inde du Sud et en Australie* (Paris, Mouton, 1975).

———, *Homo Hierarchicus: The Caste System and its Implications*, complete revised English edition, trans. M. Sainsbury, L. Dumont and B. Gulati (Chicago, University of Chicago Press, 1970); translated from the French, *Homo hierarchicus. Essai sur le système des castes* (Paris, Gallimard, 1966).

———, 'The Dravidian Kinship Terminology as an Expression of Marriage', *Man* 53, n° 54 (1953), pp. 34–9.

Dunis, S., *L'Ile aux femmes. 8000 ans d'un seul et même mythe d'origine en Asie-Pacifique-Amérique* (Paris, CNRS Éditions, 2016).

Durkheim, E., 'Compte rendu de *Zur Urgeschichte der Ehe. Prof. J. Kohler*', *Année sociologique* I (1987), pp. 306–19.

Elkin, A. P., 'Sections and Kinship in Some Desert Tribes', *Man* 40 (1940).

———, 'Studies in Australian Totemism', *Oceania* 4, nos 1–2 (1933–34).

Engels, F., *Dialectic of Nature* (New York, 1940).

Ferchiou, S., *Hasab wa nasab. Parenté, alliance et patrimoine en Tunisie* (Paris, CNRS Éditions, 1992).

Firth, R., 'Totemism in Polynesia', *Oceania* 1, n° 3 (1930), pp. 291–321.

Fletcher, A. C. and J. R. Murie, *The Hako, a Pawnee Ceremony*, 22nd Annual Report of the Bureau of American Ethnology (1900–1901), part II, 1904.

Fortes, M., ed., *Social Structure* (Oxford, Oxford University Press, 1949).

Frazer, J. G., *Totemism and Exogamy* (London, Macmillan, 1910), 4 volumes.

Freeman, J., 'On the Concept of the Kindred', *Journal of the Royal Anthropological Institute of Great Britain and Ireland* 91, n° 2 (1961), pp. 192–220.

———, 'The family of Iban of Borneo', in J. Goody, ed., *The Development Cycle in Domestic Groups* (New York, Cambridge University Press, 1958).

Freud, S., *Totem and Taboo* (Boston, MA, Beacon Press, 1913).

Gell, A., *Metamorphosis of the Cassowaries: Umeda Society, Language and Ritual* (London, Athlone Press, 1975).

Gentner, D., K. Holyoak and S. Kokinov, eds, *The Analogical Mind: Perspectives from Cognitive Science* (Cambridge, MA, MIT Press, 2001).

Gernet, L., *Recherches sur le développement de la pensée juridique et morale en Grèce, étude sémantique* (Paris, Albin Michel, 2001) (1st ed., 1917).

Gilhodes, C., *The Kachins: Religion and Customs* (Calcutta, Catholic Mission Press, 1922).

————, *The Kachins: Their Religion and Mythology* (Calcutta, 1922).

Girard, R., *La Violence et le sacré* (Paris, Grasset, 1972).

Godelier, M. and J. Hassoun, eds, *Meurtre du père, sacrifice de la sexualité. Approches anthropologiques et psychanalytiques* (Paris, Arcanes, 1996).

————, 'Économie marchande, fétichisme, magie et science selon Marx dans *Le Capital*', *Nouvelle Revue de Psychanalyse* 2 (1970), pp. 197–213.

————, 'Afterword: Transformations and Lines of Evolution', in M. Godelier, F. Tjon Sie Fat and T. Trautmann, eds, *Transformations of Kinship*, trans. N. Scott (Washington, DC, Smithsonian Institution Press, 1998), pp. 386–413.

————, *In and Out of the West: Reconstructing Anthropology*, trans. N. Scott (Charlottesville, University of Virginia Press and Verso, 2009); translated from the French, *Au fondement des sociétés humaines. Ce que nous apprend l'anthropologie* (Paris, Albin Michel, 2007).

————, 'Les structures de la méthode du *Capital*, I, II, III', *Économie et politique*, nos 70, 71, 80 (1960 and 1961).

————, *Metamorphoses of Kinship*, trans. N. Scott (London and New York, Verso, 2012); translated from the French, *Métamorphoses de la parenté* (Paris, Fayard, 2004).

————, 'Mythe et histoire: réflexions sur les fondements de la pensée sauvage', *Annales*, year 26, nos 3–4 (1971).

————, *The Enigma of the Gift*, trans. N. Scott (Chicago, University of Chicago Press; Cambridge, Polity Press, 1998); translated from the French, *L'Énigme du don* (Paris, Fayard, 1996).

————, *The Making of Great Men: Male Domination and Power among the New Guinea Baruya*, trans. R. Swyer (Cambridge, Cambridge University Press, 1986); translated from the French, *La production des grands homes. Pouvoir et domination masculine chez les Baruya de Nouvelle-Guinée* (Paris, Fayard, 1982).

————, and M. Strathern, *Big Men and Great Men: Personifications of Power in Melanesia* (Cambridge, Cambridge University Press, 1991).

Goldenweiser, A. A., 'Remarks on the Social Organization of the Crow', *American Anthropologist* 15 (1913).

————, 'Totemism: An Analytical Study', *Journal of American Folklore* 23 (1910).

Goldstein, K., *La structure de l'organisme* (Paris, Gallimard, 1951).

Goudineau, Y., 'Lévi-Strauss, la Chine de Granet, l'ombre de Durkheim. Retour aux sources de l'analyse structurale de la parenté', *Cahiers de L'Herne*, n° 82 (2004), pp. 165–78.

Granet, M., *Catégories matrimoniales et relations de proximité dans la Chine ancienne* (Paris, Alcan, 1939).

——, *Danses et légendes de la Chine ancienne* (Paris, Presses Universitaires de France, 1926).

——, *La Civilisation chinoise* (Paris, Albin Michel, 1994; 1st ed., 1929).

——, *La Pensée chinoise* (Paris, Albin Michel, 1988; 1st ed., 1934).

Hage, P., 'Dravidian Kinship Systems', *L'Homme*, nos 177–178 (2006), pp. 395–408.

Hartog, F., *Les Régimes d'historicité. Présentisme et expériences du temps* (Paris, Seuil, 2003).

Héran, F., 'De Granet à Lévi-Strauss', *Social Anthropology* 6, n° 1, pp. 1–60; n° 2, pp 169–201; n° 3, pp. 309–30.

——, *Figures de la parenté* (Paris, Presses Universitaires de France, 2009).

Héritier, F., *L'Exercice de la parenté* (Paris, Gallimard/Seuil, 1981).

Herrenschmidt, C., 'Le Xwêtôdas ou "mariage incestueux" en Iran ancien', in P. Bonte, ed., *Épouser au plus proche. Inceste, prohibition et stratégies matrimoniales autour de la Méditerranée* (Paris, Éditions de l'EHESS, 1994).

Hocart, A. M., *Social Origins* (London, Watts, 1954).

——, 'The Indo-European Kinship System', *Ceylon Journal of Science*, section G, vol. 1 (1928), p. 203 ff.

Hodson, T. C., *The Primitive Culture of India* (London, Royal Asiatic Society, 1922; James G. Furlong Fund, volume 1).

Homans, G. C. and D. M. Schneider, *Marriage, Authority and Final Causes: A Study of Unilateral Cross-Cousin Marriage* (Glencoe, Free Press, 1955).

Honigmann, J., ed., *Handbook of Social and Cultural Anthropology* (Chicago, Rand McNally, 1973), pp. 579–607.

Hornborg, A., 'Social Redundancy in Amazonian Social Structure', in M. Godelier, F. Tjon Sie Fat and T. Trautmann, eds, *Transformations of Kinship*, trans. N. Scott (Washington DC, Smithsonian Institution Press, 1998), pp. 168–86.

Hua, C., *Une société sans père ni mari. Les Na de Chine* (Paris, Presses Universitaires de France, 1997).

Hutchins, E., 'Material Anchors for Conceptual Blends', *Journal of Pragmatics*, n° 37 (2005), pp. 1555–77.

Jacob, F., *La Logique du vivant* (Paris, Gallimard, 1970).

Joyce, R. A. and S. D. Gillespie, eds, *Beyond Kinship: Social and Material Reproduction in House Societies* (Philadelphia, University of Pennsylvania Press, 2000).

Juillerat, B., 'Terminologie de parenté yafar. Étude formelle d'un système dakota-iroquois', *L'Homme* 17, n° 4 (1977), pp. 71–81.

Karvé, I., *Kinship Organization in India* (Bombay, Asia Publishing House, 1953).

Kirchhoff, P., 'Verwandschaftsbezeichnungen und Verwandtenheirat', *Zeitschrift für Ethnologie* 64 (1932), pp. 41–72.

Klapisch-Zuber, C., *La Maison et le nom. Stratégies et rituels dans l'Italie de la Renaissance* (Paris, Éditions de l'EHESS, 1990).

Kohler, J., *On the Prehistory of Marriage, Totemism, Group Marriage, Mother Right* (Chicago, University of Chicago Press, 1975; 1st ed., 1897).

Kroeber, A.L., ed., *Anthropology Today* (Chicago, University of Chicago Press, 1953).

Kronenfeld, D., 'Crow- (and Omaha-) Type Kinship Terminology: The Fanti Case', in T. Trautmann and P. M. Whiteley, eds, *Crow-Omaha: New Light on a Classic Problem of Kinship Analysis* (Tucson, University of Arizona Press, 2012), chap. VIII.

———, *Fanti Kinship and the Analysis of Kinship Terminologies* (Urbana and Chicago, University of Illinois Press, 2009).

———, 'Fanti Kinship: The Structure of Terminology and Behavior', *American Anthropologist*, n° 75 (1973), pp. 1577–95.

Kryukov, M. V., 'Development of the Chinese Kinship System', in M. Godelier, F. Tjon Sie Fat and T. Trautmann, eds, *Transformations of Kinship*, trans. N. Scott (Washington DC, Smithsonian Institution Press, 1998), pp. 296–8.

Lane, B. S., 'Structural Contrasts between Symmetric and Asymmetric Marriage Systems: A Fallacy', *South Western Journal of Anthropology* 17, n° 1 (1961), pp. 49–55.

Leach, E., *Culture and Communication* (Cambridge, Cambridge University Press, 1976).

———, 'Jinghpaw Kinship Terminology', *Journal of the Royal Anthropological Institute*, n° 75 (1945), pp. 59–72.

———, *Political Systems of Highland Burma: A Study of Kachin Social Structure* (Cambridge, MA, Harvard University Press, 1954).

———, *Rethinking Anthropology* (London, Athlone Press, 1961).

———, 'The Structural Implications of Matrilateral Cross-Cousin Marriage), *Journal of the Royal Anthropological Institute*, n° 81 (1951), pp. 23–55.

Lefébure, C., 'Le Mariage des cousins parallèles patrilatéraux et l'endogamie de lignée agnatique: L'Anthropologie de la parenté face à la question de l'endogamie', in C.-H. Breteau and C. Lacoste-Dujardin, eds, *Production, pouvoir et parenté dans le monde méditerranéen, de Sumer à nos jours* (Paris,

AECLAS, Librairie Orientaliste Paul Geuthner, 1981), pp. 195–207).

Lemonnier, P., *Le Sabbat des lucioles. Sorcellerie, chamanisme et imaginaire cannibale en Nouvelle-Guinée* (Paris, Stock, 2006).

——, *Mundane Objects. Materiality and Non-Verbal Communication* (Walnut Creek, Left Coast Press, 2012).

——, 'Mythe et rite chez les Anga', *Journal de la Société des Océanistes*, nos 130–131 (2010), pp. 67–77.

*Les Cahiers de L'Herne*, n° 24, special issue devoted to Lévi-Strauss, 2004.

Lesser, A., 'Kinship Origins in the Light of Some Distributions', *American Anthropologist* 31, n° 4 (1929), pp. 710–30.

Lévi-Strauss, C., 'Answers to Some Investigations: The Three Humanisms', *Structural Anthropology, Volume 2*, trans. M. Layton (Chicago, The University of Chicago Press, 1983), pp. 271–4; translated from the French, 'Les Trois humanismes' (1956), in *Anthropologie structurale deux* (Paris, Plon, 1973), pp. 312–22; first published in *Demain*, n° 35 (1956).

——, *Anthropology and Myth: Lectures, 1951–1982*, trans. R. Willis (Oxford, Basil Blackwell, 1987); translated from the French, *Paroles données* (Paris, Plon, 1984).

——, *Anthropology Confronts the Problems of the Modern World*, foreword M. Olender, trans. J. M. Todd (Cambridge, MA, The Belknap Press of Harvard University Press, 2013); translated from the French, *L'Anthropologie face aux problèmes du monde moderne* (Paris, Seuil, 2011).

——, 'Apologue des amibes', in J.-L. Jamard, M. Xanthakou and E. Terray, eds, *En substances: Textes pour Françoise Héritier* (Paris, Fayard, 2000), pp. 493–6.

——, Article in *Arts*, n° 60 (1966), marking the inauguration of the exhibition 'Hommage à Picasso' at the Grand and Petit Palais in Paris.

——, Article in *Renaissance* 2 and 3 (1944–45), New York, pp. 168–86.

——, 'Cultural Discontinuity and Economic and Social Development', *Structural Anthropology, Volume 2*, trans. M. Layton (Chicago, University of Chicago Press, 1983), pp. 312–22.

——, 'De Grées ou de force?' *L'Homme*, n° 163 (2002).

——, 'Du mariage dans un degré rapproché', in J.-C. Galey, ed., *Différences, valeurs, hiérarchie. Textes offerts à Louis Dumont* (Paris, Éditions de l'EHESS, 1984), pp. 79–89.

——, *Entretiens multidisciplinaires sur les sociétés musulmanes* (Paris, École des Hautes Études, 6th section, 1959).

——, 'Four Winnebago Myths', *Structural Anthropology, Volume 2*, trans. M. Layton (Chicago, The University of Chicago Press, 1983), pp. 198–210.

———, 'Four Winnebago Myths: A Structural Sketch', in S. Diamond, ed., *Culture in History. Essays in honor of Paul Radin* (New York, Columbia University Press, 1960).

———, *From Honey to Ashes: Introduction to a Science of Mythology 2*, trans. J. and D. Weightman (Chicago, University of Chicago Press, 1973); translated from the French, *Du miel aux cendres* (Paris, Plon 1966).

———, 'From Mythical Possibility to Social Existence', *The View from Afar*, trans. J. Neugroschel and P. Hoss (Chicago, University of Chicago Press, 1985).

———, 'Histoire et ethnologie', *Annales ESC* 38, n° 6 (1983).

———, 'Hourglass Configurations', in P. Maranda, ed., *The Double Twist: From Ethnography to Morphodynamics* (Toronto, University of Toronto Press, 2001).

———, 'How Myths Die', *Structural Anthropology, Volume 2*, trans. M. Layton (Chicago, University of Chicago Press, 1983), pp. 256–68.

———, *Introduction to the Work of Marcel Mauss*, trans. F. Baker (London, Routledge & Kegan Paul, 1987); translated from the French, 'Introduction', in M. Mauss, *Sociologie et anthropologie* (Paris, Presses Universitaires de France, 1950).

———, 'La Notion de maison', interview with Lévi-Strauss by P. Lamaison, *Terrain*, n° 9 (October 1987).

———, 'La Sexualité féminine et l'origine de la société', *Les Temps modernes*, n° 598 (1998), pp. 78–84; first published in *La Repubblica*, 3 November 1995, under the title 'Quell'intenso profumo di donna'.

———, 'La Vie familiale et sociale des Indiens Nambikwara', *Journal de la Société des Américanistes* 37, n° 1 (1948), pp. 1–132.

———, 'Le Problème des relations de parenté', *Entretiens multidisciplinaires sur les sociétés musulmanes* (Paris, École Pratique des Hautes Études, 6th section, 1959; mimeo), pp. 13–20.

———, 'Le Retour de l'oncle maternel', first published in *La Repubblica*, 24 December 1995 (reprinted in *Nous sommes tous des cannibales*, Paris, Le Seuil, 2013).

———, 'Le Sentiment de la nature. Un besoin fondamental', *Ethnies*, nos 29–30 (2003), pp. 88–94.

———, 'Le Triangle culinaire', *L'Arc*, n° 26 (1965), pp. 19–29.

———, 'Les Mathématiques de l'homme', *Bulletin international des sciences sociales* 6, n° 4 (1954), pp. 653–76.

———, *Look, Listen, Read*, trans. B. Singer (New York, Basic Books, 1997);

translated from the French, *Regarder, écouter, lire* (Paris, Plon, 1993).

——, 'Musique et identité culturelle', *in Harmoniques*, n° 2 (1987), pp. 8–14.

——, 'On Manipulated Sociological Models', *Bijdragen tot de Taal-, Land-, en Volkenkunde* 116, n° 1 (1960), pp. 45–54.

——, 'Postface', *L'Homme*, special issue, *Question de parenté*, nos 154–155 (2000), p. 717.

——, 'Productivité et condition humaine', *Études rurales*, nos 159–160 (2001), pp. 129–44.

——, 'Race and History', *Structural Anthropology, Volume 2*, trans. M. Layton (Chicago, University of Chicago Press, 1976), pp. 323–62.

——, 'Rapports de symétrie entre rites et mythes de peuples voisins', in T. Beidelman, ed., *The Translation of Culture: Essays to E. E. Evans-Pritchard* (London, Tavistock, 1971), pp. 161–78.

——, 'Réflexions sur l'atome de parenté', *L'Homme* 13, n° 3 (1973), pp. 5–30.

——, 'Relations of Symmetry between Rituals and Myths of Neighboring Peoples', *Structural Anthropology, Volume 2*, trans. M. Layton (Chicago, University of Chicago Press, 1976).

——, 'Réponse à Edmund Leach', *L'Homme* 17, nos 2–3 (1977), pp. 131–3.

——, 'Social Structure', in A. L. Kroeber, ed., *Anthropology Today* (Chicago, University of Chicago Press, 1953); also in *Structural Anthropology*, trans. C. Jacobson and B. Grundfest Schoepf (New York, Basic Books, 1963), pp. 277–323.

——, 'Social Structure', presented at the Wenner-Gren Foundation International Symposium on Anthropology, New York, 1952, in A. L. Kroeber, ed., *Anthropology Today* (Chicago, University of Chicago Press, 1953), pp. 524–53.

——, 'Split Representation in the Art of Asia and America', *Structural Anthropology*, trans. C. Jacobson and B. Grundfest Schoepf (New York, Basic Books, 1963), pp. 245–68.

——, 'Structural Analysis in Linguistics and in Anthropology', *Structural Anthropology*, trans. C. Jacobson and B. Grundfest Schoepf (New York, Basic Books, 1963), pp. 31–54; translated from the French, 'L'Analyse structurale en linguistique et en anthropologie', *Word, Journal of the Linguistic Circle of New York* I, n° 2 (August 1945), pp. 1–21; reprinted in *Anthropologie structurale* (Paris, Plon, 1968), pp. 37–62.

——, *Structural Anthropology*, trans. C. Jacobson and B. Grundfest Schoepf (New York, Basic Books, 1963); translated from the French, *Anthropologie structurale* (Paris, Plon, 1968).

——, *Structural Anthropology, Volume 2*, trans. M. Layton (Chicago, University of Chicago Press, 1976, reprinted 1983); translated from the French, *Anthropologie structurale deux* (Paris, Plon, 1973).

——, 'Structuralism and Ecology', Gildersleeve Lecture, Barnard College, New York, 1972, published in *The View from Afar*, trans. J. Neugroschel and P. Hoss (Chicago, University of Chicago Press, 1985), pp. 143–66.

——, 'Structure and Dialectics', *Structural Anthropology*, trans. C. Jacobson and B. Grundfest Schoepf (New York, Basic Books, 1963), pp. 232–41.

——, 'The Bear and the Barber', text of the 1960 Henry Meyers Memorial Lecture, *Journal of the Royal Anthropological Institute of Great Britain and Ireland* 93, n° 1, pp. 1–11.

——, 'The Concept of Archaism in Anthropology', *Structural Anthropology*, trans. C. Jacobson and B. Grundfest Schoepf (New York, Basic Books, 1963), pp. 101–19; translated from the French, 'La Notion d'archaïsme en ethnologie', *Cahiers internationaux de sociologie* 12 (1952), pp. 32–55.

——, 'The Deduction of the Crane', in P. Maranda and E. Köngäs Maranda, eds, *Structural Analysis of Oral Tradition* (Philadelphia, University of Pennsylvania Press, 1971), pp. 3–21.

——, *The Elementary Structures of Kinship*, trans. J. H. Bell and J. R. von Sturmer and R. Needham, ed. (Boston, Beacon Press, 1969); translated from the French, *Les Structures élémentaires de la parenté* (Paris, Presses Universitaires de France, 1949).

——, 'The End of the West's Cultural Supremacy', *Anthropology Confronts the Problems of the Modern World*, foreword M. Olender, trans. J. M. Todd (Cambridge, MA, The Belknap Press of Harvard University Press, 2013), pp. 1–44.

——, 'The Family', in H. L. Shapiro, ed., *Man, Culture, and Society* (London, Oxford University Press 1956), pp. 332–57.

——, 'The Future of Kinship Studies', Huxley Memorial Lecture, in *Proceedings of the Royal Institute of Great Britain and Ireland*, 1965, pp. 13–22.

——, *The Jealous Potter*, trans. B. Chorier (Chicago, University of Chicago Press, 1988); translated from the French, *La Potière jalouse* (Paris, Plon, 1985).

——, *The Naked Man: Mythologiques, Volume 4*, trans. J. and D. Weightman, (Chicago, University of Chicago Press, 1981); translated from the French, *L'Homme nu* (Paris, Plon, 1971).

——, *The Origin of Table Manners: Mythologiques, Volume 3*, trans. J. and D. Weightman, (Chicago, University of Chicago Press, 1990); translated from the French *L'Origine des manières de table* (Paris, Plon, 1968).

———, 'The Place of Anthropology in the Social Sciences and Problems Raised in Teaching It', *Structural Anthropology*, trans. C. Jacobson and B. Grundfest Schoepf (New York, Basic Books, 1963), pp. 346–81.

———, *The Raw and the Cooked: Introduction to a Science of Mythology 1*, trans. J. and D. Weightman (Harmondsworth, Penguin, 1986); translated from the French, *Le Cru et le cuit* (Paris, Plon, 1964).

———, *The Savage Mind* (no translator mentioned) (Chicago, University of Chicago Press, 1966); translated from the French, *La Pensée sauvage* (Paris, Plon, 1962).

———, 'The Scope of Anthropology', *Structural Anthropology, Volume 2*, trans. M. Layton (Chicago, University of Chicago Press, 1976), pp. 3–32; first published by the Collège de France under the title *Chaire d'anthropologie sociale: Leçon inaugurale faite le mardi 5 janvier 1960 par M. Claude Lévi-Strauss, Professeur* (Paris, Collège de France, 1960, n° 31).

———, 'The Story of Asdiwal', *Structural Anthropology, Volume 2*, pp. 146–97.

———, *The Story of Lynx*, trans. C. Tihanyi (Chicago, University of Chicago Press, 1995); translated from the French, *Histoire de Lynx* (Paris, Plon, 1991).

———, 'The Structural Study of Myth', *Journal of American Folklore* 68, n° 270 (Oct–Dec 1955), pp. 428–44; also in *Structural Anthropology*, trans. C. Jacobson and B. Grundfest Schoepf (New York, Basic Books, 1963), pp. 206–31.

———, *The View from Afar*, trans. J. Neugroschel and P. Hoss (Chicago, University of Chicago Press, 1985); translated from the French, *Le Regard éloigné* (Paris, Plon, 1983).

———, *The Way of the Masks*, trans. S. Modelski (Seattle, University of Washington Press, 1982); translated from the French *La Voie des masques* (Paris, Plon, 1975).

———, *Totemism*, trans. R. Needham (Boston, Beacon Press, 1963); translated from the French, *Le Totémisme aujourd'hui* (Paris, Presses Universitaires de France, 1962).

———, 'Toward a General Theory of Communication', paper presented before the International Conference of Linguists and Anthropologists, Bloomington, Indiana, 1952.

———, *Voir l'autre face de la lune* (Paris, Seuil, 2011).

———, and C. Charbonnier, ed., *Conversations with Claude Lévi-Strauss*, trans. J. and D. Weightman (London, Jonathan Cape, 1969); translated from the French, *Entretiens avec Claude Lévi-Strauss* (Paris, Plon & Éditions René

Julliard, 1961).

——, and D. Eribon, ed., *Conversations with Claude Lévi-Strauss*, trans. P. Wissing (Chicago, University of Chicago Press, 1991); translated from the French, *De près et de loin* (Paris, Odile Jacob, 1988).

Levine, N., 'Fathers and Sons: Kinship Value and Validation in Tibetan polyandry', *Man* 22, n° 2 (1987), pp. 267–86.

Long, J. L., *Voyages and Travels of an Indian Interpreter and Trader* (A. H. Clark, 1791; re-issued Chicago, 1922).

Loraux, N., *Les Enfants d'Athéna* (Paris, Maspero, 1981).

Lounsbury, F. G., 'A Formal Account of the Crow and Omaha Kinship Terminologies', in W. Goodenough, ed., *Explorations in Cultural Anthropology: Essays in Honor of George Peter Murdock* (New York, McGraw-Hill, 1964), pp. 352–94.

——, 'The Structural Analysis of Kinship Semantics', in H. G. Lunt, ed., *Proceedings of the Ninth International Congress of Linguistics* (The Hague, Mouton, 1964), pp. 1073–90.

Lowie, R. M., 'A Note on Relationship Terminologies', *American Anthropologist*, n° 30 (1928), pp. 263–7.

Lyotard, J. F., *The Postmodern Condition: A Report on Knowledge*, trans. G. Bennington and B. Massumi, foreword F. Jameson (Minneapolis, University of Minnesota Press, 1984); translated from the French, *La Condition postmoderne. Rapport sur le savoir* (Paris, Minuit, 1979).

Maine, H. J. S., *Ancient Law: Its Connection with the Early History of Society, and Its Relation to Modern Ideas* (London, John Murray, 1861).

Malinowski, B., *Sex and Repression in Savage Society* (New York, Harcourt, Brace & Co., 1927).

——, *The Father in Primitive Psychology* (New York, Norton Library, 1928).

Maranda, P. and E. Köngäs, 'Structural Models in Folklore', *Midwest Folklore*, XII, Indiana University (1962), pp. 133–92.

——, *The Double Twist: From Ethnography to Morphodynamics* (Toronto, University of Toronto Press, 2001).

Marx, K., *Capital*, volume 1, chapter II.

Massenzio, M., ed., *Claude Lévi-Strauss. Un itinéraire* (Paris, L'Échoppe, 2000).

Maurice, P., *La Famille en Gévaudan au XVe siècle (1380–1483)* (Paris, Publications de la Sorbonne, 1988).

Mauss, M., *Sociologie et anthropologie* (Paris, Presses Universitaires de France, 1950).

——, *The Gift: The Form and Reason for Exchange in Archaic Societies*, trans. W. D. Halls, foreword by M. Douglas (New York, W.W. Norton, 1990);

translated from the French, 'Essai sur le don', *L' Année sociologique* (1923–24), and *Sociologie et anthropologie* (Paris, Presses Universitaires de France, 1973), pp. 149–279.

McCauley, R. and T. E. Lawson, *Bringing Ritual to Mind* (Cambridge, Cambridge University Press, 2002).

Meyers, F., *Pintupi Country, Pintupi Self: Sentiment, Place and Politics Among Western Aborigines* (Washington, DC, Smithsonian Institution Press, 1986).

Montberg, T., 'Fathers Were Not Genitors', *Man* 10, n° 1 (1975), pp. 81–113.

Moore, J. and R. Ali, 'Are Dispersal and Inbreeding Avoidances Related?' *Animal Behaviour*, n° 32 (1984), pp. 94–112.

Morava, J., 'From Lévi-Strauss to Chaos and Complexity', in M. S. Mosko and F. H. Damon, eds, *On the Order of Chaos* (New York, Berghahn Books, 2005).

——, 'Une interprétation mathématique de la formule canonique de Claude Lévi-Strauss', *Lévi-Strauss, Cahiers de L'Herne*, 2004.

Morgan, L. H., *Ancient Society or Research in the Lines of Human Progress from Savagery through Barbarism to Civilization* (Tucson, University of Arizona Press, 1985; 1st ed. 1887).

——, *Systems of Consanguinity and Affinity of the Human Family* (Washington DC, Smithsonian Institution, 1871).

Mosko, M. S. and F. H. Damon, eds, *On the Order of Chaos* (New York, Berghahn Books, 2005).

Munn, N., 'Symbolism in a Ritual Context', in J. Honigmann, ed., *Handbook of Social and Cultural Anthropology* (Chicago, Rand McNally, 1973), pp. 579–607.

Murdock, G. P., 'Double Descent', *American Anthropologist* 42, n° 4 (1942), pp. 555–61.

——, *Social Structure* (New York, Free Press, 1949).

Nash, J., *Matriliny and Modernization: The Nagovisi of South Bougainville* (Canberra, Australian National University Press, 1974).

Nattiez, J-J., *Lévi-Strauss musicien. Essai sur la tentation homologique* (Paris, Actes Sud, 2008).

Olender, M., interview with Claude Lévi-Strauss by Maurice Olender in 1976, *Le Point*, 30 September 2010, pp. 75–7.

Parkin, R., *The Munda of Central India: An Account of Their Social Organization* (Delhi, Oxford University Press, 1992).

Petitot, J., 'Approche morphodynamique de la formule canonique du mythe, *L'Homme*, nos 106–107 (1988), pp. 24–50.

Propp, V., *The Historical Roots of Fairy-tales* (North Holland Publishing Company, 1982).

Radcliffe-Brown, A. R., 'The Comparative Method in Social Anthropology', Huxley Memorial Lecture for 1951, *Journal of the Royal Anthropological Institute* 81, nos 1–2, parts I and II, pp. 15–22.

——, 'The Sociological Theory of Totemism', *Structure and Function in Primitive Society: Essays and Addresses* (Glencoe, Free Press, 1952).

——, 'The Study of Kinship Systems', *Journal of the Royal Anthropological Institute* 71, n° 1 (1941), pp. 1–18.

Raheja, G. G., *The Poison in the Gift: Ritual, Prestation and the Dominant Caste in a North Indian Village* (Chicago, University of Chicago Press, 1988).

Ricœur, P., 'Symbole et temporalité', *Archivio di filosofia*, nos 1–2 (1963).

Rivers, W. H. R., 'Marriage of Cousins in India', *Journal of the Royal Asiatic Society of Great Britain and Ireland* (July 1907), pp. 623–4.

Rogers, G., 'The Father's Sister Futa-Helu is Black: A Consideration of Female Rank and Power in Tonga', *Journal of the Polynesian Society* 86 (1977), pp. 157–82.

Roudinesco, É., *Jacques Lacan. Esquisse d'une vie, histoire d'un système de pensée* (Paris, Fayard, 1993).

Sahlins, M., *Islands of History* (Chicago, University of Chicago Press, 1984).

Sartre, J.-P., *Critique of Dialectical Reason*, trans. Q. Hoare, foreword F. Jameson (New York, Verso, 2009).

Scheid, J., *Quand faire c'est croire. Les Rites sacrificiels des Romains* (Paris, Aubier, 2005).

Schmid, K., 'Zur Problematik von Familie, Sippe und Geschlecht, Haus und Dynastie beim mittelalterlichen Adel', *Zeitschrift für die Geschichte des Oberrheins* 105, n° 1 (1957), pp. 56 ff.

Scubla, L., *Lire Lévi-Strauss* (Paris, Odile Jacob, 1998).

——, 'Structure, transformation et morphogénèse', *Cahiers de L'Herne*, n° 82 (2004).

Seligman, B., 'The Incest Taboo as Social Regulation', *Sociological Review* 27, n° 1 (1935), pp. 75–110.

Shannon, C. and W. Weaver, *The Mathematical Theory of Communication* (Urbana, University of Illinois Press, 1949).

Shternberg, L. I., 'The Social Organization of the Gilyak', *Anthropological Papers of the American Museum of Natural History*, n° 82 (June 1999).

Stanner, W. E. H., 'Murinbata Kinship and Totemism', *Oceania* 7, n° 2 (1936–37).

Stoczkowski, V., *Anthropologies rédemptrices* (Paris, L'Harmattan, 2008).

Swanton, J. R., 'The Social Organization of American Tribes', *American*

*Anthropologist* 7, n° 4 (1905), pp. 663–73.

Tambiah, S. J., 'Forms and Meaning of Magical Acts: A Point of View', in R. Horton and R. Finnegan, eds, *Modes of Thought* (London, Faber & Faber, 1979), pp. 199–229.

Tax, S., 'The Social Organization of the Fox Indians', in F. Eggan, ed., *Social Anthropology of North American Tribes* (Chicago, University of Chicago Press, 1937), pp. 243–84.

Thom, R., *Structural Stability and Morphogenesis* (Boulder, Westview Press, 1994; 1st ed., 1972).

Thompson, D'Arcy Wentworth, *Forme et croissance* (Paris, Seuil, 2009).

Thompson, S., *Tales of the North American Indians* (Bloomington, Indiana University Press, 1929).

——, 'The Star Husband Tale', *Studia Septentrionalia*, n° 4 (1953), pp. 93–163.

Tjon Sie Fat, F., 'On the Formal Analysis of Dravidian, Iroquois and Generational Varieties as Nearly Associative Combinations', in M. Godelier, F. Tjon Sie Fat and T. Trautmann, eds, *Transformations of Kinship*, trans. N. Scott (Washington DC, Smithsonian Institution Press, 1998), pp. 50–93.

Trautmann, T., 'Crossness and Crow-Omaha', in T. Trautmann and P. M. Whiteley, eds, *Crow-Omaha: New Light on a Classic Problem of Kinship Analysis* (Tucson, University of Arizona Press, 2012), pp. 31–50.

——, *Dravidian Kinship* (Cambridge, Cambridge University Press, 1981).

——, T. and P. Whiteley, eds, *Crow-Omaha: New Light on a Classic Problem of Kinship Analysis* (Tucson, University of Arizona Press, 2012).

——, and R. Barnes, '"Dravidian", "Iroquois" and "Crow-Omaha" in North American Perspective', in M. Godelier, F. Tjon Sie Fat and T. Trautmann, eds, *Transformations of Kinship*, pp. 27–58.

Turner, V., *The Ritual Process: Structure and Anti-Structure* (Chicago, Aldine, 1969).

Tuzin, D., 'Art, Ritual and the Crafting of Illusion', *Asia Pacific Journal of Anthropology* 3, n° 1 (2002), pp. 1–23.

Tylor, E. B., 'On a Method of Investigating the Development of Institutions, Applied to Laws of Marriage and Descent', *Journal of the Royal Anthropological Institute*, n° 18 (1889).

Van Gennep, A., *L'État actuel du problème totémique* (Paris, Leroux, 1920).

Van Wouden, F. A. E., *Sociale Structuurtypen in de Groote Oost* (Leiden, J. Ginsberg, 1935).

Vernant, J.-P., *Mythe et pensée chez les Grecs* (Paris, Maspero, 1965).

———, *Mythe et religion en Grèce ancienne* (Paris, Seuil, 1990).

———, *Mythe et tragédie en Grèce ancienne* (with Pierre Vidal-Naquet), vol. 1. (Paris, Maspéro, 1972; vol. 2, Paris, La Découverte, 1986).

———, *Raisons du mythe*, II: *Le Mythe aujourd'hui. Œuvres* (Paris, Seuil, 2007).

Viveiros de Castro, E., 'Dravidian and Related Kinship Systems', in M. Godelier, F. Tjon Sie Fat and T. Trautmann, eds, *Transformations of Kinship*, pp. 332–85.

———, *Métaphysiques cannibales* (Paris, Presses Universitaires de France, 2009).

Von Neumann, J. and O. Morgenstern, *Theory of Games and Economic Behavior* (Princeton, Princeton University Press, 1944).

Wagner, R., 'The Practical Person', in M. Godelier and M. Strathern, eds, *Big Man and Great Men: Personifications of Power in Melanesia* (Cambridge, Cambridge University Press, 1991), pp. 159–73.

Whitehouse, H. and R. N. McCauley, eds, *Mind and Religion: The Psychological and Cognitive Foundations of Religiosity* (Walnut Creek, AltaMira Press, 2005).

Whiteley, P., 'Crow-Omaha Kinship in North America: A Pueblo Perspective', in T. Trautmann and P. Whiteley, eds, *Crow-Omaha: New Light on a Classic Problem of Kinship Analysis*, (Tucson, University of Arizona Press, 2012), pp. 83–108.

Wiener, N., *Cybernetics or Control and Communication in the Animal and the Machine* (Cambridge, MA, MIT Press, 1948).

Yi Feng, H., 'The Chinese Kinship System', *Harvard Journal of Asiatic Studies* 2, n° 2 (1937).

# Acknowledgements

I would like to thank all those without whom this translation would not have been possible. First of all, the translator, Nora Scott, not only for this long translation but for the immense labour of documentation and collation required. And then all those who contributed their financial aid: Georges Demathas who, on behalf of our kinship ties, generously offered to ensure half of the expense of the translation; the Centre National du Livre and the Centre de Recherche et de Documentation sur l'Océanie, who took on the financing of the other half. My heartfelt thanks to them all.

# Indexes

## Index of Names

## Index of Subjects